FACTOR ANALYSIS:
AN APPLIED APPROACH

FACTOR ANALYSIS: AN APPLIED APPROACH

Edward E. Cureton
University of Tennessee

Ralph B. D'Agostino
Boston University

LEA

LAWRENCE ERLBAUM ASSOCIATES, PUBLISHERS

1983   Hillsdale, New Jersey   London

Lawrence Erlbaum Associates, Inc., Publishers
365 Broadway
Hillsdale, New Jersey 07642

Library of Congress Cataloging in Publication Data

Cureton, Edward Eugene, 1902–
  Factor analysis: an applied approach.

  Bibliography: p.
  Includes indexes.
  1. Factor analysis. I. D'Agostino, Ralph B.,
joint author. II. Title.
QA278.5.C87   519.5'354   80-20760
ISBN 0-89859-048-5

Printed in the United States of America
10 9 8 7 6 5 4 3 2

To the memory of
Truman Lee Kelley

Contents

Tables and Figures

Preface

This book is written primarily as a text for a course in factor analysis at the advanced undergraduate or graduate level. It is most appropriate for students of the behavioral and social sciences, though colleagues and students in other disciplines also have used preliminary copies. It does not pretend to be a comprehensive treatise. It presents only those methods and procedures which the writers are able to recommend for practical use. Other methods are either ignored or mentioned only briefly. We have not hesitated, moreover, to include rules of thumb from the common lore and our own experience. Factor analysis is partly a mathematical science and partly an art.

We have tried to develop understanding by presenting models and theories, but without the use of advanced mathematics. Almost everything that can be derived by elementary algebra is so derived. The rudiments of analytical geometry and trigonometry are used sparingly, but calculus and advanced analysis are almost entirely avoided. Some elements of matrix algebra are used extensively, but these are discussed explicitly in Chapter III. Propositions requiring more mathematics than we have assumed or presented are merely stated without proof, and acknowledged to be beyond the scope of our treatment.

We begin with a description of Spearman-type procedures. All of the necessary theorems can be derived by elementary algebra, which clarifies basic concepts and definitions. Back-references are inserted later wherever appropriate, to show how modern methods are related to these earlier methods.

Computational procedures are treated in some detail along with discussions of theory. It is our belief that the student should not use an electronic computer to solve a large factor-analysis problem until he has solved a similar but much smaller problem using a hand or desk calculator. This requires him to go through all the successive steps in logical order, entering all of the intermediate results on a work sheet. Procedures for the reduction of overflow and rounding error when using an electronic computer are described. Sources of computer programs for factor analysis, including a complete set based on the procedures discussed in this book, are given in Appendix 2.

Materials for students' practice are of two types. Each *problem* is complete in itself and in most cases short. *Exercises,* on the other hand, are usually longer, and come in series. The data for some of the later ones come from the solutions of earlier ones. Hence the writers assume that all or almost all exercises will be assigned. Problems and exercises are more numerous in the earlier chapters than in the later ones.

For illustrative examples and for exercises we have used only a few very simple sets of data, and most of these have been used over and over. Thus the student should come to see how the same data can be analyzed in a number of different ways.

We are indebted to the many factor-analysts whose published works we have consulted in the preparation of this book: most particularly to the late Louis Leon Thurstone, whose basic viewpoints we share. Several generations of graduate students have used earlier drafts of this book as texts, and their comments and questions have led to improvements in the treatment of a number of topics. Henry F. Kaiser, Bert F. Green, Jr., and Louise Witmer Cureton read the entire manuscript and made a host of valuable suggestions leading to considerable revision of the original manuscript. Not all of their suggestions were incorporated, however, and we take full responsibility for the contents of this book.

We are grateful to a number of publishers for permission to reprint tables and portions of tables of correlations for use as examples, exercises, and problems: the American Association for the Advancement of Science (and Henryk Misiak), the American Institutes for Research, the Institute of Mathematical Statistics, The Psychological Corporation, the Psychometric Society, and The University of Chicago Press. The use of data from two unclassified reports from the Department of the Army is also acknowledged. We appreciate permission of Roger K. Blashfield to quote from a letter to the senior author some remarks on the literature of cluster analysis.

Some of the procedures of factor analysis (and cluster analysis) described in this book were developed in connection with substantive as well as theoretical studies by Louise Witmer Cureton and Edward E. Cureton, supported by Grant No. MH-07274 from the National Institute of Mental Health to the American Institutes for Research, by Contract No. OE-6-10-065 between the U.S. Office of Education and the American Institutes for Research and the School of Education, University of Pittsburgh, and by Grant No. GJ-36029 from the National Science Foundation to the University of Tennessee.

We acknowledge with thanks computer services supplied by the University of Tennessee Computing Center and the Oak Ridge National Laboratory, the programming services and computer-use supervision of Richard C. Durfee and Virginia Patterson, and the clerical assistance and duplicating services of the Department of Psychology, University of Tennessee. We are indebted for the typing of several drafts to Gail Brown, Evelyn Ottaway, Lyn Simmons, and especially Jerry Warwick, who typed the final draft.

We wish to thank our wives for their support, encouragement, and forbearance during the writing and revision of this book.

Edward E. Cureton
Ralph B. D'Agostino

49   Last line: (N = 84) should be (N = 841).

80   3 lines up: $1\sigma_1$ should be $1/\sigma_1$.

81   Right hand equation in third row of matrices:

$(BA)' = AB$ should be $(BA)' = AB$

$$\begin{bmatrix} 5 & 5 \\ 9 & 8 \end{bmatrix} = AB \qquad \begin{bmatrix} 5 & 5 \\ 9 & 8 \end{bmatrix} = AB$$

98   Formula at top should be preceded by equal sign.

99   Eq (3-28): $\sum_{j=1}^{p} d_{ij} c_{ih}$ should be $\sum_{j=1}^{p} d_{ij} c_{jh}$

108 Table 4.1, last panel: line under X should be removed and X = should be moved further to right.

119 Eq (4-26): Last number at lower right should be .2 not .3.

276 Table 10.3, panel 2, eq (1), col Σ: 1.3075 should be 1.3076.

276 Table 10.3, test (11), col V_{33}: .058 should be $-.058$.

282 Table 11.1, test (7), col II of Matrix $P = VD^{-1}$: .275) should be .275.

282 Table 11.1, last section, panel 1, eq (2), col Σ + 1: $-.1.8110$ should be -1.8110.

303 Table 12.2 (continued), second panel, row (3), col (5): = .041 should be $-.041$.

323 Table 12.5, fourth line from bottom, col (3): $1/\sqrt{\Sigma^{2b}}$ should be $1/\sqrt{\Sigma^{2b}}$ with b referring to footnote b.

331 Line 7 up: $r = r_2|$ should be $|r = r_2|$.

349 Formula (14-1), numerator: $\overline{nh^2}$ should be $n\overline{h^2}$.

391 Formula (16-2): letters l in denominator should be script ℓs as in numerator and in first line of following text.

404 Line 2 up: $\bar{r}^2$ = .1945 should be $\overline{r^2}$ = .1945 and $\bar{r}^2 - \bar{r}^2 = ...$ should be $\overline{r^2} - \bar{r}^2 = ...$

426 Fig. P8.3:1: vertical axis should be labelled w_i.

433 Last panel, row (3), col (6): #.122 should be +.122.

434 First panel, row (3), col (5) (Refl 2): #.043 should be +.043.

434 First panel, row (4), col (5) (Refl 2): +.087 should be #.087.

434 First panel, row (5), col (4) (Refl 1): +.087 should be #.087.

438 Third table heading, first letter: italic p should be Greek ϱ (rho).

440 Line 4: 1982 should be 1983.

443 Cureton, E. E. Studies of the Promax....: 1976, 4 should be 1976,11.

1 Introduction and Spearman Approach

1.1 INTRODUCTION

Factor analysis consists of a collection of procedures for analyzing the relations among a set of random variables observed or counted or measured for each individual of a group.

An *individual* may be a person, some other organism, an object, or in general any entity. The *group* consists of one class of such entities, for example, sixth-grade pupils, college students, members of a legislative body, a particular species, white rats of a given strain, plots of ground in a forest or field, counties in a state or nation, or boxes. It may be a *population* (*all* entities of the defined class) or more commonly a *sample* from such a defined population.

The *random variables* of the set to be analyzed may consist of any attributes on which the members of the group differ. For example, with groups of humans the random variables may be sex, age, vote (yes or no) on an issue, time to solve a particular problem, height, weight, or score on an aptitude, personality, or educational achievement test. With agricultural problems the group may consist of counties, and the random variables may be average yields per acre of different crops. With botanical problems the groups may be plots in different kinds of terrain, and the random variables may be numbers of plants of different species per plot. In experimental psychology, the group may consist of white rats, and the random variables may be the number of seconds required to solve each of a number of problems using different types of apparatus. For a group consisting of a collection of boxes, the random variables might be perimeters (of top, side, and end), diagonals (of top, side, and end), squares (of length, width, and height),

1

and the like. For a factor analysis, *several* different random variables must be observed or counted or measured for each member of the group.

Because factor analysis deals with the *relations* among the random variables, we must first obtain a *score* on each variable, and then compute the *correlation* between the scores on each pair of variables. Two-point variables are scored arbitrarily by assigning the number 0 or 1 to each individual of the group, for example, 0 for no or 1 for yes on a vote; and 0 for failure or 1 for success with a problem. The number of plants of a particular species found in a plot is recorded directly as a score. Average yields are often scored as bushels per acre. Age may be scored in years (for adults), in months (for children), or in weeks or even days (for infants or small animals). Aptitude and achievement test scores are usually the number of right answers, or perhaps the number right minus a fraction of the number wrong, to minimize the effects of differences in guessing tendency on scores that are intended to represent aptitude or achievement. Height may be scored in centimeters or inches; weight in pounds or grams. Measures of boxes (perimeter, diagonal of top, and the like) will also be scored in centimeters or inches.

In the case of ordered categories (e.g., strongly agree, agree, neutral, disagree, or strongly disagree with a proposition), the assignment of the scores 5, 4, 3, 2, 1 may be insufficient. In this case, substitution of normalized standard scores is recommended. And in general, wherever the distribution of a set of raw scores is substantially skewed, substitution of either normalized standard scores or ranks is recommended (Section 4.6.1).

The scores on any variable will be treated as interval-scale measurements, that is, as measurements whose successive scale-intervals are equal, as are inches or pounds, even though they may in fact be scores on variables whose units are larger at the extremes than near the middle. With such scores, as with ranks, Baker, Hardyck, and Petrinovich (1966) have shown that normalization is unnecessary; and ranking, where this can be done without many ties and particularly without any large multiple ties, may be acceptable as an approximation, to substitute for normalization in order to get rid of skewness.

The original variables, representing actual observations or counts or measurements, are termed the *manifest variables*. Historically, the first manifest variables to be studied by the methods of factor analysis were psychological and educational test scores. We use the terms "variable" and "test" (often interchangeably) throughout this book rather than the more cumbersome "manifest variable."

The purpose of a factor analysis is to account for the *intercorrelations* among *n* variables, by postulating a set of *common factors,* considerably fewer in number than the number, *n,* of these variables. There will also be *n unique factors,* one for each variable, which do not help to account for the intercorrelations, but which do help to account for the fact that these intercorrelations are less than unity.

The *factors* are random variables that cannot be observed or counted or measured directly, but which are presumed to exist in the population and hence in the experimental sample. They, as well as the manifest variables, are presumed to vary from individual to individual. Because they are not observed or counted or measured directly, they are sometimes termed *latent variables*. We use the term "factors" to designate latent variables; the term "variable" (or "test") will *always* designate a manifest variable. The factors are actually hypothetical or explanatory *constructs*. Their reality in the individuals of the population or sample is always open to argument. At the conclusion of a factor analysis we can only say of the factors that *if* they were real, *then* they would account for the correlations found in the sample. The converse does not necessarily follow, and different sets of factors can account for the same set of observed or counted or measured variables and their intercorrelations.

1.1.1 Interpretation of Factors

In a factor analysis, interest centers mainly on the common factors, which are interpreted with reference to the observed or counted or measured variables. The unique factor in each variable is merely whatever part of that variable is uncorrelated with all the other variables in the experimental battery (the total collection of observed variables), including its error of measurement. If to an original set of variables others are added, part of the unique factor in one of the original variables may become a common factor that it shares with one or more of the added variables.

If the variables are psychological and/or educational tests, the common factors will be interpreted as the principal underlying abilities. Examples are verbal comprehension, numerical ability, abstract reasoning ability, visual space manipulatory ability, knowledge of the natural sciences, knowledge of the social sciences, and mathematical knowledge and ability.

If the variables are athletic and gymnastic measures, the common factors will be such things as static strength (as in chinning or push-ups), explosive strength (as in hitting or jumping), speed of movement, eye–hand coordination, endurance, and the like.

If the variables are the items of an opinion questionnaire, the common factors will be the main underlying attitudes.

If the variables are the record votes of members of a legislative body, the common factors will again be the underlying attitudes, such as attitudes toward agricultural issues, monetary issues, social-service issues, big-business issues, foreign-policy issues, and economic issues. Each of these attitudes will run on a scale from conservative to liberal, and they will be more or less distinct. Descriptions of legislators on a single scale, running from conservative through middle-of-the-road to liberal, will be found to be too simplistic. The most pervasive "attitude" is likely to be party membership.

If the variables are yields per acre of various crops, the common factors will be such things as grains, fruits, vegetables, and the like.

The variables may be such things as complex measurements of a collection of boxes, for example:

(1) Perimeters (of top, side, end)
(2) Diagonals (of top, side, end)
(3) Squares (of length, width, height)
(4) Logarithms (of length, width, height)
(5) Squares of diagonals (of top, side, end)
(6) Volume
(7) Longest diagonal (from northwest top corner to southeast bottom corner)

In this case the common factors will be length, width, and height in relative terms, with a general factor interpretable as *size*, best represented by volume and longest diagonal but not identical with either.

If the variables are the items of a self-description personality inventory, the common factors will be the major underlying *personality traits*, such as aggressiveness–submissiveness, introversion–extraversion, stolidity–ebullience, self-assurance–anxiety, and so on.

1.1.2 Example

A simple example illustrates the problem of factor analysis and the point that different sets of postulated factors, based on different assumptions, may account equally well for the same set of intercorrelations. As a part of a large study, Thurstone and Thurstone (1941),[1] gave to 710 eighth-grade children in 15 Chicago elementary schools the following four tests (along with 59 others):

(1) Sentence Reading
(2) Paragraph Reading
(3) Multiplication
(4) Addition

The intercorrelations were

$$r_{12} = .68 \qquad r_{14} = .18 \qquad r_{24} = .19$$

$$r_{13} = .17 \qquad r_{23} = .16 \qquad r_{34} = .50$$

Inspection shows immediately that r_{12} and r_{34} are larger than the other intercorrelations. Looking back at the tests we see that r_{12} is the correlation between the

---

[1]From Appendix Table 1, pp. 83–87, Thurstone and Thurstone, 1941. Copyright 1941 by The University of Chicago. Reprinted by permission.

two reading tests, and that r_{34} is the correlation between the two arithmetic tests. We can conclude at once that something we might term "reading ability" accounts for the high correlation between the sentence reading test and the paragraph reading test, that something we could call "arithmetical ability" accounts for the high correlation between the multiplication test and the addition test, and that these abilities are distinct.

Now the other four correlations, though much lower than r_{12} and r_{34}, are all positive and significantly greater than zero. How do we account for them? There are at least *four* alternative explanations:

Alternative 1. "Reading ability" and "arithmetical ability" are correlated.

Alternative 2. All four of the tests draw partly on one general ability: call it "intelligence." The two reading tests draw also on "reading ability"; the two arithmetic tests draw also on "arithmetical ability." The three factors are all uncorrelated.

Alternative 3. "Intelligence" is essentially verbal in character; reading tests draw heavily on it and arithmetic tests only slightly. "Arithmetical ability" is a special skill accounting for the high correlation between the two arithmetic tests. The two factors are uncorrelated.

Alternative 4. "Intelligence" is essentially quantitative in character; arithmetic tests draw heavily on it and reading tests only slightly. "Reading ability" is a special skill accounting for the high correlation between the two reading tests. The two factors are uncorrelated.

These four alternative explanations illustrate the point that the factors or latent variables are *never* uniquely determined by the intercorrelations among the tests or manifest variables. The factors are *constructs:* they are merely postulated in order to arrive at a reasonable explanation of the intercorrelations.

When the decision as to which alternative to use has been made, we go on to further problems. Suppose we accept Alternative 2, above. We then want answers to the following questions:

Question 1. What proportion of the score variability on each test is due to "intelligence"?

Question 2. What proportion is due to "reading ability," and what proportion to "arithmetical ability"?

Question 3. What proportion is due to factors unique to each test?

Questions such as these cannot be answered precisely from the intercorrelations among only four tests, but if each factor appears in at least three (preferably four or more) tests, they *can* be answered. Factor analysis techniques which do this will be presented as we proceed.

Problem 1.1.2:1. Gitter, D'Agostino, and Graffman (1975),[2] in a study of leadership and quality of life in the army, obtained from 130 enlisted men ratings of their satisfaction with how

---

[2]From Appendix 7, p. 63, Gitter, D'Agostino, and Graffman, 1975.

(1) Leader backs you up
(2) Leader respects you
(3) Leader keeps discipline
(4) Leader knows his job

The leader is defined as the individual who originates orders. Variables 1 and 2 are termed *consideration* variables; 3 and 4, *structure* variables. The intercorrelations were

$$r_{12} = .70 \qquad r_{14} = .31 \qquad r_{24} = .47$$

$$r_{13} = .50 \qquad r_{23} = .52 \qquad r_{34} = .61$$

Give four alternative explanations of the nature of leadership to account for these intercorrelations.

1.2   THE LINEAR MODEL

A *factor pattern* is a set of equations relating the scores on n tests to the scores on m postulated common factors ($m < n$) and n unique factors. Each test score is considered to be a *weighted sum* of the m common-factor scores and one unique-factor score; hence the term "linear model."

Let $X_1, X_2, \ldots, X_n$ represent standard scores on n manifest random variables.

Let $A, B, \ldots, M$ represent standard scores on m common factors ($m < n$).

Let $a_i, b_i, \ldots, m_i$ ($i = 1, 2, \ldots, n$) represent the weights or common-factor loadings of the n variables on the m common factors.

Let $U_1, U_2, \ldots, U_n$ represent standard scores on n unique factors.

Let $u_1, u_2, \ldots, u_n$ represent the weights or unique-factor loadings of the n variables on the n unique factors.

The generalized factor pattern of the linear model is then

$$X_1 = a_1 A + b_1 B + \ldots + m_1 M + u_1 U_1$$

$$X_2 = a_2 A + b_2 B + \ldots + m_2 M + u_2 U_2 \qquad (1\text{-}1)$$

$$X_n = a_n A + b_n B + \ldots + m_n M + u_n U_n$$

There will be a different set of scores $(X_1, X_2, \ldots, X_n; U_1, U_2, \ldots, U_n)$ for each individual of the sample. The weights or factor loadings $(a_1, a_2, \ldots, a_n; b_1, b_2, \ldots, b_n; \ldots; m_1, m_2, \ldots, m_n; u_1, u_2, \ldots, u_n)$, however, will be the same for all individuals.

If the X_i, $A, B, \ldots, M$, and the U_i form a multivariate normal system or a good approximation to such a system, the linear model is appropriate. But if some of the variables have skew distributions and/or nonlinear regressions, the linear model may be only a first approximation to some more complex model. Nonlinear and nonmetric models have been proposed, in which the variables are represented by rank orders or dichotomies (two-point variables). In this book we use only the linear model, and hence discuss only *linear* factor analysis. Ordinal and two-point data *can* be treated by linear procedures, with some restrictions, and for most types of data limitation to linear relations yields quite good approximations.

The n unique factors of (1-1) are *always* taken to be uncorrelated with one another and with the common factors. These common factors may or may not be uncorrelated. Because each unique factor is present in one and only one test, the Us in (1-1) have subscripts tying each of them to a different test. Each common factor must be present in at least two and usually more than two tests, so the common-factor scores $(A, B, \ldots, M)$ do not have subscripts. In (1-1) these common-factor scores are written as though the factors are present in all tests, but as many as $n - 2$ (usually fewer) of the a's, b's, $\ldots$, and/or m's may be zero, leaving at least two non-zero for a common factor. In this case the corresponding A's, B's, $\ldots$, and/or M's are absent from the tests on which their loadings are zero.

If a common factor is present with nonzero loadings on *all* n tests, it is termed a *general factor*. If it has nonzero loadings on two or more but fewer than all n of the tests, it is termed a *group factor*. If a group factor has nonzero loadings on only *two* tests, it is termed a *doublet*. Doublet loadings are not well determined, and doublets should be avoided as far as possible. In factor analyses with moderate to large numbers of variables, the variables should be chosen so that no two of them appear to resemble each other more closely than they resemble at least one other variable.

Because interest centers mainly on the loadings, the common *factors* are designated $a, b, \ldots, m$ (without subscripts). The common factor a has loadings $a_1, a_2, \ldots, a_n$ on the n variables, and similarly for the factors $b, \ldots, m$. The whole *set* of unique factors is designated u (without subscript), and $u_1, u_2, \ldots, u_n$ designate both the individual unique factors and their loadings, the context indicating which meaning is intended.

Problem 1.2:1. The following four equations represent a factor pattern such as (1-1), with numerical coefficients:

$$X_1 = .60A + .00B + .70C + .39U_1$$

$$X_2 = .55A + .40B + .65C + .34U_2$$

$$X_3 = .00A + .45B + .55C + .70U_3$$

$$X_4 = .00A + .35B + .75C + .56U_4$$

Which is a general factor? Which are the unique factors? Which is a doublet? Which is a group factor that is *not* a doublet?

1.3   THE PRINCIPLES OF PARSIMONY

The main objective of a factor analysis is to find the *simplest* (most parsimonious) factor pattern, among all possible patterns of the type represented by (1-1), which can account for the n $(n - 1)/2$ intercorrelations among n tests. There are several criteria of parsimony, which are usually inconsistent with one another.

Parsimony 1.   The number m of common factors should be as small as possible. According to this criterion we should eliminate Alternative 2 (a general factor plus two group factors) as an interpretation of the reading–arithmetic problem.

Parsimony 2.   The common factors should be uncorrelated. This criterion would eliminate Alternative 1 (correlated common factors) also, leaving only Alternative 3 ("intelligence" is essentially verbal) and Alternative 4 ("intelligence" is essentially quantitative). But on substantive grounds (here psychological), we might refuse to accept either Alternative 3 or Alternative 4: we might insist that so far as these data go, "intelligence" is demonstrated solely by the fact that "reading ability" and "arithmetical ability" are either correlated or the result of an additional general factor. In this case Parsimony 1 and Parsimony 2 are incompatible with each other for these data, and we must choose between Alternative 1 and Alternative 2 on other grounds.

Parsimony 3.   Each common factor should have as many zero loadings as possible, but it should have at least two and preferably three or more nonzero loadings. This eliminates Alternative 2 (a general factor plus two group factors), because one (general) factor has nonzero loadings on all n variables.

Parsimony 4.   The common factors should have minimum overlap. Two common factors have one element of overlap for every variable that has nonzero loadings on both of them. This again eliminates Alternative 2, since all group factors have total overlap with the general factor.

Having found a particular version of the linear model which accords with those principles of parsimony most acceptable to the investigator in the light of his knowledge of the nature of the variables (tests), and consistent with the experimental data (the inter-test correlations), the rest of a factor analysis consists in finding the numerical values of the loadings: $a_1, \ldots, a_n; b_1, \ldots, b_n; \ldots;$ $m_1, \ldots, m_n;$ and $u_1, \ldots, u_n$. The data are then said to have been *factor-analyzed,* or *factored.*

1.4   SPEARMAN'S THEORY

Factor analysis started with the work of Spearman (1904), who thought originally that all intercorrelations among mental tests could be explained by assuming one general factor, along with a unique factor in each test. He called this the *theory of two factors* (two factors in each test). Later it became evident that the theory of two factors did not hold generally, and he modified it to include group factors (Spearman, 1927). The postulate of a single general factor in tests of cognitive abilities is appealing because this general factor can be interpreted as "general intelligence." Spearman's theory emphasized Parsimony 2 (uncorrelated factors) first of all. He *always* postulated a general factor. He preferred solutions such as Alternative 3 or Alternative 4, with a subgroup of tests having nonzero loadings on only the general factor. But because this usually resulted in strained interpretations of the factors, he was quite willing to relax Parsimony 1 and add the general factor without reducing (by one) the number of group factors, as in Alternative 2, thus violating Parsimony 3 and Parsimony 4. In place of Parsimony 1, Parsimony 3, and Parsimony 4, he proposed these modifications:

Parsimony 1a.   The number of *group* factors should be as small as possible.

Parsimony 3a.   Each *group* factor should have as many zero loadings as possible.

Parsimony 4a.   The *group* factors should have minimum overlap among themselves.

Because correlated group factors were not allowed, some overlap among them had to be tolerated whenever necessary. The amount of overlap was reduced and in some cases eliminated, however, by the presence of a general factor.

1.5   ELEMENTARY THEOREMS[3]

We next prove some elementary theorems relating to factor patterns which include a general factor, and solve a relatively simple problem by these methods.

1.5.1   Factor Pattern and Correlation

Consider first the correlation between two tests, and assume that this correlation can be accounted for by one factor common to the two tests. There will also be one factor *unique* to each of the two tests. Then equations (1-1) reduce to

$$X_1 = a_1 A + u_1 U_1$$
$$X_2 = a_2 A + u_2 U_2 \qquad (1\text{-}2)$$

From the first of these equations,

$$\sigma_1^2 = a_1^2 \sigma_A^2 + u_1^2 \sigma_{U_1}^2 + 2 a_1 u_1 \sigma_{A U_1}. \qquad (1\text{-}3)$$

Here σ^2 with *one* subscript represents a variance (of X_1 or A or U_1), and σ with two subscripts represents a covariance, so that $\sigma_{A U_1} = r_{A U_1} \sigma_A \sigma_{U_1}$. We can

---

[3]In this section, the debt to Kelley (1928, Chapter 3) is great.

assume without loss of generality that all variables are in standard-score form (i.e., $\sigma^2 = 1$), so that

$$\sigma_1^2 = \sigma_2^2 = \sigma_A^2 = \sigma_{U_1}^2 = \sigma_{U_2}^2 = 1. \tag{1-4}$$

Also, taking square roots,

$$\sigma_1 = \sigma_2 = \sigma_A = \sigma_{U_1} = \sigma_{U_2} = 1. \tag{1-5}$$

We assume also, in accordance with the definition of unique factors, that A, U_1, and U_2 are uncorrelated, and in particular that $r_{AU_1} = \sigma_{AU_1} = 0$. Then (1-3) reduces to

$$a_1^2 + u_1^2 = 1, \tag{1-6}$$

and similarly,

$$a_2^2 + u_2^2 = 1. \tag{1-7}$$

In (1-6) and (1-7), the terms on the left are squares and are therefore intrinsically nonnegative. Hence the limits of a_1^2, a_2^2, u_1^2, and u_2^2 are 0 and 1, and the limits of a_1, a_2, u_1, and u_2 are ± 1.

From (1-2), the correlation between X_1 and X_2 is

$$r_{12} = S(a_1A + u_1U_1)(a_2A + u_2U_2)/N\sigma_1\sigma_2,$$

where S means $\sum_{1}^{N}$.[4] Expanding the numerator,

$$r_{12} = (a_1a_2SA^2 + a_1u_2SAU_2 + u_1a_2SU_1A + u_1u_2SU_1U_2)/N\sigma_1\sigma_2.$$

Carrying out the division by N,

$$r_{12} = (a_1a_2\sigma_A^2 + a_1u_2\sigma_{AU_2} + u_1a_2\sigma_{U_1A} + u_1u_2\sigma_{U_1U_2})/\sigma_1\sigma_2.$$

Because the factors are all uncorrelated, the last three terms in the numerator vanish, and by (1-4) and (1-5), $\sigma_A^2 = \sigma_1 = \sigma_2 = 1$, so

$$r_{12} = a_1a_2. \tag{1-8}$$

The reader should familiarize himself thoroughly with these preliminary derivations, because hereafter we jump directly from factor–pattern equations such as (1-2) to results such as (1-6), (1-7), and (1-8), which depend on the properties of standard scores and uncorrelated factors.

---

[4] We use S rather than Σ to denote a summation over the N values of a random variable in a sample, because in later chapters Σ is used to denote $\sum_{1}^{n}$, a summation over the n variables of a factor analysis.

1.5.2 Sample and Population

The equations in Section 1.5.1 refer ordinarily to a sample, as do most of the equations in the other sections of this book. We could instead have presented the derivations in terms of a population. In this case the σ^2's and σ's of (1-3), (1-4) and (1-5) would represent population variances, covariances, and standard deviations, and the r of (1-8) would be replaced by ρ. Also the equations following (1-7) would become

$$\rho_{12} = E(a_1 A + u_1 U_1)(a_2 A + u_2 U_2)/\sigma_1 \sigma_2$$

$$= [a_1 a_2 E(A^2) + a_1 u_2 E(AU_2) + u_1 a_2 E(U_1 A) + u_1 u_2 E(U_1 U_2)]/\sigma_1 \sigma_2$$

$$= (a_1 a_2 \sigma_A^2 + a_1 u_2 \sigma_{AU_2} + u_1 a_2 \sigma_{U_1 A} + u_1 u_2 \sigma_{U_1 U_2})/\sigma_1 \sigma_2,$$

and (1-8) would become

$$\rho_{12} = a_1 a_2.$$

The operator E (mathematical expectation) means "to average over all individuals of the population." If the population is theoretically infinite, $E(XY)$, say, would be defined as

$$E(XY) = SXY/N \text{ as } N \text{ approaches infinity.}$$

In this treatment we use a mixed (sample-population) notation, for example, in equations (1-4), (1-5), and (1-8). with r_{ij} for a correlation and σ_i^2, σ_{ij}, and σ_i for a variance, a covariance, and a standard deviation, for four reasons:

1. We regard the statistics of factor analysis primarily as a branch of descriptive statistics, with interest centering mainly on the sample, though vague generalizations to a population "such as" the individuals of the sample are not infrequently implied. Such a population is regarded as one from which the given sample might well be considered to be a *random* sample.

2. For dependable results, factor-analysis procedures require large samples, ideally samples of several hundred. Inferential procedures are used for only a few problems, and most of the formulas are large-sample approximations for which the distinctions between sample statistics and population parameters are lost, and the sample statistics are inserted into the formulas to represent the population parameters. Multivariate normal distributions of the variables are assumed, usually with little knowledge of robustness against nonnormality, in the hope that the Central Limit Theorem will prevent us from making intolerable errors by using this normality assumption. The Central Limit Theorem, roughly stated, says that the sampling distributions of most statistics approach the normal distribution as the sample size increases without limit, for almost all distributions of the variables.

3. Students with statistical backgrounds limited to one or two courses in

applied statistics may not be familiar with the notion of mathematical expectation and the use of the operator E.

4. It is conventional in factor analysis to use the symbols s and s^2 for another purpose (see Section 1.6.6).

1.5.3 Theorems on a Single Correlation Coefficient

Theorem 1.1.   The correlation between two tests can *always* be accounted for by a factor pattern with one common factor and two unique factors.

Proof.   This theorem implies the factor pattern of (1-2), and hence the results (1-6), (1-7), and (1-8). From the discussion following (1-7), the limits of a_1 and a_2 are ± 1. Hence the limits of $a_1 a_2$ are also ± 1. But from elementary correlation theory, the limits of r_{12} are also ± 1. Hence (1-8) is true for all possible values of r_{12}: the factor pattern (1-2) imposes no restriction upon its numerical value, and the theorem is proved.

The point of this theorem is that no possible value of a single correlation coefficient can be inconsistent with the assumed factor pattern (1-2), which is the simplest of all possible factor patterns.

Note also that although (1-8) gives the *product* of the two general-factor loadings, we cannot estimate separately the numerical values of a_1 and a_2 from the single correlation r_{12}, and we are therefore unable to estimate the values of u_1 and u_2 from (1-6) and (1-7). This argument proves the corollary,

Corollary 1.1.   Two variables *cannot* be factor-analyzed.

Theorem 1.2.   The correlation between two variables can *always* be accounted for by a factor pattern with one general factor and one unique factor.

Proof.   This theorem implies the factor pattern,

$$X_1 = a_1 A + u_1 U_1$$
$$X_2 = A \tag{1-9}$$

Then

$$r_{12} = r_{1A} = \frac{S(a_1 A + u_1 U_1)A}{N\sigma_1 \sigma_2}$$

$$= \frac{a_1 \sigma_A^2 + u_1 \sigma_{AU1}}{\sigma_1 \sigma_2} ,$$

$$r_{12} = r_{1A} = a_1 . \tag{1-10}$$

The limits of a_1 are ± 1, as are also the limits of r_{12}, which proves the theorem.

Problem 1.5.3:1.   Show that if

$$X_1 = a_1 A + u_1 U_1$$

$$X_2 = a_2 A$$

then $r_{12} = a_1 a_2$, and that this also proves Theorem 1.2.

1.5.4 Definition of Triad

When we have three intercorrelations among three tests (r_{12}, r_{13}, and r_{23}), we define three triads as follows:

$$t_{123} = r_{12} r_{13} / r_{23}$$

$$t_{213} = r_{12} r_{23} / r_{13} \qquad\qquad (1\text{-}11)$$

$$t_{312} = r_{13} r_{23} / r_{12}$$

The first subscript of each triad designates the variable that is present in both numerator correlations and absent in the denominator correlation. The order of the second and third subscripts is immaterial: we arbitrarily write first the one that is numerically smaller.

1.5.5 Theorems on Triads

We next proceed to prove several additional theorems. The "if" part of the statement of each theorem implies a factor pattern, and from this factor pattern we derive the relations that must hold among the correlation coefficients, as stated in the "then" part of the statement. When, in a set of actual data, the derived "then" relations do *not* hold, the factor pattern is inadequate, and we must try a more complicated pattern.

Theorem 1.3.   *If* the correlations among three tests can be accounted for by a factor pattern with one general factor and three unique factors, *then* all three triads must be positive or zero and not greater than unity.

Proof.   From the "if" part of the statement the factor pattern is

$$X_1 = a_1 A + u_1 U_1$$

$$X_2 = a_2 A + u_2 U_2 \qquad\qquad (1\text{-}12)$$

$$X_3 = a_3 A + u_3 U_3$$

Then from the argument leading to (1-8),

$$r_{12} = a_1 a_2$$

$$r_{13} = a_1 a_3 \qquad\qquad (1\text{-}13)$$

$$r_{23} = a_2 a_3$$

Substituting from (1-13) into (1-11),

$$t_{123} = a_1^2 a_2 a_3 / a_2 a_3 = a_1^2$$

$$t_{213} = a_1 a_2^2 a_3 / a_1 a_3 = a_2^2 \qquad (1\text{-}14)$$

$$t_{312} = a_1 a_2 a_3^2 / a_1 a_2 = a_3^2$$

From (1-14) it is clear that all three triads must be positive or zero, because each one is equal to an a^2, which is intrinsically nonnegative. Each a^2, moreover, must have limits 0 and 1 by the argument following (1-7), and the theorem is proved.

Theorem 1.3 provides *boundary conditions* for the factor pattern (1-12), and they are *weak* boundary conditions. In actual data the intercorrelations among almost *any* three tests lead to triads all of which are nonnegative and not greater than unity.

Theorem 1.4. If the correlations among three tests can be accounted for by a factor pattern with one general factor and three unique factors, *then* the general-factor loadings are the square roots of the corresponding triads.

Proof. The triad *corresponding* to each test is the one whose first subscript is the same as that of the test. The "if" part of Theorem 1.4 implies that of Theorem 1.3, and hence that (1-14) holds. The a's are the square roots of the a^2's of (1-14), which proves Theorem 1.4, apart from the signs.

The signs of the a-factor loadings are obtained as follows:

1. If all three correlations in (1-13) are positive, the signs of all three a-factor loadings are positive.

2. If two correlations are negative and one is positive, the three triads will be positive. From (1-13), we can have two negative correlations and one positive correlation if either one or two of the a's are negative. We assume that only one a is negative,[5] then the two positive a's are those whose subscripts are the same as the subscripts of the positive correlation. All unique-factor loadings are arbitrarily taken to be positive.[5]

A positive triad cannot be made from two positive correlations and one negative correlation, nor from three negative correlations: these combinations violate the first boundary condition of Theorem 1.3 (all traids positive or zero), and Theorem 1.4 does not hold.

Theorem 1.5. If the correlations among three tests can be accounted for by a factor pattern with one general factor and three unique factors, *then* the correlations between the general factor and the tests are the square roots of the corresponding triads.

Proof.

$$r_{1A} = \frac{S(a_1 A + u_1 U_1)A}{N\sigma_1 \sigma_A} = \frac{a_1 \sigma_A^2 + u_1 \sigma_{AU_1}}{\sigma_1 \sigma_A}.$$

---

[5]Quite generally, when the signs of the factor loadings are not determined by the data, we assume a pattern that maximizes the number of positive loadings.

All variances and standard deviations are unity, and $\sigma_{AU_1} = 0$, so $r_{1A} = a_1$, and similarly $r_{2A} = a_2$ and $r_{3A} = a_3$. The "if" part of Theorem 1.5 implies the "if" part of Theorem 1.3 and hence (1-14), from which each a is the square root of the corresponding triad, and Theorem 1.5 is proved. The signs of r_{1A}, r_{2A} and r_{3A} are taken to be the same as those of a_1, a_2, and a_3.

Quite generally, when factors are uncorrelated, the loadings of the variables on a common (here general) factor are *both* the coefficients of the common factor in the factor pattern [(1-1) or here (1-12)] *and* the correlations between the tests and the common factor. If we have two or more *correlated* common factors, the coefficients of a common factor in the factor pattern and the correlations between the tests and that common factor are different. This case is treated in later chapters. The elementary Spearman-type procedures considered in this chapter deal only with uncorrelated common factors. Because unique factors are uncorrelated both with one another and with the common factors, their loadings are always both pattern coefficients and correlations with the corresponding tests.

Theorem 1.6. If the correlations among three tests can be accounted for by a factor pattern with one general factor and three unique factors, *then* the proportion of the variance of each test which is due to the general factor is equal to the corresponding triad.

Proof. The "if" part of Theorem 1.6 implies that of Theorem 1.3, and hence (1-12) and (1-14). From (1-12), by the argument leading to (1-6) and (1-7),

$$a_1^2 + u_1^2 = 1$$
$$a_2^2 + u_2^2 = 1$$
$$a_3^2 + u_3^2 = 1$$

In each of these equations a_i^2 is the proportion of the variance of test i which is due to the general factor, and by (1-14) this is equal to the corresponding triad, which proves the theorem.

When we have the numerical values of the a^2's, we find at once from these equations,

$$u_1 = \sqrt{1 - a_1^2}$$
$$u_2 = \sqrt{1 - a_2^2} \tag{1-15}$$
$$u_3 = \sqrt{1 - a_3^2}$$

Problem 1.5.5:1. For the following set of three correlations, $r_{12} = .16$, $r_{13} = .08$, $r_{23} = .32$, compute the triads, t_{123}, t_{213}, and t_{312}. Verify that Theorem 1.3 is satisfied, compute a_1, a_2, and a_3 by Theorem 1.4, and then compute u_1, u_2, and u_3 by (1-15).

1.5.6 Tests of Significance for Triads

A triad computed from a sample may be negative or greater than unity due merely to sampling error, in which case the boundary conditions of Theorem 1.3 are not violated. In testing significance, however, we should be *very* conservative, because the theorem asserts a null hypothesis, and we must *accept* this null hypothesis rather than reject it when the computed value of the triad lies outside of but close to the theoretical limits 0 or 1. For this reason we recommend that the tests of significance be made at the one-sided .20 level rather than at some lower level, making it harder to accept the null hypothesis when it is really false.

If the population value corresponding to $t_{123} = r_{12}r_{13}/r_{23}$ is 0, either r_{12} or r_{13} (or both) must differ only randomly from 0, and we test this hypothesis only if the computed value of t_{123} is negative and of small magnitude. To make the test, we select r_{12} or r_{13}, whichever is smaller in absolute value, and perform the t-test.

$$t_r = |r| \sqrt{(N - 2)/(1 - r^2)} \qquad (DF = N - 2). \qquad (1\text{-}16)$$

The null hypothesis (and Theorem 1.3) is accepted if the value of t_r is *not* significant at the one-sided .20 level. If N is large (say $N > 122$), we accept the hypothesis if the value of t_r is less than .8416. If $N \leq 122$, we will use that column of the t-table whose bottom entry (t_∞) is .8416 (or .842), and use instead of .8416 the entry at $N - 2$ degrees of freedom as the critical value.

To test the hypothesis that the population value of $t_{123} = 1$ against the one-sided alternative that $t_{123} > 1$, we note that if $r_{12}r_{13}/r_{23} > 1$ and r_{23} is positive, then $r_{23} - r_{12}r_{13} < 0$. If $t_{123} > 1$ and r_{23} is negative, then r_{12} or r_{13} (but not both) must also be negative, and in this case $-(r_{23} - r_{12}r_{13}) < 0$. But $r_{23} - r_{12}r_{13}$, or $-(r_{23} - r_{12}r_{13})$, is the numerator of the partial correlation $r_{23\cdot1}$, and vanishes with this partial correlation. To perform the test, therefore, we compute the partial correlation by the usual formula,

$$r_{23\cdot1} = \frac{r_{23} - r_{12}r_{13}}{\sqrt{(1 - r_{12}^2)(1 - r_{13}^2)}} \, .$$

The t-test for significance is then

$$t_{r_{23\cdot1}} = |r_{23\cdot1}| \sqrt{(N - 3)/(1 - r_{23\cdot1}^2)} \qquad (DF = N - 3), \qquad (1\text{-}17)$$

and we test the hypothesis that $r_{23\cdot1} = 0$ against the one-sided alternative that $r_{23\cdot1}$ is negative if r_{23} is positive, or that $r_{23\cdot1}$ is positive if r_{23} is negative. As in the previous test, we accept the null hypothesis (and conclude that t_{123} is not significantly greater than unity) if $t_{r_{23\cdot1}} < .8416$, or is less than the tabled value of t at $(N - 3)$ DF in the column of the t-table whose bottom entry is $t = .8416$ (or $.842$) if $N \leq 123$. This is again the one-sided $.20$ significance level.

1.5.7 The Tetrads

We consider next the case of *four* tests and one common (general) factor.

Theorem 1.7. *If* the correlations among four tests can be accounted for by a factor pattern with one general factor and four unique factors, *then* $r_{12}r_{34} = r_{13}r_{24} = r_{14}r_{23}$.

Proof. The "if" part of this statement implies the factor pattern,

$$
\begin{aligned}
X_1 &= a_1 A + u_1 U_1 \\
X_2 &= a_2 A + u_2 U_2 \\
X_3 &= a_3 A + u_3 U_3 \\
X_4 &= a_4 A + u_4 U_4
\end{aligned}
\tag{1-18}
$$

The correlations, by the argument leading to (1-8), are

$$
\begin{array}{ll}
r_{12} = a_1 a_2 & r_{23} = a_2 a_3 \\
r_{13} = a_1 a_3 & r_{24} = a_2 a_4 \\
r_{14} = a_1 a_4 & r_{34} = a_3 a_4
\end{array}
\tag{1-19}
$$

and

$$
r_{12}r_{34} = r_{13}r_{24} = r_{14}r_{23} = a_1 a_2 a_3 a_4,
\tag{1-20}
$$

which proves the theorem.

From the first three terms of (1-20), we can form the three *tetrad differences* (commonly shortened to *tetrads*),

$$
\begin{aligned}
t_{1234} &= r_{12}r_{34} - r_{13}r_{24} \\
t_{1243} &= r_{12}r_{34} - r_{14}r_{23} \\
t_{1342} &= r_{13}r_{24} - r_{14}r_{23}
\end{aligned}
\tag{1-21}
$$

and all three will equal zero if Theorem 1.7 holds. Three more tetrads could be formed also, but each of them would be merely the negative of one of the equations (1-21), for example, $t_{1324} = r_{13}r_{24} - r_{12}r_{34} = -t_{1234}$.

Each tetrad is the product of the r's defined by its *end pairs* of subscripts (r_{12} and r_{34} for t_{1234}), minus the product of the correlations defined by its *alternate pairs* of subscripts (r_{13} and r_{24} for t_{1234}).

If we subtract the first of equations (1-21) from the second, we obtain the third. If we add the first to the third, we obtain the second. And if we subtract the third from the second we obtain the first. Hence any two of equations (1-21) are *linearly independent,*[6] while the other is not. These equations provide two linearly independent explicit conditions for the adequacy of the factor pattern (1-18); it is *adequate* if any *two* of them equal zero (within sampling error).

When the tetrad criterion is satisfied we can form from (1-19), using (1-11) and (1-14), the triads,

$$t_{123} = t_{124} = t_{134} = a_1^2$$

$$t_{213} = t_{214} = t_{234} = a_2^2$$

$$t_{312} = t_{314} = t_{324} = a_3^2 \qquad (1\text{-}22)$$

$$t_{412} = t_{413} = t_{423} = a_4^2$$

The three estimates of each of the four a^2 values are linearly independent, because the denominator of each of the three triads is a correlation that does not appear in either of the other two. Hence each a^2 is *overdetermined* by the data, and we can improve the accuracy of estimation by averaging the numerical values of the three triads.

> **Problem 1.5.7:1.** Verify that the conditions of Theorem 1.7 hold by computing tetrads by formula (1-21), and find the a's and u's by (1-14) and (1-15) for the set of correlations,
>
> $r_{12} = .400 \qquad r_{14} = .150 \qquad r_{24} = .150$
>
> $r_{13} = .200 \qquad r_{23} = .200 \qquad r_{34} = .075$
>
> Note that for each a^2 we have *three* triads, for example, $a_1^2 = t_{123} = t_{124} = t_{134}$.

1.5.8 Negative Triads; Heywood Case

Occasionally a case arises in which Theorem 1.7 holds but the conditions of Theorem 1.3 do not. Thus if r_{12} and r_{34} are negative while r_{13}, r_{14}, r_{23}, and r_{24} are positive, Theorem 1.7 can hold if the numerical values of the correlations are appropriate, but t_{123} ($= r_{12}r_{13}/r_{23}$) will be negative, contrary to Theorem 1.3. For example,

$$r_{12} = -.20 \qquad r_{23} = .20 \qquad r_{12}r_{34} = r_{13}r_{24} = r_{14}r_{23} = .08$$

$$r_{13} = .25 \qquad r_{24} = .32$$

$$r_{14} = .40 \qquad r_{34} = -.40 \qquad t_{123} = t_{124} = t_{134} = -.25$$

---

[6]Two or more equations are linearly independent if no one of them is a multiple or fraction of any other, and if no one of them can be formed from some or all of the others by multiplying or dividing each of these others by *any* positive or negative constant (usually a different constant for each of the others), and then adding them algebraically.

In this example, in fact, all 12 of the triads are negative.

There are also combinations of numerical values of the correlations which will satisfy Theorem 1.7 but will yield one set of three equal triads greater than unity (the so-called *Heywood case;* Heywood, 1931), again contrary to Theorem 1.3. One such set is as follows:

$$r_{12} = .945 \qquad r_{23} = .720 \qquad t_{123} = t_{124} = t_{134} = 1.1025$$

$$r_{13} = .840 \qquad r_{24} = .630 \qquad t_{213} = t_{214} = t_{234} = .81$$

$$r_{14} = .735 \qquad r_{34} = .560 \qquad t_{312} = t_{314} = t_{324} = .64$$

$$t_{412} = t_{413} = t_{423} = .49$$

$$r_{12}r_{34} = r_{13}r_{24} = r_{14}r_{23} = .5292$$

Hence before we can be sure that the model of (1-18) is acceptable, we should compute the values of the three tetrads by (1-21), check this computation by adding the first and third to obtain the second, see that none of them is significantly different from zero (Section 1.6.1), compute the 12 triads indicated by (1-22), and check to be sure that all of them are positive and not greater than unity. For example,

$$r_{12} = -.72 \qquad r_{23} = -.56$$

$$r_{13} = .63 \qquad r_{24} = -.48$$

$$r_{14} = .54 \qquad r_{34} = .42$$

$$r_{12}r_{34} = r_{13}r_{24} = r_{14}r_{23} = -.3024,$$

and all three tetrads are exactly zero. The triads, and the positive correlations entering into each of them, are

$t_{123} = .81$	$t_{213} = .64$	$t_{312} = .49$	$t_{412} = .36$
$(r_{13}\ +)$	$(r_{13}\ +)$	$(r_{13}\ +)$	$(r_{14}\ +)$
$t_{124} = .81$	$t_{214} = .64$	$t_{314} = .49$	$t_{413} = .36$
$(r_{14}\ +)$	$(r_{14}\ +)$	(all r's +)	(all r's +)
$t_{134} = .81$	$t_{234} = .64$	$t_{324} = .49$	$t_{423} = .36$
(all r's +)	$(r_{34}\ +)$	$(r_{34}\ +)$	$(r_{34}\ +)$

In each column, the same triads have the same first subscript, so

$$a_1^2 = .81 \qquad a_2^2 = .64 \qquad a_3^2 = .49 \qquad a_4^2 = .36$$

In columns 1, 3, and 4, above, the first subscript of each triad appears in the positive correlation in its formula (1-22). Hence a_1, a_3, and a_4 are positive. In column 2, the first subscript of each triad does *not* appear in the positive correlation in its formula, so a_2 is negative (recall part 2 of proof of Theorem 1.4). Then

$$a_1 = .9 \qquad a_2 = -.8 \qquad a_3 = .7 \qquad a_4 = .6$$

Problem 1.5.8:1. Verify that the conditions of Theorem 1.7 hold by computing tetrads by (1-21), and find the a's and u's by (1-14) and (1-15) for the set of correlations,

$$r_{12} = .18 \qquad r_{14} = -.15 \qquad r_{24} = -.30$$

$$r_{13} = -.12 \qquad r_{23} = -.24 \qquad r_{34} = .20$$

Note that the method of allocating signs to the a's used in the immediately preceding example breaks down. Noting that $r_{ij} = a_i a_j$ for every i and j, allocate signs to the a's in such a manner that all the correlations have the correct signs. You will find that this can be done in two different ways.

1.5.9 Limiting Conditions

When we seek to account for the intercorrelations among n tests by postulating one general factor and n unique factors, all uncorrelated, we obtain no limiting conditions when $n = 2$ (Theorem 1.1); and from equation (1-8) we can estimate the product $a_1 a_2$; but there is no way to estimate a_1 and a_2 separately. Theorem 1.2 is trivial, for every test has a unique factor.

When $n = 3$ we obtain three weak boundary conditions by Theorem 1.3, and a single explicit estimate of the numerical value of each factor loading by (1-14).

When $n = 4$ we obtain three *explicit* conditions for the applicability of the postulated factor pattern by Theorem 1.7 (two of which are linearly independent) and twelve *boundary* conditions (four sets of three each) by Throem 1.3. If these conditions are met, we also obtain three linearly independent explicit estimates of the numerical value of each factor loading by (1-22) and (1-14).

Mathematically, both the boundary conditions of Theorem 1.3 and the explicit conditions of Theorem 1.7 are *necessary* conditions for the postulated model of (1-18), but whether or not they are together *sufficient* conditions is not apparent, though it seems probable that they are. It is of course always possible to postulate more complicated factor patterns which are consistent with the data.

1.5.10 Theorem on Group Factors

Theorem 1.8. *If* the correlations among four tests can be accounted for by a factor pattern with one general factor, a group factor in X_1 and X_2 *or* in X_3 and X_4 *or* in both of these pairs, and four unique factors, *then* $t_{1234} = t_{1243} \neq 0$, *and* $t_{1342} = 0$.

Proof. The "if" part of this statement implies any one of three factor patterns,

Pattern I	Pattern II	Pattern III

$$X_1 = a_1A + b_1B + u_1U_1 \qquad X_1 = a_1A \qquad\quad + u_1U_1 \qquad X_1 = a_1A + b_1B + u_1U_1$$
$$X_2 = a_2A + b_2B + u_2U_2 \qquad X_2 = a_2A \qquad\quad + u_2U_2 \qquad X_2 = a_2A + b_2B + u_2U_2$$
$$X_3 = a_3A \qquad\;\; + u_3U_3 \qquad X_3 = a_3A + c_3C + u_3U_3 \qquad X_3 = a_3A + c_3C + u_3U_3$$
$$X_4 = a_4A \qquad\;\; + u_4U_4 \qquad X_4 = a_4A + c_4C + u_4U_4 \qquad X_4 = a_4A + c_4C + u_4U_4$$

$$(1\text{-}23)$$

From these patterns the correlations, by arguments analogous to the one leading to (1-8) near the end of Section 1.5.1, are

Pattern I	Pattern II	Pattern III

$$r_{12} = a_1a_2 + b_1b_2 \qquad\qquad r_{12} = a_1a_2 \qquad\qquad\qquad r_{12} = a_1a_2 + b_1b_2$$
$$r_{13} = a_1a_3 \qquad\qquad\qquad\; r_{13} = a_1a_3 \qquad\qquad\qquad r_{13} = a_1a_3$$
$$r_{14} = a_1a_4 \qquad\qquad\qquad\; r_{14} = a_1a_4 \qquad\qquad\qquad r_{14} = a_1a_4$$
$$r_{23} = a_2a_3 \qquad\qquad\qquad\; r_{23} = a_2a_3 \qquad\qquad\qquad r_{23} = a_2a_3 \qquad (1\text{-}24)$$
$$r_{24} = a_2a_4 \qquad\qquad\qquad\; r_{24} = a_2a_4 \qquad\qquad\qquad r_{24} = a_2a_4$$
$$r_{34} = a_3a_4 \qquad\qquad\qquad\; r_{34} = a_3a_4 + c_3c_4 \qquad\qquad r_{34} = a_3a_4 + c_3c_4$$

From these correlations and equations (1-21), we have:

Tetrad	Pattern I	Pattern II	Pattern III
t_{1234}	$b_1b_2a_3a_4$	$a_1a_2c_3c_4$	$a_1a_2c_3c_4 + b_1b_2a_3a_4 + b_1b_2c_3c_4$
t_{1243}	$b_1b_2a_3a_4$	$a_1a_2c_3c_4$	$a_1a_2c_3c_4 + b_1b_2a_3a_4 + b_1b_2c_3c_4$ (1-25)
t_{1342}	0	0	0

Thus from each pattern we see that $t_{1234} = t_{1243}$ and $t_{1342} = 0$, which proves the theorem. When these relations are found among the tetrads, we know that there is at least one group factor of *extent* 2 (having nonzero loadings for two tests), and that its nonzero loadings are in tests 1 and 2 or tests 3 and 4, or that there are two such group factors, one with nonzero loadings in tests 1 and 2 and the other with nonzero loadings in tests 3 and 4. The tetrads of only four tests do not provide the information necessary for distinguishing among these three alternative patterns.

An obvious example of Theorem 1.8 is the one used previously, based on the Thurstones' data (Section 1.1.2). Here

$$t_{1234} = r_{12}r_{34} - r_{13}r_{24} = (.68)(.50) - (.17)(.19) = .3077 \doteq .31$$

$$t_{1243} = r_{12}r_{34} - r_{14}r_{23} = (.68)(.50) - (.18)(.16) = .3112 \doteq .31$$

$$t_{1342} = r_{13}r_{24} - r_{14}r_{23} = (.17)(.19) - (.18)(.16) = .0035 \doteq .00$$

Note that the two "equal" tetrads need be near-equal only in absolute value. If in this example we merely interchange the variable-numbers of tests 2 and 3, the intercorrelations become

$$r_{12} = .17 \qquad r_{14} = .18 \qquad r_{24} = .50$$

$$r_{13} = .68 \qquad r_{23} = .16 \qquad r_{34} = .19$$

The tetrads are then

$$t_{1234} = r_{12}r_{34} - r_{13}r_{24} = (.17)(.19) - (.68)(.50) = -.3077$$

$$t_{1243} = r_{12}r_{34} - r_{14}r_{23} = (.17)(.19) - (.18)(.16) = .0035$$

$$t_{1342} = r_{13}r_{24} - r_{14}r_{23} = (.68)(.50) - (.18)(.16) = .3112$$

The two "equal" tetrads now have opposite signs. The rule, $t_{1234} + t_{1342} = t_{1243}$, still holds for the three tetrads *with* their signs.

Problem 1.5.10:1. Prove that if the intercorrelations among four tests can be accounted for by a factor pattern with one general factor, one group factor in tests 1, 2, and 3, and four unique factors, then $t_{1234} = a_3a_4b_1b_2 - a_2a_4b_1b_3$, $t_{1243} = a_3a_4b_1b_2 - a_1a_4b_2b_3$, $t_{1342} = a_2a_4b_1b_3 - a_1a_4b_2b_3$, and that no one of these tetrads will necessarily equal zero.

1.6 TETRAD-TRIAD ANALYSIS

A method of factor analysis based on the theorems of the previous section will be illustrated with a five-test problem. Note that each theorem applies to *any* two, three, or four tests, regardless of the presence or absence of other tests in the same battery. We can test the applicability of Theorem 1.7 and Theorem 1.8 with every subset of four tests; and we can test the applicability of Theorem 1.3, Theorem 1.4, Theorem 1.5, and Theorem 1.6 with every subset of three tests.

Five verbal tests, each having 40 items, were given to 841 high school students (Cureton et al., 1944). Table 1.1 gives the intercorrelations among these tests, and also their reliabilities (of which more later). Brief descriptions of these tests are given in notes below the table.

The analysis will consist of the following steps:

1. Compute the tetrads, and set up the symbolic factor pattern.
2. Compute the appropriate triads, and estimate the first-factor loadings.
3. Compute the *residual correlations*

$$r_{ij \cdot a} = r_{ij} - a_i a_j.$$

By equations (1-24), if r_{ij} is accounted for entirely by the general factor, $r_{ij \cdot a}$ will equal zero. But if r_{ij} depends in part on a group factor also, $r_{ij \cdot a} = b_i b_j$ and

TABLE 1.1
Intercorrelations and Reliabilities of Five Verbal Tests ($N = 841$)

Test	Test (1)	(2)	(3)	(4)	Reliability[a]
(1) Paragraph Meaning					.653
(2) Same–Opposite	.585				.690
(3) Proverb Matching	.658	.663			.810
(4) Verbal Analogies	.616	.634	.697		.839
(5) Vocabulary	.555	.689	.626	.598	.715

(1) Paragraph followed by five *four-choice* questions
(2) Two words to be identified as synonyms, opposites, class and member of the class, or none of these (*four-choice*)
(3) Stem proverb followed by four answer proverbs: two to be identified as teaching the same lession as the stem proverb (*six-choice*)
(4) Two stem words followed by six alternative words: two to be selected and arranged in correct order to complete the analogy (*30-choice*)
(5) One stem word: synonym to be selected from among five alternatives (*five-choice*)

[a] The numerical values of the reliability coefficients are roughly proportional to the numbers of alternatives per item, that is, at least their rank orders are the same.
Note. From Table 1, p. 3, Cureton et al, 1944.

is not equal to zero. In this case $r_{ij \cdot a}$ is that part of r_{ij} which is *not* accounted for by the general factor. For this problem there is only one such nonzero residual correlation, indicating a doublet common factor in addition to the general factor.

4. Using the reliability data and a reasonable assumption (to be described later), estimate the second-factor (doublet) loadings.

5. Compute the unique-factor loadings, by (1-15) or for the doublet variables by the analogous equation

$$u_i = \sqrt{1 - a_i^2 - b_i^2},$$

and compute the *communality* ($h_i^2 = a_i^2$ or $h_i^2 = a_i^2 + b_i^2$) for each variable. Then set up the numerical factor pattern: the table of coefficients for the symbolic factor pattern.

6. Interpret the results in terms of the descriptions of the tests.

1.6.1 Standard Error of a Tetrad

In order to know when to consider a tetrad near-zero, we need a test of the null hypothesis that its population value is zero. To make this test we have only large-sample approximations to the standard error of a tetrad. Such approximations have been derived by Spearman and Holzinger (1924, 1925), by Pearson and Moul (1927), by Kelley (1928), and by Wishart (1928). The best of these approximations appears to be Wishart's. It is the square root of

$$\sigma_t^2 = \frac{1}{N-2}\left[\frac{N+1}{N-1}(1 - r_a^2)(1 - r_b^2) - |R| \right],$$ (1-26)

where r_a and r_b are the two correlations that do *not* enter into the tetrad whose standard error is being computed, and $|R|$ is the determinant of the 4 by 4 correlation matrix. The computation of the numerical value of a determinant is described in Chapter 4.

When the intercorrelations among a set of more than four variables do not differ too greatly among themselves, it is usually sufficient to compute a single average standard error for the whole set of tetrads. Spearman and Holzinger (1929) have derived such an average standard error. It is the square root of

$$\bar{\sigma}_t^2 = \frac{4}{N}\left[\bar{r}^2(1 - \bar{r})^2 + (\overline{r^2} - \bar{r}^2)\left(1 - 3\bar{r}\frac{n-4}{n-2} + 2\bar{r}^2\frac{n-6}{n-2} \right) \right],$$ (1-27)

where $\bar{r}$ is the mean of the $n(n-1)/2$ intercorrelations among n tests, $\bar{r}^2$ is the square of this mean correlation, and $\overline{r^2}$ is the mean of the squares of the $n(n-1)/2$ correlations.

In using either (1-26) or (1-27), it is usually sufficient to compare the absolute value of each tetrad with 1.282 times its standard error: this gives the .20 significance level against a two-sided alternative.

Note again that when a theorem says *if* a certain factor pattern applies, *then* a condition holds within sampling error, there is the implication that if the condition is *not* met within sampling error, the assumed factor pattern does not apply to the data under consideration.

If the tetrad, among a set of three, having the *smallest* absolute value is statistically significant (i.e., different from zero), none of the factor patterns of Theorem 1.7 or Theorem 1.8 apply, and we must assume that the four tests require two general factors, or one general factor and a group factor which has nonzero loadings on three tests.

If the *median* (in absolute value) of the three tetrads is statistically significant but the smallest is not, we assume that Theorem 1.8 applies, and that two of the variables have nonzero loadings on a group factor. The allocation of variables to group factors is discussed in Section 1.6.2.

If the *median* (in absolute value) of the three tetrads is *not* statistically significant, we *may* assume that all three are near-zero, even though the largest may appear marginally significant. This is true because, by the relations described in the paragraph preceding (1-22) in Section 1.5.7, the sum of the two smallest (in absolute value) *must* equal the absolute value of the largest, and it is not entirely reasonable to assume that the sum of two insignificant values is significant. This argument is weak, however, and a more conservative statement might be that the data do not tell us whether the largest of the three is or is not significant.

Problem 1.6.1:1. Compute the three tetrads for the army leadership data of Problem 1.1.2:1. Test the significance of the smallest by formula (1-26) to see if Theorem 1.8 holds. In (1-26) the value of the determinant $|R|$ is .2051 for this problem. If Theorem 1.8 is rejected at the two-sided .20 level, compare the tetrad with $1.96\,\sigma_t$ to see if it holds at the two-sided .05 level, i.e. if it *almost* holds.

1.6.2 Tetrad Analysis

For each four variables, say a, b, c, d in that order, there are three tetrads. Call the correlations r_{ab} and r_{cd} the *end pairs*, and r_{ac} and r_{bd} the *alternate pairs*, as in Section 1.5.7, and call r_{ad} and r_{bc} the *symmetric pairs*. Each of the three tetrads is the difference between the products of two of these pairs, and if one tetrad is near-zero (i.e., not significantly different from zero) and the other two are not, the group factor, by Theorem 1.8, is in one or other or both of the pairs of variables represented by the subscripts of the third pair. Thus:

Tetrad	= Product of	− Product of	Group factor location if $t = 0$
t_{abcd}	$= r_{ab}r_{cd}$ (end pr)	$- r_{ac}r_{bd}$ (alt pr)	a,d or b,c (sym pr)
t_{abdc}	$= r_{ab}r_{cd}$ (end pr)	$- r_{ad}r_{bc}$ (sym pr)	a,c or b,d (alt pr)
t_{acdb}[7]	$= r_{ac}r_{bd}$ (alt pr)	$- r_{ad}r_{bc}$ (sym pr)	a,b or c,d (end pr)

Check: $t_{abcd} + t_{acdb} = t_{abdc}$ (within rounding error unless tetrads are computed to twice the number of decimals in the correlations).

Note again that the two "equal" tetrads of a set need be near-equal only in absolute value; they may have opposite signs. The check given above, however, is correct for each set of three tetrads *including* their signs.

For the example of Table 1.1, $\bar{\sigma}_t = .01607$ by (1-27), and $1.282\,\bar{\sigma}_t = .021$. The tetrads and the group-factor allocations, computed as indicated above, are shown in Table 1.2. None of the results are in doubt: the largest near-zero tetrad is .009, and the smallest nonzero tetrad is .073, neither of which is close to the critical value $1.282\,\bar{\sigma}_t = .021$. In cases of doubt, where the smallest or the median of three tetrads is close to $1.282\,\bar{\sigma}_t$, it is probably safest to use (1-26) to test the significance of the smallest or the median tetrad.

[7]Proved in detail for $a = 1$, $b = 2$, $c = 3$, $d = 4$ under Theorem 1.8.

TABLE 1.2
Tetrads for Five Verbal Tests ($N = 841$)

Tests				Tetrad			
a	b	c	d	t_{abcd} (Sym pr)[a]	t_{abdc} (Alt Pr)[a]	t_{acdb} (End Pr)[a]	Group Factor and Location
1	2	3	4	$-.009$	$-.001$	.009	None
1	2	3	5	$-.087$	$-.002$	.085	1, 3 or 2, 5
1	2	4	5	$-.075$	$-.002$	.073	1, 4 or 2, 5
1	3	4	5	.008	.007	$-.001$	None
2	3	4	5	.000	$-.084$	$-.083$	3, 4 or 2, 5

[a] Group factor location if this tetrad is nonzero and the other two are not. The critical value for near-zero is .021.

1.6.3 The Factor Pattern

From rows 2, 3, and 5 of Table 1.2, we can assume, in addition to a general factor, a group factor in either tests 2 and 5 or tests 1, 3 and 4, or three separate group factors: one in tests 1 and 3, one in tests 1 and 4, and one in tests 3 and 4. The last possibility we discard because too many common factors (four) are required, and because there would be no clear interpretation. A group factor in tests 2 and 5, however, can be interpreted as a word meaning factor, and a group factor in tests 1, 3, and 4 as a verbal reasoning factor. We discard this last explanation for three reasons: (1) it requires one more non-zero loading (a weak reason); (2) it requires somewhat improbable combinations of the loadings to account for all the 1–2–3–4 and 1–3–4–5 tetrads being so close to zero; (3) verbal reasoning is a more general concept than word meaning and may well include the latter, so verbal reasoning is more easily regarded as a general factor than is word meaning.

The symbolic factor pattern is then

$$X_1 = a_1A \qquad\qquad + u_1U_1$$
$$X_2 = a_2A + b_2B + u_2U_2$$
$$X_3 = a_3A \qquad\qquad + u_3U_3 \qquad\qquad (1\text{-}28)$$
$$X_4 = a_4A \qquad\qquad + u_4U_4$$
$$X_5 = a_5A + b_5B + u_5U_5$$

From this factor pattern, each correlation except r_{25} is

$$r_{ij} = a_ia_j, \qquad\qquad (1\text{-}29)$$

and

$$r_{25} = a_2a_5 + b_2b_5. \qquad\qquad (1\text{-}30)$$

TABLE 1.3
Triads for Five Verbal Tests ($N = 841$)

		Test		
(1)	(2)	(3)	(4)	(5)
$t_{123} = .581$	$t_{213} = .589$	$t_{312} = .746$	$t_{412} = .668$	
$t_{124} = .568$	$t_{214} = .602$	$t_{314} = .745$	$t_{413} = .653$	$t_{513} = .528$
		$t_{315} = .742$	$t_{415} = .664$	$t_{514} = .539$
$t_{134} = .582$	$t_{234} = .603$	$t_{324} = .729$	$t_{423} = .667$	
$t_{135} = .583$				
$t_{145} = .572$		$t_{345} = .730$	$t_{435} = .666$	$t_{534} = .537$
$\Sigma_1 = 2.886$	$\Sigma_2 = 1.794$	$\Sigma_3 = 3.692$	$\Sigma_4 = 3.318$	$\Sigma_5 = 1.604$
$a_1^2 = .5772$	$a_2^2 = .5980$	$a_3^2 = .7384$	$a_4^2 = .6636$	$a_5^2 = .5347$
$a_1 = .760$	$a_2 = .773$	$a_3 = .859$	$a_4 = .815$	$a_5 = .731$

Note. At this point it would be well for the reader to complete the tetrad portion of the analysis of Exercise 1.1 in Section 1.6.8, using note 1 of that exercise.

1.6.4 Triad Analysis

The triads used in estimating the a-factor loadings, and the computation of these loadings are shown in Table 1.3, with column headings the same as the first subscripts of all triads in a given column. Triads involving both tests 2 and 5 are not shown: these triads include factor b as well as factor a, and hence cannot be used in estimating the a-factor loadings.

At the bottom of each column, the sum of the five or three entries is recorded as Σ_i, the mean as a_i^2, and the square root of this mean as a_i, the estimate of the general-factor loading by Theorem 1.4.

1.6.5 The Residuals

Now that we have estimates of all the a's, we have from (1-29), for all correlations except r_{25},

$$r_{ij \cdot a} = r_{ij} - a_i a_j \doteq 0, \tag{1-31}$$

and from (1-30)

$$r_{25 \cdot a} = r_{25} - a_2 a_5 = b_2 b_5. \tag{1-32}$$

The quantities $r_{ij \cdot a}$ (including $r_{25 \cdot a}$) are the *residuals:* the correlations remaining after removal of the correlation-producing effects of the general factor. The reader should take care to avoid confusing a residual correlation such as $r_{ij \cdot a}$

with the corresponding partial correlation, $r_{ij \cdot A}$. For our example the residuals are

$$r_{12 \cdot a} = -.002 \qquad r_{23 \cdot a} = -.001 \qquad r_{34 \cdot a} = -.003 \qquad r_{45 \cdot a} = .002$$

$$r_{13 \cdot a} = .005 \qquad r_{24 \cdot a} = .004 \qquad r_{35 \cdot a} = -.002$$

$$r_{14 \cdot a} = -.003 \qquad r_{25 \cdot a} = .124$$

$$r_{15 \cdot a} = -.001$$

All of these residuals except $r_{25 \cdot a}$ are close to zero, as (1-31) indicates they should be if the factor pattern (1-28) is appropriate. Hence (1-31) is correct within sampling error for all of the residual correlations except $r_{25 \cdot a}$.

1.6.6 Estimation of Group-Factor Loadings

From (1-32) and the numerical value of $r_{25 \cdot a}$ we see that $b_2 b_5 = .124$. This estimate may be in error by as much as $\pm .005$, judging by the other residuals, but we have no means of knowing the actual sign or magnitude of the error, so we take it to be zero.

Because the group factor is a doublet, we cannot estimate the values of b_2 and b_5 separately from the one residual correlation $r_{25 \cdot a}$ (see proof of Theorem 1.1). The residual correlations among three tests would be needed to form a triad.

For these data, however, we have the reliability coefficients as well as the intercorrelations, and we can use them along with a somewhat crude but still serviceable assumption to estimate the doublet (group factor) loadings. We do not discuss the *computation* of reliability coefficients; procedures for doing this are taken up in treatments of mental measurement theory. To *interpret* them in a factor-analysis context, we note that any unique factor can be subdivided into two uncorrelated parts, a nonchance *specific* factor s_i and an error-of-measurement factor e_i, with factors scores S_i and E_i. For X_2 and X_5, the corresponding equations of the factor pattern (1-28) then become

$$X_2 = a_2 A + b_2 B + s_2 S_2 + e_2 E_2$$

$$X_5 = a_5 A + b_5 B + s_5 S_5 + e_5 E_5$$

Then remembering that all test and factor scores are in standard-score form with variances unity,

$$a_2^2 + b_2^2 + s_2^2 + e_2^2 = 1$$

$$\tag{1-33}$$

$$a_5^2 + b_5^2 + s_5^2 + e_5^2 = 1$$

The reliability coefficient is defined as the nonchance variance divided by the total variance and is designated r_{ii}. s_i^2 is a part of the nonchance variance along with a_i^2 and b_i^2, while the chance or error variance is e_i^2. Then from (1-33)

$$r_{22} = 1 - e_2^2$$

$$r_{55} = 1 - e_5^2 \tag{1-34}$$

Then from (1-34) and Table 1.1

$$e_2^2 = 1 - r_{22} = 1 - .690 = .310$$

$$e_5^2 = 1 - r_{55} = 1 - .715 = .285$$

Substituting these values into (1-33) along with the values of a_2^2 and a_5^2 from Table 1.3, we have

$$.598 + b_2^2 + s_2^2 + .310 = 1$$

$$.535 + b_5^2 + s_5^2 + .285 = 1$$

From these equations,

$$b_2^2 + s_2^2 = 1 - .598 - .310 = .092$$

$$b_5^2 + s_5^2 = 1 - .535 - .285 = .180$$

The values .092 and .180 are the upper bounds of b_2^2 and b_5^2 respectively, and it is evident that they can be reached only if $s_2^2 = s_5^2 = 0$, that is, if there is *no* nonchance specific variance, all unique variance being error variance.

We know also from (1-31) and the following table of residuals that $b_2 b_5$ = .124, whence $b_2^2 b_5^2 = .0154$. Not knowing the relative values (or the actual values) of s_2^2 and s_5^2, we assume that they are equal: this assumption is about as reasonable as any we can make in the absence of knowledge, and certainly more reasonable than the assumption that one of them is zero (the only assumption under which one of these equations and the equation $b_2 b_5 = .124$ could be solved exactly). If we assume then that $s_2^2 = s_5^2$, we can subtract .000, .001, and so on successively from .092 and .180 until we reach the pair whose product is most nearly .0154, at which point we obtain the best available estimates of b_2^2 and b_5^2. Thus

If	*Then*		
$s_2^2 = s_5^2 =$	$b_2^2 =$	$b_5^2 =$	$b_2^2 b_5^2 =$
.000	.092	.180	.0166
.001	.091	.179	.0163
.002	.090	.178	.0160
.003	.089	.177	.0158
.004	.088	.176	.0155
.005	.087	.175	.0152

Because .0155 is closer to .0154 than is .0152, we take $b_2^2 = .088$ and $b_5^2 = .176$. Taking square roots,

$$b_2 = .297$$

$$b_5 = .420$$

Check: $b_2 b_5 = .125 \doteq .124$

If we do not have reliability data, and know only that $b_2 b_5 = .124$, we must make much cruder assumptions in trying to estimate b_2 and b_5 (Corollary 1.1, Section 1.5.3). If we assume that $b_2 = b_5 = \sqrt{.124} = .352$, this result is quite far from the result obtained from the reliability data: $b_2 = .297$ and $b_5 = .420$. Thus without the reliability data corollary 1.1 stands: two variables *cannot* be factor-analyzed when the data consist of only one correlation.

The five-verbal-tests problem is quite unusual. The writers have seen only one other study in the literature in which reliabilities consistent with the intercorrelations were reported (Davis, 1968).

1.6.7 The Numerical Factor Pattern

The factor pattern of (1-28) can now be supplied with numerical coefficients throughout. The general-factor loadings are found in Table 1.3, and the group-factor loadings are given above as $b_2 = .297$ and $b_5 = .420$. Generalizing (1-6) and (1-7), or rewriting (1-33) with $s_i^2 + e_i^2 = u_i^2$,

$$a_i^2 + b_i^2 + u_i^2 = 1, \tag{1-35}$$

from which

$$u_i = \sqrt{1 - a_i^2 - b_i^2}, \tag{1-36}$$

which gives the unique-factor loadings. Table 1.4 gives the results.

TABLE 1.4
Factor Pattern for Five Verbal Tests ($N = 841$)

Test	Factor			h^2	Reliability
	a	b	u		
(1) Paragraph Meaning	.760	.000	.650	.578	.653
(2) Same–Opposite	.773	.297	.560	.686	.690
(3) Proverb Matching	.859	.000	.512	.738	.810
(4) Verbal Analogies	.815	.000	.580	.664	.839
(5) Vocabulary	.731	.420	.538	.711	.715

The column headed h^2 gives the communalities. The communality of a test, with relation to a given battery, is the sum of squares of its common-factor loadings (here a^2 or $a^2 + b^2$), when the factors are uncorrelated, or the proportion of its variance which it holds in common with the other tests in the battery. Hence

$$h_i^2 + u_i^2 = 1, \tag{1-37}$$

u_i^2 is the unique-factor variance, and u_i is the unique-factor loading. If we consider (1-33) and (1-34), we note this important point: *The upper limit of the communality of a test is the reliability of that test.* In Table 1.4 the last column gives the reliabilities. Each of them is larger than the corresponding value of the communality in column h^2.

We have noted in Section 1.5.8 that in the one-common-factor case there can arise (rarely) a situation in which one triad exceeds unity whereas all tetrads are zero (or with real data, near-zero). But by Theorem 1.6 and the definition of communality, this triad is the communality of the test, and this situation is termed a Heywood case (Heywood, 1931). In general, with any number of common factors, a Heywood case is any case in which the fitted factor pattern gives one communality greater than unity. But as we have just seen, the upper limit of a communality is less than unity whenever (as with all mental and educational tests) the reliability of a variable is less than unity. If the fitted factor pattern gives one communality greater than the reliability of the variable but still less than unit y, we term this situation a *quasi-Heywood case*.

Problem 1.6.7:1. Estimate new group-factor loadings under the radical assumption that $s_2 = 0$. Then complete a table analogous to Table 1.4 under this assumption (omitting reliabilities), and compare with Table 1.4 to show the maximum errors in b_2 and b_5 that can occur because of the assumption that $s_2 = s_5$ in (1-33).

1.6.8 Interpretation

From the nature of the tests and Table 1.4, it is evident that factor a is a general verbal factor with highest loadings on test 3 (Proverb Matching) and test 4 (Verbal Analogies), the two tests that most clearly involve reasoning content. Factor b is a word-meaning group factor (doublet), with nonzero loadings only on test 2 (Same–Opposite) and test 5 (Vocabulary).

Exercise 1:1. The data of Table 1.5 come from the study by Thurstone and Thurstone (1941) cited previously, and include two of the same tests used in the reading–arithmetic example of Section 1.1.2. The first three tests are reading tests; the last three are tests of spatial visualization. Make a complete tetrad–triad factor analysis of these intercorrelations. There are no reliability coefficients.

TABLE 1.5
Intercorrelations among Six Psychological Tests ($N = 710$)

Test	(1)	(2)	(3)	(4)	(5)
(1) Vocabulary					
(2) Sentence Meaning	.769				
(3) Paragraph Meaning	.671	.681			
(4) Cards	.158	.189	.144		
(5) Figures	.211	.268	.207	.621	
(6) Flags	.231	.242	.159	.623	.510

Note. From Appendix Table 1, pp. 83–87, Thurstone and Thurstone, 1941. Copyright 1941 by The University of Chicago. Reprinted by permission.

Notes:

1. It is evident from Table 1.5 that the group factor should lie either in tests 1, 2, and 3 (verbal) or in tests 4, 5, and 6 (spatial) or in both. We assume that there is only one group factor. Make up a table like Table 1.2 (Section 1.6.2), circle the median tetrads for variables 1-2-3-4; 1-2-3-5; and 1-2-3-6; and for variables 1-4-5-6; 2-4-5-6; and 3-4-5-6. The group factor lies in the set having larger median tetrads, because *all* the tetrads in the other set must be treated as near-zero. Check by counting the 1-2, 1-3, and 2-3 allocations and the 4-5, 4-6, and 5-6 allocations. The group factor should lie in the set having the larger number of such allocations.

2. After deciding where the group factor lies, compute only those triads that can be used in estimating the a-factor loadings, that is, those that use not more than one of the variables included in the group factor.

3. If a group factor has nonzero loadings on more than two variables, triads can be formed from the nonzero residual correlations to obtain the b-factor loadings. Thus if the group factor is in tests 1, 2, and 3, we have

If		Then
$X_1 = a_1A + b_1B + u_1U_1$		$r_{12} = a_1a_2 + b_1b_2$
$X_2 = a_2A + b_2B + u_2U_2$		$r_{13} = a_1a_3 + b_1b_3$
$X_3 = a_3A + b_3B + u_3U_3$		$r_{23} = a_2a_3 + b_2b_3$
$X_4 = a_4A \qquad + u_4U_4$		
$X_5 = a_5A \qquad + u_5U_5$		$r_{12\cdot a} = r_{12} - a_1a_2 = b_1b_2$
$X_6 = a_6A \qquad + u_6U_6$		$r_{13\cdot a} = r_{13} - a_1a_3 = b_1b_3$
		$r_{23\cdot a} = r_{23} - a_2a_3 = b_2b_3$

and

$$t_{123\cdot a} = \frac{r_{12\cdot a}r_{13\cdot a}}{r_{23\cdot a}} = \frac{b_1b_2b_1b_3}{b_2b_3} = b_1^2, \text{ etc.}$$

4. Save your results for use in a later exercise (in Chapter 2).

2

Centroid Method; Rotation in Two Dimensions

2.1 INTRODUCTION

As the number of variables increases, and especially as the number of common factors increases, the Spearman approach, based on explicit theorems and the tetrad–triad procedures, becomes increasingly complex and soon becomes impractical. We require, therefore, a procedure that can be generalized to any number of common factors. This number, m, is usually not even known at the outset of the analysis, and the procedure must enable us to obtain a reasonable estimate of m. The first factor-analyst who recognized these problems fully, and who devised procedures to solve them, was Thurstone, though some of his early work was foreshadowed by the studies of Webb (1915) and Garnett (1919).

2.1.1 The Two-Step Procedure

To solve the factor-analysis problem in the general case, Thurstone adopted a two-step procedure. At the first step he obtained an *arbitrary* factor matrix, with *orthogonal* (uncorrelated) factors of decreasing magnitude. Because each factor had loadings smaller on the average than those of the preceding factor, the last (m-th) factor would then be the last one whose loadings were larger than those one would expect to obtain as a result of the sampling errors and the errors of measurement of the variables. This step was termed the *initial factoring* step.

The second step consisted in applying to the initial arbitrary factor matrix a *linear transformation* designed to yield *interpretable* factors. Because this transformation was equivalent to a rotation of the original axes in a geometric model, this step was termed the *rotational* step.

The purpose of this chapter is to describe and illustrate the two-step procedure, using only two-factor data and the same example and exercise used in Chapter 1.

2.1.2 The Transformation

The linear model of (1-1) is

$$X_1 = a_1 A + b_1 B + \ldots + m_1 M + u_1 U_1$$

$$X_2 = a_2 A + b_2 B + \ldots + m_2 M + u_2 U_2 \qquad (2\text{-}1)$$

$$X_n = a_n A + b_n B + \ldots + m_n M + u_n U_n$$

The scores $X_1, X_2, \ldots, X_n$, for any one of the N individuals of the experimental group, are standard scores on the tests or manifest random variables. The scores $A, B, \ldots, M$, and U_i $(i = 1, 2, \ldots, n)$, also for any one of the N individuals, are standard scores on the factors or latent random variables, and their values for any given individual are unknown. The values $a_i, b_i, \ldots, m_i, u_i$ are the factor loadings or weights or coefficients. The linear model of (2-1) states that the standard score X_i on each test, for any one individual, is a weighted sum of his standard scores on m postulated common factors and one postulated factor unique to that particular test. By definition, a common factor is one that appears with nonzero loadings on two or more tests, while a unique factor has a nonzero loading on only one test.

The factor a consists of the loadings $a_1, a_2, \ldots, a_n$, the factor b of the loadings $b_1, b_2, \ldots, b_n, \ldots$, the factor m of the loadings $m_1, m_2, \ldots, m_n$, and the whole *set* of unique factors u of the loadings $u_1, u_2, \ldots, u_n$, each with its corresponding nonzero loading on only one test. If we were to write the unique-factor loadings in common-factor notation, they would be $u_1, 0, 0, \ldots, 0; 0, u_2, 0, \ldots, 0; \ldots; 0, 0, \ldots, 0, u_n$. We do not do this ordinarily because we know that by definition each unique factor has a nonzero loading on only one test. Each *test* (or random variable) is designated by the *subscript* of the corresponding X in (2-1); sometimes written in parentheses. Thus in (2-1) the tests are $1, 2, \ldots, n$ or $(1), (2), \ldots, (n)$.

By arguments similar to those leading to (1-6), (1-7), (1-8), (1-29), and (1-30), we have, in the case of *uncorrelated* factors,

$$a_i^2 + b_i^2 + \ldots + m_i^2 + u_i^2 = 1 \qquad (2\text{-}2)$$

$$r_{ij} = a_i a_j + b_i b_j + \ldots + m_i m_j \qquad (2\text{-}3)$$

The initial data for a factor analysis are the intercorrelations r_{ij} $(i, j = 1, 2, \ldots, n; i \neq j)$. There are an infinite number of sets of equations such as (2-1), each with a different set of common factors and a different set of common-factor loadings but the same unique factors and unique-factor loadings, which will satisfy (2-2) and (2-3). Thus in place of (2-1) we could write another set of equations specifying a different set of common factors, with common-factor standard scores I*, II*, ... , Z*, and loadings I_1, II_1, ... , Z_1; I_2, II_2, ... , Z_2; ... ; I_n, II_n, ... , Z_n. We use Roman numerals (and Z) with stars to represent common-factor standard scores, corresponding to the $A, B, \ldots, M$ of (2-1); and Roman numerals (and Z) with subscripts to represent factor loadings, corresponding to the $a_1, b_1, \ldots, m_1; a_2, b_2, \ldots, m_2; \ldots; a_n, b_n, \ldots, m_n$ of (2-1). A Roman numeral without either a star or a subscript represents a common factor $(I, II, \ldots, Z)$ as does a lower-case letter $(a, b, \ldots, m)$ for the model of (2-1). Thus I_1 is the loading of test 1 on factor I, just as in (2-1), a_1 is the loading of test 1 on factor a. We use this notation for two reasons: (1) it is common practice to use lower-case letters, $a, b, \ldots, m$ to designate the arbitrary common factors of step 1, and Roman numerals to designate the transformed common factors of step 2; (2) we use this notation (capital Roman numerals with stars and capital Roman numerals with subscripts), instead of a notation strictly comparable to that of (2-1), in order to avoid the use of lower-case Roman numerals. In many type faces, the lower-case Roman numeral i is not readily distinguished from the lower-case letter i. In this notation the transformed set of equations is

$$X_1 = I_1 I^* + II_1 II^* + \ldots + Z_1 Z^* + u_1 U_1,$$

$$X_2 = I_2 I^* + II_2 II^* + \ldots + Z_2 Z^* + u_2 U_2, \tag{2-4}$$

$$X_n = I_n I^* + II_n II^* + \ldots + Z_n Z^* + u_n U_n.$$

The unique factor loadings, $u_1, u_2, \ldots, u_n$ and the unique factor standard scores, $U_1, U_2, \ldots, U_n$, are the same in (2-4) as in (2-1). The number of common factors in (2-4) is also the same (m) as the number in (2-1). The m common factors I, II, ... , Z of (2-4) are linear combinations (linear transformations) of the common factors $a, b, \ldots, m$ of (2-1). The transformation equations are

$$
\begin{aligned}
I_i &= (Ia)a_i + (Ib)b_i + \cdots + (Im)m_i \\
II_i &= (IIa)a_i + (IIb)b_i + \cdots + (IIm)m_i
\end{aligned}
\tag{2-5}
$$

$$Z_i = (Za)a_i + (Zb)b_i + \cdots + (Zm)m_i$$
$$i = 1, 2, \ldots, n$$

In expanded form, equations (2-5) become

$$
\left.
\begin{aligned}
I_1 &= (Ia)a_1 + (Ib)b_1 + \cdots + (Im)m_1 \\
I_2 &= (Ia)a_2 + (Ib)b_2 + \cdots + (Im)m_2 \\
&\quad\text{------------------------------} \\
I_1 &= (Ia)a_n + (Ib)b_n + \cdots + (Im)m_n
\end{aligned}
\right\} \quad \text{for } I_i
$$

$$
\left.
\begin{aligned}
II_1 &= (IIa)a_1 + (IIb)b_1 + \cdots + (IIm)m_1 \\
II_2 &= (IIa)a_2 + (IIb)b_2 + \cdots + (IIm)m_2 \\
&\quad\text{------------------------------} \\
II_n &= (IIa)a_n + (IIb)b_n + \cdots + (IIm)m_n
\end{aligned}
\right\} \quad \text{for } II_i
$$

$$\left.\begin{array}{l} Z_1 = (Za)a_1 + (Zb)b_1 + \cdots + (Zm)m_1 \\ Z_2 = (Za)a_2 + (Zb)b_2 + \cdots + (Zm)m_2 \\ \text{--} \\ Z_n = (Za)a_n + (Zb)b_n + \cdots + (Zm)m_n \end{array}\right\} \quad \text{for } Z_i$$

The symbols in parentheses are the transformation coefficients. They are to be determined by the step-2 rotational procedures, to be described in Section 2.5. The first symbol of each transformation coefficient (I, II, . . . , Z) designates the transformed factor, and the second symbol (a, b, . . . , m) designates the initial factor. For any one transformed factor (I, II, . . . , Z), the coefficients are the same for every variable, that is, they are the same for every column of any one set of the expanded equations. Thus to find the loading I_1 on the first transformed factor I, we use the first equation of I_i, giving I_1 as a linear combination of the loadings of variable 1 on the initial common factors a, b, . . . , m.

Note that the transformation equations, (2-5) and their expansions, apply only to the *loadings*, giving the I_i, II_i, . . . , Z_i in terms of the a_i, b_i, . . . , m_i. The initial factors, a, b, . . . , m, are always obtained from the original intercorrelations in such a manner that they are uncorrelated. The transformed factors, I, II, . . . , Z, however, may be either correlated or uncorrelated. If they are uncorrelated, equations (2-4) represent the transformed factor pattern. If they are correlated, equations (2-4) do *not* represent the transformed factor pattern. But in this case the coefficients, I_i, II_i, . . . , Z_i are still the *correlations* between the factors and the original variables. With more than two factors, a model based on correlated factors (Alternative 1 of Section 1.1.2) is almost always preferred because it increases the number of near-zero correlations between the factors and the tests or original variables. A few writers, most notably Guilford, disagree with this statement and prefer to use only transformations which leave the factors uncorrelated.

Note again that in equations (2-5) and their expansion, the number of *sets* of equations (for the I_i, II_i, . . . , Z_i) is the same as the number of factors of equations (2-1), namely m, and each equation applies to all of the n variables in turn. Thus the total number of transformation coefficients is m^2, the square of the number of common factors. We emphasize again that the number of possible transformations is infinite, so additional conditions must be imposed to specify at step 2 the particular transformation that will lead to an interpretable transformed factor matrix.

2.2 ELEMENTARY THEORY OF INITIAL FACTORING

At step 1, in order to solve equations (2-1) in such a manner as to be able to estimate as accurately as possible the number of common factors m, we first impose, as in Chapter 1, the condition that the factor scores A, B, . . . , M, and all the U's shall be uncorrelated. Then remembering that all variables are in standard-score form, with variances and standard deviations all unity, the variance of variable i, from (2-2), is

$$\sigma_i^2 = a_i^2 + b_i^2 + \ldots + m_i^2 + u_i^2 = 1, \tag{2-6}$$

and by (2-3)

$$r_{ij} = a_i a_j + b_i b_j + \ldots + m_i m_j. \tag{2-7}$$

We define r_{ii} (r_{ij} when $j = i$), *not* as the unity of elementary correlation theory, but in such a manner that (2-7) still holds, that is,

$$r_{ii} = a_i^2 + b_i^2 + \ldots + m_i^2 = h_i^2. \tag{2-8}$$

Thus r_{ii} is the *communality* of test i, because by definition the communality of test i is the sum of squares of its common-factor loadings. Then, from (2-6) and (2-8),

$$h_i^2 + u_i^2 = 1 \tag{2-9}$$

in the general case as well as in the special case of (1-37).

The objective of initial factoring is to factor in such a manner that the loadings on the first factor a shall be in aggregate as large as possible, the loadings on the second factor b shall be as large as possible given factor a, and the loadings on each successive factor shall be as large as possible given the larger loadings on all previous factors. When we reach a factor with loadings so small that they can be ascribed to the sampling errors and the errors of measurement which by chance are correlated, we can discard it and all later factors, which can also be attributed to chance effects. The number of previous factors is then m, the number of common factors which can be transformed and interpreted.

The best procedure would be to use the method of least squares: choose the a's in such a manner that, if $\Sigma\Sigma r$ represents a summation over the n^2 entries in the complete square correlation table, then

$$\Sigma\Sigma(r_{ij} - a_i a_j)^2$$

will be a minimum. Then choose the b's in such a manner that

$$\Sigma\Sigma(r_{ij \cdot a} - b_i b_j)^2 = \Sigma\Sigma(r_{ij} - a_i a_j - b_i b_j)^2$$

will be a minimum, and so on. In this case m will be the factor derived from the last [the $(m - 1)$-th] residual matrix whose elements,

$$r_{ij \cdot (m-1)} = r_{ij} - a_i a_j - b_i b_j - \ldots - (m-1)_i (m-1)_j,$$

are appreciably greater than zero. This method is termed the *principal-axes* method. It is the method of choice, and is described in Chapter 5. It is mathematically complicated and computationally cumbersome, however, and is only practical when the computations are done on a high-speed electronic digital computer.

In order to illustrate the two-step procedure, we first describe briefly the centroid method for step 1, which can be used with a hand or desk calculator, and illustrate it with a very small problem to show the general principles of initial factoring and to provide data for step 2. Then for step 2 we describe and illustrate a graphic procedure for rotation when there are only two common factors. Historically the centroid method (in several variants) was commonly used for initial factoring until the advent of high-speed electronic computers permitted the more accurate but computationally much longer principal-axes method to supersede it.

2.3   THE CENTROID METHOD

2.3.1 Centroid Equations

Writing (2-7) in expanded form, we have for the first column of the correlation matrix (the complete n by n table of correlations),

$$
\begin{aligned}
r_{11} &= a_1 a_1 + b_1 b_1 + \cdots + m_1 m_1 \\
r_{21} &= a_2 a_1 + b_2 b_1 + \cdots + m_2 m_1 \\
\hline
r_{n1} &= a_n a_1 + b_n b_1 + \cdots + m_n m_1 \\
\end{aligned}
\tag{2-10}
$$

$$
\Sigma r_{i1} = a_1 \Sigma a + b_1 \Sigma b + \cdots + m_1 \Sigma m
$$

The column sums form the first equation of the following set:

$$
\begin{aligned}
\Sigma r_{i1} &= a_1 \Sigma a + b_1 \Sigma b + \cdots + m_1 \Sigma m \\
\Sigma r_{i2} &= a_2 \Sigma a + b_2 \Sigma b + \cdots + m_2 \Sigma m \\
\hline
\Sigma r_{in} &= a_n \Sigma a + b_n \Sigma b + \cdots + m_n \Sigma m \\
\end{aligned}
\tag{2-11}
$$

$$
\Sigma \Sigma r = (\Sigma a)^2 + (\Sigma b)^2 \quad \cdots + (\Sigma m)^2
\tag{2-12}
$$

Now instead of trying to minimize first $\Sigma\Sigma(r_{ij} - a_i a_j)^2$, which implies that Σa^2 shall be as large as possible, we merely try to maximize Σa. To do this we require (temporarily) that all of the a's be nonnegative, and that $\Sigma b, \ldots, \Sigma m$ all be zero. Then from (2-12)

$$
\Sigma a = \sqrt{\Sigma\Sigma r},
\tag{2-13}
$$

and from (2-11) and (2-13)

$$
\begin{aligned}
a_1 &= \Sigma r_{i1} / \sqrt{\Sigma\Sigma r} \\
a_2 &= \Sigma r_{i2} / \sqrt{\Sigma\Sigma r} \\
\hline
a_n &= \Sigma r_{in} / \sqrt{\Sigma\Sigma r} \\
\end{aligned}
\tag{2-14}
$$

From these equations it is evident that $a_1, a_2, \ldots, a_n$ can be found from the column sums and the total sum of the entries in the correlation matrix. It is evident also that all the column sums must be positive and as large as possible if Σa is to be a maximum.

2.3.2 Reflection

If the correlation matrix contains a substantial number of negative correlations, some (occasionally all) of the column sums may be quite low or even negative. Then if Σa is to be a maximum, we require some procedure for making them all positive and as large as possible.

We cannot change arbitrarily the numerical values of any of the individual correlations in order to maximize the column sums: these numerical values are given by the data. Nor can we change the signs of any one or more such correlations arbitrarily for this purpose. But we *can* arbitrarily reverse the *scale* of a *variable* (temporarily or permanently), so that for every score X_i we substitute a score $X_i'' = -X_i$. The system by which we score a variable is essentially arbitrary. Thus if the score X_i on a test is the number of right answers (or the number right minus a fraction of the number wrong), the "good" score is a high score, and the "poor" score is a low score. But if, on another variable, the score is the number of minutes required to complete a task, the "good" score is a low score and the "poor" score is a high score. If the intrinsic correlation between the two performances is positive, the computed correlation between the two sets of scores will be negative. In this situation we can reverse the score scale for one of the variables. If we reverse the scale of a test scored number right (or number right minus a fraction of number wrong), a "good" score becomes a low score, and the *name* of the variable is reversed. Thus if X_i is "dominance," X_i'' becomes "submission." If X_i is "paragraph reading ability," X_i'' becomes "paragraph reading deficiency," and so on. Or we may, instead, reverse the scale of a variable scored in minutes. If this variable is a typing test, the number of minutes required to type a given passage (with, say, a penalty of one minute for every error), the original score in minutes is a measure of "typing deficiency," If we reverse the scale it becomes a measure of "typing ability." In either case (one variable scored in reverse but not the other), if the intrinsic relation between the two performances is positive, so that "good" performances on one variable tend to go with "good" performances on the other and "poor" performances on one with "poor" performances on the other, the computed correlation between the two sets of scroes (with one score scale reversed) will also be positive.

Because the direction of any score scale is arbitrary, we can arbitrarily reverse the scale of any variable in order to increase a column sum or change this sum from negative to positive. If the change is permanent, we must reverse the *name* of the variable, as noted above. If the change is temporary, we can rereverse it later and the name of the original variable remains the same. If

$$r_{ij} = Sx_ix_j/N\sigma_i\sigma_j$$

where S represents a summation from 1 to N, $x_i = X_i - \bar{X}_i$, X_i is now a raw score on variable i, $\bar{X}_i$ is the mean of these raw scores, and x_i is a deviation from the mean, it follows that

$$r_{ij}'' = Sx_i''x_j/N\sigma_i''\sigma_j = S(-x_i)x_j/N\sigma_i\sigma_j = -r_{ij},$$

for $\sigma_i = \sigma_i''$ since $S(-x_i)^2 = Sx_i^2$ and $S(-x_i)x_j = -Sx_ix_j$. The effect on the correlation matrix of reversing the scale of X_i is merely to reverse the sign of the correlation between variable i and every other variable, that is, to reverse the sign of every r_{ij} in row i *and* column i except the diagonal element $r_{ii} = h_i^2$. The sign of r_{ii} remains the same because $S(-x_i)(-x_i) = Sx_ix_i = Sx_i^2$, and $\sigma_{-i}^2 = \sigma_i^2$. We can regard the sign of r_{ii} as having been reversed twice, once for the row and once again for the column. This sign-reversal procedure is termed *reflection* of variable i.

We can continue to reflect variables, including rereflection of some of them, until so far as possible we have maximized $\Sigma r_{i1}, \Sigma r_{i2}, \ldots, \Sigma r_{in}$, and hence also $\Sigma\Sigma r$. It appears that by reflection of enough variables, these column sums can always be made equal to or greater than their diagonal entries, $r_{11}, r_{22}, \ldots, r_{nn}$ respectively, that is, that every column sum of a correlation matrix, exclusive of its diagonal element, can be made nonnegative (positive or zero). The writers have not seen an algebraic proof of this proposition, but they have never seen a set of data for which it failed to hold.

2.3.3 Residual Matrices and Later Factors

To determine the loadings on the second factor, we form the first residual correlation matrix (commonly termed simply the first residual matrix) with elements,

$$r_{ij\cdot a} = r_{ij}' - a_ia_j, \tag{2-15}$$

where $r_{ij\cdot a}$ is the residual correlation after the extraction of factor a, r_{ij}' is an element of the original correlation matrix, after reflection if any: $r_{ij}' = r_{ij}$ or r_{ij}''; including $r_{ii\cdot a} = r_{ii} - a_i^2$. Then from (2-7) and (2-8)

$$r_{ij\cdot a} = b_ib_j + c_ic_j + \ldots + m_im_j \tag{2-16}$$

for all i and j, including the n cases in which $i = j$.

From (2-10), noting again that to obtain the first-factor loadings we let $\Sigma b = \Sigma c = \ldots = \Sigma m = 0$, we have

$$\Sigma r_{i1}' = a_1\Sigma a = \Sigma a_ia_1.$$

But from this equation and (2-15)

$$\Sigma r_{i1 \cdot a} = \Sigma r'_{i1} - \Sigma a_i a_1 = 0,$$

and similarly

$$\Sigma r_{i2 \cdot a} = \Sigma r'_{i2} - \Sigma a_i a_2 = 0$$

$$\Sigma r_{in \cdot a} = \Sigma r'_{in} - \Sigma a_i a_n = 0$$

Thus the sum of every row (and column) of the residual matrix will be zero, within rounding error. In the computing system to be described, this fact is used as a check on the computations for each row of the residual matrix.

We can now treat the first residual matrix in the same way we did the original correlation matrix, thus obtaining the b-factor loadings.

The second residual matrix has elements

$$r_{ij \cdot b} = r_{ij \cdot a} - b_i b_j = c_i c_j + \ldots + m_i m_j. \tag{2-17}$$

In $r_{ij \cdot k}$ (here $k = a$ or b), the letter after the dot in the subscript indicates the last factor previously extracted. Thus $r_{ij \cdot k}$ designates an element of the k-th residual matrix: the residual matrix after k factors have been extracted.

The process of forming residual matrices and extracting factors from them continues until we reach a residual matrix whose elements are small enough to be ascribed to the chance errors, or a factor based on such a residual matrix whose loadings are all small. At this point the immediately preceding factor is factor m, the last factor to be retained for the transformation of step 2.

An initial correlation matrix may consist entirely or mainly of positive correlations, so that little or no reflection is required in obtaining the a's. But with every residual matrix, having initial column sums all 0, extensive reflection will be necessary. With the computing procedure described below, each residual matrix is formed from the entries of the previous matrix (original or residual) *after reflection,* and the all-positive factor loadings computed from that matrix.

2.3.4 Effects of Reflection

We have noted that reflecting a test, say test i, merely reverses its scale of measurement, replacing each X_i by $-X_i$, and that this has the effect of reversing the signs of all r_{ij} (and all r_{ji}) except r_{ii}. Then if $k (= a, b, \ldots, m)$ is the factor resulting from this reflection, the loading k_i of test i on factor k is actually the loading on that factor of test $-i$. Hence for test i itself, the loading will be $-k_i$. *When a test has been reflected, the loading of the reflected test will be the same numerically as that of the unreflected test, but with opposite sign.*

We do *not* reverse the signs of any reflected first-factor loadings before extracting the second factor, nor the signs of any reflected second-factor loadings before extracting the third factor, and so on. When all substantial factors have been extracted, with all loadings temporarily positive, the proper signs are attached all at once as follows.

1. If reflections are necessary in the initial correlation matrix, the signs of the corresponding a-factor loadings are ordinarily *not* changed. The *names* of the reflected tests are changed instead. This is done in order to keep the loadings on this first and largest factor all positive, which facilitates the step-2 transformation and simplifies the subsequent interpretation of the transformed factor.

2. For all factors *after* the first, the signs of some of the loadings are changed. Consider the loading of the i-th test on the k-th factor ($i = 1, 2, \ldots,$ n; $k = 2, 3, \ldots, m$). If the number of reflections of this test, on the k-th and all previous factors except the first, is zero or even, its sign remains positive. If the number of reflections is odd, the sign of its loading is changed to negative. The signs of all factors then apply to all variables, as originally named or as renamed if there were reflections of the original correlation matrix.

2.4   CENTROID COMPUTATIONS

Table 2.1 gives the intercorrelations among the five verbal tests which we used for illustration in Chapter 1. We shall not consider in this chapter the further problem raised by the fact that in most actual cases we do not know in advance the numerical values of the communalities and must estimate them. In Table 2.1 we have inserted (in parentheses) on the diagonal the communalities ($r_{ii} =$ estimated h_i^2) computed previously by the tetrad–triad method and recorded in column h^2 of Table 1.4. The matrix is all-positive, so there are no initial reflections and hence no changes in the names of the tests.

2.4.1 Computational Accuracy and Checks

Factor-analytic procedures are fairly long, so we need a systematic method for setting up work sheets and checking the calculations as we go along.

Intercorrelations and residuals are ordinarily recorded to three decimals, even though their sampling errors usually affect the second decimal. Whenever we factor-analyze intercorrelations from the literature, which are often *reported* to only two decimals, we proceed as though each of them were a three-decimal value with the last decimal exactly zero.

Factor loadings are computed to four decimals, so that their products, in equations such as (2-15), are not likely to be in error by more than 1 in the third decimal. If the fourth decimal of a factor loading is 5, it is followed by a + or a − to show whether it is a little larger or a little smaller than the recorded value. This permits correct rounding to three decimals in the factor matrix.

Computed constants, such as $\Sigma\Sigma r$, $\sqrt{\Sigma\Sigma r}$, and $\sqrt{1/\Sigma\Sigma r}$, which are to be used to multiply every element of a row, are computed to at least five *significant*

TABLE 2.1
Intercorrelations among Five Verbal Tests, and Computations for
First-Factor Loadings ($N = 841$)

Test	(1)	(2)	(3)	(4)	(5)	Σ	Ch
(1)	(.578)	.585	.658	.616	.555	2.992	
(2)	.585	(.686)	.663	.634	.689	3.257	
(3)	.658	.663	(.738)	.697	.626	3.382	
(4)	.616	.634	.697	(.664)	.598	3.209	
(5)	.555	.689	.626	.598	(.711)	3.179	
Σ	2.992	3.257	3.382	3.209	3.179	16.019	16.019
a	.7476	.8138	.8450	.8018	.7943	4.0025	4.0024

figures (or to machine capacity) and recorded to five significant figures or four decimals, whichever is greater.

At the right of the correlation matrix of Table 2.1 we have columns headed Σ and Ch (for check). Every entry in column Σ is the actual sum of the preceding entries in the row. In column Ch we record values calculated in a different manner. Pairs of entries in columns Σ and Ch (with exceptions to be noted) should agree, either exactly or within the accumulated rounding error for one row. For later calculations, we *always* use the entries in column Σ, *never* those in column Ch.

2.4.2 First-Factor Loadings

In Table 2.1, the row sums are recorded in column Σ and the column sums in row Σ. The sum of the entries in row Σ is recorded in column Σ (here $\Sigma\Sigma r$ = 16.019), and the sum of the entries in column Σ is recorded in row Σ, column Ch. The check is exact.

The square root of $\Sigma\Sigma r$ is recorded in row a column Ch (here 4.0024) to five significant figures. Its reciprocal (or $\sqrt{1/\Sigma\Sigma r}$) is multiplied by each entry in row Σ, including the entry in column Σ, to give the four-decimal value of a, just below. These a's are the first-factor loadings. Their sum is recorded in column Σ. The check is correct within rounding error.

2.4.3 Residuals

Table 2.2 shows the residuals, $r_{ij} - a_i a_j = r_{ij \cdot a}$. Note that for any one row of residuals, a_i is always the same. Store a_i in memory. Then to form each residual in row i, recall a_i, multiply negatively by a_j, and add r_{ij} from Table 2.1. It is convenient to set a ruler just above row i in Table 2.1 to cover the immediately preceding row or rows. Then r_{ij} is the entry just below the ruler in the same column as that in which a_j appears. Thus

TABLE 2.2
First Residual Matrix for Five Verbal Tests ($N = 841$)

Test	(1)	(2)	(3)	(4)	(5)	Σ
(1)	(.019)	−.023	.026	.017	−.039	.000
(2)	−.023	(.024)	−.025	−.019	.043	.000
(3)	.026	−.025	(.024)	.019	−.045	−.001
(4)	.017	−.019	.019	(.021)	−.039	−.001
(5)	−.039	.043	−.045	−.039	(.080)	.000

$$r_{11 \cdot a} = (.7476)(-.7476) + .578 = .019$$

$$r_{12 \cdot a} = (.7476)(-.8138) + .585 = -.023, \text{ etc.}$$

When the first row has been completed, its algebraic sum is computed. If this sum is zero within rounding error, it is recorded in column Σ, and the entries in row (1) are copied into column (1).

The second row begins with the calculation of $r_{22 \cdot a}$, the third with the calculation of $r_{33 \cdot a}$, and so on. As each row is completed, the *entire* row sum is calculated and entered in column Σ. It should be zero within rounding error.

2.4.4 Reflection

The first test to be reflected is the one whose column sum, *exclusive of the diagonal entry,* is largest negative. Because all diagonal entries are positive, and all total row sums (and hence column sums) are zero within rounding error, each column sum, exclusive of the diagonal entry, will be negative and numerically equal, apart from rounding error, to the diagonal entry. The largest diagonal entry, in Table 2.2, is $r_{55 \cdot a} = .080$. We therefore reflect test 5 first. Put a 1 after the column heading (5) to show that test 5 was the first test reflected. Then change the signs of all entries in row (5) *and* column (5) except that of the diagonal entry. Table 2.3 shows the result of the first reflection.

TABLE 2.3
First Residual Matrix for Five Verbal Tests after First Reflection
($N = 841$)

Test	(1)	(2)	(3)	(4)	(5)1	Σ
(1)	(.019)	—.023	.026	.017	╫.039	.000
(2)	—.023	(.024)	—.025	—.019	═.043	.000
(3)	.026	—.025	(.024)	.019	╫.045	—.001
(4)	.017	—.019	.019	(.021)	╫.039	—.001
(5)	╫.039	═.043	╫.045	╫.039	(.080)	.000

The sign changes are made with *double* lines so we can tell which minus and plus signs were original and which are the results of reflection. This permits checking a reflection if necessary.

In columns (1), (3), and (4), the effect of changing the sign from $-$ to $+$ in row (5) is to add twice the row (5) entry to the former column sum exclusive of the diagonal entry. Because twice any of these row (5) entries is larger than the diagonal entry, the sums of columns (1), (3), and (4), exclusive of the diagonal entries, are already positive. In column (2), however, the effect of changing the sign in row (5) from $+$ to $-$ is to add $2(-.043)$ to the already negative sum, so the next test to be reflected is test 2. In the first residual matrix of the next table (Table 2.4) we will therefore put a 1 in column (5) and a 2 in column (2), both in the row labeled Refl.

Ordinarily we use a single work sheet for the whole centroid analysis. The intercorrelations are in the first section, the first residuals and all their reflections

TABLE 2.4
Centroid Analysis of Five Verbal Tests (N = 841)

Test	(1)	(2)	(3)	(4)	(5)	Σ	Ch
(1)	(.578)	.585	.658	.616	.555	2.992	
(2)	.585	(.686)	.663	.634	.689	3.257	
(3)	.658	.663	(.738)	.697	.626	3.382	
(4)	.616	.634	.697	(.664)	.598	3.209	
(5)	.555	.689	.626	.598	(.711)	3.179	
Σ	2.992	3.257	3.382	3.209	3.179	16.019	16.019
a	.7476	.8138	.8450	.8018	.7943	4.0025	4.0024
Refl		2			1		
(1)	(.019)	‖ .023	.026	.017	‖ .039	.000	.124
(2)	‖ .023	(.024)	‖ .025	‖ .019	≡ .043	.000	.134
(3)	.026	‖ .025	(.024)	.019	‖ .045	−.001	.139
(4)	.017	‖ .019	.019	(.021)	‖ .039	−.001	.115
(5)	‖ .039	‖ .043	‖ .045	‖ .039	(.080)	.000	.246
Σ	.124	.134	.139	.115	.246	.758	.758
b	.1424	≡ .1539	.1597	.1321	≡ .2826	.8707	.87063

Second residual matrix

	(1)	(2)	(3)	(4)	(5)	
(1)	(−.001)	.001	.003	−.002	−.001	.000
(2)	.001	(.000)	.000	−.001	.000	.000
(3)	.003	.000	(−.002)	−.002	.000	−.001
(4)	−.002	−.001	−.002	(.004)	.002	.001
(5)	−.001	.000	.000	.002	(.000)	.001

are in the second section, and following each section we have a Σ-row and an a-row or b-row of factor loadings. We know already that for this problem there are only two factors, but we add a third section showing the second residuals, $r_{ij \cdot b} = r_{ij \cdot a} - b_i b_j$, to clinch this argument. The complete analysis is shown in Table 2.4.

The second section of Table 2.4 shows the results of the two reflections. All entries are now positive, though in general reflections can only guarantee that the column sums (and row sums) will be nonnegative, and stop when this result has been achieved. The row sums in column Σ are all zero within rounding error. Note that in the second section the sign of $r_{52 \cdot a} = r_{25 \cdot a} = .043$ has been changed twice.

In row Σ, just below the second section, we have the column sums after reflection, and their sum (here $\Sigma\Sigma r = .758$) is recorded in the same row in column Σ. We use column Ch to record the row sums after reflection. They are the same as the column sums, and their sum (again $.758$) is recorded in row Σ.

The second-factor loadings in row b are computed in the same manner as were the first-factor loadings in row a. Because tests 2 and 5 were reflected, we show that their b-factor loadings are negative, using double lines to indicate that this is due to their having been reflected.

The third section of Table 2.4 shows the second residuals. In computing them we take b_2 and b_5 as positive. These residuals are all so small, the largest being $r_{44 \cdot b} = .004$, that it is evident that we cannot extract a third factor from them. The sum of the diagonal entries in this panel (the residual communalities) is $.001$, or zero within rounding error. This shows that the total estimated communality (the sum of the diagonal entries in the first section) has been accounted for almost exactly by two factors.

2.4.5 Factor Matrix

The results are gathered together in the factor matrix of Table 2.5, with the entries in columns a and b rounded to three decimals from the entries in row a and row b of Table 2.4. At this point the b-entries for tests 2 and 5 are recorded with their final minus signs. In column h^2 we have the computed communalities,

$$h_i^2 = a_i^2 + b_i^2.$$

To check them, compute the sums of squares of the entries in columns a and b, and record them in row Σf^2. Their sum is 3.377, which is recorded in row Ch, column h^2. Add the entries in column h^2. Their sum, here 3.378, is recorded in row Σ just above the row–sum 3.377. These two entries agree within rounding error.

In this table we show in the last column, labeled h_0^2, the original communality estimates obtained from the tetrad–triad procedure and recorded on the diagonal in the first section of tables 2.1 and 2.4. The agreement is quite close, the largest

TABLE 2.5
Centroid Factor Matrix for Five Verbal Tests ($N = 841$)

Test	Factor a	b	h^2	h_0^2
(1) Paragraph Meaning	.748	.142	.580	.578
(2) Same–Opposite	.814	−.154	.686	.686
(3) Proverb Matching	.845	.160	.740	.738
(4) Verbal Analogies	.802	.132	.661	.664
(5) Vocabulary	.794	−.283	.711	.711
Σf^2	3.210	.167	3.378	3.377
Ch			3.377	

discrepancy (for test 4) being .003, and $\Sigma h_0^2 = 3.377$. Without this previous tetrad–triad analysis we would have had to estimate communalities by a less accurate procedure, and the agreement would not have been this good. Procedures for communality estimation are discussed in Chapter 5.

Exercise 2:1. Table 1.5 gives the correlations among six psychological tests. A tetrad–triad analysis of these correlations was performed in Exercise 1:1. Factor this correlation matrix to two factors by the centroid method, and compute the second residual matrix as in Tables 2.4 and 2.5. Take as initial communality estimates the communalities computed by the tetrad–triad method in Exercise 1:1. Reflect either variables 1, 2, and 3 or 4, 5, and 6, whichever set of three includes the variable with the largest diagonal entry in the first residual matrix. Save the results.

2.5 ROTATION IN TWO DIMENSIONS

The centroid factor matrix of Table 2.5 bears little resemblance to the tetrad–triad factor matrix of Table 1.4, and is not too readily interpreted. Factor a is a general factor (verbal ability), and factor b is some sort of *contrast* between word meaning (tests 2 and 5) and verbal reasoning (tests 1, 3 and 4). Some of the earlier writers, mainly in Great Britain, did stop here and present interpretations such as this. But with more than two or three factors, interpretations of this type become increasingly obscure. We desire interpretations based on explicit factors rather than contrasts, so we proceed to the transformation procedures of step 2. With this example (five verbal tests), one such transformation will give a result closely comparable to that of Table 1.4, and two others will also give easily interpretable results.

From equations (2-1), with five tests and two factors, we have the initial (step 1) factor pattern.

$$X_1 = a_1 A + b_1 B + u_1 U_1$$
$$X_2 = a_2 A + b_2 B + u_2 U_2$$
$$X_3 = a_3 A + b_3 B + u_3 U_3 \qquad (2\text{-}18)$$
$$X_4 = a_4 A + b_4 B + u_4 U_4$$
$$X_5 = a_5 A + b_5 B + u_5 U_5$$

The numerical values of the a's and b's are given in Table 2.5. If we want the u's, they are easily obtained from the equation,

$$u_i = \sqrt{1 - h_i^2} \quad (i = 1, 2, \ldots, n; \text{ here } n = 5). \qquad (2\text{-}19)$$

We know that equations (2-18) are the correct version of the general equations (2-1) for this example because we found from Table 2.4 that the number of substantial factors (m) is two.

The final desired result is represented by a set of equations such as (2-2), namely,

$$X_1 = I_1 I^* + II_1 II^* + u_1 U_1$$
$$X_2 = I_2 I^* + II_2 II^* + u_2 U_2$$
$$X_3 = I_3 I^* + II_3 II^* + u_3 U_3 \qquad (2\text{-}20)$$
$$X_4 = I_4 I^* + II_4 II^* + u_4 U_4$$
$$X_5 = I_5 I^* + II_5 II^* + u_5 U_5$$

To get from (2-18) to (2-20), we need to determine a transformation such as the one indicated by (2-5). For two factors the equations of the transformation are

$$I_i = (Ia)a_i + (Ib)b_i$$
$$II_i = (IIa)a_i + (IIb)b_i \qquad (2\text{-}21)$$
$$(i = 1, 2, \ldots, n; \text{ here } n = 5)$$

To use these equations, we must find some reasonable procedure for determining the transformation coefficients (Ia), (Ib), (IIa), and (IIb).

2.5.1 Geometric Model

Each pair of initial common-factor loadings may be thought of as the coordinates of a point in a plane. Each point, 1, 2, 3, 4, 5, represents the two loadings on one variable. The plot, from Table 2.5, is shown in Fig. 2.1, with axes labeled a and b, and arrows indicating the positive direction of each axis at the distance $+1$ from the origin 0. The distance from the origin to each of the points (i.e., the length of the vector from the origin to the point, drawn as a dashed line with an arrow for point 5 in Fig. 2.1) is h_i. For by (2-8), when $m = 2$ (two factors), $h_i^2 = a_i^2 + b_i^2$. But in the figure, the coordinates a_i and b_i (a_5 and b_5 for point 5) are the legs of a right triangle, h_i is its hypotenuse, and $h_i^2 = a_i^2 + b_i^2$ is a statement of the Pythagorean theorem. This is why we designate a communality by the symbol h_i^2 (the square on the hypotenuse).

Note. In the geometric model of factor analysis it is convenient, though not actually necessary, to let the first initial axis a be vertical, and the second axis b horizontal. The coordinates of any point i are then a_i, b_i in that order. This reverses a common practice in mathematics, in which the horizontal axis is likely to be labeled x and the vertical axis y, with the coordinates of a point i labeled x_i, y_i in that order.

Note also that the a-coordinate is measured *parallel* to the axis a *from* the axis b, and that the b-coordinate is measured *parallel* to the axis b *from* the axis a. This is a general rule. Axes are designated by letters or Roman numerals, coordinates by letters or Roman numerals with Arabic numerical subscripts designating the points of which they are coordinates, and points simply by Arabic numerals. Then for *any* axis and *any* point, the coordinate bearing the same designation as the axis is measured *parallel* to that axis, *from* the axis at right angles to it.

It can be seen in Fig. 2.1 that test points 1, 3, and 4 lie almost on a line through the origin. This line, when extended to unit length, with an arrow on the bounding semicircle, is labeled II. Suppose we move the axis b to this line II, and draw the line RII at right angles to it; that is, rotate axes b and a counterclockwise about the origin 0 to the positions II and RII. The coordinates of the

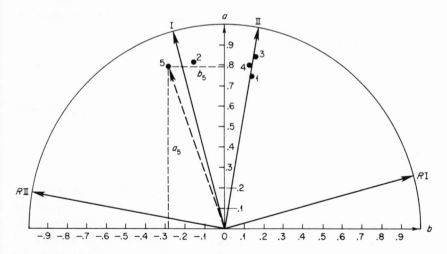

FIG. 2.1.   Plot of factor loadings from Table 2.5 for five verbal tests, and rotation of axes ($N = 84$).

points on the rotated axes II and RII will then represent the loadings of the corresponding variables on the transformed factors of (2-20), just as the coordinates of these points on the original axes a and b represent the loadings of the corresponding variables on the original factors of (2-18). We state also here without proof that the coordinates of the rotated axes II and RII on the original axes a and b represent the transformation coefficients of (2-21). The termini of these axes. II and RII, lie on the unit circle. The proof is outlined at the end of Section 2.5.3. Let us also, *for this rotation only*, re-label axis II as axis I, and axis RII as axis II. The result is shown in Fig. 2.1.a. (The labeling of Fig. 2.1 applies to the oblique rotation, discussed later in Section 2.5.5.)

From Fig. 2.1.a, when we measure the coordinates of the five points parallel to axis I (from axis II), they will all be positive and fairly large, so factor I will be a general factor, with loadings (I-coordinates) all positive and large. And when we measure the coordinates parallel to axis II (from axis I), those of points 1, 3, and 4 will be near-zero, while those of points 2 and 5 will be positive and moderately large: positive because as axis a moves to II its positive direction is to the left. Hence factor II will be a group factor, with substantial loadings (II-coordinates) only on tests 2 and 5. The new loadings will now resemble more or less closely those on factors a and b of Table 1.4. The relabeling of axes used in Fig. 2.1.a is designed to make factor I a general (here verbal-reasoning) factor and factor II a group (here word-meaning) factor. When the initial axes a and b are rotated, we are free to assign the numbers I and II to the rotated axes in either order. If one of the rotated factors is a general factor, with substantial loadings on all of the variables, it is usual to call this general factor factor I.

We term this rotation the large counterclockwise orthogonal rotation. A rotation is defined as orthogonal whenever the two rotated axes remain at right angles to each other.

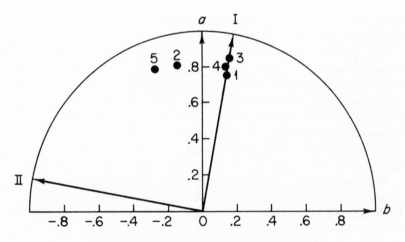

FIG. 2.1.a.   Large counterclockwise orthogonal rotation.

2.5.2. Centroid Vectors

We wish to define the new axis I as a line from the origin passing as nearly as possible through the three points 1, 3, and 4 of Fig. 2.1.a. One way to do this is to use the averages of the three a-coordinates and of the three b-coordinates to define a single point with coordinates a_c and b_c. This point is termed the *centroid* of the points 1, 3, and 4. It is a two-dimensional average of the positions of the three points on the graph. In a physical model, the centroid would be the center of gravity of the three points. This centroid is not shown on Fig. 2.1.a but is easily visualized as lying just barely to the right of point 4 on the line 0I.

The point of real interest is the point I, where a line from the origin through the centroid reaches the unit semicircle, rather than the centroid point itself. The coordinates of this point must be *proportional* to a_c and b_c, and by the Pythagorean theorem the sum of their squares must be unity because the line 0I is of unit length and is the hypotenuse of the triangle whose sides are the a and b coordinates of the point I. If the coordinates are proportional to a_c and b_c, they are also proportional to $3a_c$ and $3b_c$, the column sums $a_1 + a_3 + a_4$ and $b_1 + b_3 + b_4$ of Table 2.5. The computation of the coordinates of axis I, which are the values of the coefficients (Ia) and (Ib) of (2-21), is as follows, using the data from Table 2.5:

Var.	a	b	
			$2.395^2 + .434^2 = 5.9244$
(1)	.748	.142	$\sqrt{5.9244} = 2.4340$
(3)	.845	.160	$1/2.4340 = .41085$
(4)	.802	.132	$(.41085)(2.395) = .984 = (Ia)$
Σ	2.395	.434	$(.41085)(.434) = .178 = (Ib)$
			Check: $(Ia)^2 + (Ib)^2 = 1.000$

In the intermediate computations at the right, the results are carried to five significant figures to avoid accumulation of rounding errors.

This procedure is termed *normalizing* the sums (or the averages) of the a-loadings and the b-loadings of the three tests. When two or more numbers (here two column sums) are normalized, each of them is multiplied by the reciprocal of the square root of the sum of their squares. If the numbers are a and b, the corresponding normalized numbers are $a/\sqrt{a^2 + b^2}$ and $b/\sqrt{a^2 + b^2}$, and the sum of squares of these normalized numbers is $(a^2 + b^2)/(a^2 + b^2) = 1$. The extension to more than two such numbers is obvious. Note that normalizing, as defined here, has no reference to the normal distribution.

Note on geometry: In this book only two theorems from Euclidean geometry are used, namely: (1) the Pythagorean theorem: in a right triangle, the square on the hypotenuse is equal to the sum of the squares on the sides; (2) the similar-triangles theorem: if the angles of any two triangles are equal, the sides are proportional; and if the sides are proportional, the angles are equal.

It is of interest to note that all of the theorems of trigonometry can be developed from these two theorems and the definitions of the sine, cosine, tangent, cotangent, secant, and cosecant.

2.5.3 The Transformation Equations and the Rotated Factor Matrix

For the data of our example, the terminus I of the line (vector) OI in Fig. 2.1.a has coordinates $(Ia) = .984$ and $(Ib) = .178$. (Ia) is the a-coordinate of point I, and (Ib) is its b-coordinate, as given by the normalized centroid procedure.

We now have the coefficients, (Ia) and (Ib), of the first equation of (2-21). The second equation calls for (IIa) and (IIb), the a and b coordinates of the point II. Because the axes I and II are at right angles, as are also the axes a and b, the a-coordinate of point II (measured parallel to axis a and upward from axis b) is the same as the b-coordinate of point I, or $(IIa) = (Ib) = .178$. The b-coordinate of point II (measured parallel to axis b and leftward from axis a) is the same length as the a-coordinate of point I, but its leftward direction parallel to axis b is negative, so that $(IIb) = -(Ia) = -.984$.

Gathering these results together, equations (2-21) become, for the large counterclockwise orthogonal rotation,

$$I_i = (Ia)a_i + (Ib)b_i$$

$$II_i = (Ib)a_i - (Ia)b_i \tag{2-22}$$

or for the data of Table 2.5

$$I_i = .984a_i + .178b_i$$

$$II_i = .178a_i - .984b_i$$

The first two columns of Table 2.6 are the same as the first two columns of Table 2.5. Applying to each pair of loadings in columns a and b the transformations above, we obtain the figures in columns I and II of Table 2.6. Thus for variable (1), $(.984)(.748) + (.178)(.142) = .761$, and $(.178)(.748) - (.984)(.142) = -.007$. In practice, we write the coefficients .984 and .178 at the top of a small card, hold the card just below each pair of numbers in columns a and b, perform the two multiplications accumulatively, and enter the result, rounded to three decimals, in column I. This procedure is repeated for column II with the coefficients .178 and $-.984$ written on the card.

The entries in row Σ are the column sums, and the entries in row Ch of columns I and II are computed from those in row Σ of columns a and b. Thus $(.984)(4.003) + (.178)(-.003) = 3.938$, and $(.178)(4.003) - (.984)(-.003) = .715$. These check-values should agree with the column sums just above them within rounding error.

TABLE 2.6
Large Counterclockwise Orthogonal Rotation of Centroid Factor Matrix
for Five Verbal Tests (N = 841)

Test	Centroid a	Centroid b	Rotated I	Rotated II	Tetrad–Triad I_0	Tetrad–Triad II_0
(1)	.748	.142	.761	−.007	.760	.000
(2)	.814	−.154	.774	.296	.773	.297
(3)	.845	.160	.860	−.007	.859	.000
(4)	.802	.132	.813	.013	.815	.000
(5)	.794	−.283	.731	.420	.731	.420
Σ	4.003	−.003	3.939	.715	3.938	.717
Ch			3.938	.715		

Because this is an orthogonal transformation, leaving factors I and II uncorrelated, the entries in columns I and II of Table 2.6 represent the coefficients of a transformed factor pattern. Hence in each row i of columns I and II, $I_i^2 + II_i^2 = h_i^2$, which should agree within rounding error with the corresponding value of h_i^2 in column h^2 of Table 2.5.

In columns I_0 and II_0 we have entries copied from columns a and b of Table 1.4. Comparing these with the corresponding entries in columns I and II, we see that the centroid method with this rotation gives essentially the same results as did the tetrad–triad method. The only appreciable discrepancies are in rows (1), (3), and (4) of factors II and II_0: in column II the arbitrarily exact zeros of column II_0 are replaced by near-zeros.

The primary object of this rotational procedure was to find one factor, here factor II, with elements II_i (i = 1, 2, 3, 4, 5) several of which (here three) are near-zero, so that this factor becomes a group factor rather than a general factor. We did this by passing the line 0I through a cluster of points at the right boundary of the configuration of all the test points. The factor I emerged as a general factor because the I-coordinates of all the points, measured parallel to axis I from axis II, were far from the line 0II. With highest loadings on the tests having greatest reasoning content, 3 (Proverb Matching) and 4 (Verbal Analogies), this is a general (verbal-reasoning) factor.

The axis II was required to be at right angles to the axis I. Factor II emerged as a word-meaning group factor (doublet) because the II-coordinates of points 1, 3, and 4, measured parallel to axis II from axis I, gave near-zero loadings (−.007, −.007, .013), whereas those of points 2 and 5 gave substantial loadings: .296 for variable 2 (Same–Opposite) and .420 for variable 5 (Vocabulary).

Note on doublets: In Chapter 1 we first showed that a single correlation (original or residual) gives the *product* of the loadings on a doublet but does not give their separate values. Some writers, noting only this fact, tend to reject all doublets as having indeterminate loadings. Later we showed that in those very rare cases in which reliabilities are available (the five-verbal-tests example is one such case), we can estimate the two loadings on a second-factor doublet with fair accuracy. It was shown also (in Problem 1.6.7:1) that, by using the least reasonable assumption, the maximum errors in the estimates of the two doublet loadings given by the more reasonable assumption are not excessively large. In this chapter we then obtained estimates of these doublet loadings by the centroid method and rotation without using the data on reliability. In Table 2.6 the agreement between the two pairs of estimates is striking: .296 and .297 for test 2, and .420 by both methods for test 5. We must conclude that the estimates of these loadings given by the two-step procedure are good estimates, and that the "reasonable assumption" used in Chapter 1 was in fact a good assumption. The agreement in Table 2.6 is well within the limits of two different sets of rounding errors and is highly unlikely to be a coincidence.

There is probably no such thing as a perfect doublet in real data. The near-zero loadings are too small to contribute to the *interpretation* of a doublet, but in toto they have some validity, and enable us to obtain good estimates of the substantial loadings on the doublet. In larger studies, therefore, doublet loadings need not be rejected as indeterminate: they are probably almost as well determined as are those of common factors with more than two substantial loadings. In a larger sense, a common factor defined by only two substantial loadings is not as well defined as is one defined by at least three or four. In selecting the variables for a larger study, the investigator should avoid as far as possible sets of only two similar variables. If doublets do appear, however, they should not be rejected, but should be interpreted as well as possible given only two substantial loadings.

The complete proof that the coordinates of the points I and II on the unit semicircle are in fact the correct coefficients for the transformation equations of (2-22) is not attempted, but for those well acquainted with analytic geometry and trigonometry we give herewith an *outline* of this proof. If, in Fig. 2.1.a, we let the angle of rotation $b \ 0 \ I = \phi$, the a-coordinate of I is $(Ia) = \sin \phi$, and its b-coordinate is $(Ib) = \cos \phi$. The counterclockwise orthogonal rotation from $0b$ and $0a$ to $0I$ and $0II$ gives new coordinates specified by

$$I_i = a_i \sin \phi + b_i \cos \phi$$

$$II_i = a_i \cos \phi - b_i \sin \phi$$

These equations are then identical with (2-22). The proof of these relations uses in turn the theorems giving the sine and cosine of the sum and difference of two angles, one of them ϕ and the other, say ϕ_i, the angle between the b-axis and a line of unit length from the origin through the test-point i.

For those not thoroughly familiar with analytic geometry and trigonometry, the method given previously, for finding the coordinates of axes I and II directly from the plot, is recommended.

2.5.4 Alternative Orthogonal Rotation

In Chapter 1 we rejected the alternative hypothesis of a general factor and a group factor in tests 1, 3, and 4. But when we use the two-step procedure, and do not know the test reliabilities, we lack some of the data on which that decision was based. We therefore describe another orthogonal rotation designed to give a general factor and a group factor with nonzero loadings on tests 1, 3, and 4. We rotate the axis a to the original axis I of Fig. 2.1, with axis b moving to RI, which *for this rotation* we relabel axis II. Because this rotation moves the a and b axes through smaller angles than did the previous rotation, we term it the small counterclockwise orthogonal rotation. The result is shown in Fig. 2.1.b.

When we measure the I_i coordinates of the test points parallel to axis I from axis II, they will all be large, and factor I will be a general factor. And when we measure the II_i coordinates parallel to axis II from axis I, those of points 2 and 5 will be near-zero, whereas those of points 1, 3, and 4 will be moderately large, so factor II will be a group factor with nonzero loadings on tests 1, 3, and 4.

We locate axis I by passing the line 0I through the centroid of points 2 and 5. Then from Table 2.5, we have

Var.	a	b	
(2)	.814	−.154	
(5)	.794	−.283	
Σ	1.608	−.437	

$1.608^2 + .437^2 = 2.7766$

$\sqrt{2.7766} = 1.6663$

$1/1.6663 = .60013$

$(.60013)(1.608) = .965 = (Ia)$
$(.60013)(-.437) = -.262 = (Ib)$
Check: $(Ia)^2 + (Ib)^2 = 1.000$

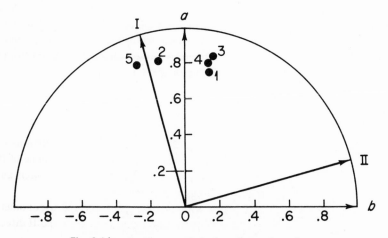

Fig. 2.1.b. Small counterclockwise orthogonal rotation.

Then from Fig. 2.1.b, noting that (Ib) is negative, $(IIa) = -(Ib) = .262$, and $(IIb) = (Ia) = .965$. Making these substitutions in equations (2-21), we have

$$I_i = (Ia)a_i + (Ib)b_i$$
$$II_i = -(Ib)a_i + (Ia)b_i \tag{2-23}$$

or for the data of Table 2.5

$$I_i = .965a_i - .262b_i$$
$$II_i = .262a_i + .965b_i$$

Applying these transformations to the figures in columns a and b of Table 2.7 (which are the same as those in columns a and b of Table 2.5), we obtain the results shown in columns I and II of Table 2.7. Here again these values represent the coefficients of a transformed factor pattern.

Factor I is now a general (word-meaning) factor, with highest loadings on 2 (Same–Opposite) and 5 (Vocabulary), but still quite substantial loadings on the other three tests. Factor II is a verbal-reasoning group factor, with nonzero loadings on 1 (Paragraph Meaning), 3 (Proverb Matching), and 4 (Verbal Analogies). The near-zero loadings on factor II, .065 for 2 (Same–Opposite) and $-.065$ for 5 (Vocabulary), are not as low as were the near-zeros of Table 2.6 ($-.007$, $-.007$, and $.013$), but they are still well below the commonly accepted critical value $\pm.100$ for near-zeros. Values as high as $\pm.110$ or even $\pm.120$ are not too infrequently accepted as near-zeros.

2.5.5 Oblique Rotation

A third rotation is often used when we do not wish to define a general factor in terms of either of the effectively bounding clusters. The aim is instead to maximize the number of near-zero loadings on *each* of the factors, by allowing them to be *correlated* rather than orthogonal or uncorrelated. The rotation that accomplishes this aim is termed a *simple-structure* rotation. It corresponds to Alternative 1 of the reading-arithmetic example of Chapter 1.

Consider the axes as designated in Fig. 2.1. Suppose we move axis a to I and axis b to II. The lines at right angles to the axes I and II are the axes RI and RII. When we measure the distances of the test points *parallel* to the axes I and II *from* the axes RI and RII, both factors are *general* factors, with all loadings on both factors positive and large. Factor I is the factor I of Table 2.7, and factor II is the factor I of Table 2.6.

To obtain two *group* factors we move axis b to RI and axis a to RII. Then when we measure the test points *parallel* to the axes RI and RII *from* the axes I and II we obtain the two group factors. The coordinates of RI are equal to $-(Ib)$ and (Ia) of axis I, and hence equal to those of the second equation of (2-23). The coordinates of RII are equal to (IIb) and $-(IIa)$ of axis II, and hence equal numerically to those of the second equation of (2-22) but without the change of

Table 2.7
Small Counterclockwise Orthogonal Rotation of
Centroid Factor Matrix for Five Verbal Tests
($N = 841$)

Test	Centroid		Rotated	
	a	b	I	II
(1)	.748	.142	.685	.333
(2)	.814	−.154	.826	.065
(3)	.845	.160	.774	.376
(4)	.802	.132	.739	.338
(5)	.794	−.283	.840	−.065
Σ	4.003	−.003	3.864	1.047
Ch			3.864	1.046

designation (I for II) of Fig. 2.1.a and (2-22). The transformation equations are then

$$I_i = -(Ib)a_i + (Ia)b_i$$

$$II_i = (IIb)a_i - (IIa)b_i \tag{2-24}$$

or for the data of this example

$$I_i = .262a_i + .965b_i$$

$$II_i = .178a_i - .984b_i$$

Applying these transformations to factors a and b of Table 2.8, which are the same as factors a and b of Table 2.5, we obtain the entries in columns I and II of Table 2.8. The figures are the same as those in column II of Table 2.7 and column II of Table 2.6.

TABLE 2.8
Oblique Rotation of Centroid Factor Matrix for
Five Verbal Tests ($N = 841$)

Test	Centroid		Rotated	
	a	b	I	II
(1)	.748	.142	.333	−.007
(2)	.814	−.154	.065	.296
(3)	.845	.160	.376	−.007
(4)	.802	.132	.338	.013
(5)	.794	−.283	−.065	.420
Σ	4.003	−.003	1.047	.715
Ch			1.046	.715

Here both of the factors are group factors, as we desired. Factor I is the verbal-reasoning factor, and factor II is the word-meaning factor.

The axes RI and RII are termed the *reference vectors,* and are defined as the lines at right angles to the axes I and II. In the orthogonal case, where the axes I and II are at right angles to each other, RI is the same as II and RII is the same as I (see Figs. 2.1.a and 2.1.b again). Because in the oblique case we measured the coordinates of the test points parallel to these reference vectors (RI and RII), the solution of Table 2.8 is termed the *reference-vector structure.* When, as in this case, and quite generally when we rotate obliquely, the reference vectors are so located as to maximize the number of near-zero loadings on each of the reference-vector factors, with at least as many near-zero loadings on each factor as the number of factors (here two), this reference-vector structure is a *simple structure.*

In the oblique case, the axes 0I and 0II, near the boundaries of the configuration of test points, are termed the *primary factors.* These primary factors represent "ideal" tests, each of which measures one and only one common factor, with no unique factors because their vector lengths of unity imply that their communalities are 1.000. It is the reference vectors RI and RII, however, which determine the excellence of the simple structure.

The reader should note that the column (rotated factor) labels I and II of Table 2.8 do *not* refer to the axes 0I and 0II of Fig. 2.1 but rather to the reference vectors RI and RII. Note also that the axis 0II is correlated with the reference vector RI (angle II 0 RI acute) but uncorrelated with RII (angle RII 0 II a right angle). Similarly the axis 0I is correlated with the reference vector RII but uncorrelated with RI. Because each reference vector is correlated with the *corresponding* primary factor and uncorrelated with the other, axis 0II is the primary factor PI, and 0I is the primary factor PII. In higher-dimensional cases (three or more factors), the axes 0I and 0II become planes or *hyperplanes,* but the primary axes remain vectors.

The transformed factor pattern, in the oblique case, has coefficients that are the projections of the test points on the primary axes. The loadings on the reference-vector axes, given in columns I and II of Table 2.8, are the *correlations* between the tests and the oblique reference-vector factors, but they are *not* the coefficients of the primary-factor pattern, which are discussed in Chapter 6; and in each row (i) of this table, $\text{I}_i^2 + \text{II}_i^2$ is not equal to the communality h_i^2.

The reference-vector factors are *initially* the factors of interest for an oblique rotation, because they are the factors the numbers and magnitudes of whose near-zero loadings determine the excellence of the simple structure. The primary factors, however, are of greater theoretical interest, because they can be interpreted as "ideal" tests.

In the two-factor case, the correlation between the primary factors is given by

$$r_{\text{I II}} = (\text{I}a)(\text{II}a) + (\text{I}b)(\text{II}b). \qquad (2\text{-}25)$$

For the present problem this is

$$r_{I\ II} = (.965)(.984) + (-.262)(.178) = .903.$$

This correlation, which is quite high, is the correlation between the two "ideal" tests, I and II in Fig. 2.1. It tells us that in our data knowledge of word meanings and verbal-reasoning ability are highly correlated. Geometrically, this correlation is also the cosine of the angle I 0 II of Fig. 2.1. This angle is highly acute, so its cosine is high. From a table of cosines we find that the angle whose cosine is .903 is quite close to 25.5°.

If the two outer clusters were so far apart, in Fig. 2.1, that the angle I 0 II was greater than 90°, the "small clockwise orthogonal rotation" would be through a greater angle than the "large counterclockwise orthogonal rotation," and the correlation between the primary factors would be negative. This case is relatively rare with most types of real data. It occurs only when, in the original correlation matrix, the correlations are mostly negative.

In the oblique case, the sum of squares of the elements in one row of the rotated factor matrix is *not* the communality of the test represented by that row. This can be verified from Table 2.8, in which for any row the sum of squares of the unrotated loadings, $a^2 + b^2$, is the communality, while the sum of squares of the rotated loadings, $I^2 + II^2$, is not.

The matters discussed in this section are treated in detail in Chapter 6, including the general case of more than two factors.

2.5.6 Efficient Computation

For practical computation, much of the foregoing procedure can be bypassed. From the centroid factor matrix of Table 2.5, or from any similar table for another problem, we merely plot the test points from the coordinates a and b. The effectively bounding clusters (possibly only single points if we do not have a good simple structure) can be identified by inspection of the plot. Any points or clusters that are not near an effective boundary are ignored. The effectively bounding clusters (or points) are labeled I (for the left cluster or point) and II (for the right cluster or point). The normalized centroids (or normalized coordinates of a single point) then yield (Ia), (Ib), (IIa), and (IIb).

Alternatively, the points may be plotted as accurately as possible (to about .005 instead of .01 or .02) on millimeter or 1/20-inch cross-section paper, the upper part of the unit semicircle may be drawn with a compass, the lines 0I and 0II may be drawn in "by eye," and their coordinates, (Ia), (Ib), (IIa), and (IIb), may be read from the plot. This procedure yields coordinates accurate to about two decimals, which is quite sufficient for most two-factor problems.

If we now rewrite (2-22), (2-23), (2-24), and (2-25) without any relabeling of the axes I and II, and without including RI and RII on the plot, we can substitute the values of (Ia), (Ib), (IIa), and (IIb) directly into these equations. Fig. 2.2

shows the procedures. In this figure the locations of the points 1–7 are arbitrary: they do not represent the plot of a real initial factor matrix. The axis I goes through the single point 4 at the left. The axis II goes through the centroid of the cluster consisting of points 2, 6, and 7 at the right. The cluster consisting of points 1, 3, and 5 is ignored, because it is not near either of the effective boundaries.

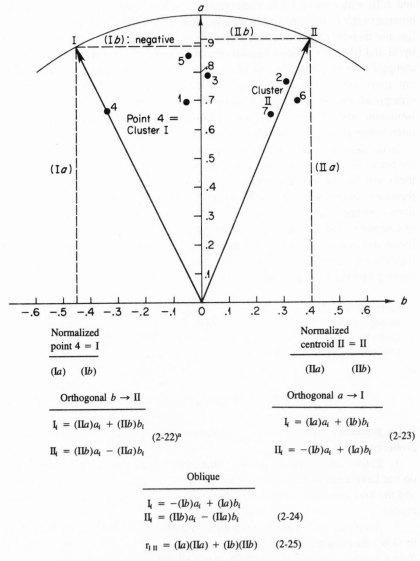

Normalized
point 4 = I
_____

(Ia)   (Ib)

Orthogonal $b \to$ II
_____

$I_i = (IIa)a_i + (IIb)b_i$
$II_i = (IIb)a_i - (IIa)b_i$ (2-22)[a]

Normalized
centroid II = II
_____

(IIa)   (IIb)

Orthogonal $a \to$ I
_____

$I_i = (Ia)a_i + (Ib)b_i$
$II_i = -(Ib)a_i + (Ia)b_i$ (2-23)

Oblique
_____

$I_i = -(Ib)a_i + (Ia)b_i$
$II_i = (IIb)a_i - (IIa)b_i$ (2-24)

$r_{I\ II} = (Ia)(IIa) + (Ib)(IIb)$ (2-25)

[a] Axes I and II not interchanged here.

FIG. 2.2. Summary of rotations in two dimensions.

Below the figure, the equations (2-22), (2-23), (2-24), and (2-25) are written, with notation revised to agree with the figure.

The *structure* of the points in the plane of Fig. 2.1 or 2.2 is determined by the locations of the effectively bounding lines 0I and 0II, and the reference vectors 0RI and 0RII (not shown in Fig. 2.2) are at right angles to them. If both reference vectors lie *outside* the bounded region, the structure is *acute* (as it is in Figs. 2.1 and 2.2), with angle I 0 II an acute angle. If both reference vectors lie *inside* the bounded region, the structure is *obtuse,* and the angle I 0 II is an obtuse angle (greater than 90 degrees). If one reference vector lies inside the region bounded by 0I and 0II and the other lies outside this region, the structure is partly acute and partly obtuse, regardless of whether the angle I 0 II is acute or obtuse. In the rare transition case, where the angle I 0 II is a right angle, the structure itself is orthogonal; the oblique transformation of (2-24) becomes an orthogonal transformation; and (2-22), (2-23), and (2-24) all give the same result (apart from interchange of the factors in the $b \rightarrow$ II solution).

In the two-factor case, with the all-positive-loadings rule for factor a, some of the points will always lie to the left of the axis a and some to the right, and all of them will lie above (very rarely one or two *on*) the axis b. The rotation can therefore always be performed by using (2-22) or (2-23) or (2-24). These rotations correspond to Alternatives 3, 4, and 1 for the reading–arithmetic example of Chapter 1. The numerical procedure corresponding to Alternative 2, a general factor and two group factors all orthogonal to one another, must be delayed to a later chapter. The geometry shifts from two dimensions to three, with the axis a moving upward from the plane of the two-dimensional plot.

Exercise 2:2. In Exercise 2:1 you obtained a centroid solution of the correlations among six psychological tests. Plot the loadings of the centroid factor matrix, and rotate by (2-22), (2-23), and (2-24), using Fig. 2.2. Compare the results of the rotation by (2-22) with the tetrad–triad results of Exercise 1:1. Save the results.

2.6 FURTHER PROBLEMS

In the preceding sections we have omitted or discussed only briefly a number of problems.

1. *Estimation of communalities.* Ordinarily, at the beginning of step 1, we do not have a tetrad–triad analysis giving good estimates of the communalities, and the best available procedures, even in the two-factor case, are considerably cruder.

2. *Reestimation in residual matrices.* If an original communality estimate is too low, the corresponding diagonal element of a residual matrix, say the $(k-1)$-th (not necessarily the first if $m > 2$), may become near-zero or negative. But this diagonal entry represents all of the residual communality that remains to be accounted for by the k-th factor (derived from the $(k-1)$-th residual matrix) and

any later salient factors. We therefore restore some of the original underestimated communality by replacing this too-low diagonal residual by an entry which is at least appreciably positive, before computing the loadings on the k-th factor. All salient factors should be computed from correlation matrices (original or residual) all of whose diagonal entries are appreciably positive.

The residual matrix after the last factor retained (the m-th) should ideally have diagonal entries some of which are positive and some negative and adding to a value close to zero as in Table 2.4.

If an original communality estimate is too high, little harm is done. Most of the surplus communality will go into a too-high diagonal entry in the m-th residual matrix, though some of it will inflate slightly the loadings of the variable on the salient factors.

3. *Systematic reflection.* With more than five or six variables, the method of reflection described in Section 2.4.4 is impractical, and a systematic procedure is needed. We start by computing the column sums exclusive of the diagonal entries, and reflect the variable having the largest negative sum. New column sums (exclusive of the diagonal entries) are then computed, and the variable whose new sum is largest negative is reflected. This process is repeated until we reach a set of new sums all of which are positive or zero. Procedures which minimize the computations needed to obtain the new column sums are described in older texts, but we omit them here because the centroid method is now seldom used, even when $m = 2$, when n is greater than 5 or 6.

4. *Estimation of the number of factors.* Only in rare cases do we reach a residual matrix, such as the second residual matrix of Table 2.4, whose entries are so obviously insubstantial. Exercise 2:1 is a more typical case. Ordinarily several methods are used to estimate the number of salient (substantial) factors. No one method is satisfactory, but by using several we can usually arrive at the correct or almost-correct number. Occasionally the various methods yield answers so inconsistent that we must rotate m and then $m + 1$ or even $m + 2$ to see which rotation gives the most sensible result in terms of the substantive nature of the variables.

5. *Refactoring.* The initial communality estimates are entered on the diagonal of the original correlation matrix. Their sum should be close to (ideally equal to) the sum of the final communalities: the row sums-of-squares of the loadings on the factors retained. If the initial estimates are so poor that these sums differ appreciably (say by more than about 5%), the computed communalities should be inserted on the diagonal of the correlation matrix as new estimates, and the matrix should then be refactored. If the number of factors has been correctly estimated, one refactoring is all that is required to bring the two sums (of initial estimated communalities and final computed communalities) into substantial agreement.

Some of these problems are discussed in more detail in Chapter 5, along with the discussion of the principal-axes method of initial factoring. Systematic reflection is not discussed. Reflection is not used with the principal-axes method unless the original correlation matrix has one or more negative column sums (exclusive of the diagonal entries) in which case it is used only with this original matrix.

2.6.1 Example

Table 2.9 shows, at the top, the intercorrelations among seven reasoning and perseveration tests, from a study by Misiak and Loranger (1961). The subjects were 86 older adults, and with N this small the correlations were reported to only two decimals, so the third figure of every entry in the correlation matrix is 0.

When we look at this correlation matrix it is evident that variables 6 and 7 must be reflected. Thus variable 6 becomes "Avoidance of Perseverative Errors" and variable 7 becomes "Youngness." The fact that these variables were reflected in the original correlation matrix and not rereflected is indicated by placing minus signs before the variable-*numbers* (6) and (7) of the factor matrices below the correlation matrix in Table 2.9. The signs of the loadings in the factor matrices are those which apply when these variables are not rereflected.

We have omitted the details of communality estimation and the centroid factoring procedure, including systematic reflection of residual matrixes and communality reestimation in these residual matrices.

The first solution (at the left) includes three centroid factors. In each row, the h^2-value is the sum of squares: $a^2 + b^2 + c^2$. The sum of the entries in column h^2 is recorded in row Σ. Each entry in row Σf^2 is the sum of *squares* of the elements in the column above it. The sum of these sums of squares, $2.918 + .556 + .273 = 3.747$, agrees with the sum 3.746 of column h^2 witin rounding error.

In column h_0^2 we have the initial communality estimates, which were placed on the diagonal of the original correlation matrix for the centroid analysis. Their sum is termed the *trace* of this correlation matrix, shown as 3.677 at the bottom of the column. If we recall that the communality of a variable is the proportion of its variance which it holds in common with the other variables, the trace can be interpreted as the total common variance of all the variables. The *initial* trace is an estimate of the final trace, which is the sum of communalities computed from the factor loadings. In the last row, labeled % tr, we have the values of 2.918/3.677, (2.918 + .556)/3.677, and (2.918 + .556 + .273)/3.677, reduced in each case to a percentage. Thus factor a accounts for 79% of the initial estimated variance (the trace), factors a and b for 94%, and all three factors for 102%. Note that Σh^2 does *not* have an upper bound equal to the initial trace; reestimation of the diagonal entries in the residual matrices (the residual communalities) adds 2% in this case.

It is not clear in this problem whether factor c is *salient* (substantial) or not. Tests of salience are discussed in Chapter 5. The various tests for the salience of this factor were inconclusive. Hence we tried a two-factor solution. In this two-factor initial solution the same initial communality estimates (h_0^2) were used

TABLE 2.9
Intercorrelations among Seven Reasoning and Perseveration Tests,
and Three Centroid Factor Matrices (N = 86)

Correlation Matrix

Test	(1)	(2)	(3)	(4)	(5)	(6)	(7)
(1)		.370	.230	.230	.120	−.490	−.120
(2)	.370		.430	.650	.550	−.530	−.270
(3)	.230	.430		.440	.480	−.450	−.200
(4)	.230	.650	.440		.670	−.400	−.180
(5)	.120	.550	.480	.670		−.380	−.320
(6)	−.490	−.530	−.450	−.400	−.380		.340
(7)	−.120	−.270	−.200	−.180	−.320	.340	

Factor Matrices

Test	3-Factor					Initial 2-Factor			Refactored 2-Factor		
	a	b	c	h^2	h_0^2	a	b	h^2	a	b	h^2
(1)	.443	−.374	−.317	.437	.391	.443	−.328	.304	.426	−.319	.283
(2)	.792	.057	−.192	.667	.688	.792	.028	.628	.784	.036	.616
(3)	.609	.051	.063	.377	.451	.609	.025	.372	.595	.037	.355
(4)	.738	.380	−.167	.717	.677	.738	.381	.690	.745	.403	.717
(5)	.725	.345	.232	.698	.670	.725	.328	.633	.721	.345	.639
−(6)	.711	−.353	−.003	.630	.538	.711	−.381	.651	.741	−.424	.729
−(7)	.384	−.148	.224	.220	.262	.384	−.110	.160	.363	−.078	.138
Σ				3.746	3.677[a]			3.438			3.477
Σf^2	2.918	.556	.273			2.918	.519		2.906	.572	
% tr	79	94	102			79	93		85	101	

(1) Critical Flicker Frequency
(2) Digit Symbol (WAIS)
(3) Porteus Maze
(4) Thurstone PMA Reasoning (untimed)

(5) Raven Progressive Matrices
(6) Wisconsin Card Sorting (perseverative errors)
(7) Age

[a] 3.677 = initial trace.

Note. From Table 2, p. 1519, Misiak and Loranger, 1961. Copyright 1961 by the American Association for the Advancement of Science. Reprinted by permission.

as in the three-factor solution. The loadings on factor a are the same as those of the three-factor solution. The loadings on factor b are a little smaller in most cases. When factor b is taken to be the last factor, we usually use lower reestimates of the residual communalities than when it is not, and this results in slightly lower factor loadings, on the average. The sum of squares of the b-factor loadings is .556 for the three-factor solution and .519 for the initial two-factor solution.

TABLE 2.10
Oblique Rotation of Centroid Factor Matrix
for Seven Reasoning and Perseveration Tests (N = 86)

| | Centroid | | | Rotated | |
Test	a	b	h^2	I	II
(1)	.426	−.319	.283	−.080	.478
(2)	.784	.036	.616	.403	.324
(3)	.595	.037	.355	.314	.237
(4)	.745	.403	.717	.707	−.021
(5)	.721	.345	.639	.645	.020
−(6)	.741	−.424	.729	−.023	.714
−(7)	.363	−.078	.138	.103	.234
Σ	4.375	.000	3.477	2.069	1.986
Ch				2.069	1.986

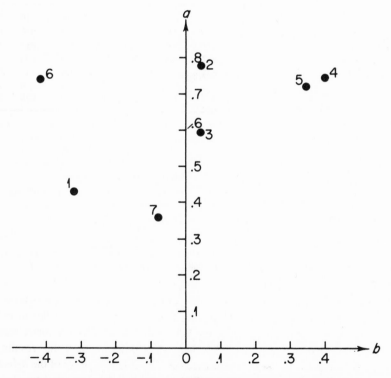

FIG. 2.3. Plot of factor loadings from Table 2.9 for seven reasoning and perseveration tests (N = 86).

In the initial two-factor solution, the per cent of trace accounted for by two factors is only 93%. Ideally it should be 100%, and a discrepancy of 7% is a little too great. For two factors, the estimated communalities are too large. For three factors they were satisfactory, with discrepancy only 2%. So for the two-factor solution we reestimate the initial communalities and refactor. The results are shown in the factor matrix at the far right of Table 2.9.

For the refactoring, the h^2 values of the initial two-factor solution become the h_0^2 values for the refactoring; and the final h^2 values are $a^2 + b^2$. At the refactoring $\Sigma h^2 = 3.477$ is 101% of $\Sigma h_0^2 = 3.438$, which is satisfactorily close.

The refactored two-factor solution was rotated obliquely using the procedure of Fig. 2.2. A general factor including both reasoning tests and tests of resistance to perseveration would have no meaning, so an oblique rotation is used. Figure 2.3 shows the plot of the a and b loadings from the last factor matrix of Table 2.9, and Table 2.10 shows the loadings of the rotated factor matrix. For this rotation, the centroid of variables 1, 6, and 7 was used to define axis I, and the centroid of variables 4 and 5 to define axis II.

We can interpret the results by reference to the variable names in Table 2.9. Factor I is the reasoning factor, with highest loadings on variable 4 (Thurstone PMA Reasoning, untimed) and 5 (Raven Progressive Matrices). Factor II is the resistance-to-perseveration factor, with its highest loading on variable 6 (Wisconsin Card Sorting, perseverative errors, reversed) and a moderately high loading on variable 1 (Critical Flicker Frequency). Variables 2 (Digit Symbol, WAIS) and 3 (Porteus Maze) have intermediate loadings on both common factors. Variable 7 (Age reversed: "Youngness") has an intermediate loading on factor II and a loading (.103) just at the border between a near-zero and a low nonzero on factor I. Thus resistance to perseveration increases with "youngness," or perseveration with age, and there is just a hint that reasoning increases with "youngness," or decreases with age, in this group of older adults.

For the interpretation of the three-factor solution, we must await the treatment of rotation in three dimensions in Chapter 7.

3

Elements of Matrix Algebra

3.1 INTRODUCTION

In order to proceed much further with the study of factor analysis, it is necessary to have some knowledge of matrix algebra, linear computation procedures, and a few results from m-dimensional Euclidean geometry. This chapter is intended to provide the essential background in matrix algebra, Chapter 4 discusses the necessary elements of linear computations, and m-dimensional Euclidean geometry is considered in Chapter 6, where it is used in the treatment of rotation of axes in more than two dimensions. The treatment of all these topics will be selective; topics irrelevant to factor analysis are touched on only lightly or omitted entirely, and applications to factor analysis and related problems are pointed out.

3.2 ELEMENTARY MATRIX ALGEBRA

We consider here only matrices over the field of real numbers, which consists of the positive and negative integers, fractions, and irrationals. The *elements* of this matrix algebra are the same as the elements of ordinary algebra, namely the real numbers. Many of the rules of ordinary algebra carry over directly to matrix algebra, but some do not. The rules of matrix algebra are derived from a set of *definitions,* plus the axioms and the rules of ordinary algebra.

67

3.2.1 Preliminary Definitions, and Rules of Addition and Subtraction

Definition of a Matrix.   A matrix is a rectangular array of numbers:

Literal examples	Numerical examples

$$A = \begin{bmatrix} a_{11} & a_{12} & a_{13} \\ a_{21} & a_{22} & a_{23} \end{bmatrix} \qquad A = \begin{bmatrix} 2 & 1 & 3 \\ 4 & 7 & 7 \end{bmatrix}$$

$$B = \begin{bmatrix} b_1 \\ b_2 \\ b_3 \end{bmatrix} \qquad B = \begin{bmatrix} 2 \\ 4 \\ 3 \end{bmatrix}$$

$$C' = \begin{bmatrix} c_{11} & c_{12} & c_{13} & c_{14} \end{bmatrix} \qquad C' = \begin{bmatrix} 3 & 4 & 2 & 6 \end{bmatrix}$$

$$D = \begin{bmatrix} d_{11} & d_{12} & d_{13} \\ d_{21} & d_{22} & d_{23} \\ d_{31} & d_{32} & d_{33} \end{bmatrix} \qquad D = \begin{bmatrix} 1 & 2 & 3 \\ 3 & 4 & 2 \\ 4 & 3 & 1 \end{bmatrix}$$

Notation.   In the *expanded* form, a matrix is written as a rectangular array, enclosed by brackets (as here), by *double* vertical lines, or by parentheses or braces. When the elements are indicated by letters, each letter ordinarily carries *two* subscripts. The *first* subscript designates the *row* in which the element is found; the *second* subscript designates the *column*. Thus d_{23}, in the last example is the element in the second row (from the top) and the third column (from the left). When a matrix has only one column or row, its elements are sometimes written with single subscripts, as in the second example above.

In the *compact* form a matrix is represented by a single capital letter. The corresponding small letter with appropriate subscripts represents an element of this matrix written in the expanded form. Thus the first matrix above is A, and its upper left element is a_{11}.

Definition of the Order of a Matrix.   The order of a matrix is defined by the number of its rows and the number of its columns. Thus, in the examples above, A is of order 2 by 3, B is of order 3 by 1, C' is of order 1 by 4, and D is of order 3 by 3. The order designation (e.g., 2 by 3) specifies first the row order, and then the column order. A *square* matrix, such as D above, is a matrix whose row order is equal to its column order. When it is quite clear that a matrix is square, its order may be indicated by a single number. Thus the matrix D of the previous examples might be described as of order 3 rather than 3 by 3.

Definition of Matrix Equality.   Two matrices are equal if and only if every element of the first is equal to the corresponding element of the second. Hence two matrices cannot be equal unless they are of the same order.

Definition of Matrix Addition. The *sum* of two matrices is a matrix every element of which is the sum of the corresponding elements of the matrices added: $a_{ij} + b_{ij} = c_{ij}$. Example:

$$
\begin{array}{ccccc}
A & + & B & = & C
\end{array}
$$

$$
\begin{bmatrix} 1 & 2 & 3 \\ 2 & 3 & 4 \end{bmatrix} + \begin{bmatrix} 2 & 1 & 3 \\ 2 & 4 & 3 \end{bmatrix} = \begin{bmatrix} 3 & 3 & 6 \\ 4 & 7 & 7 \end{bmatrix}
$$

It follows that two matrices do not have a sum unless they are of the same order.

Definition of a Zero Matrix. A zero matrix is a matrix every element of which is zero.

Definition of Matrix Subtraction. The *difference* between two matrices is a matrix every element of which is the difference between the corresponding elements of the first (minuend) matrix and the second (subtrahend) matrix: $a_{ij} - b_{ij} = c_{ij}$. Example:

$$
\begin{array}{ccccc}
A & - & B & = & C
\end{array}
$$

$$
\begin{bmatrix} 1 & 2 & 3 \\ 2 & 3 & 4 \end{bmatrix} - \begin{bmatrix} 2 & 1 & 3 \\ 2 & 4 & 3 \end{bmatrix} = \begin{bmatrix} -1 & 1 & 0 \\ 0 & -1 & 1 \end{bmatrix}
$$

It follows that two matrices do not have a difference unless they are of the same order.

From these definitions, it is evident that all the rules of ordinary algebra dealing with addition and subtraction apply also to matrix algebra, so long as the matrices considered are of the same order.

3.2.2 Transpose of a Matrix

The transpose, A', of a matrix A is defined as a matrix whose *columns*, in order from left to right and with elements in order in each column from top to bottom, are identical to the *rows* of A, in order from top to bottom and with elements in each row in order from left to right. If the elements of A are a_{ij} and the elements of A' are a'_{ij}, then $a'_{ij} = a_{ji}$. Example:

$$
\text{If } A = \begin{bmatrix} 1 & 2 & 3 \\ 2 & 3 & 4 \end{bmatrix} \quad \text{then } A' = \begin{bmatrix} 1 & 2 \\ 2 & 3 \\ 3 & 4 \end{bmatrix}
$$

Problem 3.2.2:1. Prove the four following relations, using the previously given definitions:

1. If A is of order n by m, then A' is of order m by n.
2. If $A \pm B = C$, then $A' \pm B' = C'$.

3. $(A')' = A$.
4. $(A \pm B)' = A' \pm B'$.

3.2.3 Vectors

A vector is defined, in matrix algebra, as a matrix of one column or one row. Thus in the examples of Section 3.2.1, the matrices B and C' are vectors. The elements of a vector may specify the coordinates of the terminus of a geometric vector from the origin in a Euclidean space of m dimensions, where m is the nonunit order of the vector. Because either the column order or the row order of a vector is always 1, *the* order of a vector is often stated as a single number indicating its nonunit order. But if we say a vector is m by 1, this also defines it as a column vector, whereas 1 by m defines it as a row vector, in case this distinction is not apparent otherwise. It is common practice, however, to designate a row vector as the transpose of the corresponding column vector. Thus in the examples at the beginning of Section 3.2.1, B is a column vector of order 3 and C' is a row vector of order 4. The transpose of a column vector is a row vector, and the transpose of a row vector is a column vector.

Where it is important to distinguish between vectors and other matrices, it is common usage to designate a vector by a boldface small letter rather than a capital letter. We do not employ this convention in the present treatment, but the student should remember it in reading other literature.

Scalar Product of Two Vectors. If A' and B are vectors of the same order, the product $A'B$ is a *scalar:* a single number. Example:

$$
\begin{array}{ccccc}
A' & \cdot & B & = & c \\
[2 \quad 3 \quad 4] & \cdot & \begin{bmatrix} 1 \\ 2 \\ 3 \end{bmatrix} & = & 20
\end{array}
$$

This product is $2 \cdot 1 + 3 \cdot 2 + 4 \cdot 3 = 20$. The scalar product is the *sum of products* of the elements of A' (taken from left to right) and the elements of B (taken from top to bottom). The scalar product is also termed the *inner* product or the *dot* product of the two vectors (written $A \cdot B$).

Matrix Product of Two Vectors. For the example above, consider the product AB'. It is

$$
\begin{array}{ccccc}
A & \times & B' & = & C \\
\begin{bmatrix} 2 \\ 3 \\ 4 \end{bmatrix} & \times & [1 \quad 2 \quad 3] & = & \begin{bmatrix} 2 & 4 & 6 \\ 3 & 6 & 9 \\ 4 & 8 & 12 \end{bmatrix}
\end{array}
$$

The rule for this product is $a_i b_j = c_{ij}$. Thus the elements of the first row of C are 2×1, 2×2, and 2×3; the elements of the second row of C are

$3 \times 1, 3 \times 2$, and 3×3; the elements of the third row of C are $4 \times 1, 4 \times 2$, and 4×3. The matrix product is also termed the *outer* product or the *cross* product (written $A \times B'$).

The terms "inner" and "outer" products, or "dot" and "cross" products, are required when we do not adhere to the convention that a row vector will *always* be written as the transpose of the corresponding column vector.

If two vectors are not of the same order, they do not have a scalar product. For a matrix product to exist, the two vectors need not be of the same order. Thus

$$
\begin{array}{ccccc}
A & \times & B' & = & C \\
\end{array}
$$

$$
\begin{bmatrix} 2 \\ 3 \\ 4 \end{bmatrix} \times \begin{bmatrix} 1 & 2 \end{bmatrix} = \begin{bmatrix} 2 & 4 \\ 3 & 6 \\ 4 & 8 \end{bmatrix} \text{ and } \begin{bmatrix} 2 \\ 3 \end{bmatrix} \times \begin{bmatrix} 1 & 2 & 3 \end{bmatrix} = \begin{bmatrix} 2 & 4 & 6 \\ 3 & 6 & 9 \end{bmatrix}
$$

Problem 3.2.3:1. Show that for the scaler product example, if $A' \cdot B = c$, then $B' \cdot A = c$ also. And for the matrix product example, show that if $A \times B' = C$, *then* $B \times A' = C'$.

3.2.4 Matrix Multiplication

In contrast to matrix addition and subtraction, the definition of matrix multiplication leads to several rules that do not parallel the rules of ordinary algebra. It is precisely this definition, however, which gives matrix algebra its considerable power in handling simultaneous linear equations, linear transformations, and the relations of m-dimensional Euclidean geometry.

Definition of Matrix Multiplication. The matrix product $A \cdot B = C$ can be defined by the rule that *each element c_{ij}* of the product matrix C is the *sum of products* of the elements in the i-th *row* of the *left* matrix A (taken from left to right) and the elements in the j-th *column* of the *right* matrix B (taken from top to bottom). Or considering each row of A and each column of B as a vector, each element of C is the scalar product of the row vector i of A and the column vector j of B. This is illustrated in the schematic picture:

The arrow i indicates the elements of one row of A (here the middle row). The arrow j of B indicates the elements of one column of B (here the left column). The scalar product of these vectors is the element c_{ij} of C, in row i (here the middle row) and column j (here the left column) of C.

The product of two 2 by 2 matrices, with numerical elements, might be

$$
\underset{A}{\begin{bmatrix} 4 & 2 \\ 3 & 1 \end{bmatrix}} \cdot \underset{B}{\begin{bmatrix} 5 & 7 \\ 6 & 8 \end{bmatrix}} = \underset{AB}{\begin{bmatrix} 4 \cdot 5 + 2 \cdot 6 & 4 \cdot 7 + 2 \cdot 8 \\ 3 \cdot 5 + 1 \cdot 6 & 3 \cdot 7 + 1 \cdot 8 \end{bmatrix}} = \underset{C}{\begin{bmatrix} 32 & 44 \\ 21 & 29 \end{bmatrix}}
$$

For the general matrix product $A \cdot B = C$, each element of C is thus defined as

$$
c_{ij} = \sum_{k=1}^{m} a_{ik} b_{kj}. \tag{3-1}
$$

The rules for the scalar and matrix products of two vectors are special cases. For the scalar product the left matrix has only one row and the right matrix has only one column. For the matrix product, each row of the left matrix and each column of the right matrix has only one element.

Common Order; Existence of the Product of Two Matrices.   The number m, in (3-1) above, is called the *common order* of the matrices A and B: it is the column order of A and row order of B. If the number of *columns* of A (the left matrix) and the number of *rows* of B (the right matrix) are not the same, A and B do not have a common order. The product of two matrices exists if and only if they have a common order. And if A is of order n by m, and B is of order m by p, with m the common order, the product matrix $C = AB$ will be of order n by p ($i = 1, 2, \ldots, n; j = 1, 2, \ldots, p$). Examples:

$$
\begin{array}{cccccc}
A \text{ (2 by 3)} & \cdot & B \text{ (3 by 2)} & = & C \text{ (2 by 2)} \\
\begin{bmatrix} 1 & 2 & 3 \\ 2 & 3 & 4 \end{bmatrix} & \cdot & \begin{bmatrix} 1 & 3 \\ 4 & 2 \\ 2 & 2 \end{bmatrix} & = & \begin{bmatrix} 15 & 13 \\ 22 & 20 \end{bmatrix}
\end{array} \tag{a}
$$

$$
\begin{array}{cccccc}
B \text{ (3 by 2)} & \cdot & A \text{ (2 by 3)} & = & C \text{ (3 by 3)} \\
\begin{bmatrix} 1 & 3 \\ 4 & 2 \\ 2 & 2 \end{bmatrix} & \cdot & \begin{bmatrix} 1 & 2 & 3 \\ 2 & 3 & 4 \end{bmatrix} & = & \begin{bmatrix} 7 & 11 & 15 \\ 8 & 14 & 20 \\ 6 & 10 & 14 \end{bmatrix}
\end{array} \tag{b}
$$

$$
\begin{array}{cccccc}
A \text{ (2 by 3)} & \cdot & B \text{ (3 by 1)} & = & C \text{ (2 by 1)} \\
\begin{bmatrix} 1 & 2 & 3 \\ 2 & 3 & 4 \end{bmatrix} & \cdot & \begin{bmatrix} 3 \\ 4 \\ 5 \end{bmatrix} & = & \begin{bmatrix} 26 \\ 38 \end{bmatrix}
\end{array} \tag{c}
$$

$$
\begin{array}{cccccc}
A' \text{ (1 by 3)} & \cdot & B \text{ (3 by 2)} & = & C' \text{ (1 by 2)} \\
\begin{bmatrix} 3 & 4 & 5 \end{bmatrix} & \cdot & \begin{bmatrix} 1 & 3 \\ 4 & 2 \\ 2 & 2 \end{bmatrix} & = & \begin{bmatrix} 29 & 27 \end{bmatrix}
\end{array} \tag{d}
$$

$$
\begin{array}{cccccc}
A \text{ (3 by 3)} & \cdot & B \text{ (3 by 3)} & = & C \text{ (3 by 3)} \\
\begin{bmatrix} 1 & 2 & 2 \\ 3 & 2 & 1 \\ 2 & 1 & 1 \end{bmatrix} & \cdot & \begin{bmatrix} 2 & 3 & 2 \\ 1 & 2 & 1 \\ 3 & 1 & 2 \end{bmatrix} & = & \begin{bmatrix} 10 & 9 & 8 \\ 11 & 14 & 10 \\ 8 & 9 & 7 \end{bmatrix}
\end{array} \tag{e}
$$

$$B \text{ (3 by 3)} \quad \cdot \quad A \text{ (3 by 3)} \quad = \quad C \text{ (3 by 3)}$$

$$\begin{bmatrix} 2 & 3 & 2 \\ 1 & 2 & 1 \\ 3 & 1 & 2 \end{bmatrix} \cdot \begin{bmatrix} 1 & 2 & 2 \\ 3 & 2 & 1 \\ 2 & 1 & 1 \end{bmatrix} = \begin{bmatrix} 15 & 12 & 9 \\ 9 & 7 & 5 \\ 10 & 10 & 9 \end{bmatrix} \qquad \text{(f)}$$

Matrix Multiplication is in General not Commutative.   In general, the matrix product AB is *not* equal to the matrix product BA, and the existence of one product does not in general imply the existence of the other. In examples (a) and (b), above, the products AB and BA are different and of different orders. In examples (c) and (d) the products BA and BA' do not exist, because B and A (in that order) and B and A' (in that order) do not have a common order. In examples (e) and (f), the matrix products AB and BA both exist and are both of the same order, but have different elements and hence are unequal.

Because the products AB and BA of matrix multiplication are in general different, we say in discussing a matrix product such as AB, in any one of the examples above, that B is *premultiplied* by A or that A is *postmultiplied* by B. For the same reason, any rule of ordinary algebra that requires the commutative axiom of multiplication, $ab = ba$, for its proof, will in general not have a parallel rule in matrix algebra. In special cases, matrices may be commutative, and in such cases the rules of ordinary algebra based on the commutative axiom of multiplication may have parallel rules in matrix algebra applying to these special matrices. We give next three examples of rules of ordinary algebra which do not have parallels in matrix algebra because they depend (in ordinary algebra) on the commutative axiom of multiplication.

1. $AB = 0$ *does not imply in general that* $A = 0$ *and/or* $B = 0$.

$$A \qquad \cdot \qquad B \qquad = \qquad 0$$

$$\begin{bmatrix} a & 0 \\ b & 0 \end{bmatrix} \cdot \begin{bmatrix} 0 & 0 \\ c & d \end{bmatrix} = \begin{bmatrix} 0 & 0 \\ 0 & 0 \end{bmatrix}$$

Here a, b, c, and d can take *any* values, and AB is still equal to 0.

2. $AB = AC$ *does not imply in general that* $B = C$.

$$A \qquad \cdot \qquad B \qquad = \qquad AB$$

$$\begin{bmatrix} 0 & 0 \\ 2a & 2a \end{bmatrix} \cdot \begin{bmatrix} 0 & 2a \\ 0 & 0 \end{bmatrix} = \begin{bmatrix} 0 & 0 \\ 0 & 4a^2 \end{bmatrix}$$

$$A \qquad \cdot \qquad C \qquad = \qquad AC$$

$$\begin{bmatrix} 0 & 0 \\ 2a & 2a \end{bmatrix} \cdot \begin{bmatrix} 0 & a \\ 0 & a \end{bmatrix} = \begin{bmatrix} 0 & 0 \\ 0 & 4a^2 \end{bmatrix}$$

Here $AB = AC$, but B does not equal C for any value of a except $a = 0$.

3. *A square matrix with all elements positive or zero may have any number of square roots.*   The square root of a matrix is defined as is the square root of a number: if $A \cdot A = B$, then A is a square root of B. Thus in ordinary algebra it is proved that any positive real number has exactly two square roots, one of which

is the complement of the other, and that zero has exactly one square root: itself. But the matrix equality

$$
\begin{matrix} A & & A & = & B \end{matrix}
$$
$$
\begin{bmatrix} 1 & 2a \\ 1/a & -1 \end{bmatrix} \cdot \begin{bmatrix} 1 & 2a \\ 1/a & -1 \end{bmatrix} = \begin{bmatrix} 3 & 0 \\ 0 & 3 \end{bmatrix}
$$

is true for all real numbers a except $a = 0$, so B has an infinite number of square roots. A square zero matrix, however, has only one square root: itself.

Multiplication by a Zero Matrix. If a matrix A is premultiplied or post-multiplied by a zero matrix with which it has a common order, the product is a zero matrix. This is evident as soon as we note that a sum of products will be zero if one factor of every product is zero.

Elementary Operation of Matrix Multiplication. If $A = B$ and $C = D$, then $AC = BD$, if A and C have a common order. Because A and B are equal element by element, as are also C and D, this proposition follows immediately from the definitions of matrix multiplication and matrix equality.

We state two further theorems without formal proof, because the proofs are rather complex, and illustrate them. The proofs are given in Section 3.5 at the end of this chapter.

Matrix Multiplication is Associative. $(AB)C = A(BC) = ABC$. For the product

$$
\begin{matrix} A & & B & & C \end{matrix}
$$
$$
\begin{bmatrix} 2 & 3 & 4 \\ 1 & 2 & 3 \end{bmatrix} \cdot \begin{bmatrix} 1 & 3 \\ 4 & 2 \\ 2 & 2 \end{bmatrix} \cdot \begin{bmatrix} 1 & 2 \\ 3 & 2 \end{bmatrix}
$$

we have

$$
\begin{matrix} AB & & C & = & ABC \end{matrix}
$$
$$
\begin{bmatrix} 22 & 20 \\ 15 & 13 \end{bmatrix} \cdot \begin{bmatrix} 1 & 2 \\ 3 & 2 \end{bmatrix} = \begin{bmatrix} 82 & 84 \\ 54 & 56 \end{bmatrix}
$$

$$
\begin{matrix} A & & BC & = & ABC \end{matrix}
$$
$$
\begin{bmatrix} 2 & 3 & 4 \\ 1 & 2 & 3 \end{bmatrix} \cdot \begin{bmatrix} 10 & 8 \\ 10 & 12 \\ 8 & 8 \end{bmatrix} = \begin{bmatrix} 82 & 84 \\ 54 & 56 \end{bmatrix}
$$

Corollary: If A and B have a common order, and if AB and C have a common order, then B and C have a common order, and A and BC have a common order.

Matrix Multiplication is Distributive over Matrix Addition and Subtraction. $A(B \pm C) = AB \pm AC;$ $(A \pm B)C = AC \pm BC.$ Examples:

$$A \quad\quad \cdot \quad (B \quad + \quad C) \quad = \quad A \quad\quad \cdot \quad (B + C) \quad = \quad A\,(B + C)$$

$$\begin{bmatrix} 2 & 3 & 4 \\ 1 & 2 & 3 \end{bmatrix} \cdot \left\{ \begin{bmatrix} 2 & 1 \\ 2 & 1 \\ 2 & 2 \end{bmatrix} + \begin{bmatrix} 1 & 2 \\ 2 & 1 \\ 1 & 1 \end{bmatrix} \right\} = \begin{bmatrix} 2 & 3 & 4 \\ 1 & 2 & 3 \end{bmatrix} \cdot \begin{bmatrix} 3 & 3 \\ 4 & 2 \\ 3 & 3 \end{bmatrix} = \begin{bmatrix} 30 & 24 \\ 20 & 16 \end{bmatrix}$$

$$AB \quad + \quad AC \quad = \quad A(B + C)$$

$$\begin{bmatrix} 18 & 13 \\ 12 & 9 \end{bmatrix} + \begin{bmatrix} 12 & 11 \\ 8 & 7 \end{bmatrix} = \begin{bmatrix} 30 & 24 \\ 20 & 16 \end{bmatrix}$$

$$A \quad\quad \cdot \quad (B \quad - \quad C) \quad = \quad A \quad\quad \cdot \quad (B - C) \quad = \quad A(B - C)$$

$$\begin{bmatrix} 2 & 3 & 4 \\ 1 & 2 & 3 \end{bmatrix} \cdot \left\{ \begin{bmatrix} 2 & 1 \\ 2 & 1 \\ 2 & 2 \end{bmatrix} - \begin{bmatrix} 1 & 2 \\ 2 & 1 \\ 1 & 1 \end{bmatrix} \right\} = \begin{bmatrix} 2 & 3 & 4 \\ 1 & 2 & 3 \end{bmatrix} \cdot \begin{bmatrix} 1 & -1 \\ 0 & 0 \\ 1 & 1 \end{bmatrix} = \begin{bmatrix} 6 & 2 \\ 4 & 2 \end{bmatrix}$$

$$AB \quad - \quad AC \quad = \quad A(B - C)$$

$$\begin{bmatrix} 18 & 13 \\ 12 & 9 \end{bmatrix} - \begin{bmatrix} 12 & 11 \\ 8 & 7 \end{bmatrix} = \begin{bmatrix} 6 & 2 \\ 4 & 2 \end{bmatrix}$$

$$(A \quad + \quad B) \quad \cdot \quad C \quad = \quad (A + B) \quad \cdot \quad C \quad = \quad (A + B)C$$

$$\left\{ \begin{bmatrix} 2 & 1 \\ 3 & 2 \\ 4 & 3 \end{bmatrix} + \begin{bmatrix} 1 & 2 \\ 2 & 1 \\ 1 & 1 \end{bmatrix} \right\} \cdot \begin{bmatrix} 1 & 2 \\ 3 & 4 \end{bmatrix} = \begin{bmatrix} 3 & 3 \\ 5 & 3 \\ 5 & 4 \end{bmatrix} \cdot \begin{bmatrix} 1 & 2 \\ 3 & 4 \end{bmatrix} = \begin{bmatrix} 12 & 18 \\ 14 & 22 \\ 17 & 26 \end{bmatrix}$$

$$AC \quad + \quad BC \quad = \quad (A + B)C$$

$$\begin{bmatrix} 5 & 8 \\ 9 & 14 \\ 13 & 20 \end{bmatrix} + \begin{bmatrix} 7 & 10 \\ 5 & 8 \\ 4 & 6 \end{bmatrix} = \begin{bmatrix} 12 & 18 \\ 14 & 22 \\ 17 & 26 \end{bmatrix}$$

$$(A \quad - \quad B) \quad \cdot \quad C \quad = \quad (A - B) \quad \cdot \quad C \quad = \quad (A - B)C$$

$$\left\{ \begin{bmatrix} 2 & 1 \\ 3 & 2 \\ 4 & 3 \end{bmatrix} - \begin{bmatrix} 1 & 2 \\ 2 & 1 \\ 1 & 1 \end{bmatrix} \right\} \cdot \begin{bmatrix} 1 & 2 \\ 3 & 4 \end{bmatrix} = \begin{bmatrix} 1 & -1 \\ 1 & 1 \\ 3 & 2 \end{bmatrix} \cdot \begin{bmatrix} 1 & 2 \\ 3 & 4 \end{bmatrix} = \begin{bmatrix} -2 & -2 \\ 4 & 6 \\ 9 & 14 \end{bmatrix}$$

$$AC \quad - \quad BC \quad = \quad (A - B)C$$

$$\begin{bmatrix} 5 & 8 \\ 9 & 14 \\ 13 & 20 \end{bmatrix} - \begin{bmatrix} 7 & 10 \\ 5 & 8 \\ 4 & 6 \end{bmatrix} = \begin{bmatrix} -2 & -2 \\ 4 & 6 \\ 9 & 14 \end{bmatrix}$$

Transpose of a Product.   The transpose of the product of two matrices is the product of their transposes in reverse order: $(AB)' = B'A'$. Example:

$$A \quad\quad \cdot \quad B \quad = \quad AB$$

$$\begin{bmatrix} 1 & 2 & 3 \\ 2 & 3 & 4 \end{bmatrix} \cdot \begin{bmatrix} 1 & 3 \\ 4 & 2 \\ 2 & 2 \end{bmatrix} = \begin{bmatrix} 15 & 13 \\ 22 & 20 \end{bmatrix} \quad (AB)' \quad = \quad \begin{bmatrix} 15 & 22 \\ 13 & 20 \end{bmatrix}$$

$$B' \quad\quad \cdot \quad A' \quad = \quad B'A'$$

$$\begin{bmatrix} 1 & 4 & 2 \\ 3 & 2 & 2 \end{bmatrix} \cdot \begin{bmatrix} 1 & 2 \\ 2 & 3 \\ 3 & 4 \end{bmatrix} = \begin{bmatrix} 15 & 22 \\ 13 & 20 \end{bmatrix} = (AB)'$$

In general, the transpose of the product of several matrices is the product of their transposes in reverse order. Thus $(ABCD)' = (CD)'(AB)' = D'C'B'A'$.

Note that in the example above, $A'B'$ would be of order 3 by 3, as would also BA, whereas AB and $B'A'$ are of order 2 by 2. If AB exists, then $B'A'$ exists also, but $A'B'$ may not exist. Thus:

$$
\begin{array}{ccccc}
A & \cdot & B & = & AB \\
\begin{bmatrix} 1 & 2 & 3 \\ 2 & 3 & 4 \end{bmatrix} & \cdot & \begin{bmatrix} 1 \\ 4 \\ 2 \end{bmatrix} & = & \begin{bmatrix} 15 \\ 22 \end{bmatrix}
\end{array}
$$

and

$$
\begin{array}{ccccccc}
B' & \cdot & A' & = & B'A' & = & (AB)' \\
[1 \quad 4 \quad 2] & \cdot & \begin{bmatrix} 1 & 2 \\ 2 & 3 \\ 3 & 4 \end{bmatrix} & = & [15 \quad 22] & = & (AB)'
\end{array}
$$

but

$$
\begin{array}{ccc}
A' & \cdot & B' \\
\begin{bmatrix} 1 & 2 \\ 2 & 3 \\ 3 & 4 \end{bmatrix} & \cdot & [1 \quad 4 \quad 2]
\end{array}
$$

does not exist, because A' and B' (in that order) do not have a common order.

3.2.5 Application to Nonhomogeneous Linear Equations

One major reason for the definition of matrix multiplication may be seen in the application of matrix methods to systems of nonhomogeneous linear equations. Consider first the simple algebraic equation

$$ ax = c \tag{3-2} $$

in which a is a coefficient, x is an unknown, and c is a constant. A set of three analogous nonhomogeneous linear equations is

$$
\begin{aligned}
a_{11}x_1 + a_{12}x_2 + a_{13}x_3 &= c_1 \\
x_{21}x_1 + a_{22}x_2 + a_{23}x_3 &= c_2 \\
a_{31}x_1 + a_{32}x_2 + a_{33}x_3 &= c_3
\end{aligned} \tag{3-3}
$$

These equations are nonhomogeneous if at least one constant (c_1 or c_2 or c_3) is not zero, and an exact and unique solution exists if the number of equations is equal to the number of unknowns (here x_1, x_2, and x_3), and the equations are all *linearly independent*. Linear independence exists when *no one* of the equations is a multiple or fraction of any other, nor any combination of sums or differences of multiples or fractions of any two others (two or more others if there are more than three equations).

Equations (3-3) may be written in matrix form:

$$\begin{bmatrix} a_{11} & a_{12} & a_{13} \\ a_{21} & a_{22} & a_{23} \\ a_{31} & a_{32} & a_{33} \end{bmatrix} \cdot \begin{bmatrix} x_1 \\ x_2 \\ x_3 \end{bmatrix} = \begin{bmatrix} c_1 \\ c_2 \\ c_3 \end{bmatrix} \tag{3-4}$$

Performing the matrix multiplication indicated on the left of the equality sign,

$$\begin{bmatrix} a_{11}x_1 + a_{12}x_2 + a_{13}x_3 \\ a_{21}x_1 + a_{22}x_2 + a_{23}x_3 \\ a_{31}x_1 + a_{32}x_2 + a_{33}x_3 \end{bmatrix} = \begin{bmatrix} c_1 \\ c_2 \\ c_3 \end{bmatrix} \tag{3-5}$$

Note that if the matrix multiplication of (3-4) were carried out with actual numbers, the matrix on the left of (3-5) would be a column vector of three elements. Then by the definition of matrix equality (equal element by element), we come back at once to (3-3). In compact matrix notation, we could write (3-3) simply as

$$AX = C, \tag{3-6}$$

where A is a square matrix of coefficients, X is a column vector of unknowns, and C is a column vector of constants, as in (3-4). The actual solution of sets of nonhomogeneous linear equations by matrix methods will be taken up in Chapter 4.

3.2.6 Application to Linear Transformations

We consider only transformations that do not include a constant; such transformations correspond geometrically to *rotations* about a fixed origin. Inclusion of constants implies *translations,* that is, shifts of origin. In the one-variable case, the general equation is

$$y = a_0 + a_1 x,$$

but we consider only cases analogous to

$$y = a_1 x.$$

Thus if

$$y_1 = a_{11}x_1 + a_{12}x_2; \quad y_2 = a_{21}x_1 + a_{22}x_2$$

and $\hspace{10cm}$ (3-7)

$$z_1 = b_{11}y_1 + b_{12}y_2; \quad z_2 = b_{21}y_1 + b_{22}y_2$$

we have a system of two linear equations in two unknowns transforming x_1 and x_2 into y_1 and y_2, and two more equations transforming y_1 and y_2 into z_1 and z_2. By substituting the values of the y's in terms of the x's into the equations for the z's, we have

$$z_1 = b_{11}(a_{11}x_1 + a_{12}x_2) + b_{12}(a_{21}x_1 + a_{22}x_2)$$

$$z_2 = b_{21}(a_{11}x_1 + a_{12}x_2) + b_{22}(a_{21}x_1 + a_{22}x_2)$$

Collecting coefficients of x_1 and x_2,

$$z_1 = (b_{11}a_{11} + b_{12}a_{21})x_1 + (b_{11}a_{12} + b_{12}a_{22})x_2$$
$$z_2 = (b_{21}a_{11} + b_{22}a_{21})x_1 + (b_{21}a_{12} + b_{22}a_{22})x_2 \qquad (3\text{-}8)$$

It is evident that if the systems of equations were large, involving $x_1, x_2, \ldots,$ x_n; $y_1, y_2, \ldots, y_n$; $z_1, z_2, \ldots, z_n$; with n greater than 4 or 5, expressing the transformations in this manner would become quite cumbersome.

In matrix notation we can write (3-7) as:

$$X = \begin{bmatrix} x_1 \\ x_2 \end{bmatrix} \quad A = \begin{bmatrix} a_{11} & a_{12} \\ a_{21} & a_{22} \end{bmatrix} \quad Y = \begin{bmatrix} y_1 \\ y_2 \end{bmatrix} \quad B = \begin{bmatrix} b_{11} & b_{12} \\ b_{21} & b_{22} \end{bmatrix} \quad Z = \begin{bmatrix} z_1 \\ z_2 \end{bmatrix} \quad (3\text{-}9)$$

The first pair of equations (3-7) is then

$$Y = AX, \qquad (3\text{-}10)$$

and the second pair is

$$Z = BY. \qquad (3\text{-}11)$$

The matrix A is the *transformation matrix* for transforming X into Y, and the matrix B is the transformation matrix for transforming Y into Z. To transform X directly into Z, we substitute the value of Y from (3-10) into (3-11), obtaining

$$Z = B(AX). \qquad (3\text{-}12)$$

Then by the associative law of matrix multiplication

$$Z = (BA)X, \qquad (3\text{-}13)$$

and BA is the transformation matrix for transforming X directly into Z.

Problem 3.2.6:1. Form the expanded matrix BA from the values of B and A given by (3-9). Then postmultiply BA by X, and show that the result is precisely (3-8).

If we write the coefficients of the *rows* of (2-22) as the *columns* of a transformation matrix denoted by Λ, we have

$$\Lambda = \begin{bmatrix} (Ia) & (Ib) \\ (Ib) & -(Ia) \end{bmatrix} \qquad (3\text{-}14)$$

Then if F is the unrotated factor matrix of Table 2.6, with columns headed a and b, and V is the rotated factor matrix, with columns headed I and II, the rotation is given by

$$F\Lambda = V, \qquad (3\text{-}15)$$

or explicitly, from Table 2.6 and the pair of numerical equations following (2-22),

$$
\begin{array}{ccc}
F & \Lambda & V
\end{array}
$$

$$
\begin{bmatrix}
.748 & .142 \\
.814 & -.154 \\
.845 & .160 \\
.802 & .132 \\
.794 & -.283
\end{bmatrix}
\cdot
\begin{bmatrix}
.984 & .178 \\
.178 & -.984
\end{bmatrix}
=
\begin{bmatrix}
.761 & -.007 \\
.774 & .296 \\
.860 & -.007 \\
.813 & .013 \\
.731 & .420
\end{bmatrix}
$$

Problem 3.2.6:2. Verify this result by performing the numerical operations implied by $F \cdot \Lambda$ for these data, to obtain V.

From (3-10) and the rule for the transpose of a product,

$$X'A' = Y',$$

and from (3-9)

$$
\begin{array}{ccc}
X' & A' & = Y'
\end{array}
$$

$$
[x_1 \quad x_2] \cdot
\begin{bmatrix}
a_{11} & a_{21} \\
a_{12} & a_{22}
\end{bmatrix}
= [y_1 \quad y_2]
\tag{3-16}
$$

This procedure turns the *rows* of A into the *columns* of A', X' and Y' become row vectors, and X' is *post*multiplied by A'. The expansion agrees again with the first two equations of (3-7). Here (by analogy) X' corresponds to one row of the unrotated factor matrix F, Y' corresponds to one row of the rotated factor matrix V, and A' corresponds to the transformation matrix Λ, which was in turn the transpose of the coefficient matrix of (2-22). This correspondence will be clearer if instead of the first two equations of (3-7) we consider the two *sets* of pairs of such equations implied by the expanded matrix equation

$$
\begin{array}{ccc}
X' & A' & = Y'
\end{array}
$$

$$
\begin{bmatrix}
x_{11} & x_{21} \\
x_{12} & x_{22} \\
x_{13} & x_{23} \\
x_{14} & x_{24} \\
x_{15} & x_{25}
\end{bmatrix}
\cdot
\begin{bmatrix}
a_{11} & a_{21} \\
a_{12} & a_{22}
\end{bmatrix}
=
\begin{bmatrix}
y_{11} & y_{21} \\
y_{12} & y_{22} \\
y_{13} & y_{23} \\
y_{14} & y_{24} \\
y_{15} & y_{25}
\end{bmatrix}
\tag{3-17}
$$

Substituting x_1 and x_2 for x_{11} and x_{21}, and y_1 and y_2 for y_{11} and y_{21}, the transformation of the first row of X' into the first row of Y' is identical with (3-16). When each of a whole *set* of rows is to be subjected to the same transformation, the transformation matrix must be arranged to *post*multiply the matrix representing these rows in order to preserve the common order of the rows of X' and the columns of A'. We show in a later chapter that these transformations represent, in the case of the geometric model of factor analysis, a rotation of the axes b and a of Fig. 2.1.a to positions I and II.

Problem 3.2.6:3.

1. Given the following matrices

$$A = \begin{bmatrix} 1 & 5 & 8 \\ 3 & 2 & 1 \end{bmatrix} \qquad B = \begin{bmatrix} 6 & 4 & 2 \\ 0 & 5 & 6 \end{bmatrix} \qquad C = \begin{bmatrix} 1 & 5 \\ 8 & 3 \\ 4 & 2 \end{bmatrix}$$

which of the following do not exist? State why.

a) $A + B$ e) AB i) $A + C'$
b) $A - B$ f) AC j) AB'
c) $A + C$ g) BC k) BA'
d) $A - C$ h) $A + B'$ l) AC'

2. Write the transposes of the following matrices:

$$A = \begin{bmatrix} 6 & 9 & 3 \\ 10 & 4 & 6 \end{bmatrix} \qquad B = \begin{bmatrix} 5 & 4 & 3 \\ 6 & 7 & 8 \\ 8 & 4 & 2 \\ 2 & 0 & 1 \end{bmatrix} \qquad C = \begin{bmatrix} 6 \\ 5 \\ 2 \end{bmatrix}$$

3. Write the following system of linear equations in matrix form similar to (3-4):

$$5x_1 + 6x_2 + 3x_3 = 7$$
$$9x_1 + 10x_2 + 2x_3 = 4$$
$$3x_1 + 8x_2 + 3x_3 = 10$$

4. The following two systems of linear equations are linearly dependent. For each system, why is this so?

$$2x_1 + 4x_2 = 10$$
$$4x_1 + 8x_2 = 20$$

$$3x_1 + 2x_2 + 5x_3 = 4$$
$$6x_1 + 3x_2 + 4x_3 = 6$$
$$9x_1 + 5x_2 + 9x_3 = 10$$

5. A raw-score matrix for two random variables and five pairs of scores is

$$X = \begin{bmatrix} 3 & 4 & 5 & 2 & 1 \\ 10 & 9 & 7 & 6 & 8 \end{bmatrix}$$

a. If $y_i = x_i - \bar{x}_i$ ($i = 1, 2$), write the matrix Y of deviation scores.

b. Show that the variance-covariance matrix of the scores is $\dfrac{YY'}{5}$. Why is it not $\dfrac{Y'Y}{5}$? Note: When a matrix is divided by a scalar (a single number), every element of the matrix is divided by that scalar (Section 3.2.9).

c. Find the reciprocals of the *standard deviations* of the two variables. Set up a matrix

$$D = \begin{bmatrix} 1\sigma_1 & 0 \\ 0 & 1/\sigma_2 \end{bmatrix}$$

and verify that the correlation matrix is $D \dfrac{YY'}{5} D$

3.2.7 Symmetric Matrices

A matrix is symmetric if and only if it is its own transpose. It is clear that only a square matrix can be symmetric, because the order, say m by n, of A' must be the same as the order, n by m, of A. Example:

$$A = \begin{bmatrix} 6 & 2 & 1 \\ 2 & 4 & 3 \\ 1 & 3 & 5 \end{bmatrix} = A'$$

The *principal diagonal,* often called simply "the diagonal," of a square matrix consists of the elements along the diagonal from upper left to lower right: 6, 4, 5 in the example above. In a symmetric matrix it is the elements symetrically located with respect to the diagonal which are equal: $a_{ji} = a_{ij}$ for all i and j, and when $j = i$ the element is on the diagonal. In the example above the equal elements are $a_{21} = a_{12} = 2$, $a_{31} = a_{13} = 1$, $a_{32} = a_{23} = 3$. In regression analysis the coefficients of a set of normal equations form a symmetric matrix, with sums of squares on the diagonal and sums of products elsewhere. A variance-covariance matrix is symmetric, with variances on the diagonal and covariances elsewhere. A correlation matrix is symmetric, with unities on the diagonal (or communalities, in factor analysis), and correlation coefficients elsewhere.

If Two Square Matrices, A and B, of the Same Order, are Symmetric, then AB = (BA)'.   For if A and B are symmetric, $A' = A$ and $B' = B$ by definition. Then $AB = A'B'$ by the elementary operation of matrix multiplication, and $A'B' = (BA)'$ by the rule for the transpose of a product. Example:

$$\begin{array}{ccccc} A & \cdot & B & = & AB \\ \begin{bmatrix} 1 & 2 \\ 2 & 3 \end{bmatrix} & \cdot & \begin{bmatrix} 3 & 1 \\ 1 & 2 \end{bmatrix} & = & \begin{bmatrix} 5 & 5 \\ 9 & 8 \end{bmatrix} \end{array}$$

$$\begin{array}{ccccccc} B & \cdot & A & = & BA & (BA)' & = AB \\ \begin{bmatrix} 3 & 1 \\ 1 & 2 \end{bmatrix} & \cdot & \begin{bmatrix} 1 & 2 \\ 2 & 3 \end{bmatrix} & = & \begin{bmatrix} 5 & 9 \\ 5 & 8 \end{bmatrix} & & \begin{bmatrix} 5 & 5 \\ 9 & 8 \end{bmatrix} = AB \end{array}$$

The Product of Two Symmetric Matrices is not in General Symmetric.   This property also is illustrated by the examples above.

If A is Symmetric and B is a Column Vector, then AB = (B'A)', and B'A = (AB)'.   Example:

$$\begin{array}{ccccc} A & \cdot & B & = & AB \\ \begin{bmatrix} 1 & 2 \\ 2 & 3 \end{bmatrix} & \cdot & \begin{bmatrix} 4 \\ 5 \end{bmatrix} & = & \begin{bmatrix} 14 \\ 23 \end{bmatrix} \end{array} \qquad (AB)' = [14 \quad 23]$$

$$\begin{array}{ccccc} B' & \cdot & A & = & B'A \\ [4 \quad 5] & \cdot & \begin{bmatrix} 1 & 2 \\ 2 & 3 \end{bmatrix} & = & [14 \quad 23] \end{array} \qquad (B'A)' = \begin{bmatrix} 14 \\ 23 \end{bmatrix} = AB.$$

The Product of any Matrix by its Transpose (in either order) is a Symmetric Matrix.   For the product of the i-th row of A (or A') by the j-th column of A' (or A), $i \neq j$, will be the same as the product of the j-th row of A (or A') by the i-th column of A' (or A). Hence the ij-th and ji-th elements of AA' (or $A'A$) will be the same. If A (or A') is of order m by n, then A' (or A) will be of order n by m, and the product AA' (or $A'A'$) will be of order n by n. Examples:

$$\begin{array}{ccccc} A' & \cdot & A & = & A'A \text{ (sym)} \\ \begin{bmatrix} 1 & 2 & 3 \\ 2 & 3 & 4 \end{bmatrix} & \cdot & \begin{bmatrix} 1 & 2 \\ 2 & 3 \\ 3 & 4 \end{bmatrix} & = & \begin{bmatrix} 14 & 20 \\ 20 & 29 \end{bmatrix} \end{array}$$

$$\begin{array}{ccccc} A & \cdot & A' & = & AA' \text{ (sym)} \\ \begin{bmatrix} 1 & 2 \\ 2 & 3 \\ 3 & 4 \end{bmatrix} & \cdot & \begin{bmatrix} 1 & 2 & 3 \\ 2 & 3 & 4 \end{bmatrix} & = & \begin{bmatrix} 5 & 8 & 11 \\ 8 & 13 & 18 \\ 11 & 18 & 25 \end{bmatrix} \end{array}$$

$$\begin{array}{ccccc} A & \cdot & A' & = & AA' \text{ (sym)} \\ \begin{bmatrix} 1 & 2 \\ 3 & 4 \end{bmatrix} & \cdot & \begin{bmatrix} 1 & 3 \\ 2 & 4 \end{bmatrix} & = & \begin{bmatrix} 5 & 11 \\ 11 & 25 \end{bmatrix} \end{array}$$

$$\begin{array}{ccccc} A' & \cdot & A & = & A'A \text{ (sym)} \\ \begin{bmatrix} 1 & 3 \\ 2 & 4 \end{bmatrix} & \cdot & \begin{bmatrix} 1 & 2 \\ 3 & 4 \end{bmatrix} & = & \begin{bmatrix} 10 & 14 \\ 14 & 20 \end{bmatrix} \end{array}$$

Note that *in general* $AA' \neq A'A$ even when A is square. In particular cases, AA' *may* equal $A'A$ when A is not symmetric.

If A is symmetric, then $A'A = AA'$ (because $A = A'$).

Problem 3.2.7:1.

1. Which of the following matrices are symmetric?

$$A = \begin{bmatrix} 4 & 3 & 2 \\ 2 & 4 & 3 \\ 3 & 2 & 4 \end{bmatrix} \quad B = \begin{bmatrix} 1 & 1 & 0 \\ 1 & 1 & 0 \\ 0 & 0 & 1 \end{bmatrix} \quad C = \begin{bmatrix} 5 & 2 & 3 \\ 2 & 5 & 4 \\ 4 & 3 & 5 \end{bmatrix} \quad D = \begin{bmatrix} 1 & 2 & 3 \\ 2 & 4 & 4 \\ 3 & 4 & 2 \end{bmatrix}$$

2. For each matrix which is *not* symmetric, check the equality of GG' and $G'G$, where G is A or B or C or D.

3.2.8 Diagonal Matrices

A diagonal matrix is a symmetric matrix with all diagonal elements nonzero and all off-diagonal elements zero. A diagonal matrix is usually designated D in compact notation.

Consider the matrix product,

$$
\begin{array}{ccc}
D & A & DA \\
\begin{bmatrix} 3 & 0 \\ 0 & 4 \end{bmatrix} \cdot & \begin{bmatrix} 1 & 2 & 3 \\ 2 & 3 & 4 \end{bmatrix} = & \begin{bmatrix} 3 & 6 & 9 \\ 8 & 12 & 16 \end{bmatrix}
\end{array}
$$

It may be seen that *premultiplication* of a matrix A by a diagonal matrix D multiplies all elements in each *row* by the diagonal element in the same row of D.

Consider again,

$$
\begin{array}{ccc}
A & D & AD \\
\begin{bmatrix} 1 & 3 \\ 4 & 2 \\ 2 & 2 \end{bmatrix} \cdot & \begin{bmatrix} 3 & 0 \\ 0 & 4 \end{bmatrix} = & \begin{bmatrix} 3 & 12 \\ 12 & 8 \\ 6 & 8 \end{bmatrix}
\end{array}
$$

Postmultiplication of a matrix A by a diagonal matrix D multiplies all elements in each *column* of A by the diagonal element in the same column of D.

Problem 3.2.8:1. If A is a symmetric variance-covariance matrix, and D is a diagonal matrix with diagonal elements $d_{ii} = 1/\sigma_i$, show that the corresponding correlation matrix is DAD.

The *product* of two diagonal matrices is a diagonal matrix each diagonal element of which is the product of the two corresponding diagonal elements of the original matrices. Examples:

$$
\begin{bmatrix} 1 & 0 & 0 \\ 0 & 2 & 0 \\ 0 & 0 & 3 \end{bmatrix} \cdot \begin{bmatrix} 2 & 0 & 0 \\ 0 & 3 & 0 \\ 0 & 0 & 4 \end{bmatrix} = \begin{bmatrix} 2 & 0 & 0 \\ 0 & 6 & 0 \\ 0 & 0 & 12 \end{bmatrix}
$$

$$
\begin{bmatrix} 2 & 0 & 0 \\ 0 & 3 & 0 \\ 0 & 0 & 4 \end{bmatrix} \cdot \begin{bmatrix} 1 & 0 & 0 \\ 0 & 2 & 0 \\ 0 & 0 & 3 \end{bmatrix} = \begin{bmatrix} 2 & 0 & 0 \\ 0 & 6 & 0 \\ 0 & 0 & 12 \end{bmatrix}
$$

From these examples and the preceding discussion (back to the definition of a diagonal matrix), it is evident that *multiplication of diagonal matrices is commutative: $AB = BA$ if both A and B are diagonal and of the same order.* Also, *every diagonal matrix is its own transpose,* because every diagonal matrix is symmetric.

3.2.9 Scalar Matrices and Scalar Multiplication

A scalar matrix is a diagonal matrix all of whose diagonal elements are equal.

From the previous observations on premultiplication and postmultiplication by a diagonal matrix, it is evident that if we premultiply or postmultiply a matrix B by a scalar matrix A of appropriate order, the product will be a matrix of the same order as B, with elements ab_{ij}, where a is the value of the diagonal elements of A.

Definition of Scalar Multiplication. A scalar is a single number (Section 3.2.3), and we can define the product of a matrix B and a scalar a as a matrix aB, every element of which is a times the corresponding element of B.

The rule that the existence of a matrix product requires that the number of columns of the left matrix equal the number of rows of the right matrix is not violated, because any scalar may be represented by a scalar matrix of appropriate order. The following three theorems are then essentially self-evident.

Scalar multiplication is commutative. $aB = Ba$

Scalar multiplication is associative. $a(BC) = (aB)C$, and $a(bC) = (ab)C$.

Scalar multiplication is distributive over both scalar and matrix addition and subtraction. $(a \pm b)C = aC \pm bC$, and $a(B \pm C) = aB \pm aC$.

Division of a matrix by a scalar is multiplication of that matrix by the reciprocal of the scalar. Thus when a matrix is divided by a scalar, every element of the matrix is divided by that scalar.

3.2.10 The Identity Matrix

For every nonzero matrix A, there are two square identity matrices, I_1 and I_2, equal if and only if A is square, such that $I_1 A = AI_2 = A$.

An identity matrix I is a scalar matrix all of whose diagonal elements are 1. The statement above follows from this definition and the conclusions about premultiplication and postmultiplication of a matrix A by a diagonal matrix.

From the definition above, it is clear that the identity matrix has the same significance in matrix algebra as has the number 1 in ordinary algebra. (For every number a, there is a number 1 such that $1 \cdot a = a \cdot 1 = a$.)

Examples:

$$
\begin{array}{ccccc}
A & \cdot & I & = & A
\end{array}
$$

$$
\begin{bmatrix} 1 & 2 & 3 \\ 2 & 3 & 4 \end{bmatrix} \cdot \begin{bmatrix} 1 & 0 & 0 \\ 0 & 1 & 0 \\ 0 & 0 & 1 \end{bmatrix} = \begin{bmatrix} 1 & 2 & 3 \\ 2 & 3 & 4 \end{bmatrix}
$$

$$
\begin{array}{ccccc}
I & \cdot & A & = & A
\end{array}
$$

$$
\begin{bmatrix} 1 & 0 \\ 0 & 1 \end{bmatrix} \cdot \begin{bmatrix} 1 & 2 & 3 \\ 2 & 3 & 1 \end{bmatrix} = \begin{bmatrix} 1 & 2 & 3 \\ 2 & 3 & 1 \end{bmatrix}
$$

3.3 THE INVERSE OF A SQUARE MATRIX

In ordinary algebra there is a theorem which states that for every number a except $a = 0$, there is a number $a^{-1} = 1/a$, its *reciprocal*, such that $aa^{-1} = a^{-1}a = a/a = 1$, and division of a by b is defined as $ab^{-1} = a(1/b) = a/b$, or as $b^{-1}a = (1/b)a = a/b$. In matrix algebra, the inverse plays the same role as does the reciprocal in ordinary algebra; matrix *inversion* is analogous to the formation of a reciprocal; and matrix *division* is represented by premultiplication or postmultiplication by an inverse.

3.3.1 Definition and Properties of the Inverse

For every *square nonsingular* matrix A, there is a matrix A^{-1}, of the same order, such that $AA^{-1} = A^{-1}A = I$, an identity matrix. Examples:

$$
\begin{matrix} A \end{matrix} \qquad\qquad \begin{matrix} A^{-1} \end{matrix} \qquad = \qquad \begin{matrix} I \end{matrix}
$$

$$
\begin{bmatrix} 1 & 3 & 3 \\ 1 & 4 & 3 \\ 1 & 3 & 4 \end{bmatrix} \cdot \begin{bmatrix} 7 & -3 & -3 \\ -1 & 1 & 0 \\ -1 & 0 & 1 \end{bmatrix} = \begin{bmatrix} 1 & 0 & 0 \\ 0 & 1 & 0 \\ 0 & 0 & 1 \end{bmatrix}
$$

$$
\begin{matrix} A^{-1} \end{matrix} \qquad\qquad \begin{matrix} A \end{matrix} \qquad = \qquad \begin{matrix} I \end{matrix}
$$

$$
\begin{bmatrix} 7 & -3 & -3 \\ -1 & 1 & 0 \\ -1 & 0 & 1 \end{bmatrix} \cdot \begin{bmatrix} 1 & 3 & 3 \\ 1 & 4 & 3 \\ 1 & 3 & 4 \end{bmatrix} = \begin{bmatrix} 1 & 0 & 0 \\ 0 & 1 & 0 \\ 0 & 0 & 1 \end{bmatrix}
$$

A square matrix is nonsingular if no row (or column) consists entirely of zeros, or is a multiple or fraction of any other row (or column), and is not the algebraic sum of positive and/or negative multiples or fractions of any two or more of the other rows (or columns). Consider the matrices

$$
\begin{matrix} A \end{matrix} \qquad\qquad \begin{matrix} B \end{matrix} \qquad\qquad \begin{matrix} C \end{matrix}
$$

$$
\begin{bmatrix} 2 & 4 & 0 \\ 3 & 2 & 0 \\ 4 & 8 & 0 \end{bmatrix} \quad \begin{bmatrix} 2 & 4 & 0 \\ 3 & 2 & 2 \\ 4 & 8 & 0 \end{bmatrix} \quad \begin{bmatrix} 2 & 4 & 0 \\ 3 & 2 & 2 \\ 4 & 6 & 1 \end{bmatrix}
$$

The matrix A is singular because all elements in the third column are 0. The matrix B is singular because every element in the bottom row is twice the corresponding element in the top row. The matrix C is singular because every element in the third column is the element in the first column minus one-half the element next to it in the second column.

We merely state without proof four further propositions:

1. The product of two singular matrices is singular.
2. The product of a singular matrix and a nonsingular matrix is singular.
3. The product of two nonsingular matrices may or may not be singular.
4. The product of two *square* nonsingular matrices is nonsingular.

These propositions are considered further in Section 3.4.2.

Comparing the definition of a singular matrix with the definition of a set of linearly independent nonhomogeneous simultaneous equations in Section 3.2.5, we see that such a set of equations is linearly independent if its coefficient matrix is nonsingular.

Proof of the existence of an inverse of every square nonsingular matrix is beyond the scope of this treatment. But assuming such existence, we can show that the left inverse and the right inverse are the same, that is, that *every nonsingular square matrix is commutative with its inverses*. Assume that both exist, and define

$$A_1^{-1}A = I \qquad (3\text{-}18)$$

$$AA_2^{-1} = I \qquad (3\text{-}19)$$

Then start with the identity,

$$A_1^{-1}A = A_1^{-1}A. \qquad (3\text{-}20)$$

Postmultiply both sides of (3-20) by A_2^{-1}, and invoke the associative law:

$$(A_1^{-1}A)A_2^{-1} = A_1^{-1}(AA_2^{-1}).$$

Then from (3-18) and (3-19)

$$IA_2^{-1} = A_1^{-1}I.$$

Then from the definition of I

$$A_2^{-1} = A_1^{-1} = A^{-1}.$$

The inverse of a product is the product of the inverses in reverse order: $(AB)^{-1} = B^{-1}A^{-1}$. Because by definition $BB^{-1} = AA^{-1} = I$,

$$(AB)(B^{-1}A^{-1}) = A(BB^{-1})A^{-1} = AIA^{-1} = AA^{-1} = I$$

or

$$I = (AB)(B^{-1}A^{-1}). \qquad (3\text{-}21)$$

Premultiply both sides of (3-21) by $(AB)^{-1}$. Then

$$(AB)^{-1}I = (AB)^{-1}(AB)(B^{-1}A^{-1}). \qquad (3\text{-}22)$$

But $(AB)^{-1}(AB) = I$, so from (3-22)

$$(AB)^{-1}I = I(B^{-1}A^{-1})$$

and, by the definition of I,

$$(AB)^{-1} = (B^{-1}A^{-1}).$$

The inverse of a diagonal matrix is a diagonal matrix each diagonal element of which is the reciprocal of the corresponding element of the original matrix. This follows from the definition of the inverse as $AA^{-1} = A^{-1}A = I$, the proposition that the product of two diagonal matrices is a diagonal matrix each diagonal element of which is the product of the two corresponding diagonal elements of the original matrices and the fact that $a(1/a) = 1$ for all a except $a = 0$.

The Identity Matrix is Its Own Inverse.   This follows at once from the proposition above when we note that $1/1 = 1$.

The Transpose of an Inverse is the Inverse of the Transpose: $(A^{-1})' = (A')^{-1}$. *Proof:*

$$(A')^{-1}A' = (AA^{-1})' = I.$$

By the definition of an inverse, $(A')^{-1}A' = I$. Also $AA^{-1} = I$, and $(AA^{-1})' = I' = I$ because I is symmetric and is therefore its own transpose. Then, applying the rule for the transpose of a product to $(AA^{-1})'$,

$$(A')^{-1}A' = (A^{-1})'A'.$$

Postmultiply both sides by $(A')^{-1}$:

$$(A')^{-1}A'(A')^{-1} = (A^{-1})'A(A')^{-1}.$$

Noting that $A'(A')^{-1} = I$,

$$(A')^{-1}I = (A^{-1})'I$$

and, by the definition of I,

$$(A')^{-1} = (A^{-1})'.$$

The Inverse of an Inverse is the Original Matrix: $(A^{-1})^{-1} = A$. By the definition of an inverse,

$$(A^{-1})(A^{-1})^{-1} = I.$$

Premultiplying both sides by A,

$$A(A^{-1})(A^{-1})^{-1} = AI = A$$

and, because $AA^{-1} = I$,

$$I(A^{-1})^{-1} = A,$$

and

$$(A^{-1})^{-1} = A.$$

Simultaneous Equations and the Inverse.   Referring back to (3-6) in Section 3.2.5, we note that a system of n linearly independent nonhomogeneous linear equations in n unknowns can be represented by the matrix equation,

$$AX = C.$$

Premultiplying both sides by A^{-1},

$$A^{-1}AX = A^{-1}C.$$

Then because $A^{-1}A = I$ and $IX = X$, the solution to the set of equations is

$$X = A^{-1}C.$$

3.3.2 Matrix Inversion

The matrix equation $AA^{-1} = I$ may be written in the longer form (using a 3 by 3 matrix for illustration),

$$
\underset{A}{\begin{bmatrix} a_{11} & a_{12} & a_{13} \\ a_{21} & a_{22} & a_{23} \\ a_{31} & a_{32} & a_{33} \end{bmatrix}} \cdot \underset{A^{-1}}{\begin{bmatrix} a^{11} & a^{12} & a^{13} \\ a^{21} & a^{22} & a^{23} \\ a^{31} & a^{32} & a^{33} \end{bmatrix}} = \underset{I}{\begin{bmatrix} 1 & 0 & 0 \\ 0 & 1 & 0 \\ 0 & 0 & 1 \end{bmatrix}}
$$

with a_{ij} an element of A and a^{ij} an element of A^{-1}. The matrix multiplication of the rows of A by the first column of A^{-1} to give the first column of I are exactly the same as those which would follow if we were to write

$$
\begin{bmatrix} a_{11} & a_{12} & a_{13} \\ a_{21} & a_{22} & a_{23} \\ a_{31} & a_{32} & a_{33} \end{bmatrix} \cdot \begin{bmatrix} a^{11} \\ a^{21} \\ a^{31} \end{bmatrix} = \begin{bmatrix} 1 \\ 0 \\ 0 \end{bmatrix}
$$

and these represent three nonhomogeneous simultaneous equations in three unknowns. If we then write

$$
\begin{bmatrix} a_{11} & a_{12} & a_{13} \\ a_{21} & a_{22} & a_{23} \\ a_{31} & a_{32} & a_{33} \end{bmatrix} \cdot \begin{bmatrix} a^{12} \\ a^{22} \\ a^{32} \end{bmatrix} = \begin{bmatrix} 0 \\ 1 \\ 0 \end{bmatrix}
$$

and

$$
\begin{bmatrix} a_{11} & a_{12} & a_{13} \\ a_{21} & a_{22} & a_{23} \\ a_{31} & a_{32} & a_{33} \end{bmatrix} \cdot \begin{bmatrix} a^{13} \\ a^{23} \\ a^{33} \end{bmatrix} = \begin{bmatrix} 0 \\ 0 \\ 1 \end{bmatrix}
$$

we see that solving for the inverse is equivalent to solving three (or n) *sets*, each of three (or n) nonhomogeneous simultaneous linear equations in three (or n) unknowns, the coefficient matrix A being the same for each set. In each set, the column of constants is one column of the identity matrix I.

Elementary Transformations. Operations that change every element of just one row or column of a matrix are called elementary transformations. We consider here only elementary *row* transformations. These transformations are based on the two rules of ordinary algebra: (1) if equals are added to (or subtracted from) equals, the results are equal; (2) if equals are multiplied (or divided) by equals, the results are equal.

From these rules are obtained the two commonly used elementary transformations: (3) multiplication (or division) of the elements of a row (equation) by a nonzero constant (rule 2); (4) adding to (or subtracting from) the elements of one row the same multiple (or fraction) of the elements of another row (rule 2 and then rule 1).

These transformations are clearly permissible in ordinary algebra. Performing an elementary transformation upon the coefficients and constant of a true equation produces another true equation (see rules 1 and 2 above). Hence elementary transformations are used in solving systems of linear equations. But we have shown that matrix inversion is equivalent to the solution of such systems of linear equations. Hence, elementary transformations may be used for matrix inversion.

Suppose we perform upon the rows of a square, nonsingular matrix A some sequence of elementary transformations which reduce it to I. Because $I = A^{-1}A$, such a set of transformations is equivalent to premultiplying A by A^{-1}. Then if we perform this identical sequence of transformations upon I, the result is $A^{-1}I = A^{-1}$.

It has also been shown that, for a set of nonhomogeneous linear equations with nonsingular coefficient matrix A, $X = A^{-1}C$, where C is a column vector of constants. If now we perform upon C the sequence of elementary transformations that reduces A to I, the result is $A^{-1}C = X$. These are the essential principles on which matrix inversion and the solution of systems of nonhomogeneous linear equations are based. The procedures may be diagrammed as follows:

$$
\begin{array}{ccc}
A & I & C \\
\downarrow & \downarrow & \downarrow \\
I & A^{-1} & X
\end{array}
$$

The arrows stand for the sequence of elementary transformations: the same sequence in each column of the diagram above. In matrix inversion we omit the last column; in the solution of systems of nonhomogeneous linear equations we omit the middle column.

If A^{-1} is computed initially from a coefficient matrix A, then for *any* column vector of constants C, $X = A^{-1}C$. The computation of $A^{-1}C$ is easy. For three variables, for example, the computation of X is

$$
\begin{array}{ccc}
A^{-1} & \cdot\quad C & = \quad X
\end{array}
$$
$$
\begin{bmatrix} a^{11} & a^{12} & a^{13} \\ a^{21} & a^{22} & a^{23} \\ a^{31} & a^{32} & a^{33} \end{bmatrix} \cdot \begin{bmatrix} c_1 \\ c_2 \\ c_3 \end{bmatrix} = \begin{bmatrix} x_1 \\ x_2 \\ x_3 \end{bmatrix}
$$

and

$$x_1 = a^{11}c_1 + a^{12}c_2 + a^{13}c_3$$

$$x_2 = a^{21}c_1 + a^{22}c_2 + a^{23}c_3 \qquad (3\text{-}23)$$

$$x_3 = a^{31}c_1 + a^{32}c_2 + a^{33}c_3$$

The actual solution of sets of nonhomogeneous simultaneous linear equations, and the detailed procedures of matrix inversion, using elementary row transformations, are discussed in Chapter 4.

3.4 SOME FURTHER MATRIX ALGEBRA

3.4.1 Orthogonal and Orthonormal Matrices

These matrices, especially the latter, play an important role in factor analysis as transformation matrices for orthogonal rotation of factor matrices.

Definition of Orthogonal Vectors.   Two vectors of the same order are orthogonal if and only if their scalar product is zero. Example:

$$[3 \quad -2 \quad 3] \cdot \begin{bmatrix} 3 \\ 3 \\ -1 \end{bmatrix} = 0$$

Definition of a Normal Vector.   A normal vector V is a vector such that $V'V = 1$, that is, it is a vector the sum of squares of whose elements is unity. Example:

$$[.7 \quad .5 \quad .1 \quad .5] \cdot \begin{bmatrix} .7 \\ .5 \\ .1 \\ .5 \end{bmatrix} = 1$$

Definition of Orthonormal Vectors.   Two vectors of the same order are orthonormal if and only if they are orthogonal *and* each of them is a normal vector. Example:

$$[.7 \quad .6 \quad -.3 \quad .2 \quad .1 \quad -.1] \cdot \begin{bmatrix} .6 \\ -.4 \\ .6 \\ .2 \\ -.2 \\ .2 \end{bmatrix} = 0$$

It is easily verified that the sum of squares of the elements of each of these vectors is unity.

Normalization of a Vector. Any vector, V or V', may be normalized by dividing each of its elements by the square root of the sum of their squares. This sum of squares is the scalar product $V'V$. Then if U or U' is the normalized vector,

$$U = \frac{V}{\sqrt{V'V}}; \quad U' = \frac{V'}{\sqrt{V'V}}. \tag{3-24}$$

Then

$$U'U = \frac{V'V}{V'V} = 1.$$

Example:

$$V = \begin{bmatrix} 6 \\ 8 \end{bmatrix}$$

$$V'V = 6^2 + 8^2 = 36 + 64 = 100$$

$$\sqrt{V'V} = 10$$

$$U = \frac{1}{10} \cdot \begin{bmatrix} 6 \\ 8 \end{bmatrix} = \begin{bmatrix} .6 \\ .8 \end{bmatrix}$$

$$U'U = .6^2 + .8^2 = .36 + .64 = 1.00$$

The numerical procedure for normalization, based directly on the verbal definition, was illustrated in Chapter 2, where it was used to find unit vectors through a centroid.

Definition of a Matrix that is Orthogonal by Columns. A matrix A is orthogonal by columns if and only if $A'A = D$, a diagonal matrix.

If each column of A is considered a column vector, the scalar products of all pairs of *different* column vectors will be 0 if D is diagonal. Then by the definition of orthogonal vectors, all columns of A are orthogonal to one another.

Definition of a Matrix that is Orthogonal by Rows. A matrix A is orthogonal by rows if and only if $AA' = D$, a diagonal matrix. All the row vectors of A are orthogonal to one another.

Definition of a Matrix that is Orthonormal by Columns. A matrix A is orthonormal by columns if and only if it is orthogonal by columns *and* every column vector is a normal vector. Then $A'A = I$, an identity matrix.

Definition of a Matrix that is Orthonormal by Rows. A matrix A is orthonormal by rows if and only if it is orthogonal by rows *and* every row vector is a normal vector. Then $AA' = I$, an identity matrix.

Normalization. Any matrix, whether orthogonal or not, may be normalized by columns (rows) by dividing the elements of each column (row) by the square root of the sum of their squares.

1. *Post*multiplication of an *n* by *m* matrix *A* by a diagonal matrix *D* of order *m*, with diagonal elements

$$d_{jj} = 1/\sqrt{a_{1j}^2 + a_{2j}^2 + \ldots + a_{nj}^2} \qquad (j = 1, 2, \ldots, m)$$

for *m* columns, normalizes *A* by columns.

2. *Pre*multiplication of an *n* by *m* matrix *A* by a diagonal matrix *D* of order *n*, with diagonal elements

$$d_{ii} = 1/\sqrt{a_{i1}^2 + a_{i2}^2 + \ldots + a_{im}^2} \qquad (i = 1, 2, \ldots, n),$$

for *n* rows, normalizes *A* by rows.

Note that the matrix that normalizes the *rows* of *A* can be written

$$D = [\text{diag } (AA')]^{-1/2}.$$

The diagonal elements of AA' are the sums of squares of the elements of its rows. Their reciprocals are $[\text{diag } (AA')]^{-1}$, and the square root of a diagonal matrix has elements which are the square roots of its elements, so

$$D = \{[\text{diag } (AA')]^{-1}\}^{1/2} = [\text{diag } (AA')]^{-1/2}.$$

Similarly the matrix that normalizes the *columns* of *A* is

$$D = [\text{diag } (A'A)]^{-1/2}.$$

Definition of an Orthonormal Matrix. A matrix *A* is orthonormal if it is *square* and if (and only if) $A'A = AA' = A^{-1}A = AA^{-1} = I$.

If *A* is orthonormal by columns, $A'A = I$, and if *A* is orthonormal by rows, $AA' = I$. But $A^{-1}A = AA^{-1} = I$; therefore it follows for square matrices that if $A'A = I$, then $AA' = I$ also. Hence if a square matrix is orthonormal by either rows or columns it is *orthonormal* (by *both* rows and columns).

Most writers call *A*, as defined above, an orthogonal matrix. But clearly, it is also orthonormal. We do not consider here orthogonal matrices that are not orthonormal.

It has been shown that if *D* is a diagonal matrix, D^{-1} is a diagonal matrix with diagonal elements $1/d_{ii}$. Also $D' = D$. Then, if $D^{-1} = D' = D$, the diagonal elements of *D* must be their own reciprocals. And, because the number 1 is the only number that is its own reciprocal, it follows that the identity matrix is the *only* diagonal orthonormal matrix.

Problem 3.4.1:1. If [2/3 2/3 1/3] and [$1/\sqrt{2}$ $-1/\sqrt{2}$ 0] are the first two rows of a 3 by 3 matrix *A*, find a third row such that *A* is orthonormal. Hint: if the third row is orthogonal to the second, it must be of the form [*x* *x* *y*]. Why?

Then what form must it take to be orthogonal to the first row, and what must be the value of y in terms of x? Finally, what must be the numerical values of its elements if A is to be orthonormal?

3.4.2 Rank of a Matrix

Any given matrix A may be expressed as the product of two other matrices of the same or lower order, and in fact by an infinite number of such products. The rank of A is the lowest common order of any pair of matrices B and C whose product is the matrix A, that is, $BC = A$ or $CB = A$. Thus if B or C or both are vectors, and $BC' = A$ or $CB' = A$, A has rank 1. An example of a square matrix A, of order 4 by 4 and rank 2 is

$$
\underset{B}{\begin{bmatrix} 1 & 0 \\ 0 & 1 \\ 2 & 0 \\ 1 & 1 \end{bmatrix}} \cdot \underset{C}{\begin{bmatrix} 1 & 2 & 3 & 4 \\ 3 & 4 & 3 & 2 \end{bmatrix}} = \underset{A}{\begin{bmatrix} 1 & 2 & 3 & 4 \\ 3 & 4 & 3 & 2 \\ 2 & 4 & 6 & 8 \\ 4 & 6 & 6 & 6 \end{bmatrix}} \tag{3-25}
$$

In factor analysis, we are interested mainly in the ranks of square matrices, and particularly in the rank of a correlation matrix with communalities on the diagonal.

Singularity and Linear Restraints. A square matrix is *singular* (Section 3.3.1) if its rank is lower than its order. The matrix A above is singular.

A *linear restraint* exists whenever one row (or column) of a matrix can be formed by a finite number of elementary transformations of the elements of any one or more of the other rows (or columns). In the matrix A above, the elements of the third row are twice those of the first row, and those of the fourth row are the sums of those in the first and second rows, so there are two linear restraints. Two rows are linearly independent of each other.

Note that we do *not* specify *which* two rows are linearly independent. In the matrix A above, *any* pair of rows except the first and third may be considered linearly independent. If we label the rows a, b, c, and d, and designate by asterisks the two rows considered linearly independent, we have the five possible sets of relations indicated in the five columns below:

	1	2	3	4	5
$a =$	a^*	a^*	$c/2$	$d - b$	$c/2$
$b =$	b^*	$d - a$	b^*	b^*	$d - c/2$
$c =$	$2a$	$2a$	c^*	$2d - 2b$	c^*
$d =$	$a + b$	d^*	$b + c/2$	d^*	d^*

The first column represents the construction described in the previous paragraph, with rows a and b considered linearly independent, but we could equally well construct the matrix A by taking any other two rows except a and c as the independent pair, as in the last four columns above. We cannot take rows a and c as the linearly independent pair because they are linearly dependent to begin with.

The rank of a square matrix is also reduced by one for every row (or column) which consists entirely of zeros. This is most easily appreciated if we consider a set of n simultaneous equations in n unknowns, and one equation is

$$0x_1 + 0x_2 + \ldots + 0x_n = 0.$$

No matter what values the x's take, this equation reduces to $0 = 0$, and hence provides no information about the values of the x's. We have then effectively only $n - 1$ equations in n unknowns, and the matrix of coefficients is singular, with rank $n - 1$ or lower.

The rank of a square matrix of order n, then, is n minus the number of linear restraints minus the number of zero rows (or columns), or the number of nonzero linearly independent rows (or columns). We state without proof that in a square matrix the number of linear restraints on the rows is equal to the number of linear restraints on the columns, each all-zero row (or column) being counted as a linear restraint. Thus in the matrix

$$\begin{bmatrix} 1 & 2 & 3 \\ 2 & 4 & 6 \\ 2 & 0 & 4 \end{bmatrix}$$

the linear restraint on the rows is at once apparent: the elements of the second row are twice those in the first row. For the columns, twice each element in the first plus one-half the element in the second is equal to the third. And in the matrix

$$\begin{bmatrix} 2 & 1 & 3 \\ 0 & 0 & 0 \\ 4 & 3 & 1 \end{bmatrix}$$

each element in the third column is four times the element in the first minus five times the element in the second.

Equality of the numbers of linear restraints in rows and columns (including any rows and/or columns which are all-zero) leads at once to the proposition that *the rank of A' is equal to the rank of A.*

The lowest common order of any two matrices whose product is a given square matrix A is 1. Hence the rank of a square matrix cannot be less than 1, and we have seen that this rank cannot exceed its order. *Exception:* the zero matrix (and no other) is said to have rank 0, because all n rows (and columns) have all elements zero.

The rank of a nonsquare matrix cannot exceed its *lower* (row or column) order.

The row rank is equal to the column rank. Thus if a matrix A is of order 3 by 6 and rank 2, its rows must have one linear restraint and its columns must have four linear restraints (taking any all-zero column or row as one linear restraint). Example:

$$A = \begin{bmatrix} 1 & 2 & 3 & 4 & 5 & 6 \\ 2 & 3 & 4 & 5 & 1 & 6 \\ 3 & 5 & 7 & 9 & 6 & 12 \end{bmatrix}$$

It is fairly evident that the row rank is 2: each element in the third row is the sum of those in the first two rows. To show that the column rank is also 2 is somewhat more difficult. If we take the first two columns as linearly independent, we can set up from A the equations

$$x + 2y = 3, \quad 4, \quad 5, \quad 6$$

$$2x + 3y = 4, \quad 5, \quad 1, \quad 6$$

$$3x + 5y = 7, \quad 9, \quad 6, \quad 12$$

and solve for x and y, taking each column to the right of the equal signs in turn as the column of constants. When we do this, letting x be the multiplier for the first column of A and y the multiplier for the second column, we find that the third column is twice the second minus the first, the fourth column is three times the second minus twice the first, the fifth column is nine times the second minus 13 times the first, and the sixth column is six times the second minus six times the first.

If the rank of a matrix is 1, its rows and columns (if nonzero) are proportional. Thus

$$A = \begin{bmatrix} 1 & 2 & 3 & 0 & 4 \\ 2 & 4 & 6 & 0 & 8 \end{bmatrix}$$

is of rank 1, with proportional rows and columns. The rows and columns must be proportional because any one of them whose elements are not all zero must be linearly dependent on any one other. Before he invented the tetrad, Spearman used this property to test the hypothesis that one general factor is sufficient to account for a set of intercorrelations. For if the correlations are proportional by columns (or rows), omitting the two pairs one of each of which is an unknown diagonal element (a communality), the $n(n-1)/2$ *intercolumnar correlations* must all be unity within sampling error. He abandoned this criterion in favor of the tetrad criterion as soon as he and Holzinger had derived the standard error of a tetrad (Spearman and Holzinger, 1924) because he had not found an accurate test of the hypothesis that $n(n-1)/2$ correlations all differ from unity only by sampling error.

If the rank of a matrix is equal to its lower order, all rows (and columns) have at least one nonzero element and are linearly independent, and the matrix is *nonsingular*. Any correlation matrix with unities on the diagonal is non-singular unless the multiple corelation of at least one variable with some or all of the others is unity. Every diagonal matrix (including the identity matrix) is nonsingular. Every orthonormal matrix is nonsingular, for if A is such a matrix, $A' = A^{-1}$, and if A were singular, A^{-1} would not exist. A general method for determining the rank of a matrix, and hence whether it is singular or non-singular, is described and illustrated in Chapter 4.

Problem 3.4.2:1. Find the ranks of the following matrices by examining rows and columns:

$$\begin{bmatrix} 1 & 2 & 3 \\ 1 & 0 & 5 \\ 2 & 4 & 6 \end{bmatrix} \quad \begin{bmatrix} 1 & 2 & 3 \\ 1 & 0 & 5 \\ 2 & 2 & 8 \end{bmatrix} \quad \begin{bmatrix} 1 & 2 & 3 \\ 4 & 5 & 6 \\ 7 & 8 & 9 \end{bmatrix}$$

$$\begin{bmatrix} 3 & 1 & 2 \\ 6 & 2 & 4 \\ 9 & 3 & 6 \end{bmatrix} \quad \begin{bmatrix} 3 & 2 & 1 \\ 6 & 3 & 3 \\ 9 & 4 & 5 \end{bmatrix} \quad \begin{bmatrix} 2 & 3 & 1 \\ 3 & 5 & 2 \\ 5 & 8 & 3 \end{bmatrix} \quad \begin{bmatrix} 2 & 0 & 4 \\ 1 & 0 & 2 \\ 3 & 0 & 6 \end{bmatrix}$$

Rank of the Product of Two Matrices. The following three propositions are stated without proof.

1. The rank of the product of two matrices cannot be greater than that of the matrix of lower rank. Thus, if $A = BC$, $r_A \leq \min(r_B, r_C)$, where r_A, r_B, and r_C are the ranks respectively of the matrices A, B, and C.

2. The rank of the product of two matrices cannot be less than the sum of their ranks minus their common order: $r_A \geq r_B + r_C - m$, where m is the common order of B and C.

3. The rank of AA' and $A'A$ is the rank of A.

This last proposition is used occasionally in the following manner. If $AX = C$ (where A is a square coefficient matrix, X is a solution vector, and C is a vector of constants), we have seen that the solution is $X = A^{-1}C$. Premultiply $AX = C$ by A', yielding

$$A'AX = A'C. \qquad (3\text{-}26)$$

The solution is

$$X = (A'A)^{-1}A'C. \qquad (3\text{-}27)$$

Some authors have suggested the use of (3-27) in solving systems of non-homogeneous simultaneous equations because $A'A$ is symmetric, and the solution is simpler when the coefficient matrix is symmetric. In most cases, however, the gain in solution time is more than offset by the time required for pre-multiplication by A', and this procedure also increases the accumulated rounding error in the computations. A still more serious difficulty arises in some cases: $A'A$ may become *almost singular,* causing a drastic drop in the accuracy of the results (see Chapter 4), even though A is not so close to singular. For these reasons, we do not recommend this procedure.

3.4.3 Gramian Matrices

Definition: if B is a real symmetric matrix (a symmetric matrix all of whose elements are real numbers), and there exists a real matrix A such that $AA' = B$ or $A'A = B$, then B is a *Gramian matrix*.

Problem 3.4.3:1. Verify that

$$B = \begin{bmatrix} 4 & 6 & 8 \\ 6 & 9 & 12 \\ 8 & 12 & 16 \end{bmatrix}$$

is Gramian by showing that $AA' = B$, where $A' = [2 \quad 3 \quad 4]$.

Every correlation matrix (with unities on the diagonal) is a Gramian matrix. Consider a set of scores on n variables for each of N individuals. If the scores are expressed as deviations from the mean of each variable, the score matrix may be written as

$$X = \begin{bmatrix} x_{11} & x_{12} & \ldots & x_{1N} \\ x_{21} & x_{22} & \ldots & x_{2N} \\ \hline x_{n1} & x_{n2} & \ldots & x_{nN} \end{bmatrix}$$

If we now normalize the rows of X, that is, divide the elements of each row by the square root of the sum of their squares, we obtain a matrix

$$W = \begin{bmatrix} w_{11} & w_{12} & \ldots & w_{1N} \\ w_{21} & w_{22} & \ldots & w_{2N} \\ \hline w_{n1} & w_{n2} & \ldots & w_{nN} \end{bmatrix}$$

Then

$$WW' = R.$$

Each element of R is

$$\sum_{k=1}^{N} w_{ik} w_{jk} = \sum_{k=1}^{N} \left(\frac{x_{ik}}{\sqrt{\sum_{k=1}^{N} x_{ik}^2}} \right) \left(\frac{x_{jk}}{\sqrt{\sum_{k=1}^{N} x_{jk}^2}} \right)$$

$$\frac{\sum\limits_{k=1}^{N} x_{ik}\, x_{jk}}{\sqrt{\sum\limits_{k=1}^{N} x_{ik}^2}\ \sqrt{\sum\limits_{k=1}^{N} x_{jk}^2}} = r_{ij},$$

where $i = 1, 2, \ldots, n;\ j = 1, 2, \ldots, n;\ k = 1, 2, \ldots, N$. Thus the scalar product of any row i of W and any column j of W' is r_{ij}. Also, if $j = i$,

$$\sum\limits_{k=1}^{N} \left(\frac{x_{ik}}{\sqrt{\sum\limits_{k=1}^{N} x_{ik}^2}} \right) \left(\frac{x_{ik}}{\sqrt{\sum\limits_{k=1}^{N} x_{ik}^2}} \right) = \frac{\sum\limits_{k=1}^{N} x_{ik}^2}{\sum\limits_{k=1}^{N} x_{ik}^2} = 1.$$

Hence R is Gramian, because $WW' = R$ and every element of R and of W is real.

In initial factoring, the reduced correlation matrix R^*, with estimated communalities on the diagonal, must also be Gramian (Chapter 5).

Problem 3.4.3:2. Given the Gramian matrix

$$G = \begin{bmatrix} .13 & .14 & .05 \\ .14 & .20 & .06 \\ .05 & .06 & .02 \end{bmatrix}$$

find the first residual matrix if the first factor is $A' = [.2 \quad .4 \quad .1]$. Then, if the second factor is $B' = [.3 \quad .2 \quad .1]$, show that the second residual matrix is a zero matrix. Verify the result by showing that if the factor matrix is

$$F = \begin{bmatrix} .2 & .3 \\ .4 & .2 \\ .1 & .1 \end{bmatrix}$$

then $FF' = G$.

3.5 NOTES

3.5.1 Matrix Multiplication is Associative

We are to show that $(AB)C = A(BC)$. We first prove compatibility of common orders.

$$A(n \text{ by } m) \cdot B(m \text{ by } p) = AB(n \text{ by } p)$$

$$AB(n \text{ by } p) \cdot C(p \text{ by } q) = ABC(n \text{ by } q)$$

With A, B, and C having the same orders as above,

$$B(m \text{ by } p) \cdot C(p \text{ by } q) = BC(m \text{ by } q)$$

$$A(n \text{ by } m) \cdot BC(m \text{ by } q) = ABC(n \text{ by } q)$$

Hence if A and B have a common order and AB and C have a common order, then B and C have a common order and A and BC have a common order.

Now let $i = 1, \ldots, n; j = 1, \ldots, p; k = 1, \ldots, m; h = 1, \ldots, q$. Then

$$A(n \text{ by } m) = [a_{ik}]; \ B(m \text{ by } p) = [b_{kj}]; \ C(p \text{ by } q) = [c_{jh}].$$

The [ ] notation is another abbreviation of the expanded notation, showing subscripts of the typical element as well as the letter that identifies the matrix.

Let

$$AB = D(n \text{ by } p) = [d_{ij}]$$

$$BC = E(m \text{ by } q) = [e_{kh}]$$

$$ABC = F(n \text{ by } q) = [f_{ih}]$$

The proof of associativity is as follows:

$$[d_{ij}] = [a_{ik}] \cdot [b_{kj}], \text{ where } d_{ij} = \sum_{k=1}^{m} a_{ik} b_{kj}$$

$$[f_{ih}] = [d_{ij}] \cdot [c_{jh}], \text{ where } f_{ih} = \sum_{j=1}^{p} d_{ij} c_{ih} = \sum_{j=1}^{p} \left(\sum_{k=1}^{m} a_{ik} b_{kj} \right) c_{jh} \quad (3\text{-}28)$$

$$[e_{kh}] = [b_{kj}] \cdot [c_{jh}], \text{ where } e_{kh} = \sum_{j=1}^{p} b_{kj} c_{jh}$$

$$[f_{ih}] = [a_{ik}] \cdot [e_{kh}], \text{ where } f_{ih} = \sum_{k=1}^{m} a_{ik} e_{kh} = \sum_{k=1}^{m} a_{ik} \left(\sum_{j=1}^{p} b_{kj} c_{jh} \right) \quad (3\text{-}29)$$

But the expressions (3-28) and (3-29) are equal by the associative and distributive axioms of ordinary algebra, which proves the proposition.

3.5.2 Matrix Multiplication is Distributive over Matrix Addition and Subtraction

$$1. \ A(B \pm C) = AB \pm AC \qquad 2. \ (A \pm B)C = AC \pm BC$$

Note that because matrix multiplication is not in general commutative, the two distributive laws, 1 and 2, are distinct.

To prove 1 for addition, let $A(n \text{ by } m) = [a_{ik}]$, and $B(m \text{ by } p) = [b_{kj}]$.

Then if $B + C$ exists, C must be m by p also, and $C(m$ by $p) = [c_{kj}]$. Let $B + C = G$. Then

$$G = B + C; [g_{kj}] = [b_{kj} + c_{kj}]$$

and

$$A(B + C) = AG = H(n \text{ by } p) = [h_{ij}]$$

But

$$h_{ij} = \sum_{k=1}^{m} a_{ik} g_{kj} = \sum_{k=1}^{m} a_{ik}(b_{kj} + c_{kj})$$

Then by the distributive axiom of ordinary algebra,

$$h_{ij} = \sum_{k=1}^{m} a_{ik} b_{kj} + \sum_{k=1}^{m} a_{ik} c_{kj},$$

or

$$H = AG = A(B + C) = AB + AC.$$

The proof for subtraction, and the proof of 2 for both addition and subtraction, are similar.

4

Linear Computations

4.1 INTRODUCTION

In connection with the rotational step of factor analysis, we frequently find it necessary to solve small sets of simultaneous nonhomogeneous linear equations, and to find the inverses of small square matrices, of orders equal to the numbers of salient factors. The first part of this chapter deals with these problems.

Factor analysis proper starts with a correlation matrix. But in computing a set of intercorrelations, usually on an electronic computer, other problems arise, especially when N is large and/or when the numbers of digits to which the original scores are given exceed two or three, and further problems arise when the correlation matrix is almost singular and when the score matrix has missing scores. These problems are considered in later sections of this chapter. It should be noted that many of the older programs in the computer literature do not deal adequately with these problems (Longley, 1967), yielding standard deviations, correlations, solutions of simultaneous equations, and inverses which are quite inaccurate.

For solving sets of linear equations and computing inverses, we describe only one procedure: the single-division method of complete elimination with diagonal pivots, which avoids the need for any "back solutions." This method has two advantages. The first is that for desk calculation it is the simplest and most easily learned of all procedures, though it does involve a little more computing and considerably more recording of intermediate results than do the more complicated "abbreviated" and "compact" methods. But because electronic computers are now used for all but the smallest problems (of, say, three to five variables), the saving in learning (and relearning) time becomes more important than the saving in computing and recording time when more complicated methods are used.

The second advantage is that this procedure can be programmed directly for electronic digital computers; the programs are shorter than those using most other procedures; and, with proper initial conditioning of the scores (also described in this chapter), the results are quite accurate.

4.2 ELIMINATION PROCEDURE

We use directly the two elementary row transformations of Section 3.3.2, in a sequence which reduces A to I and at the same time reduces C to X in the equation $AX = C$, or I to A^{-1} in the equation $AA^{-1} = I$. For the first problem we start with the matrix A and the column vector C.

4.2.1 Algebra of Elimination

We work with detached coefficients and constants, the x's being understood. Then for $n = 3$ we have

$$
\begin{bmatrix} (a_{11}) & a_{12} & a_{13} \\ a_{21} & a_{22} & a_{23} \\ a_{31} & a_{32} & a_{33} \end{bmatrix} \begin{bmatrix} c_1 \\ c_2 \\ c_3 \end{bmatrix} \tag{4-1}
$$

The upper left element, a_{11}, is enclosed in parentheses. It is termed the *pivotal element*, the first row is termed the *pivot row*, and for reasons that will shortly become apparent, the first column is termed the *multiplier column*.

Using elementary transformations, we start by reducing the first column of A to the first column of I, and apply these same elementary transformations to C.

Multiply the pivot row by the reciprocal of the pivotal element. This row is then

$$
\begin{bmatrix} 1 & \dfrac{a_{12}}{a_{11}} & \dfrac{a_{13}}{a_{11}} \end{bmatrix} \begin{bmatrix} \dfrac{c_1}{a_{11}} \end{bmatrix} \tag{4-2}
$$

To obtain the other rows, multiply (4-2) by the element in the first (multiplier) column of each row of (4-1) except the first (pivot) row, and subtract the product from the same row. For the second row, the product is

$$
\begin{bmatrix} a_{21} & a_{21}\dfrac{a_{12}}{a_{11}} & a_{21}\dfrac{a_{13}}{a_{11}} \end{bmatrix} \begin{bmatrix} a_{21}\dfrac{c_1}{a_{11}} \end{bmatrix}
$$

and when we subtract this product from the second row we obtain

$$\begin{bmatrix} 0 & a_{22} - a_{21}\dfrac{a_{12}}{a_{11}} & a_{23} - a_{21}\dfrac{a_{13}}{a_{11}} \end{bmatrix} \begin{bmatrix} c_2 - a_{21}\dfrac{c_1}{a_{11}} \end{bmatrix} \quad (4\text{-}3)$$

Similar operations applied to row 3 of (4-1) will again give zero in the first column of this row.

We now introduce two changes of notation. For the first, let $c_1 = a_{14}$, $c_2 = a_{24}$, $c_3 = a_{34}$, and in general $c_i = a_{i(n+1)}$. Here $n = 3$. For the second, call the elements of (4-2), including the constant as redefined, $a_{1j \cdot 1}$, and the elements of (4-3) and the following rows $a_{ij \cdot 1}(i \neq 1)$. Then the elements of (4-2) are given by

$$a_{1j \cdot 1} = a_{1j}(1/a_{11}), \qquad (4\text{-}4)$$

and those of (4-3) and the following rows are given by

$$a_{ij \cdot 1} = a_{ij} - a_{i1}a_{1j \cdot 1} \qquad (i \neq 1). \qquad (4\text{-}5)$$

Following these operations, the matrix and vector of (4-1) are reduced to

$$\begin{bmatrix} 1 & a_{12 \cdot 1} & a_{13 \cdot 1} \\ 0 & (a_{22 \cdot 1}) & a_{23 \cdot 1} \\ 0 & a_{32 \cdot 1} & a_{33 \cdot 1} \end{bmatrix} \begin{bmatrix} a_{14 \cdot 1} \\ a_{24 \cdot 1} \\ a_{34 \cdot 1} \end{bmatrix} \qquad (4\text{-}6)$$

with elements defined by (4-4) for the first row and (4-5) for the other rows. The first row of (4-6), derived from the first (pivot) row of (4-1), is termed a *unit* row, because its first entry is always unity. All other rows begin with 0.

The second diagonal element of (4-6) now becomes the pivotal element for a similar set of operations. In place of (4-4) we have

$$a_{2j \cdot 2} = a_{2j \cdot 1}(1/a_{22 \cdot 1}). \qquad (4\text{-}7)$$

Row 2 of (4-6) is the pivot row, and (4-7) yields the unit row (row 2) of the next matrix. In place of (4-5) we now have

$$a_{ij \cdot 2} = a_{ij \cdot 1} - a_{i2 \cdot 1}a_{2j \cdot 2} \qquad (i \neq 2). \qquad (4\text{-}8)$$

The matrix and vector are now

$$\begin{bmatrix} 1 & 0 & a_{13 \cdot 2} \\ 0 & 1 & a_{23 \cdot 2} \\ 0 & 0 & (a_{33 \cdot 2}) \end{bmatrix} \begin{bmatrix} a_{14 \cdot 2} \\ a_{24 \cdot 2} \\ a_{34 \cdot 2} \end{bmatrix} \qquad (4\text{-}9)$$

The subscript after the dot defines the *cycle* of operations: (4-6) is the matrix and vector after the first cycle and (4-9) is the matrix and vector after the second cycle.

It is easily verified that if we multiply the elements of row 2 of (4-6) by $1/a_{22 \cdot 1}$, we obtain row 2 of (4-9), and if we multiply each element of row 2 of (4-9) by the element in column 2 of each other row of (4-6) and subtract the product from the corresponding element of the same row of (4-6), we obtain the corresponding row of (4-9).

For the third cycle

$$a_{3j \cdot 3} = a_{3j \cdot 2}(1/a_{33 \cdot 2}) \tag{4-10}$$

$$a_{ij \cdot 3} = a_{ij \cdot 2} - a_{i3 \cdot 2}a_{3j \cdot 3} \quad (i \neq 3) \tag{4-11}$$

and the matrix and vector after the third cycle are

$$\begin{bmatrix} 1 & 0 & 0 \\ 0 & 1 & 0 \\ 0 & 0 & 1 \end{bmatrix} \begin{bmatrix} a_{15 \cdot 3} \\ a_{25 \cdot 3} \\ a_{35 \cdot 3} \end{bmatrix} \tag{4-12}$$

The matrix on the left is now an identity matrix, and the vector on the right is therefore the solution vector X, with elements $a_{i4 \cdot 3} = c_{i \cdot 3} = x_i$ for $i = 1, 2, 3$, with c_i as given in (4-1).

4.2.2 Numerical Example

Solve the system of nonhomogeneous equations

$$2x_1 - x_2 - x_3 = 1$$

$$x_1 + x_2 - 2x_3 = 2$$

$$x_1 - x_2 + 3x_3 = 3$$

With detached coefficients these equations are represented by

$$\begin{bmatrix} (2) & -1 & -1 \\ 1 & 1 & -2 \\ 1 & -1 & 3 \end{bmatrix} \quad \begin{bmatrix} 1 \\ 2 \\ 3 \end{bmatrix}$$

Using (4-4) and (4-5) we have

$$\begin{bmatrix} 1 & -1/2 & -1/2 \\ 0 & (3/2) & -3/2 \\ 0 & -1/2 & 7/2 \end{bmatrix} \quad \begin{bmatrix} 1/2 \\ 3/2 \\ 5/2 \end{bmatrix}$$

Using next (4-7) and (4-8)

$$\begin{bmatrix} 1 & 0 & -1 \\ 0 & 1 & -1 \\ 0 & 0 & (3) \end{bmatrix} \quad \begin{bmatrix} 1 \\ 1 \\ 3 \end{bmatrix}$$

Using finally (4-10) and (4-11)

$$\begin{bmatrix} 1 & 0 & 0 \\ 0 & 1 & 0 \\ 0 & 0 & 1 \end{bmatrix} \quad \begin{bmatrix} 2 \\ 2 \\ 1 \end{bmatrix}$$

so $x_1 = 2$, $x_2 = 2$, and $x_3 = 1$.

Problem 4.2.2:1. Solve the following two sets of simultaneous equations, using detached coefficients and matrix notation as above:

$$\begin{aligned} 4x_1 + 2x_2 &= 2 \\ 6x_1 - x_2 &= 1 \end{aligned} \qquad \begin{aligned} x_1 + x_2 - x_3 &= 3 \\ x_1 + 2x_2 - x_3 &= 5 \\ 2x_2 + 2x_3 &= 8 \end{aligned}$$

Check your results by substituting the x-values into the original equations.

4.2.3 Matrix Inversion

In matrix inversion we use the same sequence of row operations as in the solution of simultaneous equations, but we start with an identity matrix on the right in place of the column of constants. Corresponding to (4-1), (4-6), (4-9), and (4-12), and using superscripts instead of subscripts to identify elements of the right matrices, we then have

$$\begin{bmatrix} (a_{11}) & a_{12} & a_{13} \\ a_{21} & a_{22} & a_{23} \\ a_{31} & a_{32} & a_{33} \end{bmatrix} \begin{bmatrix} 1 & 0 & 0 \\ 0 & 1 & 0 \\ 0 & 0 & 1 \end{bmatrix} \qquad (4\text{-}13)$$

$$\begin{bmatrix} 1 & a_{12\cdot1} & a_{13\cdot1} \\ 0 & (a_{22\cdot1}) & a_{23\cdot1} \\ 0 & a_{32\cdot1} & a_{33\cdot1} \end{bmatrix} \begin{bmatrix} a^{11\cdot1} & 0 & 0 \\ a^{21\cdot1} & 1 & 0 \\ a^{31\cdot1} & 0 & 1 \end{bmatrix} \qquad (4\text{-}14)$$

$$\begin{bmatrix} 1 & 0 & a_{13\cdot2} \\ 0 & 1 & a_{23\cdot2} \\ 0 & 0 & (a_{33\cdot2}) \end{bmatrix} \begin{bmatrix} a^{11\cdot2} & a^{12\cdot2} & 0 \\ a^{21\cdot2} & a^{22\cdot2} & 0 \\ a^{31\cdot2} & a^{32\cdot2} & 1 \end{bmatrix} \qquad (4\text{-}15)$$

$$\begin{bmatrix} 1 & 0 & 0 \\ 0 & 1 & 0 \\ 0 & 0 & 1 \end{bmatrix} \begin{bmatrix} a^{11\cdot3} & a^{12\cdot3} & a^{13\cdot3} \\ a^{21\cdot3} & a^{22\cdot3} & a^{23\cdot3} \\ a^{31\cdot3} & a^{32\cdot3} & a^{33\cdot3} \end{bmatrix} \qquad (4\text{-}16)$$

and the last matrix on the right, with elements $a^{ij\cdot3} = a^{ij}$, is A^{-1}.

4.2.4 Numerical Example

Find the inverse of

$$A = \begin{bmatrix} 1 & 2 & 3 \\ -1 & 3 & 4 \\ 2 & 1 & 3 \end{bmatrix}$$

Setting this matrix up with an identity matrix on the right as in (4-13) we have

$$\begin{bmatrix} (1) & 2 & 3 \\ -1 & 3 & 4 \\ 2 & 1 & 3 \end{bmatrix} \begin{bmatrix} 1 & 0 & 0 \\ 0 & 1 & 0 \\ 0 & 0 & 1 \end{bmatrix}$$

Then using (4-4) and (4-5) we obtain

$$\begin{bmatrix} 1 & 2 & 3 \\ 0 & (5) & 7 \\ 0 & -3 & -3 \end{bmatrix} \begin{bmatrix} 1 & 0 & 0 \\ 1 & 1 & 0 \\ -2 & 0 & 1 \end{bmatrix}$$

Now using (4-7) and (4-8)

$$\begin{bmatrix} 1 & 0 & 1/5 \\ 0 & 1 & 7/5 \\ 0 & 0 & (6/5) \end{bmatrix} \begin{bmatrix} 3/5 & -2/5 & 0 \\ 1/5 & 1/5 & 0 \\ -7/5 & 3/5 & 1 \end{bmatrix}$$

Using finally (4-10) and (4-11)

$$\begin{bmatrix} 1 & 0 & 0 \\ 0 & 1 & 0 \\ 0 & 0 & 1 \end{bmatrix} \begin{bmatrix} 5/6 & -1/2 & -1/6 \\ 11/6 & -1/2 & -7/6 \\ -7/6 & 1/2 & 5/6 \end{bmatrix}$$

and the matrix on the right is A^{-1}.

Problem 4.2.4:1. Find the inverse of each of the following matrices:

$$A = \begin{bmatrix} 1 & 0 & 1 \\ 0 & 1 & 0 \\ 0 & 0 & 1 \end{bmatrix} \quad A = \begin{bmatrix} 3 & 2 & 6 \\ 2 & 2 & 5 \\ 1 & 1 & 2 \end{bmatrix}$$

Check your work by showing that in each case $AA^{-1} = I$.

4.2.5 Value of a Determinant

In this treatment, we have only occasional use for determinants, for example, in the formula for the standard error of a tetrad, (1-26), and in the formula for the Bargmann test of the hypothesis that m factors are sufficient (Section 5.5.2). For these uses, and for those readers who are familiar with determinants, we note without proof that the elimination procedure can be used to find the numerical value of the determinant of a nonsingular square matrix. The value of this determinant is simply the product of all the pivotal elements. If we call this determinant D, then for a matrix of order 3, as in the coefficient matrix of (4-1), its value is

$$D = a_{11}a_{22\cdot1}a_{33\cdot2}$$

or in general, for a matrix of order n,

$$D = a_{11}a_{22\cdot1}a_{33\cdot2} \cdots a_{nn\cdot(n-1)} \tag{4-17}$$

For the example of 4.2.4, of order 3, the value of the determinant of A is

$$D = (1)(5)(6/5) = 6.$$

Note: The reader who is not interested in hand- and desk-calculator procedures may omit or skip over most of Sections 4.3, 4.4, and 4.5. He should read enough of Sections 4.3.1 and 4.3.2 to understand these procedures when he encounters them in later chapters. He should know enough of Section 4.4 to recognize the cases in which conditioning and deconditioning are needed, and he should read Section 4.5.2 with some care.

4.3   COMPUTATIONAL PROCEDURES

Although the computations of the examples of 4.2.2 and 4.2.4 used common fractions to obtain exact values, computations are ordinarily performed with decimal entries. We illustrate these computations using an example with a coefficient matrix of order 3.

4.3.1 Computation: Simultaneous Linear Equations

For our first example we use a matrix derived (and reduced to $n = 3$) from one considered by Waugh and Dwyer (1945) and used by Dwyer (1951) to illustrate a number of other methods for linear computations. This matrix,[1] including a column of constants, is

	Variable			Constant	
Eq	(1)	(2)	(3)	(4)	
(1)	.26	−.10	.15	.27	
(2)	.19	.45	−.14	.97	(4-18)
(3)	−.12	.16	.27	−.35	

[1]From Table 1, p. 264, Waugh and Dwyer, 1945. Copyright 1945 by the Institute of Mathematical Statistics. Reprinted by permission.

When working with an electronic desk or hand calculator (or an old mechanical calculator), we adopt the rule of rounding each entry to *four decimals* for recording on the work sheet and for further computations. *Exception:* the reciprocal of a pivotal element, used in computing all the entries of a unit row, should be carried to at least *five significant figures* or to machine capacity. When *recorded* (in matrix inversion) it is recorded to four decimals.

Table 4.1 shows the solution of the equations represented by (4-18). On this work sheet, the record of a cycle of operations is termed a *panel*. Each panel is separated from the one below it on the work sheet by a horizontal line. In panel 0, we set up the problem to be solved: a matrix of coefficients and a column vector of constants (A, C). We retain the convention of letting $c_i = a_{i(n+1)}$ (here a_{i4}). A vertical line on the work sheet, between columns (3) and (4), separates the coefficients from the constants. There will be $n + 1$ panels: panels 0, 1, 2, . . . , n.

In order to simplify and regularize the computing, we adopt the device of moving the top row to the bottom as we go from each panel to the next. Thus for $n = 3$, as we go from panel 0 to panel 3 the row numbers are 1, 2, 3; 2, 3, 1; 3, 1, 2; and 1, 2, 3. With this device, the top row of every panel (except the last) is the pivot row, and the bottom row of every panel (except the first) is the unit row.

We do not compute or record the entries on the left which we know to be 0s. As we form each unit row, however, we do compute its initial entry, 1.0000, as a

TABLE 4.1
Solution of Simultaneous Equations[a]

Panel	Eq	Variable (1)	(2)	(3)	Constant (4)	Σ	Ch
0	(1)	(.26)	−.10	.15	.27	.58	.2700
	(2)	.19	.45	−.14	.97	1.47	.9700
	(3)	−.12	.16	.27	−.35	−.04	−.3500
1	(2)		(.5231)	−.2496	.7727	1.0462	1.0461
	(3)		.1138	.3392	−.2254	.2276	.2277
	(1)	1	−.3846	.5769	1.0385	2.2308	2.2308
2	(3)			(.3935)	−.3935	.0000	.0000
	(1)	1		.3934	1.6066	3.0000	3.0000
	(2)		1	−.4772	1.4772	2.0000	2.0000
3	(1)	1			2.0000	3.0000	3.0000
	(2)		1	$X =$	1.0000	2.0000	2.0000
	(3)			$\overline{1}$	−1.0000	.0000	.0000

[a] Determinant of coefficients = .05352.

check on the computation of the reciprocal. As soon as it is checked and recorded (as merely 1), we copy it, in the same column, into the row of the same number in every following panel. It is recorded there because it is a necessary part of the row sum.

We add on the right a row–sum column headed Σ, and a check column headed Ch. Each entry in column Σ is the sum of the entries to its left in the same row. The blank spaces in the panels below panel 0 (here panels 1–3) would contain zeros if they were computed and entered. As each row operation is performed to obtain the entries of a row in the following panel, this same operation is performed on the entry in column Σ of that row, and the result is entered in the corresponding row of the following panel in column Ch. The entries in the new row of the following panel are then added, and their sum is recorded in column Σ. The adjacent entries in column Σ and column Ch must agree within the accumulated rounding error for the one set of row operations.

The first row of (4-18) represents the equation

$$.26x_1 - .10x_2 + .15x_3 = .27,$$

and each of the other rows of (4-18) represents another equation in the same x's. If the equations are linearly independent, each equation is a *true* equation, and elementary row transformations performed on it lead to true equations. If now we forget the x's, and write the row–sum equation,

$$.26 - .10 + .15 + .27 = .58,$$

this numerical identity is also a true equation, and elementary operations performed upon it lead to true equations. This is the basis for the row–sum checking procedure.

In panel 0, the entries in column Ch are separated from those in column Σ by a vertical line. They are the final substitution-check values. The computed values of the x's are multiplied by the coefficients of each equation, and the algebraic sums of products are recorded in column Ch. The entries in column Ch must agree with the corresponding entries in column (4), or in general with those in column $(n + 1)$, within the accumulated rounding error, if the x's have been determined correctly.

In each panel, the pivotal element is enclosed in parentheses, and a vertical line separates the multiplier column from those to its right.

The procedure is given in equations (4-4), (4-5), (4-7), (4-8), (4-10) and (4-11). Because this procedure is essentially the same as we form each panel from the previous panel, it can be summarized in the following manner:

1. Enclose the upper left element of the previous panel (the pivotal element) in parentheses. Draw a vertical line between the column containing the pivotal element and the column to its right. The other entries in this column are the multipliers.

2. Find the reciprocal of the pivotal element to *five significant figures*, or to

machine capacity, and set it in memory as a repeat multiplier. Recall and multiply by each element in the pivot row, and record each product (except the last), rounded to *four decimals,* directly below in the last row (the unit row) of the new panel. The product of the reciprocal times the element in column Σ is recorded in column Ch of the new panel. Add algebraically the other entires in the new unit row, and record the sum in the same row in column Σ. The adjacent entries in columns Σ and Ch must agree within rounding error. Copy the 1 at the beginning of the row into all rows of the same number in later panels, in the same column. The zeros in the left columns of (4-6), (4-9), and (4-12) are neither computed nor recorded on the work sheet.

3. To form each other row of the new panel, set the multiplier of the same row in the previous panel in memory as a repeat multiplier. Recall and multiply negatively by each entry in the new unit row, and then add algebraically the number directly above it in the row of the previous panel. Thus the number in row 2, column 2 of panel 1 is

$$-(-.3846)(.19) + .45 = .5231.$$

Note that the product of the negative multiplication will be *negative* if the numbers in the unit row and the multiplier column have the *same* sign, or *positive* if they have *opposite* signs (as above where they are $-.3846$ and $.19$). Record the result of each multiplication and addition (or subtraction if the $.45$ had been $-.45$) to *four* decimals, in the row and column having the same numbers in the new panel, except that if the unit-row and previous-panel entries are in column Σ, the product is entered in column Ch. Thus in row 2, column Σ, of panel 1 we have,

$$-(2.2308)(.19) + 1.47 = 1.0461.$$

Add algebraically the other entries in the new row and record in the same row in column Σ. Thus for row 2 of panel 1,

$$.5231 - .2496 + .7727 = 1.0462.$$

The adjacent entries in columns Σ and Ch (here 1.0462 and 1.0461) must agree within rounding error.

The solution is given in column $(n + 1)$, here (4), of the last panel. The final check consists in verifying that $AX = C$. Form the sum of products of the entries in column $(n + 1)$ of the last panel and the entries in each row of panel 0, and record in the same row in column Ch. For the first row of Table 4.1 we have,

$$(2.0000)(.26) + (1.0000)(-.10) + (-1.0000)(.15) = .2700.$$

Each entry in column Ch of panel 0 should agree within the total accumulated rounding error with the corresponding entry in column $(n + 1)$, here column (4).

For this problem, the solution happens to be exact: $x_1 = 2$, $x_2 = 1$, $x_3 = -1$. This occurred because reciprocals were taken to machine capacity and because the other rounding errors balanced out. In general, this will not be the case. A fairly safe rule is that the x's can be trusted to the number of *significant figures* indicated by the largest discrepancy in panel 0, columns $(n + 1)$ and Ch.

The value of the determinant of the coefficients is the product of all the n pivotal elements, here

$$(.26)(.5231)(.3935) = .05352.$$

In general, the value of a determinant can be trusted to the number of significant figures retained in the computations, minus one for every initial zero (between a decimal point and the first significant digit) in all the pivotal elements (here none) plus or minus about 3 in the last. This rule assumes that all of the initial coefficients are either exact or correct to at least the number of significant figures retained in the computations, and that all of these coefficients have absolute values between .1 and 1.0. If one or more of them have absolute values between 0 and .1, subtract one further significant figure of accuracy for each initial 0 in the smallest. And if one or more of them include integral digits, no further accuracy can necessarily be assumed. For our present problem, we assume that the coefficients are exact. In this case the value of the determinant probably lies between .05355 and .05349. But had there been two pivotal elements each with one initial 0, or one pivotal element with two initial 0s, or one coefficient with two initial 0s, we could only have said that the value of the determinant probably lies between .057 and .051 (.054 ± .003).

Problem 4.3.1:1. Solve the system of nonhomogeneous simultaneous linear equations whose coefficients and constants are given by (4-19), below, and compute the value of the determinant of the coefficients. Assume that the coefficients are exact.

	Variable			*Constant*
Eq	(1)	(2)	(3)	(4)
(1)	.4	.1	−.3	−.2
(2)	.1	.3	.2	.5
(3)	.2	.2	.3	.9

(4-19)

4.3.2 Computation of Inverse

The computation of the inverse on a desk or hand calculator, for the coefficients of Table 4.1, is shown in Table 4.2.

In equations (4-13), (4-14), (4-15), and (4-16), it may be observed that every row contains a 1 either on the left or on the right but not both. Hence in computing the inverse we record neither the 1s nor the 0s of these equations, but label the sum column $\Sigma + 1$ instead of Σ to indicate that each entry is the actual sum of the recorded entries in the row plus the 1 not written.

Also, in forming each unit row from the pivot row of the previous panel, the unity at the right of the pivot row is the last nonzero entry of that row, and the last nonzero entry of the next unit row is the reciprocal of the pivotal element times this unity. Thus $a^{11\cdot1} = (1/a_{11})1$, $a^{22\cdot2} = (1/a_{22\cdot1})1$, and $a^{33\cdot3} = (1/a_{33\cdot2})1$. Each unit row is formed as before, except that its last entry is the reciprocal of the pivotal element used in forming it from the pivot row of the previous panel.

Note also in these equations that, apart from the 1s and 0s omitted on the work sheet, each successive panel loses one column on the left and gains one on the right.

In Table 4.2, all entries to the left of the center vertical line are identical with those of Table 4.1, and are formed in the same way. In rows other than the unit row, each entry in the last column is of the form, $0 - (\text{multiplier})(\text{entry in unit row})$, though the 0 has not been written.

TABLE 4.2
Calculation of Inverse: Data from Table 4.1

Panel	Eq	Variable (1)	(2)	(3)	Variable (1)	(2)	(3)	$\Sigma + 1$	Ch
0	(1)	(.26)	−.10	.15				1.31	
	(2)	.19	.45	−.14	$= A$			1.50	
	(3)	−.12	.16	.27				1.31	
1	(2)		(.5231)	−.2496	−.7308			.5427	.5427
	(3)		.1138	.3392	.4615			1.9145	1.9146
	(1)		−.3846	.5769	3.8462			5.0385	5.0385
2	(3)			(.3935)	.6205	−.2176		1.7964	1.7964
	(1)			.3934	3.3089	.7352		5.4375	5.4375
	(2)			−.4772	−1.3971	1.9117		1.0374	1.0375
3	(1)				2.6885	.9528	−.9997	3.6416	3.6416
	(2)			$A^{-1} =$	−.6446	1.6478	1.2127	3.2159	3.2159
	(3)				1.5769	−.5530	2.5413	4.5652	4.5652
				$I_r =$	1.0000	.0000	.0000		
					.0000	1.0000	.0000		
					.0000	.0000	1.0001		
				C'	.27	.97	−.35		
				X	2.0000	.9999	−1.0001	1.9998	1.9998
				Σ	3.6208	2.0476	2.7543		

As each row is completed, the same operation is performed on the entry in column $\Sigma + 1$, and the result is entered in the next panel in the row of the same number, column Ch.

In the last panel we have the elements of A^{-1}. The final check consists in forming numerically the elements of $I_r = AA^{-1}$, and I_r is termed the *reproduced identity matrix*. In Table 4.2 its first element is

$$(.26)(2.6885) + (-.10)(-.6446) + (.15)(1.5769) = 1.0000.$$

The only element of I_r which is not precisely an element of an identity matrix, to four decimals, is $r^{33} = 1.0001$. In general, the elements of I_r should be those of an identity matrix within the accumulated rounding error.

4.3.3 Simultaneous Equations from Inverse

To solve the equations of Table 4.1 from the inverse in Table 4.2, we make use of the relation $X = A^{-1}C$. The column vector C, from column (4), panel 0 of Table 4.1, is written as a row vector C' just below I_r in Table 4.2. Then row by row multiplications of C' with the rows of A^{-1} give the successive values of row X. Here, with more accumulated rounding errors, the values of the Xs are not exact but are correct within these accumulated rounding errors.

In the last row, row Σ, we record the sum of the entries in each column of A^{-1}. In row X, the row sum (here 1.9998) is recorded in column $\Sigma + 1$. The sum of products of the entries in rows C and Σ is recorded in row X, column Ch. The two sums must agree within rounding error, thus checking the arithmetic used in finding the Xs.

Problem 4.3.3:1. Find the inverse of the transpose of the matrix of Table 4.2, and verify that it is the transpose of the inverse of the original matrix (A^{-1} of Table 4.2), within the limits of a different set of rounding errors. Because this is an adequate check, I_r need not be computed.

4.3.4 General Equations and Computer Programming

Equations (4-4), (4-5), (4-7), (4-8), (4-10), and (4-11) are complete, giving values for all elements of every row. But from (4-6), (4-9), and (4-12), we know that the results on the left in each row will be 0 or 1, and that the 1s in Table 4.1 were recorded only because they were needed for the row–sum checks. In the actual computations, each successive panel loses a column. Modifying the equations to leave out the unnecessary computations, we have

$$a_{1j\cdot1} = a_{1j}/a_{11} \quad (j > 1) \tag{4-4a}$$

$$a_{ij\cdot1} = a_{ij} - a_{i1}a_{1j\cdot1} \quad (i \neq 1, j > 1) \tag{4-5a}$$

$$a_{2j\cdot2} = a_{2j\cdot1}/a_{22\cdot1} \quad (j > 2) \tag{4-7a}$$

$$a_{ij\cdot2} = a_{ij\cdot1} - a_{i2\cdot1}a_{2j\cdot2} \qquad (i \neq 2, j > 2) \tag{4-8a}$$

$$a_{3j\cdot3} = a_{3j\cdot2}/a_{33\cdot2} \qquad (j > 3) \tag{4-10a}$$

$$a_{ij\cdot3} = a_{ij\cdot2} - a_{i3\cdot2}a_{3j\cdot3} \qquad (i \neq 3, j > 3) \tag{4-11a}$$

etc.

Each *pair* of these equations is used in forming the next successive panel. If we designate the successive panels, after panel 0, by the subscript k ($k = 1, 2, \ldots, n$), the first equation of every pair can be written

$$a_{kj\cdot k} = a_{kj\cdot(k-1)}/a_{kk\cdot(k-1)} \qquad (j > k). \tag{4-20}$$

The second equation of every pair can likewise be written,

$$a_{ij\cdot k} = a_{ij\cdot(k-1)} - a_{ik\cdot(k-1)}a_{kj\cdot k} \qquad (i \neq k, j > k). \tag{4-21}$$

Note also that, as each new row is formed, the corresponding elements of the same row in the previous panel are never used again. Hence as each element of a new panel is computed, we could erase the value of the corresponding element in the previous panel and replace it by the new element just computed. The indication $(j > k)$ in (4-20) and (4-21) means that after we have computed the first element of a new row and replaced the corresponding element of the previous panel by it, the element in the multiplier column will still remain for the computation of the other elements in that row. With a sufficient number of erasures and replacements, all results could be recorded in one panel, and at the finish the entries to the left of the vertical line would be the successive multiplier columns, and the entries to its right would be the x's.

For programming, then, the required memory is only that needed for an n by $n + 1$ matrix. The original augmented matrix of coefficients and constants must be entered by *rows*.

In computing an inverse, we wish to transfer each numbered column to the right of the center vertical line to the position of the same numbered column to the left of this line, in order to record all entries for each cycle in the same n by n matrix in the memory. To do this, we must first detach the multiplier column and record it elsewhere in the memory, and then set the elements of this column, other than the pivotal element, to zero. Programs for matrix inversion often use this procedure.

4.4 CONDITIONING AND DECONDITIONING

Sets of simultaneous equations and matrices to be inverted are often *conditioned*, or modified prior to solution, for two main reasons: (1) to bring decimal accuracy and significant-figure accuracy into agreement; (2) to avoid relatively small numbers on the diagonal of a square matrix.

With either a desk calculator, where we ordinarily record each entry on a work sheet to a fixed number of decimals, or an electronic computer, which normally computes at a fixed number of significant figures (in what is termed floating-point arithmetic), the original entries should be so modified that throughout the computations the number of decimals after each operation will equal or almost equal the number of significant figures. The reason is that the accuracy in addition and subtraction is the decimal accuracy, whereas the accuracy in multiplication and division is the significant-figure accuracy. If the original entries (coefficients and constants) all lie between .1 and 1 in absolute value *they,* at least, all have decimal accuracy equal to their significant-figure accuracy. Then if the elements of the solution are of the same general order of magnitude as the coefficients and constants, the intermediate operations will usually not lose too much accuracy of either type.

Sometimes allowable preliminary adjustments still leave some of the coefficients and/or constants more than ten times as large in absolute value as some others. It is usually better to permit several of them to take values between 1 and 10 than it is to permit more than a *very* few to take values less than .1. Values less than .01 are likely to cause more trouble than are values above 100.

If the data are least-squares normal equations, it is usually advisable to perform the matrix calculations on the *correlation* matrix rather than on the variance–covariance matrix or the matrix of sums of squares and sums of products of deviations from the means. Correlations always have absolute values between 0 and 1, and in most cases the majority of them will have absolute values between .1 and 1.0.

For other types of data, conditioning to keep decimal accuracy and significant-figure accuracy approximately equal is most easily accomplished by multiplying each *row* of the original matrix by some appropriate power of 10 (integral or fractional). When this type of conditioning is employed, no deconditioning is required for simultaneous linear equations. To prove this we note first that the original equations are

$$AX = C. \tag{4-22}$$

If we multiply each row of A by a constant d_i (for the i-th row), the conditioned equations are

$$(DA)Y = DC, \tag{4-23}$$

where D is a diagonal matrix with diagonal elements d_i, and Y takes the place of X as the solution vector. The solution is

$$Y = (DA)^{-1}DC = A^{-1}D^{-1}DC = A^{-1}C.$$

But $A^{-1}C = X$, the solution of the original equations $AX = C$, so $Y = X$, and the solution of (4-23) is the same as the solution of (4-22).

For the inverse we have

$$(DA)^{-1} = A^{-1}D^{-1}$$

$$(DA)^{-1}D = A^{-1}D^{-1}D$$

$$A^{-1} = (DA)^{-1}D \tag{4-24}$$

Hence deconditioning consists in multiplying each *column* of $(DA)^{-1}$ by the corresponding diagonal element d_i of D.

If the *columns* of A (and/or C) contain elements of quite different orders of magnitude, this procedure is inadequate. We omit discussion of this case, which can be found in more extended treatments of linear computations.

A second type of conditioning may also be required. If the coefficient matrix, whether symmetric or nonsymmetric, does not already have a numerically large element in every *column* on the diagonal, pairs of *rows* should be interchanged in such a manner as to bring elements to the diagonal which have large absolute values, relative to those of the other elements in the same columns. Ideally, the largest element in every column of the coefficient matrix should lie on the diagonal, but this ideal is often not attainable in practice. When it is not, it is more important to avoid having a relatively small element on the diagonal of *any* column than it is to maximize the mere number of columns whose largest elements are on the diagonal. Bringing large elements to the diagonal is necessary to insure that the pivotal elements in the elimination procedure will not become too small. If a pivotal element contains a zero between its decimal point and its first significant figure, the accuracy of *all* later computations will be reduced by about one significant figure.

Row interchanges to bring relatively large elements to the diagonal should be made *after* any multiplication of rows by constants (powers of 10).

After row interchanges, the rows should be renumbered $1, 2, 3, \ldots, n$ before beginning the elimination procedure.

The last step in deconditioning is correcting for initial row interchanges, if any. For simultaneous linear equations, there are *no* corrections. The x_i of the equations are related to the *column* numbers of the detached coefficients, these column numbers remain in the order $1, 2, \ldots, n$, and the row order of the *equations* is immaterial. When we reach an identity matrix on the left, the elements of the solution, in column $n + 1$ of the last panel, are in the correct order (from the top to bottom) in that panel.

For the inverse, the *original row* numbers are restored to the *columns* of the inverse. Thus if *rows* 1 and 2 were interchanged initially, the *column* numbers of the inverse would be (2) (1) (3). The result is the inverse of the original matrix before the row interchanges.

To decondition a *determinant*, after multiplying each column of the original matrix by a constant d_i, the determinant of the original matrix is the determinant of the conditioned matrix times the reciprocals of all the d_i. And *each* interchange of two rows of the original matrix changes the sign of the determinant. If the number of row interchanges is *even*, the sign of the determinant is not affected. If the number of row interchanges is *odd*, the sign of the determinant of the original matrix is the reverse of that of the determinant of the rowinterchanged matrix.

Suppose that the original equations, from which those of (4-18) were derived by conditioning, were

	Variable			*Constant*	
Eq	(1)	(2)	(3)	(4)	
(1)	19	45	−14	97	
(2)	26	−10	15	27	(4-25)
(3)	−12	16	27	−35	

To condition these equations we would multiply each row by .01 and then interchange rows (1) and (2) to bring larger elements to the diagonal. Then from Table 4.1 the solution is still $x_1 = 2$, $x_2 = 1$, $x_3 = -1$. The determinant of (4-25), with one row interchange, is

$$-(.05352)(100)(100)(100) = -53520.$$

The inverse of (4-25) from Table 4.2, multiplying each column by .01 and interchanging columns (1) and (2), is

	(1)	(2)	(3)
(1)	.009528	.026885	−.009997
(2)	.016478	−.006446	.012127
(3)	−.005530	.015769	.025413

In moving the first (pivot) row of each panel (after division by the pivotal element) to the bottom of the following panel to form the next unit row, we are not really interchanging any rows. We are merely writing them in different orders in the successive panels to regularize the computing procedures, so that the unit row will be the last row of every panel, and the pivot row the first row. If we were to write them in the natural order (1, 2, 3, 4) in every panel, the elements of every row (by number) would be exactly the same.

4.5   THE ALMOST-SINGULAR CASE

A case of this type occurs when one row or equation is *almost* equal to a multiple or fraction of another, or to an algebraic sum of multiples and/or fractions of two or more others.

Note: The reader who wishes only to recognize an almost-singular case, and to know what to do about it, may skip or skim this section. Section 4.5.2, however, is important for all readers.

4.5.1 Example

Table 4.3 shows the solution of a set of three equations in three unknowns. The fact that the matrix is almost singular is not evident until we see the privotal element .0008 at the beginning of panel 2. Its reciprocal multiplies all other entries in the same row to form the entries in the unit row [row (3)] of the last panel, and these entries enter into all the entries in the other rows of the last panel. Hence *all* the entries in the last panel will be accurate to only one significant figure. Completing the computations, however, still at four decimals, we obtain the solution $x_1 = .1935$, $x_2 = .4505$, $x_3 = .2500$. The row checks of the last two panels are all correct to four decimals, and the substitution check [rows (4) and Ch of panel 0] shows only one discrepancy of .0001. These checks

TABLE 4.3
Solution of Equations: Almost-Singular Case[a]

Panel	Eq	Variable			Constant		
		(1)	(2)	(3)	(4)	Σ	Ch
	(1)	(.5204)	.4892	−.5100	.1936	.6932	.1936
0	(2)	.4892	.7116	−.7300	.2328	.7036	.2327
	(3)	−.5100	−.7300	.7500	−.2400	−.7300	−.2400
	(2)		(.2518)	−.2506	.0508	.0520	.0520
1	(3)		−.2506	.2502	−.0503	−.0507	−.0507
	(1)	1	.9400	−.9800	.3720	1.3320	1.3321
	(3)			(.0008)	.0002	.0010	.0010
2	(1)	1		−.0445	.1824	1.1379	1.1379
	(2)		1	−.9952	.2017	.2065	.2065
	(1)	1			.1935	1.1935	1.1935
3	(2)		1	$X =$	.4505	1.4505	1.4505
	(3)			1	.2500	1.2500	1.2500

[a] Determinant = (.5204)(.2518)(.0008) = .0001

tell us that the arithmetic of the calculations is correct, but fail to warn us that the solution in column (4) of the last panel may be radically wrong. The only warning of almost-singularity is the near-zero pivotal element.

The exact solution is $x_1 = .2$, $x_2 = .6$, $x_3 = .4$. With these values, the substitution check is exact, with no rounding error.

This example was contrived in the following manner:

$$x_1 = .2 \quad x_2 = .6 \quad x_3 = .4$$

$$\begin{bmatrix} 1 & 1 & -1 \\ 1.04 & .92 & -1 \\ 0 & 1 & -1 \end{bmatrix} \begin{bmatrix} .4 \\ .36 \\ .3 \end{bmatrix} \tag{4-26}$$

Here the second row is quite clearly almost equal to the first row. We next premultiply both the coefficient matrix and the vector of constants by the transpose of the coefficient matrix. For if $AX = C$,

$$A'AX = A'C, \tag{4-27}$$

then

$$X = (A'A)^{-1}A'C$$

$$= A^{-1}(A')^{-1}A'C$$

$$= A^{-1}C$$

so the solution of (4-27) is the same as the solution of $AX = C$. We then have

$$\begin{bmatrix} 2.0816 & 1.9568 & -2.0400 \\ 1.9568 & 2.8464 & -2.9200 \\ -2.0400 & -2.9200 & 3.0000 \end{bmatrix} \begin{bmatrix} .7744 \\ .9312 \\ -.9600 \end{bmatrix} \tag{4-28}$$

The coefficient matrix is now symmetric, and every element in it and in the column of constants is an exact multiple of 4. Dividing every element by 4, we obtain panel 0 of Table 4.3, with entries that are properly conditioned for computation, and with no added rounding error.

Note that if we solve directly the equations from which those of Table 4.3 were contrived, namely (4-26), four-decimal computations will give the correct answer: $x_1 = .2000$, $x_2 = .6000$, $x_3 = .4000$. Premultiplication by the transpose of the coefficient matrix increases the almost-singularity quite drastically.

In the almost-singular case, we can select x_3 almost arbitrarily. Then if x_2 and x_1 are consistent with it in terms of the equations, the substitution check will be satisfied approximately. Suppose we let $x_3 = .1$. To obtain consistent values of x_2 and x_1, we will use the unit rows of panel 2 and panel 1 of Table 4.3. From the former

$$1x_2 - .9952x_3 = .2017$$

$$x_2 = .2017 + .9952(.1) = .3012$$

Then from the unit row of panel 1

$$1x_1 + .9400x_2 - .9800x_3 = .3720$$

$$x_1 = .3720 - (.9400)(.3012) + (.9800)(.1) = .1869$$

Using $x_1 = .1869$, $x_2 = .3012$, and $x_3 = .1000$, the substitution check gives $c_1 = .1936$, $c_2 = .2328$, $c_3 = -.2402$, as compared with the exact values .1936, .2328, and $-.2400$. The one discrepancy, of .0002 in the third equation, could easily be attributed to accumulated rounding error.

Problem 4.5.1:1. Solve the equations of (4-29), below, completely at four decimals, and complete the substitution check. Compare your solution with the exact answer: $x_1 = .1$, $x_2 = .2$, $x_3 = .3$.

	Variable			Constant	
Eq	(1)	(2)	(3)	(4)	
(1)	.2256	.3552	.2320	.1632	
(2)	.3552	.5684	.3640	.2584	(4–29)
(3)	.2320	.3640	.2400	.1680	

4.5.2 Recognition of Almost-Singular Case, and Remedy

When the initial equations, or the rows of an initial matrix to be inverted, are properly conditioned, the pivotal elements should lie between .1 and 1, or at worst between .1 and 10, if the matrix of coefficients or the initial matrix to be inverted is *not* almost singular. If it *is* almost singular, the loss of accuracy in the elements of the solution (the xs), due to almost-singularity, can be taken roughly as the total number of zeros between the decimal points and the first significant figures of all the pivotal elements. Thus in Table 4.3, with three initial zeros in the third pivotal element, the x's can be trusted to only one decimal (or one significant figure), ± about .2 or .3 for accumulated rounding error. Rounding to one decimal, the solution of Table 4.3 becomes .2, .5, .2, as compared to the exact values, .2, .6, .4. In computing the inverse of an almost-singular matrix, the errors in the elements of the computed inverse are of the same order of magnitude as are the errors in the xs of a set of simultaneous equations.

Computer programs should be arranged to print out the pivotal elements so they can be examined for almost-singularity.

This rule (reduce the estimated accuracy of the results by one significant figure for every initial zero in all the pivotal elements) is conservative: it *may* indicate more loss of accuracy than has in fact occurred. Better methods for estimating the loss of accuracy due to almost-singularity are described in treatments of numerical mathematics, but they are much more complicated, requiring about as much additional computing as does the solution of the problem itself.

When an almost-singular case is encountered, the most practical method for finding an almost-correct solution is usually to repeat the computations, using as many significant figures as the original number plus the number of initial zeros in the pivotal elements. With an electronic computer, if the number of initial zeros does not exceed the number of decimals in single-precision computing, double-precision computing will yield at least single-precision accuracy. If the coefficient matrix, or the initial matrix to be inverted, is exactly singular, there is of course no solution.

4.5.3 Determination of Rank

The rank of a square matrix is *usually* the number of panels (including panel 0) preceding the one in which a pivotal element zero first appears. But a zero pivotal element *may* be due to an accident resulting from less than optimal arrangement of the rows. We therefore use a procedure which will *always* give the correct rank. This procedure consists in detaching the unit rows, and computing *all* of the n^2 elements in each panel. The rows remain in the original order in every panel. If the diagonal element in any panel is zero, we pivot on any convenient non-zero element in the row, so long as it is not in any column previously used as a multiplier column, and the new multiplier column is then the column containing this pivotal element. Let k be the column containing the i-th pivotal element. This k will be different for every panel. Equations (4-4a) through (4-11a) then become

$$u_{1j} = a_{1j}/a_{1k} \tag{4-4b}$$

$$a_{ij\cdot1} = a_{ij} - a_{ik}u_{1j} \qquad (i \neq 1) \tag{4-5b}$$

$$u_{2j} = a_{2j\cdot1}/a_{2k\cdot1} \tag{4-7b}$$

$$a_{ij\cdot2} = a_{ij\cdot1} - a_{ik\cdot1}u_{2j} \qquad (i \neq 2) \tag{4-8b}$$

$$u_{3j} = a_{3j\cdot2}/a_{3k\cdot2} \tag{4-10b}$$

$$a_{ij\cdot3} = a_{ij\cdot2} - a_{ik\cdot2}u_{3j} \qquad (i \neq 3) \tag{4-11b}$$

In each pair of these equations, u is the unit row and k is the column containing the pivotal element. The rank of the matrix is then the number of panels preceding the one all of whose elements are zero.

Table 4.4 shows the procedure, using the example of (3-25), Section 3.4.2. We use $k = 1$ to form row u_1 because, since the pivotal element is 1, row u_1 is

TABLE 4.4
Determination of the Rank of a Square Matrix

Panel	Var	(1)	(2)	(3)	(4)	Σ	Ch
	(1)	(1)	2	3	4	10	
0	(2)	3	4	3	2	12	
	(3)	2	4	6	8	20	
	(4)	4	6	6	6	22	
	u_1	1	2	3	4	10	10
	(1)	0	0	0	0	0	0
1	(2)	0	-2	-6	(-10)	-18	-18
	(3)	0	0	0	0	0	0
	(4)	0	-2	-6	-10	-18	-18
	u_2	0	.2	.6	1	1.8	1.8
	(1)	0	0	0	0	0	0
2	(2)	0	0	0	0	0	0
	(3)	0	0	0	0	0	0
	(4)	0	0	0	0	0	0

$$
\begin{bmatrix} 1 & 0 \\ 3 & -10 \\ 2 & 0 \\ 4 & -10 \end{bmatrix}
\begin{bmatrix} 1 & 2 & 3 & 4 \\ 0 & .2 & .6 & 1 \end{bmatrix}
=
\begin{bmatrix} 1 & 2 & 3 & 4 \\ 3 & 4 & 3 & 2 \\ 2 & 4 & 6 & 8 \\ 4 & 6 & 6 & 6 \end{bmatrix}
$$

simply copied from row (1) of panel 0. Row (1) of panel 1 has all elements zero by (4-5b), that is $1 - 1 \cdot 1, 2 - 1 \cdot 2, 3 - 1 \cdot 3$, and $4 - 1 \cdot 4$. Row (3) of panel 1 is also all-zero because row (3) of panel 0 is linearly dependent on row (1). The elements of row (3), panel 1, are $2 - 2 \cdot 1, 4 - 2 \cdot 2, 6 - 2 \cdot 3$, and $8 - 2 \cdot 4$.

The second pivotal element would normally be the -2 in row (2), column (2) of panel 1. We chose instead the -10 in row (2), column (4) to show how we would have proceeded if this -2 had been 0. Then $k = 4$ for panel 1, and column (4) is the multiplier column. We chose the -10 instead of the -6 in column (3) because its reciprocal is more easily computed and used. The elements of row u_2 are then $0/-.1 = 0, -2/-.1 = .2, -6/-.1 = .6$, and $-10/-.1 = 1$. The first row of panel 2 is then $0 - 0 \cdot 0 = 0, 0 - .2 \cdot 0 = 0, 0 - .6 \cdot 0 = 0$, and $0 - 1 \cdot 0 = 0$. The second row is $0 - (-10)0 = 0, -2 - (-10).2 = 0, -6 - (-10).6 = 0$, and $-10 - (-10)1 = 0$. The other rows are computed in a similar manner.

Panel 2 has all elements zero. There are two previous panels, so the rank of the matrix is 2. The factors of the 4 by 4 matrix are the 4 by 2 matrix whose columns are the multiplier columns, postmultiplied by the 2 by 4 matrix whose rows are the unit rows. These matrices are shown at the bottom of Table 4.4, and their product is the original matrix. Note that these matrices are not the same as those of (3-25). They are merely one of the infinite number of pairs of 4 by 2 and 2 by 4 matrices whose product is the original 4 by 4 matrix.

Determination of the rank of a nonsquare matrix is exactly similar. We can start with either the original matrix or its tranpose. Table 4.5 shows the procedure for the matrix derived from that of Table 4.4 by deleting the last column. The upper part of Table 4.5 shows this procedure for the original matrix, the lower

TABLE 4.5
Determination of the Rank of a Nonsquare Matrix

Panel	Var	(1)	(2)	(3)	Σ	Ch
	(1)	(1)	2	3	6	
0	(2)	3	4	3	10	
	(3)	2	4	6	12	
	(4)	4	6	6	16	
	u_1	1	2	3	6	6
	(1)	0	0	0	0	0
1	(2)	0	(−2)	−6	−8	−8
	(3)	0	0	0	0	0
	(4)	0	−2	−6	−8	−8
	u_2	0	1	3	4	4
	(1)	0	0	0	0	0
2	(2)	0	0	0	0	0
	(3)	0	0	0	0	0
	(4)	0	0	0	0	0

Panel	Var	(1)	(2)	(3)	(4)	Σ	Ch
	(1)	(1)	3	2	4	10	
0	(2)	2	4	4	6	16	
	(3)	3	3	6	6	18	
	u_1	1	3	2	4	10	10
	(1)	0	0	0	0	0	0
1	(2)	0	(−2)	0	−2	−4	−4
	(3)	0	−6	0	−6	−12	−12
	u_2	0	1	0	1	2	2
	(1)	0	0	0	0	0	0
2	(2)	0	0	0	0	0	0
	(3)	0	0	0	0	0	0

part for its transpose. In either case the factors are the matrix whose columns are the multiplier columns post-multiplied by the matrix whose rows are the unit rows.

4.6   INITIAL COMPUTATIONS

A factor analysis ordinarily starts with a correlation matrix, and conditioning as described in Section 4.4 is unnecessary. Initial conditioning is necessary mainly with certain matrices that arise in connection with problems of rotation discussed later. But in computing the correlations from the original scores, especially when this is done on an electronic computer, certain safeguards are necessary to be sure that these correlations will be sufficiently accurate as input data for a factor analysis.

Today whole sets of intercorrelations (and criterion correlations) among n (or $n + 1$) variables are so seldom computed on hand or desk calculators that we omit discussion of these computations. Older books on elementary statistics discuss appropriate methods.

Electronic digital computers use mainly *binary* arithmetic, based on powers of two, rather than decimal arithmetic, based on powers of ten. Thus we have in decimal and binary arithmetic the equivalent numbers

Decimal	1	2	3	4	5	6	7	8	
Binary	0	1	10	11	100	101	110	1000	
Decimal	9	10	11	12	13	14	15	16	etc.
Binary	1001	1010	1011	1100	1101	1110	1111	10000	

In binary notation the number of digits increases by one every time we reach the next power of two, whereas in decimal notation the number of digits increases by one only every time we reach the next power of ten. Some computers also use *octal* arithmetic, based on powers of eight, and/or *hexadecimal* arithmetic, based on powers of sixteen. The main computing, however, is usually done in binary, because the digits 0 and 1 can be represented mechanically or magnetically or electronically by devices such as relay open, relay closed; spot magnetized, spot not magnetized or pole north, pole south; spot charged, spot not charged or spot charged negatively, spot charged positively; and the like.

In binary arithmetic there is no rounding. When a computation has been carried out, the result is simply truncated at the machine precision, that is, the number of binary digits carried in the hardware.

Computers ordinarily use *floating-point* arithmetic. In multiplication, division, raising to a power, extracting a root, and finding a trigonometric function, every result is carried to the same number of *significant figures* (in binary digits the machine precision), and a parallel computation gives the exponent which locates the decimal (or binary) point. In addition and subtraction, however, decimal (or binary) accuracy may be lost if the numbers added or subtracted have different exponents.

When using a computer, formulas should be modified to take account of binary truncation and floating-point arithmetic in such a manner as to minize loss of accuracy.

1. If the original scores of any variable contain decimals, convert them to integers *before punching*. Let the original scores of any such variable be X_i'. Then, if these scores are given to d decimals, replace them by the integral scores

$$X_i = 10^d X_i', \tag{4-30}$$

that is, move all decimal points d places to the right. An integer is an exact number in binary notation, but a decimal usually is not. Converting to integers avoids having most of the scores turned into repeating binaries and truncated at machine precision, thus introducing truncation errors into most of the original scores before any computing takes place. This conversion to integers will have no effect on the intercorrelations, but the means and standard deviations of the X_i as computed will need to be divided by 10^d to give the means and standard deviations of the X_i'.

2. If N is large and/or the number of digits in the integral X_i exceeds two or three, it is necessary to use some procedure which will avoid or minimize *overflow* in the initial accumulations: sums of products and especially sums of squares which exceed machine precision. Single precision computing amounts to truncating at the binary equivalent of 7 to 10 significant decimal figures after each addition, subtraction, multiplication, or division. Suppose $N = 999$, and the X_i are four-figure numbers. The X_i^2 will be eight-figure numbers, and their sum might be something on the order of

47,262,436,989.

Truncated at eight significant figures, this would be

47,262,436,000

with an appreciable loss in accuracy. The machine, it is true, truncates in binary rather than decimal arithmetic, with errors only one-fifth as large, on the average, as those resulting from truncation in decimal arithmetic, but these errors should still be avoided or minimized.

To avoid or minimize overflow in the initial accumulations, coding by subtraction should be employed. Let M_i be an integer as close as is reasonably possible to $\bar{X}_i$, and define

$$x_i = X_i - M_i. \tag{4-31}$$

M_i may be merely a "guessed mean," or for extreme accuracy $\bar{X}_i$ may actually be computed for each variable in a preliminary run, and M_i chosen as the integer nearest to it. With M_i and X_i both integers, x_i is also an integer. We do *not* define x_i as

$$x_i = X_i - \bar{X}_i$$

because in this case every x_i would contain the truncation error in $\bar{X}_i$. With the x_i defined by (4-31) replacing the X_i, Sx_i^2 and Sx_ix_j will be as small as possible, thus avoiding or minimizing overflow without introducing any additional truncation errors in the process.

3. In the final computations we wish (1) to use as few divisions and square roots as possible because each of them introduces a truncation error; (2) to avoid any product as large as Sx_i^2 or Sx_ix_j, which may exceed machine precision and hence lead again to overflow and truncation. Starting with the accumulations Sx_i, Sx_i^2, and Sx_ix_j, the best compromise appears to be the use of the following formulas:

$$\bar{x}_i = Sx_i/N \tag{4-32}$$

$$S_{ii} = Sx_i^2 - \bar{x}_i\, Sx_i \tag{4-33}$$

$$S_{ij} = Sx_ix_j - \bar{x}_i Sx_j \tag{4-34}$$

$$r_{ij} = S_{ij}/\sqrt{S_{ii}S_{jj}} \tag{4-35}$$

The means are then

$$\bar{X}_i = \bar{x}_i + M_i, \tag{4-36}$$

and, if (4-30) was used,

$$\bar{X}'_i = \bar{X}_i/10^d. \tag{4-37}$$

The standard deviations are

$$\sigma_i = \sqrt{S_{ii}/(N-1)}, \tag{4-38}$$

and, if (4-30) was used,

$$\sigma'_i = \sigma_i/10^d. \tag{4-39}$$

With electronic computers coding by division (as in using grouped X_i) is never employed. If N is so large and/or the number of digits in one or more of the X_i (or X'_i) is so large that one or more Sx_i^2 will exceed machine precision by an intolerable amount, the most useful procedure is to go to double precision computing, or in a very few rare cases to extended precision.

Some standard computer programs, unfortunately, use formulas such as

$$L_{11} = NSX_1^2 - (SX_1)^2$$

$$L_{22} = NSX_2^2 - (SX_2)^2$$

$$L_{12} = NSX_1X_2 - (SX_1)(SX_2)$$

$$r_{12} = L_{12}/\sqrt{L_{11}L_{22}}$$

which are useful mainly with mechanical calculators having 20 places in the accumulator dials. These formulas, moreover, are often used without coding by subtraction. If N and/or the number of digits in the X_i are even moderately large, use of these equations results in severe overflow and drastic loss of accuracy in some cases.

4.6.1 Normalization of Scores, and Ranking

In factor analysis we are interested in the analysis of the intrinsic relations among the variables.

The product-moment correlation, however, is a measure of the intrinsic relation between two variables only if the joint distribution of the scores is bivariate normal (each distribution normal, with linear regressions). Mild leptokurtosis (distributions in which the central region is a little higher and the tails are a little longer than in the normal distribution) makes little difference. Mild to moderate platykurtosis (flat-topped distributions, in which the central region is lower and the tails are shorter than in the normal distribution, down to the rectangular and rank distributions which have completely flat tops) also makes little difference. Thus if the scores on two normally distributed variables are replaced by their ranks, the product-moment correlation does not change by more than .02.

In substantially skew distributions, however, the product-moment correlation measures the skewness relations along with the strength of the intrinsic relation. If both variables are skewed in the same direction, the correlation is lower than the strength of the intrinsic relation. If the variables are skewed in opposite directions, the correlation is higher than the strength of the intrinsic relation. In this latter case the regressions are likely to be S-curves rather than straight lines, but mild nonlinearity of this type usually has only a small effect on the correlation. For factor analysis, normalization (or ranking as a first approximation) is recommended for variables whose distributions are substantially skew, even when substantive considerations suggest that the skewness is real rather than an artifact of scaling.

Normalization becomes particularly important when we are factor-analyzing questionnaire data from Likert-type scales, with only, say, three to six steps. Two examples of five-step scales are:

The personal sensitivity of my supervisor is

1. very high   2. above average   3. average
4. below average   5. quite low

Capital punishment should be abolished.

1. agree strongly   2. agree moderately   3. neutral

4. disagree moderately   5. disagree strongly

The *mean* method of normalizing a set of scores is shown in Table 4.6, starting with five-step original X-values 1, 2, 3, 4, 5, and the corresponding frequencies f_1, f_2, f_3, f_4, f_5, with which the alternatives represented by the X-values were checked by the N respondents.

Note that "normalizing," as used here, must be distinguished carefully from "normalizing" as used previously to denote a score divided by the square root of the sum of squares of the scores on the same variable. A more accurate but more cumbersome term for this conversion of a set of scores to equivalent scores in a normal distribution would be "normal-standardizing."

In normalizing, we first divide a unit-normal distribution into segments with areas proportional to the frequencies of the original score-groups. The mean method of normalizing puts each z at the mean of the corresponding segment, where z is the standard-score distance from the mean of the whole distribution (standard scores have mean 0) to the mean of the segment. Hence z will be negative if the mean of the segment is below the mean of the whole normal

TABLE 4.6
Mean Normalizing Procedure

						Σ	Note
X	1	2	3	4	5		
f	22	35	64	128	110	359	1
p	.061	.098	.178	.357	.306	1.000[a]	2
pc	.061	.159	.337	.694	1.000		3
y	.121	.242	.365	.351	.000		4
yd	−.121	−.121	−.123	.014	.351	.000	5
z	−2.0	−1.2	−.7	0.0	1.1		6
T	30	38	43	50	61		7

1. $\Sigma f = N$. Here $N = 359$.
2. $p = f/N$. $\Sigma p = 1.000^a$.
3. p-cumulative. $.061 + .098 = .159 + .178 = .337$, etc. Last pc must equal 1.000.
4. Normal ordinate corresponding to pc = area (Table 4.8).
5. y-difference. $y_0 = .000$; $.000 − .121 = −.121$, $.121 − .242 = −.121$, $.242 − .365 = −.123$, $.365 − .351 = .014$, $.351 − .000 = .351$. Σyd must equal .000.
6. $z = yd/p$. $z_1 = −.121/.061 = −2.0$ (to one decimal), etc.
7. $T = 10z + 50$. The T-scores (two-digit, integral) replace the X-scores for the computation of the correlation matrix.

[a] Force the sum to equal 1.000 by rounding one p (rarely two) the wrong way: that one (or two) for which misrounding will introduce the smallest errors. Here, for P_2, $35/359 = .09749$, misrounded to .098 so sum will equal 1.000 instead of .999.

distribution, or positive if the mean of the segment is above the mean of the whole distribution. The general formula is

$$z = \frac{y_1 - y_2}{Q_2 - Q_1} = \frac{y_1 - y_2}{p} \tag{4-40}$$

where y_1 is the unit-normal ordinate at the left boundary of the segment; y_2 is the unit-normal ordinate at the right boundary of the segment; Q_1 is the area from $-\infty$ to the left boundary (i.e., the relative frequency below the given segment); Q_2 is the area from $-\infty$ to the right boundary (i.e., the relative frequency below plus the relative frequency *in* the given segment); and $p = Q_2 - Q_1$ is the relative frequency *in* the given segment. Derivations of formula (4-40) can be found in Kelley (1923) and in Peters and Van Voorhis (1940).

For the segment at the extreme left, $y_1 = 0$, $Q_1 = 0$, $Q_2 - Q_1 = Q_2 = p$, so

$$z = \frac{-y_2}{p}. \tag{4-41}$$

For the segment at the extreme right, $y_2 = 0$, $Q_2 = 1$, and $Q_2 - Q_1 = 1 - Q_1 = p$, so

$$z = \frac{y_1}{p}. \tag{4-42}$$

In Table 4.6 the skewness of the distribution

X	1	2	3	4	5
f	22	35	64	128	110

is $-.795$ $[Sk = \Sigma f(X - \bar{X})^3 / N\sigma^3]$. But, for the normalized distribution

T	30	38	43	50	61
f	22	35	64	128	110

$Sk = -.314$. The skewness has not been reduced to zero because a five-group distribution, even with optimum unequally spaced scale values, is still not a good approximation to a distribution with many equal intervals and normally distributed frequencies.

If the X-scale has more than six steps, the slightly cruder midpoint method of normalizing will be sufficiently accurate. The midpoint method of normalizing places each z at the midpoint of the corresponding segment. Using (improperly) the same example, in Table 4.7, we see that even with only five segments the T-scores, rounded to two figures, are the same except at the extremes, where they are one score-point closer to the mean of the whole distribution.

To use these normalizing procedures, we need inverse tables of the ordinates and deviates of the normal distribution. Computation at three decimals, as illus-

TABLE 4.7
Midpoint Normalizing Procedure

	1	2	3	4	5	Σ	Note
X	1	2	3	4	5		
f	22	35	64	128	110	359	1
2fc	22	79	178	370	608	718	2
pr	.031	.110	.248	.515	.847	1.000	3
z	−1.9	−1.2	−.7	0.0	1.0		4
T	31	38	43	50	60		5

1. $\Sigma f = N$. Here $N = 359$.
2. $2fc = 2$ times f-cumulative to midpoint of group. Each $2fc$ = previous $2fc$ + f above + next f. Thus $2fc_1 = 0 + 0 + 22 = 22$, $2fc_2 = 22 + 22 + 35 = 79, \ldots$, $2fc_5 = 370 + 128 + 110 = 608$. Last $2fc$ (in column Σ) = $608 + 110 + 0 = 718 = 2N = 2(359)$.
3. Find $1/2N$ and set in memory at machine capacity. Here $1/718 = .00139275766$. Multiply by each value of $2fc$ and record to three decimals in row pr (for percentile rank). In column Σ the result must be 1.000 (not equal to Σpr).
4. z = normal deviate (to one decimal) for lower tail area pr. If $pr < .5$, z is negative (Table 4.9).
5. $T = 10z + 50$. Substitute the Ts, rounded to the nearest integral numbers, for the Xs as the normalized scores.

trated in Table 4.6 and Table 4.7, is sufficient for all practical purposes to give values of z to one decimal and hence values of T to two figures. And a T-score scale with two-digit values provides 60 steps from -3σ to $+3\sigma$. Also the reliability of a test must reach .96 before the standard error of measurement is as little as twice the scale unit. For practical purposes Table 4.8 and Table 4.9 can be used without interpolation to find values of y or z, given pc or pr.

Normalizing scores reduces artificial nonlinear regressions due to differences in direction of skewness. If, however, the regressions of the normalized scores on one another are not linear, there is no more to be done. The product-moment r then measures the intrinsic strength of the least-squares best fitting *linear* relation. To the extent that some nonlinear relation has greater intrinsic strength, the linear model itself is inappropriate.

Problem 4.6.1:1.

X	1	2	3	4	5	Σ
f	71	137	181	53	58	500 = N

Normalize this distribution by the mean method, and again by the midpoint method.

When we have an original score distribution that is continuous or quasi-continuous (with many different values of X_i), and fairly highly skew, the X_i may be grouped into 12 to 20 groups with equal score-intervals, and normalized as in Table 4.7, arranging the scores in a column instead of in a row, and letting

TABLE 4.8
Ordinates (y) of the Unit-Normal Distribution

	9	8	7	6	5	4	3	2	1	0	pc
pc	0	1	2	3	4	5	6	7	8	9	
.00	.000	.003	.006	.009	.012	.014	.017	.019	.022	.024	.027	.99
.01	.027	.029	.031	.033	.036	.038	.040	.042	.044	.046	.048	.98
.02	.048	.050	.052	.054	.056	.058	.060	.062	.064	.066	.068	.97
.03	.068	.070	.072	.074	.075	.077	.079	.081	.083	.084	.086	.96
.04	.086	.088	.090	.091	.093	.095	.096	.098	.100	.101	.103	.95
.05	.103	.105	.106	.108	.110	.111	.113	.114	.116	.118	.119	.94
.06	.119	.121	.122	.124	.125	.127	.128	.130	.131	.133	.134	.93
.07	.134	.136	.137	.139	.140	.142	.143	.144	.146	.147	.149	.92
.08	.149	.150	.151	.153	.154	.156	.157	.158	.160	.161	.162	.91
.09	.162	.164	.165	.166	.168	.169	.170	.172	.173	.174	.175	.90
.10	.175	.177	.178	.179	.181	.182	.183	.184	.186	.187	.188	.89
.11	.188	.189	.190	.192	.193	.194	.195	.196	.198	.199	.200	.88
.12	.200	.201	.202	.204	.205	.206	.207	.208	.209	.210	.212	.87
.13	.212	.213	.214	.215	.216	.217	.218	.219	.220	.221	.223	.86
.14	.223	.224	.225	.226	.227	.228	.229	.230	.231	.232	.233	.85
.15	.233	.234	.235	.236	.237	.238	.239	.240	.241	.242	.243	.84
.16	.243	.244	.245	.246	.247	.248	.249	.250	.251	.252	.253	.83
.17	.253	.254	.255	.256	.257	.258	.259	.260	.261	.261	.262	.82
.18	.262	.263	.264	.265	.266	.267	.268	.269	.270	.270	.271	.81
.19	.271	.272	.273	.274	.275	.276	.277	.277	.278	.279	.280	.80
.20	.280	.281	.282	.282	.283	.284	.285	.286	.287	.287	.288	.79
.21	.288	.289	.290	.291	.291	.292	.293	.294	.295	.295	.296	.78
.22	.296	.297	.298	.298	.299	.300	.301	.301	.302	.303	.304	.77
.23	.304	.304	.305	.306	.307	.307	.308	.309	.309	.310	.311	.76
.24	.311	.312	.312	.313	.314	.314	.315	.316	.316	.317	.318	.75
.25	.318	.318	.319	.320	.320	.321	.322	.322	.323	.324	.324	.74
.26	.324.	.325	.326	.326	.327	.328	.328	.329	.329	.330	.331	.73
.27	.331	.331	.332	.332	.333	.334	.334	.335	.335	.336	.337	.72
.28	.337	.337	.338	.338	.339	.340	.340	.341	.341	.342	.342	.71
.29	.342	.343	.343	.344	.344	.345	.346	.346	.347	.347	.348	.70
.30	.348	.348	.349	.349	.350	.350	.351	.351	.352	.352	.353	.69
.31	.353	.353	.354	.354	.355	.355	.356	.356	.357	.357	.358	.68
.32	.358	.358	.359	.359	.359	.360	.360	.361	.361	.362	.362	.67
.33	.362	.363	.363	.363	.364	.364	.365	.365	.366	.366	.366	.66
.34	.366	.367	.367	.368	.368	.368	.369	.369	.370	.370	.370	.65
.35	.370	.371	.371	.372	.372	.372	.373	.373	.373	.374	.374	.64
.36	.374	.374	.375	.375	.376	.376	.376	.377	.377	.377	.378	.63

(*continued*)

TABLE 4.8 (continued)

		9	8	7	6	5	4	3	2	1	0	pc
pc	0	1	2	3	4	5	6	7	8	9		
.37	.378	.378	.378	.379	.379	.379	.380	.380	.380	.380	.381	.62
.38	.381	.381	.381	.382	.382	.382	.383	.383	.383	.383	.384	.61
.39	.384	.384	.384	.385	.385	.385	.385	.386	.386	.386	.386	.60
.40	.386	.387	.387	.387	.387	.388	.388	.388	.388	.389	.389	.59
.41	.389	.389	.389	.389	.390	.390	.390	.390	.390	.391	.391	.58
.42	.391	.391	.391	.391	.392	.392	.392	.392	.392	.393	.393	.57
.43	.393	.393	.393	.393	.393	.394	.394	.394	.394	.394	.394	.56
.44	.394	.395	.395	.395	.395	.395	.395	.395	.396	.396	.396	.55
.45	.396	.396	.396	.396	.396	.396	.397	.397	.397	.397	.397	.54
.46	.397	.397	.397	.397	.397	.397	.397	.398	.398	.398	.398	.53
.47	.398	.398	.398	.398	.398	.398	.398	.398	.398	.398	.398	.52
.48	.398	.398	.399	.399	.399	.399	.399	.399	.399	.399	.399	.51
.49	.399	.399	.399	.399	.399	.399	.399	.399	.399	.399	.399	.50

TABLE 4.9
Deviates (z) of the Unit-Normal Distribution

(z −)		9	8	7	6	5	4	3	2	1	0	pr
pr	0	1	2	3	4	5	6	7	8	9		(z +)
.00	∞	3.1	2.9	2.7	2.7	2.6	2.5	2.5	2.4	2.4	2.3	.99
.01	2.3	2.3	2.3	2.2	2.2	2.2	2.1	2.1	2.1	2.1	2.1	.98
.02	2.1	2.0	2.0	2.0	2.0	2.0	1.9	1.9	1.9	1.9	1.9	.97
.03	1.9	1.9	1.9	1.8	1.8	1.8	1.8	1.8	1.8	1.8	1.8	.96
.04	1.8	1.7	1.7	1.7	1.7	1.7	1.7	1.7	1.7	1.7	1.6	.95
.05	1.6	1.6	1.6	1.6	1.6	1.6	1.6	1.6	1.6	1.6	1.6	.94
.06	1.6	1.5	1.5	1.5	1.5	1.5	1.5	1.5	1.5	1.5	1.5	.93
.07	1.5	1.5	1.5	1.5	1.4	1.4	1.4	1.4	1.4	1.4	1.4	.92
.08	1.4	1.4	1.4	1.4	1.4	1.4	1.4	1.4	1.4	1.3	1.3	.91
.09	1.3	1.3	1.3	1.3	1.3	1.3	1.3	1.3	1.3	1.3	1.3	.90
.10	1.3	1.3	1.3	1.3	1.3	1.3	1.2	1.2	1.2	1.2	1.2	.89
.11	1.2	1.2	1.2	1.2	1.2	1.2	1.2	1.2	1.2	1.2	1.2	.88

continued

TABLE 4.9 (continued)

(z −)	9	8	7	6	5	4	3	2	1	0	pr
pr	0	1	2	3	4	5	6	7	8	9	(z +)
.12	1.2	1.2	1.2	1.2	1.2	1.2	1.1	1.1	1.1	1.1	1.1	.87
.13	1.1	1.1	1.1	1.1	1.1	1.1	1.1	1.1	1.1	1.1	1.1	.86
.14	1.1	1.1	1.1	1.1	1.1	1.1	1.1	1.0	1.0	1.0	1.0	.85
.15	1.0	1.0	1.0	1.0	1.0	1.0	1.0	1.0	1.0	1.0	1.0	.84
.16	1.0	1.0	1.0	1.0	1.0	1.0	1.0	1.0	1.0	1.0	1.0	.83
.17	1.0	1.0	.9	.9	.9	.9	.9	.9	.9	.9	.9	.82
.18	.9	.9	.9	.9	.9	.9	.9	.9	.9	.9	.9	.81
.19	.9	.9	.9	.9	.9	.9	.9	.9	.8	.8	.8	.80
.20	.8	.8	.8	.8	.8	.8	.8	.8	.8	.8	.8	.79
.21	.8	.8	.8	.8	.8	.8	.8	.8	.8	.8	.8	.78
.22	.8	.8	.8	.8	.8	.8	.8	.7	.7	.7	.7	.77
.23	.7	.7	.7	.7	.7	.7	.7	.7	.7	.7	.7	.76
.24	.7	.7	.7	.7	.7	.7	.7	.7	.7	.7	.7	.75
.25	.7	.7	.7	.7	.7	.7	.7	.7	.6	.6	.6	.74
.26	.6	.6	.6	.6	.6	.6	.6	.6	.6	.6	.6	.73
.27	.6	.6	.6	.6	.6	.6	.6	.6	.6	.6	.6	.72
.28	.6	.6	.6	.6	.6	.6	.6	.6	.6	.6	.6	.71
.29	.6	.6	.5	.5	.5	.5	.5	.5	.5	.5	.5	.70
.30	.5	.5	.5	.5	.5	.5	.5	.5	.5	.5	.5	.69
.31	.5	.5	.5	.5	.5	.5	.5	.5	.5	.5	.5	.68
.32	.5	.5	.5	.5	.5	.5	.5	.4	.4	.4	.4	.67
.33	.4	.4	.4	.4	.4	.4	.4	.4	.4	.4	.4	.66
.34	.4	.4	.4	.4	.4	.4	.4	.4	.4	.4	.4	.65
.35	.4	.4	.4	.4	.4	.4	.4	.4	.4	.4	.4	.64
.36	.4	.4	.4	.4	.3	.3	.3	.3	.3	.3	.3	.63
.37	.3	.3	.3	.3	.3	.3	.3	.3	.3	.3	.3	.62
.38	.3	.3	.3	.3	.3	.3	.3	.3	.3	.3	.3	.61
.39	.3	.3	.3	.3	.3	.3	.3	.3	.3	.3	.3	.60
.40	.3	.3	.2	.2	.2	.2	.2	.2	.2	.2	.2	.59
.41	.2	.2	.2	.2	.2	.2	.2	.2	.2	.2	.2	.58
.42	.2	.2	.2	.2	.2	.2	.2	.2	.2	.2	.2	.57
.43	.2	.2	.2	.2	.2	.2	.2	.2	.2	.2	.2	.56
.44	.2	.1	.1	.1	.1	.1	.1	.1	.1	.1	.1	.55
.45	.1	.1	.1	.1	.1	.1	.1	.1	.1	.1	.1	.54
.46	.1	.1	.1	.1	.1	.1	.1	.1	.1	.1	.1	.53
.47	.1	.1	.1	.1	.1	.1	.1	.1	.1	.1	.1	.52
.48	.1	.0	.0	.0	.0	.0	.0	.0	.0	.0	.0	.51
.49	.0	.0	.0	.0	.0	.0	.0	.0	.0	.0	.0	.50

$X, f, 2fc, pr, z,$ and T designate successive columns. Note again that the intervals between the successive Ts are not usually equal.

When the X_i take on more than 10 or 12 different values, normalizing by these procedures may become an onerous job. Then, if N is not too large, ranking becomes an acceptable alternative to normalizing to get rid of skewness, with tied ranks resolved by the average-rank method.

Normalization (or ranking) is also recommended for cases of extreme platykurtosis, such as bimodal distributions. Extremely leptokurtic distributions can also be usefully normalized.

When N is very large, ranking of a continuous or quasi-continuous skew or very platykurtic distribution may be more trouble than grouping and normalizing. Then, if the number of variables is also fairly large, it may be desirable to program a computer to perform the normalization. It is easier to program a computer for the mean method than for the midpoint method. Instead of putting the whole of Table 4.8 into the memory, an approximation devised by Hamaker (1978) may be used to obtain the normal deviates x_i from pc_i. The approximation is

$$x_i = \pm[1.238t_i(1 + .0262t_i)]\begin{cases} + \text{ if } pc_i \geqq .5 \\ - \text{ if } pc_i < .5 \end{cases}$$

$$t_i = \sqrt{-\ell n\ [4\ pc_i(1 - pc_i)]}.$$

The maximum absolute error of this approximation is about .003, which is sufficient for the present purpose. The normal ordinates y_i are given by

$$y_i = (1/\sqrt{2\pi})\ \exp(-x_i^2/2).$$

Hastings (1955) gives a more accurate but longer approximation to x_i.

4.6.2 Two-Point Variables

The most extreme case of platykurtosis is represented by the two-point distribution, and such distributions will be highly skew also if the frequencies in the two categories are greatly unequal. Normalization, by either the mean method or the midpoint method, or ranking with two large multiple ties, has no effect. It appears best to leave two-point variables as they stand and simply use product-moment correlations, giving each such variable the arbitrary scores 0 and 1. The phi-coefficient (fourfold-point correlation) and the point-biserial correlation between a two-point variable and a continuous or several-point variable (possibly normalized), are both literally product-moment correlations. The special formulas for them which appear in statistics texts are merely convenient condensations for desk calculation. In most cases they are not worth special computer programming.

It has been pointed out by various authors that with two-point data, difficulty or popularity factors may appear, for example, a factor with nonzero loadings for all easy items and a factor with nonzero loadings for all hard items. In practice such factors seldom if ever rise above the error level; they seem almost always to be overshadowed by the substantive factors. We must simply recognize and tolerate the fact that, with two-point data, the limits of a correlation are narrower than -1 to $+1$, and that these correlations will in general be lower than the intrinsic relations.

The alternative would be to use tetrachoric correlations and Pearson biserial correlations. This usually introduces worse difficulties. The correlation matrix is no longer strictly consistent; it may be non-Gramian; its statistical rank may be increased, leading to over-factoring; and some of the communalities are likely to be inflated, leading quite often to a quasi-Heywood case and occasionally to an actual Heywood case.

4.6.3 Missing Data

When a large battery of tests is administered to a large sample of examinees, several testing sessions are required, and some examinees may miss one or more sessions. If questionnaires are included in the battery, with interitem correlations to be factor-analyzed, some respondents may omit some items, and some may fail to finish even when the time limits are generous. Comparable difficulties often arise with other types of data, leading to score matrices with missing elements.

If the number of missing scores is not too great, one solution is to delete from the sample every examinee or respondent for whom there are one or more missing scores. This not only reduces the size of the sample, but may also bias it in various ways: the examinees or respondents with missing scores are seldom a random subgroup of the whole sample.

A second procedure is to compute each separate correlation using all subjects for whom both scores are available, and to compute each mean and standard deviation using all the subjects having scores on the given variable. Reduction of the sample size is thus minimized, but the reduction *could* be different for every variable and every pair of variables. In any case the correlation matrix is to some extent inconsistent; it may become non-Gramian so that there is no F such that $FF' = R^*$. If, however, the number of missing scores is not too great for any pair of variables (say less than 5% to 10%), the inconsistency may not be too great to invalidate the factor analysis.

A third procedure is to "force" consistency, thus preserving the Gramian property of the correlation matrix, by entering for every missing score the integer nearest to the mean of the given variable, computed from all the integral scores present for that variable. This procedure is likely to be better than the second procedure if for each variable the missing scores are more or less randomly distributed over the score distribution. Also as compared with that procedure the means will be the same, but the covariances and standard deviations will be reduced.

A fourth procedure starts with the third. Then for each variable pick the one other variable with which it correlates highest, compute the raw-score regression of the given variable on the other variable, and use this regression equation to estimate or reestimate each missing score on the given variable.

The best method by far, but one that requires a very great deal of computation, is as follows:

1. For each missing score enter the integer nearest to the mean of the given variable, computed from the scores which are present.

2. For each variable set up a parallel dummy variable with scores 2 for data present and 1 for data missing.

3. For each of the n original variables compute the raw-score multiple regression equation, using all $2n - 1$ other variables (including the n dummy variables) as predictors. As a practical matter, if the number of variables is large, stepwise regression may be used so that each variable is predicted by those few others which do most of the work of prediction anyhow.

4. For each original variable predict each missing score from the regression equation for that variable, and replace the mean by the regression estimate rounded to the nearest integer.

5. For the greatest possible accuracy repeat steps 3 and 4 iteratively until two successive predictions of each missing score agree. In practice, this last refinement seldom yields enough improvement to justify the great amount of computing which it involves, and it is rarely if ever used.

This method not only yields a complete score matrix and hence a consistent correlation matrix; it also yields for each missing score the least-squares best estimate based on all the information available in the incomplete score matrix.

5 The Principal-Axes Method

5.1 INTRODUCTION

The principal axes method is the method of choice for initial factoring. It requires the use of an electronic digital computer for all but *very* small problems and, because computers are now generally available, it is likely to be used even with small correlation matrices as well as with larger ones. In connection with this method we also discuss some problems that were passed over lightly in Chapter 2: initial communality estimation, reestimation in residual matrices, estimation of the number of salient factors, and refactoring to improve the solution.

The principal-axes method gives a least-squares solution. The sum of squares of the first-factor loadings is a maximum, and the sum of squares of the first residuals is a minimum. Then, given the first factor, the sum of squares of the second-factor loadings is a maximum and the sum of squares of the second residuals is a minimum. For each successive factor, given the previous factors, the sum of squares of its loadings is a maximum and the sum of squares of the following residuals is a minimum.

Before discussing the principal-axes method itself, we consider some preliminary problems.

5.2 COMMUNALITY ESTIMATION

5.2.1 Squared Multiple Correlations

Guttman (1940) showed that the communality of a test is the value that its squared multiple correlation with all the other tests would approach as the number of tests is increased without limit while the number of common factors remains fixed.

With a finite battery of tests, therefore, the squared multiple correlation of each test with all the others is a *lower bound* to its communality.

In factor analysis we consider the tests to be a fixed finite population of n, *not* a sample of n from an infinite universe of tests measuring the same m factors. It is well known, however, that adding more predictors to the first four or five increases the multiple correlation only slightly unless the criterion test is of greater complexity than this, that is, has substantial loadings on more than four or five common factors. If the test battery is at least moderately large and well balanced, therefore, so that every rotated common factor has at least four or five substantial loadings, the squared multiple correlations are usually *close* lower bounds. But if this is not the case the squared multiple correlations may give substantial underestimates of the communalities.

On the other hand, there is no reason to suppose that the *total* number of "real" common factors is less even than the number of variables. In addition to the major factors, there may be all sorts of weak relations among two or three variables, generating small common factors with no very substantial loadings. In addition to these, small common factors may be generated by chance nonzero correlations between sampling errors, by chance nonzero correlations between the errors of measurement of the variables, and especially by real nonzero correlations between these errors of measurement. With psychological and educational test data the correlation between two tests will be highest if they are administered one right after the other: ideally if they are administered *simultaneously* (by alternating items or small groups of items from the two tests in one booklet). As the time interval between the two tests is increased, and as the number of intervening tests is increased, this correlation is attenuated. Thus when tests are administered at several sittings, and especially when these sittings come on different days, small or even not-so-small factors may arise which reflect only the fact that some of the tests were administered at the same sitting, apart altogether from their substantive contents.

If the number of common factors exceeds the number of variables, some of the small common factors must coalesce both with one another and with the major common factors, because we cannot *extract* more common factors than the number of variables; and we cannot *usefully* extract more than one-third to one-half this number.

If the variables are highly unreliable and fairly numerous, (for example, single items of a questionnaire or inventory), the small "real" common factors and the error factors, taken together, may account for a substantial proportion of the total variance. In this case the *effective* communalities, which are based only on the *salient* (or major) factors, may even be *less* than the squared multiple correlations. The squared multiple correlation between one variable and all the others is based on *all* the variance which that variable has in common with all the others. This includes that of the error common factors as well as the real (substantive) common factors too small to be separated from these error common factors, as well as the variance of the salient factors. While most of the error-of-measurement variance of a variable is a part of its unique variance, some of it, especially the nonchance time-associated variance, joins the correlated sampling and chance error-of-measurement variance and the variance of the small substantive factors to inflate the squared multiple correlations as estimates of the effective communalities.

The effective communalities, based on only the salient factors, are the communalities of interest. Our purpose in factor analysis is to find these salient factors (the common factors large enough to be separated from the error factors) and to estimate the proportion of the total variance of each variable (its effective communality) which is contributed by these salient factors. Because the total estimated communality (the initial trace) may not be a very good estimate of the total final effective communality computed from the loadings on the salient factors, we recommend *one* refactoring, with the computed m-factor communalities from the first factoring used as the estimated communalities for the refactoring. At the refactoring, the final total computed communality should be almost equal to the total estimated communality, and the number m of salient factors should be the same as the number estimated from the initial factoring, and usually more clearly this number. If the refactoring suggests a different m (one more or one less salient factor), new communality estimates should be made from the revised m-factor loadings and used as initial estimates for a second refactoring. With careful estimation of m at the first factoring, this situation will arise only rarely unless the first communality estimates are seriously in error.

Repeated refactoring to "stabilize the communalities" is *not* recommended, though a few writers do advocate it. When it is used, convergence is to the *exact sample communalities* for m factors. The diagonal of the residual matrix Δ ($R^* = FF' + \Delta$), after m factors, consists entirely of exact zeros, and subject to this the sum of squares of the elements of Δ is a minimum. But the elements of Δ are supposed to represent the small nonsalient common factors that are not extracted, including those generated by correlations among the errors. It would seem logical, therefore, that these diagonal elements should be of the same order of magnitude as the side entries of Δ, but with some positive and some negative and with *sum* close to zero. If they are all *exactly* zero, the variance associated with the small common factors has all been forced into the salient factors, whose numerical values are thereby somewhat inflated.

The real reason for our objection to repeated refactoring, however, is empirical. It has been observed repeatedly, by the present writers and by others, that repeated refactoring leads all too frequently to a Heywood case and even more frequently to a quasi-Heywood case, with one communality greater than the reliability of the variable. When the variance properly associated with the small (including error) common factors is forced into the salient factors, it appears that there is some tendency for this variance to concentrate on one variable. The reason for this effect is unclear.

With one refactoring, when m is correctly determined, the final total communality is close to the initial trace, the elements of the diagonal of Δ are reduced to the error level with *sum* not far from zero, the sum of squares of the elements of Δ is fairly close to a minimum, and the probability of a Heywood or quasi-Heywood case is greatly reduced.

Returning to the problem of initial communality estimation, we note again that, as the number of variables increases while the number of common factors remains constant, the squared multiple correlations approach the communalities. With a well-selected finite battery, the squared multiple correlations should be approximately *proportional* to the communalities. And because the squared multiple correlation of one variable with all the others is in fact that part of its total variance which it holds in common with all the others of the finite battery, it might well be termed the "finite communality" of the variable.

5.2.2 Modification Using $|r|max$ Values

The value $|r|max$ is the absolute value of the numerically highest off-diagonal element in one column of the correlation matrix. The $|r|max$ values have long been used as initial estimates of the communalities. Some $|r|max$ values are overestimates and some are underestimates of the corresponding effective communalities; experience indicates, however, that these two sets of errors balance out fairly well in the sum. With most matrices, where the sums of the squared multiple correlations (*SMCs*) usually give underestimates of the total effective communalities, the sums of the $|r|max$ values still give fairly good estimates. Also, with large matrices based on unreliable variables, in which the sums of the *SMCs* may give overestimates, the errors of measurement attenuate the $|r|max$ values, and their sums still seem to give reasonably good estimates.

We conclude, then, that the best practical initial communality estimates should be *proportional* to the *SMCs*, but with sum equal to $\Sigma|r|max$. The formula for initial communality estimation is then

$$r_{ii} = SMC_i \frac{\Sigma|r|\max}{\Sigma\ SMC}. \tag{5-1}$$

The *SMCs* can be readily computed on an electronic digital computer. It is shown in treatments of multiple correlation that, if R is the correlation matrix with unities on the diagonal,

$$SMC_i = 1 - 1/R_{ii}, \tag{5-2}$$

where R_{ii} is a diagonal element of R^{-1}.

For our small example of five verbal tests we have the following results:

Var	SMC	$|r|max$	$SMC \dfrac{\Sigma|r|max}{\Sigma\,SMC}$	h^2
(1)	.505	.658	.611	.580
(2)	.591	.689	.716	.686
(3)	.622	.697	.753	.741
(4)	.571	.697	.691	.658
(5)	.544	.689	.659	.711
Σ	2.833	3.430	3.430	3.376

The h^2 values are the computed communalities from the principal-axes solution of this problem. The *SMC* values are clearly underestimates (not very close lower bounds). The $|r|max$ values and the values given by (5-1) give slight overestimates on the average. For variables 1, 3, and 4, the values given by (5-1) are a little closer to the h^2 values than are those given by $|r|max$. For variables 2 and 5 the reverse is true.

5.2.3 Reestimation in Residual Matrices

If an initial communality estimate is too high, we shall do nothing about it, trusting to the refactoring to rectify the result. But if an initial estimate is too low, a diagonal element of a residual matrix (not necessarily the first) may become near-zero or negative. We should therefore restore some of this underestimated communality wherever it appears in a residual matrix. All of the diagonal elements of all the residual matrices (except the residual matrix after m factors) should be appreciably positive. To this end we first compute the mean of the absolute values of the off-diagonal elements in each column of every residual matrix. Then, if a diagonal element of a residual matrix is negative, or positive and also lower than one-half the corresponding column mean of absolute values of off-diagonal elements, we replace it by the latter. This is a pure rule of thumb, but it is a conservative rule, giving much lower reestimates than does the rule proposed by Thurstone, which calls for replacing each diagonal element of a residual matrix by the absolute value of the numerically highest element in the column (the $|r|max$ value).

Thurstone's rule was quite good, on the average, for the original correlation matrix, and we used it in developing the estimate of (5-1). But in each successive residual matrix, the values of the diagonal elements become smaller relative to the absolute values of the side entries, so that in the residual matrix Δ, after the last salient factor (the m-th), they should ideally be about half positive and half negative, with sum close to zero.

There is no way to recognize an initially overestimated communality by examining the residual matrices, and no reestimation is used to correct for any such overestimation. Therefore, even with our conservative rule to correct for communalities originally underestimated, the sum of the diagonal elements of Δ (the residual matrix after m factors) is likely to be positive rather than near-zero. The diagonal residuals are used throughout, except when one or more of them becomes negative or so small, if positive, that one-half the column mean of absolute values of the off-diagonal elements is larger. Thus the reduced correlation matrix, with estimated communalities on the diagonal and revisions in residual matrices for any that may have been underestimated, remains Gramian to m factors (Section 3.4.3).

5.2.4 Alternative Procedure

There are two situations in which the SMCs are not used as the basis for initial communality estimation:

1. When the correlation matrix is so large ($n > 100$, say) that their computation requires more time than the improvement in the estimates warrants. With very large matrices, errors in initial communality estimation have little effect on the final factor matrix (F).

2. When the correlation matrix, with unities on the diagonal, is singular or almost singular, and the inverse either does not exist or is determined so poorly that the SMCs, adjusted by (5-1), give poorer estimates of the communalities than do the individual $|r|max$ values. The main cause of a singular correlation matrix is the case when $n \geqq N$: the number of variables is greater than or equal to the number of individuals. Such matrices *can* be factored, though interpretation is sometimes difficult because the factorial fit to the errors is too good. Almost-singular cases arise mainly with nontest data, in which some of the SMCs may approach unity, leading to approximate linear restraints.

In these cases the $|r|max$ values are taken as the initial communality estimates, and reestimation is again used only if a residual diagonal element becomes too small or negative. In the second case (singular or almost-singular R), care must be taken not to include error factors among those retained, and refactoring once with revised communality estimates is almost always advisable.

5.3   RANK REDUCTION, EIGENVALUES AND EIGENVECTORS, AND PRINCIPAL-AXES FACTORING

5.3.1 Rank Reduction

Some sequences of elementary row (and column) operations are *rank-reducing* sequences: each residual matrix is of rank exactly one less than the preceding (original or residual) matrix. The sequence used in the elimination procedure for solving simultaneous linear equations and in computing an inverse by reducing an original square matrix to an identity matrix is a rank-reducing sequence. In each successive panel (on the left) the rank of the matrix is exactly one less than the rank of the matrix in the immediately preceding panel. That is why the elimination procedure can be used to find the rank of a matrix. When we reach a panel consisting entirely of zeros, the rank of that matrix is zero, and the rank of the original matrix is the number of previous panels (Tables 4.4 and 4.5, Section 4.5.3). Not all sequences of elementary operations are rank-reducing sequences, however.

For initial factor analysis we also require a rank-reducing sequence. The sequences of operations for the complete principal-axes method, the centroid method, and the diagonal method (Section 5.5.1) are all rank-reducing sequences. With the principal-axes method, some iterative procedures are rank-reducing when the iterations are terminated short of complete convergence, and some are not (Section 5.4.1).

The general rank-reduction theorem was given originally by Guttman (1944) and has been discussed at some length by Horst (1963, 1965).

When we terminate a factor analysis of real data at $m < n$ factors, so that

$$R^* = FF' + \Delta,$$

we assume in effect that Δ is of rank 0, that is, that its elements differ only negligibly from zero. Then the effective or useful rank of R^* is its *salient rank* m. If the sequence of operations leading to F were not a rank-reducing sequence, the factoring procedure would not determine this salient rank.

The number of statistically significant factors is the *statistical rank* of R^*, and in this case the set of elements of Δ will as a whole be statistically insignificant.

The salient rank will be less than the statistical rank if the last one or more statistically significant factors are too small for effective rotation and interpretation. And if the factorial structure is unusually clear, the number of salient factors may exceed the number of statistically significant factors, though only rarely by more than one. Hence tests of the number of statistically significant factors, even when these tests are accurate, are not sufficient tests of the number of salient factors.

5.3.2 Eigenvalues and Eigenvectors

If R is any real symmetric matrix (e.g., a correlation matrix with either unities or estimated communalities on the diagonal), there exists a real matrix E, orthonormal by columns (so that $E'E = I$), and a real diagonal matrix D, such that

$$EDE' = R. \tag{5-3}$$

This relation holds under permutations of the diagonal elements of D, with corresponding permutations of the columns of E and the rows of E'. Hence the diagonal elements of D can be arranged in descending order of magnitude.

The diagonal elements of D are termed the *eigenvalues* (or latent roots or characteristic roots or proper values) of R. The columns of E are termed the *eigenvectors* (or latent vectors or characteristic vectors or proper vectors) of R.

If R is of rank $m < n$, then D is an incomplete diagonal matrix with its last $n - m$ diagonal entries equal to 0, and the last $n - m$ columns of E (and hence the last $n - m$ rows of E') consist entirely of zeros. In practice we may take E as an n by m rectangular matrix, D as an m by m diagonal matrix, and E' as an m by n rectangular matrix.

The proofs of these propositions are beyond the scope of this treatment. They can be found in more extensive treatments of matrix algebra (e.g., Murdoch, 1957), which start with more fundamental definitions of eigenvalues and eigenvectors and derive (5-3) as a theorem from these definitions.

In (5-3) we can factor D into $(D^{1/2})(D^{1/2})$, since $(D^{1/2})' = D^{1/2}$ because a diagonal matrix is symmetric, and $D^{1/2}$ will have diagonal elements $\sqrt{d_i}$. Then (5-3) can be written

$$(ED^{1/2})(ED^{1/2})' = R. \tag{5-4}$$

If the nonzero elements of D are all positive, R will be Gramian, and in this case we know that

$$FF' = R.$$

and F is real. Then from (5-4)

$$F = ED^{1/2}. \tag{5-5}$$

But if an eigenvalue of R, say d_j, is negative, $\sqrt{d_j}$ will be imaginary, and the column vector F_j of F will be

$$F_j = E_j \sqrt{d_j}.$$

Then because E_j is real, the elements of F_j are imaginary and R is not Gramian.

There are an infinite number of real matrices F for which $FF' = R$, any real symmetric matrix. Any one of them differs from any other only by an orthogonal transformation. Among these, the one defined by (5-5) is unique and has special properties:

1. If R (or R^*) is a Gramian *correlation* matrix, with unities (for R) or communalities (for R^*) on the diagonal, then F is the *principal-components matrix* of R or the *principal-axes factor matrix* of R^*.

2. The trace of R (or R^*), that is, the sum of its diagonal elements, is equal to the sum of its eigenvalues.

The proofs of properties 1 and 2 are beyond the scope of this treatment.

3. The sum of squares of the elements of each column of F is equal to the corresponding eigenvalue. One *column* of F, say F_j, will have elements

$$e_{1j} \sqrt{d_j}, \; e_{2j} \sqrt{d_j}, \ldots, \; e_{nj} \sqrt{d_j}.$$

The sum of squares of these elements will be

$$e_{1j}^2 d_j + e_{2j}^2 d_j + \cdots + e_{nj}^2 d_j = d_j \sum_{i=1}^{n} e_{ij}^2 .$$

But because E is ortonormal, E_j is a normal vector, $\sum_{i=1}^{n} e_{ij}^2 = 1$, and the sum of squares of the elements of F_j equals d_j, the corresponding eigenvalue.

4. The matrix F is *orthogonal by columns*, so that $F'F = D$. Thus from (5-5)

$$F'F = D^{1/2} E'ED^{1/2} = D^{1/2} ID^{1/2} = D,$$

because E is orthonormal by columns and hence $E'E = I$. This D is the diagonal matrix whose diagonal elements are the eigenvalues of R (or R^*).

5. If R (or R^*) is Gramian and of rank $m < n$, its first m eigenvalues will all be positive, and its last $n - m$ eigenvalues will all be zero. The Gramian property implies that a real F exists such that $FF' = R$ (or R^*) and, if the rank of R (or R^*) is m, F has m real nonzero columns and may be considered to have $n - m$ additional all-zero columns, because in this latter case FF' still equals R (or R^*). Then by property 3, above, the first m eigenvalues are all positive if F is real, and the last $n - m$ are all zero.

6. If R (or R^*) is Gramian and of rank $m < n$, the original matrix and the first $m - 1$ residual matrices will have all diagonal elements nonnegative. We consider only R^*, because the argument for R is identical.

By the definition of a Gramian matrix

$$R^* = FF',$$

and both R^* and F are real. The j-th diagonal element of R^* is the sum of squares of the elements in the j-th row of F, and these squares must all be positive or zero if F is real. Therefore the diagonal elements of R^* are all positive. If one were zero this would imply that the corresponding variable had nothing in common with any other variables and should not be included in a battery to be factored.

The diagonal elements of the successive residual matrices are

$$r_{ii.1} = r_{ii} - f_{i1}^2$$

$$r_{ii.2} = r_{ii} - f_{i1}^2 - f_{i2}^2$$

$$\text{------------------------------------}$$

$$r_{ii.(m-1)} = r_{ii} - f_{i1}^2 - f_{i2}^2 - \cdots - f_{i(m-1)}^2$$

$$r_{ii.m} = r_{ii} - f_{i1}^2 - f_{i2}^2 - \cdots - f_{i(m-1)}^2 - f_{im}^2 = r_{ii} - h_i^2 = 0,$$

because $r_{ii} = h_i^2$ if h_i^2 is an exact communality and the rank of R^* is exactly m. The i-th diagonal element of each successive residual matrix is the same as or smaller than that of the preceding residual matrix by the square of a real number

f_{ij}^2 ($j = 1, 2, \ldots, m$), which is positive or zero: zero only if all elements of the corresponding row (and column) of the residual matrix are zero, that is, if all of the variance of variable i is accounted for by the preceding factor(s). Thus, in the exact (no error) case, a salient factor can sometimes be extracted from a residual matrix that has one or more rows (and columns) the elements of which, including the diagonal element, are all exactly zero. But in the real case, which includes errors, any such column will consist of near-zeros rather than exact zeros, and the estimate of the residual communality must be sufficiently positive to be consistent with these near-zero but not exactly zero elements.

5.3.3 Principal-Axes Factoring

In a factor analysis based on actual data, the elements r_{ij} of R^* will contain sampling errors, errors of measurement, and errors of communality estimation. The actual (mathematical) rank of R^* will be n, no matter what values we place on the diagonal, except in those rare cases in which one row of R^* is linearly dependent on one or more others, so that the multiple correlation of that variable with all the others is unity. If a communality is *overestimated,* the correlation matrix remains Gramian, but some of the unique variance will be injected into the salient common factors. This is not serious unless the overestimation is severe, for example, as in factoring with unities on the diagonal. But if a communality is *underestimated,* the last residual matrix may have off-diagonal elements still large enough to yield a salient factor, but with some diagonal elements near-zero or negative, contrary to property 6, above. For this reason we restore some of the underestimated communality by arbitrarily increasing the diagonal residual by an amount sufficient to make it appreciably positive, that is, a plausible estimate of the residual communality. Hence the rule of thumb: substitute for the diagonal residual one-half the mean of the absolute values of the off-diagonal elements in the column if the diagonal residual is numerically smaller or negative.

If we are to retain m salient factors we should *like* to have communality estimates, adjusted where necessary by revision of diagonal residuals, such that the rank of R^* is m, with the first m eigenvalues positive and the last $n - m$ eigenvalues all zero. This situation is unattainable because of the sampling errors and the errors of measurement of the variables, so we try to approximate it as best we can. To do this, we estimate the number of salient factors m, compute new communality estimates from the loadings on these first m factors, and refactor once. After doing so, the sum of the first m eigenvalues will be closely equal to the initial trace, the *sum* of the last $n - m$ eigenvalues will be close to zero, and the sum of the first m eigenvalues will be close to the sum of all n. Thus we can say that R^* is *Gramian to m factors,* and that m is the *salient rank* of R^*.

If the number of salient factors m is estimated correctly at the first factoring, this number should be even more clearly m at the refactoring. In fairly rare cases

m may appear to be different at the refactoring. When this situation occurs, m should be reestimated from the refactored factor matrix, new communalities should be computed, and these new communalities should be used as estimates for a second refactoring.

If $R*$ is based on actual data and has only *salient* rank m, the equation

$$R* = FF'$$

will not hold exactly. Instead we will have

$$R* = FF' + \Delta,$$

and Δ, which would be a zero matrix if the rank were exactly m, will have nonzero elements which differ randomly from zero. With one refactoring, as described above, the *sum* of the diagonal elements of Δ will be close to zero, and so also will be the sum of its eigenvalues. These eigenvalues will also differ only randomly from zero, and about half of them will be negative, with corresponding factors imaginary. With diagonal elements summing to approximately zero, the sum of squares of all the elements of Δ will be close to a minimum.

5.4   FACTORING PROCEDURE

There are a number of methods for obtaining the eigenvalues and eigenvectors of a square matrix on an electronic computer, and hence the factor loadings by (5-5). The method most favored as this is written is the Householder-Ortega-Wilkinson method (Wilkinson, 1965), and improvements are still being made to speed up the computations. This method, along with most others, gives all the eigenvalues and eigenvectors at once; and it does not include the computation of residual matrices. In factor analysis we are interested only in the larger factors; and more importantly we may need to reestimate diagonal elements in the residual matrices to keep the solution Gramian to m factors, if some of the initial communality estimates are too low. We therefore describe the older and slower Hotelling method, which gives the factors one at a time in descending order of magnitude of the eigenvalues, using a program which includes reestimation of diagonal values in residual matrices wherever necessary. The additional computing time required is usually only a few minutes even with fairly large matrices ($n \doteq 100$), and with small matrices ($n < 20$) only a few seconds.

The essential procedure is iterative for each factor. At each iteration we postmultiply $R*$ by a vector of trial factor loadings V_i and then rescale the product vector $R*V_i$ to obtain an improved vector of trial factor loadings V_{i+1} (Hotelling, 1933). This procedure converges for each factor to the largest eigenvalue and to a vector proportional to the corresponding vector of factor loadings if (1) the initial vector of trial factor loadings is not exactly orthogonal to the final vector; (2) the two or more largest eigenvalues are not equal.

Hotelling's original procedure was to rescale each product vector $R*V_i$ by multiplying each of its elements by the reciprocal of the absolute value of the largest. This largest element of $R*V_i$ converges to the eigenvalue. When two successive values of the vector are equal to a sufficiently close approximation, this vector is rescaled so that the sum of squares of its elements will equal the eigenvalue. A residual matrix is then formed, and the process is repeated to obtain the next factor.

5.4.1 Horst's Scaling Factor

Horst (1962) showed that Hotelling's scaling procedure does not lead to rank reduction exactly one for each successive factor unless the number of iterations is sufficient to determine each eigenvector exactly. He proposed instead the iteration formula

$$V_{i+1} = \frac{R*V_i}{\sqrt{V_i'(R*V_i)}}. \tag{5-6}$$

To see the meaning of this result we recall that by (5-3), substituting $R*$ for R because we have communality estimates on the diagonal and neglecting the resulting final residual matrix Δ,

$$EDE' = R*$$

with E orthonormal by columns, so that $E'E = I$ (m by m), and D is an m by m diagonal matrix of the first m eigenvalues: $d_1, d_2, \ldots, d_m$. Then, postmultiplying each side of this equation by E,

$$EDE'E = ED = R*E,$$

because E is orthonormal by columns so that $E'E = I$. This implies that, for a particular eigenvector E_j and the associated eigenvalue d_j,

$$E_j d_j = R*E_j.$$

Note that d_j here is a scalar. Then if $d_j > 0$,

$$E_j d_j = E_j \sqrt{d_j} \sqrt{d_j} = R*E_j = R*E_j \frac{\sqrt{d_j}}{\sqrt{d_j}}.$$

Setting $E_j \sqrt{d_j} = F_j$ (the j-th column of the principal-axes factor matrix), we have, from the second and fourth expressions above,

$$F_j \sqrt{d_j} = R*F_j/\sqrt{d_j}$$

and, postmultiplying both sides of this equation by $\sqrt{d_j}$,

$$F_j d_j = R*F_j.$$

Also $F_j'F_j = d_j$, since E_j is a normal vector, so that $E_j'E_j = 1$ and $F_j = E_j\sqrt{d_j}$. Now (5-6) becomes reasonable, for, if V_i were exactly F_j, then

$$V_{i+1} = \frac{R*V_i}{\sqrt{V_i'(R*V_i)}} = \frac{F_j d_j}{\sqrt{F_j'(F_j d_j)}} = \frac{F_j d_j}{\sqrt{d_j d_j}} = \frac{F_j d_j}{d_j} = F_j.$$

The proof that (5-6) converges so that its denominator is the *largest* eigenvalue (next-to-last expression above), with F_j ($= V_{i+1}$) the associated column of the factor matrix, is beyond the scope of this treatment.

Formation of the scalar product $V_i'(R*V_i)$ adds one vector product to each iteration, and finding the square root is a little more trouble than finding the largest element of $R*V_i$, but this scaling factor $1/\sqrt{V_i'(R*V_i)}$ has advantages that greatly outweigh the disadvantages. Horst shows that:

1. If the sequence is terminated at any iteration after the first, that is, if even V_2 is taken as the final vector of factor loadings, the residual matrix

$$R* - V_i V_i'$$

will be of rank exactly one less than $R*$.

2. In each successive iteration after the first the denominator of (5-6) increases in value and approaches the eigenvalue.

If two eigenvalues are fairly near equal, convergence of the denominator of (5-6) to the larger is much faster than is convergence of V_{i+1} to the exact vector of factor loadings. Thus if ϵ is a small fixed number (e.g., .00001), and if after k iterations the difference between the denominator of (5-6) and the true d_j is ϵ, there may still be a number of elements of V_{i+1} which differ from the corresponding elements of F_j by more than ϵ; and many more iterations would be required before every element of V_{i+1} differs from the corresponding element of F_j by no more than ϵ. But, if we stop the iterations for each of two successive factors as soon as the approach to the *eigenvalue* (d_j) is satisfactory, the two obtained factors will be linear combinations of the corresponding exact factors, and this is all that is required for rotation. It follows, however, that if two eigenvalues are almost equal, *both* of the corresponding factors should either be retained for rotation or omitted.

As this procedure is rank-reducing for any number of iterations greater than one, it is not necessary to continue iterating until even the exact eigenvalue is approximated very closely. Whatever variance is thereby lost from one factor will be picked up by the next. In practice, using an electronic computer, we merely continue iterating until the increase in the denominator of (5-6) from one iteration to the next falls short of .00001. This does *not* mean that at this point the eigenvalue is approximated within .00001, but only that if iterations were continued, each increase in the denominator would be less than .00001. In fact, if two eigenvalues are *quite* close together, it may happen that the approach to the larger is terminated before the value of the smaller is reached. In this case the computed value of the second may even exceed that of the first, and this also is tolerable so long as either both or neither of them are retained for rotation.

5.4.2 Matrix Squaring

Hotelling (1936) showed that, if iterations are performed on R^{*2}, only half as many will be required as would be needed to achieve the same amount of convergence if performed on R^*; that, if performed on R^{*4}, only one-fourth as many would be required, and so on.

With a symmetric matrix, squaring requires $n(n + 1)/2$ vector products: $n(n - 1)/2$ for the off-diagonal entries and n for the diagonal entries. One iteration requires $n + 1$, namely n for the product R^*V_i and 1 for $V_i'(R^*V_i)$. If k iterations would be required without squaring to reach a given criterion of convergence, this would require $k(n + 1)$ vector products: n for R^*V_i and 1 for $V_i'(R^*V_i)$ at each of k iterations. We can reduce this number by $k(n + 1)/2$ at a cost of $n(n + 1)/2$ for squaring the matrix. Equating these values,

$$k(n + 1)/2 = n(n + 1)/2, \text{ or } k = n.$$

Thus squaring the matrix R^* will save time if, but only if, the number of required iterations without squaring exceeds the number of variables. Experience indicates that, with large or moderately large matrices, the number of iterations required to reach our criterion of denominator increase less than .00001 is usually less than the number of variables, so matrix squaring is not used.

5.4.3 Initial Trial Vector, V_0

The most obvious suggestion is to use a unit vector, and this is indeed often excellent for the first factor. The elements of R^*V_0 are then the column sums, and if all of these sums are positive the first iteration yields the centroid solution. With every residual matrix, however, and even with R^* if half or more of its off-diagonal entries are negative, the unit vector is almost orthogonal to the final vector of factor loadings, because reflection is not employed; and convergence will be quite slow at first. An even greater difficulty arises occasionally. In a later residual matrix, wherein the diagonal entries are smaller on the average than the side entries, it is possible for the sum of all the entries to be negative. But, with a unit vector as the initial trial vector, $V_0'(R^*V_0)$ is this negative sum; its square root is imaginary; and the procedure breaks down completely.

A satisfactory and sufficiently simple initial trial vector is a zero–one vector, with a one in the position of the largest diagonal entry, and all other elements zero. In this case R^*V_0 is simply the column of R^* whose diagonal element is largest; $V_0'(R^*V_0)$ is this diagonal element; and the denominator of (5-6) is its square root. To find V_1, then, we merely multiply all elements of the column whose diagonal element is largest by the reciprocal of the square root of this diagonal element.

5.4.4 Example

For the five-verbal-tests example the principal-axes factor matrix is shown in Table 5.1, along with the four-decimal centroid solution from the a and b rows of Table 2.4. Though the principal-axes solution was computed for this example on a desk calculator, we omit the description of the steps, because desk calculators are no longer used for principal-axes factoring, even for problems as small as this.

The first thing to note is the remarkable similarity of the results of the two analyses. If we round the entries to three decimals, the largest discrepancies are .001 in column a, .003 in column b, and .002 in column h^2. With larger problems ($n > 5$, $m > 2$) the similarity of the centroid solution to the principal-axes solution decreases.

The superiority of the principal-axes solution to the centroid solution is barely apparent. The communality sum for the principal-axes solution is 3.3763 or 3.3764, and for the centroid solution it is 3.3758. The principal-axes solution yields the larger total communality, but the difference is only .0005 or .0006.

The principal-axes factor matrix must be an orthogonal matrix ($F'F = D$, a diagonal matrix). We show the two $F'F$ matrices at the bottom of Table 5.1. For

TABLE 5.1
Factor Matrices for Five Verbal Tests ($N = 841$)

Test	Principal Axes			Centroid		
	Factor			Factor		
	a	b	h^2	a	b	h^2
(1)	.7481	−.1436	.5803	.7476	.1424	.5792
(2)	.8138	.1536	.6859	.8138	−.1539	.6860
(3)	.8454	−.1628	.7212	.8450	.1597	.7395+
(4)	.8010	−.1295+	.6584	.8018	.1321	.6603
(5)	.7943	.2823	.7106	.7943	−.2826	.7108
Σ	4.0026	.0000	3.3764	4.0025	−.0023	3.3758
Σf^2	3.2091[a]	.1672[a]	3.3763	3.2090	.1668	3.3758
	$F'F$			$F'F$		
	3.2091	.0004		3.2090	−.0024	
	.0004	.1672		−.0024	.1668	

[a] Eigenvalues

the principal-axes solution the off-diagonal elements of $F'F$ are .0004, which is close enough to zero to be ascribed to accumulated rounding error. For the centroid solution they are $-.0024$. The centroid factor matrix is not an orthogonal matrix, though it is *approximately* orthogonal; $-.0024$ is close to zero, but not close enough to ascribe to rounding error. In both solutions the *axes* are orthogonal, however, and so therefore are the factors.

A centroid factor matrix *can* be orthogonal, in which case this matrix is also the principal-axes factor matrix. The probability that this will occur with real data, however, is so low that the writers have never seen or heard of a case in which it did occur.

In the principal-axes solution the negative b-loadings are b_1, b_3, and b_4, while in the centroid solution they are b_2 and b_5. Any *factor* may be reflected at will by changing the signs of all its elements, without reflecting any of the tests. If, in the centroid solution, we had reflected tests 1, 3, and 4 instead of tests 2 and 5, we would have obtained the same sign pattern as in the principal-axes solution. If we plot this factor matrix, the plot will be a mirror-image of Fig. 2.1, with two points to the *right* of the a-axis and three to its left. The rotated factors will be the same, but factor I will be factor II and factor II will be factor I. In the oblique rotation the order of the rotated factors is arbitrary, depending on the sign pattern in the initial F-matrix. In the orthogonal rotations we arbitrarily arranged the solutions so that the general factor would be factor I.

5.5   NUMBER OF COMMON FACTORS

5.5.1 Upper Limits

We start with the two basic equations (2-7) and (2-8):

$$r_{ij} = a_i a_j + b_i b_j + \ldots + m_i m_j \tag{5-7}$$

$$r_{ii} = a_i^2 + b_i^2 + \ldots + m_i^2 = h_i^2 \tag{5-8}$$

The correlation matrix, assuming all communalities r_{ii} correctly determined, is

$$
\left[
\begin{array}{cccccc}
r_{11} & r_{12} & r_{13} & \cdots & r_{1n} \\
r_{21} & r_{22} & r_{23} & \cdots & r_{2n} \\
r_{31} & r_{32} & r_{33} & \cdots & r_{3n} \\
\hline
r_{n1} & r_{n2} & r_{n3} & \cdots & r_{nn}
\end{array}
\right]
\tag{5-9}
$$

We first show that it is *always* possible to derive from this correlation matrix a factor matrix with $n - 1$ common factors and at most one unique factor, namely

$$\begin{bmatrix} a_1 & 0 & 0 & \cdots & 0 \\ a_2 & b_2 & 0 & \cdots & 0 \\ a_3 & b_3 & c_3 & \cdots & 0 \\ \hline a_n & b_n & c_n & \cdots & n_n \end{bmatrix} \qquad (5\text{-}10)$$

Because a_1 is the only nonzero loading in the first row of (5-10), we have from (5-8)

$$r_{11} = a_1^2; \, a_1 = \sqrt{r_{11}} \qquad (5\text{-}11)$$

and from (5-7)

$$r_{12} = a_1 a_2 ; \, a_2 = r_{12}/a_1$$

$$r_{13} = a_1 a_3 ; \, a_3 = r_{13}/a_1$$

$$\text{-------------------------------} \qquad (5\text{-}12)$$

$$r_{1n} = a_1 a_n ; \, a_n = r_{1n}/a_1$$

Then from the second row of (5-10), by (5-8),

$$r_{22} = a_2^2 + b_2^2; \, b_2 = \sqrt{r_{22} - a_2^2}, \qquad (5\text{-}13)$$

and from (5-7)

$$r_{2j} = a_2 a_j + b_2 b_j ; \, b_j = (r_{2j} - a_2 a_j)/b_2 \qquad (j > 2). \qquad (5\text{-}14)$$

We could also derive (5-13) and (5-14) from the residual matrix having elements

$$r_{ij \cdot a} = r_{ij} - a_i a_j. \qquad (5\text{-}15)$$

By the first equation of (5-11) and the first set of equations (5-12), all entries in the first row and column of the residual matrix will be zero. By (5-15) $r_{22 \cdot a} = r_{22} - a_2^2$, whose square root is b_2 by (5-13). Also, for the rest of row 2, $r_{2j \cdot a} = r_{2j} - a_2 a_j$ $(j > 2)$; and by (5-14) $b_j = r_{2j \cdot a}/b_2$. Thus the b-factor loadings are obtained from the residual matrix by the same procedure used to obtain the a-factor loadings from the original correlation matrix, but starting with the diagonal element $r_{22 \cdot a}$; and the second factor is orthogonal to the first.

From the third row of (5-10), by (5-8),

$$r_{33} = a_3^2 + b_3^2 + c_3^2; \, c_3 = \sqrt{r_{33} - a_3^2 - b_3^2} \qquad (5\text{-}16)$$

and from (5-7)

$$r_{3j} = a_3 a_j + b_3 b_j + c_3 c_j; \, c_j = (r_{3j} - a_3 a_j - b_3 b_j)/c_3 \qquad (j > 3). \quad (5\text{-}17)$$

We could also obtain these values from the second residual matrix by the same method used previously, starting with $r_{33 \cdot b}$ and using the succeeding entries in row 3 of (5-10). In this second residual matrix all entries in both rows and columns 1 and 2 would be zero.

This procedure continues until finally

$$n_n = \sqrt{r_{nn} - a_n^2 - b_n^2 - c_n^2 - \ldots - (n-1)_n^2}, \qquad (5\text{-}18)$$

where $(n-1)_n^2$ is the last loading on the next-to-last factor. The last residual matrix has only one nonzero entry, $r_{nn\cdot(n-1)}$, and the final loading n_n is its square root. But because factor n has only one nonzero entry, it is unique factor. Then, if the r_{ii} are a set of exact communalities for $m = n - 1$, $r_{nn\cdot(n-1)}$ and hence n_n will be exactly zero. If these diagonal entries are not exact communalities for $n - 1$ factors, n_n will be a final unique factor.

This procedure is termed the diagonal or square-root method of factoring. It is a Gram-Schmidt orthogonalization of the reduced correlation matrix (Chapter 8). It is not a practical method for initial factoring in common factor analysis because, when the communalities must be estimated, the full error in estimating each r_{ii} affects every loading on the corresponding factor. It is useful, however, in other applications in which the diagonal elements are given data (e.g., unities or reliabilities) rather than estimates.

If now there are only $m < n - 1$ common factors, and the r_{ii} are exact communalities for m factors, every column of (5-10) after the m-th will consist entirely of zeros. The first m columns will contain $m(m-1)/2$ zeros, and the whole factor matrix will contain $mn - m(m-1)/2$ nonzero entries.

The point of this demonstration is that *any* initial factor matrix with the same communalities differs from (5-10), or (5-10) with the last $n - m$ columns all-zero, only by a linear transformation. Hence of the mn entries in *any* factor matrix, only $mn - m(m-1)/2$ are linearly independent.

Returning now to the problem of the maximum number of common factors that can be derived from the intercorrelations among n variables, we note first that the correlation matrix contains $n(n-1)/2$ linearly independent entries r_{ij} $(i < j)$; the communalities as well as the factor loadings must ultimately be determined from these intercorrelations. The number of degrees of freedom for the determination of the factor loadings is the number of linearly independent correlations minus the number of linearly independent factor loadings derived from them. Note again that the communalities are functions of the loadings by (5-8). Thus,

$$DF = n(n-1)/2 - [mn - m(m-1)/2],$$

which may be written

$$DF = [n(n-1) - 2mn + m(m-1)]/2,$$

and expanding we obtain

$$DF = (n^2 - n - 2mn + m^2 - m)/2.$$

Noting that $n^2 - 2mn + m^2 = (n - m)^2$, this becomes

$$DF = [(n - m)^2 - (n + m)]/2. \tag{5-19}$$

If $(n - m)^2 > (n + m)$, the number of degrees of freedom is positive, m common factors may or may not account for the intercorrelations among n variables, and tests of significance and salience are in order to see if they do. Thus, if $n = 4$ and $m = 1$, $DF = [(4 - 1)^2 - (4 + 1)]/2 = 2$, and one common factor will account for the intercorrelations if and only if two linearly independent tetrads are each equal to zero within sampling error. The number of degrees of freedom specifies the number of explicit conditions that must be met if the intercorrelations among n variables are to be accounted for by m common factors.

If $(n - m)^2 = (n + m)$, the number of degrees of freedom is zero, and there are no explicit conditions whose violation would require more than m common factors. There may, however, be weak boundary conditions. Thus, if $n = 3$ and $m = 1$, $DF = [(3 - 1)^2 - (3 + 1)]/2 = 0$, and one common factor will be sufficient if and only if each of three triads is positive or zero and not greater than 1. For cases in which n and m are larger, the boundary conditions are not fully worked out, but Theorem 1.3 generalizes in part to the proposition that no communality may be negative or greater than unity.

If $(n - m)^2 < (n + m)$, the number of degrees of freedom is negative, and n variables are insufficient to determine the loadings on m common factors. Then, if the hypothesis that $m - 1$ common factors are sufficient has been rejected, we must conclude that the set of variables in question is unsuitable for factor analysis. Suppose, for example, we have a test battery consisting of two verbal tests, two numerical tests, two abstract (nonverbal) reasoning tests, and two space tests. One test of each pair is a power test and one is a speed test. Thus with eight tests we have five common factors: verbal, numerical, abstract reasoning, space, and speed. The first four are doublets. Here $[(8 - 5)^2 - (8 + 5)]/2 = -2$, and it will not be possible to extract five common factors.

For several small values of n the following tabulation shows the largest value of m for which the number of degrees of freedom is positive or zero, and the number of degrees of freedom.

							n					
	3	4	5	6	7	8	9	10	11	12	13	14
m	1	1	2	3	3	4	5	6	6	7	8	9
DF	0	2	1	0	3	2	1	0	4	3	2	1

It is sometimes possible and useful to find a set of reasonable loadings for m factors when $DF = 0$, and this may be necessary when the hypothesis of $m - 1$ factors is clearly rejected.

The upper bounds specified by the preceding analysis do not guarantee that a *unique* solution exists. In some cases there may be two or more different sets of nm factor loadings, with different sets of n communalities, which will account for the intercorrelations among the n variables.

The number of common factors m is equal to the rank of the reduced correlation matrix, and this rank has been defined as the smallest number of nonzero rows and columns that can be reached by performing elementary transformations upon the rows of that matrix. If the diagonal entries are considered unknown, the *ideal rank* is defined as the rank determined by the known intercorrelations alone. In this case pivotal reductions can use only nondiagonal pivots, and every resulting entry that includes a diagonal element as a term or factor must also be considered unknown. Each pivot "uses up" directly one row and a different column, namely row i and column j if the pivot is r_{ij}. But in this case there will be an unknown value in column i of the unit row (where the reciprocal of the pivotal element multiplies the unknown r_{ii}), and an unknown value r_{jj} in the multiplier column. In consequence, the residual matrix will have zeros or unknowns in *both* rows i and j and in *both* columns i and j. Hence for every reduction we lose *two* rows and *two* columns.

If n is even, we can therefore make at most $n/2$ reductions, and if n is odd, we can make at most $(n - 1)/2$. And if, within these numbers of reductions, we do not reach an all-zero row and column in a residual matrix, the ideal rank is not determined. Hence, for n even, the largest determinate ideal rank must be less than $n/2$, and for n odd it must be less than $(n - 1)/2$.

If the rank is exactly $n/2$ (n even) or $(n - 1)/2$ (n odd), there *may* still be a unique set of communalities, even though in this case it cannot be proved by elementary transformations that the rank is not greater (Albert, 1944a). But if the actual rank is greater than the ideal rank, there is always the possibility that two or more different sets of factor loadings and communalities may yield that actual rank, which is now no longer wholly determined by the intercorrelations. The only proof that the factor loadings and communalities *will* be unique, moreover, requires that m be less than or equal to $n/3$ (Albert, 1944b). The mathematical complexities of his proof are beyond the scope of this treatment. Albert also gives exact solutions for the communalities, on the assumption that the rank of R^* is exact and not greater than the ideal rank, but they are of theoretical interest only: correlation matrices based on real data subject to sampling errors and errors of measurement do not have exact rank less than n, and the writers have not seen a factor analysis in the literature in which they were actually used.

We conclude, then, that sets of variables for factor analysis should be so chosen that the probable number of common factors will not exceed $n/3$, or at most will fall short of $n/2$ (n even) or $(n - 1)/2$ (n odd). Every variable in such a battery should be more or less similar, as judged by its substantive content, to at least two other variables.

5.5.2 Estimation of m

With real data, based on a properly selected set of n variables, the number m of salient common factors will usually be appreciably less than the upper bounds discussed above, and we use these upper bounds only as guides. With an electronic computer, it is usual to *overfactor* initially, that is, to extract more common factors than any reasonable preliminary estimate of the number that are likely to be salient: say $n/2$ (n even), or $(n - 1)/2$ (n odd), or the last common factor corresponding to a positive eigenvalue. Even with reestimation of diagonal values in successive residual matrices, a negative eigenvalue *may* be reached before we have extracted as many as $n/2$ or $(n - 1)/2$, in which case the actual rank of R^* *must* be less than the ideal rank. We then perform a number of tests on the successive common factors in order to judge which is the last salient factor. No one of these tests is conclusive, but when several of them agree, the number on which they agree is probably correct. In cases in which there is no substantial agreement among the tests, we may need to rotate k, $k + 1$, or even $k + 2$ in addition, and take as m the largest of these which leads to an interpretable rotated factor matrix. It is highly undesirable to underestimate the number of salient factors, because in this case we will obtain a rotated factor matrix that does not include one or more determinable common factors. But it is almost equally undesirable to overestimate the number of salient factors, because in this case we *may* obtain one or more rotated factors that *seem* to be interpretable but are in fact due only to fortuitous relationships among the variables, for example, correlated sampling errors or correlated errors of measurement.

1. *Bargmann test.* This is a test of statistical significance: a test of the hypothesis that k factors are sufficient against the alternative that more than k are required (Bargmann, 1957; Bargmann & Brown, 1961). It is a modification of the Bartlett test (Bartlett, 1950, 1951), and it assumes that the variables have a multivariate normal distribution. It applies strictly only to factoring by the maximum-likelihood method (Section 5.6.2), but it applies fairly well to principal-axes factoring, and Bargmann reports good results even when it is used with centroid factoring.

The test is made successively with $k = 1, 2, \ldots$, and the number of statistically significant factors is the first value of k for which the hypothesis is *not* rejected. The formula is

$$\chi^2 = \left[N - \frac{2n + 1}{6} - k \right] \left[\sum^n \ell n(1 - h_k^2) - \ell n |I_k - F_k' R^{-1} F_k| - \ell n |R| \right],$$

(5-20)

$$DF = n(n - 1)/2,$$

for N individuals, n variables, and k factors. In this formula, h_k^2 is a computed communality for the first k factors of R^* ($h_{ki}^2 = a_i^2 + b_i^2 + \ldots + k_i^2$) in the i-th row of F, I_k is an identity matrix of order k, F_k is the first k columns of the principal-axes factor matrix (computed from R^* with communality estimates on the diagonal), and R^{-1} and $|R|$ are the inverse and determinant of the correlation matrix with *unities* on the diagonal. The inverse is required also to obtain the $SMCs$, and the natural logarithm of the determinant is computed, at the same time, as the sum of the natural logarithms of the pivotal elements in the computation of R^{-1}.

Computation of $\ell n|I_k - F_k' R^{-1} F_k|$ is not as formidable as it might seem at first glance. If p is the number of factors computed initially ($n/2$, $(n-1)/2$, or the number corresponding to positive eigenvalues), the matrix $[I_p - F_p' R^{-1} F_p]$ is computed first. The elimination procedure is applied to it and, for each successive value of k, $\ell n|I_k - F_k' R^{-1} F_k|$ is the sum of the natural logarithms of the first k pivotal elements.

For $DF > 70$ the Fisher approximation,

$$x/\sigma = \sqrt{2\chi^2} - \sqrt{2DF - 1}, \tag{5-21}$$

is adequate for all practical purposes. The probability that m factors are enough is then given by the area in *one tail* of the unit-normal distribution beyond the normal deviate x/σ. If $n < 13$ (hence $DF < 70$), the probability may be obtained directly from a table of the chi-square distribution with χ^2 as computed from (5-20) and $DF = n(n-1)/2$ (Pearson & Hartley, 1954, Table 7).

Because we terminate this test with the acceptance rather than the rejection of a null hypothesis (k factors are enough), significance levels larger than usual (e.g., the .20 level or some higher level) should be used. This guards against errors of Type II (here rejecting a factor when it is in fact significant). One can even argue that the next factor should be retained whenever the test on the current factor rejects it beyond the .50 level. This would say that the last factor should be the first for which the x/σ value, by (5-21), is *negative*. Such an argument is probably a little extreme, but one should certainly consider retaining the next factor whenever x/σ for the current factor is as great as 1 (the .16 level).

Statistical significance is only one evidence of salience, and not the best. It depends too greatly on N. If N is large (say more than 800 or 1000), one or several of the later factors may be significant but with loadings so small that they are of no practical value. And when N is small (say less than 80 or 100), one or two of the later factors may be clearly salient but statistically insignificant. The salience of a factor depends more on its *clarity* of structure than on its statistical significance. A later factor is clearest when it has a small number of fairly high loadings with the rest quite low.

With a singular, almost singular, or very large correlation matrix (say $n > 100$), where the alternative procedure for communality estimation ($r_{ii} = |r_i|max$) is used, the data for the Bargmann test are not available.

2. *Scree test*. When the correlation matrix has been appreciably over-factored initially, examination of the eigenvalues (in order of magnitude) and their differences often provides excellent evidence of the number of salient factors. When the differences decrease regularly up to a point, followed by a substantially larger difference, and the later differences are all small (usually less than .10), this scree test suggests that the last salient factor is the one immediately preceding the substantially larger difference. Consider first the data for girls in Table 5.2 (Cureton, 1968). The differences decrease regularly from 26.16 to .06, then there is a substantially larger difference (.16), and all the later differences are well below .10. This suggests clearly that the first eight factors are salient and the last eight are not.

For the boys the issue is less clear. There is a similar indication for eight salient factors, but an almost equally clear indication for ten. In this situation, more weight must be given to other evidence on the number of salient factors, and it may be necessary to rotate eight, nine, and ten factors to see which result leads to the clearest interpretation.

Instead of examining the successive differences, we can plot eigenvalues against factor numbers. Figure 5.1 shows such a plot for the girls' data of Table

TABLE 5.2
Eigenvalues and Differences for Two Groups Taking a 91-Test Battery

	Boys (N = 257)			Girls (N = 286)		
Factor	Eigenvalue	Difference[a]	Per Cent of Trace	Eigenvalue	Difference[a]	Per Cent of Trace
1	33.28		58	31.55		58
2	5.87	27.41	68	5.40	26.16	68
3	4.31	1.56	76	3.52	1.88	74
4	2.54	1.77	80	2.23	1.29	78
5	1.65	.89	83	1.57	.66	81
6	1.37	.28	85	1.28	.29	84
7	1.22	.15	88	1.14	.14	86
8	1.15	.07	90	1.08	.06	88
9	.98	(.17)	91	.91	(.16)	89
10	.91	.06	93	.87	.04	91
11	.76	(.15)	94	.81	.05	93
12	.73	.03	96	.75	.06	94
13	.70	.03	97	.68	.07	95
14	.61	.09	98	.63	.05	96
15	.59	.02	99	.63	.01	97
16	.56	.03	100	.57	.06	99

[a] Eigenvalues and eigenvalue differences were rounded separately. In consequence the reported differences will sometimes differ from the differences between rounded eigenvalues by ±.01.

Note. From Table 3, p. 32, Cureton, 1968. Reprinted by permission.

5.2. A smooth curve fits the first eight points and another—almost a straight line—fits the last eight, but the two curves do not join. The name "scree test" (Cattell, 1966) comes from the resemblance of such a plot to the rock slope of a mountain with a mass of rubble called the scree or talus at the bottom. Cattell factors a matrix with unities on the diagonal, makes the scree test by plotting as in Fig. 5.1, retains one factor from the scree (e.g., factor 9 in this case), and then refactors with estimated communalities on the diagonal. The writers see no need for factoring twice, prefer to stop at the last factor *not* on the scree, and find that examination of a difference column is in most cases just as clear as is examination of a plot.

In some cases the last substantial difference is not preceded by a smaller difference, but there may be a point above which the differences are generally large and below which they are generally small. In these cases the last salient factor is the one just preceding the last substantial difference.

There is no precise definition of "substantial." The last "substantial" difference is one which is distinctly larger than all or almost all of those which follow it and are fairly clearly on the scree. Usually, however, the distinction will occur somewhere near the values .10 to .15; a difference of .15 or greater is likely to be "substantial," and a difference less than .10 is likely not to be "substantial." This critical region (about .10 to .15) is essentially independent

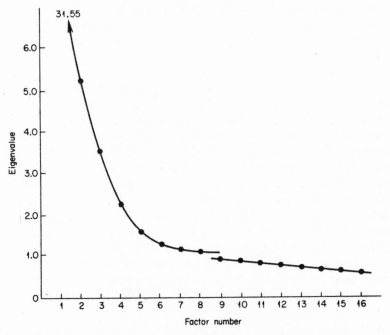

FIG. 5.1.   Plot of eigenvalues against factor numbers for girls' data of Table 5.2 (*N*=286).

of the number of variables, n. As n increases, however, the eigenvalues and differences above the critical region become larger. In the case of the boys, in Table 5.2, the substantial loadings on the ninth rotated factor were on a group of disparate tests administered at the same sitting; the tenth made no sense and was interpreted as another error factor; so the eight-factor solution was accepted.

In Table 5.2, the last column on each side is labeled "Per Cent of Trace." The per cent of trace (often termed also per cent of variance), at the m-th factor, is the sum of the first m eigenvalues divided by the initial trace (the sum of the estimated communalities). If the initial trace is too high, the per cent of trace at the m-th factor will be less than 100. If the initial trace is too low, the per cent of trace at the m-th factor will exceed 100. If this percentage is close to 100 for the number m of factors retained, say 95 to 105, no refactoring is necessary. If it is further from 100 than this, m-factor computed communalities should be used as new initial communality estimates for refactoring. At the refactoring the initial trace should agree closely with the sum of the m-factor communalities. Exact agreement, which is seldom attainable, is the condition under which the residual matrix after m factors is almost a minimum.

If, in Table 5.2, we stop at eight factors, the per cent of trace is 90 for the boys and 88 for the girls. In these cases we should refactor, using as initial communality estimates the communalities computed from the first eight columns of the first factor matrix.

When the scree test is clear, as in the case of the girls in Table 5.2 and Fig. 5.1, it is probably the best single test for the number of salient factors. When it is not clear, as in the case of the boys, other methods of estimation become relatively more important.

3. *Critical eigenvalue.* Some factor analysts, most notably Kaiser, recommend retaining as salient all factors corresponding to eigenvalues greater than unity, and discarding all those with lower eigenvalues. This rule works well for both the boys and the girls in Table 5.2. For factor 8 the eigenvalues are 1.15 for the boys and 1.08 for the girls. And for factor 9 they are .98 for the boys and .91 for the girls. But the rule does *not* work well for the five-verbal-tests example. There (Table 5.1) the second factor was clearly salient, with eigenvalue only .167. Also for a very large matrix ($n = 372$, $m = 19$: Cureton, 1970, II, B-19b), the 19-th factor had eigenvalue 2.17 and the 20-th had eigenvalue 1.92, a difference of .25, with all later differences below .10. Here the critical value is about 2. Thus the critical eigenvalue varies considerably with the number of variables n. The writers propose instead the rule: the last salient factor is the last one whose eigenvalue exceeds $(n^{.6})/15$. By this rough empirical rule the critical value is about .175 when $n = 5$, about .998 when $n = 91$, and about 2.324 when $n = 372$. Even with this modification the rule is less dependable than most of the others.

4. *Examination of factor matrix.* The number of common factors m can also be inferred from certain features of the over-factored factor matrix. It is generally observed that common-factor loadings have similar numerical values for both

small and large values of n. They are generally a little larger, however, for highly reliable variables, in which the error-of-measurement parts of the unique factors are small. And for very unreliable variables, such as single items of a test or questionnaire, the loadings on the common factors have somewhat lower absolute values. For variables whose reliabilities are moderate, say .60 to .90, Thurstone quite generally ignored loadings below .20. The rules here are imprecise and often conflicting, but they do provide useful guides. We start with the over-factored factor matrix, with $n/2$ or $(n-1)/2$ factors, or all factors corresponding to positive eigenvalues if this number is less.

a. We can usually require that enough factors of F be retained to include the highest loading in every row, if this loading is above .20.

b. If the first m columns of F include both the highest and second highest loadings in every row, m factors are likely to be enough or more than enough.

c. If a given column contains even one loading as high as $\pm.40$, or as many as 3% of its loadings as high as $\pm.30$, this column and all previous columns of F should usually be retained. This rule is weakened if, in every row containing such a loading, the highest and second highest loadings are in previous columns.

d. If as many as 10% to 20% of the loadings in a column are as high as $\pm.20$, with at least one or two as high as $\pm.25$, this column and all previous columns should usually be retained.

e. Enough columns should be retained to include in almost every row a sum of absolute values of loadings at least twice the sum in the columns not retained, provided the total number of columns is $n/2$ or $(n-1)/2$ or all columns corresponding to positive eigenvalues.

5.5.3 Example

Swineford (1948, p. 14) gives the intercorrelations among nine aptitude tests administered to 504 children aged 12-0 to 14-5 in grades 5-10. The correlation matrix was factored by the principal-axes method on an electronic computer, with initial communality estimates by (5-1). Table 5.3 gives the data needed to estimate the number of factors to be retained.

The first section of the table shows the correlation matrix, the pivotal elements in the computation of the inverse, the estimated communalities by (5-1), and the reliabilities as estimated by Swineford. These reliability estimates are a little higher than would be estimates strictly consistent with the correlations.

There are no near-zero pivotal elements, so the correlation matrix is not almost singular.

The estimated communalities look at least reasonable. Even allowing for some overestimation of the reliabilities, the estimated communalities are all smaller, so we do not have a quasi-Heywood case.

The second section of the table gives the data for the scree test, the Bargmann

TABLE 5.3
Principal-Axes Factor Analysis of Nine Aptitude Tests ($N = 504$)

Test	(1)	(2)	(3)	(4)	(5)	(6)	(7)	(8)	(9)	Pivotal Element	Est Com	Rel
							Correlation Matrix					
(1)		.511	.498	.542	.509	.445	.372	.333	.281	1.000	.544	.874
(2)	.511		.473	.436	.462	.426	.435	.370	.414	.739	.500	.934
(3)	.498	.473		.504	.462	.418	.372	.330	.354	.687	.469	.915
(4)	.542	.436	.504		.654	.764	.439	.449	.455	.621	.841	.897
(5)	.509	.462	.462	.654		.645	.405	.417	.406	.514	.660	.851
(6)	.445	.426	.418	.764	.645		.376	.376	.458	.375	.787	.874
(7)	.372	.435	.372	.439	.405	.376		.686	.589	.718	.700	.905
(8)	.333	.370	.330	.449	.417	.376	.686		.535	.497	.642	.903
(9)	.281	.414	.354	.455	.406	.458	.589	.535		.552	.557	.895

Initial trace $= 5.700$

Factor	Eigenvalue	Eig Diff	Eig Sum	Per Cent of Trace	Chi-Square	Normal Deviate
a	4.36		4.36	76	487.5	22.80
b	.79	3.57	5.15	90	166.3	9.81
c	.41	.38	5.56	97[a]	44.0	.96
d	.13	.28	5.69	100	19.2	−2.22
e	.09	.04	5.78	101	6.6	−4.80

Test	K	a	b	c	d	e	h_3^2
				Factor			
(1)	1	.645	−.185	−.319	.110	−.005	.552
(2)	1	.639	−.004	−.293	−.152	.014	.494
(3)	1	.619	−.106	−.259	−.027	−.086	.461
(4)	1	.826	−.285	.201	.141	−.151	.804
(5)	1	.746	−.216	.035	.028	.227	.604
(6)	1	.765	−.307	.304	−.114	.016	.772
(7)	1	.692	.483	−.004	.056	−.011	.712
(8)	1	.658	.438	.080	.145	.054	.631
(9)	1	.645	.305	.124	−.203	−.059	.524
Σ							5.554

(1) Arithmetic Computation   (4) General Information   (7) Punched Holes
(2) Number Series   (5) Reading Comprehension   (8) Drawings (mirror image)
(3) Deductions (syllogisms)   (6) Word Meaning   (9) Visual Imagery

[a] Computed from eigenvalue sum to eight decimals. Two-decimal value shown would give 98.

Note. Correlation matrix from Table 4, p. 14, Swineford, 1948. Copyright 1948 by The University of Chicago. Reprinted by permission.

test, and the critical eigenvalue. The last substantial eigenvalue difference is the .28 between the third and fourth eigenvalues. This suggests three salient factors. The correlation matrix was factored to $(n + 1)/2 = 5$ factors to show that the fourth eigenvalue difference is small.

By the formula $(n^{.6})/15$, the critical eigenvalue is .25. This again suggests three factors. To obtain $n^{.6}$ we use logarithms: $n^{.6} = $ antilog$(.6 \log n)$.

The third normal deviate is a little below 1.00 but is still clearly positive. The Bargmann test is not conclusive as between three and four factors, but the three-factor hypothesis is rejected at only the .17 significance level.

The third section of the table shows the over-factored factor matrix. If a row of this factor matrix had had a negative first-factor loading, the entry in column K would have been -1 instead of 1. Column K shows that there were no negative first-factor loadings (in fact, the correlation matrix was all-positive).

The highest loading in every row is in column a, and the second highest in column b or column c except in row (5), where it is in column e. Three salient factors are suggested.

Column c contains two loadings higher than $\pm.300$, while columns d and e contain none. This also suggests three salient factors.

Columns d and e each contain one loading above $\pm.20$ (just over 10%), but neither is as high as .25. Column c contains five loadings above $\pm.20$, four of which are above .25. Again three factors are suggested.

In every row, the sum of absolute values of the loadings in the first three columns is more than twice that in the last two, so three salient factors should be enough.

With the per cent of trace accounted for by three factors equal to 97, there is no need to refactor. The first three factors are ready for rotation as they stand. The three-factor communalities are shown in the last column of the factor matrix.

This is a particularly clear case. The nine variables were in fact selected by Swineford to yield three common factors.

5.6   OTHER METHODS FOR
INITIAL FACTOR ANALYSIS

Aside from the Spearman-type procedures, which were described first because they are based on explicit algebraic theorems and do not require the two-step procedure or the use of a geometric model, and the centroid method, which was used only to illustrate step 1 of the two-step procedure and to provide data for the illustration of step 2 in the two-factor case, we have described and recommended only the principal-axes method for initial factoring, using an electronic computer for the computations. We next consider briefly some methods simpler than the complete centroid method, some methods more complex than the principal-axes method, and some methods based on models which are different from the usual linear model of common-factor analysis.

5.6.1 The Simpler Methods

Thurstone (1947) described three variants of the centroid procedure which are simpler than the complete centroid method described briefly in Chapter 2: the grouping method, the group centroid method, and the multiple-group method. The multiple-group method has been used fairly extensively in substantive research in the past, to bring the analysis of fairly large matrices within the practical limits of computing time on desk calculators.

By all of these methods the loadings on each factor are determined from a subgroup of tests rather than from all the tests. In consequence, the errors in the loadings are larger, the separation of common-factor variance from unique variance is less precise, and there is less opportunity for the positive and negative errors to balance out. With these methods, moreover, communality reestimation in successive factors is not employed, so the errors in initial estimation have a slightly larger influence on the final results. Refactoring with improved communality estimates is still possible, though it has seldom been used.

Because electronic computers are now generally available, these simpler methods, including the complete centroid method, are now mainly of historic interest and are not described further in this treatment. Other methods that fall in this category are the diagonal method, the Wherry-Winer (1953) procedure, and the bi-factor method (Holzinger & Harman, 1941; Harman, 1976). The diagonal method is useful for problems that are allied to those of common-factor analysis but do not require the use of estimated communalities. The bi-factor method is essentially a method of cluster analysis followed by factor analysis of the clusters. It gives results essentially equivalent to the centroid method or the principal-axes method followed by rotation if, but only if, all or most of the tests fall in exactly m clusters centered on the primary axes. In other cases it may underestimate, or more commonly overestimate, the number of salient factors, because it is constrained to find a factor corresponding to every cluster.

5.6.2 The More Complex Methods

These include Lawley's *maximum-likelihood method* (Lawley, 1940, 1941), Rao's *cannonical method* (Rao, 1955), which is another maximum-likelihood method, the *minres method* (Harman & Jones, 1966; Harman, 1976), and Comrey's *minimum-residual method* (Comrey, 1962; Comrey & Ahumadra, 1964, 1965).

The maximum-likelihood methods (Lawley, Rao) assume that the variables have the multivariate normal distribution, and under this assumption these methods yield estimates of the population loadings which, for a specified number of factors, maximize the likelihood that a sample drawn at random from the population will be the given sample. They are scale-invariant; for example, factoring a variance-covariance matrix will give the same result as factoring the corresponding correlation matrix.

The minres method, like the maximum-likelihood methods, determines the loadings on all m factors simultaneously, with m specified initially, and minimizes the sum of squares of the off-diagonal entries in the final residual matrix Δ. Unlike the maximum-likelihood methods it includes a side condition that prohibits any communality from exceeding unity.

The maximum-likelihood methods and the minres method are complex, partly in that they use more complicated iterative procedures than does the principal-axes method, and partly in that if the specified value of m turns out to be wrong the whole process must be repeated with a revised estimate of m. The loadings on m factors are not the same as the loadings on the first m factors in an $(m + 1)$-factor solution. These methods tend to rely heavily on tests of statistical significance, because asymptotic tests (tests appropriate for use with large samples) are available. We have noted that the Bargmann test is an appropriate test for maximum-likelihood factoring. We must add, however, that there is nothing in these methods per se which requires that statistical significance be considered the only or even the main evidence of salience.

The major criticism of the maximum-likelihood and minres methods is that their iterations converge to the exact sample communalities for any specified number of factors, so that the diagonal of the residual matrix after m factors has exact zeros on the diagonal. This represents over-fitting of the model to the data. The sampling errors and the errors of measurement, as well as the general factorial trends, are fitted exactly. As a result, Heywood cases result not too infrequently from maximum-likelihood analysis (Kaiser, 1976) and communalities equal to unity from minres analysis. Quasi-Heywood cases arise fairly frequently. Harman (1976) shows that the maximum-likelihood methods, the minres method, and the principal-axes method iterated to stable communalities are equivalent.

In Comrey's minimum-residual method, the first-factor loadings minimize the sum of squares of the off-diagonal elements of the first residual matrix, the second-factor loadings minimize the sum of squares of the off-diagonal elements of the second residual matrix, and so on. The process is sequential, and factoring is stopped when a factor is reached whose loadings can be considered nonsalient. The procedure is iterative for each factor. Successive iterations alternate between overestimates and underestimates of the correct loadings, and the loadings from successive pairs of iterations are averaged to accelerate convergence. The minimum-residual procedure *may* over-fit the data, but the writers have not seen evidence that it actually does so. The only objections to it are that the iterative procedures are somewhat complicated and that it has not been shown to reduce the rank by exactly one for each factor extracted, if the iterations are stopped short of complete convergence (though it *may* do this). For a given number of factors m the minimum-residual procedure does not give the same loadings as the minres procedure, so it does not converge to the exact sample communalities.

5.6.3 Methods Based on Different Models

The model of ordinary factor analysis regards the group measured as a sample from an infinite population and, for the statistical tests, as a sample from a multivariate normal population. The variables, however, are regarded as a fixed finite group, chosen by the investigator to cover some area or areas of substantive interest or importance.

For *alpha factor analysis* (Kaiser & Caffrey, 1965), these assumptions are reversed. The individuals measured are regarded as a fixed finite group, and the variables are regarded as a sample from an infinite universe of variables with common variance accounted for by the same factors. This reversal of roles leads to weighting the variables by their communalities, and the test for the number of factors becomes a test of the hypothesis that the m-th factor might have reliability zero instead of the hypothesis that it might be due to sampling error.

Image factor analysis (Harris, 1962) is based on Guttman's (1953) image theory. Here both the individuals measured and the variables are regarded as fixed finite groups.

A fourth possibility would be to regard both the individuals measured and the variables as samples, respectively, from an infinite population of individuals and an infinite universe of variables with common variance accounted for by the same factors. So far as the writers are aware, this model has not been developed into a working method of factor analysis. With two varieties of sampling to complicate the situation, the problems are likely to be intractable.

The computing procedures for alpha factor analysis and image factor analysis are both somewhat more complicated than are those of principal-axes analysis, approaching in complexity those of the maximum-likelihood and minres methods. Because the usual model seems to fit best the purposes of most factor analyses, these alternative methods should be used only when the logic of a substantive problem demands one or other of their models.

Alpha factor analysis is indicated when we are investigating the factorial structure of a *defined universe* of possible tests, the tests actually used being a random sample (usually fairly large) from this universe. The results, however, do not generalize to any population of examinees beyond the group actually tested.

Image factor analysis is appropriate when the experimental group consists of all members of a class (e.g., all members of a legislative body), and the data consist of all observations that are relevant (e.g., all record votes at one session). The results do not generalize at all. For the legislative body the factors would be the general attitudes underlying all record votes of one particular set of legislators at one given session.

6

Rotation of Axes

6.1 *m*-DIMENSIONAL VECTOR SPACE

In considering rotation, the discussion is mainly in terms of the geometric model. In the two-factor case, we used a geometric model in Section 2.5. We first consider this model in more formal terms, generalize it to three dimensions, and then generalize it further to any number *m* of dimensions.

In Fig. 6.1 we show the plot of Fig. 2.1 for the five-verbal-tests example in a slightly different form, and reproduce Table 2.8 as Table 6.1. In Fig. 6.1 the axes *a* and *b* intersect at the origin 0 and are of unit length. In this two-dimensional space we plot five points, for the five verbal tests. The coordinates of each point are its *a* and *b* centroid factor loadings from Table 6.1. A line is drawn from the origin to each plotted point. These lines, with arrows at their termini (the plotted points) to indicate the directions of the vectors (*from* the origin *to* the plotted points), are the *test vectors*.

The geometric test and axis vectors are directed lines in the vector space. The corresponding algebraic vectors are pairs of numbers specifying the coordinates of the vector termini. The *a*-coordinate of each vector terminus is measured *from* the *b*-axis, *parallel* to the *a*-axis. The *b*-coordinate is measured *from* the *a*-axis, *parallel* to the *b*-axis. The *length* of the vector, by the Pythagorean theorem, is the square root of the sum of squares of its coordinates: $\sqrt{a_i^2 + b_i^2} = \sqrt{h_i^2}$.

Alternatively, we can drop perpendiculars from each vector terminus to the axes. The *a*-coordinate is then the distance from the origin along the *a*-axis to the point where the perpendicular from the vector terminus meets this axis. It is

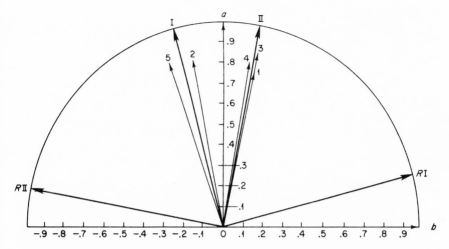

Fig. 6.1.   Axis vectors, test vectors, rotated axis vectors, and reference vectors for five verbal tests ($N = 841$).

termed the *projection* of the vector on the *a*-axis. The *b*-coordinate is the distance along the *b*-axis from the origin to the point where the perpendicular meets it, or the projection of the vector on the *b*-axis. If a test vector terminus lies to the left of the *a*-axis, its *b*-coordinate is negative.

TABLE 6.1
Oblique Rotation of Centroid Factor Matrix for Five Verbal Tests
($N = 841$)

Test	Centroid		Rotated	
	a	*b*	I	II
(1)	.748	.142	.333	−.007
(2)	.814	−.154	.065	.296
(3)	.845	.160	.376	−.007
(4)	.802	.132	.338	.013
(5)	.794	−.283	−.065	.420
Σ	4.003	−.003	1.047	.715
Ch			1.046	.715

(1) Paragraph Meaning
(2) Same-Opposite
(3) Proverb Matching
(4) Verbal Analogies
(5) Vocabulary

Problem 6.1:1. Given the two factor matrices,

	I				II	
Var	a	b		Var	a	b
(1)	.3	.4		(1)	−.1	.3
(2)	.0	.9		(2)	.9	.2
(3)	.8	.2		(3)	.2	−.4
(4)	.9	.1		(4)	.0	.8

Plot each of these sets of points on a sheet of cross-section paper, labelling the axes *a* and *b* as in Fig. 6.1. The half circle may be omitted. Draw the vector from the origin to each plotted point, with an arrow at the terminus.

In general, a geometric vector may be any directed line in a vector space. In this limited treatment, however, we are concerned only with vectors from the origin. The common-factor space is of dimensionality m. In more extended treatments of factor analysis, consideration is given also to the individual space of dimensionality N, the test space of dimensionality n, the unique-factor space also of dimensionality n, and the total-factor space of dimensionality $m + n$. In this treatment, however, we consider only the common-factor space.

Consider next a three-dimensional vector space (see Fig. 6.2). Visualize first a cubical room with origin 0 at, say, the lower southwest corner. The axis *a* goes up from 0 along the intersection of the south and west walls. The axis *b* goes north from 0 along the intersection of the west wall and the floor. The axis *c* goes east from 0 along the intersection of the south wall and the floor.

The terminus of a vector from the origin to any point inside the room will have three positive coordinates. The *a*-coordinate will be the distance from the floor to the vector terminus. If we drop a perpendicular from the vector terminus to the floor, it will be parallel to the *a*-axis (vertical), and its length will be the *a*-coordinate. Similarly the *b*-coordinate will be the distance from the south wall to the vector terminus, measured parallel to the *b*-axis, and the *c*-coordinate will be the distance from the west wall to the vector terminus, measured parallel to the *c*-axis.

Alternatively, once again, we can drop perpendiculars from the vector terminus to the axes. Then because, in the previous definitions, each coordinate was measured parallel to the corresponding axis, the projections of the vector terminus on the axes are its coordinates. Note that a coordinate, measured perpendicularly from a plane (here the floor or a wall) is equal to its projection on an axis only if the axis is *orthogonal* (perpendicular) to the plane. We are dealing here with planes orthogonal to one another, and the axes lie along the intersections of the plans taken two at a time, with each axis orthogonal to the plane which it meets or intersects at the origin 0.

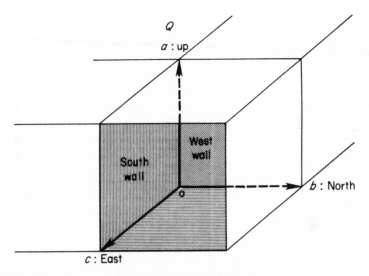

Fig. 6.2.   Illustration of a three-dimensional vector space.

If the b-coordinate is negative, the vector terminus will lie south of the south wall (outside the room). If the c-coordinate is negative, the vector terminus will lie west of the west wall. If the b-coordinate and the c-coordinate are both negative, the vector terminus will lie outside the room in the region below Q in the figure. And if the a-coordinate is negative, the vector terminus will lie below the floor.

The length of a vector in three-space, as given by the generalized Pythagorean theorem, is $\sqrt{a_i^2 + b_i^2 + c_i^2}$.

For vector spaces of $m > 3$ dimensions, we cannot visualize corresponding physical spaces, so we shall proceed with this discussion by analogy. (A more rigorous treatment would proceed from a set of axioms, which reduce to those of plane and solid geometry in the case of two and three dimensions.) The terminus of any vector from the origin, in such an m-space, can be specified by m coordinates

$$a_i, b_i, \ldots, m_i.$$

Instead of three planes (walls and floor in Fig. 6.2), we now have m *hyperplanes*, each of dimensionality $m - 1$, all intersecting at the origin, and each axis is orthogonal (perpendicular) to one of these hyperplanes. In three-space each hyperplane becomes a plane (of dimensionality $3 - 1 = 2$). In two-space each hyperplane becomes a line (of dimensionality $2 - 1 = 1$) and, because the axes are orthogonal to each other and each axis is orthogonal to a hyperplane (here a line), the hyperplane orthogonal to each axis is the other axis.

In a space of any dimensionality, the m hyperplanes all intersect at the origin. In three-space, the three planes, taken *two* at a time, intersect in three lines: the three axes. In m-space ($m > 3$) the m hyperplanes, taken $m - 1$ at a time, intersect in m lines, again the axes. In two-space the two lines, taken *one* at a time, do not form intersections, and this case is degenerate: instead of intersecting to form the axes, they *are* the axes.

In a space of any dimensionality each axis is orthogonal to a hyperplane. The length of one coordinate of a vector terminus in the space is its distance from one hyperplane, measured orthogonally from that hyperplane, and hence parallel to the axis which is orthogonal to that hyperplane. Because hyperplanes cannot be visualized directly, whereas projections on axes can, the projection definition of coordinate length is somewhat clearer when $m > 3$.

The length of a vector in m-space, by a further generalization of the Pythagorean theorem, is

$$\|V_i\| = \sqrt{a_i^2 + b_i^2 + \cdots + m_i^2}.$$

The symbol $\|V_i\|$ is to be read as "the length of the vector V_i."

6.1.1 Scalar Product of Two Vectors

In geometric terms the scalar product of two vectors is the product of their lengths times the cosine of the angle between them. If they are *unit* vectors representing normalized variables, their scalar product is the correlation between the two variables. These relations are shown below.

Consider two vectors X and Y in m-space, and let K be a line joining their termini. By the generalized Pythagorean theorem

$$\|X\|^2 = a_1^2 + b_1^2 + \ldots + m_1^2 \tag{6-1}$$

$$\|Y\|^2 = a_2^2 + b_2^2 + \ldots + m_2^2 \tag{6-2}$$

If we project the two vectors on the a-axis, the projection of the length of K will be $|a_1 - a_2|$, that is, $a_1 - a_2$ if $a_1 > a_2$, or $a_2 - a_1$ if $a_2 > a_1$. The projections of the length of K on the other axes will be $|b_1 - b_2|, \ldots, |m_1 - m_2|$. Then again by the generalized Pythagorean theorem, the length of K will be the square root of

$$K^2 = |a_1 - a_2|^2 + |b_1 - b_2|^2 + \ldots + |m_1 - m_2|^2. \tag{6-3}$$

These relations are illustrated for the case $m = 2$ in Fig. 6.3.

Expanding (6-3)

$$K^2 = a_1^2 + a_2^2 - 2a_1a_2 + b_1^2 + b_2^2 - 2b_1b_2 + \ldots + m_1^2 + m_2^2 - 2m_1m_2,$$

and from (6-1) and (6-2)

$$K^2 = \|X\|^2 + \|Y\|^2 - 2a_1a_2 - 2b_1b_2 - \ldots - 2m_1m_2. \tag{6-4}$$

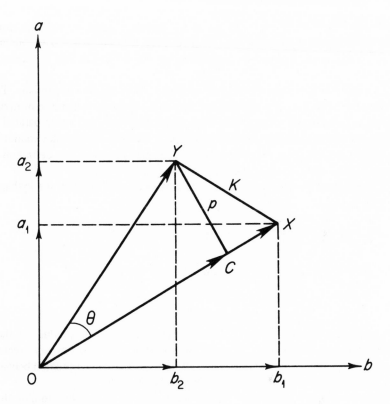

$$\|X\|^2 = a_1^2 + b_1^2 \tag{6-1a}$$

$$\|Y\|^2 = a_2^2 + b_2^2 \tag{6-2a}$$

$$K^2 = |\, a_1 - a_2 \,|^2 + |\, b_1 - b_2 \,|^2$$

$$= a_1^2 + a_2^2 - 2a_1 a_2 + b_1^2 + b_2^2 - 2b_1 b_2 \tag{6-3a}$$

$$K^2 = \|X\|^2 + \|Y\|^2 - 2a_1 a_2 - 2b_1 b_2 \tag{6-4a}$$

Fig. 6.3. Illustration of formulas (6-1), (6-2), (6-3), and (6-4) for the case $m = 2$, and of the law of cosines.

By the law of cosines, however,

$$K^2 = \|X\|^2 + \|Y\|^2 - 2\|X\| \cdot \|Y\| \cdot cos\ \theta, \tag{6-5}$$

where θ is the angle between the vectors X and Y. To demonstrate this, consider only the plane containing the vectors X and Y, the plane of the page in Fig. 6.3. Drop a perpendicular from Y to X intersecting X at C, and let the length of this perpendicular be p. Then by definition $cos\ \theta = \|C\|/\|Y\|$: in the right triangle

$0CY$, the length of the side adjacent to θ (namely $0C$ or $\|C\|$) divided by the length of the hypotenuse ($0Y$ or $\|Y\|$). Then from Fig. 6.3

$$\|Y\|^2 - \|C\|^2 = p^2 = K^2 - (\|X\| - \|C\|)^2$$

$$\|Y\|^2 - \|C\|^2 = K^2 - \|X\|^2 + 2\|C\|\cdot\|X\| - \|C\|^2$$

$$K^2 = \|X\|^2 + \|Y\|^2 - 2\|C\|\cdot\|X\| \tag{6-6}$$

Then, from the definition $cos\ \theta = \|C\|/\|Y\|$,

$$\|C\| = \|Y\|\cdot cos\ \theta,$$

and substituting in (6-6)

$$K^2 = \|X\|^2 + \|Y\|^2 - 2\|X\|\cdot\|Y\|\cdot cos\ \theta,$$

which is (6-5), the law of cosines. Then, equating the right sides of (6-4) and (6-5),

$$\|X\|^2 + \|Y\|^2 - 2a_1a_2 - 2b_1b_2 - \ldots - 2m_1m_2$$

$$= \|X\|^2 + \|Y\|^2 - 2\|X\|\cdot\|Y\|\cdot cos\ \theta,$$

$$\|X\|\cdot\|Y\|\cdot cos\ \theta = a_1a_2 + b_1b_2 + \ldots + m_1m_2. \tag{6-7}$$

The right side of this equation is the algebraic scalar product $X\cdot Y$ ($= X'Y = Y'X$) as defined in Section 3.2.3, and the left side is the corresponding geometric definition. The cosine of the angle between the two vectors, letting $X\cdot Y = a_1a_2 + b_1b_2 + \ldots + m_1m_2$ in (6-7), is

$$cos\ \theta = \frac{X\cdot Y}{\|X\|\cdot\|Y\|} : \tag{6-8}$$

the scalar product of two vectors divided by the product of their lengths is the cosine of the angle between them. And if X and Y are normal (unit) vectors, $\|X\| = \|Y\| = 1$, and

$$X\cdot Y = cos\ \theta: \tag{6-9}$$

the scalar product of two *unit* vectors is the cosine of the angle between them. And if these unit vectors represent *normalized variables*, with x and y deviations from their respective means,

$$X\cdot Y = \Sigma(x/\sqrt{\Sigma x^2})(y/\sqrt{\Sigma y^2})$$

$$= \frac{\Sigma xy}{\sqrt{\Sigma x^2}\ \sqrt{\Sigma y^2}} = r_{xy};$$

the cosine of the angle between the unit vectors is equal to the correlation between the normalized variables.

6.1.2 Applications to Factor Analysis

From the definition of the linear model, if X and Y are two test vectors in the common-factor space with orthogonal axes of unit length (orthonormal axes),

$$r^\dagger_{xy} = a_1 a_2 + b_1 b_2 + \ldots + m_1 m_2 = X \cdot Y, \tag{6-10}$$

and $\|X\| = h_x = \sqrt{h_x^2}$ and $\|Y\| = h_y = \sqrt{h_y^2}$. In (6-10) $r^\dagger_{xy}$ is the *reproduced* correlation between the variables x and y, and h_x^2 and h_y^2 are communalities. The original correlation is

$$r_{xy} = X \cdot Y + \delta_{xy}, \tag{6-11}$$

where δ_{xy} is the corresponding element of the final residual matrix Δ. Then in the common-factor space (ignoring the δs) we have from (6-10) and (6-8)

$$\cos\theta = \frac{r^\dagger_{xy}}{h_x h_y} \tag{6-12}$$

and

$$r^\dagger_{xy} = h_x h_y \cos\theta. \tag{6-13}$$

The whole reproduced correlation matrix is given by

$$FF' = R^\dagger, \tag{6-14}$$

and if we normalize each row of F (i.e., divide each element by h_i) and call the row-normalized reproduced factor matrix F_n

$$C = F_n F'_n, \tag{6-15}$$

and C is the matrix of cosines of angles between pairs of test vectors.

At the outset of a factor analysis the data give us only the correlation matrix with unknown diagonal entries. If the communalities were known, their square roots would be the test vector lengths, and by (6-12) and a cosine table we could find (within the errors $\delta_{ij}/h_i h_j$) the angle between each pair of test vectors. The combination of the test vector lengths and the angles between these vectors is termed the *configuration* of the test vectors. This configuration is independent of any set of axes from which we measure the coordinates of the test vector termini.

In initial factoring, we insert into the configuration an arbitrary set of orthogonal axes. Preliminary reflection is employed if necessary. Reflection of a test vector rotates it through an angle of 180°, so that it follows the same straight line and has the same length, but with terminus in the opposite direction from the origin. After reflection all test vector termini are on the same side of the hyperplane orthogonal to the first axis as is the terminus of this axis.

In principal-axes factoring after any necessary reflections of test vectors, the first axis is so placed that the sum of squares of the projections of the test-vector termini on it (the first-factor loadings) will be a maximum. The second axis, in the subspace orthogonal to the first axis, is then so placed that the sum of squares of the projections of the test vectors on it in this subspace (the second-factor loadings) will be a maximum. The third axis, in the residual subspace orthogonal to the first two axes, is again so placed that the sum of squares of the projections of the test vector termini in this subspace (the third-factor loadings) will be a maximum. Factoring continues until we reach a factor m such that, in the following residual subspace (the m-th), the test vectors are all so short that they can be attributed to error.

If after initial reflection (if any) all angles between pairs of test vectors are less than 90°, with positive cosines, the configuration is termed *acute*. But if some angles are still greater than 90°, with some cosines still negative, the configuration is *obtuse* in some dimensions.

6.1.3 Rotation and Transformation

The configuration of the test vectors (their lengths and the angles between them) is determined by the data. Initial factoring determines the dimensionality m of the common-factor space, revises the communality estimates and hence the estimates of the test-vector lengths ($\|X_i\| = h_i = \sqrt{h_i^2}$), and inserts into the configuration a set of arbitrary orthonormal axes the coordinates of whose termini are represented by the rows of an identity matrix. These arbitrary axes are designed to lend greatest accuracy to the determination of m and the revision of the communality estimates. The configuration cannot be changed except by reflection, but the axes can be placed anywhere in the common-factor space so long as they all start from the origin. From their initial positions the axes may be rotated about the origin to reach any other positions.

In the usual language of factor analysis we say that we rotate the initial factor matrix F into the final factor matrix V by means of the transformation $F\Lambda = V$. This language is not precise. What we actually do is first rotate the *axes* of F into the *axes* of V. From this rotation we construct the transformation matrix Λ, which is then used to *transform* the matrix F into the matrix V by the transformation $F\Lambda = V$.

Note first that it is the *rows* of F which are the test vectors. The *axes* of F are also row vectors (of unit length) in the common-factor space. They are the rows of the identity matrix I, or more properly the rows of I' ($= I$). The projections of the test vectors (row vectors of F) on the *axes* of F are given by the transformation

$$F(I')' = FI = F.$$

The transformation matrix $(I')'$ is the transpose of the axis matrix I'.

The projections of the *axes* of F on themselves are given by the same transformation applied to the axis matrix I', instead of the factor matrix F,

$$I'(I')' = I'I = I.$$

In the general (usually oblique) case, when we transform F into V, the axes of V are the *rows* of Λ'. The rotation of axes is from I' to Λ'. The transformation matrix is $(\Lambda')' = \Lambda$. The *transformation* is

$$F(\Lambda')' = F\Lambda = V,$$

and V gives the projections of the test vectors on the axes of V. These projections are the *correlations* between the tests and the factors represented by the row vectors of Λ'.

The projections of the axes of F on the axes of V are obtained by substituting I' for F in the previous equation,

$$I'(\Lambda')' = I'\Lambda = I\Lambda = \Lambda,$$

and the elements of Λ are the correlations between the factors (axes) of F, namely I', and the factors (axes) of V, given by Λ'.

The rows of Λ', and hence the columns of Λ, are of unit length. If the new axes are the *reference vectors* (RI and RII in Fig. 6.1), the projections of the test vector termini on them (equal numerically to the elements of V) are also the *perpendicular distances* of these test vector termini (points) from the hyperplanes (lines 0I and 0II in Fig. 6.1), because each reference vector is orthogonal to the corresponding hyperplane. When one of these distances is short (usually .100 or less), the corresponding element of V is termed a *near-zero* loading. It is this property which lends importance to the reference-vector structure represented by the matrix V.

6.2 SIMPLE STRUCTURE

We have seen that given a configuration of test vectors, specified by a correlation matrix and a set of n communalities, we can place the axes anywhere we wish, so long as the dimensionality of the space is not reduced by placing two or more axes too close to one another. For the initial factoring problem we imposed first the condition that the axes should be orthogonal and of unit length, and second the condition that the first-factor loadings should be as large as possible, the second-factor loadings as large as possible given the first, and so on. By "large" we mean in principal-axes analysis that the sum of squares of the loadings on each factor, given the previous factor or factors, shall be a maximum. The first condition gives uncorrelated factors, and this condition along with the second enables us to find the number m of salient common factors when factor m + 1 has loadings so low that they do not rise substantially above the error level. It was recommended that the initial factoring be repeated once, if necessary, to insure that the sum of the communalities computed from the rows of the m factors of F should be closely equal to the sum of the communality estimates placed on the diagonal of R^*. Whenever factoring is based on successive residual matrices and leads to $R^* \doteq FF'$, the axes will be orthogonal and their unit vectors will form an identity matrix, because each residual matrix represents the intercorrelations in a subspace orthogonal to the factor or factors extracted previously. And if for each successive factor we maximize the loadings, the factors will become progressively smaller, enabling us to obtain the value of m. When the axes are orthonormal, moreover, the sum of squares of the loadings in each row of the factor matrix is the communality of the corresponding test. If the axes are of unit length but *not* orthogonal, each communality is given by

$$h_i^2 = a_i^2 + b_i^2 + c_i^2 + \ldots + (m - 1)_i^2 + m_i^2 + 2ab\ cos(ab)$$

$$+ 2ac\ cos(ac) + \ldots + 2am\ cos(am) + 2bc\ cos(bc)$$

$$+ \ldots + 2bm\ cos(bm) + \ldots + 2(m - 1)\ m\ cos[(m - 1)m],$$

and similar formulas with $m(m + 1)/2$ terms, including $m(m - 1)/2$ with cosines, replace (6-10) to give the reproduced correlations $r^\dagger_{ij}$. The cosines in this formula are the cosines of the angles between pairs of axes in the common-factor space. In the orthogonal case they are all zero, and only the first m terms remain.

With respect to the final rotated axes, the positions of the axes of F are arbitrary, dictated by the need to determine m and the communalities before proceeding further.

In order to find the final or "true" factors, we need to rotate the axes of F and then transform F itself according to some reasonable criteria that will yield a unique and interpretable result. In most substantive areas of investigation to which factor analysis is applied, there is no compelling reason why the "true" factors should be uncorrelated, so for rotation and transformation we abandon the restriction of orthogonality and use oblique transformations.

Initial interest centers on the *reference-vector structure:* the matrix of correlations between the tests and the reference-vector factors, or the projections of the test-vector termini on the reference vectors, because it is in terms of this structure that the necessary conditions can be stated most simply. The basic equation for this transformation is $F\Lambda = V$.

We impose on the transformed factor matrix V the apparently fewest, simplest, and most generally reasonable conditions. The result is that V is a *simple structure*. In practice, almost all rotations of the axes of F are guided by the conditions of simple structure. Various authors give different reasons for preferring these conditions. The present writes prefer them merely because they *are* the fewest, simplest, most generally reasonable, and most widely applicable conditions that lead to unique and interpretable results. There are no other sets of conditions which are simpler and which lead so frequently to unique and substantively acceptable interpretations in almost all areas to which factor analysis can properly be applied.

Each of the conditions of simple structure can be stated in terms of

(a) the correlations between the tests and the reference-structure factors;
(b) the transformed factor matrix V (whose elements are these correlations);
(c) the geometric model.

1. The first condition is based on the general proposition that most of the tests will be factorially less complex than is the experimental battery as a whole. The factorial complexity of a test is the number of common factors on which it has nonzero loadings.

(1a) There are at least m tests that correlate near-zero with each factor, and usually several more than m.
(1b) In every column of V there are at least m near-zero elements, and usually several more than m.
(1c) There are at least m test vectors, and usually several more than m, which lie on or close to each hyperplane.

This requirement (1a, 1b, 1c) is termed the criterion of *overdetermination*. The position of each hyperplane in the common-factor space is *overdetermined* by at least m test vectors, and usually several more than m. Note that m points ($m - 1$ test-vector termini and the origin) are required to fix the position of a hyperplane in m-space. If we do not have more than $m - 1$ points, however, the evidence that the hyperplane represents a real factor is usually weak. With real data, including sampling errors and errors of measurement, the position of each hyperplane in the m-space should be overdetermined by more than the geometrically minimum number of test-vector termini.

In the oblique solution of the five-verbal-tests problem, condition 1a says that the word-meaning tests should correlate near-zero with the verbal-reasoning factor, and that the verbal-reasoning tests should correlate near-zero with the word-meaning factor. Condition 1b is verified in Table 6.1, in which variables 2 and 5 have near-zero loadings in column I, while variables 1, 3, and 4 have near-zero loadings in column II. Condition 1c is verified in Fig. 6.1: two test-vector termini are near the degenerate "hyperplane" (line) 0I, and three test-vector termini are close to the degenerate "hyperplane" 0II.

In connection with this first general proposition, Thurstone added another condition:

(a) Every test should correlate near-zero with at least one factor;
(b) Every *row* of V should include at least one near-zero entry;
(c) every test vector should lie on or close to at least one hyperplane.

This condition as stated is too strong. If a test has nonzero loadings on all factors so that its test vector does not lie on or close to any hyperplane, it is merely useless in helping to determine the hyperplane positions. *Most* of the tests must correlate near-zero with at least one factor, but if enough of them do so to provide good overdetermination for every hyperplane, a few others may have nonzero loadings on every factor. If every factor has only m or a very few more than m test vectors lying on or close to its hyperplane (i.e., if every factor is overdetermined only weakly), the locations of the hyperplanes may be poorly determined by the test vectors, and the battery is not really suitable for factor analysis.

A marginal case is the two-factor oblique solution of the example of seven reasoning and perseveration tests, shown in Table 2.10 and Fig. 2.3. We reproduce Table 2.10 as Table 6.2 and Fig. 2.3 as Fig. 6.4 with the "hyperplanes" (lines) and reference vectors added.

Here tests 2 (WAIS Digit Symbol) and 3 (Porteus Maze) are both affected by reasoning and also by perseveration, leaving condition 1 (overdetermination) rather weak. In Table 6.2 these tests both have nonzero loadings in column I and also in column II; and in Fig. 6.4 their test-vector termini both lie near the a-axis. One "hyperplane" is barely overdetermined by points 4 and 5; the other is fairly

TABLE 6.2

Oblique Rotation of Centroid Factor Matrix for Seven Reasoning and Perseveration Tests ($N = 86$)

	Centroid			Rotated	
Var	a	b	h^2	I	II
(1)	.426	−.319	.283	−.080	.478
(2)	.784	.036	.616	.403	.324
(3)	.595	.037	.355	.314	.237
(4)	.745	.403	.717	.707	−.021
(5)	.721	.345	.639	.645	.020
−(6)[a]	.741	−.424	.729	−.023	.714
−(7)[a]	.363	−.078	.138	.103	.234
Σ	4.375	.000	3.477	2.069	1.986
Ch				2.069	1.986

(1) Critical Flicker Frequency
(2) Digit Symbol (WAIS)
(3) Porteus Maze
(4) Thurstone PMA Reasoning (untimed)
(5) Raven Progressive Matrices
(6) Wisconsin Card Sorting (perseverative errors)
(7) Age

[a] Scale reversed: −(6) is "avoidance of perseverative errors" instead of "perseverative errors;" −(7) is "Youngness" instead of "Age" (= "Oldness").

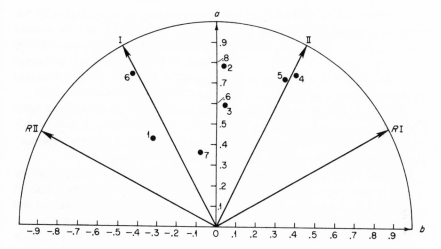

Fig. 6.4. Plot of factor loadings from Table 6.2 for seven reasoning and perseveration tests ($N = 86$).

well overdetermined by points 1, 6, and 7, though variable 7 (reversed) has loading .103, just barely near-zero, on factor I (Table 6.2). But variables 2 and 3 do not lie close to either the "hyperplane" (line) 0II from the origin through the centroid of points 4 and 5, or the "hyperplane" (line) 0I from the origin through the centroid of points 1, 6, and 7. The simple structure is, nevertheless, fairly clear. With only seven tests high overdetermination of two factors is not to be expected.

2. The second condition is not so readily expressed except in terms of the geometric model. The general idea is that the factors should be maximally distinct from one another, and that the factorial structure should be unique.

(2a) Among the subset of m or more tests having near-zero correlations with any one factor, there is at least one and usually more than one having nonzero correlation with each of the other factors.

(2b) Among the subset of m or more rows of V having near-zero entries in any one column, there is at least one and usually more than one nonzero entry in every other column. Every one of these rows must have at least one nonzero entry, and these nonzero entries are distributed over all the other columns. For if two columns should have *all* their near-zero entries in the same rows, the factors represented by these columns would be almost identical rather than unique.

If the sum of squares of the loadings on the first factor of F is large in comparison with the sums of squares of the loadings on all the later factors, and if we reflect temporarily any test whose first-factor loading is negative, condition 2b has an interesting corollary.

(2b) Corollary: In every column of V, the number of negative nonzero loadings should be a minimum. These negative nonzero loadings, if any, are the ones that cannot be made near-zero by widening the boundaries without loss or drastic reduction of overdetermination.

(2c) The hyperplanes lie at the *effective boundaries* of the configuration of test vectors in the common-factor space. In Fig. 6.4 the effective boundaries are the "hyperplanes" (here lines) 0I and 0II. The test vectors that define them lie close to them, and have near-zero loadings on the corresponding factors. Some of these near-zeros are positive and some are negative: each hyperplane is so fitted as to minimize the perpendicular distances of a subgroup of test vector termini from it, and these perpendicular distances are the absolute values of the near-zero loadings on the corresponding factor. Thus for 0I the corresponding factor is I in Table 6.2, with near-zero loadings $-.080$ on test 1, $-.023$ on test -6, and .103 on test -7. For 0II, the corresponding factor is II in Table 6.2, with near-zero loadings $-.021$ on test 4 and .020 on test 5.

Note that if a primary axis is passed through the *centroid* of a subgroup of test vectors, the algebraic sum of the near-zero loadings will be zero within rounding error. Thus in Table 6.2, the sum of the near-zero loadings on factor I is $-.080 + (-.023) + .103 = .000$, and the sum of the near-zero loadings on factor II is $-.021 + .020 = -.001$.

A very few test vectors may lie substantially outside the effective boundaries of a simple structure, leading to negative nonzero loadings. Thus if there were a single test vector about half-way between 0II and 0RI in Fig. 6.1 at the beginning of this chapter, the effective right boundary would still be 0II as shown in this figure. We could not move 0II out to coincide with such a test vector because overdetermination would then be lost. "Effectively bounding" is thus a compromise: we seek hyperplanes as nearly bounding as is consistent with good overdetermination.

Thurstone (1947) expressed this second condition in terms of several criteria, but it is not clear that any of them are really necessary for the existence of simple structure as he envisioned it. In terms of the columns of V, his formulations were:

(2x) For every pair of columns of V, there should be several tests whose loadings are near-zero in one column but not in the other. This is essentially our 2b above, except that in our formulation the minimum value of "several" is one.

(2y) For every pair of columns of V, a large proportion of the tests should have near-zeros in both columns. This condition is entirely unnecessary. A test will have near-zeros in two columns of V only if its vector lies at or close to the intersection of two hyperplanes. If every test has complexity $m - 1$ (with only one near-zero in every row of V), *no* test will have near-zeros in *any* two columns, yet simple structure may still exist. Ideally, of course, as many tests as possible should have complexity less than $m - 1$, in which case this condition will be met at least partially.

(2z) For every pair of columns of V, there should preferably be only a small number of tests which have nonzero entries in both columns. This is essentially condition 2y stated in terms of nonzeros instead of near-zeros. In the ideally perfect situation, however, every test would have complexity one (correlate substantially with only one factor), in which case there would not be any tests having nonzero entries in two columns.

Thurstone apparently tried to incorporate into his rules some elements of the criterion of *simplicity* (the opposite of complexity), as well as of simple structure per se. Simple structure is defined by imposing conditions on the *columns* of V. Simplicity is defined by imposing a condition on the *rows* of V: each row (test) shall have as many near-zero loadings as possible (ideally all but one). The writers prefer the "pure" simple-structure criterion. A procedure based on a "pure" criterion of simplicity, alternative to that based on the criteria of simple structure, has been proposed by Bentler (1977). The results given by his procedure are not very different from those based on simple structure in several examples given by him.

Thurstone recognized our condition 2c only partially. Originally he used graphic rotations such as those of Fig. 6.4, rotating axes two at a time iteratively until a satisfactory simple structure was reached. With reference to these graphic pairwise rotations he said (1947):

> The identification of a positive simple structure is done by noting the bounding hyperplanes if they are found in the rotations. If a positive manifold is not postulated or suspected in the test battery, the rotations are made toward linear concentrations of points in the diagrams without reference to the question of whether the hyperplanes are bounding planes [p. 343].

(A positive manifold is one in which the rotated factor matrix V has no negative nonzero loadings.)

In attempting to generalize, we have substituted "effectively bounding" for "bounding" in 2c) and have used the procedure of reflecting temporarily any test vectors having negative loadings on the first factor of F before rotating (see variables -6 and -7 in Table 6.2). We return to the principles of simple structure and try to clarify them further in Chapter 7. The method of extended vectors for the three-factor case, which is described in Chapter 7, includes the preparation of a plot from which the principles of simple structure can be visualized.

6.3   AXES AND HYPERPLANES

6.3.1 Model

In the two-dimensional case of Figs. 6.1 and 6.4, the common-factor vector space was bounded by a circle of radius unity. Any tests having negative first-factor loadings were reflected (e.g., tests 6 and 7 in Fig. 6.4) and their *names* were reversed, so that the *effective* vector space was bounded by a half-circle and the *b*-axis. The effective boundaries of the configuration of test vectors (vectors *from* the origin *to* the plotted points) were the two unit vectors I and II passing through the centroids of the outer clusters. The reference vectors corresponding to these "hyperplanes" (lines) were the vectors. *R*I and *R*II in Fig. 6.4, which were orthogonal to I and II.

In the three-dimensional case the common-factor space is bounded by a sphere of unit radius. If, again, tests having negative first-factor loadings are reflected and their names reversed, the effective vector space is bounded by a hemisphere. The first-factor axis rises vertically from the origin, and the other perpendicular axes are on the "floor."

Figure 6.5 shows this model. The initial axes are *a*, *b*, and *c*. The shaded ellipse is the "floor." The effectively bounding hyperplanes (here planes) are *H*I (at the left), *H*II (at the right), and *H*III (at the back). These planes form an inverted triangular pyramid with apex at the origin *O*. They generate a spherical triangle at the top, where they meet the surface of the hemisphere. They meet (intersect) in pairs at the lines (unit vectors) whose termini are *P*I, *P*II, and *P*III. These unit vectors are the *primary axes*. The *reference vectors* are unit vectors orthogonal to the planes. The reference vector *R*III (greatly foreshortened) is orthogonal to the plane *H*III. The reference vectors *R*I and *R*II, orthogonal, respectively, to *H*I and *H*II, are hidden behind the plane *H*III. Most of the test vectors (not shown) should lie on or close to the planes *H*I, *H*II, and *H*III. A few may lie inside the subspace bounded by these planes and the hemisphere, and a *very* few may lie outside this subspace. The number outside must be so few that, if one or more of the planes were moved out (away from the axis *a*) to include any of them, overdetermination (the number of test vectors on or close to such a plane) would be substantially reduced.

Note that because *P*III is in the intersection of *H*I and *H*II, it lies in both of these hyperplanes. Similarly *P*II lies in *H*I and *H*III, and *P*I lies in *H*II and *H*III. Note also that *R*III, which is orthogonal to the plane *H*III, is therefore orthogonal to *P*I and *P*II, both of which lie in *H*III. However, *R*III is correlated with (*not*

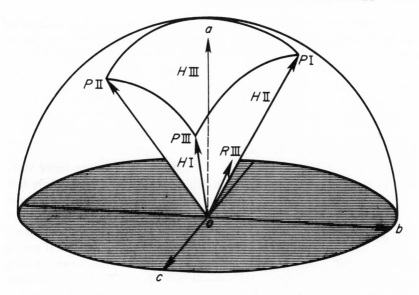

Fig. 6.5. Geometric model for the three-factor case.

orthogonal to) PIII, which is *not* in HIII. Similar descriptions apply to RI and RII; each reference vector is correlated with the *corresponding* primary axis (the one having the same number) and orthogonal to the other two.

If the parts of the test vectors lying in the common-factor space (rows of F not including unique factors) were normalized, their extended termini would lie on the hemisphere, and could actually be plotted on a physical hemisphere. Their coordinates would be their projections on the axes a, b, and c, or their perpendicular distances from the "floor" and two vertical walls erected on the axes b and c and intersecting in the axis a. In this model the hyperplanes (here planes) could be located by drawing a spherical triangle on the surface of the hemisphere at the effective boundaries of the configuration of plotted unit-length test-vector termini.

In the m-dimensional case ($m > 3$), the sphere becomes a hypersphere, and the m planes become hyperplanes of dimensionality $m - 1$. The m hyperplanes all intersect at the origin. Taken $m - 1$ at a time, they intersect in m lines, again the primary axes. Considering only the hyperhemisphere wherein all a-coordinates are positive, and terminating each hyperplane at its $m - 1$ intersections and at the surface of the hyperhemisphere, these hyperplanes form an inverted hyperpyramid. This system cannot be visualized, but if we consider Fig. 6.4 and then Fig. 6.5, we can "see" it roughly by analogy.

In the two-dimensional case the relations described above must still hold. The sphere becomes a circle or, after reflection of test vectors to make all a-coordinates positive, a semicircle. The "hyperplanes" become lines. Taken m

($= 2$) at a time, they intersect at the origin. In Fig. 6.4 these "hyperplanes" are I and II, or more properly HI and HII. The reference vectors, RI and RII, are orthogonal to the "hyperplanes" I and II (or HI and HII). These "hyperplanes," taken $m - 1$ ($= 1$) at a time, "intersect" to form the primary axes. But how does one line "intersect" with itself? It doesn't, so the primary axes *are* the "hyperplanes." But which is which? The clue here is that each primary axis is correlated only with the *corresponding* reference vector, and orthogonal to all other reference vectors (here the one other reference vector). In Fig. 6.4, I is correlated with RII (angle I 0 RII is acute), and orthogonal to RI (angle I 0 RI is a right angle). Also II is correlated with RI and orthogonal to RII. Hence I ($= H$I) is PII, and II ($= H$II) is PI. Each "hyperplane" is the *other* primary axis.

6.3.2 Equations of Hyperplanes and Their Intersections

Consider an m-dimensional vector space, with orthonormal axes $a, b, \ldots, m$ (a, b, c, in Fig. 6.5). We propose to rotate the m axes to new positions, not necessarily orthogonal, specified by a transformation matrix Λ, normal by columns. The elements of Λ' are the coordinates of RI, RII, and RIII in Fig. 6.5, although only RIII is actually shown.

The equation of the hyperplane orthogonal to the unit vector Λ_1 (the first column of Λ) is

$$\lambda_{a1}a_1 + \lambda_{b1}b_1 + \ldots + \lambda_{m1}m_1 = 0, \tag{6-16}$$

where the vector

$$\Lambda_1 = \begin{bmatrix} \lambda_{a1} \\ \lambda_{b1} \\ \cdot \\ \cdot \\ \cdot \\ \lambda_{m1} \end{bmatrix}$$

is the first column of Λ, and $a_1, b_1, \ldots, m_1$ are the coordinates of any point P_1 on the hyperplane. Equation (6-16) is termed the *scalar equation of the hyperplane*, and its coefficients (λ_{i1}; $i = a, b, \ldots, m$) are the coordinates of the terminus of the column vector Λ_1.

We demonstrate this relation only for the case $m = 2$. Figure 6.6 pictures this situation. The hyperplane HI (here a line) is orthogonal to the vector Λ_1, whose coordinates are λ_{a1} and λ_{b1}. The point P_1 is any arbitrary point on HI, with coordinates a_1 and b_1.

Because HI is orthogonal to Λ_1, the triangles whose sides are a_1 and b_1 are

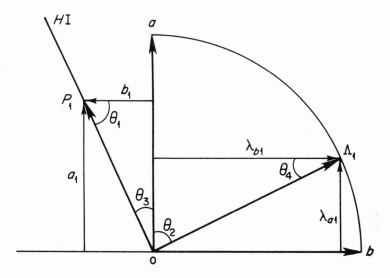

Fig. 6.6. Demonstration that $\lambda_{a1}a_1 + \lambda_{b1}b_1 = 0$.

similar to the triangles whose sides are λ_{b1} and λ_{a1}, the angle $\theta_1 = \theta_2$ and the angle $\theta_3 = \theta_4$. It follows that

$$\frac{a_1}{\lambda_{b1}} = \frac{-b_1}{\lambda_{a1}} ,$$

because a_1, λ_{a1}, and λ_{b1} are all positive, and b_1 is negative. Then from this equation, multiplying means and extremes,

$$\lambda_{a1}a_1 = -\lambda_{b1}b_1,$$

and transposing,

$$\lambda_{a1}a_1 + \lambda_{b1}b_1 = 0,$$

which is (6-16) when $m = 2$. If

$$\Lambda = \begin{bmatrix} \lambda_{a1} & \lambda_{a2} \\ \lambda_{b1} & \lambda_{b2} \end{bmatrix}$$

there would also be a hyperplane (line) H_2, orthogonal to the second column Λ_2 of Λ, and any point P_2 on this hyperplane would have coordinates a_2 and b_2 satisfying the relation

$$\lambda_{a2}a_2 + \lambda_{b2}b_2 = 0.$$

In the general case, (6-16) is simply the first of the m scalar equations

$$
\begin{aligned}
\lambda_{a1}\, a_1 + \lambda_{b1}\, b_1 + \cdots + \lambda_{m1}\, m_1 &= 0 \\
\lambda_{a2}\, a_2 + \lambda_{b2}\, b_2 + \cdots + \lambda_{m2}\, m_2 &= 0 \\
&\ \ \vdots \\
\lambda_{am}\, a_m + \lambda_{bm}\, b_m + \cdots + \lambda_{mm}\, m_m &= 0
\end{aligned}
\tag{6-17}
$$

$$
\Lambda = \begin{bmatrix}
\lambda_{a1} & \lambda_{a2} & \cdots & \lambda_{am} \\
\lambda_{b1} & \lambda_{b2} & \cdots & \lambda_{bm} \\
\hline
\lambda_{m1} & \lambda_{m2} & \cdots & \lambda_{mm}
\end{bmatrix}
$$

and each scalar equation is the equation of a hyperplane orthogonal to a column vector of Λ.

If we invert Λ,

$$\Lambda^{-1}\Lambda = I.$$

Then the i-th row vector of Λ^{-1} is orthogonal to every column vector of Λ except the i-th, because the scalar product of the i-th row vector of Λ^{-1} and any column vector of Λ except the i-th is zero. But each hyperplane H_i contains all vectors orthogonal to Λ_i, so the i-th row vector of Λ^{-1} is in every hyperplane *except H_i*, the one orthogonal to Λ_i. Hence the row vectors of Λ^{-1} are at the intersections of the hyperplanes taken $m - 1$ at a time and so also are the primary axes.

If, therefore, we normalize the row vectors of Λ^{-1}, we have

$$T' = D\Lambda^{-1} \tag{6-18}$$

where D is the diagonal matrix that normalizes the rows of Λ^{-1}, and T is the matrix whose column vectors represent the coordinates of the primary axes.

If we premultiply both sides of (6-18) by $(T')^{-1}$,

$$(T')^{-1}T' = (T')^{-1}D\Lambda^{-1} = I.$$

Then postmultipying the last two expressions above by Λ,

$$(T')^{-1}D = \Lambda, \tag{6-19}$$

and the same diagonal matrix that normalizes the rows of Λ^{-1} to give T' also normalizes the columns of $(T')^{-1}$ to give Λ.

We can find T directly from (6-18). Thus

$$T = (T')' = (D\Lambda^{-1})' = (\Lambda^{-1})'D'.$$

Then noting that $D' = D$, because D is diagonal, and that $(\Lambda^{-1})' = (\Lambda')^{-1}$,

$$T = (\Lambda')^{-1}D, \tag{6-20}$$

and D is also the matrix that normalizes the columns of $(\Lambda')^{-1}$ to give T.

Remember that when we postmultiply F by a matrix whose columns represent the coordinates of a set of unit axes, we obtain a *structure*, whose row vectors are the correlations between the tests and the factors defined by these axes, as when $F\Lambda = V$ is the structure on the reference vectors. Thus

$$FT = S, \tag{6-21}$$

and S is the *structure on the primary factors*, or the matrix of correlations between the real tests and the "ideal" tests represented by these primary axes.

The rows of T', like the rows of F, represent vectors in the common-factor space. Hence by analogy with (6-21)

$$T'T = R_s, \tag{6-22}$$

and R_s is the matrix of correlations between the primary factors or "ideal" tests, each of which measures one and only one common factor. There are no unique factors because the row-vectors of T' are of unit length, and hence the communalities of the "ideal" tests are all unity.

Problem 6.3.2:1. If $V = F\Lambda$ is an orthogonal transformation, then Λ is orthonormal. Show by matrix algebra that in this case $T = \Lambda$ and $S = V$.

6.4 STRUCTURES AND PATTERNS

The terms *rotated factor* and *rotated factor matrix* can have four distinct meanings. They can refer to (1) the structure on the reference vectors; (2) the structure on the primary factors; (3) the pattern on the reference vectors; and (4) the pattern on the primary factors.

We have defined a structure as a matrix of correlations between tests and factors. The structure on the reference vectors is the one that is almost always obtained first, because it is the one on which simple structure is defined. The transformation matrix is Λ, and the transformed factor matrix is $V = F\Lambda$. The structure on the primary factors and the two patterns are derived from the structure on the reference vectors, and then only after V has been so determined that it is a satisfactory or near-optimum simple structure.

Because Λ', like T', defines a set of unit vectors in the common-factor space,

$$\Lambda'\Lambda = C, \tag{6-23}$$

and C is the matrix of correlations between the reference vectors. And because the rows of Λ' (and the columns of Λ) are unit vectors, their scalar products, which give these correlations, are also the cosines of the angles between the reference vectors in the common-factor space. This is also the case with $T'T = R_s$; R_s is not only the matrix of correlations between the primary factors but also the matrix of cosines of angles between the primary axes. It is usual to refer to

C as a matrix of cosines, but to R_s as a matrix of correlations. Some authors routinely report the matrix C, but it is of little interest in itself, whereas R_s is of considerably more interest because the primary factors are the factor-pure "ideal" tests. Also R_s is the starting point for second-order and hierarchical analysis.

The structure on the primary factors $S = FT$ is usually of little interest in itself; but the transformation matrix T is required for the equation $R_s = T'T$; and the diagonal matrix D, which normalizes the rows of Λ^{-1} to give T', the columns of $(T')^{-1}$ to give Λ, and the columns of $(\Lambda')^{-1}$ to give T, is required also in the equations for the patterns.

Because Λ and T are normal by columns, $\Lambda'T$ or $T'\Lambda$ is the matrix of correlations (and cosines) between the reference vectors and the primary factors. But from (6-20), premultiplying both sides by Λ',

$$\Lambda'T = \Lambda'(\Lambda')^{-1}D = D, \tag{6-24}$$

and from (6-19), premultiplying by T',

$$T'\Lambda = T'(T')^{-1}D = D. \tag{6-25}$$

Thus D is the matrix of correlations (and of cosines) between the reference vectors and the primary axes. But because D is diagonal, it follows that only the *corresponding* reference vectors and primary axes have nonzero correlations or cosines. Each reference vector is orthogonal to all but the *corresponding* primary axis, because the cosine of a right angle is zero. This follows from the fact that each reference vector is orthogonal to a hyperplane containing all primary axes except the one corresponding to it, and each primary axis lies in all but one hyperplane and is thus orthogonal to all reference vectors which are orthogonal to these $m - 1$ hyperplanes.

A *pattern* consists of the *coefficients* of the standardized factor scores in a *specification equation* defining the test scores as weighted sums of the factor scores. A typical specification equation is

$$X_i = a_iA + b_iB + \ldots + m_iM + u_iU_i \qquad (i = 1, 2, \ldots, n).$$

In double-subscript notation this can be written

$$X_i = p_{i1}A_1 + p_{i2}A_2 + \ldots + p_{im}A_m + u_iB_i \qquad (i = 1, 2, \ldots, n).$$

Here the U_i of the previous equation has been changed to B_i so that in matrix notation U and B will represent different matrices: U the matrix of coefficients and B the matrix of unique-factor scores. Then writing this equation in matrix form

$$X = PA + UB. \tag{6-26}$$

Here $X(n$ by $N)$ is the matrix of standard scores on the observed variables, $P(n$ by $m)$ is the factor-pattern matrix or matrix of common-factor coefficients, $A(m$

by N) is the matrix of common-factor standard scores, $U(n$ by $n)$ is the diagonal matrix of unique-factor coefficients, and $B(n$ by $N)$ is the matrix of unique-factor standard scores. If we draw this matrix equation out, we have

$$n\ \boxed{\overset{N}{X}} = n\boxed{\overset{m}{P}}\cdot m\boxed{\overset{N}{A}} + n\boxed{\overset{n}{\diagdown U}}\cdot n\boxed{\overset{N}{B}}$$

from which it can be seen that the common-order requirements are met. The diagonal line in U indicates that it is a diagonal matrix, because there is only one unique-factor loading for each test.

In (6-26) the part of X which is in the common-factor space of m dimensions is PA, while UB is in a unique-factor space of n dimensions orthogonal to the common-factor space: orthogonal because the unique factors are uncorrelated with the common factors.

The matrix X consists of standard scores, and in these units

$$r_{ij} = \sum_{}^{N} x_i x_j /N,$$

and the correlation matrix is the n by n matrix

$$R = (1/N)XX'. \tag{6-27}$$

A structure matrix S is also a correlation matrix, consisting of the correlations between the tests and the factors with typical correlation coefficients

$$r_{ik} = \sum_{}^{N} x_i a_k /N,$$

so in matrix notation

$$S = (1/N)XA'.$$

Then from (6-26)

$$S = (1/N)(PA + UB)A'$$
$$= (1/N)(PAA' + UBA').$$

But because the unique-factor scores b_k ($k = 1, 2, \ldots, N$) and the common-factor scores a_{jk} ($j = 1, 2, \ldots, m; k = 1, 2, \ldots, N$) are uncorrelated, $BA' = 0$, so $UBA' = 0$ also and

$$S = (1/N)PAA'.$$

Because $1/N$ is a scalar, we can rewrite this as

$$S = P(1/N)AA'.$$

Here $(1/N)AA'$ is the matrix of correlations between the standard scores on the factors. Call this correlation matrix C. Then

$$S = PC. \tag{6-28}$$

Now postmultiply both sides by C^{-1}, so

$$P = SC^{-1}. \tag{6-29}$$

In this derivation S may be the structure on either the reference vectors or the primary factors, and P is the corresponding pattern. For the reference vectors $S = V$, $C \equiv C$ (symbol unchanged), and let $P = W$. Then from (6-29)

$$W = VC^{-1}.$$

But $V = F\Lambda$, and by (6-23) $C = \Lambda'\Lambda$. Hence

$$W = F\Lambda(\Lambda'\Lambda)^{-1}$$
$$= F\Lambda\Lambda^{-1}(\Lambda')^{-1}$$
$$W = F(\Lambda')^{-1} \tag{6-30}$$

which is the pattern on the reference vectors. This pattern is seldom of any particular interest.

For the primary factors $S \equiv S$, $P \equiv P$ (symbols unchanged), and $C = R_s$. Then from (6-29)

$$P = SR_s^{-1}.$$

But by (6-21) and (6-20) $S = FT = F(\Lambda')^{-1}D$; and from (6-22), (6-18), and (6-20) $R_s = T'T = D\Lambda^{-1}(\Lambda')^{-1}D$, so

$$P = F(\Lambda')^{-1}D[D\Lambda^{-1}(\Lambda')^{-1}D]^{-1}$$
$$= F(\Lambda')^{-1}D \, D^{-1}\Lambda'\Lambda D^{-1}$$
$$= F(\Lambda')^{-1}\Lambda'\Lambda D^{-1}$$
$$P = F\Lambda D^{-1} \tag{6-31}$$

which is the pattern on the primary factors. This pattern is often of considerable interest: it specifies the coefficients of the equations which define the test scores as weighted sums of the scores on the factor-pure "ideal" tests.

From (6-21) and (6-20)

$$S = F(\Lambda')^{-1}D, \tag{6-32}$$

which is the structure on the primary factors.

Gathering together the previously known result $V = F\Lambda$ and those of (6-30), (6-31), and (6-32), we obtain the results shown in Table 6.3. Thus all of the transformation matrices are functions of Λ, and each of the four factor matrices is F postmultiplied by the corresponding transformation matrix.

TABLE 6.3
Structures and Patterns on the Reference Vectors and the Primary Factors

		Structure	Pattern
Reference vectors	{ Transformation matrix	Λ	$Y = (\Lambda')^{-1}$
	{ Factor matrix	$V = F\Lambda$	$W = FY = F(\Lambda')^{-1}$
Primary factors	{ Transformation matrix	$T = (\Lambda')^{-1}D$	$Q = \Lambda D^{-1}$
	{ Factor matrix	$S = FT = F(\Lambda')^{-1}D$	$P = FQ = F\Lambda D^{-1}$

The symbols F, V, S, P, Λ and T are more or less standard. There are no standard symbols for the pattern on the reference vectors, the corresponding transformation matrix, and (curiously) the transformation matrix for the pattern on the primary factors. Hence the symbols Y, W, and Q are arbitrary with the present writers.

Looking at the diagonally opposite pairs of equations in Table 6.3, we see that the elements of each column of the primary-factor pattern are proportional to those of the corresponding column of the reference-vector structure: $V = F\Lambda$ and $P = F\Lambda D^{-1}$, the proportionality factor being a diagonal element of D^{-1}. Similarly the elements of each column of the primary-factor structure are proportional to those of the corresponding column of the reference-vector pattern: $W = F(\Lambda')^{-1}$ and $S = F(\Lambda')^{-1}D$, the proportionality factor being a diagonal element of D.

Note that when we normalize the columns of $(\Lambda')^{-1}$ or the rows of Λ^{-1}, we obtain the diagonal elements of D^{-1} first, as the square roots of the column or row sums of squares. The diagonal elements of D are then the reciprocals of those of D^{-1}.

The interfactor correlation matrices are:

Between pairs of reference vectors	$C = \Lambda'\Lambda$
Between pairs of primary factors	$R_s = T'T = D\Lambda^{-1}(\Lambda')^{-1}D$
Between a reference vector and the corresponding primary factor	$diag\,(D)$

The specification equation of test score X_i in terms of the primary factors, from the equation just preceding (6-26), is

$$X_i = p_{i1}A_1 + p_{i2}A_2 + \ldots + p_{im}A_m + u_iB_i. \tag{6-33}$$

Here p_{ij} ($i = 1, 2, \ldots, n$; $j = 1, 2, \ldots, m$) is an element of the primary-factor-pattern matrix P; $A_1, A_2, \ldots, A_m$ are the common-factor scores of an individual; $u_i = (1 - f_{i1}^2 - f_{i2}^2 - \ldots - f_{im}^2)^{1/2}$ is a unique-factor coefficient computed from the i-th row of the unrotated factor matrix F; and B_i is the unique-factor score of the individual on the i-th test. Note that in (6-33) we have not used a third subscript to identify the k-th individual in the sample ($k = 1$, $2, \ldots, N$). Had we done so, this equation would be

$$X_{ik} = p_{i1}A_{1k} + p_{i2}A_{2k} + \ldots + p_{im}A_{mk} + u_iB_{ik}.$$

Note again that in the oblique case, the sum of squares $p_{i1}^2 + p_{i2}^2 + \ldots + p_{im}^2$ is *not* the communality of test i, and that u_i^2 is therefore *not* equal to $1 - p_{i1}^2 - p_{i2}^2 - \cdots - p_{im}^2$ (see the equation for h_i^2 in the oblique case near the beginning of Section 6.2).

In this discussion we have ignored the distinction between R^* and $R^\dagger$, which latter was treated in Section 6.1.2. We have proceeded as though

$$R = FF' + U^2 = R^\dagger + U^2,$$

where $R^\dagger = FF'$ is the *reproduced* correlation matrix (reproduced from F), and U^2 is a diagonal matrix of the squares of the unique-factor loadings, with $h_i^2 + u_i^2 = 1$. But in actual computation

$$R = FF' + \Delta + U^2 = R^* + U^2,$$

where Δ is the residual matrix after the last factor retained. In these derivations we have assumed that Δ is negligible.

6.4.1 Example

For the oblique solution of the five-verbal-tests example, the centroid factor matrix F and the reference-vector structure matrix V are given in Table 2.8. The transformation matrix Λ is obtained by turning the rows of equations (2-24), or rather the rows of the immediately following equations with numerical coefficients, into columns. These matrices appear in Table 6.4 with Λ just below V, and it can readily be verified that $V = F\Lambda$. $(\Lambda')^{-1}$ is found by a short method (for the case $m = 2$) described in Section 9.2.1. Then T is found by normalizing the columns of $(\Lambda')^{-1}$, this procedure yielding D^{-1} as well as D. In Table 6.4, we show only the diagonals of D^{-1} and D. The products T and Q are obtained by multiplying the elements of each column of $(\Lambda')^{-1}$ by the corresponding diagonal element of D, and the elements of each column of Λ by the corresponding diagonal element of D^{-1}. Note that the elements of the primary-factor pattern P are proportional to those of the reference-vector structure V, the factors of proportionality being the elements of *diag* D^{-1}. Also the elements of the primary-factor structure S are proportional to those of the reference-vector pattern W, the factors of proportionality being the elements of *diag* D.

Because the elements of each column of P are proportional to those of the corresponding column of V, some authors attempt to evaluate the excellence of the simple structure by examining the columns of P. But in this case the rough rule of thumb for V, that a loading is to be regarded as near-zero if it is equal to or less than .100, breaks down. The critical values for P become .100 *diag* D^{-1},

TABLE 6.4
Structures and Patterns for Five Verbal Tests ($N = 841$)

Test	F a	b	$V = F\Lambda$ I	II	$W = FY$ I	II	$S = FT$ I	II	$P = FQ$ I	II
(1)	.748	.142	.333	−.007	1.772	1.593	.761	.685	.775	−.016
(2)	.814	−.154	.065	.296	1.801	1.922	.774	.826	.151	.690
(3)	.845	.160	.376	−.007	2.002	1.800	.860	.774	.875	−.017
(4)	.802	.132	.338	.013	1.892	1.721	.813	.739	.786	.030
(5)	.794	−.283	−.065	.420	1.702	1.956	.731	.840	−.151	.977
Σ	4.003	−.003	1.047	.715	9.169	8.992	3.939	3.864	2.436	1.664
Ch			1.046	.715	9.170	8.993	3.938	3.864	2.435	1.664

	Λ I	II	$Y = (\Lambda')^{-1}$ I	II	$T = (\Lambda')^{-1}D$ I	II	$Q = \Lambda D^{-1}$ I	II
a	.262	.178	2.291	2.246	.984	.965	.610	.414
b	.965	−.984	.414	−.610	.178	−.262	2.246	−2.291

$$\text{diag } D^{-1} \quad 2.328 \quad 2.328$$
$$\text{diag } D \quad .4296 \quad .4296$$

Test	h^2	$1 - h^2$	$u = \sqrt{1 - h^2}$
(1)	.5797	.4203	.648
(2)	.6863	.3137	.560
(3)	.7396	.2604	.510
(4)	.6606	.3394	.583
(5)	.7105	.2895	.538

Values of h^2 come from the rows of F:
$$a_i^2 + b_i^2 = h_i^2.$$

$$
\begin{array}{c}
P \\
\begin{bmatrix}
.775 & -.016 \\
.151 & .690 \\
.875 & -.017 \\
.786 & .030 \\
-.151 & .977
\end{bmatrix}
\end{array}
\quad
\begin{array}{c}
A \\
\begin{bmatrix}
1.235 \\
-.859
\end{bmatrix}
\end{array}
+
\begin{array}{c}
U \\
\begin{bmatrix}
.648 & 0 & 0 & 0 & 0 \\
0 & .560 & 0 & 0 & 0 \\
0 & 0 & .510 & 0 & 0 \\
0 & 0 & 0 & .583 & 0 \\
0 & 0 & 0 & 0 & .538
\end{bmatrix}
\end{array}
\begin{array}{c}
B \\
\begin{bmatrix}
-.982 \\
-1.321 \\
.756 \\
-.613 \\
-1.824
\end{bmatrix}
\end{array}
$$

$$
\begin{array}{c}
PA \\
\begin{bmatrix}
.971 \\
-.406 \\
1.095 \\
.945 \\
-1.026
\end{bmatrix}
\end{array}
+
\begin{array}{c}
UB \\
\begin{bmatrix}
-.636 \\
-.740 \\
.386 \\
-.357 \\
-.981
\end{bmatrix}
\end{array}
=
\begin{array}{c}
X \\
\begin{bmatrix}
.335 \\
-1.146 \\
1.481 \\
.588 \\
-2.007
\end{bmatrix}
\end{array}
\begin{array}{c}
= x_1 \\
= x_2 \\
= x_3 \\
= x_4 \\
= x_5
\end{array}
$$

and may be different for every column of P. Thus for column I of V the near-zeros are .065 and $-.065$, which are less in absolute value than .100, while for column I of P the near-zeros are .151 and $-.151$, and these loadings are less in absolute value than .2328. For column II of V the near-zeros are $-.007$, $-.007$, and .013, while for column II of P they are $-.016$, $-.017$, and .030. Note that the elements of $diag\ D^{-1}$ (and $diag\ D$) are equal in general only in the two-factor case.

Suppose that an individual has common-factor standard scores on primary factors I and II of 1.235 and $-.859$, and unique-factor scores on the five tests of $-.982$, -1.321, .756, $-.613$, and -1.824. The computation of his standard scores on the five tests by (6-26) is shown in the lower part of Table 6.4. For a single individual, $N = 1$, and A, B, and X each have only one column. In the usual case N would be the number of individuals in the sample, A would be m by N (here 2 by 841), and B and X would be n by N (here 5 by 841).

Computation of test scores by this procedure is mainly of theoretical interest, because the test scores are the original data for factor analysis, whereas the factor scores are unknown. Methods for *estimating* them (they *cannot* be computed directly) are discussed in Chapter 13. Computing a few test scores from such estimated factor scores, by the methods illustrated in Table 6.4, and comparing them with the original measured test scores, will give the investigator some feeling about the magnitudes of the errors of estimation in the factor scores.

Exercise 6:1. In exercise 2:2 you obtained the F and oblique V matrices for the six-psychological-tests problem. From that exercise and from Fig. 2.2 (oblique case) the transformation matrix is

		I	II			I	II
$\Lambda =$	a	$-(Ib)$	(IIb)	$=$	a	.615	.559
	b	(Ia)	$-(IIa)$		b	.789	$-.829$

Compute from these data Y and W, T and S, and Q and P, as in Table 6.4. An individual has primary-factor standard scores on factors I and II which are .782 and $-.431$. His unique-factor standard scores, from U_1 to U_6, are .613, $-.729$, .212, .314, $-.456$, and $-.824$. Calculate his test standard scores on the six tests.

6.4.2 Note on Geometry

We have seen in Chapter 2 that the projections of the test points on the reference vectors are the reference-vector loadings: the correlations between the tests and the reference-vector factors. From a given test point we drop a perpendicular on a reference vector. The distance from the origin along the reference vector to the point where the perpendicular meets it is the loading of the given test on the reference vector.

Figure 6.7 shows two unrotated axes *a* and *b*, two primary axes *P*I and *P*II, two reference vectors *R*I and *R*II, and one test point *X*. Dashed lines show the projections of the point *X* on the reference vectors and the primary axes. The vectors 0*c* and 0*d* are the projections on *R*I and *R*II; they are the reference-vector structure loadings: the correlations between the test *X* and the reference-vector factors. The vectors 0*e* and 0*f* are the projections on *P*II and *P*I; they are the primary-structure loadings: the correlations between the test *X* and the primary factors. Note again that all of these projections, like all of those discussed previously, are *perpendicular* projections: each dashed line (*Xe*, *Xd*, *Xc*, *Xf*) makes a right angle with the axis on which it is dropped.

There is a second system of projections, however, illustrated by the same figure. Here the projection on each reference vector is made parallel to the other reference vector, and the projection on each primary axis is made parallel to the other primary axis. The vectors 0*g* and 0*h* are the parallel projections on the reference vectors *R*I and *R*II; they are the reference-vector pattern loadings: the coefficients of the specification equations for the reference-vector factors. The vectors 0*i* and 0*j* are the parallel projections on the primary axes *P*II and *P*I; they are the primary-factor pattern loadings: the coefficients of the specification equations for the primary factors.

Because the reference vectors are perpendicular to the primary axes, a line parallel to a reference vector is perpendicular to the corresponding primary axis, and a line parallel to a primary axis is perpendicular to the corresponding refer-

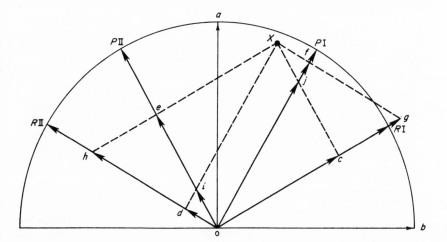

Fig. 6.7. Geometric relations between structures and patterns on the reference vectors and the primary axes.

ence vector. Hence the same dashed lines are used for the parallel projections that were used for the perpendicular projections, either lengthened or shortened. Note, for example, how the reference-structure loading on RI (vector $0c$) is related to the primary-pattern loading on PI (vector $0j$). Note also that the projection of X on RI is greater than unity. The angles between primary axes are usually acute; they can be obtuse only when a substantial proportion of the intercorrelations among the variables is negative. Therefore, in the case of primary patterns, the pattern coefficients of the specification equations exceed unity fairly infrequently.

We are usually interested only in the reference-vector *structure* and the primary-factor *pattern*, corresponding to the inner pair of dashed lines in Fig. 6.7 (Xd and Xc).

In higher-dimensional cases the parallel projection on PI, say, is made parallel to *all* the other primary axes, that is, parallel to the hyperplane which includes them (the plane HI in Fig. 6.5). And each parallel projection on a reference vector would be parallel to *all* the other reference vectors, that is, parallel to one of another set of hyperplanes intersecting $m - 1$ at a time in the reference vectors. These latter hyperplanes are not shown in Fig. 6.5, but for an acute structure such as that of Fig. 6.5 they would lie outside the hyperplanes shown; they would make obtuse angles with one another and would be orthogonal to the primary axes.

7
Extended Vectors; Varieties of Simple Structure

7.1 THE METHOD OF EXTENDED VECTORS

7.1.1 Model

The spherical model for the three-factor case is shown in Fig. 6.5. But for practical use this model is somewhat awkward. Not only do we require a physical hemisphere on which to plot but the plotting itself must be done along great circles rather than along straight lines. We therefore seek a procedure that will simplify the plotting. Thurstone (1938b, 1947) described such a procedure and termed it the method of extended vectors. This procedure is clearest, most direct, and most useful in the three-factor case, and it can be used to illustrate graphically the varieties of simple structure.

In Fig. 6.5, Section 6.3.1, imagine a horizontal plane sitting on top of the hemisphere and tangent to it at the point a: the terminus of the first unrotated factor. The test vectors are extended right on through the surface of the hemisphere to meet this plane. Figure 7.1 shows a two-dimensional cross-section. The plane and the "floor" are seen edge-on. The a-axis is vertical. The b-axis, on the "floor," runs from left to right. The c-axis runs straight out from the origin, perpendicular to the page, and is visible only as the dot at the origin. Some test vectors are shown with dotted-line extensions to the plane. The effectively bounding planes (lines) and reference vectors are not shown.

On the extended-vector plane the a-coordinates of all the test vector termini will be unity, and the b and c coordinates will be stretched proportionally.

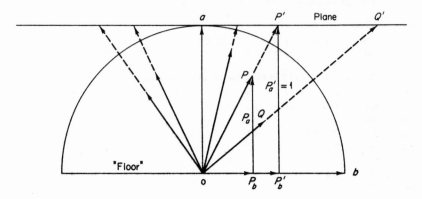

Fig. 7.1. Cross-section of the extended-vector picture.

Consider the test vector P with a-coordinate P_a and b-coordinate P_b. If we extend this vector to P' on the plane, the a-coordinate P'_a is unity, and the b-coordinate is P'_b. The two triangles $0PP_b$ and $0P'P'_b$ are similar, so their sides are proportional, and

$$1/P_a = P'_b/P_b$$

$$P'_b = P_b(1/P_a) \tag{7-1}$$

If we viewed the configuration from the left of Fig. 7.1, the axis b would be replaced by the axis c, and by similar reasoning we would find that

$$P'_c = P_c(1/P_a). \tag{7-2}$$

Note that the test vector Q, when extended to Q' on the plane, has a b-coordinate greater than unity. If Q were almost on the "floor," the extension would run almost to infinity. This is the main limitation of the extended-vector method: it does not handle tests whose first-factor loadings in F are near-zero.

If the axes b and c are projected upward (raised vertically) to the plane as horizontal lines, the plot of the extended vectors can be made in terms of ordinary rectangular coordinates. The a-coordinates will all be unity and hence need not be plotted. The extended-vector projection from the spherical model of Fig. 6.5 is precisely the polar projection of the map-maker, used frequently in making maps of the polar regions.

7.1.2 Preliminary Computations and Plot

From (7-1) and (7-2) it can be seen that to form the extended-vector factor matrix from the F-matrix, we merely multiply the elements of each row of F by the reciprocal of the first. Table 7.1 shows at the top the principal-axes F-matrix and the extended-vector matrix for the eleven subtests of the Wechsler Adult Intelligence Scale (WAIS), computed from the correlation matrix for a sample of 150

TABLE 7.1
Extended-Vector Rotation for Eleven WAIS Subtests, Age-Group 25–34
($N = 300$)

Test	Principal Axes F				F-Extended			Rotated $V = F\Lambda$		
	a	b	c	h^2	a	b	c	I	II	III
(1)	.886	−.183	−.029	.819	1	−.21	−.03	.215	.003	(.304)
(2)	.761	−.141	.249	.661	1	−.19	.33	−.082	.066	(.480)
(3)	.698	−.085	−.262	.563	1	−.12	−.38	(.384)	.018	.012
(4)	.775	−.182	.030	.635	1	−.23	.04	.140	−.009	(.322)
(5)	.588	−.098	−.263	.425	1	−.17	−.45	(.371)	−.018	−.012
(6)	.878	−.282	.134	.868	1	−.32	.15	.081	−.066	(.485)
(7)	.657	.023	−.037	.434	1	.04	−.06	.136	.152	.135
(8)	.756	.176	.070	.607	1	.23	.09	.014	(.339)	.176
(9)	.730	.361	−.044	.665	1	.49	−.06	.074	(.492)	−.016
(10)	.744	.130	−.012	.571	1	.17	−.02	.101	(.278)	.127
(11)	.615	.433	.075	.571	1	.70	.12	−.075	(.558)	.016
Σ	8.088	.152	−.089	6.819		Σ		1.359	1.813	2.029
Eig	6.036	.549	.233	6.818		Ch		1.359	1.813	2.028

Panel	Eq	Variable			Variable			$\Sigma + 1$	Ch
		(1)	(2)	(3)	(1)	(2)	(3)		
0	(1)	(1)	−.1423	−.4082	$=E'$			1.4495	
	(2)	1	.5903	.0230				2.6133	
	(3)	1	−.2581	.2337				1.9756	
1	(2)		(.7326)	.4312	−1			1.1638	1.1638
	(3)		−.1158	.6419	−1			.5261	.5261
	(1)		−.1423	−.4082	1			1.4495	1.4495
2	(3)			(.7101)	−1.1581	.1581		.7101	.7101
	(1)			−.3244	.8058	.1942		1.6756	1.6756
	(2)			.5886	−1.3650	1.3650		1.5886	1.5886
3	(1)				.2767	.2664	.4569	2.0000	2.0000
	(2)	$(E')^{-1} =$			−.4050	1.2339	−.8289	1.0000	1.0000
	(3)				−1.6310	.2227	1.4083	1.0000	1.0000
	Σ^2				2.9007	1.6431	2.8791		
	$\sqrt{\Sigma^2}$				1.7031	1.2818	1.6968		
	$1/\sqrt{\Sigma^2}$				.5872	.7802	.5893	$= diag\ (\Delta^{-1}D)$	
	$\Lambda =$				.162	.208	.269		
					−.238	.963	−.488		
					−.958	.174	.830		
	Σ^2				1.001	1.001	.999		

Note. Computed from the correlation matrix, Table 8, p. 16, Wechsler, 1955. Copyright 1955 by The Psychological Corporation. Used by permission.

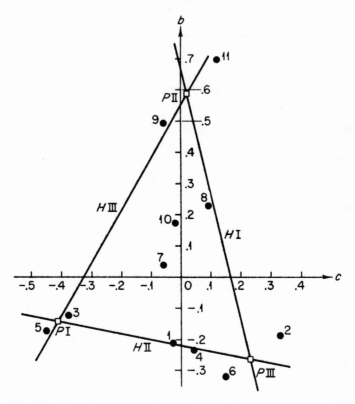

Fig. 7.2. Extended-vector plot for eleven WAIS subtests, age-group 25–34 (*N* = 300).

men and 150 women aged 25–34 (Wechsler, 1955, p. 16). Each reciprocal (not shown) is computed to at least four significant figures. It is taken as a repeat multiplier, and multiplied first by the *a*-factor loading of *F* to obtain 1.000 as a check. Then it is multiplied by the *b* and *c* loadings of *F* to give the *b* and *c* loadings of the extended-vector matrix. These loadings are recorded to only two decimals, because two are sufficient for plotting.

The plot of the extended-vector *b* and *c* loadings for the WAIS data, made from columns *b* and *c* of the extended-vector matrix of Table 7.1, is shown in Fig. 7.2. The original working plot is made on 8½ by 11 inch cross-section paper with 1/20-th inch or one-millimeter squares, so that 1/20-th of an inch or one millimeter represents a graph distance of .01.

7.1.3 The Simple Structure

The effectively bounding hyperplanes (here planes) will meet the extended-vector plane in straight lines, whereas they would meet the hemisphere of Fig. 6.5 in great circles. The extended-vector projection preserves directions, but distances are stretched as we go out radially from the origin. Thus in Fig. 7.1 compare the distance $P'Q'$ on the plane with the corresponding great-circle distance on the unit circle. The unit circle where the hemisphere of Fig. 6.5 meets the "floor" would in fact be projected on the extended-vector plane as a circle of infinite radius, as would the equator on a polar-projection map.

From the plot of Fig. 7.2 we are to determine the three effectively bounding lines where the effectively bounding planes intersect the extended-vector plane. In doing so we must take account of the stretching of distances between points as we go farther away from the origin.

When we examine the plotted points of Fig. 7.2, the centroids of points 3 and 5, 9 and 11, and 2 and 6 appear to lie close to the effective corners of the configuration, and can be used to define the locations of the primary axes, where the projections of the effectively bounding planes intersect in pairs. From the F-matrix of Table 7.1, we have for these centroids:

Test	a	b	c
(3)	.698	−.085	−.262
(5)	.588	−.098	−.263
Σ	1.286	−.183	−.525
Ext	1	−.1423	−.4082 (PI)

Test	a	b	c
(9)	.730	.361	−.044
(11)	.615	.433	.075
Σ	1.345	.794	.031
Ext	1	.5903	.0230 (PII)

Test	a	b	c
(2)	.761	−.141	.249
(6)	.878	−.282	.134
Σ	1.639	−.423	.383
Ext	1	−.2581	.2337 (PIII)

The extensions are made directly from the sums. In making them, we take the reciprocals to five significant figures and compute the extended-vector coordinates to four decimals, to avoid unnecessary rounding error in later computations in which they are used, though only two decimals are used in plotting them.

These computed points $PI = -.1423$ and $-.4082$ (points 3 and 5), $PII = .5903$ and $.0230$ (points 9 and 11), and $PIII = -.2581$ and $.2337$ (points 2 and 6) are the primary axes; they are represented by squares in Fig. 7.2 to distinguish them from the test-vector points.

The pairs of points PI and PII, PI and $PIII$, and PII and $PIII$ are connected by lines on the plot. These lines are the projections of the effectively bounding planes $HIII$, HII, and HI, on the extended-vector plane. Note that each effectively bounding plane (line) lies *opposite* the primary axis having the same number (PI, PII, or $PIII$).

The plane HI is overdetermined by points 2, 6, 8, 9, 11, and possibly 10. The plane HII is overdetermined by points 3, 5, 1, 4, 6, and 2. The plane $HIII$ is overdetermined (less completely) by points 5, 3, 9, and 11. The origin contributes one more element of overdetermination to each of the three planes.

In Fig. 6.5 the planes are shown in perspective, intersecting the hemisphere in great circles. When we extend them (and the test vectors) upward to intersect the horizontal extended-vector plane tangent to the hemisphere at a, and look down from above on this extended-vector plane, we have the picture of Fig. 7.2. Vertical planes on the axes b and c of Fig. 6.5, intersecting each other in the axis a, intersect the extended-vector plane of Fig. 7.2 in the axes b and c. The vector terminus a of Fig. 6.5 is the origin 0 of Fig. 7.2.

We have now determined the locations of the effectively bounding planes, and the coordinates of the primary axes on the extended-vector plane. These latter are the coordinates of the three extended-vector centroids PI, PII, and $PIII$.

7.1.4 The Reference Vectors and the Transformed Factor Matrix

Let E' be an m by m matrix, the elements of whose row vectors are the coordinates of the primary axes on the extended-vector plane. If we normalize these vectors we obtain the corresponding unit vectors forming the matrix T': the transpose of the transformation matrix for the structure on the primary axes, as was shown in Section 6.3.2. Thus

$$\Delta E' = T', \tag{7-3}$$

where each diagonal element of Δ shortens the corresponding row vector of E' to unit length. But by (6-19)

$$(T')^{-1}D = \Lambda.$$

Substituting from (7-3)

$$(\Delta E')^{-1}D = \Lambda,$$

$$(E')^{-1}(\Delta^{-1}D) = \Lambda, \tag{7-4}$$

and because the columns of Λ are of unit length, the diagonal elements of $(\Delta^{-1}D)$ normalize the columns of $(E')^{-1}$ to give Λ.

For the WAIS data the computations are shown in the lower part of Table 7.1. In panel 0 we have E', with row vectors that are the coordinates of the extended primary-axis vectors obtained from the three centroids. E' is already a fairly well-conditioned matrix, and because its first column consists entirely of unities, the computations for panel 1 are simplified. As soon as we find $(E')^{-1}$, we normalize its columns to obtain Λ. Then $F\Lambda = V$, and V is recorded in the last three columns of the upper part of Table 7.1. The numbering of the rotated factors is arbitrary, depending on the arbitrary numbering of the primary axes and planes in Fig. 7.2.

It should be noted that the use of centroids to define the coordinates of the primary axes is possible only because there is a cluster of test vectors at each of the effective corners of the configuration. When one of these effective corners is not defined by either a cluster or a single test vector, it is necessary to draw in two of the lines by eye, and then to read from the plot the coordinates of their point of intersection to obtain the b and c elements of the corresponding row of E' (the first being unity). Each of these lines should be at an effective boundary of the configuration, and should be overdetermined by at least two points lying close to it, and usually more than two. It should be drawn so that about half of these points lie on one side of the line and about half on the other side, with the largest perpendicular distance of any one of them from the line a minimum, allowing slightly greater distances for points far from the origin.

Problem 7.1.4:1. Given the following artificial F-matrix (whose axes may not actually be orthogonal, but assume that they are):

Var	a	b	c
(1)	.60	−.06	−.12
(2)	.80	.08	−.16
(3)	.70	.14	−.14
(4)	.80	.24	.00
(5)	.60	.12	.06
(6)	.70	.07	.14
(7)	.80	−.16	.16
(8)	.60	−.18	.00

Form the extended-vector matrix and plot its b and c entries. Draw lines representing the hyperplanes, and find at their intersections the extended-vector coordinates of the primary factors $P\mathrm{I}$ (at bottom), $P\mathrm{II}$ (at top), and $P\mathrm{III}$ (at right), forming the matrix E'. Compute $(E')^{-1}$, Λ, and V, as in Table 7.1.

7.1.5 Interpretation

The subtests of the WAIS are as follows:

(1)   Information (mostly "what" questions)
(2)   Comprehension (mostly "why" questions)
(3)   Arithmetic (problems stated verbally)
(4)   Similarities (in what way are two objects alike?)
(5)   Digit Span (3-9 forward; 2-8 backward)
(6)   Vocabulary (tell meaning of word)
(7)   Digit Symbol (draw symbol according to key)
(8)   Picture Completion (name missing part)
(9)   Block Design (arrange blocks to duplicate design on card)
(10) Picture Arrangement (in order to tell a story)
(11) Object Assembly (form board)

In Table 7.1 loadings larger than $\pm .250$ are enclosed in parentheses to aid in interpretation.

Factor I, with highest loadings on 3 (Arithmetic) and 5 (Digit Span), is some sort of numerical or quantitative reasoning factor. The loading .215 on 1 (Information) may reflect the fact that some of the questions of this test call for numerical information.

Factor II, with substantial loadings on 8 (Picture Completion), 9 (Block Design), 10 (Picture Arrangement), and 11 (Object Assembly), is a non-verbal reasoning factor. If we add 7 (Digit Symbol), with loading .152, we have precisely the tests of Wechsler's Performance (nonverbal) Scale.

Factor III, with substantial loadings on 1 (Information), 2 (Comprehension), 4 (Similarities), and 6 (Vocabulary), is clearly the well-known verbal relations factor. Factors I and III taken together form Wechsler's Verbal Scale, but in our analysis Arithmetic and Digit Span separate from it entirely, and Information partially, to form the smaller numerical or quantitative factor.

The two tests with lowest communalities are 5 (Digit Span) and 7 (Digit Symbol). The former is a numerical memory test, and its numerical content permits it to have a substantial loading on Factor I (and no other). It is the only memory test in the battery, so there is no memory factor. Test 7 (Digit Symbol) is a coding or perceptual speed test; because there are no other tests of this type in the battery (and its numerical content for adults is essentially irrelevant to the task), it has no really substantial loading on any of the three rotated factors, though no one of its three loadings is near-zero.

Exercise 7.1. Columns *a*, *b*, and *c* of the factor matrix of Table 5.3 give the principal-axis loadings on the salient factors for the nine-aptitude-tests problem. Rotate this *F*-matrix to simple structure by the method of extended vectors, and interpret the factors in terms of the tests as described at the bottom of Table 5.3. Hint: Use two three-test centroids to locate two of the primary axes, and tests 4 and 6 (but not 5) to locate the third. Save the results.

7.2   VARIETIES OF SIMPLE STRUCTURE

In Chapter 6 we considered only the *criteria* of simple structure. But with the extended-vector plot we are able to visualize both overdetermination, effectively bounding hyperplanes, and the primary axes at their intersections, in the three-factor case; so we can now treat the concept of simple structure in more detail.

The criteria of simple structure define the overdetermined, essentially bounding planes or hyperplanes. In the rotated factor matrix V (the structure on the reference vectors) they specify the *near-zero* loadings. Thus each factor is *defined* by a subgroup of tests which do *not* measure it. The reference vectors are orthogonal to the hyperplanes defined by these near-zero loadings. The primary factors are the unit vectors at the intersections of the hyperplanes taken $m - 1$ at a time. From the V-matrix each factor is *interpreted* in terms of whatever is common to the variables that have high loadings on that factor. If the interpretation is correct and consistent, the variables that have low but not near-zero loadings on the factor should then be interpretable as being *somewhat* affected by that factor.

7.2.1 The Positive Manifold

The positive manifold of a vector space is the subregion within which any vector terminus will have all coordinates positive or near-zero. A V-matrix represents a positive-manifold solution if all loadings that are not near-zero are positive. In Fig. 6.5 the positive manifold is the subspace of the hemisphere which is bounded by the three planes.

If the axes are orthogonal, the positive manifold of a circle (in two-space) is a quadrant, that of a sphere (in three-space) is an octant, and so on. But if the axes are oblique, this is no longer the case. Thus in Fig. 6.1 the positive manifold of the oblique solution is the segment I 0 II that is very much less than a quadrant. I and II are the "hyperplanes" at the effective boundaries of the configuration, and RI and RII are the reference vectors orthogonal to I and II. The structure is highly acute, and the oblique factors correlate positively and substantially.

Figure 7.3 shows a contrasting structure. Here the "hyperplanes" are labeled I and II and the reference vectors RI and RII. The positive manifold is the segment I 0 II, which is considerably larger than a quadrant. Here the structure is obtuse (defined by the angle I 0 II), the reference vectors are *inside* the effective boundaries instead of outside as in Fig. 6.1, and the correlation between the primary factors is negative. In the three-factor case a similar situation would exist

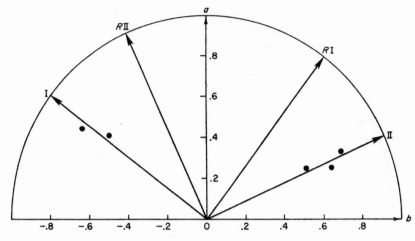

Fig. 7.3. Illustration of an obtuse simple structure.

if some or all of the angles between the primary axes (*P*I, *P*II, and *P*III in Fig. 6.5) were obtuse. Obtuse structures, however, are somewhat less common than acute structures, because for most types of data the primary factors tend to be positively correlated.

7.2.2 Bipolar Factors

A bipolar factor is any rotated factor that has one or more *negative nonzero* loadings in the column of *V* which represents it. There are two types of bipolarity. A test contributes a *nominal* bipolarity to at least one factor when its test-vector terminus lies below the "floor," that is, the hyperplane orthogonal to the first factor (*a*) of *F* (Fig. 6.5). It contributes an *intrinsic* bipolarity to at least one factor if it lies outside the subspace bounded by the hyperplanes.

Any nominal bipolarity is easily recognized, and corrected if this seems desirable. It is recognized by the fact that a test vector has a negative nonzero loading on the first factor of *F*. It is corrected by reflecting the test vector (reversing the signs of all elements in the given row of *F*) *and* reversing the scale and the name of the test, so that, for example, a "typing proficiency" test becomes a "typing deficiency" test. An intrinsic bipolarity can be recognized only in *V*, and it cannot be corrected.

Figure 7.4 illustrates nominal and intrinsic bipolarity in the two-factor case, and Table 7.2 shows two *F*-matrices, the Λ-matrix, and two *V*-matrices for these artificial data. In Fig. 7.4, *a* and *b* are the unrotated *F*-axes, *H*I and *H*II are the oblique "hyperplanes" (here lines) of the simple structure, and *R*I and *R*II are the corresponding reference vectors. There are eleven numbered test vectors. *H*I goes through the centroid of test vectors 4, 5, 6, and 7, and the coordinates of its

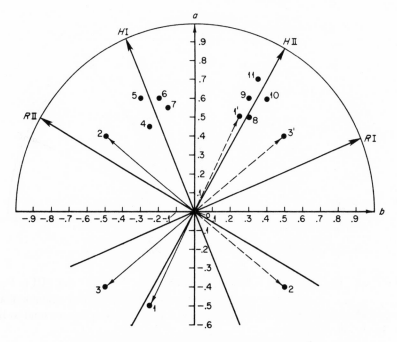

Fig. 7.4. Illustration of bipolar factors: Two-factor case.

unit vector (on the semicircle) are $(Ia) = .926, (Ib) = -.379$. HII goes through the centroid of test vectors 8, 9, 10, and 11, and the coordinates of its unit vector (also on the semicircle) are $(IIa) = .871, (IIb) = .490$. From the coordinates of HI and HII, by the oblique case of Fig. 2.2, we derive the Λ of Table 7.2.

Matrix F of Table 7.2 comes directly from the coordinates of the eleven test-vector termini (the numbered points in Fig. 7.4). The actual test vectors are drawn in only for points 1, 2, and 3. From the F-matrix of Table 7.2, we see at once that there are two nominal bipolarities: the a-loadings of variables 1 and 3 are negative and nonzero. In $V = F\Lambda$ (Table 7.2), variables 1 and 3 have negative nonzero loadings on factor I. In this matrix, variable 2 also has a negative nonzero loading on factor I, so we conclude that this variable contributes an intrinsic bipolarity to factor I, because its a-factor loading in F is positive.

Going back to Fig. 7.4, it is seen that the test vectors for variables 1 and 3 lie below the b-axis (the "hyperplane" orthogonal to the a-axis). This implies that these test vectors will contribute nominal bipolarities to one of the factors of V, as we have seen that they do (here to factor I). When we reflect variable 1, it goes to the position $1'$, with its test vector shown as a dashed line to indicate that it has been reflected. It now joins the 8, 9, 10, 11 cluster, and increases by one the overdetermination of HII.

TABLE 7.2
F, Λ, and V Matrices Illustrating Bipolar Factors: Two-Factor Case

	F			F_r				
Var	a	b	Var	a	b	Var	a	b
(1)	−.50	−.25	(1′)	.50	.25			
(2)	.40	−.50	(2)	.40	−.50	(2′)	−.40	.50
(3)	−.40	−.50	(3′)	.40	.50			
(4)	.45	−.25	(4)	.45	−.25			
(5)	.60	−.30	(5)	.60	−.30			
(6)	.60	−.20	(6)	.60	−.20			
(7)	.55	−.15	(7)	.55	−.15			
(8)	.50	.30	(8)	.50	.30			
(9)	.60	.30	(9)	.60	.30			
(10)	.60	.40	(10)	.60	.40			
(11)	.70	.35	(11)	.70	.35			

	Λ	
	I	II
a	.379	.490
b	.926	−.871

	$V = F\Lambda$			$V_r = F_r\Lambda$				
Var	I	II	Var	I	II	Var	I	II
(1)	−.421	−.027	(1′)	.421	.027			
(2)	−.311	.632	(2)	−.311	.632	(2′)	.311	−.632
(3)	−.615	.240	(3′)	.615	−.240			
(4)	−.061	.438	(4)	−.061	.438			
(5)	−.050	.555	(5)	−.050	.555			
(6)	.042	.468	(6)	.042	.468			
(7)	.070	.400	(7)	.070	.400			
(8)	.467	−.016	(8)	.467	−.016			
(9)	.505	.033	(9)	.505	.033			
(10)	.598	−.054	(10)	.598	−.054			
(11)	.589	.038	(11)	.589	.038			

The test vector of variable 3 is intrinsically as well as nominally bipolar. It lies not only below the b-axis, but also outside the subspace bounded by the downward extensions of the "hyperplanes" HI and HII. When it is reflected to the position 3′, removing the nominal bipolarity by placing its terminus above the b-axis (the "hyperplane" orthogonal to the a-axis), its intrinsic bipolarity remains. The vector terminus 3′ lies outside the subspace HI 0 HII bounded by the "hyperplanes."

The test vector of variable 2 is intrinsically bipolar, but not nominally bipolar. Its terminus lies above the b-axis (the "hyperplane" orthogonal to the a-axis), but outside the subspace HI 0 HII bounded by the "hyperplanes."

The matrix F_r is the F-matrix with variables 1 and 3 reflected to remove their nominal bipolarities. All a-factor loadings are now positive. If these reflections had been made before plotting, the centroid from which HII was plotted would have included the test vector 1' along with 8, 9, 10, and 11; the second column of Λ would have been .483, $-$.876 instead of .490, $-$.871; and the difference in the location of the vector 0HII would have been hardly visible in Fig. 7.4. In $V_r = F_r\Lambda$ variable 2 now contributes an intrinsic bipolarity to Factor I, and variable 3' contributes an intrinsic bipolarity to factor II. If after rotation we rereflect the nominally bipolar variables 1 and 3 (in order, say, to retain their original scale directions and names), V_r becomes precisely V, as may be seen in Table 7.2.

At the right of Table 7.2, in rows (2') of F_r and V_r, we show the effect of trying to remove the intrinsic bipolarity of variable 2 by reflection. The bipolarity in V_r is transferred from factor I to factor II, and, as may be seen in Fig. 7.4, the vector 2' is now nominally as well as intrinsically bipolar.

To remove the intrinsic bipolarity of test 2, we would have to move HI to coincide approximately (or exactly) with test vector 2. Then RI would lie between HII and test vector 3', and the projections of all the test vector termini except 2 would be nonzero, destroying the overdetermination of factor I. Similarly to remove the intrinsic bipolarity of test 3, we would have to move HII to coincide (approximately or exactly) with test vector 3', and this would destroy the overdetermination of factor II (HII).

Nominal bipolarity has been seen in the two-factor solution of the seven reasoning and perseveration tests, in which variables 6 and 7 were reflected in finding the centroid F. If we rereflect variables 6 and 7 in the rotated factor matrix of Table 2.10, we obtain

Variable	I	II
(1) Critical Flicker Frequency	$-$.080	.478
(2) Digital Symbol (WAIS)	.403	.324
(3) Porteus Maze	.314	.237
(4) Thurstone PMA Reasoning (untimed)	.707	$-$.021
(5) Raven Progressive Matrices	.645	.020
(6) Wisconsin Card Sorting (perseverative errors)	.023	$-$.714
(7) Age	$-$.103	$-$.234

Factor I is still reasoning, and factor II is still nonperseveration. But Wisconsin Card Sorting and Age now have substantial negative loadings on factor II. The only gain in interpretation (if any) is that the original scales of Wisconsin Card Sorting and Age are restored. In this situation we might be inclined to reverse *all* the signs in factor II, and relabel this factor perseveration instead of nonperseveration. Reflecting a *factor* is *always* permissible: this merely represents a reversal or a 180-degree rotation of the corresponding axis. Wisconsin Card Sorting, the best perseveration test, would now have a positive loading. We would conclude that perseveration increases with age, and that the Critical Flicker Frequency score, the Digit Symbol score, and the Porteus Maze score tend to indicate resistance to perseveration.

For a further illustration we rotate by the extended-vector method the *three-factor* solution of the seven reasoning and perseveration tests. The F-matrix is that of Table 2.12, with variables 6 and 7 already reflected to eliminate nominal bipolarities. The computations are shown in Table 7.3 and the extended-vector plot in Fig. 7.5. Each plane is barely overdetermined by three points. We pass HIII through point 1 in such a manner that points 2 and 4 are about equidistant from it. HII is a rough fit ("by eye") to points 1, 6, and 7, somewhat closer to points 1 and 7 on one side than to the single point 6 on the other side. HI is about equidistant from points 4, 3, and 7. The coordinates of PI, PII, and PIII for the E'-matrix are merely read from the plot.

Point 5 contributes an intrinsic bipolarity to factor I, lying outside the subspace bounded by the lines HI, HII, and HIII. If we had moved HI far enough away from the origin to try to include point 5 as a near-zero (see dashed line in Fig. 7.5), all four of these points (4, 5, 3, 7) would be too far from it to be acceptable near-zeroes.

Writing the V-factor names and loadings with the names of variables 6 and 7 reversed, we have

	Variable	I	II	III
(1)	Critical Flicker Frequency	.543	−.012	.004
(2)	Digit Symbol	.214	.478	.058
(3)	Porteus Maze	.004	.315	.226
(4)	Thurstone PMA Reasoning[a]	−.026	.715	−.059
(5)	Raven Progressive Matrices	−.299	.568	.298
−(6)	Wisconsin Card Sorting[b]	.335	.045	.353
−(7)	Youngness	−.013	−.003	.371

[a] Untimed
[b] Avoidance of perseverative errors

Factor I is nonperseveration, but its highest loading is now on variable 1 (Critical Flicker Frequency), with 6 (Wisconsin Card Sorting) second. The loading −.299 on 5 (Raven Progressive Matrices) makes this factor intrinsically bipolar. Variable 3 (Porteus Maze) now has a near-zero loading, but variable 2 (Digit Symbol) still has a nonzero loading.

TABLE 7.3
Extended-Vector Rotation for Seven Reasoning and Perseveration Tests
(N = 86)

Var	Centroid F				F-Extended			Rotated V = FΛ		
	a	b	c	h²	a	b	c	I	II	III
(1)	.443	−.374	−.317	.437	1	−.84	−.72	.543	−.012	.004
(2)	.792	.057	−.192	.667	1	.07	−.24	.214	.478	.058
(3)	.609	.051	.063	.377	1	.08	.10	.004	.315	.226
(4)	.738	.380	−.167	.717	1	.51	−.23	−.026	.715	−.059
(5)	.725	.345	.232	.698	1	.48	.32	−.299	.568	.298
−(6)	.711	−.353	−.003	.630	1	−.50	.00	.335	.045	.353
−(7)	.384	−.148	.224	.220	1	−.39	.58	−.013	−.003	.371
Σ	4.402	−.042	−.160	3.746		Σ		.758	2.106	1.251
Σf²	2.918	.556	.273	3.747		Ch		.757	2.105	1.250

Panel	Eq	Variable			Variable			Σ + 1	Ch
		(1)	(2)	(3)	(1)	(2)	(3)		
0	(1)	(1)	−.81	−.71				.48	
	(2)	1	.41	−.18	= E'			2.23	
	(3)	1	−.39	.54				2.15	
1	(2)	(1.22)	.53		−1.00			1.75	1.75
	(3)		.42	1.25	−1.00			1.67	1.67
	(1)		−.81	−.71	1.00			.48	.48
2	(3)			(1.0676)	−.6557	−.3443		1.0676	1.0676
	(1)			−.3581	.3360	.6640		1.6419	1.6419
	(2)			.4344	−.8197	.8197		1.4344	1.4344
3	(1)				.1161	.5485	.3354	2.0000	2.0000
	(2)		(E')⁻¹ =		−.5529	.9598	−.4069	1.0000	1.0000
	(3)				−.6142	−.3225	.9367	1.0000	1.0000
	Σ²				.6964	1.3261	1.1555		
	√Σ²				.8345	1.1516	1.0749		
	1/√Σ²				1.1983	.8684	.9303	= diag (Δ⁻¹D)	
	Λ =				.139	.476	.312		
					−.663	.833	−.379		
					−.736	−.280	.871		
	Σ² =				1.001	.999	1.000		

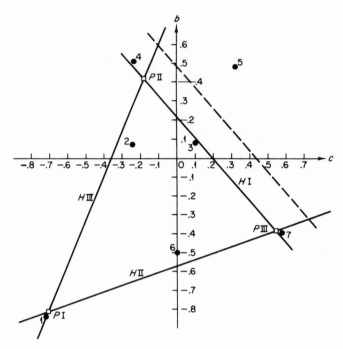

Fig. 7.5. Extended-vector plot for seven reasoning and perseveration tests ($N =$ 86).

Factor II is the reasoning factor, with loadings not too greatly different from those of factor I of the two-variable solution.

Factor III is youngness (age with scale reversed). Variable 6 (Wisconsin Card Sorting) has had a considerable part of its common variance "drained away" from the nonperseveration factor because of its correlation with -7 (Youngness). Variable 3 (Porteus Maze) has a substantial loading. From its near-zero loading on factor I, we conclude that its substantial loading on the corresponding factor II of the two-factor solution was due to its correlation with youngness. Variable 5 (Raven Progressive Matrices) has a substantial loading also. Its near-zero loading on factor II of the two-factor solution suggests that its negative correlation with nonperseveration and its positive correlation with youngness have cancelled each other in factor II of the two-factor solution.

Remembering that the third factor of F may represent some over-factoring (Section 2.6.1), this three-factor rotation illustrates what has been termed *factor fission,* which is a not-too-uncommon effect when over-factored F-matrices are rotated. Here inclusion of the youngness factor has split the nonperseveration factor into two factors. The nonperseveration factor is blurred in the three-factor rotation, and the inclusion of age as a separate factor does little to clarify the situation; though as we have just seen, the comparison of the *two* solutions does shed some light on the relationships. For the basic problem of the analysis, the two-factor solution is somewhat the clearer.

7.2.3 Types of Simple Structure

We have already encountered two of the main types of simple structure (paragraphs 1 and 2 below).

1. *Primary cluster structure.* There is a cluster at each corner of the configuration, with or without other points along the hyperplanes, and perhaps a very few in the interior. The WAIS subtests (Fig. 7.2) and the nine psychological tests are examples. In the two-factor case there are two outer clusters, with or without other points lying close to the a-axis. The five verbal tests and the exercise of six psychological tests are examples. A variant of this structure includes one or more nominally bipolar factors with test vectors below the "floor," but which fall either in the clusters or along the hyperplanes or occasionally inside the subspace bounded by the hyperplanes, when they are reflected. There may also be one or a very few outside of this subspace (before or after reflection), contributing intrinsic bipolarities.

2. *Complete linear structure.* Most of the points lie close to the hyperplanes, with a single point near each corner of the configuration. A variant includes one or more nominally bipolar factors with test vectors below the "floor," but which after reflection fall along the hyperplanes or possibly inside the subspace bounded by the hyperplanes. There may again be one or a very few that lie outside of this subspace (before or after reflection). The three-factor rotation of the seven reasoning and perseveration tests furnishes an example (see Fig. 7.5). Tests 6 and 7 contribute nominal bipolarities if we rereflect them after rotation to preserve the original scale directions, and test 5 contributes an intrinsic bipolarity to factor I. Note that a nominal bipolarity affects *all* factors on which the test has

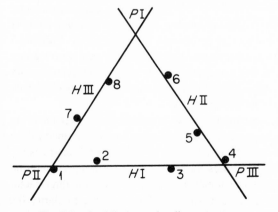

	I	II	III
(1)	0	+ +	0
(2)	0	+	+
(3)	0	+	+
(4)	0	0	+ +
(5)	+	0	+
(6)	+	0	+
(7)	+	+	0
(8)	+	+	0

Fig. 7.6.   Partially incomplete linear structure.

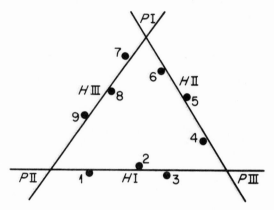

	I	II	III
(1)	0	+	+
(2)	0	+	+
(3)	0	+	+
(4)	+	0	+
(5)	+	0	+
(6)	+	0	+
(7)	+	+	0
(8)	+	+	0
(9)	+	+	0

Fig. 7.7. Entirely incomplete linear structure.

nonzero loadings: *all* signs in the corresponding row of V are reversed. If test 5 (Raven Progressive Matrices) had been scored number wrong instead of number right, it would have contributed both nominal and intrinsic bipolarity. It would have been reflected to yield row 5 of Table 7.3, and rereflection of this row of V would then make factor I all positive and factors II and III intrinsically as well as nominally bipolar.

3. *Incomplete linear structure.* Figure 7.6 illustrates a partially incomplete linear structure, with no test vector close to primary axis PI, and Fig. 7.7 illustrates an entirely incomplete linear structure, with no test vector close to any of the primary axes. In the V-factor patterns accompanying the extended-vector figures, a 0 designates a near-zero loading, a + designates a positive nonzero loading, and a ++ designates the high positive nonzero loading of a test vector close to the primary axis opposite a hyperplane.

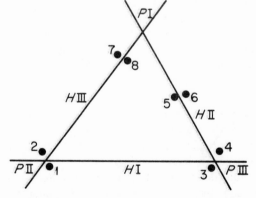

	I	II	III
(1)	0	+ +	0
(2)	0	+ +	0
(3)	0	0	+ +
(4)	0	0	+ +
(5)	+	0	+
(6)	+	0	+
(7)	+	+	0
(8)	+	+	0

Fig. 7.8. Incomplete nonprimary cluster structure.

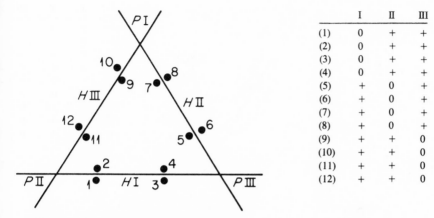

	I	II	III
(1)	0	+	+
(2)	0	+	+
(3)	0	+	+
(4)	0	+	+
(5)	+	0	+
(6)	+	0	+
(7)	+	0	+
(8)	+	0	+
(9)	+	+	0
(10)	+	+	0
(11)	+	+	0
(12)	+	+	0

Fig. 7.9. Complete nonprimary cluster structure.

4. *Nonprimary cluster structure.* Figure 7.8 illustrates an incomplete non-primary cluster structure. There are two clusters on primary axes and two more not on primary axes. Figure 7.9 illustrates a complete nonprimary cluster structure, with no clusters on the primary axes but two along each hyperplane.

It is evident from these figures that various combinations of clusters, isolated points, and linear streaks of points along the hyperplanes may occur.

Figure 7.10 shows a case that may cause trouble when computer rotation systems based on overdetermination alone are employed, neglecting condition 2 of Section 6.2 for which 2c says that the hyperplanes should lie at the *effective boundaries* of the configuration of test vectors in the common-factor space. In Fig. 7.10 the primary axes are clearly PI, PII, and $PIII$, and each bounding hyperplane is overdetermined by *five* points, leading to the structure whose columns are labeled I, II, and III. The dashed lines, however, designate non-bounding hyperplanes, each overdetermined by *six* points. Mechanical hyperplane fitting guided by overdetermination alone may yield these hyperplanes, with the incorrect primary axes labeled A, B, and C. In the A, B, C factor pattern, all three factors are intrinsically bipolar, the minus sign in each column indicating a *negative* nonzero loading. Figure 7.9 might also give rise to a situation of this type.

In all of the cases represented by these figures and the ones that follow, there may have been nominal bipolarities that were resolved by reflection before rotation, with or without rereflection after rotation.

5. *Perfect intrinsic bipolar simple structure.* In Fig. 7.5 and in the A, B, C structure of Fig. 7.10, the intrinsically bipolar points were not on the hyperplanes. A perfect simple structure (defined as a structure in which every test vector is close to a hyperplane), however, may still be intrinsically bipolar. Figure 7.11 shows such a case, and incidentally illustrates a mixed cluster-linear

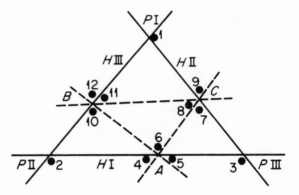

Fig. 7.10.   Nonprimary cluster structure with primary points.

	I	II	III	A	B	C
(1)	++	0	0	−	+	+
(2)	0	++	0	+	+	−
(3)	0	0	++	+	−	+
(4)	0	+	+	++	0	0
(5)	0	+	+	++	0	0
(6)	0	+	+	++	0	0
(7)	+	0	+	0	0	++
(8)	+	0	+	0	0	++
(9)	+	0	+	0	0	++
(10)	+	+	0	0	++	0
(11)	+	+	0	0	++	0
(12)	+	+	0	0	++	0

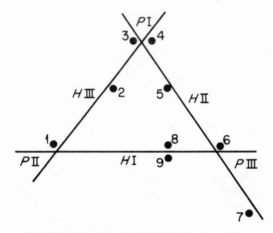

	I	II	III
(1)	0	++	0
(2)	+	+	0
(3)	++	0	0
(4)	++	0	0
(5)	+	0	+
(6)	0	0	++
(7)	−	0	+
(8)	0	+	+
(9)	0	+	+

Fig. 7.11.   Perfect intrinsic bipolar simple structure.

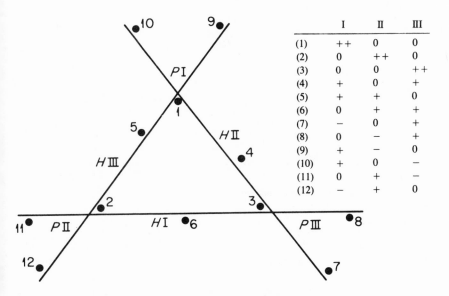

	I	II	III
(1)	++	0	0
(2)	0	++	0
(3)	0	0	++
(4)	+	0	+
(5)	+	+	0
(6)	0	+	+
(7)	−	0	+
(8)	0	−	+
(9)	+	−	0
(10)	+	0	−
(11)	0	+	−
(12)	−	+	0

Fig. 7.12. Perfect extreme intrinsic bipolar simple structure.

structure. Point 7 lies on the *H*II plane (which runs from primary axis *P*I to primary axis *P*III), but is outside the subspace bounded by the three planes. The plane *H*I, running from axis *P*II to axis *P*III, must be where it is to preserve over-determination. If we ran it from point 1 to point 7 in order to keep it strictly at the boundary of the configuration, overdetermination would be lost. In the most extreme case, represented by Fig. 7.12, every plane has an intrinsically bipolar point at each end.

6. *Incomplete simple structure.* Figure 7.13 shows an incomplete simple structure, with *H*I (running from axis *P*II to axis *P*III) not overdetermined. In a

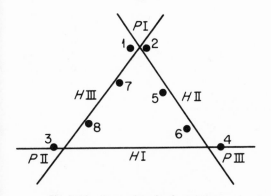

	I	II	III
(1)	++	0	0
(2)	++	0	0
(3)	0	++	0
(4)	0	0	++
(5)	+	0	+
(6)	+	0	+
(7)	+	+	0
(8)	+	+	0

Fig. 7.13. Incomplete simple structure.

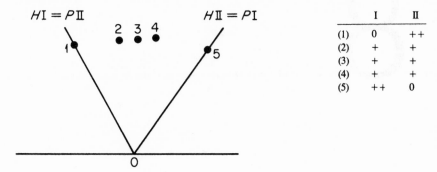

Fig. 7.14. Two-factor incomplete simple structure.

case as clear as this, bridging the two extreme points, 3 and 4, usually gives a satisfactory solution. In the analogous two-factor case of Fig. 7.14, either or both "hyperplanes" (here lines) may pass from the origin through a single outer point rather than a cluster.

7. *Nonsimple structure.* The commonest case in which a factor analysis breaks down is the one in which the number of tests of each type is insufficient, leading to nonuniqueness of communalities ($m > n/2$) and factors too many of which are doublets. There is another case, which, though rare, does occur occasionally. This case is illustrated in its simplest form in Fig. 7.15. We have four clusters, essentially at the corners of a rectangle, in a three-dimensional space, and we cannot rotate three axes into four clusters. The solution in this case is usually to refactor to four (or in general $m + 1$) factors, even though the last factor fails the salience and significance tests, and then rotate the four (or $m + 1$) factors.

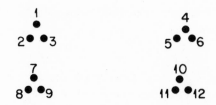

Fig. 7.15. Nonsimple structure.

8

Orthogonal Transformations

When there are more than three factors, and even when there are only three but the number of variables is fairly large, transformations based on rotation of axes will usually be carried out on an electronic computer. In this case it is usually convenient to start with an orthogonal approximation to simple structure, and then to transform this orthogonal approximation into an oblique simple structure. The first procedure yields

$$F\Lambda_0 = V_0,$$

with Λ_0 constrained to be orthonormal and V_0 the orthogonal approximation. The second procedure then gives

$$V_0 B = F\Lambda_0 B = F\Lambda_p = V_p,$$

where B and $\Lambda_0 B = \Lambda_p$ are *not* orthonormal, and V_p is an oblique reference-vector structure. Still further procedures are often used to refine V_p into the final optimum oblique simple structure V. In this chapter we deal only with the initial orthogonal transformation.

8.1 VARIMAX ORTHOGONAL TRANSFORMATIONS

Restriction to orthogonality is not serious if V_0 is fairly close to the best possible orthogonal approximation to oblique simple structure, and if there are good methods for transforming V_0 into the oblique simple-structure factor matrix V_p.

But in the usual procedures for orthogonal transformation, a less-than-optimal criterion of simple structure is employed to permit this criterion to be expressed analytically and hence computed automatically. In consequence, V_0 itself will be only an approximation to the best possible orthogonal approximation to simple structure.

First we must agree to let overdetermination be the sole criterion of simple structure, neglecting the criterion that the hyperplanes must lie at the effective boundaries of the configuration of the test vectors in the common-factor space. This restriction is serious only in relatively rare cases such as those illustrated in Fig. 7.9 and Fig. 7.11. But because a machine cannot readily be programmed to distinguish between variables having near-zero loadings and variables having substantial loadings on a factor before these loadings are computed (as can a factor analyst when he examines a plot), we must modify the definition of overdetermination.

We note first that in an overdetermined simple-structure V-matrix, unlike say an F-matrix, every factor has several (at least m) near-zero loadings, usually but not necessarily some low nonzero loadings, and at least a few high or fairly high loadings, some of which *may* be negative. In other words, the *dispersion* of the *absolute values* of the loadings will be fairly high in every column of V_0, and the dispersion of the *squares* of these loadings will be *relatively* higher still (relative to their mean values). This suggests that we might approximate simple structure by some procedure which maximizes the *variance* of the *squared* loadings in each column of V_0. When we apply this criterion to the columns of V_0 itself, we have the *raw varimax* criterion (Kaiser, 1958).

Kaiser goes one step further. First he notes that the raw varimax transformation gives not too infrequently one almost-general factor in V_0, though the loadings on this factor will still have considerably greater dispersion than do those of the first factor of F. The other factors are appreciably smaller. The raw varimax transformation does not distribute the total variance of the elements of V_0 very well over the factors. So instead of maximizing the variances of the squared loadings of the columns of V_0, he maximizes the variances of the squared loadings of the columns of U_0, where the test vectors of U_0 are those of V_0 *normalized*, that is, $u_{0ik} = v_{0ik}/h_i$; $i = 1, 2, \ldots, n$ (tests or variables); $k = 1, 2, \ldots, m$ (factors), and h_i is the length of the i-th test vector before normalization or the square root of the communality of test i. This is done most conveniently by normalizing the test vectors (rows) of F to yield F_n (F row-normalized) with elements $f_{nik} = f_{ik}/h_i$. The varimax transformation is applied to F_n, yielding U_0; and the rows of U_0 are then *denormalized* to obtain V_0 ($v_{0ik} = h_i u_{0ik}$). This amounts to considering only the *directions* of the test vectors in the common-factor space and ignoring their lengths, because normalizing stretches them all to unit length. This procedure is termed the *normal varimax* transformation.

The normal varimax transformation distributes the total variance more evenly over the rotated factors than does the raw varimax transformation, avoiding the development of an almost-general factor, and giving usually a fairly good orthogonal approximation to simple structure. Kaiser shows also that, if the test vectors form a primary cluster structure (Section 7.2.3, Paragraph 1), the fit of the orthogonal structure is invariant under changes in the *numbers* of test vectors in the outer clusters. This explains in part why an almost-general factor does not appear. With the raw varimax rotation, which does not have this property, any outer cluster having several more test vectors than any of the others tends to become such an almost-general factor. The normal varimax rotation, however, still tends to fit the hyperplanes more closely to those outer clusters that are farthest from the center of the whole configuration, that is, in most cases from the first principal axis or the first centroid axis of F.

The criterion equation for the normal varimax rotation is

$$Q = \sum_{k=1}^{m} \left[\frac{\sum_{i=1}^{n} (u_{Oik}^2)^2}{n} - \left(\frac{\sum_{i=1}^{n} u_{Oik}^2}{n} \right)^2 \right] = max. \tag{8-1}$$

The expression in brackets is the usual formula for a variance: here the variance of the squared loadings in one column of the row-normal transformed factor matrix U_0. To obtain Q we sum the m column variances. The criterion $Q = max$ means that we form U_0 from the unrotated row-normal F_n by an orthogonal rotation of the axes in such a manner as to make Q as large as possible.

The mathematical and computational details of the normal varimax rotation are beyond the scope of this treatment. The usual procedure is iterative. Axes are rotated two at a time in such a manner as to maximize Q for the pair of columns at each iteration. At the first cycle the pairs of columns are rotated in the order 1-2, 1-3, . . . , 1-m; 2-3, 2-4, . . . , 2-m; . . . ; $(m - 1)$-m. The process continues through successive cycles until, at the last cycle, no one of the pairwise rotations is greater than one-fourth of one degree, or for greater accuracy one minute.

Table 8.1 shows the results of a normal-varimax rotation of the nine-aptitude-tests problem. The principal-axes factoring was first repeated once, using as estimated communalities the h_3^2 values computed in Table 5.3.

The F-matrix loadings and final communalities are not very different from those of Table 5.3. Refactoring with revised communality estimates has resulted in only a slight improvement of the F-matrix. In addition to the V_0 matrix we show also an oblique simple-structure factor matrix V, derived from V_0 by the Promax method, which is discussed in Chapter 9. Note that although the normal-varimax loadings are all larger than the corresponding Promax loadings because the oblique structure is acute, the rank orders of the nonzero loadings in

TABLE 8.1
Normal-Varimax Rotation for Nine Aptitude Tests ($N = 504$)

Test	Principal Axes F				Normal Varimax V_0			Promax V		
	a	b	c	h^2	A	B	C	I	II	III
(1)	.648	−.193	−.320	.559	.301	.222	.648	−.042	.021	.491
(2)	.639	−.011	−.286	.491	.425	.137	.540	.133	−.051	.414
(3)	.619	−.112	−.251	.459	.343	.207	.546	.038	.026	.400
(4)	.820	−.276	.195	.787	.402	.692	.381	.013	.525	.061
(5)	.738	−.206	.041	.589	.382	.511	.427	.030	.342	.173
(6)	.764	−.305	.308	.771	.349	.755	.281	−.014	.616	−.051
(7)	.696	.491	−.008	.725	.837	.061	.143	.667	−.080	.044
(8)	.658	.433	.077	.626	.776	.131	.086	.614	.008	−.031
(9)	.642	.291	.117	.511	.668	.230	.108	.482	.112	−.039

corresponding columns are almost the same. Thus in both V_0 and V the highest loadings are on variables 7, 8, and 9 for factors A and I, on 4, 5, and 6 for factors B and II, and on 1, 2, and 3 for factors C and III. Thus we could name the factors, given the variable names, from the orthogonal rotation V_0. But from V_0 it would be impossible to deduce that variable 4 has a near-zero loading on factor I, or that variable 5 has a nonzero loading on factor III. In the normal-varimax factor matrix the near-zeros are not clearly distinguished from the low nonzeros, and the excellence of fit of the simple structure is not apparent.

It may be of some interest, especially after reading the section on the Promax rotation, to compare the Promax factor matrix of Table 8.1 with the extended-vector factor matrix of Exercise 7.1. Note that in Table 8.1, factors I and III correspond to factors III and I, respectively, of Exercise 7.1. By the normal-varimax procedure and the Promax procedure based on it, the rotated factors come out in a different order, which is quite irrelevant to the solution of the problem.

8.2   DIFFICULTIES WITH THE NORMAL-VARIMAX TRANSFORMATION

There are two situations, both relatively rare with real data, in which the normal-varimax procedure fails to arrive at an orthogonal approximation to the oblique simple structure. The first is the situation in which there is a cluster of several test vectors near the middle of each hyperplane, with only one or two test vectors near each primary axis. This situation is illustrated schematically in Fig. 7.10 and discussed briefly in Section 7.2.3, Paragraph 4. An illustration based on actual though artificial data is given in Table 8.2.

TABLE 8.2
Box Problem with Nonbounding Normal-Varimax Hyperplanes

Var		*Principal Axes F*			*Oblique V*			*Varimax V_0*		
		a	b	c	I	II	III	A	B	C
(1)	x	.618	.012	.766	.933	.000	.000	−.205	.817	.509
(2)	y	.744	.563	−.288	.000	.888	.000	.507	−.089	.830
(3)	z	.782	−.521	−.278	.000	.000	.887	.824	.532	−.002
(4)	xy	.851	.410	.283	.569	.603	−.035	.186	.417	.874
(5)	xy^2	.847	.489	.014	.317	.763	−.002	.363	.200	.885
(6)	$2x + 2y$	.838	.475	.207	.495	.678	−.066	.218	.326	.904
(7)	$\sqrt{x^2 + y^2}$	.834	.462	.191	.478	.671	−.051	.230	.321	.888
(8)	xz	.878	−.368	.280	.560	−.031	.605	.420	.856	.275
(9)	xz^2	.863	−.481	.103	.386	−.068	.753	.575	.797	.145
(10)	$2x + 2z$	.868	−.411	.258	.535	−.063	.643	.444	.860	.230
(11)	$\sqrt{x^2 + z^2}$	.851	−.411	.231	.504	−.061	.645	.453	.834	.216
(12)	yz	.911	.002	−.396	−.055	.532	.569	.844	.240	.466
(13)	yz^2	.895	−.183	−.377	−.047	.364	.704	.872	.345	.313
(14)	$2y + 2z$	.918	.013	−.386	−.043	.540	.560	.838	.244	.480
(15)	$\sqrt{y^2 + z^2}$	.908	.034	−.362	−.023	.545	.530	.809	.242	.495

Note. Computed from portions of the correlation matrix, Table 1, p. 370, Thurstone, 1947. Copyright 1947 by The University of Chicago. Used by permission.

Thurstone (1947)[1] measured the dimensions x, y, and z of a random collection of 30 boxes. Thus x, y, and z are the physical factors, corresponding to the length, width, and height of each box. He next devised a set of 26 variables consisting of functions of these measurements. A subset of these variables is shown in column Var of Table 8.2. For the dimensions x and y, xy is the area of the side x by y; xy^2 is the volume of a hypothetical box erected on the side x by y with height y; $2x + 2y$ is the perimeter of the side x by y; and $\sqrt{x^2 + y^2}$ is the diagonal of the side x by y. Similar variables are included for the sides x by z and y by z. Thurstone then reduced the 30 "scores" on each variable to normalized standard scores and computed the intercorrelations. For this subset of 15 variables (Thurstone actually used 26), the writers factored the intercorrelations twice by the principal-axes method, the first time with communality estimates all 1.000, and the second time with communality estimates computed from the first three factors of the first factoring. The result was the principal-axes factor matrix F of Table 8.2, columns a, b, and c.

---

[1]This paragraph condensed from p. 369, Thurstone, 1947. Copyright 1947 by The University of Chicago. Paraphrased by permission.

In columns I, II, and III of Table 8.2, we have an oblique simple-structure rotation (the reference-vector structure). The first three variables, x, y and z, are the actual (physical) primary factors. The rows of F are the coordinates of the variables on the F-axes, so the first three rows of F are the F-coordinates of the primary factors. But in Section 6.3.2, just below (6-18), it was shown that T is the matrix whose unit *column* vectors are the coordinates of the primary factors, so the first three rows of F should form the matrix T'. The first three rows of F are in fact the coordinates of vectors of lengths a little less than unity because most of the other variables are nonlinear functions of x, y, and z, leading to communalities a little less than unity. But these rows do form an E' matrix, with row-vectors collinear with the primary axes. Then by (7-4)

$$\Lambda = (E')^{-1}(\Delta^{-1}D),$$

where $(\Delta^{-1}D)$ is the diagonal matrix which normalizes the columns of $(E')^{-1}$, and $F\Lambda = V$. The oblique matrix V of Table 8.2, with columns I, II, and III, was formed in this manner. The near-zeros in each column, other than those in the first three rows, are all negative because those in the first three rows were forced to be eactly .000 by the method used in constructing Λ, and because the variables are nonlinear combinations of the factors.

Applying Kaiser's iterative algorithm for the normal-varimax rotation, we obtain the solution of matrix V_0, with columns A, B, and C. In each column, four of the five high loadings are on the variables that have near-zero loadings in the corresponding column of the oblique V. The fifth is on one of the primary factors but *not* the one that has a high loading in V, and the physical primary factor of each column has a low negative loading. If this varimax solution were "closed up" to an oblique solution, the primary axes would lie close to the three cluster centroid vectors; each plane would be overdetermined by 8 near-zeros (4 from each of two clusters); and variables x, y, and z (or 1, 2, and 3 in Table 8.2) would each have one fairly large negative loading.

These relations can be seen in the extended-vector picture of Fig. 8.1. The projections of the simple-structure planes are shown by the solid lines passing exactly through the primary axes: points 1, 2, and 3. The other points near each plane are outside the triangle and indicate negative near-zero loadings. The dotted lines show approximately the projections of the normal varimax planes. The figure is not large enough to show the whole triangle formed by these projections. If the planes were "closed up" into an oblique (acute) structure, they would reach positions not too far from those of the dashed lines passing through the centroids of the three clusters. The varimax algorithm behaves in this fashion because the nonbounding planes (dashed lines) are more heavily over-determined, each with eight near-zeros, than are the effectively bounding planes (solid lines), each with only six near-zeros. With large clusters not close to the primary axes, the criterion of overdetermination alone is insufficient to arrive at orthogonal planes roughly parallel to the effectively bounding planes.

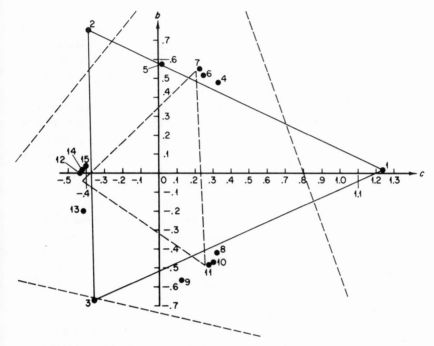

Fig. 8.1. Extended-vector plot for the box problem, with nonbounding normal-varimax hyperplanes.

The second situation is one in which there are a considerable number of test vectors (at least m but usually more) almost orthogonal to one of the axes of the initial F-matrix, usually the first. Each of them may also lie close to one of the effectively bounding hyperplanes, but all of them together overdetermine before rotation the hyperplane orthogonal to this F-axis. The varimax algorithm requires improvement of overdetermination (increases of variance of the squared factor loadings) at every iteration. But in these cases, the fit to the hyperplane orthogonal to the initial F-axis must get worse before the fit to any effectively bounding hyperplane can get better. The algorithm does not permit this, so one rotated factor is effectively "nailed" to the hyperplane orthogonal to one of the F-axes, and the varimax iterations converge to nonsense factors.

Test vectors almost orthogonal to the first axis of F will have near-zero loadings on the first factor of F. This situation is likely to arise whenever several of the original variables are essentially ratios of (or differences between) pairs of primary factors (e.g., x/y, $x - y$, etc. in the box problem). With physical measurements this may result from including several shape variables along with a majority of magnitude variables; with psychological test data, from including several ipsative measures along with a majority of normative measures, or several relative magnitudes along with a majority of absolute magnitudes. Normative data are typified by a test scored number right or by a rank or a rating on a scale with defined levels, so that the score is a comparison of the individual with others in some defined group. Ipsative data arise when the score of an individual on each of several variables is a deviation from *his own* mean for these variables, or when each individual is ranked on the same set of traits without reference to other individuals.

Table 8.3 is based on a different subset of variables from the box problem, though many of them are the same as those of Table 8.2. The same procedure as in Table 8.2 was used in obtaining the initial F-matrix. The six ratio variables, 13–18 inclusive, have very low (almost near-zero) loadings on the first factor of F, and hence overdetermine the plane orthogonal to the first principal axis before rotation starts. The first factor A of the matrix V_0 is therefore essentially the same as the first factor a of F, but with some improvement of the fit to the hyperplane orthogonal to the first F-axis, as is shown by the lower near-zero loadings on the ratio variables. Factor B has no real near-zero loadings at all; Factor C has only

TABLE 8.3
Box Problem with Overdetermined First Factor of F

		Principal Axes F			Varimax V_0		
	Var	a	b	c	A	B	C
(1)	x	.594	−.401	.682	.644	−.293	−.691
(2)	y	.768	.590	.039	.738	.624	.069
(3)	z	.771	−.356	−.497	.764	−.377	.493
(4)	xy	.857	.186	.454	.867	.275	−.385
(5)	$2x + 2y$	.849	.272	.399	.852	.354	−.321
(6)	$\sqrt{x^2 + y^2}$	.845	.264	.389	.848	.344	−.312
(7)	xz	.853	−.500	.075	.879	−.450	−.087
(8)	$2x + 2z$	.846	−.521	.025	.871	−.477	−.040
(9)	$\sqrt{x^2 + z^2}$	.830	−.495	.008	.853	−.454	−.021
(10)	yz	.921	.156	−.331	.896	.157	.394
(11)	$2y + 2z$	.929	.157	−.313	.905	.161	.377
(12)	$\sqrt{y^2 + z^2}$	.919	.162	−.281	.896	.169	.345
(13)	x/y	−.145	−.857	.484	−.080	−.800	−.585
(14)	y/x	.145	.857	−.484	.080	.800	.585
(15)	x/z	−.114	.019	.980	−.069	.128	−.976
(16)	z/x	.114	−.019	−.980	.069	−.128	.976
(17)	y/z	.021	.902	.425	−.004	.945	−.317
(18)	z/y	−.021	−.902	−.425	.004	−.945	.317

Note. Computed from portions of the correlation matrix, Table 1, p. 370, Thurstone, 1947. Copyright 1947 by The University of Chicago. Used by permission.

four, on variables 2, 7, 8, and 9; and V_0 bears no resemblance to a simple structure. The *real* simple structure would be fairly similar to that of Fig. 8.1 with variables 5, 9, and 13 omitted: each bounding plane would be overdetermined by five points showing on the plot. Each ratio variable would also lie close to one of the bounding planes with its projection-line extended far beyond the plot, and would have one high positive loading, one high negative loading, and one near-zero loading, making all three factors intrinsically bipolar as shown schematically in Fig. 7-12.

It is of course possible for a later factor of F to represent an initially overdetermined hyperplane, but this situation is so rare that we can neglect it, as indeed we must, because no analytic procedure that takes care of it is known. It can be *recognized* if it does occur, in the same manner we observed for the box problem, by the fact that one of the factors of F has m or more very low loadings, and the corresponding factor of V_0 will be quite similar but with still lower near-zeros in the same positions.

A third difficulty, very seldom as serious as the first two, occurs when one or more variables have nonzero loadings on all m rotated factors. Such variables lie well inside the subspace bounded by the simple-structure hyperplanes, and do not help to locate the positions of these hyperplanes. But they *may* distort slightly the positions of the varimax hyperplanes. Any such variable vector is likely to be almost collinear with the first unrotated axis, and may be recognized in F as having a high or at least substantial loading on the first factor and very low (near-zero) loadings on *all* of the later factors.

8.3   THE WEIGHTED-VARIMAX TRANSFORMATION

We can eliminate or at least minimize the difficulties noted above (except for a "nailed" factor of F other than the first factor) by applying the varimax rotation to a set of *weighted* test vectors (Cureton & Mulaik, 1975).

We first normalize the rows of F, and call the result F_n. The test vectors of F_n will all be of unit length, with elements $f_{nik} = f_{ik}/h_i$; $i = 1, 2, \ldots, n$ (tests); $k = 1, 2, \ldots, m$ (factors), and h_i is the vector length or the square root of the communality of test i.

We next reflect temporarily all rows of F_n whose first-factor loadings are negative and call the result A. Because the a-coordinates of all test vectors are now positive, these unit vectors will all lie on one side of the hyperplane orthogonal to the first axis of A, making angles of $90°$ or less with this axis.

In most F-matrices the sum of squares of the first-factor loadings will be much larger than the sum of squares of the loadings on any later factor, and not infrequently larger than the sum of squares of the loadings on all these later factors combined; and the sums of squares of loadings on these later factors will differ much less among themselves. This will also be true for the matrices F_n and

A. An example may be seen in the F-matrix of Table 8.2, where the sums of squares are 10.678 for factor a, 2.174 for factor b, and 1.695 for factor c. In such cases the test vectors will be distributed roughly symmetrically about the first axis of A, and this axis will lie near the middle of the whole configuration of test vectors in the common-factor space. Test vectors near the primary axes will make fairly large angles with the first axis of A. Test vectors near the hyperplanes but not near the primary axes will make somewhat smaller angles. Test vectors having near-zero loadings on all factors of F except the first, and hence lying well inside the subspace bounded by the hyperplanes, will make small angles with the first axis of A. And the test vectors of variables having very low loadings on the first factor of F (e.g., the ratio variables of Table 8.3) will make very large angles with the first axis of A: angles approaching 90°.

We can see these relations roughly in the extended-vector picture of Fig. 8.1. In this picture the first axis of F is vertical (perpendicular to the plane of the picture), with the terminus at the intersection of the axes a and b on the extended-vector plane. Test vectors from the origin (at unit distance below this intersection) have termini on the extended-vector plane at the numbered points. The test vectors on the primary axes, with termini at points 1, 2, and 3, make fairly large angles with the first axis of F. The test vectors terminating at the other plotted points lie near the planes but not near the primary axes, and make smaller angles with the first axis of F. If there were a variable drawing more or less equally on all the primary factors (e.g., xyz, the volume of the box), it would have a high loading only on the first factor of F and near-zero loadings on the other two. Its vector would make a very small angle with the first axis of F, with terminus well inside the triangle 1-2-3 and close to the intersection 0. And if there were variables such as the ratio variables of Table 8.3, with first-factor loadings near-zero, their vectors would lie almost at right angles to the first factor of F, with termini far outside the plot on the extended-vector plane.

With all unit vectors, as in the matrix A, the analogous picture would be a plot on the surface of a hemisphere, and the asymmetry represented by the location of point 1 on the extended-vector plot would be seen to be slight.

When the first factor of F is large, then, in comparison with all the later factors, we can use the angles between the test vectors and the first axis of F (or of A) to estimate whether each of these vectors lies close to a primary axis, close to a hyperplane but not to a primary axis, near the middle of the configuration, or far outside the subspace bounded by the hyperplanes.

Normalization and reflection of the test vectors of F does not change the positions of the axes. The first axis of F, and hence of F_n and A, is represented in the common-factor space by coordinates $1, 0, 0, \ldots, 0$: a one followed by $m - 1$ zeros. Each test vector of A has coordinates defined by its loadings. The scalar product of a unit test vector and the first axis of A is therefore simply a_{i1}, the loading of the test on the first factor of A, and this a_{i1} is the cosine of the angle between the test vector and the first axis of A.

The weights of the tests can be determined from these angles between the test vectors and the first axis of A. Maximum weights should be given to test vectors near the primary axes as this will improve the parallelism of the orthogonal hyperplanes to the oblique hyperplanes of the simple structure. If the first factor of A is large, and all the others are considerably smaller and do not differ very greatly in magnitude among themselves, the structure of the test vectors will be roughly symmetrical about the first axis of A, and the primary axes will lie at roughly equal angles to this first axis of A. In an orthogonal rotation that puts the rotated axes at equal angles to the first axis of A, the cosine of the angle between each rotated axis and the first axis of A is $\sqrt{1/m}$ (Landahl, 1938). Remembering that in an orthogonal rotation the primary axes and the reference vectors are the same, we can easily visualize this situation in the two-factor case. If the first axis of A is vertical and the second is horizontal, the orthogonal rotation which puts the new axes at equal angles to the vertical axis will be a 45° rotation, with each new axis at an angle of 45° to the vertical axis. Then $cos\ 45° = .70711 = \sqrt{1/2} = \sqrt{1/m}$ if $m = 2$. As the value of m increases, the angle between each primary axis and the first axis of A increases, and its cosine $\sqrt{1/m}$ becomes smaller. Thus for $m = 3$, the angle is 54°44′ with cosine $\sqrt{1/3} = .57735$, and for $m = 8$ the angle is 69°18′ with cosine $\sqrt{1/8} = .35355$. We should therefore give maximum weight to test vectors for which $a_{i1} \doteq \sqrt{1/m}$, on the assumption that the structure is roughly orthogonal and roughly symmetrical about the first axis of A.

We should give intermediate weights to variables whose test vectors are likely to lie near bounding hyperplanes but not close to any primary axis. These test vectors still make substantial angles with the first axis of A, but angles appreciably less than $cos^{-1}\sqrt{1/m}$. With these lowered weights we can reasonably hope that nonbounding hyperplanes, arising from clusters of test vectors near the middles of the hyperplanes, will be avoided in favor of those near the effective boundaries.

Test vectors near the first axis of A do not lie close to any hyperplane, and their weights should be near-zero. These test vectors make small angles with the first axis of A, with cosines (a_{i1}) approaching unity.

We should also give near-zero weights to test vectors almost orthogonal to the first axis of A, to avoid the situation of Table 8.3. These test vectors make large angles with the first axis of A, with cosines (a_{i1}) approaching zero. Giving them near-zero weights effectively removes them from consideration in determining the locations of the hyperplanes, even though each of them may lie close to one of these hyperplanes when the latter are extended beyond the boundaries of the central subspace. There seems to be no method of using them, however, without running the risk of a "nailed" hyperplane orthogonal to the first axis of A.

In summary, then, the weights should run from near-zero for test vectors almost collinear with the first axis of A $(a_{i1} \rightarrow 1)$, through maximum for test vectors likely to lie near the primary axes $(a_{i1} \rightarrow \sqrt{1/m})$, and back to near-zero for test vectors almost orthogonal to the first axis of A ($a_{i1} \rightarrow 0$). The curve relating the angle between the test vector and the first axis of A (on the abscissa) to the weight (on the ordinate) should be finite, roughly bell-shaped, and skew (symmetrical if $m = 2$), with a moderately broad top so the formula will still work when the structure is oblique. After trying out several functions having these properties, Cureton and Mulaik found that an empirically more-or-less optimum function was

$$w_i = \left[\cos^2 \left(\frac{\cos^{-1} \sqrt{1/m} - \cos^{-1} a_{i1}}{\cos^{-1} \sqrt{1/m}} \times \frac{\pi}{2} \right) \right] + .001, \text{ if } a_{i1} \geqq \sqrt{1/m};$$

$$\tag{8-2}$$

$$w_i = \left[\cos^2 \left(\frac{\cos^{-1} a_{i1} - \cos^{-1} \sqrt{1/m}}{\pi/2 - \cos^{-1} \sqrt{1/m}} \times \frac{\pi}{2} \right) \right] + .001, \text{ if } a_{i1} < \sqrt{1/m}.$$

Here $\pi/2$ is 90° in radians, and the added .001 prevents w_i from being exactly 0 when the angle is exactly 0° or 90°, so that w_i will always have a computable reciprocal. The weights then run from .001 when the angle is 0°, through the maximum 1.001 when the angle is $cos^{-1}\sqrt{1/m}$, and back to .001 when the angle is 90°. Table 8.4 shows w_i at selected angles (between a test vector and the first axis of A) for $m = 3$ and $m = 8$. Plots made from this table give curves having the desired properties.

Problem 8.3:1. From the data of Table 8.4, plot on 1/20-th inch cross-section paper the curves relating angle (abscissa) to w_i (ordinate) for $m = 3$ and $m = 8$.

Summarizing and extending the discussion above, we arrive at the following listing of the steps of the weighted varimax procedure:

1. Call the initial unrotated factor matrix F.
2. Normalize the rows of F and call the resulting matrix F_n.
3. Reflect any rows of F_n whose first-factor loadings are negative, and call the resulting matrix A.
4. Compute the weights of the test vectors by (8-2). Let W be an n by n diagonal matrix of the weights. Compute the n by m matrix WA.
5. Apply the iterative varimax algorithm to WA. This is a *raw* varimax rotation. If the rows of WA were renormalized first, the effects of the weighting would be cancelled. Call the resulting matrix V_w, the weighted reflected normal-varimax factor matrix. Call the transformation matrix (from A to V_w) Λ_0.
6. De-weight V_w: $V_r = W^{-1}V_w$. Here W^{-1} is the diagonal matrix each diagonal element of which is the reciprocal of the corresponding diagonal element of W. The matrix V_r is the reflected row-normal weighted-varimax factor matrix. Because A was row-normal, de-weighting restores row-normality to the rows of V_r.

TABLE 8.4
Values of w_i at Selected Values of $\cos^{-1} a_{i1}$
for $m = 3$ and $m = 8$ Factors

	w_i	
$\cos^{-1} a_{i1} = angle$	$m = 3$	$m = 8$
0	.001	.001
5	.021	.014
10	.081	.051
15	.175	.112
20	.296	.193
25	.436	.289
30	.576	.397
35	.713	.509
40	.833	.621
45	.925	.727
50	.983	.821
55	1.001[a]	.900
60	.947	.957
65	.806	.992
70	.606	.998[b]
75	.385	.825
80	.187	.474
85	.054	.138
90	.001	.001

[a] 1.001 exactly at 54°44′ (max).
[b] 1.001 exactly at 69°18′ (max).

7. Rereflect those rows of V_r which correspond to the rows of F_n that were reflected to form A. This restores the sign pattern corresponding to the original scale directions of the variables, and reinstates any nominal bipolarities present in the factors. The result is V_n, the weighted-varimax row-normal factor matrix.

8. Denormalize the rows of V_n by multiplying each of them by h_i, giving V_0, the weighted-varimax factor matrix. This restores the original test-vector lengths, and V_0 is the weighted-varimax orthogonal approximation to simple structure.

De-weighting, rereflecting, and denormalizing are not rotational procedures, and these procedures do not move the *axes*, so Λ_0 does not change from step 5 to step 8. Steps 6, 7, and 8 could in fact have been omitted, as could also the terms .001 in (8-2) which were needed only to insure the existence of W^{-1} for step 6. In this case, as soon as Λ_0 was available at step 5, we could have used the relations

$$V_n = F_n \Lambda_0$$

$$V_0 = F \Lambda_0$$

Steps 6, 7, and 8 and the terms .001 in (8-2) are included mainly for computing convenience. With these steps it is not necessary to hold F_n in memory: A can be formed from F_n by overlay, and F_n can even be formed from F by overlay if we do not need F for a later oblique rotation. These steps also serve to clarify the essential properties of the weighted-varimax procedure.

We have described the weighted-varimax procedure at some length because it is as yet not well known and because we believe it is to be preferred to the unweighted normal-varimax procedure, even when we do not have either heavily overdetermined nonbounding hyperplanes or an initial overdetermined hyperplane orthogonal to the first factor of F. Giving greater weights to test vectors likely to lie close to the primary axes, and giving near-zero weights to test vectors near the first axis of F, improves the parallelism of the orthogonal hyperplanes to those of the oblique simple structure. This improves the over-all excellence of the orthogonal approximation to simple structure and also takes care of the relatively rare difficulties illustrated in Table 8.2 and Table 8.3. The weighted-varimax procedure is the only analytic rotational procedure so far proposed which uses the effectively-bounding-hyperplanes criterion as well as the criterion of overdetermination in fitting the hyperplanes to the data.

Table 8.5 shows the application of the weighted-varimax procedure to the full box problem. In this problem we have (1) nonbounding hyperplanes more heavily overdetermined than those at the effective boundaries; (2) an initially overdetermined hyperplane orthogonal to the first axis of F; and (3) two test vectors (25 and 26) almost collinear with the first axis of F. Two previous attempts to rotate this F-matrix by analytic procedures had failed to reach the clear simple structure present in the data (Butler, 1964; Eber, 1968). Cureton and Mulaik (1971) succeeded in solving this problem by numerical methods, but only by a rather clumsy series of procedures which could not be programmed as a single analytic sequence.

Because Thurstone used originally a group centroid procedure to obtain F, the writers started anew from the correlation matrix and factored twice by the principal-axes method, as for Table 8.2 and Table 8.3, to obtain the F-matrix of Table 8.5. This matrix was then rotated by the weighted-varimax method to give the V_0-matrix. Because the excellence of an orthogonal approximation to simple structure is not easy to judge from the orthogonal factor matrix, we show also a Promax oblique rotation based on the weighted-varimax rotation, as described in Chapter 9. In this Promax factor matrix the near-zero loadings are enclosed in parentheses to assist the reader in judging the excellence of the oblique simple structure. It is very good. The highest near-zeros are $\pm .063$, and there are no loadings between these values and $\pm .347$. Comparing V_0 with V, we see that in V_0 all near-zero loadings are below .200, and there are no loadings between .199 and .455. This is not a general rule, however; the highest near-zero in an orthogonal approximation to simple structure is a function of the obliquity of the oblique structure.

TABLE 8.5
Complete Box Problem: Weighted-Varimax Rotation

		Principal Axes F			Weighted-Varimax V_0			Promax V		
Var		a	b	c	A	B	C	I	II	III
1)	x	.629	−.494	.579	.983	.075	.062	.953	(−.016)	(−.060)
2)	y	.751	.602	.125	.169	.941	.168	(.047)	.894	(.062)
3)	z	.765	−.230	−.572	.194	.184	.945	(.051)	(.043)	.896
4)	xy	.866	.131	.459	.699	.690	.113	.603	.609	(−.032)
5)	x^2y	.824	−.149	.528	.871	.455	.116	.797	.362	(−.028)
6)	xy^2	.859	.358	.306	.475	.841	.162	.361	.770	(.029)
7)	2x + 2y	.852	.223	.420	.616	.748	.109	.516	.674	(−.032)
8)	$\sqrt{x^2 + y^2}$	.847	.218	.405	.607	.739	.119	.507	.664	(−.020)
9)	xz	.873	−.473	−.042	.719	.139	.672	.608	(−.009)	.568
10)	x^2z	.812	−.518	.203	.862	.106	.462	.780	(−.027)	.347
11)	xz^2	.951	−.441	−.254	.612	.178	.870	.473	(.012)	.773
12)	2x + 2z	.861	−.483	−.094	.685	.116	.708	.572	(−.034)	.609
13)	$\sqrt{x^2 + z^2}$	.845	−.456	−.106	.654	.126	.700	.542	(−.021)	.604
14)	yz	.906	.250	−.323	.167	.685	.700	(.004)	.572	.611
15)	y^2z	.876	.406	−.185	.152	.812	.533	(−.003)	.721	.436
16)	yz^2	.885	.095	−.431	.172	.533	.815	(.010)	.407	.738
17)	2y + 2z	.912	.248	−.304	.183	.690	.690	(.021)	.577	.599
18)	$\sqrt{y^2 + z^2}$	.902	.246	−.272	.199	.687	.660	(.040)	.577	.568
19)	x/y	−.102	−.936	.322	.655	−.748	−.039	.729	−.789	(−.048)
20)	y/x	.102	.936	−.322	−.655	.748	.039	−.729	.789	(.048)
21)	x/z	−.081	−.163	.969	.650	−.024	−.741	.739	(.017)	−.807
22)	z/x	.081	.163	−.969	−.650	.024	.741	−.739	(−.017)	.807
23)	y/z	.006	.810	.582	−.074	.734	−.671	(−.063)	.818	−.722
24)	z/y	−.006	−.810	−.582	.074	−.734	.671	(.063)	−.818	.722
25)	xyz	.987	−.026	.043	.592	.573	.546	.454	.446	.419
26)	$\sqrt{x^2 + y^2 + z^2}$	.965	.057	−.028	.490	.614	.564	.347	.493	.445

Note. Computed from the correlation matrix, Table 1, p. 370, Thurstone, 1947. Copyright 1947 by The University of Chicago. Used by permission.

Some users of factor analysis conclude their work with a varimax transformation, although orthogonal transformations do not distinguish near-zero loadings from low nonzero loadings, and hence cannot well be used to ascertain the amount of overdetermination of each factor and thus to judge the excellence of the simple structure. They *can,* however, be used quite well to interpret the meanings of the factors because these interpretations are based on the high loadings on each factor. The high loadings are on essentially the same variables in the orthogonal solution as in any good oblique solution, though their numerical values are larger.

8.4   ARBITRARY ORTHOGONAL TRANSFORMATIONS

In most of the preceding discussions (and in most of those following), we have proceeded as though simple structure were *the* criterion for rotation. There are two situations, however, in which this is not the case. The first is the situation in which there is some over-riding theoretical or empirical consideration that indicates the presence of a general factor which is to be identified by one particular variable or cluster of variables. The consideration at issue overrides the simple-structure criterion. We wish to extract the general factor first, and only then search for a simple structure in the common-factor space of $m - 1$ dimensions orthogonal to this general factor. Consider four examples:

1. In the nine-aptitude-tests problem the original author (Swineford, 1948) argued that tests 1, 2, and 3 (reasoning tests) defined a general intelligence factor, and that the verbal and spatial factors were properly group factors. This is an example of an over-riding theoretical consideration. We are to extract first a general factor defined by the centroid of the cluster composed of variables 1, 2, and 3, and then rotate the remaining two factors in the residual plane orthogonal to this general factor to obtain the verbal and spatial group factors.

2. Suppose that, to a battery of tests measuring various aspects of abstract (figural) reasoning, quantitative reasoning, vocabulary and verbal relations, spatial visualization, memory, and numerical facility, we were to add the Stanford-Binet Intelligence Scale to define general intelligence. The clarity of the analysis of the separate aptitudes might be improved if we first extracted a general factor defined by the Stanford-Binet mental age and then rotated the remaining factors in the $(m - 1)$-space orthogonal to the Stanford-Binet intelligence dimension. It is not too clear here whether the over-riding consideration is theoretical or empirical.

3. With a battery of aptitude or school achievement tests given to a group varying widely in age (e.g., fourth to twelfth grades), it might be advisable to extract first a general factor defined by age before proceeding further. Here and in the next example we have over-riding empirical considerations.

4. Suppose we wish to determine by factor analysis the attitudes underlying the record votes of a legislative body. Because of our political system, party membership would be a general factor underlying every vote, and we might well wish to extract this general factor first and then rotate the other factors in the space orthogonal to it to determine the other attitudes.

Problems of these types are solved by using the Gram-Schmidt procedure of Section 8.4.1, below, to extract the general factor.

The second situation in which orthogonal transformations are required is a special case. We have noted that in the F-matrix the sum of squares of the elements of the first factor is commonly quite large in comparison with the sums of squares of the elements of the later factors. For graphic cluster analysis the procedures are simplified if we start from an arbitrary orthogonal rotation of F which makes the column sums of squares more nearly equal. A quick method for constructing a transformation matrix that does this is provided by the Landahl procedure of Section 8.4.2, below.

8.4.1 The Gram-Schmidt Orthogonalization

Suppose we have a square oblique matrix X, and we wish to construct an orthogonal matrix Y whose first row is the same as that of X. The Gram-Schmidt process, which is derived in books on linear algebra, does this. If the row-vectors of X are X_1', X_2', ..., X_m', and the row-vectors of Y are Y_1', Y_2', ..., Y_m', the Gram-Schmidt equations are

$$Y_1' = X_1'$$

$$Y_2' = X_2' - \left(\frac{X_2' Y_1}{Y_1' Y_1} \right) Y_1'$$

$$Y_3' = X_3' - \left(\frac{X_3' Y_1}{Y_1' Y_1} \right) Y_1' - \left(\frac{X_3' Y_2}{Y_2' Y_2} \right) Y_2'$$

$$Y_m' = X_m' - \left(\frac{X_m' Y_1}{Y_1' Y_1} \right) Y_1' - \left(\frac{X_m' Y_2}{Y_2' Y_2} \right) Y_2' - \cdots - \left(\frac{X_m' Y_{m-1}}{Y_{m-1}' Y_{m-1}} \right) Y_{m-1}'$$

In each parenthesis factor the numerator and denominator are scalar products, so each of these factors is a single number (a scalar). Hence every Y_i' is a single row-vector:

$$Y_i' = [Y_{i1} Y_{i2} \ldots Y_{im}] \qquad (i = 1, 2, \ldots, m).$$

If the Y_i' rows are then normalized, Y will be an orthonormal matrix. If the vectors X_i' are all of unit length at the outset, and we normalize each vector Y_i' as it is constructed, the denominators of the parentheses factors will all be unity, and these equations become

$$Y_1' = X_1'$$

$$Y_2' = [X_2' - (X_2' Y_1) Y_1'] / K_2$$

$$Y_3' = [X_3' - (X_3' Y_1) Y_1' - (X_3' Y_2) Y_2'] / K_3$$

$$Y_m' = [X_m' - (X_m' Y_1) Y_1' - (X_m' Y_2) Y_2' - \cdots - (X_m' Y_{m-1}) Y_{m-1}'] / K_m$$

where K_2, K_3, ... , K_m are the factors that normalize the expressions in brackets. Each equation is again a row-vector of m elements.

Suppose now that we wish to transform a factor matrix F in such a manner that a particular variable, or the centroid of a cluster of variables which have similar factorial structures, will have nonzero loadings only on the first transformed factor. This variable or cluster will thus define a general factor because every variable that has a nonzero correlation with this particular variable or cluster will have a nonzero loading on the factor defined by it. We can normalize the row of F corresponding to this variable, or form the normalized centroid of the rows of F corresponding to the variables in the cluster, and call this normalized row vector X_1'. The other rows of X are entirely arbitrary. It is convenient in this case to set up the matrix X' in the following form, with $X_1' = [a\ b\ c\ d\ e]$, say, for the five-variable case (Cureton, 1959):

$$X' = \begin{bmatrix} a & b & c & d & e \\ 1 & 0 & 0 & 0 & 0 \\ 0 & 1 & 0 & 0 & 0 \\ 0 & 0 & 1 & 0 & 0 \\ 0 & 0 & 0 & 1 & 0 \end{bmatrix}$$

The scalar products, $X_2'Y_1$, $X_3'Y_1$, $X_3'Y_2$, and so on, of the Gram-Schmidt equations then become single elements of Y, and the equations reduce to

$$Y_1' = X_1'$$

$$Y_2' = [X_2' - aY_1']/K_2$$

$$Y_3' = [X_3' - bY_1' - y_{22}Y_2']/K_3$$

$$Y_4' = [X_4' - cY_1' - y_{23}Y_2' - y_{33}Y_3']/K_4$$

$$Y_5' = [X_5' - dY_1' - y_{24}Y_2' - y_{34}Y_3' - y_{44}Y_4']/K_5$$

These equations can be solved literally for the two-factor, three-factor, four-factor, and five-factor cases. Define first

$$k_2^2 = 1 - a^2$$

$$k_3^2 = 1 - a^2 - b^2$$

$$k_4^2 = 1 - a^2 - b^2 - c^2$$

The ks as here defined are related to but not identical with the Ks above. Then after some lengthy but straightforward algebra we obtain the orthonormal transformation matrices of Table 8.6.

The system by which larger orthonormal transformation matrices can be constructed will be clear if we note that $k_1 = 1$, and that the final k (not shown as

TABLE 8.6
Orthonormal Transformation Matrices (Gram-Schmidt)

$$2\text{-}var\ Y = \begin{bmatrix} a & b \\ b & -a \end{bmatrix}$$

$$3\text{-}var\ Y = \begin{bmatrix} a & b & c \\ k_2 & -ab/k_2 & -ac/k_2 \\ 0 & c/k_2 & -b/k_2 \end{bmatrix}$$

$$4\text{-}var\ Y = \begin{bmatrix} a & b & c & d \\ k_2 & -ab/k_2 & -ac/k_2 & -ad/k_2 \\ 0 & k_3/k_2 & -bc/k_2 k_3 & -bd/k_2 k_3 \\ 0 & 0 & d/k_3 & -c/k_3 \end{bmatrix}$$

$$5\text{-}var\ Y = \begin{bmatrix} a & b & c & d & e \\ k_2 & -ab/k_2 & -ac/k_2 & -ad/k_2 & -ae/k_2 \\ 0 & k_3/k_2 & -bc/k_2 k_3 & -bd/k_2 k_3 & -be/k_2 k_3 \\ 0 & 0 & k_4/k_3 & -cd/k_3 k_4 & -ce/k_3 k_4 \\ 0 & 0 & 0 & e/k_4 & -d/k_4 \end{bmatrix}$$

General case:

$$Y = \begin{bmatrix} a & b & c & d & e \\ k_2/k_1 & -ab/k_1 k_2 & -ac/k_1 k_2 & -ad/k_1 k_2 & -ae/k_1 k_2 \\ 0 & k_3/k_2 & -bc/k_2 k_3 & -bd/k_2 k_3 & -be/k_2 k_3 \\ 0 & 0 & k_4/k_3 & -cd/k_3 k_4 & -ce/k_3 k_4 \\ 0 & 0 & 0 & k_5/k_4 & -de/k_4 k_5 \end{bmatrix}$$

such in the last element of the last row in each of the first four matrices of Table 8.6) is m, the last element of X', or the square root of

$$k_m^2 = 1 - a^2 - b^2 - \ldots - (m - 1)^2 = m^2,$$

because X' is a unit vector the sum of squares of whose elements is unity. Thus for the five-factor case, $k_5 = e$, and this matrix is shown complete under "General case" in Table 8.6. From this last matrix, extension to matrices in which $m > 5$ is quite straightforward. Because the Gram-Schmidt process operates on the rows, the actual transformation matrix is $\Lambda_g = Y'$.

We illustrate this procedure by applying it to the nine-aptitude-tests problem. The principal-axes F-matrix is given in columns a, b, and c of the factor matrix of Table 5.3, and is reproduced (without the refactoring used for Table 8.1) at the upper left of Table 8.7. The names of the tests are given in Table 5.3.

Proceeding on the original author's assumption that tests 1, 2, and 3 (reasoning tests) define a general intelligence factor, we define the arbitrary row vector as the normalized centroid vector of rows (1), (2), and (3) of F. The computations are shown just below the F-matrix of Table 8.7, and the normalized centroid vector is $X_1' = [.9004\ -.1396\ -.4121]$. The values of k_2, $1/k_2$, $-ab$, and $-ac$ are just below. Then using the second (3-var) Y-matrix of Table 8.6, we construct the Y-matrix shown just below $-ac$ in Table 8.7, and verify that the

TABLE 8.7
Orthogonal Rotation for Nine Aptitude Tests ($N = 504$)

Test	Principal Axes F			General Factor G			Transformed V			h_v^2	h_3^2
	a	b	c	$g = 1$	2	3	$g = I$	II	III		
(1)	.645	−.185	−.319	.738	−.045	.073	.738	.020	−.083	.552	.552
(2)	.639	−.004	−.293	.697	.027	−.090	.697	−.045	.083	.495	.494
(3)	.619	−.106	−.259	.679	.018	.017	.679	.025	.001	.462	.461
(4)	.826	−.285	.201	.701	.448	.334	.701	.553	.081	.804	.804
(5)	.746	−.216	.035	.687	.292	.216	.687	.359	.054	.604	.604
(6)	.765	−.307	.304	.606	.503	.388	.606	.630	.081	.771	.772
(7)	.692	.483	−.004	.557	.437	−.459	.557	−.016	.634	.712	.712
(8)	.658	.438	.080	.498	.481	−.389	.498	.065	.615	.630	.631
(9)	.645	.305	.124	.487	.485	−.249	.487	.160	.512	.525	.524
Σ	6.235	.123	−.131	5.650	2.636	−.159	5.650	1.751	1.978	5.555	5.554
Ch				5.651	2.637	−.159	5.651	1.751	1.976		

	Residual Λ_0-Matrix		Landahl $L = FL_t$		

Normalized Centroid Vector of Rows (1) + (2) + (3)

	II	III	Test	1	2	3
$\Sigma = [1.903 \quad -.295 \quad -.871]$			(1)	.221	.222	.674
2	.7071	.7071	(2)	.366	.163	.578
3	.7071	−.7071	(3)	.271	.218	.584

$$\Sigma(\Sigma^2) = 4.467,075$$
$$\sqrt{\Sigma(\Sigma^2)} = 2.113,546$$
$$1/\sqrt{\Sigma(\Sigma^2)} = .47314$$
$$X_1' = [.9004 \quad -.1396 \quad -.4121]$$
$$\Sigma(X_1')^2 = 1.0000$$

Test	1	2	3
(4)	.244	.735	.451
(5)	.254	.544	.494
(6)	.191	.782	.352
(7)	.794	.200	.205
(8)	.738	.258	.145
(9)	.621	.336	.160

$$k_2 = \sqrt{1 - .9004^2} = .43506$$
$$1/k_2 = 2.2985$$
$$-ab = .12570$$
$$-ac = .37105$$

	1	2	3
Σ	3.700	3.458	3.643
Ch	3.701	3.457	3.643
Σl^2	1.977	1.791	1.789

$Y = \Lambda_g'$

	a	b	c
1	.9004	−.1396	−.4121
2	.4351	.2889	.8529
3	0	−.9472	.3209

Landal Trf L_t

	1	2	3
a	.5774	.5774	.5774
b	.8165	−.4082	−.4082
c	0	.7071	−.7071

sum of squares of the elements of each row is 1.000 within rounding error and that the sum of products of each pair of rows is .0000 within rounding error. Then $\Lambda_g = Y'$ and G, the transformed factor matrix with factor 1 a general factor and factors 2 and 3 arbitrary, is $G = F\Lambda_g$.

In columns 2 and 3 of G, the first three (near-zero) elements sum to .000 because the general factor ($g = 1$) was derived from the *centroid* of variables 1, 2, and 3. The rest of columns 2 and 3 of G do not quite form a residual 7 by 2 principal-axes matrix: their scalar product is $-.098$, and the scalar product of the whole of columns 2 and 3 is $-.104$. These values are both too far from .000 to be due to rounding error. It appears that if F were a *centroid* factor matrix, columns 2 and 3 of G would form a residual centroid matrix, but the writers do not have an algebraic proof of this nor enough empirical evidence to assert it with any great confidence.

The transformation is finished by retaining the factor $g = 1$ as $g = I$ of the final V, and rotating factors 2 and 3. The structure of factors 2 and 3 is almost orthogonal (just barely acute), so we use an orthogonal rotation. With a larger matrix we would rotate factors $2, 3, \ldots, m$ in any appropriate (orthogonal or oblique) manner. Here the best orthogonal transformation would result from a varimax or weighted-varimax rotation of factors 2 and 3 of G, but a fair approximation results from a simple $45°$ rotation of their axes, placing the new axes II and III of V at equal angles to axis 1 of G. The transformation matrix is the 2 by 2 Landahl transformation matrix L_t (Section 8.4.2, following). This matrix is the residual matrix Λ_0 of Table 8.7, the subscript 0 indicating that the transformation is orthogonal. Postmultiplying the last two elements of each row of G by the elements of a column of Λ_0, we obtain factors II and III of V.

This type of rotation is a three-factor analog of alternatives 3 and 4 of the reading-arithmetic example of Chapter 1, wherein "intelligence" was identified first with reading tests and second with arithmetic tests.

When we examine matrix V of Table 8.7, we see that factor $g = I$ is indeed a general factor, with two of the verbal tests, 4 and 5, having loadings as high as some of the reasoning tests used to define this factor. Factor II is a verbal group factor, with high loadings only on tests 4, 5, and 6, the highest being that of test 6 (Vocabulary). Factor III is a spatial group factor, with nonzero loadings on tests 7, 8, and 9. The loading .160 of test 9 on factor II, which is a low nonzero rather than a near-zero, suggests that this test (Visual Imagery) has a little verbal content in addition to its general-factor (reasoning) content and its spatial content.

In the next to the last column of Table 8.7, we show the communalities h_v^2 computed from the rows of V. Because V is an orthogonal transformation of F, its row sums of squares should differ from those of F only by accumulated rounding error. Comparing the h_v^2 values of Table 8.7 with the h_3^2 values copied from Table 5.3, we see that there are no discrepancies greater than .001. The sum of the h_v^2 communalities, 5.555, differs also from the sum of the h_3^2 communalities of Table 5.3, 5.554, by only .001 also.

> **Exercise 8:1.** From the WAIS F-matrix of Table 7.1, define the fixed vector for a general factor as the normalized centroid of tests 8, 9, 10, and 11: the nonverbal reasoning tests. Complete the G-matrix and the V-matrix as in Table 8.7. Check the h_v^2 values against the h^2 values of Table 7.1. Interpret the factors of this matrix, using the list of test names at the beginning of Section 7.1.5. Save the results.

8.4.2 The Landahl Transformation

When an F-matrix, such as that of Table 8.7 or almost any of those we have used as examples or exercises, has a large first factor with all the others small, we may desire a simple orthogonal transformation that will make the sums of squares of the elements in the columns more nearly equal. The Landahl transformation does this by rotating the axes in such a manner that the rotated axes all lie at equal angles to the first axis of F. Thus in effect the sum of squares of the elements of the first column of F is distributed equally over all the transformed factors; and in the transformed factor matrix the column sums of squares differ only by the amounts contributed by the differences in column sums of squares of the later factors of F.

If, in the general matrix of Table 8.6, $a = b = c = d = e = \ldots = \sqrt{1/m}$ ($= \sqrt{1/5} = .4472$ when $m = 5$), every element of each matrix is determined by its order m. Hence the numerical values of the elements of the Landahl transformation matrix of any order can be computed once and for all. Note, however, that aside from being all at equal angles to the first axis of F, the positions of the rotated axes are arbitrary. If we think of them as turning rigidly about the first axis of F, like the ribs of a half-opened umbrella with its tip on the floor and its handle upright and turning, the positions of the ribs when the turning stops is arbitrary. Thus any Landahl transformation matrix constructed from one of the matrices of Table 8.6 will be only one of an infinite number of possible Landahl transformation matrices of the same order.

Table 8.8 gives the Landahl transformation matrix of order 9 (Landahl, 1938) constructed from Table 8.6, together with two others constructed differently. To obtain from the first matrix of Table 8.8 the corresponding matrix of any lower order, m, delete the first $9 - m$ columns and the first $10 - m$ rows, and add at the top a row with all elements equal to $\sqrt{1/m}$. Thus to construct the matrix of order 3, delete the first 6 columns and the first 7 rows. What is left is

$$\begin{bmatrix} .8165 & -.4082 & -.4082 \\ 0 & .7071 & -.7071 \end{bmatrix}$$

The value of $\sqrt{1/3}$ is .5774 to four decimals, so the 3 by 3 Landah transformation matrix is

TABLE 8.8
Landahl Transformation Matrices

$$
9\text{-}var\ Y =
\begin{bmatrix}
.3333 & .3333 & .3333 & .3333 & .3333 & .3333 & .3333 & .3333 & .3333 \\
.9428 & -.1179 & -.1179 & -.1179 & -.1179 & -.1179 & -.1179 & -.1179 & -.1179 \\
0 & .9354 & -.1336 & -.1336 & -.1336 & -.1336 & -.1336 & -.1336 \\
0 & 0 & .9258 & -.1543 & -.1543 & -.1543 & -.1543 & -.1543 & -.1543 \\
0 & 0 & 0 & .9129 & -.1826 & -.1826 & -.1826 & -.1826 & -.1826 \\
0 & 0 & 0 & 0 & .8944 & -.2236 & -.2236 & -.2236 & -.2236 \\
0 & 0 & 0 & 0 & 0 & .8660 & -.2887 & -.2887 & -.2887 \\
0 & 0 & 0 & 0 & 0 & 0 & .8165 & -.4082 & -.4082 \\
0 & 0 & 0 & 0 & 0 & 0 & 0 & .7071 & -.7071
\end{bmatrix}
$$

$$
4\text{-}var\ Y =
\begin{bmatrix}
.5 & .5 & .5 & .5 \\
.5 & .5 & -.5 & -.5 \\
.5 & -.5 & .5 & -.5 \\
.5 & -.5 & -.5 & .5
\end{bmatrix}
$$

$$
8\text{-}var\ Y =
\begin{bmatrix}
.3536 & .3536 & .3536 & .3536 & .3536 & .3536 & .3536 & .3536 \\
.3536 & -.3536 & .3536 & .3536 & -.3536 & -.3536 & -.3536 & .3536 \\
.3536 & .3536 & .3536 & -.3536 & -.3536 & .3536 & -.3536 & -.3536 \\
.3536 & .3536 & -.3536 & -.3536 & .3536 & -.3536 & -.3536 & .3536 \\
.3536 & -.3536 & -.3536 & .3536 & .3536 & .3536 & -.3536 & -.3536 \\
.3536 & -.3536 & .3536 & -.3536 & .3536 & -.3536 & .3536 & -.3536 \\
.3536 & -.3536 & -.3536 & -.3536 & -.3536 & .3536 & .3536 & .3536 \\
.3536 & .3536 & -.3536 & .3536 & -.3536 & -.3536 & .3536 & -.3536
\end{bmatrix}
$$

Note. Based on the table of matrices, pp. 222–223, Landahl, 1938. Used by permission.

$$
L_t = Y =
\begin{bmatrix}
.5774 & .5774 & .5774 \\
.8165 & -.4082 & -.4082 \\
0 & .7071 & -.7071
\end{bmatrix}
$$

To construct a Landahl transformation matrix of order higher than 9, it is necessary to solve numerically only the first few rows of a larger matrix like those of Table 8.6. As soon as the first nonzero element of a row is .9428, the rest of the matrix will be that of the last eight rows of the order-9 matrix apart from additional zeros at the left of each row. Thus for the matrix of order 11, we have $a = b = c = \ldots = \sqrt{1/11}$ and $ab = ac = bc = \ldots = a^2 = 1/11$. Then from Table 8.6, working at five significant figures, we have

$$a^2 = .090909 \quad a = .30151$$
$$k_2^2 = .90909 \quad k_2 = .95346 \quad k_2 k_3 = .86243$$
$$k_3^2 = .81818 \quad k_3 = .90453 \quad k_3/k_2 = .94868$$
$$k_4^2 = .72727 \quad k_4 = .85280 \quad k_4/k_3 = .94281$$

$$-a^2/k_2 = -.095346 \qquad -a^2/k_2 k_3 = -.10541$$

The Landahl transformation matrix of order 11 is then

$$
\begin{bmatrix}
.3015 & .3015 & .3015 & .3015 & \cdots \\
.9535 & -.0953 & -.0953 & -.0953 & \cdots \\
0 & .9487 & -.1054 & -.1054 & \cdots \\
0 & 0 & .9428 & -.1179 & \cdots \\
\cdot & \cdot & \cdot & \cdot & \cdots \\
\cdot & \cdot & \cdot & \cdot & \cdots \\
\cdot & \cdot & \cdot & \cdot & \cdots
\end{bmatrix}
$$

Table 8.8 also shows two alternative Landahl transformation matrices: for the cases $m = 4$ and $m = 8$ (m a power of 2). In these matrices all elements have the same absolute value, namely $\sqrt{1/m}$, and they are symmetric, so that $L_t = Y = Y'$. They do not give the same transformations as those given by the asymmetric transformation matrices of the same orders: their axes come at different points of the spin about the first axis of F.

Note that, in using an asymmetric Landahl transformation matrix to transform an F-matrix, we must use this transformation matrix as it stands, and *not* its transpose. Thus $L_t = Y_m$ (of Table 8.8), not Y'_m, and the Landahl factor matrix is

$$L = FL_t = FY_m$$

In the middle right region of Table 8.7 we show the Landahl factor matrix L for the nine-aptitude-tests problem, and below it the Landahl transformation matrix of order 3 as derived above. The sums of squares of the elements in the three columns of L are much more nearly equal than are those in the three columns of F. The difference for columns b and c of F is $.786 - .411 = .375$. For L the differences are $1.977 - 1.791 = .186$, $1.977 - 1.789 = .188$, and $1.791 - 1.789 = .002$. Adding these three differences, $.186 + .188 + .002 = .376$, which differs from the bc difference of F, $.375$, by only $.001$, which can be ascribed to rounding error. Thus the differences among the column sums of squares of L sum to the difference between the b and c column sums of squares of F. We do not have a proof that this will always be the case, but it seems probable that it will.

Problem 8.4.2:1. Apply a Landahl transformation to the F-matrix of Exercise 8.1, using the three-variable L_t-matrix of this section as the transformation matrix.

8.5 OTHER ORTHOGONAL TRANSFORMATIONS

The unweighted raw varimax transformation is one of the set of *orthomax* transformations. Some others of this set are also used occasionally in factor analysis. If we substitute v_{ik}^2 for u_{0ik}^2 in (8-1), since the 0 merely emphasizes the fact that the transformation must be orthogonal, multiply this formula by n, and insert a constant C into the second term, the result is

$$Q = \sum_{k=1}^{m} \left[\sum_{i=1}^{n} (v_{ik}^2)^2 - \frac{C}{n} \left(\sum_{i=1}^{n} v_{ik}^2 \right)^2 \right] = max.$$

This is the criterion for the general class of orthomax transformations. If $C = 0$ it is the *quartimax* transformation, the first analytical (nongraphic) transformation to be derived. Carroll (1953), Saunders (1953), Neuhaus and Wrigley (1954), and Ferguson (1954) all derived equivalent versions of the quartimax method independently.

If $C = 1$ we have the *raw varimax* transformation, since maximizing n times a function is equivalent to maximizing the function itself, and if we replace v_{ij} by u_{ij} (or u_{0ij}) the result is the *normal-varimax* transformation (Kaiser, 1958).

If $C = m/2$ we have the *equamax* transformation (Saunders, 1962). Kaiser (1974) discusses the rationale for this transformation.

Other values of C have been considered by various authors, but only these three are in common use.

9 Oblique Transformations

9.1 THE PROCRUSTES TRANSFORMATION

According to Greek legend Procrustes lived on the Corinthian isthmus, between Megara and Corinth, near the main road from Athens to Sparta. He inveigled unwary (and unguarded) passers-by into spending the night with him in his wonderful guest bed which fit exactly every traveler, whether tall or short. This exact fit, however, was attained by fitting the traveler to the bed. If he was too tall, Procrustes chopped off his feet. If he was too short, he was stretched on a rack until he was the same length as the bed.

The term "Procrustes transformation" (or "Procrustes rotation") appears to be due to Hurley and Cattell (1962), though the original idea goes back to Mosier (1939). The investigator specifies what he believes to be the approximate simple structure in a *hypothesis matrix H*, which is *not* itself a rotation of F. The Procrustes transformation then rotates the axes of F to give V_p, which is in some sense the best attainable *rotational* approximation to H. Thus the transformed factor matrix V_p (a reference-vector structure) is forced to fit as well as possible the investigator's hypothesis of what it ought to be.

9.1.1 The Algebra

The basic transformation formula is $F \Lambda = V$. But if H is an approximation to V, we can write the analogous formula

$$FL = H \tag{9-1}$$

to be solved for L. Premultiply both sides of (9-1) by F', so that

$$F'FL = F'H.$$

Then $F'F$ is a square symmetric matrix that, if nonsingular, has an inverse. Premultiply both sides by this inverse:

$$(F'F)^{-1}(F'F)L = (F'F)^{-1}F'H.$$

But $(F'F)^{-1}(F'F) = I$, and hence

$$L = (F'F)^{-1}F'H. \tag{9-2}$$

Now if F is a *principal-axes* factor matrix,

$$F'F = E,$$

where E is a diagonal matrix whose diagonal elements are the eigenvalues of R^*, then

$$(F'F)^{-1} = E^{-1},$$

which is another diagonal matrix whose diagonal elements are the reciprocals of the eigenvalues, and

$$L = E^{-1}F'H. \tag{9-3}$$

Even if F is a centroid factor matrix, we may still substitute for E a diagonal matrix whose diagonal elements are the column sums of squares of the centroid F, with little loss if the number of factors m is fairly small. For small m the centroid F is a reasonably good approximation to the principal-axes F; and the off-diagonal elements of $F'F$, though nonzero, will be small in comparison with its diagonal elements (the column sums of squares). Thus $F'F$ is *approximately* diagonal, and $(F'F)^{-1}$ will be approximated by a diagonal matrix E_c (for E-centroid) whose diagonal elements are the reciprocals of the column sums of squares.

In (9-2) and (9-3), if F is a principal-axes factor matrix, L is a transformation matrix such that FL is an actual least-squares approximation to H. The proof is beyond the scope of this treatment. The column vectors of L, however, are not of unit length, so this transformation is not simply a rotation of the axes of F.

If we normalize the columns of L, we obtain

$$\Lambda = LD \tag{9-4}$$

where D is the diagonal normalizing matrix. Then

$$F\Lambda = V_p, \tag{9-5}$$

and V_p is a matrix obtained by rotation of F which approximates H. This approximation is not strictly a least-squares fit of V_p to H, but it is close to such a least-squares fit. To obtain an actual least-squares fit we must derive equations analogous to (9-2) or (9-3) under the restriction that $diag\ (L'L) = I$, that is, that $L = \Lambda$, and this is not quite the same as the unrestricted solution of (9-2) or (9-3) *followed* by normalization of the columns of L to obtain Λ. The restricted solution has been obtained (ten Berge & Nevels, 1977), but this solution is complex both algebraically and numerically; and because H is usually a fairly crude approximation itself, the added accuracy of the exact least-squares fit is of little moment. Hence (9-2) or (9-3), (9-4), and (9-5) give an acceptable solution.

9.1.2 Computation

To illustrate the Procrustes procedure we will use it to transform the F-matrix of the WAIS subtests for the age-group 25–34, so it can be compared with the extended-vector solution of Table 7.1. The F-matrix, the same as that of Table 7.1, is given in the upper left region of Table 9.1, with column sums, eigenvalues (column sums of squares), and the reciprocals of these eigenvalues at the bottoms of the columns. The eigenvalues and reciprocals are computed to four significant figures to reduce the accumulated rounding error.

We first form the matrix FE^{-1}, (n by m), instead of the matrix $E^{-1}F'$ (m by n) of (9-3). Note that $(FE^{-1})' = E^{-1}F'$, since $(E^{-1})' = E^{-1}$ because E is diagonal and hence symmetric. Because postmultiplication of F by E^{-1} multiplies each column of F by the corresponding element of E^{-1}, we form FE^{-1} simply by multiplying the elements of each column of F by the value of 1/Eig at the bottom of the column. The value for the check row is obtained by multiplying the reciprocal by the column sum. The check should be correct within rounding error. The matrix FE^{-1} is shown in the upper central region of Table 9.1.

The elements of the H-matrix will be merely 1s and 0s: a 1 indicating the hypothesis of a nonzero loading and a 0 the hypothesis of a near-zero loading. From the list of variables given at the beginning of Section 7.1.5 and the knowledge that the F-matrix has three factors, we judge initially that we will have a verbal factor, a nonverbal (pictorial) reasoning factor, and a smaller numerical or quantitative factor.

The verbal tests are 1 (Information), 2 (Comprehension), 4 (Similarities), and 6 (Vocabulary), so in the H-matrix in the upper right region of Table 9.1 we record 1s in rows (1), (2), (4), and (6) of column I, and 0s elsewhere in this column.

The nonverbal reasoning tests are 8 (Picture Completion), 9 (Block Design), 10 (Picture Arrangement), and 11 (Object Assembly), so we record 1s in these rows in column II and 0s elsewhere in this column.

Test 3 (Arithmetic) is the clearly numerical or quantitative test, and 5 (Digit Span) may be assumed to have some numerical content, as immediate memory for numbers might be expected to correlate significantly with ability in using them. We then have only 7 (Digit Symbol) as yet unassigned. But this is essentially a perceptual and drawing speed test. The digits are used only to identify the symbols, and the task is to draw the symbol that goes with each digit rather than

TABLE 9.1
Procrustes Rotation for Eleven WAIS Subtests, Age-Group 25–34 (N = 300)

Test	Principal Axes F a	b	c	FE^{-1} a	b	c	Hypothesis H I	II	III
(1)	.886	−.183	−.029	.147	−.333	−.124	1	0	0
(2)	.761	−.141	.249	.126	−.257	1.066	1	0	0
(3)	.698	−.085	−.262	.116	−.155	−1.122	0	0	1
(4)	.775	−.182	.030	.128	−.331	.128	1	0	0
(5)	.588	−.098	−.263	.097	−.178	−1.126	0	0	1
(6)	.878	−.282	.134	.145	−.514	.574	1	0	0
(7)	.657	.023	−.037	.109	.042	−.158	0	0	0
(8)	.756	.176	.070	.125	.320	.300	0	1	0
(9)	.730	.361	−.044	.121	.657	−.188	0	1	0
(10)	.744	.130	−.012	.123	.237	−.051	0	1	0
(11)	.615	.433	.075	.102	.788	.321	0	1	0
Σ	8.088	.152	−.089	1.339	.276	−.380			
Eig	6.036	.5491	.2335	1.339	.277	−.381			
1/Eig	.1656	1.821	4.283						

Ch

	L I	II	III	Test	Rotated V_p I	II	III	Extended Vector V I	II	III
a	.546	.471	.213	(1)	(.311)	.019	.138	(.304)	.003	.215
b	−1.435	2.002	−.333	(2)	(.457)	.082	−.154	(.480)	.066	−.082
c	1.644	.382	−2.248	(3)	.032	.028	(.335)	.012	.018	(.384)
$\Sigma\ell^2$	5.0601	4.3758	5.2098	(4)	(.326)	.006	.069	(.322)	−.009	.140
$\sqrt{\Sigma\ell^2}$	2.2495	2.0918	2.2825	(5)	.013	−.010	(.328)	−.012	−.018	(.371)
$1/\sqrt{\Sigma\ell^2}$	.44454	.47806	.43812	(6)	(.491)	−.048	−.009	(.485)	−.066	.081
				(7)	.118	.163	.094	.135	.152	.136
		Λ_p		(8)	.123	(.351)	−.024	.176	(.339)	.014
	I	II	III	(9)	−.085	(.502)	.059	−.016	(.492)	.074
				(10)	.089	(.290)	.062	.127	(.278)	.101
a	.243	.225	.093	(11)	−.072	(.566)	−.080	.016	(.558)	−.075
b	−.638	.957	−.146	Σ	1.803	1.949	.818	2.029	1.813	1.359
c	.731	.183	−.985	Ch	1.803	1.949	.818	2.028	1.813	1.359
$\Sigma\lambda^2$	1.000	1.000	1.000							

even to write the digit which goes with each symbol. For adults, this test has little if any numerical or quantitative content, and little if any verbal or nonverbal reasoning content either. We therefore record 1s only in rows (3) and (5) of column III, and 0s elsewhere in this column. Row (7) then contains three 0s, indicating that no other test in the battery goes with Digit Symbol to form a coding factor.

We are now ready to proceed. By (9-3), $L = (E^{-1}F')H$. This is the usual row by column product. But for computing, with FE^{-1} written alongside H, we can use column by column multiplication to find L. And, because H is here a matrix with elements only 0 or 1, each column by column multiplication consists merely in summing, in a column of FE^{-1}, the elements that correspond to 1s in a column of H. By labeling the columns of H and L I, II, and III, and the columns of FE^{-1} and the *rows* of L a, b, and c, the particular partial sum forming each element of L is immediately apparent. Because there is no check, these partial sums should each be computed twice.

Normalize the columns of L to obtain Λ_p. The matrix L, the computations for normalizing its columns, and Λ_p are shown in the lower left region of Table 9.1. Then $F\Lambda_p = V_p$, the Procrustes transformed factor matrix, which is shown in the lower central region of Table 9.1. The loadings assumed to be substantial in H are enclosed in parentheses. The extended-vector solution of Table 7.1 is shown at its right for comparison. The columns of the extended-vector factor matrix have been rearranged in order to agree with those of V_p.

9.1.3 Interpretation and Remarks

It is at once apparent, from H and V_p, that the hypothesis represented by the H-matrix is confirmed. In each column of V_p the elements in parentheses are substantially larger than any of the others, and none of these others is as high as .200.

Comparing V_p with the extended-vector V, there seems little to choose between the two solutions. The excellence of a simple structure is commonly judged by the hyperplane count (HC): the number of loadings with absolute values .100 or lower in each column and in all columns combined. By this criterion we have:

	I	II	III	Σ
Procrustes	5	6	7	18
Extended-vector	4	6	5	15

The Procrustes solution gives three more near-zeros than does the extended-vector solution, and hence is a better solution by this criterion.

Another method of evaluating the simple structure consists first in forcing the number of near-zeros in each column of the two solutions to equality. For each column, the solution giving the larger hyperplane count is taken as the standard. Then, if the standard includes k such near-zeros, the k elements lowest in absolute value in the solution with the smaller hyperplane count are counted as near-zeros. For each column and for all columns combined, the sum of absolute values of the near-zeros thus defined are compared, and the solution having the smaller sum of absolute values is considered the better. For the WAIS data we have:

	I	II	III	Σ
Procrustes	.291	.193	.397	.881
Extended-vector	.183	.181	.563	.927

By this criterion, the extended-vector hyperplane fit is better for factors I and II, but its fit for factor III is so poor that the Procrustes fit is slightly better over all.

Exercise 9:1. Rotate the principal-axes F-matrix for the nine-aptitude-tests problem by the Procrustes method. This F-matrix is given in columns a, b, and c of the factor matrix of Table 5.3. For H, give 1s to variables 1, 2, and 3 for factor I; to variables 4, 5, and 6 for factor II; and to variables 7, 8, and 9 for factor III. Compare the results with those you obtained by the extended-vector method in Exercise 7:1 using hyperplane counts and sums of absolute values.

9.2   THE TWO-FACTOR CASE

In this case examination of the plot of the F-matrix will lead directly to the formation of the H-matrix for an oblique Procrustes rotation.

For the WAIS age-group 18–19 (Wechsler, 1955, p. 15), a principal-axes solution repeated once to give $\Sigma h^2 \doteq \Sigma r_{ii}$ yields a very good two-factor fit. Table 9.2 shows rotations by the Procrustes method and the outer-centroids method of Chapter 2, and Fig. 9.1 shows the plot.

For the outer-centroids method, from Fig. 2.2 for the oblique case, we obtain the transformation matrix Λ by converting the rows to columns:

	Λ	
	I	II
a	$-(\mathrm{I}b)$	$(\mathrm{II}b)$
b	$(\mathrm{I}a)$	$-(\mathrm{II}a)$

or for the data of this problem

	Λ	
	I	II
a	.214	.399
b	.977	$-.917$

and to agree with the Procrustes rotation we have interchanged factors I and II.

By (2-25) in Fig. 2.2, the correlation between the primary factors (the cosine of the angle between the axes I and II) is

$$r_{\text{I II}} = (\text{I}a)(\text{II}a) + (\text{I}b)(\text{II}b),$$

TABLE 9.2

Rotation by the Procrustes Method and the Outer-Centroids Method
for Eleven WAIS Subtests, Age-Group 18–19 (N = 200)

Test	Principal Axes F		FE^{-1}		H		Procrustes V_p	
	a	b	a	b	I	II	I	II
(1)	.881	−.156	.139	−.238			.517	.051
(2)	.751	−.224	.119	−.342	1	0	.523	−.045
(3)	.718	−.134	.113	−.205	1	0	.428	.035
(4)	.832	−.160	.131	−.244	1	0	.500	.036
(5)	.631	−.159	.100	−.243	1	0	.413	−.010
(6)	.875	−.271	.138	−.414	1	0	.619	−.062
(7)	.704	−.076	.111	−.116	1	0	.369	.088
(8)	.769	.251	.121	.384	0	1	.101	.421
(9)	.757	.391	.119	.597	0	1	−.030	.555
(10)	.700	.217	.110	332	0	1	.103	.372
(11)	.690	.411	.109	.628	0	1	−.076	.559
Σ	8.308	.090	1.310	.139			3.467	2.000
Eig	6.338	.6545	Ch 1.311	.138			Ch 3.466	1.998
$1/Eig$	.1578	1.528						

	L					Outer Centroids[a] V	
	I	II	Centroid 1–7		Test	I	II
a	.851	.459	a	5.392	(1)	.495	.036
b	−1.802	1.941	b	−1.180	(2)	.505	−.058
			Σ^2	30.466	(3)	.409	.023
$\Sigma\ell^2$	3.971	3.978	$\sqrt{\Sigma^2}$	5.5196	(4)	.479	.022
$\sqrt{\Sigma\ell^2}$	1.993	1.994	$1/\sqrt{\Sigma^2}$	.18117	(5)	.398	−.020
$1/\sqrt{\Sigma\ell^2}$	.5018	.5015	$(\text{I}a)$	.977	(6)	.598	−.078
			$(\text{I}b)$	−.214	(7)	.351	.076
					(8)	.077	.410
			Σ^2	1.000	(9)	−.057	.544
					(10)	.080	.362
					(11)	−.102	.549
					Σ	3.233	1.866
					Ch	3.232	1.866

(*continued*)

TABLE 9.2 (*continued*)

	Procrustes Λ_p		Centroid 8–11		Outer Centroids[a] Λ	
	I	II			I	II
a	.427	.230	a	2.916	a	.399	.214
b	−.904	.973	b	1.270	b	−.917	.977
			Σ^2	10.116		
$\Sigma\lambda^2$	1.000	1.000	$\sqrt{\Sigma^2}$	3.1806		
			$1/\sqrt{\Sigma^2}$	.31441		
			(IIa)	.917		
			(IIb)	.399		
			Σ^2	1.000		

[a] Factors I and II interchanged.

Note. Computed from the correlation matrix, Table 7, p. 15, Wechsler, 1955. Copyright 1955 by The Psychological Corporation. Used by permission.

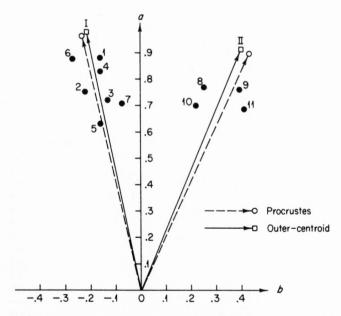

Fig. 9.1. Plot of factor loadings with Procrustes and outer-centroid axes for eleven WAIS subtests, age-group 18–19 ($N = 200$).

that is, the sum of products of the pairs of entries in columns I and II of the rows a and b of Λ_p or Λ, with the signs of the upper right and lower left elements reversed. For the Procrustes Λ_p this is

$$r_{\text{I II}} = (-.427)(.230) + (-.904)(-.973) = .781,$$

and for the outer-centroids Λ it is

$$r_{\text{I II}} = (-.399)(.214) + (-.917)(-.977) = .811.$$

The outer-centroid primary axes are a little closer together, as may be seen in Fig. 9.1.

From the normalized-centroid vectors of Table 9.2, the coordinates of the "hyperplanes" are .977, $-.214$ for factor I and .917, .399 for factor II. These reference-vector factors were then interchanged, as noted above, to agree with the Procrustes rotation, so that in Fig. 9.1 axes I and II become I = HII and II = HI. These axes are then correctly numbered as the *primary axes,* I = PI and II = PII (Section 6.3.1).

By analogy, comparing the Procrustes Λ_p with the outer-centroids Λ in Table 9.2, the coordinates of the Procrustes "hyperplanes" should be .904, .427 for factor I (or PII), and .973, $-.230$ for factor II (or PI), as indeed they are; but we need to prove this. In the general (m-factor) case, by (6-18) and (6-20), the coordinates of the primary axes are given by the rows of

$$T' = D\Lambda^{-1} \tag{9-6}$$

or the columns of

$$T = (\Lambda')^{-1}D, \tag{9-7}$$

so we need to know what $D\Lambda^{-1}$ or $(\Lambda')^{-1}D$ is in the two-factor case.

9.2.1 Inverse of a 2 by 2 Matrix

For a 2 by 2 matrix, evaluation of the inverse by a direct method described in elementary treatments of determinants is more expeditious than the methods described in Chapter 4. If A is the 2 by 2 matrix,

$$A = \begin{bmatrix} a & b \\ c & d \end{bmatrix} \tag{9-8}$$

the *determinant* of A is the scalar,

$$\Delta = ad - bc \tag{9-9}$$

and the inverse of A is

$$A^{-1} = \begin{bmatrix} d/\Delta & -b/\Delta \\ -c/\Delta & a/\Delta \end{bmatrix} \tag{9-10}$$

Consider in particular the case where $A = \Lambda$, the transformation matrix of the oblique transformation $F\Lambda = V$. We wish to obtain the T of (9-7), in which D is the diagonal matrix that normalizes the columns of $(\Lambda')^{-1}$. Then if

$$\Lambda = \begin{bmatrix} a & b \\ c & d \end{bmatrix} = \begin{bmatrix} -(Ib) & (IIb) \\ (Ia) & -(IIa) \end{bmatrix} \qquad (9\text{-}11)$$

$$\Lambda' = \begin{bmatrix} a & c \\ b & d \end{bmatrix} = \begin{bmatrix} -(Ib) & (Ia) \\ (IIb) & -(IIa) \end{bmatrix} \qquad (9\text{-}12)$$

and the value of T is given by

$$T = \begin{bmatrix} d & -c \\ -b & a \end{bmatrix} = \begin{bmatrix} -(IIa) & -(Ia) \\ -(IIb) & -(Ib) \end{bmatrix} \quad \text{if } \Delta \text{ is positive} \quad (9\text{-}13)$$

or by

$$T = \begin{bmatrix} -d & c \\ b & -a \end{bmatrix} = \begin{bmatrix} (IIa) & (Ia) \\ (IIb) & (Ib) \end{bmatrix} \quad \text{if } \Delta \text{ is negative} \quad (9\text{-}14)$$

The value of Δ can be determined by inspection, or if necessary by (9-9).

The second matrix for the Λ of (9-11) is the Procrustes Λ_p of Table 9.2. It is evident that Δ is positive for that Λ_p, for

$$\Delta = ad - bc = (.427)(.973) - (.230)(-.904)$$
$$= (.427)(.973) + (.230)(.904),$$

with all factors positive. Then by (9-13)

$$\begin{array}{cc} & \text{I} \qquad \text{II} \\ T = \begin{array}{c} a \\ b \end{array} \begin{bmatrix} .973 & .904 \\ -.230 & .427 \end{bmatrix} \end{array}$$

that is, the coordinates are .973, $-.230$ for primary factor I and .904, .427 for primary factor II, as we saw by analogy just above (9-6).

We may also need D or D^{-1}. To find D, we merely compute $\Delta = ad - bc$ from Λ or T. Thus for our example

$$\Delta = (.427)(.973) + (.230)(.904) = .623.$$

Then if Δ is positive, the diagonal elements of D are both equal to Δ, and if Δ is negative, they are both equal to $-\Delta$. The diagonal elements of D^{-1} are the reciprocals of those of D, or $1/.623 = 1.505$. Note that the diagonal elements of D and D^{-1} are always positive.

Exercise 9:2. In Exercise 2:1 the two-factor centroid factor matrix for six psychological tests was obtained, and in Exercise 2:2 the results were plotted and rotated by the outer-centroids method. Rotate the F-matrix by the Procrustes method, taking the sum of squares of the elements in each column of F as an approximation to the eigenvalue. Compare the results with those of Exercise 2:2.

9.3   THE PROMAX TRANSFORMATION

Although the Procrustes procedure has not been shown to be generally superior to the outer-centroids procedure in the two-factor case, nor to the extended-vector procedure in the three-factor case, it has the advantage that it can be generalized to any number of factors and programmed for an electronic digital computer.

Though larger numbers of factors can be rotated graphically either two at a time or three at a time, and though the computations can be programmed in either case, these graphical procedures are iterative. At each cycle it is necessary to make a number of plots, and the judgments based on them become increasingly difficult as m increases: so much so that graphical rotation becomes an art. It is the conviction of the writers, therefore, that graphical rotation when $m > 3$ is primarily of historic rather than practical interest, and methods of graphical rotation for $m > 3$ are not discussed in this book.

To use the Procrustes procedure when $m > 3$, we require an objective method for constructing an H-matrix of any order. This problem was solved by Hendrickson and White (1964) and termed by them the Promax (for Procrustes-varimax) method. In using this method, the H-matrix is formed from a varimax (the present writers prefer a weighted-varimax) factor matrix. Either the row-normal matrix V_n or the denormalized matrix V_0 (of Section 8.3) may be used for this purpose.

The elements of V_n or V_0 are then raised to some power, usually the square, cube, or fourth power, with their original signs restored if the power is 2 or 4, to form the hypothesis matrix H. Powering reduces the absolute values of all the loadings, but the low and moderately low loadings are reduced proportionally more, to become near-zeros, as can be seen in Table 9.3. This procedure yields an H-matrix whose elements are more nearly proportional in each column to those of an oblique simple structure than are those of the orthogonal approximation, V_n or V_0.

Powering the elements of a varimax or weighted-varimax factor matrix is not a rotational procedure, and the numerical reduction of the loadings by powering may be considerable. The rest of the Promax procedure therefore consists of a Procrustes rotation of F toward H. Note that the elements of a column of H need only be *proportional* to those of the corresponding column of the final oblique V-matrix for a Procrustes rotation to give good results. The proof is given in Section 9.6.1. Hendrickson and White suggest that the Procrustes rotation be from the orthogonally rotated factor matrix V_0 or V_n toward H. In Section 9.6.2 we show that rotation from F or F_n gives the same result (the same V-matrix).

TABLE 9.3
Effects of Powering Varimax
(or Weighted-Varimax) Loadings
on Relative Range

Varimax Loading	Power		
	2	3	4
.9	.81	.729	.6561
.8	.64	.512	.4096
.7	.49	.343	.2401
.6	.36	.216	.1296
.5	.25	.125	.0625
.4	.16	.064	.0256
.3	.09	.027	.0081
.2	.04	.008	.0016
.1	.01	.001	.0001

The optimum choice of the matrix to use in forming H (the row-normal V_n or the denormalized V_0) varies with the data, as does also the optimum power (2, 3, or 4). If the best simple structure is essentially orthogonal, the denormalized weighted-varimax factor matrix is itself the best analytic approximation to simple structure, the optimum power is 1, and the Procrustes transformation is simply a transformation of V_0 into itself. As the obliquity increases, so also does the optimum power.

Cureton (1976) performed six Promax rotations of each of nine sets of data, forming H from V_0 and V_n with powers 2, 3, and 4. The best results were obtained most frequently, in the absence of prior knowledge of the obliquity and other features of the data, by using the *fourth* powers of the elements of the *row-normalized* weighted-varimax factor matrix V_n in forming H.

Examples of Promax rotations are given in Tables 8.1 and 8.5, and also in Tables 9.4 and 9.5, following.

The Promax transformation tends merely to "close up" (or occasionally, for one or more factors, to "open out") the orthogonal hyperplanes to oblique positions. The oblique hyperplanes of V remain more or less parallel to the orthogonal hyperplanes of V_n or V_0, because each hyperplane of H is formed from a hyperplane of V_n or V_0 by the same powering procedure. If the orthogonal hyperplanes are not closely parallel to the best oblique hyperplanes, the Promax procedure applies to them little or no "spin" about the origin in order to attain the optimum oblique positions. Though the weighted-varimax rotation improves the *over-all* parallelism somewhat, as compared to the unweighted normal-varimax rotation, the hyperplanes of an orthogonal factor matrix *cannot* be closely parallel to those of the final oblique factor matrix unless the latter form an almost-symmetric structure, which they seldom do.

9.4 THE OPTRES TRANSFORMATION

An entirely different approach to the problem of analytic rotation to simple structure is represented by the Optres (for optimum resolution) transformation (Hakstian, 1972). It is based on the idea that in a good simple structure the near-zero loadings on each factor should be as small as possible in comparison with the high loadings. More specifically it uses, for each hyperplane j of V separately ($j = 1, 2, \ldots, m$), the criterion

$$Q_j = M(v_{j(s)}^2) - kM(v_{j(ns)}^2) = max. \tag{9-15}$$

Here $M(v_{j(s)}^2)$ is the mean of the squared loadings on the *salient*[1] variables of factor j (those that should have high loadings on this factor); $M(v_{j(ns)}^2)$ is the mean of the squared loadings on the *nonsalient* variables of factor j (those that should have near-zero loadings on this factor); and k is a constant included to give more or less equal importance to the two terms of Q_j. This leads, for each factor j, to the equation,

$$W_j = (1/p_j)F_{j(s)}'F_{j(s)} - (k/q_j)F_{j(ns)}'F_{j(ns)}, \tag{9-16}$$

where p_j is the number of salient variables; q_j is the number of nonsalient variables; $F_{j(s)}$ consists of those rows of F corresponding to salient variables; $F_{j(ns)}$ consists of those rows of F corresponding to nonsalient variables; and k, the same k as in (9-15), is a constant designed to give more or less equal importance to the salient and nonsalient variables in (9-16). Hakstian suggests the value 50 for k, but empirical studies with the nine sets of data mentioned previously (Cureton, 1976) indicate that the value 100 gives better results more frequently. To see how the use of the constant k works, suppose the root-mean-square of the salient loadings is .5. The mean-square salient loading is then .25. Suppose the root-mean-square of the nonsalient loadings is .05. The mean-square nonsalient loading is then .0025, and multiplication by 100 gives .25, which is equal to the mean-square salient loading. The value of k is not critical: quite rough equalization of the two terms of W_j is sufficient.

If there are some variables of factor j which have low nonzero loadings, and hence are neither salient nor nonsalient, they are ignored: $p_j + q_j$ may but need not equal n, the total number of variables.

The matrix W_j of (9-16) is of order m by m, where m is the number of factors. Let B_j represent the unit eigenvector of W_j corresponding to its largest eigenvalue. We must find B_j for each factor separately. Then the m by m matrix B, with unit column vectors B_j, is the Optres transformation matrix, and

$$V = FB$$

is the Optres reference-vector-structure factor matrix.

---

[1]Do not confuse with "salient" as used in "number of salient initial *factors*" (Chapters 2 and 5).

It is perhaps worth noting that the matrices W_j (one for each factor), though symmetric, tend to have most of their elements negative. In this situation the Hotelling-Horst algorithm, described in Chapter 5, often fails to converge, and the eigenvectors B_j must be determined by some more general method.

In order to use the Optres procedure we must know in advance, for each factor, the salient variables and the nonsalient variables. This is essentially the same problem we encountered in Section 9.1 in using the Procrustes transformation. This problem can be solved in various ways, and finding the exact optimum sets of salient and nonsalient variables is not crucial so long as good approximations to these optimum sets are obtained for each factor. An approximation is very good if, in the final Optres factor matrix, (1) all the loadings of the selected nonsalient variables are lower in absolute value than those of any variable not so selected, even though they are not all below $\pm.100$; and (2) if the loadings of the selected salient variables are all higher in absolute value than any others. The approximation is probably at least adequate if, among the Optres factor loadings, the variables selected as nonsalient all have numerically lower loadings than any of those selected as salient. There may be one or two reversals (cases in which the final value of a variable selected as nonsalient is higher than the final value of one selected as salient) if all or almost all of the n variables were selected as either salient or nonsalient, with none or at most only one or two which were not selected as either salient or nonsalient.

To find the lists of salient and nonsalient variables for each factor, we use the weighted-varimax-Promax procedure. When we have the Promax factor matrix V_p, we apply for each column two empirically derived rules (Cureton, 1976).

1. *Nonsalient* variables. The principle is to select as many as possible of the variables with loadings lowest in absolute value, subject to the restriction that after an optimum rotation these loadings will all lie between $\pm.100$. Select first the variable whose loading is numerically lowest, then the one whose loading is second lowest, and so on, until the sum of the highest positive loading and the absolute value of the highest negative loading is as large as possible without exceeding .200. Suppose these loadings are

Variable	4	2	9	7	13	3	18	6	etc.
Loading	−.003	.004	−.010	.021	−.063	.119	.123	.139	etc.

Here $.063 + .123 = .186 < .200$;
But $.063 + .139 = .202 > .200$.

Note that if we include any given variable we *must* include all others which are numerically lower. The nonsalient variables are therefore 4, 2, 9, 7, 13, 3, and 18.

If the low loadings all have the same sign, the last one included should be the one whose loading is largest but not greater in absolute value than .200.

2. Select as *salient* all loadings whose absolute values are at least one-half as great as that of the numerically highest loading in the column, *provided* that a loading already selected as nonsalient may not be selected as salient also. This last provision is seldom needed, but it *can* be necessary. Thus if the highest negative loading is $-.020$ and the highest positive loading is $.350$, a variable with loading $.178$ would be selected as nonsalient ($.178 + .020 = .198 < .200$), and this variable could not then be selected as salient also even though $.178 > .350/2 = .175$.

Table 9.4 compares the Promax and Optres solutions for Thurstone's 26-variable box problem. To facilitate the comparison, the loadings in each column

TABLE 9.4
Comparison of Promax and Optres Rotations
for Thurstone's Complete 26-Variable Box Problem

			Promax						Optres		
Var	I	Var	II	Var	III	Var	I	Var	II	Var	III
(1)	.953	(2)	.894	(3)	.896	(1)	.946	(2)	.898	(3)	.903
(5)	.797	(23)	.818	(22)	.807	(5)	.795	(23)	.814	(11)	.804
(10)	.780	(20)	.789	(11)	.773	(21)	.771	(20)	.784	(22)	.770
(21)	.739	(6)	.770	(16)	.738	(10)	.754	(6)	.778	(24)	.751
(19)	.729	(15)	.721	(24)	.722	(19)	.712	(15)	.727	(16)	.731
(9)	.608	(7)	.674	(14)	.611	(4)	.607	(7)	.682	(12)	.646
(4)	.603	(8)	.664	(12)	.609	(9)	.573	(8)	.672	(13)	.639
(12)	.572	(4)	.609	(13)	.604	(12)	.536	(4)	.618	(9)	.606
(13)	.542	(18)	.577	(17)	.599	(7)	.522	(18)	.585	(14)	.600
(7)	.516	(17)	.577	(9)	.568	(8)	.512	(17)	.585	(17)	.588
(8)	.507	(14)	.572	(18)	.568	(13)	.506	(14)	.580	(18)	.558
(11)	.473	(26)	.493	(26)	.445	(25)	.435	(26)	.503	(26)	.454
(25)	.454	(25)	.446	(15)	.436	(11)	.430	(25)	.457	(25)	.436
(6)	.361	(16)	.407	(25)	.419	(6)	.366	(16)	.415	(15)	.419
(26)	.347	(5)	.362	(10)	.347	(26)	.328	(5)	.372	(10)	.394
(24)	.063	(3)	.043	(2)	.062	(2)	.056	(3)	.051	(2)	.041
(3)	.051	(21)	.017	(20)	.048	(18)	.020	(11)	.024	(6)	.029
(2)	.047	(11)	.012	(6)	.029	(24)	.015	(21)	.019	(19)	.015
(18)	.040	(9)	−.009	(8)	−.020	(3)	.007	(9)	.003	(5)	.007
(17)	.021	(1)	−.016	(5)	−.028	(17)	−.001	(1)	−.005	(1)	−.006
(16)	.010	(22)	−.017	(4)	−.032	(15)	−.015	(13)	−.009	(8)	−.009
(14)	.004	(13)	−.021	(7)	−.032	(23)	−.015	(10)	−.015	(4)	−.014
(15)	−.003	(10)	−.027	(19)	−.048	(14)	−.019	(22)	−.019	(20)	−.015
(23)	−.063	(12)	−.034	(1)	−.060	(16)	−.021	(12)	−.022	(7)	−.020
(20)	−.729	(19)	−.789	(23)	−.722	(20)	−.712	(19)	−.784	(23)	−.751
(22)	−.739	(24)	−.818	(21)	−.807	(22)	−.771	(24)	−.814	(21)	−.770
$\|M\|$	.034		.022		.040		.019		.019		.017

are arranged in order from highest positive to highest negative, with the original variable-number (from Table 8.5) printed at the left of each loading. Two horizontal lines in the lower half of each column mark off the near-zero loadings, which are those of the nonsalient variables. In the Promax matrix another horizontal line about the middle of each column separates the positive salient variables (above the line) from the others. The two variables at the bottom of each column are also salient, with large negative loadings.

The hyperplane count is nine for each column of both solutions. Below each column, in a row labeled $|M|$, we show the mean absolute value of the nine near-zero loadings in the column. All three of the Optres means are lower than any one of the Promax means. Thus despite the excellence of the Promax hyperplane fits, the fits of the Optres hyperplanes are slightly better.

A final step consists in reflecting any *column* of the Optres factor matrix the sum of those loadings is negative, and along with it the corresponding column of the Optres transformation matrix. In the weighted-varimax procedure (and the unweighted normal-varimax as well), one or more columns may come out inverted, and these inversions carry over to the Promax and Optres factor matrices if they are not corrected. This happened with the box problem in column III. The original print-out of the ordered Promax factor matrix came out with variables 21 and 23 at the top, and 22 and 3 at the bottom. But because of this final step, the ordered Optres factor III came out as shown. It is usually best to report bipolar factors (such as those of the box problem) with the preponderance of loadings positive. In marginal cases, where the sum of the Promax loadings is close to zero, the sign of this sum may change as we go from the Promax to the Optres solution, so we defer column reflection to the final Optres factor matrix.

To the writers, this combination of the weighted-varimax, Promax, and Optres rotations appears to be the best procedure presently available for computer rotation to simple structure.

As a further example, we show in Table 9.5 various rotations of the F-matrix of the eleven WAIS subtests, age-group 25–34. The extended-vector rotation is that of Table 7.1, with columns rearranged to agree with the order in which the factors came out on the computer.

To assist the reader in comparing the Promax, Optres, and extended-vector solutions, all loadings below .100 have been enclosed in parentheses, and at the bottom of the table in row HC the number of these near-zeros in each column is recorded. The total hyperplane counts are 13 for the Promax solution, 16 for the Optres solution, and 15 for the extended-vector solution. Remember here that the Procrustes solution, with H-matrix derived from substantive considerations, gave 18.

With largest hyperplane counts six for factor I, five for factor II, and six for factor III, the mean absolute values of the near-zeros are given in the row labeled $|M|$. For the three factors combined, the means are .073 for the Promax solution, .053 for the Optres solution, and .049 for the extended-vector solution.

TABLE 9.5
Rotations for Eleven WAIS Subtests, Age-Group 25–34 (N = 300)

Test	Principal Axes			Weighted-Varimax			Hypothesis		
	a	b	c	A	B	C	I	II	III
(1)	.886	−.183	−.029	.571	.596	.370	.159	.188	.028
(2)	.761	−.141	.249	.532	.330	.519	.183	.027	.166
(3)	.698	−.085	−.262	.460	.588	.075	.141	.377	.000
(4)	.775	−.182	.030	.493	.499	.378	.147	.154	.051
(5)	.588	−.098	−.263	.367	.537	.046	.100	.461	.000
(6)	.878	−.282	.134	.523	.544	.547	.099	.116	.119
(7)	.657	.023	−.037	.521	.363	.175	.391	.093	.005
(8)	.756	.176	.070	.704	.264	.205	.666	.013	.005
(9)	.730	.361	−.044	.786	.218	.007	.862	.005	.000
(10)	.744	.130	−.012	.658	.334	.164	.574	.038	.002
(11)	.615	.433	.075	.755	.040	.021	.993	.000	.000

Test	Promax			Optres			Extended-Vector		
	I	II	III	I	II	III	I	II	III
(1)	.109	.251	.213	(.010)	.280	.244	(.003)	.215	.304
(2)	.152	(−.044)	.416	(.064)	(−.015)	.425	(.066)	(−.082)	.480
(3)	.104	.400	(−.068)	(.031)	.418	(−.036)	(.018)	.384	(.012)
(4)	(.084)	.175	.245	(−.004)	.202	.270	(−.009)	.140	.322
(5)	(.056)	.385	(−.082)	(−.006)	.400	(−.051)	(−.018)	.371	(−.012)
(6)	(.040)	.130	.399	(−.063)	.164	.429	(−.066)	(.081)	.485
(7)	.227	.149	(.074)	.159	.166	(.083)	.152	.136	.135
(8)	.418	(.019)	.116	.343	(.036)	.107	.339	(.014)	.176
(9)	.565	(.060)	(−.071)	.500	(.070)	(−.092)	.492	(.074)	(−.016)
(10)	.359	.108	(.063)	.285	.124	(.062)	.278	.101	.127
(11)	.614	(−.095)	(−.020)	.562	(−.089)	(−.055)	.558	(−.075)	(.016)
HC	3	4	6	6	4	6	6	5	4
$\|M\|$	.091	.065	.063	.030	.067	.063	.030	.065	.053

9.5   OTHER PROCEDURES FOR OBLIQUE NUMERICAL TRANSFORMATION

There are a number of other numerical (nongraphic) procedures for oblique transformation of an F-matrix to a V-matrix. We consider briefly the more commonly-used of these methods. All of them employ the single criterion of overdetermination, estimating this as the minimum covariance of the squared loadings in pairs of columns. If v_{ik} is a loading on the final transformed (rotated) factor matrix, and $u_{ik} = v_{ik}/h_i$, with h_i the length of the i-th test vector or the square root of the communality of the i-th variable, and if j designates a factor other than k, then one criterion is

$$Q = \sum_{j<k=1}^{m(m-1)/2} \left[n \sum_{i=1}^{n} u_{ij}^2 \, u_{ik}^2 - C\left(\sum_{i=1}^{n} u_{ij}^2 \right) \left(\sum_{i=1}^{n} u_{ik}^2 \right) \right] = min.$$

This is the formula for the *oblimin* class of transformations. The constant C defines the particular member of the class. If $C = 0$, we have the *quartimin* solution (Carroll, 1953). This solution is usually more acute than optimum. If $C = 1$, we have the *covarimin* solution (Carroll, 1953, Kaiser, 1958). This solution is usually more nearly orthogonal than optimum. Carroll (1957) proposed to take the mean of these two values and let $C = .5$. This he termed the *biquartimin* criterion. It is probably closer to optimum than either $C = 0$ or $C = 1$ but is not actually optimum in general.

A variant of these procedures is the *direct oblimin* solution (Jennrich & Sampson, 1966), that gives directly the primary factors. But in the absence of the reference-structure matrix it is difficult to judge the excellence of the simple structure. There is again an arbitrary constant, whose value determines the acuteness or obtuseness of the solution.

The *orthoblique* method (Harris & Kaiser, 1964) gives oblique solutions by applying orthogonal transformations, not to F itself, but to the matrix of retained eigenvectors of R^* pre- and/or postmultiplied by one or more diagonal (rescaling) matrices, one of which is the diagonal matrix of the retained eigenvalues. Two special cases are discussed by Harris and Kaiser. The first is the "independent cluster" case, in which the test vectors fall into exactly m clusters centered on the primary axes, each test having nonzero loadings on one and only one common factor. In this case the fit is excellent. The second case is termed "$A'A$ proportional to L," where A is the factor-pattern matrix and L is the matrix of intercorrelations among these factors. Using this second case, Harris and Kaiser obtained a good fit to Thurstone's original 20-variable box problem (Thurstone, 1940). The class of problems to which this case applies is not defined, and there is a third case which has not yet been thoroughly investigated.

All of these methods yield acceptable simple structures in most cases, but in rare cases all of them lead to poor simple structures or iterations which do not converge.

9.6   NOTES

9.6.1. Rescaling the Columns of H Has No Effect

The equations of a Procrustes rotation are

$$FL_1 = H \tag{9-17}$$

$$L_1 = (F'F)^{-1}F'H, \tag{9-18}$$

$$\Lambda_1 = L_1D_1 = (F'F)^{-1}F'HD_1 \tag{9-19}$$

where D_1 is the diagonal matrix that normalizes the columns of $(F'F)^{-1}F'H$, and Λ_1 is the transformation matrix of the Procrustes rotation $(F\Lambda_1 = V_1)$.

Now rescale the columns of H:

$$J = H\Delta$$

where Δ is any arbitrary diagonal rescaling matrix. The Procrustes rotation is then

$$FL_2 = J = H\Delta$$

$$L_2 = (F'F)^{-1}F'H\Delta$$

$$\Lambda_2 = L_2D_2 = (F'F)^{-1}F'H\Delta D_2$$

where D_2 is the diagonal matrix that normalizes the columns of $(F'F)^{-1}F'H\Delta$, and Λ_2 is the transformation matrix of the Procrustes rotation of the rescaled matrix $J = H\Delta$ (and $F\Lambda_2 = V_2$).

Now $(F'F)^{-1}F'H$ is an m by m matrix (m factors), and postmultiplication by Δ to give $(F'F)^{-1}F'H\Delta$ merely multiplies each column by a constant (a diagonal element of Δ). Therefore normalizing the columns of $(F'F)^{-1}F'H$ and of $(F'F)^{-1}F'H\Delta$ gives the same result:

$$D_1 = \Delta D_2$$

$$\Lambda_1 = \Lambda_2$$

$$V_1 = V_2 \qquad \text{QED}$$

9.6.2 Rotation from F or V_0 Gives the Same Result

When we rotate from F we have by (9-17) and (9-18),

$$FL_1 = H \tag{9-20}$$

$$L_1 = (F'F)^{-1}F'H \tag{9-21}$$

If we rotate from $V_0 = F\Lambda_0$, we have similarly

$$V_0L_2 = F(\Lambda_0L_2) = H \tag{9-22}$$

$$L_2 = (V_0'V_0)^{-1}V_0'H \tag{9-23}$$

Comparing the second expression of (9-22) with (9-20), the theorem is proved if we can show that

$$L_1 = \Lambda_0L_2 \tag{9-24}$$

or from (9-21) and (9-23) that

$$(F'F)^{-1}F' = \Lambda_0(V_0'V_0)^{-1}V_0'. \tag{9-25}$$

Rewriting V_0 as $F\Lambda_0$ in the right-hand expression of (9-25), we have

$$\Lambda_0[(F\Lambda_0)'(F\Lambda_0)]^{-1}(F\Lambda_0)'$$

$$= \Lambda_0(\Lambda_0'F'F\Lambda_0)^{-1}\Lambda_0'F'$$

$$= \Lambda_0\Lambda_0^{-1}(F'F)^{-1}(\Lambda_0')^{-1}\Lambda_0'F'$$

$$= (F'F)^{-1}F' \qquad \text{QED}$$

If we replace F by F_n and V_0 by V_n, the proof is the same.

10

Refinement Transformations

10.1 INTRODUCTION

When the objective of a factor analysis is merely to interpret the rotated factors and to judge the excellence of the simple structure by noting the overdetermination of each factor, the analysis is ordinarily concluded with the Promax or Optres transformation. But when the investigator wants really excellent estimates of the primary factors, and especially when he intends to go on to second-order analysis, hierarchical analysis, and/or the computation of factor scores, further refinement of the simple structure on the reference vectors is advisable. No initial rotation, whether it is based on an entirely numerical procedure such as the Optres transformation or on the examination of a plot as in the extended-vector procedures, leads to the best attainable simple structure.

In the past, refinement was usually accomplished by small graphic rotations of the axes taken two at a time. But there is now available a numerical procedure by which we can consider the hyperplanes one at a time, and try to improve the overdetermination of each of them separately. This method is a slight modification of Thurstone's (1954) analytic single-hyperplane procedure.

For illustration we start with the extended-vector rotation of the eleven WAIS subtests for the age-group 25–34, as shown in Table 7.1. We need the initial factor matrix F, the extended-vector factor matrix V, and the extended-vector transformation matrix Λ. Table 10.1 shows the extended-vector rotated factor matrix of Table 7.1 at the upper left. The transformation matrix Λ is just below it. At the upper right we have the matrix $[V]$. This is the V of Table 7.1 with the

266

TABLE 10.1
Preliminary Computations for Single-Hyperplane Rotations,
WAIS Age-Group 25–34 ($N = 300$)

	Matrix V			*Matrix [V]*					
Var	I	II	III	I		II		III	
(1)	.215	.003	.304	(3)	.384	(11)	.558	(6)	.485
(2)	−.082	.066	.480	(5)	.371	(9)	.492	(2)	.480
(3)	.384	.018	.012	(1)	.215	(8)	.339	(4)	.322
(4)	.140	−.009	.322	(4)	.140	(10)	.278	(1)	.304
(5)	.371	−.018	−.012	(7)	.136	(7)	.152	(8)	.176
(6)	.081	−.066	.485	(10)	.101	(2)	.066	(7)	.135
(7)	.136	.152	.135	(6)	.081	(3)	.018	(10)	.127
(8)	.014	.339	.176	(9)	.074	(1)	.003	(11)	.016
(9)	.074	.492	−.016	(8)	.014	(4)	−.009	(3)	.012
(10)	.101	.278	.127	(11)	−.075	(5)	−.019	(5)	−.012
(11)	−.075	.558	.016	(2)	−.082	(6)	−.066	(9)	−.016
Σ	1.359	1.813	2.029						

Matrix Λ

	I	II	III
a	.162	.208	.269
b	−.238	.963	−.488
c	−.958	.174	.830

	Matrix F			*Matrix B*						
Var	*a*	*b*	*c*	a^2	b^2	c^2	*ab*	*ac*	*bc*	$(a + b + c)^2$
(1)	.886	−.183	−.029	.7850	.0335	.0008	−.1621	−.0257	.0053	.4543
(2)	.761	−.141	.249	.5791	.0199	.0620	−.1073	.1895	−.0351	.7552
(3)	.698	−.085	−.262	.4872	.0072	.0686	−.0593	−.1829	.0223	.1232
(4)	.775	−.182	.030	.6006	.0331	.0009	−.1410	.0232	−.0055	.3881
(5)	.588	−.098	−.263	.3457	.0096	.0692	−.0576	−.1546	.0258	.0515
(6)	.878	−.282	.134	.7709	.0795	.0180	−.2476	.1177	−.0378	.5329
(7)	.657	.023	−.037	.4316	.0005	.0014	.0151	−.0243	−.0009	.4134
(8)	.756	.176	.070	.5715	.0310	.0049	.1331	.0529	.0123	1.0040
(9)	.730	.361	−.044	.5329	.1303	.0019	.2635	−.0321	−.0159	1.0962
(10)	.744	.130	−.012	.5535	.0169	.0001	.0967	−.0089	−.0016	.7430
(11)	.615	.433	.075	.3782	.1875	.0056	.2663	.0461	.0325	1.2611
Σ	8.088	.152	−.089	6.0362	.5490	.2334	−.0002	.0009	.0014	6.8229
Ch				6.0362+	.5490+	.2334	−.0004	+.0018	+.0028	= 6.8228

elements of each column rearranged in order from highest positive to highest negative, with the original row-numbers (of V) recorded at the left of each element.

The objectives of the refinement procedure are (1) to maximize for each factor the number of near-zero loadings, usually those between $\pm.100$; (2) to maximize the difference between the largest positive near-zero loading and the smallest positive nonzero loading, and the difference between the largest negative near-zero loading and the smallest negative nonzero loading (if any), by making the largest positive near-zero loading and the absolute value of the largest negative near-zero loading very nearly equal.

In matrix $[V]$ we examine each column and record an estimate, indicated by a horizontal line, of the point separating the near-zero loadings (below) from the nonzero loadings (above). If a factor is bipolar, with one or more nonzero negative loadings at the bottom, there will also be a second horizontal line separating the largest negative near-zero from the smallest negative nonzero, as in the ordered Optres factor matrix of Table 9.4. The judged near-zeros will then be those *between* the two horizontal lines rather than all those below the upper horizontal line. A fairly good rule of thumb is to place the horizontal line or lines so that the sum of the highest positive near-zero loading and the absolute value of the highest negative near-zero loading will be as close to .200 as possible without exceeding this value.[1] It should then be possible, by a suitable rotation, to bring the values of both of these loadings within the range $\pm.100$. If all the low loadings are positive, the horizontal line will come just above the highest of these which is less than or equal to .200, so that after rotation the highest positive loading will be below .100 and the highest negative loading above $-.100$. If all the low loadings are negative, and the lowest positive loading is above .200, the upper horizontal line will be just above the first negative loading, and the lower horizontal line will be just above the first negative loading whose absolute value exceeds .200. Then after rotation the smallest negative near-zero will become positive but less than .100, and the largest negative near-zero will be less than $-.100$.

Factor II can hardly be improved. We cannot make variable 7 near-zero, for $.152 + .066 = .218 > .200$, and any attempt to make it near-zero will result in two "near-zero" loadings appreciably greater than $\pm.100$. For the variables that are presently near-zero, we have already a minimax fit (see Section 10.4), with the largest positive near-zero equal numerically to the largest negative near-zero. The excellence of this fit may be seen in the HII line of Fig. 7.2 and the numbered points (5, 3, 1, 4, 6, 2) close to it.

In factor I, we cannot make variable 7 near-zero, for $.136 + .082 = .218 > .200$. We can, however, reduce the loading of variable 10 to a value below .100

---

[1]This procedure is similar to that in Section 9.4 for identifying nonsalient variables for the Optres rotation (numbered paragraph 1).

by letting the numerical values of variables 2 and 11 increase a little, but not beyond $-.100$. In Fig. 7.2, this would consist in moving the line HI to just the other side of point 8, and just about parallel to its present position in that figure.

The largest improvement can probably be made in factor III. Here we should be able to reduce the loadings of variables 8, 7, and 10 to values below .100 by letting the negative loadings of variables 5 and 9 increase, and letting the loadings of variables 11 and 3 become negative. In Fig. 7.2 this would consist in moving the line $HIII$ toward the origin and approximately parallel to its present position in that figure. That this much improvement is possible can be inferred from our rule of thumb: $.176 + .016 = .192 < .200$, and can be seen in factor III of the Optres solution of Table 9.5, in which variable 8 has loading .107 and the other six all have loadings below $\pm.100$, with $.107 + .092 = .199 < .200$. For an example, we attempt to improve the overdetermination of Factor III of the WAIS extended-vector V-matrix.

10.2 THE ALGEBRA

We outline this algebra without proofs, which can be found in Thurstone (1954). Let V_{0j} be *one column* of the matrix V, and let Λ_{0j} be the corresponding column of the matrix Λ. The procedure is iterative. The first subscript is the iteration number, and subscript 0 means a column of V or Λ prior to the first iteration. The second subscript is the column number of the factor at issue. For the WAIS problem of our example, $j = 3$. Let F_{0j} consist of those rows of F which correspond to the judged near-zero elements of the j-th column of $[V]$. For factor III of the WAIS problem, from Table 10.1, they are rows (3), (5), (7), (8), (9), (10), and (11). We first form the m by m matrix $F'_{0j}F_{0j}$, and then solve for the vector U_{0j} in the set of m simultaneous linear equations

$$F'_{0j}F_{0j}U_{0j} = \Lambda_{0j}. \tag{10-1}$$

In these equations the m by m matrix of coefficients is $F'_{0j}F_{0j}$, the m by 1 vector of unknowns is U_{0j}, the m by 1 vector of constants is Λ_{0j}, and m is number of factors. Then

$$\Lambda_{1j} = U_{0j} \text{ normalized} \tag{10-2}$$

$$V_{1j} = F\Lambda_{1j} \tag{10-3}$$

$$[V_{1j}] = V_{1j} \text{ ordered} \tag{10-4}$$

Then Λ_{1j} is the improved j-th column of the transformation matrix Λ, V_{1j} is the improved j-th column of the factor matrix V, and $[V_{1j}]$ is this column with elements ordered from highest positive to highest negative. This concludes the first iteration.

We can now examine $[V_{1j}]$, revise our estimates of which elements are near-zero, and proceed to a second iteration with F_{1j} now the rows of F corresponding to the revised list of near-zero elements of $[V_{1j}]$. Then

$$F'_{1j}F_{1j}U_{1j} = \Lambda_{1j} \quad \text{(solve for } U_{1j}) \tag{10-5}$$

$$\Lambda_{2j} = U_{1j} \text{ normalized} \tag{10-6}$$

$$V_{2j} = F\Lambda_{2j} \tag{10-7}$$

$$[V_{2j}] = V_{2j} \text{ ordered} \tag{10-8}$$

which completes the second iteration. Note that at any iteration (say the i-th), F_{ij} consists of a subset of rows of the original unrotated factor matrix F.

This procedure continues, possibly with a modification to be described later, until the variables we would judge to be near-zero in $[V_{ij}]$ are the same identically as those that were judged to be near-zero in $[V_{(i-1)j}]$. At this point Λ_{ij} is the j-th column of the revised transformation matrix Λ, and V_{ij} is the j-th column of the revised rotated factor matrix V.

There is nothing we can do to avoid solving a set of m simultaneous linear equations in m unknowns for each iteration of each factor. But for desk calculation the formation of all the $F'_{ij}F_{ij}$ matrices, each m by m, can be greatly facilitated by forming first what we term a B-matrix. For the WAIS data the B-matrix is shown at the bottom of Table 10.1. The first three columns show the F-matrix. The next three columns show the squares of the elements of F, rounded to four decimals, and the third set of three columns shows their products, also rounded to four decimals. If $m > 3$, there will be m columns of squares and $m(m-1)/2$ columns of products. The last column of B shows the squares of the algebraic sums of the elements in each row of F for checking purposes. The check is

$$(a_i + b_i + c_i)^2 = a_i^2 + b_i^2 + c_i^2 + 2a_ib_i + 2a_ic_i + 2b_ic_i, \tag{10-9}$$

where i refers to any one row of the B-matrix or to the row of its column sums. For four-decimal entries in the B-matrix, the check should be correct within rounding error. If we had used the full six-decimal entries (for three-decimal entries in F), the check would be exact. This check is ordinarily applied first to the column sums, and if it seems not to hold for these column sums it is applied to each row separately until the error is found and corrected.

To find any matrix of the type $F'_{ij}F_{ij}$, we consider only the rows of B corresponding to the near-zeros of $[V_{ij}]$. The sums of elements in these rows in columns a^2, b^2, and c^2 give the diagonal elements of $F'_{ij}F_{ij}$, and their sums in columns ab, ac, and bc give the off-diagonal elements. The matrix $F'_{ij}F_{ij}$ is symmetric, so $ba = ab$, $ca = ac$, $cb = bc$, and each off-diagonal element appears in two places in $F'_{ij}F_{ij}$, symmetrically located about its principal diagonal. The sum in the selected rows of the B-matrix in column $(a + b + c)^2$ must be equal within rounding error to the sum of all the m^2 elements of $F'_{ij}F_{ij}$.

10.3 SINGLE-HYPERPLANE ROTATION OF WAIS DATA, FACTOR III

In Table 10.1, we noted that the near-zero loadings of $[V]$ on factor III are those of variables 3, 5, 7, 8, 9, 10, and 11. The matrix $F'_{03}F_{03}$ in panel 0 of the first section of Table 10.2 contains the sums of the elements in these rows of the B-matrix. The sums of squares are on the diagonal. Thus from column a^2 of B, $.4872 + .3457 + .4316 + .5715 + .5329 + .5535 + .3782 = 3.3006$, the upper left diagonal element of $F'_{03}F_{03}$. The sum of the elements in these rows of B in column b^2 is .3830, and the sum in column c^2 is .1517. The sum of products in these rows in column ab is .6578, which is entered at (1)-(2) and also at (2)-(1) in $F'_{03}F_{03}$. The sum of products in these rows in column ac is $-.3038$, which is entered at (1)-(3) and also at (3)-(1). The sum of products of these rows in column bc is .0745, which is entered at (2)-(3) and also at (3)-(2). At the right of $F'_{03}F_{03}$, in column Λ_{03}, we record the entries from column III of Λ from Table 7.1. The sum of all nine of the elements of $F'_{03}F_{03}$, 4.6923, is entered as $\Sigma\Sigma(f'_{03}f_{03})$ just below the last (3)-row. The check, which is the sum of elements in the selected rows of B in column $(a + b + c)^2$, is 4.6924, which agrees within rounding error with 4.6923 and is entered below it.

The equations are solved, as they stand, by the methods of Chapter 4. We might have interchanged rows (1) and (3) of these equations to remove the low value .1517 of row (3), column (3) from the diagonal, but this seemed hardly worthwhile. The third pivotal element, .0515, indicates that the final results may be accurate to only three significant figures, but the work was continued anyhow at four decimals.

The solution vector U_{03} has elements 4.9373, -14.0746, and 22.2324 in the last panel in column Λ_{03}. The check, $r^2_{m1} = 26.64$, $r^2_{m2} = 26.65$, holds at four significant figures within rounding error, and renders the substitution check unnecessary. We next normalize the U_{03} vector as shown in the line just below the table. The sum of squares of its elements is 716.75, the square root of this sum is 26.772, and the reciprocal of the square root is .03735. Then multiplying the elements of U_{03} by .03735, we obtain the elements of Λ_{13}, which are entered in the first three rows of the check column (where we would otherwise have entered the results of the substitution check), and this column is relabeled $Ch(\Lambda_{13})$. They are probably accurate to the three figures shown, possibly $\pm.001$ or at most $\pm.002$. Their sum of squares is .999, which differs only by rounding

TABLE 10.2
Single-Hyperplane Rotations of Factor III, WAIS Age-Group 25–34
($N = 300$)

Panel	Eq	Variable (1)	(2)	(3)	Constant Λ_{03}	Σ	$Ch\,(\Lambda_{13})$	Test	V_{13}	Test	$[V_1$
0	(1)	(3.3006)	.6578	−.3038	.2690	3.9236	(.184)	(1)	.235	(2)	.4
	(2)	.6578	.3830	.0745	−.4880	.6273	(−.526)	(2)	.421	(6)	.4
	(3)	−.3038	.0745	.1517	.8300	.7524	(.830)	(3)	−.044	(4)	.
1	(2)		(.2519)	.1350	−.5416	−.1547	−.1547	(4)	.263	(1)	.
	(3)		.1350	.1238	.8548	1.1136	1.1136	(5)	−.059	(8)	.
	(1)	1	.1993	−.0920	.0815	1.1888	1.1888	(6)	.421	(7)	.(
2	(3)			(.0515)	1.1450	1.1965	1.1965	(7)	.078	(10)	.
	(1)	1		−.1988	.5100	1.3112	1.3112	(8)	.105	(3)	−.
	(2)		1	.5359	−2.1500	−.6141	−.6141	(9)	−.092	(11)	−.
3	(1)	1			4.9373	5.9373	5.9373	(10)	.059	(5)	−.
	(2)		1	$U_{03}=$	−14.0746	−13.0746	−13.0746	(11)	−.052	(9)	−.
	(3)			1	22.2324	23.2324	23.2324	Σ	1.335		
$\Sigma\Sigma$		$(f'_{03}f_{03}) = 4.6923$;			$r^2_{m1} = 26.64; r^2_{m2} = 26.65$			Ch	1.334		
		$Ch = 4.6924$									

$\Sigma u^2_{03} = 716.75$; $\sqrt{\Sigma u^2_{03}} = 26.772$; $1/\sqrt{\Sigma u^2_{03}} = .03735$; $\Sigma\lambda^2_{13} = .999$.

Panel	Eq	Variable (1)	(2)	(3)	Constant Λ_{13}	Σ	$Ch\,(\Lambda_{23})$	Test	V_{23}	Test	$[V_2$
0	(1)	(3.8721)	.7909	−.2509	.1840	4.5961	(.168)	(1)	.226	(6)	.4
	(2)	.7909	.4140	.0868	−.5260	.7657	(−.550)	(2)	.409	(2)	.4
	(3)	−.2509	.0868	.1566	.8300	.8225	(.818)	(3)	−.050	(4)	.2
1	(2)		(.2524)	.1381	−.5636	−.1731	−.1731	(4)	.255	(1)	.2
	(3)		.1381	.1403	.8419	1.1203	1.1203	(5)	−.062	(8)	.(
	(1)	1	.2043	−.0648	.0475	1.1870	1.1870	(6)	.412	(7)	.0
2	(3)			(.0647)	1.1503	1.2150	1.2150	(7)	.067	(10)	.0
	(1)	1		−.1766	.5037	1.3271	1.3271	(8)	.087	(3)	−.0
	(2)		1	.5472	−2.2330	−.6858	−.6858	(9)	−.112	(5)	−.0
3	(1)	1			3.6435	4.6435	4.6435	(10)	.044	(11)	−.0
	(2)		1	$U_{13}=$	−11.9617	−10.9617	−10.9617	(11)	−.073	(9)	−.
	(3)			1	17.7790	18.7790	18.7790	Σ	1.203		
$\Sigma\Sigma$		$(f'_{13}f_{13}) = 5.6963$;			$r^2_{m1} = 21.72; r^2_{m2} = 21.72$			Ch	1.202		
		$Ch = 5.6964$									

$\Sigma u^2_{13} = 472.45$; $\sqrt{\Sigma u^2_{13}} = 21.736$; $1/\sqrt{\Sigma u^2_{13}} = .04601$; $\Sigma\lambda^2_{23} = 1.000$.

error from unity, and this .999 is recorded at the end of the line below the table showing the normalization of U_{03}.

Using the F-matrix at the left of the B-matrix of Table 10.1, we compute $V_{13} = F\Lambda_{13}$, and record the results in column V_{13}, just to the right of the table representing the solution of the equations. Then, rearranging the elements of V_{13} in order from highest positive to highest negative, we record the entries of $[V_{13}]$ at the right of V_{13}. This completes the first iteration.

Comparing $[V_{13}]$ of Table 10.2 with column III of $[V]$ in Table 10.1, we see that the simple structure of factor III has been improved considerably: the loading of variable 8 is much lower, and the loading of variable 9 is still above $-.100$. The near-zero loadings of $[V_{13}]$ are on the same variables as those of factor III of $[V]$ in Table 10.1, and it is clear that we cannot add variable 1 to the hyperplane (here plane) without violating our rule of thumb drastically. Thus we cannot improve the simple structure further by changing the list of near-zero variables. But the rule of thumb still holds for $[V_{13}]$: $.105 + .092 = .197 < .200$. Hence it should be possible by means of another small rotation to change the values of these loadings so that they are both between $\pm.100$. The procedure for doing this is the subject of the next section.

10.4 SOME FURTHER THEORY AND ALGEBRA

The hyperplane fit of V_{13} (and hence of $[V_{13}]$) is a first approximation to a least-squares fit. If we were to continue with further iterations, using the same set of coefficients $(F'_{03}F_{03})$ at each iteration but replacing Λ_{03} by Λ_{13} at the second, by Λ_{23} at the third, and so on, the successive V_{i3}'s would converge to the least-squares fit. As we can see by comparing $[V_{13}]$ with column III of $[V]$ in Table 10.1, most of the convergence comes on the first iteration. In column III of $[V]$ the sum of squares of the near-zero elements is $.0661$, and in $[V_{13}]$ this has been reduced to $.0372$. But several more iterations would be required before the elements of $[V_{i3}]$ would agree exactly with those of $[V_{(i-1)3}]$.

The idea of simple structure, however, does not imply that the best hyperplane fit is a least-squares fit; that is, that the sum of *squares* of the near-zero loadings should be a minimum. We could argue with equal cogency for a *least-absolutes* fit, with the sum of absolute values of the near-zero loadings a minimum; or with perhaps greater cogency for a *minimax* fit, with the absolute value of the numerically *largest* near-zero loading as small as possible. This last criterion would have the virtue of maximizing the *difference* between the numerically largest near-zero and the numerically smallest nonzero, and hence sharpening the distinction between near-zeros and nonzeros and thus the *clarity* of the simple structure.

A minimax fit implies that the largest positive near-zero should be numerically equal or almost equal to the largest negative near-zero. A positive near-zero implies a test vector on one side of the hyperplane; a negative near-zero, a test vector on the other side. Then if the hyperplane is moved toward one of these test vectors to reduce the numerical value of its loading, it will almost surely move away from the other and increase the numerical value of *its* loading.

Thus in Fig. 7.2 as we move HIII toward the origin to reduce the loadings (perpendicular distances) of points 8, 10, and 7, the negative distances of points 5 and 9 must increase, while those of points 11 and 3 become negative also.

Direct methods for attaining a minimax fit, knowing which variables are close to the hyperplane, are not readily available, though this problem is probably not insoluble. We can approximate a minimax fit, however, by *weighting* one or more of the variables in the Thurstone procedure to bring the largest positive and largest negative loadings to numerical equality or near-equality. Most of the near-zeros will still have unit weights, but the numerically largest one(s) may have weight(s) greater than unity. Increasing the weight of a variable tends to draw the hyperplane toward it, and hence to reduce the absolute value of its loading.

Let W_{ij} be a k by k diagonal matrix of weights, where k is the number of near-zero variables at the i-th iteration, say $i = 2$, because weighting is rarely if ever used at the first iteration, or in general until overdetermination can no longer be improved by merely adding another variable to the near-zero list. Most of the weights will be unity, but one or a few may be greater than unity. Then in place of equations (10-5) through (10-8) we have

$$F'_{1j} W_{1j} F_{1j} U_{1j} = \Lambda_{1j} \quad \text{(solve for } U_{1j}) \tag{10-10}$$

$$\Lambda_{2j} = U_{1j} \text{ normalized} \tag{10-11}$$

$$V_{2j} = F\Lambda_{2j} \tag{10-12}$$

$$[V_{2j}] = V_{2j} \text{ ordered} \tag{10-13}$$

and further iterations may or may not include changes in the list of near-zero variables but *will* include changes in the weights of one or more variables. When a weight greater than unity has been assigned to a variable, it retains this weight at all following iterations unless the weight is changed "for cause," that is, in order to increase or decrease the loading of that variable.

When the B-matrix is used to form $F'_{ij} W_{ij} F_{ij}$, we increase the weight of a given variable in each column sum by adding in the element in the given row more than once. Thus to weight variable 5, say 2.5, we add the element in row (5) twice and then add one-half its value, in forming each column sum, instead of adding it only once. This weighting procedure in effect substitutes for the variable-5 test vector two and a half collinear test vectors. The augmented column sums are the elements of the revised coefficient matrix of (10-10).

10.5   USE OF WEIGHTS WITH THE WAIS DATA, FACTOR III

In the $[V_{13}]$ column of Table 10.2 the largest positive near-zero is the .105 of variable 8, and the largest negative near-zero is the $-.092$ of variable 9. If we increase the weight of variable 8, its loading should be decreased, but at the same time the negative loading of variable 9 on the other side of the hyperplane should be increased. We next proceed to try giving the weight 2 to variable 8. The original coefficient matrix is augmented by adding algebraically to each of its elements the corresponding element of row (8) of the B-matrix of Table 10.1. Thus

$$\begin{bmatrix} 3.3006 & .6578 & -.3038 \\ .6578 & .3830 & .0745 \\ -.3038 & .0745 & .1517 \end{bmatrix} + \begin{bmatrix} .5715 & .1331 & .0529 \\ .1331 & .0310 & .0123 \\ .0529 & .0123 & .0049 \end{bmatrix} =$$

$$\begin{bmatrix} 3.8721 & .7909 & -.2509 \\ .7909 & .4140 & .0868 \\ -.2509 & .0868 & .1566 \end{bmatrix}$$

and this last matrix is the coefficient matrix for the second iteration. For the vector of constants Λ_{03} we substitute also the new vector Λ_{13}. The result is the first panel (panel 0) of the second section of Table 10.2. The equations of this second section are solved, the solution vector is normalized, and V_{23} and $[V_{23}]$ are formed in the same manner as in the first section of Table 10.2.

The results indicate that the weight 2 for variable 8 was too large. With optimal weighting the difference between the absolute values of the largest positive and largest negative loadings should decrease almost to 0. But in this case we obtain

	$[V_{13}]$	$[V_{23}]$
(8)	$|.105|$	$|.087|$
(9)	$|-.092|$	$|-.112|$
(8) − (9)	.013	−.025

and the difference is almost twice as great for $[V_{23}]$ as for $[V_{13}]$ and in the *opposite direction*. If we used the weight 1.5, the differences would presumably be about equal (both about .013) but still in opposite directions. To obtain a difference close to zero we therefore try the weight 1.2. For the coefficient matrix this gives

$$\begin{bmatrix} 3.3006 & .6578 & -.3038 \\ .6578 & .3830 & .0745 \\ -.3038 & .0745 & .1517 \end{bmatrix} + \begin{bmatrix} .1143 & .0266 & .0106 \\ .0266 & .0062 & .0025 \\ .0106 & .0025 & .0010 \end{bmatrix} =$$

$$\begin{bmatrix} 3.4149 & .6844 & -.2932 \\ .6844 & .3892 & .0770 \\ -.2932 & .0770 & .1527 \end{bmatrix}$$

TABLE 10.3
Third Single-Hyperplane Rotation of Factor III, WAIS Age-Group 25–34 ($N = 300$)

Panel	Eq	Variable (1)	(2)	(3)	Constant Λ_{13}	Σ	$Ch\,(\Lambda_{33})$	Test	V_{33}	Test	[V
	(1)	(3.4149)	.6844	−.2932	.1840	.9901	(.180)	(1)	.233	(6)	.4
0	(2)	.6844	.3892	.0770	−.5260	.6246	(−.533)	(2)	.418	(2)	.4
	(3)	−.2932	.0770	.1527	.8300	.7665	(.827)	(3)	−.046	(4)	.2
	(2)		(.2520)	.1358	−.5629	−.1751	−.1751	(4)	.261	(1)	.2
1	(3)		.1358	.1275	.8458	1.1091	1.1091	(5)	−.059	(8)	.1
	(1)	1	.2004	−.0859	.0539	1.1684	1.1684	(6)	.419	(7)	.0
	(3)			(.0543)	1.1491	1.2034	1.2035	(7)	.075	(10)	.0
2	(1)	1		−.1939	.5015	1.3075	1.3076	(8)	.100	(3)	−.0
	(2)		1	.5389	−2.2337	−.6948	−.6948	(9)	−.097	(11)	−.0
	(1)	1			4.6048	5.6048	5.6048	(10)	.055	(5)	−.C
3	(2)		1	$U_{13} =$	−13.6380	−12.6380	−12.6380	(11)	.058	(9)	−.C
	(3)			1	21.1621	22.1621	22.1621	Σ	1.301		
$\Sigma\Sigma\,(f'_{13}f_{13}) = 4.8932$					$r^2_{m1} = 25.58$			Ch	1.301		
$Ch = 4.8932$					$r^2_{m2} = 25.59$						

$\Sigma u^2_{13} = 655.03$; $\sqrt{\Sigma u^2_{13}} = 25.594$; $1/\sqrt{\Sigma u^2_{13}} = .03907$; $\Sigma\lambda^2_{33} = 1.000$

with each element in the second matrix .2 times the value of the corresponding element in the previous second matrix. For the vector of constants we usually use Λ_{ij} from the immediately preceding iteration. But in this case this immediately preceding iteration was worse than the one before it, so we will use Λ_{13} rather than Λ_{23} as the vector of constants because it is the best current estimate of the final Λ. The results are shown in Table 10.3.

We now have close to a minimax fit, with the highest positive near-zero .100 and the highest negative near-zero −.097. This is also close to a least-squares fit because the one nonunit weight was only 1.2. The sum of squares of the near-zero loadings of $[V_{33}]$ is .0372, as compared with .0372 for $[V_{13}]$. There is an actual improvement (of .0002) in the least-squares fit, due to the added iteration, despite the effect of the weight in moving this least-squares fit toward a minimax fit.

V_{33} now replaces column III of V in Table 10.1, and Λ_{33} replaces column III of Λ.

Exercise 10:1. For the WAIS data of Table 10.1, iterate factor I of V to a minimax fit by the Thurstone procedure. The first iteration is always carried out without weighting to obtain an approximate least-squares fit, and the first weight used is almost always integral.

11

Second-Order and Hierarchical Analysis

11.1 SECOND-ORDER ANALYSIS

We have dealt so far only with the initial or first-order factors. The primary factors represent "ideal" tests, each of which measures one and only one first-order factor. In the general (oblique) case these primary factors or "ideal" tests are correlated. As we saw in Chapter 6 [formula (6-22)], their correlations are given by

$$R_s = T'T \tag{11-1}$$

where T is the primary-structure transformation matrix, and by (6-20)

$$T = (\Lambda')^{-1}D \tag{11-2}$$

where D is the diagonal matrix that normalizes the columns of $(\Lambda')^{-1}$.

Because R_s is a correlation matrix, R_s^* (with estimated communalities on the diagonal) can be factored to give the factorial structure of the "ideal" tests. In first-order analysis we factor the original reduced correlation matrix R^* to obtain F, and rotate F by means of Λ to obtain V. The factors of V are interpreted from the high V-loadings in terms of the meanings of the functions measured by the original tests. Then from Λ we can obtain T and R_s by means of (11-2) and (11-1). R_s is the *second-order* correlation matrix. We can factor R_s^* to obtain F_s, and rotate F_s to obtain V_s, the second-order reference-vector structure. The factors of V_s can be interpreted from the high V_s-loadings in terms of the meanings of the functions represented by the first-order factors. The first-order

277

primary factors have the same *interpretations* as do the corresponding first-order reference-vector factors. Thus the interpretations are pushed a step further. We interpret the first-order factors directly in terms of the tests. We interpret the second-order factors directly in terms of the first-order factors and hence indirectly in terms of the tests. In trait theory the first-order factors represent *unitary* traits, and the second-order factors represent *global* traits.

The primary factors or "ideal" tests lie entirely in the first-order common-factor space, with vector lengths and communalities unity. Each *test* has a specific factor and an error factor, and these specific factors and error factors are lumped together in the unique factors. But in the *second-order* common-factor space, we factor the correlations among the "ideal" tests. Each "ideal" test then has a unique factor as well as one or more common factors, with second-order communality less than unity. As the error factors of the tests lie entirely outside the first-order common-factor space, any error factors in the second-order analysis can be due only to imperfect first-order analysis, leading to the injection of a little of the error variance into the second-order common factors. It we neglect this, we conclude that the second-order unique factors are entirely specific factors. A similar situation would exist in first-order analysis if the original variables were perfectly or almost perfectly reliable (e.g., accurate physical measurements). In this case also the error factors would be either absent entirely or negligible, and the unique factors would be wholly or almost entirely specific factors.

In the second-order common-factor space the communalities of the "ideal" tests are less than unity, and we factor R_s^* instead of R_s, with estimated communalities on the diagonal. These estimates are made in the same manner as in first-order analysis, with one refactoring to make the initial trace closely equal to the final total communality; or the second-order correlation matrix may be factored by Spearman-type procedures as described in Sections 11.1.1, 11.1.2, and 11.1.3, below.

As we have noted, the original variables may have errors of measurement as well as specific factors, and these error factors and specific factors lie outside the first-order common-factor space in which the primary factors are defined. The second-order specific-factor space, in turn, lies outside the second-order common-factor space.

In first-order analysis we separate the original test space of n dimensions into a common-factor space of m dimensions and a unique-factor space of n dimensions orthogonal to this m-space; or into a common-factor m-space, a specific-factor n-space, and an error-factor n-space, all three orthogonal to one another. The original n-space of the tests is embedded in the $(m + n)$-space or the $(m + n + n)$-space. In second-order analysis we start with the first-order common-factor space, which becomes the m-space of the "ideal" tests. We separate this m-space into a second-order common-factor m_s-space and a second-order specific-factor m-space orthogonal to this m_s-space. The m-space of the "ideal" tests is embedded in this $(m_s + m)$-space. These second-order spaces are all orthogonal to the first-order unique-factor n-space or orthogonal to the $(n + n)$-space of the first-order specific factors and error factors.

11.1.1 The Case of Two First-Order Factors

In this case there is only one second-order correlation in R_s, and this correlation is the product of the second-order *general-factor* loadings $g_1 g_2$. This single correlation can be factored only under some *assumption* concerning the relative magnitudes of g_1 and g_2. We might assume that $g_1 = g_2$, or perhaps better that g_1 and g_2 are proportional to the mean a-loadings (in F) of the tests in the two outer clusters: these loadings should be close to the first-order general-factor loadings. For the example of five verbal tests the correlation between the primary factors, by (2-25), is .903 (.9029 to four decimals). The mean a-factor loadings, from row a of Table 2.4, are .7981 for factor I (tests 1, 3, and 4) and .8040 for factor II (tests 2 and 5). Although these mean loadings are for all practical purposes equal, we use them as they stand to illustrate the procedure. We now have two nonlinear equations in two unknowns from which to find g_1 and g_2, namely

$$\frac{g_1}{g_2} = \frac{.7981}{.8040}; \qquad g_1 g_2 = .9029.$$

From the first equation

$$g_1 = \frac{.7981}{.8040} g_2; \qquad g_1 = .9927 \, g_2$$

Then substituting in the second equation

$$.9927 g_2^2 = .9029$$

$$g_2^2 = .9029/.9927 = .9095$$

$$g_2 = \sqrt{.9095} = .9537$$

and from the equation $g_1 = .9927 g_2$

$$g_1 = (.9927)(.9537) = .9467.$$

For a check we note that

$$g_1 g_2 = (.9467)(.9537) = .9029.$$

The communalities are g_1^2 and g_2^2, or

$$h_1^2 = g_1^2 = .9467^2 = .8962; \quad h_2^2 = g_2^2 = .9537^2 = .9095.$$

The specific-factor loadings are

$$s_1 = \sqrt{1 - h_1^2} = \sqrt{.1038} = .3222$$
$$s_2 = \sqrt{1 - h_2^2} = \sqrt{.0905} = .3008$$

Gathering these results together, the second-order factor matrix is

	g	h^2	s
1	.9467	.8962	.3222
2	.9537	.9095	.3008

and for a final check we note that $g^2 + s^2 = 1.0000$ within rounding error for each row.

The additional information here is slight, though it might have a little more value if the mean a-loadings differed more markedly and if the assumption that the second-order general-factor loadings should be proportional to them is valid. Ordinarily we do not perform a second-order analysis when there are only two first-order factors.

11.1.2 The Case of Three First-Order Factors

If there are only three first-order factors, there are only three linearly independent correlations in R_s, namely r_{12}, r_{13}, and r_{23}, and the second-order analysis is performed by the methods of Chapter 1. We form the three triads

$$t_{123} = r_{12}r_{13}/r_{23} = h_1^2$$
$$t_{213} = r_{12}r_{23}/r_{13} = h_2^2 \tag{11-3}$$
$$t_{312} = r_{13}r_{23}/r_{12} = h_3^2$$

and the second-order general-factor loadings are the square roots of these triads

$$g_1 = \sqrt{t_{123}}$$
$$g_2 = \sqrt{t_{213}} \tag{11-4}$$
$$g_3 = \sqrt{t_{312}}$$

The second-order specific-factor loadings are

$$s_1 = \sqrt{1 - g_1^2} = \sqrt{1 - t_{123}}$$
$$s_2 = \sqrt{1 - g_2^2} = \sqrt{1 - t_{213}} \tag{11-5}$$
$$s_3 = \sqrt{1 - g_3^2} = \sqrt{1 - t_{312}}$$

Theorem 1.3 (Section 1.5.5) must apply to the triads of (11-3): each of them must be positive or zero and not greater than unity. And because we have only one triad to use in estimating each second-order g-loading and s-loading, we must be conservative in the use of Theorem 1.3 and require that every triad be at least .001 and not greater than .999. If one triad lies outside these limits, second-order analysis is impossible.

For second-order analysis we require a very good first-order analysis, starting ordinarily with a reference-vector-structure factor matrix refined by the methods of Chapter 10 to give a very good transformation matrix Λ for use in (11-2) and (11-1). For illustration of second-order analysis in the case of three first-order factors, we use the refined rotation of the eleven WAIS subtests for the age-group 25–34. Factor I comes from Table 10.1, factor II; factor II from the solution of Exercise 10.1; and factor III from Table 10.3. The refined V-matrix is given in the upper left region of Table 11.1, with the transformation matrix Λ just below it. The figures in this V-matrix differ slightly from those in the original tables because they have all been recomputed using four-decimal entries in the transformation matrix Λ, as shown in Table 11.1. When Λ is to be used to compute T and R_s by (11-2) and (11-1), it is advisable to retain four decimals in its elements.

The lower part of Table 11.1 shows the computation of T by (11-2), starting with Λ' in panel 0. Below the computations for the inverse, in the *second* three numbered columns, we have the computations for the normalization of the columns of $(\Lambda')^{-1}$. Row (2) shows the diagonal elements of D^{-1}, and row (3) shows the diagonal elements of D. The matrix $T = (\Lambda')^{-1}D$ is shown at the bottom of the table in the *first* three numbered columns.

At the top of Table 11.1, next to the matrix V, we show the primary-pattern factor matrix $P = VD^{-1}$, even though it is irrelevant to the second-order analysis. Each element of P is the corresponding element of V times the diagonal element of D^{-1} for the same column: 1.7751 for column I, 2.1183 for column II, and 2.0640 for column III. The near-zero elements of V and P are enclosed in parentheses. In V they are all ±.100 or lower; in P they are not. If .100 is the critical value for every column of V, the critical value for each column of P is .100 times the value of *diag* D^{-1} for that column: namely .17751 for column I, .21183 for column II, and .20640 for column III. Thus it is more troublesome to estimate the excellence of the simple structure from P than it is from V. Elements of P can exceed 1.000, though this does not happen in the present example. Also elements of *diag* D^{-1} can be less than 1.0000, though again this is not the case in the present example. When an element of *diag* D^{-1} is less than 1.0000, the critical value for a near-zero in the corresponding column of P is *less* than .100.

The elements of $R_s = T'T$ are given in Table 11.1 just below the matrix P. The diagonal elements of R_s are the sums of squares of the elements in the columns of T, and should all equal unity within rounding error. The off-diagonal elements are the sums of products (scalar products) of the elements in pairs of columns of T. In this example the second-order correlations are all positive, showing that the oblique structure is acute.

We are now ready to proceed with the second-order analysis. We continue to work at four decimals to reduce the accumulated rounding errors. We first list the three correlations of R_s.

TABLE 11.1
Primary Factors and Second-Order Analysis of Eleven WAIS Subtests,
Age-Group 25–34 (N = 300)

	Matrix V			Matrix $P = VD^{-1}$				Second-Order Matrix G		
Test	I	II	III	I	II	III		g	$g^2 = h^2$	s
(1)	(.003)	.214	.233	(.005)	.453	.481	I	.8594	.7386	.5113
(2)	(.066)	(−.081)	.418	(.117)	(−.172)	.863	II	.9333	.8710	.3592
(3)	(.018)	.380	(−.046)	(.032)	.805	(−.095)	III	.9193	.8452	.3934
(4)	(−.009)	.141	.261	(−.016)	.299	.539				
(5)	(−.018)	.367	(−.059)	(−.032)	.777	(−.122)				
(6)	(−.066)	(.085)	.419	(−.117)	(.180)	.865				
(7)	.152	.130	(.075)	.270	.275	(.155)				
(8)	.339	(.003)	(.100)	.602	(.006)	(.206)				
(9)	.492	(.057)	(−.097)	.873	(.121)	(−.200)				
(10)	.278	(.091)	(.055)	.493	(.193)	(.114)				
(11)	.558	(−.094)	(−.058)	.991	(−.199)	(−.120)				
Σ	1.813	1.293	1.301	3.218	2.738	2.686				
Ch				3.218	2.739	2.685				

	Matrix Λ				Matrix $R_s = T'T$		
	I	II	III		(1)	(2)	(3)
a	.2078	.1546	.1799	(1)	1.0000	.8021	.7901
b	.9626	−.2717	−.5328	(2)	.8021	1.0000	.8580
c	.1737	−.9499	.8268	(3)	.7901	.8580	1.0000

		Variable			Variable				
Panel	Eq	(1)	(2)	(3)	(1)	(2)	(3)	Σ + 1	Ch
0	(1)	(.2078)	.9626	.1737	= Λ′			2.3441	
	(2)	.1546	−.2717	−.9499				−.0670	
	(3)	.1799	−.5328	.8268				1.4739	
1	(2)		(−.9879)	−1.0791	−.7440			−1.8110	−1.8110
	(3)		−1.3662	.6764	−.8657			−.5555	−.5555
	(1)		4.6323	.8359	4.8123			11.2805	11.2805
2	(3)			(2,1687)	.1632	−1.3829		(.9490)	1.9490
	(1)			−4.2240	1.3237	4.6888		2.7885	2.7886
	(2)			1.0923	.7531	−1.0122		1.8332	1.8331

TABLE 11.1 (continued)

						1.6418	1.9952	1.9477	6.5847	6.5846
3	(1)			$(\Lambda')^{-1} =$		1.6418	1.9952	1.9477	6.5847	6.5846
	(2)					.6708	−.3156	−.5037	.8515	.8515
	(3)					.0753	−.6377	.4611	.8987	.8987
$T =$	(1)	.9249	.9419	.9437		3.1511	4.4871	4.2599	$= \Sigma^2$	
	(2)	.3779	−.1490	−.2440		1.7751	2.1183	2.0640	$= \sqrt{\Sigma^2} = diag\ D^{-1}$	
	(3)	.0424	−.3010	.2234		.56335	.47208	.48450	$= 1/\sqrt{\Sigma^2} = diag\ D$	
	Σt^2	1.0000	1.0000	1.0000						

$r_{12} = .8021;\ r_{13} = .7901;\ r_{23} = .8580.$

The three triads, by (11-3), are then

$$t_{123} = r_{12}r_{13}/r_{23} = (.8021)(.7901)/.8580 = .7386 = h_1^2$$

$$t_{213} = r_{12}r_{23}/r_{13} = (.8021)(.8580)/.7901 = .8710 = h_2^2$$

$$t_{312} = r_{13}r_{23}/r_{12} = (.7901)(.8580)/.8021 = .8452 = h_3^2$$

These are the second-order communalities. The second-order general-factor loadings, by (11-4), are their square roots

$$g_1 = \sqrt{.7386} = .8594$$

$$g_2 = \sqrt{.8710} = .9333$$

$$g_3 = \sqrt{.8452} = .9193$$

The second-order specific-factor loadings, by (11-5), are

$$s_1 = \sqrt{1 - g_1^2} = \sqrt{1 - t_{123}} = \sqrt{1 - .7386} = \sqrt{.2614} = .5113$$

$$s_2 = \sqrt{1 - g_2^2} = \sqrt{1 - t_{213}} = \sqrt{1 - .8710} = \sqrt{.1290} = .3592$$

$$s_3 = \sqrt{1 - g_3^2} = \sqrt{1 - t_{312}} = \sqrt{1 - .8452} = \sqrt{.1548} = .3934$$

For the final check we compute $g_1^2 + s_1^2 = 1.0000$, $g_2^2 + s_2^2 = 1.0001$, and $g_3^2 + s_3^2 = .9999$. Each of these sums of squares should equal 1.0000 within rounding error.

These results are gathered together in the second-order factor matrix G at the upper right of Table 11.1. The first-order factors, from V, are I (nonverbal [figural] reasoning), II (quantitative reasoning) and III (verbal ability). These are the unitary traits measured by the WAIS. Because the WAIS is an intelligence test, we may assume that the second-order general factor is the global trait "intelligence." It is defined by second-order factor analysis, for these data, as whatever is common to nonverbal (figural) reasoning, quantitative reasoning, and verbal ability. From the second-order factor matrix we see that II (quantitative reasoning) has slightly the highest loading, III (verbal ability) the next highest, and I (nonverbal [figural] reasoning) the lowest; though this last loading is still quite high, and the contributions of the three first-order unitary abilities to the global second-order ability (intelligence) are not very far from equal.

> ***Exercise 11:1.*** In Exercise 7:1 you obtained an extended-vector solution of the 9-aptitude-tests problem. Refine this V-matrix only by recalculating the elements of Λ to four decimals; omit any further refinement by the methods of Chapter 10. It is not necessary to invert Λ'. The elements of T' are found by normalizing the *rows* of E'. Then $R_s = T'T$, by (11-1). Carry out the second-order and primary-pattern analyses for these data.

11.1.3 The Case of Four First-Order Factors

With four first-order factors there *may* still be only one second-order general factor. The six second-order correlations are r_{12}, r_{13}, r_{14}, r_{23}, r_{24}, and r_{34}. To test the hypothesis that there is only one second-order general factor, we compute the second-order tetrads

$$t_{1234} = r_{12}r_{34} - r_{13}r_{24}$$

$$t_{1243} = r_{12}r_{34} - r_{14}r_{23} \qquad (11\text{-}6)$$

$$t_{1342} = r_{13}r_{24} - r_{14}r_{23}$$

Check: $t_{1234} + t_{1342} = t_{1243}$ within rounding errors.

The standard-error formulas (1-26) and (1-27) do not apply to second-order tetrads, whose standard errors should be somewhat larger than those of first-order tetrads, but the formulas for which are not known. A rough but reasonably conservative rule should be to take

$$\bar{\sigma}_t = 1/\sqrt{N - 1} \qquad (11\text{-}7)$$

and to consider a second-order tetrad zero within sampling error if its absolute value does not exceed this. If the absolute values of all three tetrads are less than $1/\sqrt{N - 1}$, we can assume provisionally that there is only one second-order general factor and proceed to triad analysis. There are then twelve triads, and the triad analysis is as shown in Table 11.2.

In this case we can allow one or two individual triads to lie at or outside the range 0 to 1, using the same rough rule of (11-7) to estimate significance: no triad may be lower than $-1/\sqrt{N - 1}$ nor higher than $1 + 1/\sqrt{N - 1}$. The column *means*, however, must *all* be at least .001 and not greater than .999, or one second-order general factor must be considered insufficient.

If one second-order factor is insufficient, two will usually be sufficient. If one tetrad lies within the range $\pm 1/\sqrt{N - 1}$ and two lie outside that range, we can postulate one second-order general factor and one second-order group or sub-general factor, and proceed with the triad analysis as in Sections 1.5.10 and 1.6.2 to 1.6.7. If only *one* tetrad lies outside the range $\pm 1/\sqrt{N - 1}$ (a rare occur-

TABLE 11.2
Second-Order Triad Analysis

	Second-Order Variable			
	1	2	3	4
Triads	$r_{12}r_{13}/r_{23}$ $r_{12}r_{14}/r_{24}$ $r_{13}r_{14}/r_{34}$	$r_{12}r_{23}/r_{13}$ $r_{12}r_{24}/r_{14}$ $r_{23}r_{24}/r_{34}$	$r_{13}r_{23}/r_{12}$ $r_{13}r_{34}/r_{14}$ $r_{23}r_{34}/r_{24}$	$r_{14}r_{24}/r_{12}$ $r_{14}r_{34}/r_{13}$ $r_{24}r_{34}/r_{23}$
Sum	$3h_1^2$	$3h_2^2$	$3h_3^2$	$3h_4^2$
Mean	h_1^2	h_2^2	h_3^2	h_4^2
g	$g_1 = \sqrt{h_1^2}$	$g_2 = \sqrt{h_2^2}$	$g_3 = \sqrt{h_3^2}$	$g_4 = \sqrt{h_4^2}$
s	$s_1 = \sqrt{1 - h_1^2}$	$s_2 = \sqrt{1 - h_2^2}$	$s_3 = \sqrt{1 - h_3^2}$	$s_4 = \sqrt{1 - h_4^2}$
Check	$g_1^2 + s_1^2 = 1$	$g_2^2 + s_2^2 = 1$	$g_3^2 + s_3^2 = 1$	$g_4^2 + s_4^2 = 1$

rence), the hypothesis of one second-order general factor and one second-order group or subgeneral factor becomes at least doubtful. It is always possible to postulate two second-order general factors when either *one or two* tetrads lie outside the range. When *two* tetrads lie outside the range, the investigator has the option of postulating one second-order general factor and one second-order group or subgeneral factor, rather than two second-order general factors, and using triad analysis to find their loadings. In this case none of the triads used to determine the general-factor loading may depart significantly from the range 0 to 1, and none of the *mean* triads used in determining these loadings may lie outside the range .001 to .999.

When two second-order general factors are postulated, rather than one second-order general factor and one second-order group factor or subgeneral factor, the simplest procedure is to factor the second-order correlation matrix twice by the centroid method; or by the principal-axes method if a computer is available (twice to make the sum of the final communalities very closely equal to the sum of the estimated communalities for the second analysis); and then to rotate the second-order factor matrix obliquely by the procedures of Section 2.8.6, using Fig. 2.2.

11.1.4 The Case of Five or More First-Order Factors

In this case we start with a centroid or principal-axes factoring of the *second-order* correlation matrix R_s^*. If there appears to be only *one* salient second-order factor, refactor once, using as communality estimates the squares of the first-factor loadings from the first factoring. The first factor of the second factoring is then the second-order general factor, with loadings g_i ($i = 1, 2, \ldots, m$). The second-order specific-factor loadings are

$$s_i = \sqrt{1 - g_i^2}, \tag{11-8}$$

and for each second-order available

$$g_i^2 + s_i^2 = 1 \qquad (11\text{-}9)$$

within rounding error.

With five or more first-order factors there will usually be two or more second-order factors. When the number of salient second-order factors is doubtful, we usually resolve the doubt in favor of the larger number, provided this number is less than $m/2$ (where m is the number of salient first-order factors). As in first-order analysis, the solution is indeterminate if the number of second-order factors equals or exceeds one-half the number of first-order factors. Despite this indeterminancy, however, we can still often achieve a satisfactory (though not necessarily strictly unique) solution when m_s, the number of second-order factors, is exactly one-half the number of first-order factors ($m/2$), if m is small (say not more than eight). In particular, when $m = 4$ and the tetrad–triad criteria for one general factor are not met, a two-factor second-order solution is usually satisfactory in the sense that the second-order factors permit a reasonable interpretation.

In second-order analysis a Heywood case (one second-order communality greater than unity) is more likely to arise than in first-order analysis. If this happens we may try increasing or decreasing the number of second-order factors by one. Increasing the number by one may still lead to a Heywood case, however, or to $m/2$ or $(m + 1)/2$ second-order factors. If m is even, $m_s = m/2$, and the Heywood case does not persist, a satisfactory second-order solution *may* still be possible. The chances for a satisfactory solution are not so good, however, if m is odd and $m_s = (m + 1)/2$. And decreasing the number of factors by one may result in under-factoring unless the original last factor was of doubtful salience, and again the Heywood case may still persist. In second-order analysis the quasi-Heywood case (one communality higher than the reliability of the variable but still less than unity) does not arise, because the first-order primary factors (with vector lengths unity) are assumed to be perfectly reliable.

When second-order factoring leads to a clear G-matrix, with the number of second-order common factors less than (occasionally equal to) $m/2$, and no Heywood case, we refactor once with communalities estimated as the row sums of squares of the first G. The resulting second G may be rotated in any of the usual manners to obtain a second-order reference-vector-structure V-matrix. Interpretation of this matrix must be based on quite clear interpretations of the meanings of the first-order factors.

11.2   THE HIERARCHICAL ORTHOGONAL SOLUTION

This is a solution algebraically equivalent to an oblique simple-structure solution but going one step further. The first-order solution explains the intercorrelations among the original variables in terms of the first-order factors. These factors are ordinarily correlated. Treating the primary factors as "ideal" variables, second-order analysis explains *their* intercorrelations in terms of the second-order factors. This is not enough. For example, with the WAIS problem, the infomation added by the second-order factor matrix G of Table 11.1 is not very great. We might reasonably ask two further questions:

1. What is the correlation between each test and each second-order general (and subgeneral, if any) factor?
2. What is the correlation between each test and that part of each first-order common factor not accounted for by the second-order general (and any subgeneral) factors?

The hierarchical orthogonal solution answers these questions. And because the solution is orthogonal, so that the square of each correlation is the proportion of the variance accounted for, we can also answer the two related questions:

1a. What proportion of the total variance of each test is due to each second-order general (and subgeneral, if any) factor?
2a. What proportion of the total variance of each test is due to that part of each first-order common factor that is not accounted for by the second-order general (and any subgeneral) factors?

11.2.1 Algebraic Solution

1. We note first that by (6-26)

$$X = PA + UB \tag{11-10}$$

where

X (n by N) = standard scores on original variables
P (n by m) = loadings on primary-factor *pattern*
A (m by N) = standard scores on oblique primary factors
U (n by n) = diagonal matrix of loadings on unique factors
B (n by N) = standard scores on unique factors

Note that this primary-factor-pattern solution is *oblique*. The unique factors are of course orthogonal to one another and to all of the common (primary) factors.

2. Consider now the first-order primary-factor-pattern scores A, and find an *orthogonal* solution

$$A = G_s J + G_u K \tag{11-11}$$

where

A (m by N) = standard scores on first-order primary (common) factors
G_s (m by m_s) = loadings on second-order general (and any subgeneral) factors

J (m_s by N) = standard scores on second-order general (and any subgeneral) factors

G_u (m by m) = diagonal matrix of loadings on second-order specific factors

K (m by N) = standard scores on second-order specific factors

This is the second-order factor analysis described in Section 11.1 and illustrated in Table 11.1 for the case $m_s = 1$. The solution is orthogonal: the *axes* of all the second-order general (and any subgeneral) and specific factors are all orthogonal to one another. This solution gives us G_s and G_u. In Table 11.1, G_s consists of the elements in column g of G, and G_u is the diagonal matrix whose diagonal elements are in column s of G.

3. We are now ready to find the answer to our first question: the matrix of correlations between the original test scores X and the second-order general (and any subgeneral) factor scores J. Because both of these sets of scores are *standard* scores, this matrix is

$$R_{xj} = \frac{1}{N} XJ'.$$

Then by (11-10)

$$R_{xj} = \frac{1}{N} (PA + UB)J'$$

and by (11-11)

$$R_{xj} = \frac{1}{N} [P(G_s J + G_u K) + UB]J'$$

$$= \frac{1}{N} (PG_s J + PG_u K + UB)J'$$

$$= PG_s \frac{JJ'}{N} + PG_u \frac{KJ'}{N} + U \frac{BJ'}{N}$$

Because the second-order general (and any subgeneral) factors J are orthogonal to one another, each of these sets of factor scores correlates unity with itself and zero with all others, so $JJ'/N = I$.

Because the second-order specific factors K are orthogonal to the second-order general (and any subgeneral) factors J, $KJ'/N = 0$.

Because the first-order unique factors B are orthogonal to the second-order general (and any subgeneral) factors J, $BJ'/N = 0$.

Making these substitutions,

$$R_{xj} = PG_s. \tag{11-12}$$

But from (6-31) and Table 6.3 we know that $P = F\Lambda D^{-1}$, where D^{-1} is the inverse of the diagonal matrix D which normalizes the columns of $(\Lambda')^{-1}$, and $F\Lambda = V$, so

$$R_{xj} = F\Lambda D^{-1}G_s = VD^{-1}G_s. \tag{11-13}$$

4. We next find the answer to our second question: the matrix of correlations between each test of X and that part of each first-order common factor not accounted for by the second-order general (and any subgeneral) factors. This is R_{xk}, the matrix of correlations between the original tests X and the second-order specific factors K. It is

$$R_{xk} = \frac{1}{N}XK'.$$

Then by (11-10)

$$R_{xk} = \frac{1}{N}(PA + UB)K'$$

and by (11-11)

$$R_{xk} = \frac{1}{N}[P(G_sJ + G_uK) + UB]K'$$

$$= \frac{1}{N}(PG_sJ + PG_uK + UB)K'$$

$$= \frac{1}{N}(PG_sJK' + PG_uKK' + UBK')$$

$$= PG_s\frac{JK'}{N} + PG_u\frac{KK'}{N} + U\frac{BK'}{N}$$

Because the second-order general (and any subgeneral) factors J are orthogonal to the second-order specific factors K, $JK'/N = 0$.

Because the second-order specific factors K are orthogonal to one another, each set of these specific-factor scores correlates unity with itself and zero with all others, so $KK'/N = I$.

Because the first-order unique factors B are orthogonal to the second-order specific factors K, $BK'/N = 0$.

Making these substitutions,

$$R_{xk} = PG_u. \tag{11-14}$$

Noting again that $P = F\Lambda D^{-1} = VD^{-1}$,

$$R_{xk} = F\Lambda D^{-1}G_u = VD^{-1}G_u. \tag{11-15}$$

5. The matrices R_{xj} and R_{xk} are matrices of correlations between tests and factors, here second-order general (and any subgeneral) factors and second-order specific factors. As such they are also factor-*structure* matrices. Further, substituting from (11-11) into (11-10),

$$X = P(G_s J + G_u K) + UB$$
$$= PG_s J + PG_u K + UB$$

Then from (11-12) and (11-14)

$$X = R_{xj} J + R_{xk} K + UB. \tag{11-16}$$

Recalling that J, K, and B are all factor-score matrices in standard-score form, and noting that (11-16) represents a set of specification equations for the test scores X, it follows that R_{xj} $(= PG_s)$ and R_{xk} $(= PG_u)$ represent factor-*pattern* matrices as well as factor-*structure* matrices. The factors of J, K, and B are all orthogonal to one another.

6. We can set G_s and G_u alongside each other to form the single complete second-order factor matrix

$$G = [G_s \vdots G_u]. \tag{11-17}$$

Writing out this matrix in full, and taking, for example, $m_s = 2$, g_1 is a general factor, g_2 is a general or subgeneral factor, and $s_1, s_2, \ldots, s_m$ are group factors, we have

$$
\begin{array}{cccc}
G_s : g_1 & g_2 & G_u : s_1 & s_2 \cdots s_m \\
\end{array}
$$

$$
G = \left[
\begin{array}{cccc}
g_{11} & g_{12} & s_1 & 0 \cdots 0 \\
g_{\mathrm{II}1} & g_{\mathrm{II}2} & 0 & s_2 \ldots 0 \\
\hline
g_{m1} & g_{m2} & 0 & 0 \cdots s_m \\
\end{array}
\right]
$$

Because the factors (the *axes*) of G are all orthogonal to one another, the second-order specific-factor loadings are given by

$$s_1 = \sqrt{1 - g_{\mathrm{I}1}^2 - g_{\mathrm{I}2}^2}$$
$$s_2 = \sqrt{1 - g_{\mathrm{II}1}^2 - g_{\mathrm{II}2}^2}$$
$$\text{-----------------------}$$
$$s_m \sqrt{1 - g_{m1}^2 - g_{m2}^2}$$

From (11-13), (11-15), and (11-17) we have

$$H = [R_{xj} \vdots R_{xk}] = VD^{-1}[G_s \vdots G_u] = VD^{-1}G, \tag{11-18}$$

and H is the *hierarchical orthogonal factor matrix*. The *axes* of H are orthogonal, so it is an orthogonal factor matrix in the same sense that a centroid or diagonal F is an orthogonal factor matrix: it is a matrix of loadings on orthogonal factors (axes). But H, like a centroid or diagonal F, is not itself orthogonal by columns: the sums of products of the elements in pairs of its columns do not in general equal zero. The only factor matrix having this latter property is the principal-axes F.

The elements in the first m_s column(s) of H are the loadings on the general (and any subgeneral) factor(s), or the correlations between the tests and the second-order general (and any subgeneral) factor(s). If one or more of these are subgeneral factors, the corresponding column(s) (among the first m_s) will have some zero or near-zero loadings. The last m columns of H represent m orthogonal *group* factors, with a number of near-zero elements in each column. The elements in these columns are the loadings of the tests on the corresponding group factors, or the correlations between the tests and the second-order unique factors. Each group factor corresponds to a first-order primary factor, with the effects of the correlations between these primary factors removed and accounted for by the general (and any subgeneral) factors. As we now have common factors of two orders—general (and any subgeneral) and group—the matrix H is a *hierarchical* matrix. Thus the elements in the columns of H give the answers to our first two questions. And because the factors (axes) of H are orthogonal, the answers to our second two questions are given by the squares of the elements of H.

7. For computational convenience we define the matrix

$$T_g = D^{-1}G. \tag{11-19}$$

Then from (11-18)

$$H = VT_g. \tag{11-20}$$

Because the axes of H are all orthogonal to one another, the sum of squares of the elements of each row gives the communality of the corresponding test, h_i^2. When we compute these communalities from H we designate them h_h^2. If the second-order factoring includes all salient second-order factors, the n values of h_h^2 should agree within accumulated rounding error with the corresponding values h_f^2 computed from F.

We can also compute the first-order unique-factor loading of each test as $\sqrt{1 - h_i^2}$, where h_i^2 is either h_h^2 or h_f^2.

8. In the hierarchical orthogonal solution we have, in effect, replaced the first-order common-factor space of m dimensions, in which the first-order common factors are correlated, and the second-order common-factor space of m_s dimensions, in which the second-order common factors are orthogonal, by a single common-factor space of $m + m_s$ dimensions, in which the common factors are *all* orthogonal. Because they *are* orthogonal, H is both a structure

and a pattern: its elements are both the correlations of the tests with the common factors, and the coefficients of the specification equations of (11-16). Writing out these specification equations, we have

$$X_i = g_{i1}J_1 + g_{i2}J_2 + \ldots + g_{im_s}J_{m_s} + gr_{i1}K_1 + gr_{i2}K_2 + \ldots$$
$$+ gr_{im}K_m + u_i U_i \tag{11-21}$$

for the i-th test, where

> X_i is a standard score on the i-th test
>
> $J_1, J_2, \ldots, J_{m_s}$ are standard scores on the general (and any subgeneral) factors
>
> $g_{i1}, g_{i2}, \ldots, g_{im_s}$ are the loadings of the i-th test on these general (and any subgeneral) factors
>
> $K_1, K_2, \ldots, K_m$ are standard scores on the m group factors
>
> $gr_1, gr_2, \ldots, gr_m$ are the loadings of the i-th test on these group factors
>
> U_i is a standard score on the i-th unique factor
>
> u_i is the loading of the i-th test on this i-th unique factor

Note again that the loading of the i-th test on every unique factor except the i-th is zero. There will be one such equation for every individual and every test. The coefficients (loadings) will be the same for a given test for all individuals. The standard scores will usually be different for every test or factor and every individual, though equal standard scores *may* occur for different individuals on the same test or factor, and/or for the same individual on different tests or factors.

If there are just two second-order general factors, and a plot (or a tetrad analysis) suggests that Theorem 1.8 (Section 1.5.10) may hold, the investigator may wish to consider one of them a second-order general factor and the other a second-order group factor, and to rotate them by (2-22) or (2-23) (see Fig. 2.2). In this case g_1 of H becomes a general factor, and g_2, derived from the second-order group factor, becomes a first-order subgeneral factor, with two or more near-zero loadings. Even with three second-order factors, the investigator may choose to rotate them by the methods of Section 8.4.1. In this case g_1 of H becomes a general factor, and g_2 and g_3 become subgeneral factors. The more common procedure, with three or more second-order factors and often with only two, is to rotate to an orthogonal approximation to simple structure by the weighted-varimax method (or even by a Landahl transformation if there are only two second-order common factors) to obtain the common-factor elements of the G-matrix. The investigator may go on to an oblique second-order rotation in order to clarify the *interpretation* of the second-order common factors, but the orthogonal rotation must be used in forming the G-matrix of (11-17).

11.2.2 Example

For the eleven WAIS subtests, the hierarchical orthogonal solution is shown in Table 11.3. The matrix G, from Table 11.1, is shown at the upper left. There is only one general factor. The elements of $diag\ D^{-1}$ come from the next-to-last

TABLE 11.3
Hierarchical Orthogonal Solution for Eleven WAIS Subtests,
Age-Group 25–34 (N = 300)

Factor	Matrix G				diag	Matrix $T_g = D^{-1}G$			
	g	s_1	s_2	s_3	D^{-1}	g	s_1	s_2	s_3
I	.8591	.5113	0	0	1.7751	1.5250	.9076	0	0
II	.9333	0	.3592	0	2.1183	1.9770	0	.7609	0
III	.9193	0	0	.3934	2.0640	1.8974	0	0	.8120

Test	Matrix $H = VT_g$					Communalities		
	g	gr_1	gr_2	gr_3	u_i	h_h^2	h_f^2	$h_f^2 - h_h^2$
(1)	.870	.003	.163	.189	.425	.819	.819	.000
(2)	.734	.060	−.062	.339	.581	.661	.661	.000
(3)	.691	.016	.289	−.037	.661	.563	.563	.000
(4)	.760	−.008	.107	.212	.605	.634	.635	.001
(5)	.585	−.016	.279	−.048	.760	.423	.425	.002
(6)	.862	−.060	.065	.340	.366	.866	.868	.002
(7)	.631	.138	.099	.061	.754	.431	.434	.003
(8)	.713	.308	.002	.081	.624	.610	.607	−.003
(9)	.679	.447	.043	−.079	.575	.669	.665	−.004
(10)	.708	.252	.069	.045	.654	.572	.571	−.001
(11)	.555	.506	−.072	−.047	.655	.571	.571	.000
Σ	7.788	1.646	.982	1.056		6.819	6.819	.000
Ch	7.790	1.645	.984	1.056				

(1) Information (mostly "what" questions)
(2) Comprehension (mostly "why" questions)
(3) Arithmetic (problems stated verbally)
(4) Similarities (in what way are two objects alike?)
(5) Digit Span (3–9 forward; 2–8 backward)
(6) Vocabulary (tell meaning of word)
(7) Digit Symbol (draw symbol according to key)
(8) Picture Completion (name missing part)
(9) Block Design (arrange blocks to duplicate design on card)
(10) Picture Arrangement (to tell a story)
(11) Object Assembly (form board)

row and the second three columns of Table 11.1: 1.7751, 2.1183, and 2.0640. They are recorded in the upper middle column of Table 11.3. The transformation matrix T_g is shown at the upper right. Each element of T_g is the corresponding element of G times the element of $diag\ D^{-1}$ in the same row.

The hierarchical matrix H (with orthogonal axes) is shown in the lower part of Table 11.3. The entries in column g are the sums of products of the elements in column g of T_g times those of each row of V from Table 11.1. Thus the first is

$$(1.5250)(.003) + (1.9770)(.214) + (1.8974)(.233) = .870.$$

The entries in columns gr_1, gr_2, and gr_3 are multiples of those in columns I, II, and III of V (Table 11.1). The multipliers are $s_1 = .9076$ for column I, $s_2 = .7609$ for column II, and $s_3 = .8120$ for column III, for matrix T_g of Table 11.3. Thus, for the first row of H,

$$(.003)(.9076) = .003$$

$$(.214)(.7609) = .163$$

$$(.233)(.8120) = .189$$

Because the axes of H are orthogonal, the sum of squares of the elements of each row should give the communality of the corresponding variable. These communalities are recorded in column h_h^2. Beside them we show the communalities computed from the F-matrix, h_f^2, given in Table 7.1. The discrepancies, $h_f^2 - h_h^2$, are shown in columns $h_f^2 - h_h^2$. Considering the number of computations intervening between V and H (and between F and V), the agreement is excellent and discrepancies are readily attributable to accumulated rounding error.

The matrix H is both a structure and a pattern. The unique-factor loadings are given by

$$u_i = \sqrt{1 - h_i^2} = \sqrt{1 - g_i^2 - gr_{i1}^2 - gr_{i2}^2 - gr_{i3}^2}. \qquad (11\text{-}22)$$

The u_i (using the h_h^2 values for the communalities) are shown in the last column of the H-matrix of Table 11.3.

The equations of the pattern (one for each row i of H) are given by (11-21). For one general factor and three group factors, letting $J_1 = G$, $K_1 = GR_1$, $K_2 = GR_2$, and $K_3 = GR_3$, to conform to the more common notation for a specification equation, this becomes, for the i-th test,

$$x_i = g_i G + gr_{i1} GR_1 + gr_{i2} GR_2 + gr_{i3} GR_3 + u_i U_i. \qquad (11\text{-}23)$$

The standard scores G, GR_1, GR_2, GR_3 and U_i are unknown for any given individual, so (11-23), like (11-21), is of only theoretical interest.

The matrix H provides considerable information in addition to that found in the V and G matrices. We can see at once that in every row of H, the g-factor loading is higher than the loading on any of the three group factors. Thus the battery as a whole is a better measure of its general factor (intelligence) than it is of its group factors—nonverbal (figural) reasoning, quantitative reasoning, and verbal ability. For a *multiple-aptitude battery,* as contrasted with a general-intelligence battery, the tests should if possible be so selected that the loading of each test on its own group factor exceeds its loading on the general factor.

In each row of H in Table 11.3, the sum of squares of the loadings (including u_i^2) is unity, and the contribution of each factor to the variance of X_i is the square of the factor loading. Thus for test 6 (Vocabulary), which has the highest communality, the squares of the loadings are

$$g_6^2 = .743; \ gr_{61}^2 = .004; \ gr_{62}^2 = .004; \ gr_{63}^2 = .116; \ u_6^2 = .134.$$

Thus .743 of the variance of this test is due to the general factor, .004 to the nonverbal (figural) reasoning group factor, .004 to the quantitative reasoning group factor, .116 to the verbal ability group factor, and .134 to the unique factor. Each of the other ten tests can be characterized in a similar manner. To facilitate this, the test titles, from Section 7.1.5, are repeated at the bottom of Table 11.3.

Exercise 11:2. In Exercise 11:1 you obtained a second-order analysis of the nine-aptitude-tests problem. Using these data, carry out the hierarchical orthogonal solution, and interpret the results in terms of the test titles given in Table 5.3.

12 Component Analysis

In common-factor analysis we are interested in analyzing the *common* variance of the variables. The common variance of any standardized variable X_i is its communality h_i^2, and the total common variance is the sum of the communalities. In the F-matrix or any *orthogonal* rotation of F, the proportion of the variance of any variable that is attributable to a common factor is the square of its factor loading on that factor. The proportion of its variance that is attributable to its unique factor is the square of its unique-factor loading, $1 - h_i^2$.

In component analysis, on the other hand, we are interested in analyzing the *total* variance. The total variance of any standardized variable X_i is unity, and the total variance of all the variables is n, the number of variables. In the A-matrix (corresponding to the F-matrix of factor analysis), or any *orthogonal* rotation of A, the proportion of the variance of any variable attributable to a given component is the square of its loading on that component. There are no unique components and no communalities. In consequence, the number of components is equal to the number of variables unless the correlation matrix (with unities on the diagonal) is singular, which it seldom is. We can hope, however, that the last one or a few components are insignificant or nonsalient, in which case there will be only $k < n$ salient components. The object of a component analysis is to find the $k < n$ salient components and the loadings of the variables on these components, but this object is not always attainable; in some cases the n-th component may still be salient.

Formally, initial component analysis is simply initial factor analysis with unities on the diagonal of the correlation matrix. In common-factor analysis, there are $m + n$ factors: $m < n$ (usually $m < n/2$) common factors plus n unique factors. Because $m + n$ factors are more than the n variables used to compute them, factor scores must be estimated by regression. But in component analysis there are only $k \leqq n$ components all together. Whether we use all n or only $k < n$, the number of variables is equal to or greater than the number of components. When $k = n$, the component scores can be computed exactly. When $k < n$, the component scores must be estimated, but these estimates are in general more accurate than the estimates of factor scores.

The disadvantage of component analysis is that the total variance is not separated into common variance and unique variance, and in consequence components are more complex functions of the variables than are factors, and hence are harder to interpret. If we are interested mainly in accurate description of the domain covered by the variables, we use common-factor analysis. But if, on the contrary, we are interested mainly in reducing the total number of variables under consideration and/or in obtaining more accurate estimates of the scores of individuals on this smaller number of derived variables, we use component analysis.

12.1 PRINCIPAL-COMPONENT ANALYSIS

Most users do not realize that component analysis can be anything other than principal-component analysis. As now used, this is based on Hotelling's (1933) work, though the mathematics goes back to Pearson (1901). Formally, as we noted above, initial component analysis is simply initial factor analysis with unities on the diagonal of the correlation matrix. If we use the principal-axes method, the result is principal-component analysis. If we use the centroid method, the result is centroid-component analysis. If we use the diagonal method, the result is diagonal-component analysis. And in fact *any* resolution of the original correlated variables into derived orthogonal variables is a form of component analysis.

Because the object is to make the variances of the later derived variables as small as possible, principal-component analysis is ordinarily the preferred procedure. By this method the proportion of the total variance accounted for by the first component is a maximum, the proportion of the remaining variance accounted for by the second component is a maximum, and so on. Thus the proportions of the total variance accounted for by the last few components is minimized. The resolution into components is ordinarily carried to completion: from n variables we extract initially all n components. This is a large computing job, so principal-component analysis today is always done on electronic computers.

For component analysis it is not necessary or even advisable to use Hotelling's iterative procedure, or Horst's modification of this procedure, as described in Chapter 5, because residual matrices are not required. Initial principal-component analysis can be carried out using any of the eigenvalue-eigenvector programs available in computing laboratories. Each eigenvector is the corresponding component normalized, so that the sum of squares of its elements is unity. For the corresponding principal component, the sum of squares of its loadings is the eigenvalue (see Chapter 5). To obtain the loadings on the k-th component $(k = 1, 2, \ldots, n)$, that is, the correlations between the component and the variables, or the weights of the variables in the specification equation for the component, we merely multiply each element of the k-th eigenvector by the square root of the k-th eigenvalue:

$$a_{ik} = e_{ik} \sqrt{\lambda_k}, \tag{12-1}$$

where a_{ik} is the loading of variable i on component k, e_{ik} is the coefficient of the i-th variable on the k-th eigenvector, and λ_k is the k-th eigenvalue. Note that with unities on the diagonal, the correlation matrix is mathematically Gramian: all eigenvalues will be positive or zero, and one or more of the later eigenvalues will be zero only in case the correlation matrix is singular. Its rank, if singular, will be equal to the number of positive nonzero eigenvalues.

For the five-verbal-tests data, Table 12.1 gives the loadings on the principal components, the eigenvalues, the cumulative sums of these eigenvalues for the successive components, and the cumulative per cents of trace (cumulative per cents of the total variance) accounted for by $1, 2, \ldots, n$ $(n = 5)$ components. With unities on the diagonal of the correlation matrix, the total trace is $n = 5$, the number of variables.

TABLE 12.1
Principal Components and Eigenvalues for Five Verbal Tests ($N = 841$)

Test	Component Matrix A				
	a	b	c	d	e
(1)	.8095	−.4169	.3964	−.0315	.1127
(2)	.8513	.2942	.0337	.4033	.1582
(3)	.8702	−.1465	−.1388	.0978	−.4388
(4)	.8448	−.1624	−.4227	−.1520	.2410
(5)	.8243	.4268	.1556	−.3330	−.0579
Eig	3.5304	.4903[a]	.3804	.3072	.2917
Cum Eig	3.5304	4.0207	4.4011	4.7083	5.0000 = *trace*
% Trace	71	80	88	94	100

[a] Computed value rounded to four figures. Sum of squares of rounded entries in column b rounds to .4904.

When we examine Table 12.1, we find that there is at least one component loading above $\pm$ .4000 in every column, so it is not immediately apparent that any of the components can be discarded.

12.1.1 Test of Significance

In principal-component analysis, when the first k components are significant, there is a statistical test of the hypothesis that the remaining $n - k$ components are not significant (Bartlett, 1950, 1951). The test runs as follows. We first compute

$$Q = \frac{\lambda_{k+1}\lambda_{k+2} \cdots \lambda_n}{\left(\dfrac{\lambda_{k+1} + \lambda_{k+2} + \cdots + \lambda_n}{n - k}\right)^{n-k}}, \tag{12-2}$$

that is, we divide the product of all the eigenvalues beyond the k-th by their mean raised to the power of their number. We next find a constant

$$C = -(N-1) + \frac{2n + 5}{6} + \frac{2k}{3}. \tag{12-3}$$

The natural logarithm of Q, which is 2.302,585 times its logarithm to the base 10, is then multiplied by C to give a quantity that is distributed approximately as Chi-square, namely

$$\chi^2 = C \ln Q, \tag{12-4}$$

with degrees of freedom

$$DF = (n - k - 1)(n - k + 2)/2. \tag{12-5}$$

The test is applied in sequence, with $k = 0, 1, 2, \ldots$, until a point is reached at which the last $n - k$ components are not significant. Because component $k + 1$ is the first component that is *not* significant, the significance level chosen should be fairly high: usually .2 or .1.

The null hypothesis actually tested by this procedure is the hypothesis that the last $n - k$ components are *equal* and not significantly greater than 0; that is, that they are all error components, with means 0 and equal error variances, so the procedure cannot be used to test the significance of the last (n-th) component.

For the five-verbal-tests data, we know already that the first two common factors are significant, so we can assume that the first two principal components are significant also, and start the series of tests with $k = 2$. Thus for $k = 2$, $n = 5$, $N - 1 = 840$, we have from Table 12.1 and (12-2)

$$Q = \frac{(.3804)(.3072)(.2917)}{\left(\dfrac{.3804 + .3072 + .2917}{3}\right)^3} = .979,974,$$

and by (12-3)

$$C = -840 + 15/6 + 4/3 = -836.167.$$

Also

$$\log Q = \overline{1}.99122 = -.00878,$$

so

$$lnQ = (-.00878)(2.302,585) = -.02022,$$

and by (12-4)

$$\chi^2 = (-836.167)(-.02022) = 16.9.$$

From (12-5)

$$DF = (2)(5)/2 = 5,$$

and from a table of the chi-square distribution

$$P = .00471.$$

Thus the hypothesis that two components are sufficient is rejected at the .00471 level.

Letting $k = 3$, we have

$$Q = \frac{(.3072)(.2917)}{\left(\dfrac{.3072 + .2917}{2}\right)^2} = .999,330$$

$$C = -840 + 15/6 + 6/3 = -835.5$$

$$\log Q = \overline{1}.999,709 = -.000,291$$

$$lnQ = (-.000,291)(2.302,585) = -.000,670$$

$$\chi^2 = (-835.5)(-.000,670) = .56$$

$$DF = (1)(4)/2 = 2$$

$$P = .756$$

and we cannot reject the hypothesis that the last two components are insignificant. Hence we conclude that there are three significant components in these data, even though from Table 12.1 the first three components account for only 88% of the total variance.

The Bartlett test for the significance of principal components is somewhat more accurate than is the Bargmann test for the significance of *principal-axes* factors, because the Bargmann test applies strictly only to maximum-likelihood factors. Also in the case of components there is less accumulated lore upon which to base rules of thumb for a number of salient components different from the number which are statistically significant. The scree test may still be applicable when there is a clear last substantial difference between adjacent eigenvalues, but such a difference is less likely to appear with principal-component data than with common-factor data. Thus for our present example we have

Component	Eigenvalue	Diff
1	3.5304	
		3.0401
2	.4903	
		.1099
3	.3804	
		.0732
4	.3072	
		.0155
5	.2917	

From these differences we could conclude that the last two components are not salient, but it is not too clear whether the third is or is not, so we accept the result of the Bartlett test which says it is.

The number of salient components will usually not be greater than the number that are significant by the Bartlett test, though this may depend on the arbitrary choice of a significance level. The investigator may choose, however, to consider a significant component nonsalient if it is clearly nonsalient by the scree test. For some purposes he may even choose to stop at some earlier point, retaining only the components whose eigenvalues are large in comparison with those of the later components. Some writers suggest that only those components whose eigenvalues are greater than unity be retained, and this rule often works moderately well when n is fairly large. But for small n it is too stringent: for the five-verbal-tests problem it suggests that only the first component should be retained. And for very large n (e.g., $n > 100$), one or more components with eigenvalues greater than unity may well be discarded.

The Bartlett test, like the Bargmann test for the number of significant factors, is greatly influenced by the number N of sets of observations. Hence when N is small it is likely to underestimate the number of salient components, and when N is very large it is likely to overestimate this number. Thus the scree test, which is independent of N, should be used along with the Bartlett test in arriving at a judgment concerning the number of salient components. We can sometimes use examination of the component-loading matrix also: a component which has only one substantial loading is likely to be nonsalient, though we cannot say that a component which has more than one substantial loading is likely to be salient for that reason. As this discussion shows, estimation of the number of salient components is an even less precise procedure than is estimation of salient common factors.

12.2 CENTROID COMPONENT ANALYSIS

Although principal-component analysis is the preferred method, those working with quite small problems and desk calculators may prefer to compute the centroid components. Centroid component analysis is more cumbersome than is centroid factor analysis because we must extract all n components rather than only $n/2$ or fewer, so the centroid method is seldom used with n more than 6 or 7.

For the five-verbal-tests example, the centroid-component analysis is shown in Table 12.2. The initial trace is 5.000: the sum of the five unities on the diagonal of the correlation matrix. The numbers just above each panel after the first show the order in which the columns (and rows) were reflected. The reflection symbols (successive mark-overs of the original symbols) are as follows:

	Symbol Meaning		Symbol Meaning
Original sign	none	positive	— negative
First reflection	=	now negative	╫ now positive
Second reflection	╪	now positive	⊕ now negative

Note: See page 42, paragraph number 2, for final signs of loadings.

TABLE 12.2
Centroid Component Analysis of Five Verbal Tests (N = 841)

Test	(1)	(2)	(3)	(4)	(5)	Σ	Ch
(1)	(1.000)	.585	.658	.616	.555	3.414	
(2)	.585	(1.000)	.663	.634	.689	3.571	
(3)	.658	.663	(1.000)	.697	.626	3.644	
(4)	.616	.634	.697	(1.000)	.598	3.545	
(5)	.555	.689	.626	.598	(1.000)	3.468	
Σ	3.414	3.571	3.644	3.545	3.468	17.642	17.642
a	.8128	.8502	.8676	.8440	.8257	4.2003	4.2002
Refl	1		2	3			
(1)	(.339)	╫ .106	⊕ .047	⊕ .070	╫ .116	.000	.444
(2)	╫ .106	(.277)	╫ .075	╫ .084	— .013	—.001	.529
(3)	⊕ .047	╫ .075	(.247)	⊕ .035	╫ .090	.000	.330
(4)	⊕ .070	╫ .084	⊕ .035	(.288)	╫ .099	.000	.366
(5)	╫ .116	— .013	╫ .090	╫ .099	(.318)	.000	.610
Σ	.444	.529	.330	.366	.610	2.279	2.279
b	= .2941	.3504	= .2186	= .2424	.4041	1.5096	1.5096

TABLE 12.2 (continued)

Refl	1	2					
(1)	(.253)	╫.003	╫.111	╫.141	╫.003	.001	.511
(2)	╫.003	(.154)	╫.002	╫.001	╫.155	—.001	.315
(3)	╫.111	╫.002	(.199)	— .088	.002	.000	.226
(4)	╫.141	╫.001	— .088	(.229)	.001	.000	.284
(5)	╫.003	╫.155	.002	.001	(.155)	.000	.316
Σ	.511	.315	.226	.284	.316	1.652	1.652
c	.3976	= .2451	= .1758	= .2210	.2459	1.2854	1.2853

Refl	2			1			
(1)	(.095)	╫.094	= .041	╫.053	╫.095	.000	.296
(2)	╫.094	(.094)	— .041	╫.053	.095	.001	.295
(3)	= .041	— .041	(.168)	╫.127	= .041	.000	.172
(4)	╫.053	╫.053	╫.127	(.180)	╫.053	.000	.466
(5)	╫.095	.095	— .041	╫.053	(.095)	.001	.297
Σ	.296	.295	.172	.466	.297	1.526	1.526
d	= .2396	= .2388	= .1392	.3772	.2404	1.2352	1.2353

Refl			1	2			
(1)	(.038)	.037	╫.074	— .037	.037	.001	.223
(2)	.037	(.037)	╫.074	— .037	.038	.001	.223
(3)	╫.074	╫.074	(.149)	= .074	╫.074	.001	.445
(4)	— .037	— .037	= .074	(.038)	— .038	.000	.224
(5)	.037	.038	╫.074	— .038	(.037)	.000	.224
Σ	.223	.223	.445	.224	.224	1.339	1.339
e	= .1927	=.1927	.3845+	= .1936	.1936	1.5171	1.5172

Test	Centroid Component Matrix A				
	a	b	c	d	e
(1)	.8128	−.2941	.3976	−.2396	−.1927
(2)	.8502	.3504	−.2451	−.2388	−.1927
(3)	.8676	−.2186	−.1758	−.1392	.3845
(4)	.8440	−.2424	−.2210	.3772	−.1936
(5)	.8257	.4041	.2459	.2404	.1936
Σa^2	3.5303	.4791	.3584	.3339	.2971
Cum Σa^2	3.5303	4.0094	4.3678	4.7017	4.9988 ≐ 5.0000
% Trace	71	80	87	94	100

The sum of squares of the elements of each component, the cumulative sum of squares, and the cumulative per cent of trace are shown at the bottom of the summary table.

When we compare this summary table with Table 12.1, we note first that the loadings on component a are quite similar in the two tables, whereas the loadings on the later components are not. The sums of squares (eigenvalues in Table 12.1), the cumulative sums of squares, and the per cents of trace, however, are fairly similar. For the centroid components, the scree test is

Component	Σa^2	Diff
1	3.5303	
		3.0512
2	.4791	
		.1207
3	.3584	
		.0245
4	.3339	
		.0368
5	.2971	

This scree test suggests that only the first two components are salient, but as we have noted, the scree test is not as accurate for components as it is for common factors.

The Bartlett test (designed for principal components) is *probably* about as accurate for centroid components as is the Bargmann test (designed for maximum-likelihood factors) for principal-axes factors. In the absence of any specific evidence for the applicability of the Bartlett test with centroid components, and of any accumulated lore that can lead to estimates of salience based on the component loadings, we may see what the Bartlett test suggests in this case.

For $k = 2$, $n = 5$, $N - 1 = 840$, we have

$$Q = \frac{(.3584)(.3339)(.2971)}{\left(\dfrac{.3584 + .3339 + .2971}{3}\right)^3} = .991,141$$

$$C = -840 + 15/6 + 4/3 = -836.167$$

$$\log Q = \bar{1}.996,136 = -.003,864$$

$$lnQ = (-.003,864)(2.302,585) = -.008,897$$

$$\chi^2 = (-836.167)(-.008,897) = 7.44$$

$$DF = (2)(5)/2 = 5$$

$$P = .190$$

This is a marginal result: the hypothesis that the last three components are insignificant is rejected at only the .19 level by a none-too-accurate test. The writers would be inclined to consider the third component significant (and hence salient) as a conservative decision in battery reduction, but an investigator who wants to retain the smallest possible number of components might justifiably retain only two.

> **Exercise 12:1.** Carry out a centroid-component analysis of the six-psychological-tests data. The correlations are given in Table 1.5. Save the results.

> **Exercise 12:2 (optional).** If an electronic digital computer is available, carry out a principal-components analysis of the six-psychological-tests data also, and compare the results with those of Exercise 12:1. Use a standard eigenvalue-eigenvector program, and compute the component loadings by (12-1). The first eigenvector *may* come out with all its signs negative. If it does, reverse the signs of *all* elements of *all* eigenvectors before computing the component loadings.

The procedures of Chapter 5 (with unities on the diagonal) are less efficient than the standard eigenvalue-eigenvector programs when all n components are desired, and most programs based on the Hotelling procedures terminate at about the first $n/2$ principal-axes factors or principal components and hence are not applicable when all n components are desired.

12.3   BEST COMPOSITE MEASURE

Suppose that, for a set of at least moderately similar variables, we wish to obtain a weighted sum of the n scores which will give the best single measure of whatever is common to all of the variables. Thus we might wish to obtain, for each individual tested by the five verbal tests, that weighted sum of his scores which would best represent general verbal ability as measured by all five of them. Or for each individual tested by the nine aptitude tests, we might desire a weighted composite score measuring his general intelligence as measured by all of these tests. In another context, if the individuals are counties and the variables are yield per acre in each county of wheat, barley, oats, beans, peas, potatoes, turnips, mangolds, hay (temporary grass), and hay (permanent grass), we might wish to determine for each county a relative measure of crop yield in general. By the least-squares criterion, the appropriate weights to apply to the standard scores on the variables are the loadings on the first principal component. These weights have the following properties:

1. The variance of the weighted composite scores is maximized (Horst, 1936), providing maximum discrimination among individuals.

2. The mean of the within-individuals variances of the weighted standard scores on the n variables is minimized; that is, for each individual, on the average, his weighted standard scores are as nearly equal as possible. The standard scores are those of the original n variables, and the weights are the loadings on the first principal component (Edgerton and Kolbe, 1936).

3. The domain validity of the weighted composite scores is maximized (Lord, 1958). This domain validity is the correlation between the weighted composite scores and a composite of scores on all variables in the domain or universe of variables having the same factorial structure. The sample estimate of this correlation (Meyer, 1975) is the square root of

$$R^2 = \frac{W'(\Sigma - D^2)W}{(n-1)W'\Sigma W} \qquad (W \neq 0), \tag{12-6}$$

where W is the column vector of weights, Σ is the variance-covariance matrix of the variables, D^2 is the diagonal of Σ whose elements are the variances of the variables, and n is the number of variables. The concept of domain validity is very nearly, but not exactly, the same as the concept of reliability. R^2 (not R) becomes the reliability of the composite when the variables are homogeneous, that is, when their correlation matrix with communalities on the diagonal has only one common (general) factor.

12.3.1 Composite Scores

The composite score of the j-th individual $(j = 1, 2, \ldots, N)$ is

$$C_j = a_1 X_{1j} + a_2 X_{2j} + \cdots + a_n X_{nj}, \tag{12-7}$$

where C_j is the desired composite score, $a_1, a_2, \ldots, a_n$ are the loadings of the n variables on the first principal component, and $X_{1j}, X_{2j}, \ldots, X_{nj}$ are the standard scores of the j-th individual on the n variables.

The standard score of the j-th individual on the i-th variable is

$$X_{ij} = (x_{ij} - \bar{x}_i)/\sigma_i,$$

where x_{ij} is the raw score of the j-th individual on the i-th variable, $\bar{x}_i$ is the mean score on the i-th variable, and σ_i is the standard deviation of the i-th variable. The composite score of the j-th individual is then

$$\begin{aligned} C_j = {} & (a_1/\sigma_1)x_{1j} + (a_2/\sigma_2)x_{2j} + \cdots + (a_n/\sigma_n)x_{nj} \\ & - [(a_1/\sigma_1)\bar{x}_1 + (a_2/\sigma_2)\bar{x}_2 + \cdots + (a_n/\sigma_n)\bar{x}_n], \end{aligned} \tag{12-8}$$

the term in brackets being a constant for all individuals.

For the five-verbal-tests example the basic data are

Test

	(1)	(2)	(3)	(4)	(5)
a	.8095	.8513	.8702	.8448	.8243
σ	3.9	4.4	5.9	6.4	4.2
$\bar{x}$	32.4	25.9	22.8	21.8	23.8
a/σ	.208	.193	.147	.132	.196
$(a/\sigma)\bar{x}$	6.74	5.00	3.35	2.88	4.66

The a-values are the first principal–component loadings from Table 12.1; the σ-values and $\bar{x}$-values come from the original study. The constant term of (12-8) is the sum of the terms in the last row above, $(a/\sigma)\bar{x}$, or 22.63, and (12-8) with numerical coefficients and constant is

$$C_j = .208x_{1j} + .193x_{2j} + .147x_{3j} + .132x_{4j} + .196x_{5j} - 22.63.$$

Suppose individual j has raw scores

Test	1	2	3	4	5
Raw score	30	32	28	26	25

His composite score will then be

$$C_j = (.208)(30) + (.193)(32) + (.147)(28) + (.132)(26) + (.196)(25)$$
$$- 22.63 = 2.23.$$

Note that the C_j as defined by (12-7) and (12-8) are a set of N deviation scores (with mean 0) but are *not* standard scores. To obtain the composite *standard* scores, each C_j must be divided by σ_c, which is equal to $\sqrt{\lambda_1}$, or for these data, from Table 12.1, $\sigma_c = \sqrt{3.53}$. Then for individual j

$$C_j/\sigma_c = 2.23/\sqrt{3.53} = 1.19.$$

12.3.2 Approximations

The loadings on the first centroid component are often excellent approximations to the loadings on the first principal component; they are appreciably better than are the centroid approximations to those of the later principal components. Because variables that can reasonably be combined into a composite will normally all be positively correlated, the loadings on the first centroid component can be computed easily. For the five-verbal-tests example, using the first-centroid-component loadings from Table 12.2, the basic data become

	(1)	(2)	(3)	(4)	(5)
			Test		
a	.8128	.8502	.8676	.8440	.8257
σ	3.9	4.4	5.9	6.4	4.2
$\bar{x}$	32.4	25.9	22.8	21.8	23.8
a/σ	.208	.193	.147	.132	.197
$(a/\sigma)\bar{x}$	6.74	5.00	3.35	2.88	4.69

The constant is now 22.66, and the composite standard score is still 2.23 to two decimals.

Another procedure (Kendall, 1955, Chapter 5; 1957, Chapter 2), useful when both N and n are small, is based on ranks. The N individuals are first ranked on each of the n variables, using the average-rank procedure to resolve ties. The ranks of each individual are then summed, and the rank-sums are themselves ranked to obtain the composite ranks. Thus for a small artificial example with $N = 7$ and $n = 5$ we have

				Individual			
Test	1	2	3	4	5	6	7
(1)	1	3	2	4	7	5.5	5.5
(2)	1	2.5	2.5	5	6	7	4
(3)	2	3	1	4	6	5	7
(4)	2	1	4	4	7	4	6
(5)	2	1	4	3	5	7	6
Sum	8	10.5	13.5	20	31	28.5	28.5
Rank	1	2	3	4	7	5.5	5.5

The final ranks are the composite ranks of the seven individuals on the five variables. These are the best composite ranks in the sense that they maximize the sum of the n Spearman rank correlations between the ranks on the separate variables and the composite ranks. They give a good approximation to the composite ranks that would be obtained by calculating the intercorrelations among the variables, finding the first-principal-component loadings, computing the composite-variable scores by (12-8), and ranking these N composite-variable scores to obtain the composite ranks. Kendall (1939) obtained measures of crop yield from 48 counties in England for the ten crops mentioned in the first paragraph of Section 12.3. Using both principal-component weights and sum-ranks to obtain composite ranks, he found that the Spearman rank correlation between the two sets of composite ranks for the 48 counties was .99 (Kendall, 1957, Chapter 2).

12.4   ROTATION

Initial components, like initial factors, are composite variables. Each of them is a weighted composite of all n variables. When common factors are rotated obliquely, simple structure is almost always attainable, with at least m near-zero loadings in every column of the rotated factor matrix. When they are rotated orthogonally, for example, by the varimax or weighted-varimax procedure, the result is an orthogonal approximation to simple structure. The orthogonally rotated factors can be interpreted by considering their high loadings, even though their near-zero loadings are not well identified.

Though some writers have tried to interpret unrotated components, the results are usually unsatisfactory. All unrotated components after the first, like all unrotated factors after the first, are bipolar. But like common factors, components can be rotated, either orthogonally or obliquely.

When we apply the same type of rotation to *both* the salient components and the salient common factors of the same correlation matrix, the first m rotated components (where m is the number of salient common factors) are likely to be fairly similar to the m rotated common factors. Each of the additional $k - m$ salient rotated components is likely to have only one high loading, on a variable which in the common-factor analysis would have a large unique factor (and hence a relatively low communality).

Table 12.3 shows this situation for the five verbal tests. On the left we have the A-matrix of three unrotated salient components from Table 12.1, a varimax orthogonal rotation of this matrix, and a Promax oblique rotation. On the right we have the centroid F-matrix of two unrotated salient common factors from Table 2.5, a Landahl orthogonal rotation of this matrix (fairly similar in the two-factor case to a varimax rotation), and an oblique rotation from Table 2.8 which is quite similar to a Promax rotation.

The similarities and differences are shown most clearly in the Promax and Oblique factor matrices, and with somewhat less clarity in the Varimax and Landahl orthogonal factor matrices. In both the component and common-factor oblique matrices, component or factor II has substantial loadings on variables 2 (Same–Opposite) and 5 (Vocabulary), and is the word-meaning component or factor. Component I has substantial loadings on variables 3 (Proverb Matching) and 4 (Verbal Analogies) and is some sort of verbal-reasoning component. Factor I has substantial loadings on the same two variables and also on variable 1 (Paragraph Meaning) and is the verbal-reasoning factor. Component III has only one substantial loading, on variable 1 (Paragraph Meaning). Thus in the component

TABLE 12.3
Orthogonal and Oblique Rotations of Three Principal Components
and Two Common Factors for Five Verbal Tests ($N = 841$)

	Principal Components				Common Factors		
	A-Matrix				F-Matrix		
Var	a	b	c	Var	a	b	h^2
(1)	.810	−.417	.396	(1)	.748	.142	.580
(2)	.851	.294	.034	(2)	.814	−.154	.686
(3)	.870	−.146	−.139	(3)	.845	.160	.740
(4)	.845	−.162	−.423	(4)	.802	.132	.661
(5)	.824	.427	.156	(5)	.794	−.283	.711

	Varimax Matrix				Landahl Matrix		
Var	A	B	C	Var	1	2	h^2
(1)	.310	.290	.898	(1)	.629	.429	.580
(2)	.404	.762	.260	(2)	.467	.684	.686
(3)	.669	.408	.428	(3)	.711	.484	.740
(4)	.870	.316	.248	(4)	.660	.474	.660
(5)	.260	.872	.242	(5)	.361	.762	.711

	Promax Matrix				Oblique Matrix	
Var	I	II	III	Var	I	II
(1)	.001	−.018	.699	(1)	.333	−.007
(2)	.092	.518	−.015	(2)	.065	.296
(3)	.405	.070	.132	(3)	.376	−.007
(4)	.659	−.043	−.080	(4)	.338	.013
(5)	−.071	.670	−.009	(5)	−.065	.420

Transformation Matrices

	Varimax				Promax		
	I	II	III		I	II	III
a	.603	.630	.490	a	.263	.284	.168
b	−.284	.743	−.606	b	−.347	.903	−.623
c	−.746	.227	.626	c	−.900	.323	.764

analysis the verbal-reasoning *factor* splits into two *components,* a proverb-matching and verbal-analogies component and a paragraph-meaning component. Paragraph meaning was the variable which split off, mainly because of its greater unique variance (lower communality). In the h^2 column of the factor analysis, it is the variable with the lowest communality and hence the largest unique variance.

12.4.1 Rotation for Battery Reduction

Since the objective of a component analysis is to replace n variables by $k < n$, we may wish, after determining the number k by an initial component analysis, to identify the particular subset of k *original variables* which come closest to measuring everything measured by all n. To obtain rotated components that correspond to the original variables, we can use a series of Gram-Schmidt transformations as described in Section 8.4.1. But to identify the best k out of n tests with certainty, we would have to use $k - 1$ such transformations for every different set of k out of n variables, and select that set of k variables which maximizes the proportion of the total variance accounted for. But for any practical problem the amount of computing required would be prohibitive. The number of different sets of k out of n variables is

$$\binom{n}{k} = \frac{n!}{k!(n-k)!} ,$$

so if $n = 10$ and $k = 7$ we would have six Gram-Schmidt transformations for each of 120 sets of seven variables.

We can simplify this situation very greatly by using a *stepwise assumption.* We assume that the two best tests include the one best, the three best include the two best, . . . , the k best include the $k - 1$ best. ''Best'' is evaluated in terms of the proportion of variance accounted for. When n is small, this assumption is often correct; and even when it is not correct, the k tests identified by using the stepwise assumption are usually *almost* as good as the best k. In application we find first the test that accounts for the largest proportion of the total variance, then the test that accounts for the largest residual variance given the first, then the test that accounts for the largest second-residual variance given the first two, . . . , and finally the test that accounts for the largest $(k - 1)$-th residual variance given the first $k - 1$.

The procedure consists in rotating orthogonally so that the first rotated component has a nonzero loading on only the test accounting for the largest proportion of the total variance, then rotating so that the second rotated component has nonzero loadings on only this first test and the test having the largest residual variance, then rotating so that the third rotated component has nonzero loadings on only the first two tests and the test having the largest second-residual variance, and so on. For this purpose we use a series of Gram-Schmidt transformations, the first of order k, the second of order $k - 1, \ldots$, the last of order 2. The k-th test is then the one having the largest $(k - 1)$-th residual variance.

Table 12.4 shows the procedure for the first three principal components of the five verbal tests. We start with the component matrix of Table 12.1, with the last two columns omitted, shown at the upper left of Table 12.4. The column at the right of this matrix, labeled $a^2 + b^2 + c^2$, shows the sum of squares of the loadings of each test. The sum of this column agrees within rounding error with the sum of the three eigenvalues, checking the $a^2 + b^2 + c^2$ computations.

Test 1 has the largest sum of squares, so we let test 1 load only on the first rotated component. We start with the three-variable Y-matrix of Table 8.6, namely

$$Y = \begin{bmatrix} a & b & c \\ k_2 & -ab/k_2 & -ac/k_2 \\ 0 & c/k_2 & -b/k_2 \end{bmatrix}$$

Here a, b, and c are obtained by normalizing row (1) of A, as shown at the upper right of Table 12.4. The figures .81513, $-.41980$, and .39916, rounded to four figures, are the a, b, and c in the first row of the Y_1-matrix. They are first computed to five decimals to reduce accumulated rounding errors in the other Y_1-entries.

We next compute $k_2 = \sqrt{1 - a^2}$, $1/k_2$, ab, ac, $-ab/k_2$, $-ac/k_2$, c/k_2, and $-b/k_2$, as shown just below matrix A, and copy the results into rows b and c of Y_1. The column $a^2 + b^2 + c^2$ is included as a check, because the rows of Y_1 have been normalized: $a^2 + b^2 + c^2$ must equal 1.0000 for each row, within rounding error.

The third section of Table 12.4 begins at the left with the matrix product AY_1'. The usual sum-check is used, based on the column sums of A. Note that in columns b and c, the entries in row (1) are both .0000 because the entire variance of test 1 is accounted for by rotated component a. In this matrix, component a is test 1, and components b and c are arbitrary.

We next rotate columns b and c. The column headed $b^2 + c^2$ at the right of matrix AY_1' gives the residual variances: the proportions of the variances of variables 2, 3, 4, and 5 which are not accounted for by test 1. The largest of these is that of test 5, .5780, so our next rotation will base the rotated component b on variable 5.

The normalization of variable 5 over columns b and c of AY_1' is shown at the right of AY_1'. The normalized values are given to only four figures because no further computations are required to obtain the Y_2 matrix from them. This Y_2 matrix, from the first (2 by 2) matrix of Table 8.6 (substituting b and c for a and b), is

$$Y_2 = \begin{bmatrix} b & c \\ c & -b \end{bmatrix}$$

and is shown just below the normalization computations in Table 12.4.

TABLE 12.4
Gram-Schmidt Rotation of Three Principal Components
for Five Verbal Tests ($N = 841$)

	Reduced Component Matrix A					Normalization of Row (1)		
Test	a	b	c	$a^2+b^2+c^2$			(1)	(1) Norm
(1)	.8095	−.4169	.3964	.9862		a	.8095	.81513
(2)	.8513	.2942	.0337	.8124		b	−.4169	−.41980
(3)	.8702	−.1465	−.1388	.7980		c	.3964	.39916
(4)	.8448	−.1624	−.4227	.9187		Σf_1^2	.98623	1.00000
(5)	.8243	.4268	.1556	.8858		$\sqrt{\Sigma f_1^2}$	.99309	
Σ	4.2001	−.0048	.0242	4.4011		$1/\sqrt{\Sigma f_1^2}$	1.00696	
Eig	3.5304	.4903	.3804	4.4011				

Y_1

			a	b	c	$a^2+b^2+c^2$
$k_2 = \sqrt{1 - .81513^2} = .57928 \doteq$	.5793	a	.8151	−.4198	.3992	1.0000
$1/k_2 = 1.72628$		b	.5793	.5907	−.5617	1.0000
$ab = -.34219;$		c	0	.6891	.7247	1.0000
$ac = .32537$						

$-ab/k_2 = -(1.72628)(-.34219) = .5907$
$-ac/k_2 = -(1.72628)(.32537) = -.5617$
$c/k_2 = (1.72628)(.39916) = .6891$
$-b/k_2 = -(1.72628)(-.41980) = .7247$

	AY$_1'$					Normalization of Row (5), Columns b and c		
Test	a	b	c	b^2+c^2			(5)	(5) Norm
(1)	.9931	.0000	.0000	.0000		b	.6422	.8447
(2)	.5838	.6480	.2272	.4715		c	.4069	.5352
(3)	.7154	.4955	−.2015	.2861		Σf_5^2	.57799	1.0000
(4)	.5880	.6309	−.4182	.5729		$\sqrt{\Sigma f_5^2}$	.76026	
(5)	.5548	.6422	.4069	.5780		$1/\sqrt{\Sigma f_5^2}$	1.31534	
Σ	3.4351	2.4166	.0144	1.9085				
Ch	3.4352	2.4167	.0142	1.9086				

	A Rotated					Y_2		
Test	a	b	c				b	c	b^2+c^2

Test	a	b	c
(1)	.9931	.0000	.0000
(2)	.5838	.6690	.1549
(3)	.7154	.3107	.4354
(4)	.5880	.3091	.6909
(5)	.5548	.7602	.0000
Σ	3.4351	2.0490	1.2812
Ch	3.4352	2.0490	1.2812
Σf^2	2.4924	1.2175	.6909

	b	c	b^2+c^2
b	.8447	.5352	1.0000
c	.5352	−.8447	1.0000

Summary

Comp	Σf^2	Cum Σf^2	% Trace[a]
$a = (1)$	2.4924	2.4924	50
$b = (5)$	1.2175	3.7099	74
$c = (4)$	.6909	4.4008	88

[a] Trace = 5.0000.

The final rotated component matrix is shown at the bottom left of Table 12.4. Column a is copied from column a of the AY_1' matrix. Columns b and c are obtained by postmultiplying columns b and c of AY_1' by Y_2'. Note that in column c, the entry in row (5) as well as the entry in row (1) is .0000, because the entire variance of variable 5 is accounted for by the rotated components a and b.

We do not require a c^2 column, because the largest c^2 value will be that of the variable which has the largest c-value. This is variable 4 with $c = .6909$. If we were to normalize this single number and multiply by the elements of column c, the normalized value would be unity, so column c remains unchanged. It is only a coincidence that the sum of squares of the elements in this column is also .6909.

The best three tests to measure as much as possible of whatever is measured by all five, under the stepwise assumption, are tests 1, 5, and 4. Referring to the names of these tests in Table 1.1, we see that they are 1 (Paragraph Meaning), 5 (Vocabulary), and 4 (Verbal Analogies).

At the bottom right of Table 12.4 we have a summary. The entries in the column headed Σf^2 are copied from the last row of the A-rotated matrix. The next column gives the cumulative sums of squares, and the last column gives the per cents of the total trace. Thus test 1 accounts for 50%, tests 1 and 5 for 74%, and tests 1, 5 and 4 for 88%. Comparing this last with the figure in column c of the last row of Table 12.1, we see that they are the same. The cumulative sum of squares (cumulative sum of eigenvalues) is 4.4011 in Table 12.1, and 4.4008 in Table 12.4. The difference is only .0003, which can probably be attributed to the accumulated rounding error in the computations of Table 12.4. This validates the stepwise assumption for these data. Had the figure in Table 12.4 been substantially smaller, it would indicate that the stepwise assumption had not yielded the best three tests.

12.5   COMPONENT SCORES

12.5.1   Scores in the Full-Rank Case

For all n unrotated components the basic equation is

$$X = AZ, \tag{12-9}$$

where X is the n by N matrix of standard scores on the original (measured) variables, A is the n by n matrix of component loadings, each row designating a variable and each column a component, and Z is the n by N matrix of standard scores on the components. Then unless A is singular, which is highly unlikely with real data, the solution is

$$Z = A^{-1}X. \tag{12-10}$$

This solution is exact for both principal components and centroid components: if we compute the elements of Z by (12-10) and then substitute them into (12-9), the elements of X will be reproduced exactly. The elements of Z are therefore *measurements*, not estimates.

12.5.2 Scores in the Reduced-Rank Case

If we have discarded the last $n - k$ components, so that A becomes A_k, with n rows but only k ($k < n$) columns, then Z becomes Z_k, with N columns but only k rows. In this case (12-9) is replaced by

$$X = A_k Z_k.$$

This matrix equation represents nN observation equations (one for each element of X) in only kN unknowns (one for each element of Z_k). These observation equations will be inconsistent, so we can only *estimate* the elements of Z_k. Then in place of (12-9) we have

$$X = A_k Z_k + \epsilon, \tag{12-11}$$

where A_k consists of the first k columns of A and Z_k consists of the first k rows of Z. Then

$$\epsilon = A_{n-k} Z_{n-k}, \tag{12-12}$$

where A_{n-k} consists of the last $n - k$ columns of A and Z_{n-k} consists of the last $n - k$ rows of Z.

We solve (12-11) for Z_k indirectly, by solving for B_k in the regression equations,

$$Z_k = \mathrm{B}_k X + \eta_k, \text{ or } \hat{Z}_k = \hat{\mathrm{B}}_k X. \tag{12-13}$$

From the first equation of (12-13)

$$Z_k - \mathrm{B}_k X = \eta_k, \tag{12-14}$$

where Z_k (k by N) is the matrix of true factor scores, B_k (k by n) is the matrix of true regression coefficients, X (n by N) is the matrix of standard scores on the original variables, and η_k (k by N) is the matrix of residuals. These residuals are present because, again, the first equation of (12-13) represents nN inconsistent observation equations in only kN unknowns.

Each row of (12-14) represents one component, and we can solve for the scores on each component separately, by minimizing for that row the sum of squares of the residuals. For any one row, say the i-th, (12-14) becomes

$$Z_i - \mathrm{B}_i X = \eta_i \qquad (i = 1, 2, \ldots, k).$$

There is a slight inconsistency of notation here, in that if $i = k$, Z_k, B_k, and η_k would represent the last (k-th) rows of these matrices as well as the whole k-rowed matrices. This need not cause any confusion because we use the subscript i only as a general subscript for any one row. Then for the i-th row

$$\eta_i \eta_i' = (Z_i - B_i X)(Z_i - B_i X)'.$$

Here η_i is a row vector of residuals, and $\eta_i \eta_i'$ is the sum of squares of these residuals, which is a scalar. Expanding this equation,

$$\eta_i \eta_i' = Z_i Z_i' - Z_i X' B_i' - B_i X Z_i' + B_i X X' B_i'.$$

Each term of this equation is a scalar, so

$$\eta_i \eta_i' = Z_i Z_i' - 2 B_i X Z_i' + B_i X X' B_i'.$$

The normal equations for the least-squares estimate $\hat{B}_i$ of B_i are

$$Z_i X' = \hat{B}_i X X'. \tag{12-15}$$

Dividing both sides of (12-15) by N,

$$Z_i X'/N = \hat{B}_i (X X')/N. \tag{12-16}$$

But because Z_i and each column of X' represents N standard scores,

$$Z_i X'/N = A_i',$$

where A_i' is the i-th row of A_k', or the row vector of n correlations between the i-th row of Z_k and the standard scores X on the original variables. Here again, if $i = k$, we have the same slight inconsistency of notation noted previously. Note also that

$$X X'/N = R,$$

the matrix of correlations between the original variables. Substituting these values, A_i' and R, into (12-16),

$$A_i' = \hat{B}_i R,$$

and solving for $\hat{B}_i$,

$$\hat{B}_i = A_i' R^{-1}.$$

Then for all k rows of Z_k,

$$\hat{B}_k = A_k' R^{-1}, \tag{12-17}$$

and substituting into the last equation of (12-13),

$$\hat{Z}_k = A_k' R^{-1} X. \tag{12-18}$$

This is the general equation for component scores. It applies to centroid components as well as to principal components.

If A_k is a *principal*-components matrix, there is an alternative procedure that does not require the computation of R^{-1}. Starting with (12-11) and (12-12),

$$X = A_k Z_k + A_{n-k} Z_{n-k}. \tag{12-19}$$

Premultiply both sides of this equation by $(A_k'A_k)^{-1}A_k'$. The result is

$$(A_k'A_k)^{-1}A_k'X = (A_k'A_k)^{-1}A_k'A_kZ_k + (A_k'A_k)^{-1}A_k'A_{n-k}Z_{n-k}.$$

The product $(A_k'A_k)^{-1}A_k'A_k = I$, so the first term on the right is simply Z_k. Also if A is a *principal*-components matrix, its columns are orthogonal. Then $A_k'A_{n-k}$ is equal to zero because each of its elements is a sum of products of two different columns of A, so

$$Z_k = (A_k'A_k)^{-1}A_k'X. \tag{12-20}$$

Note that the equation, $A_k'A_{n-k} = 0$, does *not* imply that $A_{n-k}Z_{n-k}$ $(= \epsilon)$ is equal to 0. If we substitute from (12-20) into (12-19), it is apparent that $A_{n-k}Z_{n-k}$ $(= \epsilon)$ still remains, so the elements of Z_k are estimates, not measurements, and $X \neq A_kZ_k$.

If A_k is a *principal*-components matrix, it can be shown that the $\hat{Z}_k$ of (12-18) is equal to the Z_k of (12-20). We omit the proof here, because it requires the use of partitioned matrices, which were not treated in Chapter 3, and uses also (3-33), which was stated without proof.

For an A which is orthogonal by columns, and in particular for a *principal*-components A,

$$A'A = D, \tag{12-21}$$

where D is the diagonal matrix whose diagonal elements are the eigenvalues of R. Then considering only the first k columns of A (and the first k rows of A'),

$$A_k'A_k = D_k,$$

where the diagonal elements of D_k are the first k eigenvalues of R. Then substituting this value of D_k into (12-20),

$$Z_k = D_k^{-1}A_k'X, \tag{12-22}$$

and the diagonal elements of D_k^{-1} are merely the reciprocals of the first k eigenvalues of R. These eigenvalues are found as a part of the solution of R for A_k.

It is often most convenient to obtain A from an eigenvalue-eigenvector solution of R, using any standard computer program for this purpose. If we generalize (12-1) in matrix notation to include *all* of the elements of A, we have

$$A = ED^{1/2},$$

where E is the matrix whose columns are the eigenvectors of R, and $D^{1/2}$ has diagonal elements that are the square roots of the eigenvalues. Then

$$A^{-1} = D^{-1/2}E^{-1},$$

with $D^{-1/2}$ having diagonal elements that are the reciprocals of the square roots of the eigenvalues. Also, because E is orthonormal, $E^{-1} = E'$, and

$$A^{-1} = D^{-1/2}E'. \qquad (12\text{-}23)$$

Substituting into (12-10),

$$Z = D^{-1/2}E'X. \qquad (12\text{-}24)$$

When we retain only the first k columns of A, we retain only the first k rows of E' and the first k diagonal elements of D. Hence, corresponding to (12-24), we have

$$Z_k = D_k^{-1/2}E_k'X, \qquad (12\text{-}25)$$

and Z_k consists precisely of the first k rows of Z. Also from (12-23) we see that $D_k^{-1/2}E_k'$ consists precisely of the first k rows of A^{-1}, or

$$\tilde{A}_k^{-1} = D_k^{-1/2}E_k'. \qquad (12\text{-}26)$$

Thus $\tilde{A}_k^{-1}$ is in effect the "inverse" of the nonsquare matrix A_k for the purpose of computing component scores. Then substituting into (12-25),

$$Z_k = \tilde{A}_k^{-1}X. \qquad (12\text{-}27)$$

If we have solved (12-10) for Z, we have at the same time solved (12-27) for Z_k for all values of k. This result has caused some writers, notably Kaiser (1962a), to maintain that the elements of Z_k are in fact measurements, as are the elements of Z in the full-rank case of (12-10).

Note again that all of the formulas after (12-18) apply only when A is a *principal*-components matrix: all of them depend on the proposition that A is orthogonal by columns, so that $A'A$ or $A_k'A_k$ is diagonal.

For centroid components, it is usually necessary to compute R^{-1} directly and use (12-18). We can, of course, assume for centroid components that $A_k'A_{n-k}$ is almost a zero matrix. Recall that in the derivation of (12-20) we obtained the solution for Z_k given there because the columns of A_k were orthogonal to the columns of A_{n-k}. If the columns of A_k are *approximately* orthogonal to those of A_{n-k} in the centroid solution, the solution for Z_k in (12-20) will be approximately correct. Also if the columns of A_k are almost orthogonal to one another, it is quite likely that they will also be almost orthogonal to those of A_{n-k}; that is, *all* the columns of A will be almost orthogonal to one another. This likelihood increases as k becomes a larger fraction of n, and the elements of A_{n-k} and hence of $A_k'A_{n-k}$ become smaller. We can test the almost-orthogonality of the columns of A_k by computing first the product $A_k'A_k$, which in this case must be almost diagonal. The assumption is justified if the off-diagonal elements of $A_k'A_k$ are all quite small in comparison with its diagonal elements. If they are, we can approximate $(A_k'A_k)^{-1}$ in (12-20) by treating it as a diagonal matrix, with elements that are the reciprocals of the diagonal elements of $A_k'A_k$, thus simplifying the computation of (12-20).

Centroid analysis is usually done on desk calculators. If an electronic computer is available, we almost always prefer to use principal-component analysis. When we use the simplifying assumptions of the previous paragraph with centroid-component analysis, the elements of Z_k will be in error beyond the least-squares approximation.

12.5.3 Scores on Transformed Components

If A has been transformed, so that

$$V = A \Lambda, \tag{12-28}$$

and if the transformation is *orthogonal*, V is the primary-pattern matrix as well as the reference-structure matrix of the transformed components. Then letting Z_t represent the matrix of component scores on the transformed components of V, we have in place of (12-10)

$$Z_t = V^{-1}X$$

and from (12-28)

$$Z_t = \Lambda^{-1}A^{-1}X.$$

But because the transformation is orthogonal, Λ is orthonormal, $\Lambda^{-1} = \Lambda'$, and

$$Z_t = \Lambda'A^{-1}X, \tag{12-29}$$

which differs from (12-10) only by the factor Λ'. In this, the full-rank case, (12-29) applies to any components matrix A, whether principal-components or centroid-components, and the elements of Z_t are measurements rather than merely estimates.

If we have retained only the first k columns of A, we have in place of (12-28)

$$V_k = A_k \Lambda_k. \tag{12-30}$$

Then if $\hat{Z}_{kt}$ is the matrix of estimated standard scores on the k transformed components, we have in place of (12-18)

$$\hat{Z}_{kt} = V_k'R^{-1}X,$$

and from this equation and (12-30)

$$\hat{Z}_{kt} = \Lambda_k'A_k'R^{-1}X, \tag{12-31}$$

which differs from (12-18) only by the factor Λ_k'.

For the case of *principal* components, we have in place of (12-20)

$$Z_{kt} = (V_k'V_k)^{-1}V_k'X$$

and from (12-30)

$$Z_{kt} = (\Lambda_k'A_k'A_k \Lambda_k)^{-1}\Lambda_k'A_k'X$$

$$= \Lambda_k^{-1}(A_k'A_k)^{-1}(\Lambda_k')^{-1}\Lambda_k'A_k'X$$

$$= \Lambda_k^{-1}(A_k'A_k)^{-1}A_k'X$$

Then noting that, because the transformation is orthogonal, $\Lambda_k^{-1} = \Lambda_k'$, and

$$Z_{kt} = \Lambda_k'(A_k'A_k)^{-1}A_k'X, \tag{12-32}$$

which differs from (12-20) only by the factor Λ_k'. And from (12-27)

$$Z_{kt} = \Lambda_k'\tilde{A}_k^{-1}X, \tag{12-33}$$

with $\tilde{A}_k^{-1}$ defined as the first k rows of A^{-1}.

Thus using any of the formulas for Z or Z_k or $\hat{Z}_k$, we have only to premultiply by Λ' or Λ_k' to obtain the corresponding formula for Z_t or Z_{kt} or $\hat{Z}_{kt}$ giving the scores on the transformed components, so long as $V = A\Lambda$ or $V_k = A_k\Lambda_k$ represents an *orthogonal* transformation.

If the transformation is *oblique*, the situation is a little more complicated. The transformation matrix is no longer orthonormal, the primary-pattern matrix differs from the reference-structure matrix, and we will need the scores on the primary components. By (6-31) the primary-components matrix (the primary pattern) is

$$P = A\Lambda\Delta^{-1}, \tag{12-34}$$

with A taking the place of the F of (6-31) and Δ taking the place of D, because in this section we have already used D to represent the diagonal matrix whose diagonal elements are the eigenvalues of R. Here Δ is the diagonal matrix that normalizes the rows of Λ^{-1} or the columns of $(\Lambda')^{-1}$. The inverse of P is

$$P^{-1} = \Delta\Lambda^{-1}A^{-1}.$$

Then in place of (12-10) we have

$$Z_t = P^{-1}X = \Delta\Lambda^{-1}A^{-1}X. \tag{12-35}$$

The last two factors are the same as those of the right-hand side of (12-10), so given any of the previous solutions for Z, we have only to premultiply by $\Delta\Lambda^{-1}$ to obtain the solution for Z_t. Note that $\Delta\Lambda^{-1}$ is simply Λ^{-1} row-normalized. But Λ is now no longer orthonormal so $\Lambda^{-1} \neq \Lambda'$, and Λ^{-1} must be computed from the oblique transformation matrix Λ and then row-normalized for use in (12-35). This formula applies to any A^{-1} matrix, centroid-components as well as principal-components.

If we have retained only the first k columns of A, namely A_k, then in the general case the regression equation corresponding to (12-13) is

$$Z_{kt} = \mathbf{B}_{kt}X + \eta_{kt}, \qquad \text{or } \hat{Z}_{kt} = \hat{\mathbf{B}}_{kt}X. \tag{12-36}$$

From the first equation of (12-36)

$$Z_{kt} - \mathbf{B}_{kt}X = \eta_{kt},$$

the i-th row of which is

$$Z_{it} - B_{it}X = \eta_{it}.$$

By the same argument leading from (12-14) to (12-15), the normal equations for the i-th row are

$$Z_{it}X' = \hat{B}_{it}XX',$$ (12-37)

and dividing by N

$$Z_{it}X'/N = \hat{B}_{it}(XX')/N.$$ (12-38)

The elements of Z_{it} are the standard scores on the elements of the i-th primary component, whose correlations with the original scores are given by the i-th row of S_k', the transpose of the primary-component structure; or

$$Z_{it}X'/N = S_i.$$

Also, once again,

$$XX'/N = R.$$

Then, substituting these results into (12-38),

$$S_i' = \hat{B}_{it}R,$$

and solving for $\hat{B}_{it}$

$$\hat{B}_{it} = S_i'R^{-1},$$

or for all rows

$$\hat{B}_{kt} = S_k'R^{-1}.$$ (12-39)

Then from the second equation of (12-36)

$$\hat{Z}_{kt} = S_k'R^{-1}X.$$ (12-40)

Using the notation of this section, it is shown in Table 6.3 that

$$S_k = A_k(\Lambda_k')^{-1}\Delta_k = A_k(\Lambda_k^{-1})'\Delta_k,$$

where Δ_k is the diagonal matrix that normalizes the columns of $(\Lambda_k')^{-1}$. Because Δ_k is diagonal, $\Delta_k' = \Delta_k$, and the transpose of S_k is

$$S_k' = \Delta_k\Lambda_k^{-1}A_k'.$$

Substituting into (12-40),

$$\hat{Z}_{kt} = \Delta_k\Lambda_k^{-1}A_k'R^{-1}X.$$ (12-41)

This differs from (12-18) only by the factor $\Delta_k\Lambda_k^{-1}$, which is Λ_k^{-1} row-normalized.

When the components are *principal* components, we have in place of (12-20)

$$Z_{kt} = (P_k'P_k)^{-1}P_k'X.$$ (12-42)

Then from (12-34)

$$P_k = A_k \Lambda_k \Delta_k^{-1},$$

whose transpose, noting that Δ_k^{-1} is diagonal so that $(\Delta_k^{-1})' = \Delta_k^{-1}$, is

$$P_k' = \Delta_k^{-1} \Lambda_k' A_k'.$$

Substituting into (12-42),

$$Z_{kt} = (\Delta_k^{-1} \Lambda_k' A_k' A_k \Lambda_k \Delta_k^{-1})^{-1} \Delta_k^{-1} \Lambda_k' A_k' X$$
$$= \Delta_k \Lambda_k^{-1} (A_k' A_k)^{-1} \underline{(\Lambda_k')^{-1} \Delta_k \Delta_k^{-1} \Lambda_k'} A_k' X.$$

The underlined factors equal I because $\Delta_k \Delta_k^{-1} = I$ and then $(\Lambda_k')^{-1} \Lambda_k' = I$, so

$$Z_{kt} = \Delta_k \Lambda_k^{-1} (A_k' A_k)^{-1} A_k' X. \tag{12-43}$$

This differs from (12-20) only by the factor $\Delta_k \Lambda_k^{-1} (= \Lambda_k^{-1}$ row-normalized). Also from (12-27) and (12-20)

$$(A_k' A_k)^{-1} A_k' = \tilde{A}_k^{-1},$$

with $\tilde{A}_k^{-1}$ the first k rows of A^{-1}, and from (12-43)

$$Z_{kt} = \Delta_k \Lambda_k^{-1} \tilde{A}_k^{-1} X, \tag{12-44}$$

which differs from (12-27) only by the factor $\Delta_k \Lambda_k^{-1} (= \Lambda_k^{-1}$ row-normalized).

Thus using any of the formulas for Z_k or $\hat{Z}_k$, following an oblique transformation, we have only to premultiply by $\Delta_k \Lambda_k^{-1} (= \Lambda_k^{-1}$ row-normalized) to obtain the corresponding formula for Z_{kt} or $\hat{Z}_{kt}$, which gives the estimated scores on the primary components.

12.5.4 Example.

For the example of five verbal tests we use (12-23) to obtain A^{-1}, because the computer gave D and E directly. Thus

$$
\text{diag } D^{-\frac{1}{2}} \cdot \qquad\qquad E'
$$

$$
A^{-1} = \begin{bmatrix} .53221 \\ 1.4282 \\ 1.6213 \\ 1.8042 \\ 1.8516 \end{bmatrix} \cdot \begin{bmatrix} .43085 & .45306 & .46312 & .44964 & .43869 \\ -.59538 & .42010 & -.20926 & -.23191 & .60948 \\ .64275 & .05467 & -.22497 & -.68532 & .25220 \\ -.05681 & .72763 & .17642 & -.27425 & -.60082 \\ .20864 & .29294 & -.81240 & .44628 & -.10722 \end{bmatrix}
$$

$$
A^{-1} = \begin{bmatrix} .2293 & .2411 & .2465 & .2393 & .2335 \\ -.8503 & .6000 & -.2989 & -.3312 & .8705 \\ 1.0421 & .0886 & -.3647 & -1.1111 & .4089 \\ -.1025 & 1.3128 & .3183 & -.4948 & -1.0840 \\ .3863 & .5424 & -1.5042 & .8263 & -.1985 \end{bmatrix}
$$

And if only the first three components are significant, $\tilde{A}_k^{-1}$ will consist of the first three rows of A^{-1}.

If individual p, say, has standard scores

Variable	1	2	3	4	5
Standard score	1.22	$-.25$	1.34	.85	$-.19$

his scores on the five components by (12-10) will be

Component	1	2	3	4	5
Score	.71	-2.03	$-.26$	$-.24$	$-.94$

and if we have retained only the first three components, his scores on these components by (12-27) will be the first three of these, namely .71, -2.03, and $-.26$.

After orthogonal rotation of the first three components, using the transpose of the varimax transformation matrix of Table 12.3,

TABLE 12.5

Calculation of $\Delta_k \Lambda_k^{-1}$ for Promax Transformation
for Five Verbal Tests ($N = 841$)

Eq	Variable (1)	(2)	(3)	Variable (1)	(2)	(3)	$\Sigma + 1$	Ch
(1)	(.2630)	.2840	.1680				1.7150	
(2)	$-.3470$	.9030	$-.6230$	$= \Lambda_k$			.9330	
(3)	$-.9000$	.3230	.7640				1.1870	
(2)		(1.2777)	$-.4013$	1.3194			3.1958	3.1958
(3)		1.2949	1.3389	3.4221			7.0559	7.0559
(1)		1.0799	.6388	3.8023			6.5210	6.5209
(3)			(1.7456)	2.0850	-1.0135		3.8171	3.8171
(1)			.9780	2.6872	$-.8452$		3.8200	3.8200
(2)			$-.3141$	1.0326	.7827		2.5012	2.5012
(1)				1.5191	$-.2774$	$-.5603$	1.6814	1.6814
(2)		$\Lambda_k^{-1} =$		1.4078	.6003	.1799	3.1880	3.1880
(3)				1.1944	$-.5806$	.5729	2.1867	2.1867
	$(\Sigma^2)^a$	$\sqrt{\Sigma^2}$	$1/\sqrt{\Sigma^2}^b$	(1)	(2)	(3)		
(1)	2.69855	1.64273	.60874	.925	$-.169$	$-.341$	$=$ matrix	
(2)	2.37462	1.54098	.64894	.914	.390	.117	$[\Delta_k \Lambda_k^{-1}]^c$	
(3)	2.09190	1.44634	.69140	.826	$-.401$	.396		

[a] Sum of squares of elements of each row of Λ_k^{-1}.

[b] Diagonal elements of Δ_k. Each one multiplies one row of Λ_k^{-1} to give the corresponding row of $\Delta_k \Lambda_k^{-1}$.

[c] Ch: sum of squares of elements in each row $= 1.000$ within rounding error.

$$\Lambda'_k \tilde{A}_k^{-1} = \begin{bmatrix} -.398 & -.091 & .506 & 1.067 & -.411 \\ -.251 & .618 & -.150 & -.348 & .887 \\ 1.280 & -.190 & .074 & -.378 & -.157 \end{bmatrix}$$

and the component scores of individual p on the rotated components by (12-33) are

Orthogonal rotated component	1	2	3
Estimated score	1.20	−1.13	1.42

For oblique rotation, using the Promax transformation matrix of Table 12.3, Table 12.5 shows the computation of $\Delta_k \Lambda_k^{-1}$. Then,

$$\Delta_k \Lambda_k^{-1} \tilde{A}_k^{-1} = \begin{bmatrix} .000 & .091 & .403 & .656 & -.071 \\ .000 & .465 & .066 & -.040 & .601 \\ .943 & -.006 & .179 & -.110 & .006 \end{bmatrix}$$

and by (12-44) the scores of individual p on these rotated components are

Oblique rotated component	1	2	3
Estimated score	1.09	−.18	1.30

12.6   REDUCED-RANK REGRESSION

Assume that we have a criterion or dependent variable y and n predictors, x_1, $x_2, \ldots , x_n$, with data from a sample of N. The nuber of degrees of freedom for fitting the regression function is

$$DF = N - n - 1 = N - (n + 1), \tag{12-45}$$

and if N is not much larger than $n + 1$, the regression coefficients will have large sampling errors. If N is *less* than $n + 1$, the regression is impossible.

Suppose that x_1 and x_2 are two of the best predictors of y, that in the population their correlations with y are almost equal, and that they correlate fairly highly with each other. Then in the sample whether x_1 or x_2 has the higher criterion correlation will be due mainly to the two sets of sampling errors. If x_1 has the higher criterion correlation it will have a large regression coefficient and the regression coefficient of x_2 will be near-zero or possibly negative. If x_2 has the higher criterion correlation, this situation will be reversed. More complicated situations of this general type occur when several pairs or subsets of predictors have high intercorrelations and almost equal criterion correlations, and in fact these criterion correlations need not be *very* closely equal if DF as given by (12-45) is not large. Thus in these cases the sample regression coefficients become exceedingly unstable.

When n is fairly large as compared with N, so that the DF of (12-45) is not large, we may resort to rank-reduction procedures. To do this, we reduce the number of variables from n to $k < n$, so that $DF = N - k - 1$ instead of $N - n - 1$. This can be done in several ways. One way is to use *stepwise regression,* whereby we determine the best $k < n$ of the original predictors, and do not use the others at all. By this procedure, the multiple correlation of y with the k predictors retained is always lower in the sample than is its multiple correlation with all n, but it may not be significantly lower. In the case of the two predictors, x_1 and x_2, described previously, the one with the higher criterion correlation in the sample would be retained and the other would be eliminated. But if we had formed one variable $x_1 + x_2$ from both, its weight would be higher than that of *either* x_1 or x_2 alone, because it would be more reliable. In any event, reduction of DF by stepwise regression is always accompanied by loss of the information contained in the variables eliminated.

A better procedure, when DF is too small to give stable regression coefficients and/or some pairs or subsets of variables have high intercorrelations, is to perform a principal-component analysis of the n predictors; then perform a stepwise regression of the y-standard scores on the *components,* and retain only the k components whose multiple correlation with the criterion is highest (Burket, 1964). The components enter in the order of their contributions to the multiple correlation, which may or may not be the same as their order of magnitude (the order of magnitude of their eigenvalues). We stop when adding another component does not increase the multiple correlation significantly. If we wish to retain only a few components, we can set the significance level low (e.g., .01 or even .001); if we can tolerate more components, we can set the significance level higher (e.g., .05 or .10).

The general solution of a set of n normal equations in standard-score form is

$$B = R^{-1}R_c, \qquad (12\text{-}46)$$

where B is the vector of standard regression coefficients, R^{-1} is the inverse of the matrix of correlations between the predictor variables, and R_c is the vector of correlations between the predictors and the criterion variable. The multiple correlation is then the square root of

$$R_n^2 = \beta_1 r_{1y} + \beta_2 r_{2y} + \cdots + \beta_n r_{ny}, \qquad (12\text{-}47)$$

where y designates the criterion variable and n specifies the number of predictors. If the predictors are principal components, (12-46) becomes

$$B = R_p^{-1}R_y \qquad (12\text{-}48)$$

where R_y (replacing R_c) indicates that the predictor variables are the principal components rather than the original variables, and R_p^{-1} (replacing R^{-1}) is the inverse of the matrix of correlations between the principal components. In this case (12-47) becomes

$$R_n^2 = \beta_1 r_{y1} + \beta_2 r_{y2} + \cdots + \beta_n r_{yn}. \qquad (12\text{-}49)$$

Reversing the order of the subscripts as we go from (12-47) to (12-49), which is otherwise immaterial, indicates again that the predictors are the principal components rather than the original variables.

Because the principal components are orthogonal, their intercorrelations are all zero. Their self-correlations are all unity as with any set of variables, so $R_p^{-1} = R_p = I$, I is the identity matrix, and from (12-48),

$$B = R_y,$$ (12-50)

the vector of correlations between the principal components and the criterion variable. Then (12-49) becomes

$$R_n^2 = r_{y1}^2 + r_{y2}^2 + \cdots + r_{yn}^2.$$ (12-51)

Summarizing in tabular form,

	Predictors	
	Original Variables	Principal Components
Predictor-criterion correlation	r_{iy}	r_{yi}
Vector of predictor-criterion correlations	R_c	R_y
Vector of regression coefficients	B (12-46)	R_y
Matrix of intercorrelations	R	R_p

When the number of predictor variables is less than the number of original variables, we use the subscript k instead of n to designate the number of predictors retained. It is evident from (12-51) that R_k^2 will increase with every component added to the predictor set. But if we add predictors in the order of their contributions to R_k^2, that is, in the order of their r_{yi}^2 values, the contributions of the later components may be negligible.

It is not necessary to compute all nN component scores in order to obtain their correlations with the criterion. Consider the equation

$$ZY/N = R_y,$$ (12-52)

where Z is the n by N matrix of standard scores on the components, Y is the N by 1 column vector of criterion standard scores, and R_y is the n by 1 column vector of correlations between the criterion and the components. But by (12-10)

$$Z = A^{-1}X,$$

and substituting into (12-52)

$$R_y = A^{-1}XY/N.$$

But $XY/N = R_c$, the vector of n correlations between the original variables and the criterion, so

$$R_y = A^{-1}R_c.$$ (12-53)

For the five-verbal-tests example we do not have criterion correlations, so for purposes of illustration we invent some. A not unreasonable set of correlations between these tests and grades in English composition might be

Variable	1	2	3	4	5
Criterion correlation R_c	.483	.424	.547	.533	.398

assuming that the verbal-reasoning tests (1, 3, 4) should correlate a little higher with these grades than should the word-meaning tests (2 and 5), and that all the tests should correlate somewhat lower with the criterion grades than with one another. Then by (12-53), using the whole of A^{-1} as given near the beginning of Section 12.5.4, we have

Variable	1	2	3	4	5
$R_y = A^{-1}R_c$	.568	−.150	−.088	−.014	−.045

Note that the absolute values of these component-criterion correlations are in the same order as the order of the eigenvalues except for variables 4 and 5, in which this latter order is reversed.

To test the incremental significance of the multiple correlation obtained by adding each successive component (in order of decreasing magnitude of r_{yi}) to the set of predictors, we can use a series of F-tests. The basic formula is

$$F_k = \frac{R_k^2 - R_{k-1}^2}{(1 - R_k^2)/(N - k - 1)}, \qquad (12\text{-}54)$$

with degrees of freedom $n_1 = 1$; $n_2 = N - k - 1$, where R_k^2 is the squared multiple correlation of the criterion with the first k components, and R_{k-1}^2 is the squared multiple correlation of the criterion with the first $k - 1$ components. In the series of tests k takes the successive values $1, 2, \ldots, n$.

Because components are orthogonal, we can simplify (12-54) to

$$F_k = \frac{r_{yk}^2 (N - k - 1)}{1 - \sum_{i=1}^{k} r_{yi}^2}, \qquad (12\text{-}55)$$

where r_{yi}^2 is the square of the correlation between the i-th component ($i = 1, 2, \ldots, k$) and the criterion, and r_{yk}^2 is the square of the correlation between the k-th component and the criterion. F_k tests the null hypothesis that the multiple correlation is not increased significantly when we add the k-th component to the first $k - 1$. Note again that r_{yi} and r_{yk} are *component*-criterion correlations, *not* test-criterion correlations.

If, as here, $n_1 = 1$ because we add the components one at a time, then $t_k = \sqrt{F_k}$; and by taking the square root of F_k we can use the t-table, which is larger than the $n_1 = 1$ column of the F table, and in which linear interpolation is more accurate, to find significance values. Then returning to our numerical example, and arranging the components in the order of magnitude of the absolute values of their criterion correlations, the computation of the successive t-tests is shown in Table 12.6.

Because the intercorrelations between the principal components are all zero, the squared multiple correlations, by (12-51) are given in row $\sum_{i=1}^{k} r_{yi}^2$. The multiple correlations are given in the last row.

When we compare the entries in row $t_k = \sqrt{F_k}$ with those in rows $t_{.05}$ and $t_{.01}$, we see that the first three t-values are significant at the .01 level, whereas the last two are not significant at the .05 level. We conclude that only the first three components need to be retained to predict the criterion. Ignoring the last two components reduces the multiple correlations by only $.596 - .594 = .002$, and even if we had retained only two components, the reduction would have been only $.596 - .587 = .009$.

When we use all n components, the result is exactly the same (aside from different rounding errors) as the result we would obtain without using component analysis. The regression coefficients are the same as those given by the usual formula,

$$B = R^{-1}R_c,$$

TABLE 12.6

Calculation of Tests of Significance for Component-Criterion
Correlations of Five Verbal Tests ($N = 841$)

	k				
	1	2	3	4	5
Variable	(1)	(2)	(3)	(5)	(4)
r_{yi} $(i = 1, 2, \ldots, k)$	.568	$-.150$	$-.088$	$-.045$	$-.014$
r_{yi}^2	.3226	.0225	.0077	.0020	.0002
$N - k - 1$	839	838	837	836	835
$r_{yk}^2 (N - k - 1)$	270.66	18.855	6.4449	1.6720	.1670
$\sum_{i=1}^{k} r_{yi}^2$	.3226	.3451	.3528	.3548	.3550
$1 - \sum_{i=1}^{k} r_{yi}^2$	.6774	.6549	.6472	.6452	.6450
F_k *(formula 12-55)*	399.56	28.791	9.9581	2.5914	2.5891
$t_k = \sqrt{F_k}$	19.989	5.366	3.156	1.610	.509
$t_{.05}{}^a$	1.963	1.963	1.963	1.963	1.963
$t_{.01}{}^a$	2.852	2.852	2.852	2.852	2.852
R_k	.568	.587	.594	.596	.596

^{a} Computed by linear reciprocal interpolation. In each row, the three-decimal values do not change because the change in *relative* magnitude of $N - k - 1$ (from 839 to 835) is slight.

where B is the vector of standard regression coefficients (the β's), and the multiple correlation is the same as that given by (12-47), namely the square root of

$$R_n^2 = \beta_1 r_{1y} + \beta_2 r_{2y} + \ldots + \beta_n r_{ny},$$

as described in Chapter 4.

12.6.1 Estimation of Criterion Scores

For individual j, say, the regression of the criterion standard score y_j on the k principal-component scores retained, $\hat{z}_{1j}, \hat{z}_{2j}, \ldots, \hat{z}_{kj}$, is

$$\hat{y}_j = \beta_1 \hat{z}_{1j} + \beta_2 \hat{z}_{2j} + \cdots + \beta_k \hat{z}_{kj} \qquad (j = 1, 2, \ldots, N). \qquad (12\text{-}56)$$

For all N individuals, this becomes

$$\hat{Y}' = B_k' \hat{Z}_k, \qquad (12\text{-}57)$$

where $\hat{Y}'$ is the row vector of N estimated criterion standard scores, B_k' is the row vector of k β's, and $\hat{Z}_k$ is the k by N matrix of estimated component standard scores. It has been shown, however, that $B = R_y$, so B_k consists of the first k elements of R_y', say R_{yk}', the vector of correlations between the criterion and the components retained, arranged in the order of their absolute values; and (12-57) becomes

$$\hat{Y}' = R_{yk}' \hat{Z}_k. \qquad (12\text{-}58)$$

Then for the j-th individual we have in place of (12-56),

$$\hat{y}_j = r_{y1} \hat{z}_{1j} + r_{y2} \hat{z}_{2j} + \cdots + r_{yk} \hat{z}_{kj}. \qquad (12\text{-}59)$$

In our previous example, individual j has estimated component standard scores

Component	1	2	3
Standard scores $\hat{z}_{ij}$	.71	-2.03	$-.26$

on the first three components. The first thee component-criterion correlations r_{yi} are

Component	1	2	3
r_{yi}	.568	$-.150$	$-.088$

Using these values in (12-59),

$$\hat{y}_j = (.568)(.71) + (.152)(2.03) + (.088)(.26) = .73$$

The component standard scores by (12-27) are given by

$$\hat{Z}_k = \tilde{A}_k^{-1} X.$$

If we wish to obtain the reduced-rank estimated standard scores directly from the original x's, we substitute $\tilde{A}_k^{-1} X$ for $\hat{Z}_k$ in (12-58), giving

$$\hat{Y}' = R_{yk}' \tilde{A}_k^{-1} X. \qquad (12\text{-}60)$$

The product $R'_{yk}\bar{A}_k^{-1}$ is a row vector of n elements. Call these elements $\hat{\beta}_{yi}$ ($i = 1, 2, \ldots, n$); they are the standard regression coefficients for predicting the y_j scores from the original x's, using reduced-rank regression. Then for individual j ($j = 1, 2, \ldots, N$),

$$\hat{y}_j = \hat{\beta}_{y1}x_{1j} + \hat{\beta}_{y2}x_{2j} + \cdots + \hat{\beta}_{yn}x_{nj}. \tag{12-61}$$

the x_{ij} being the standard scores of individual j on the original variables.

For the five-verbal-tests example, the vector R'_{yk}, with elements r_{yi}, is given above; and $\bar{A}_k^{-1}$ consists of the first three rows of A^{-1}, given near the beginning of Section 12.5.4. Then premultiplying the columns of $\bar{A}_k^{-1}$ by the vector R'_{yk}, we obtain

Variable	1	2	3	4	5
$\hat{\beta}_{yi}$	.166	.039	.217	.283	$-.034$

For individual j, whose standards scores on the original variables are given just below A^{-1} near the beginning of Section 12.5.4, we have

Variable	1	2	3	4	5
Standard score	1.22	$-.25$	1.34	.85	$-.19$

Then by (12-61)

$$\hat{y}_j = (.166)(1.22) - (.039)(.25) + (.217)(1.34) + (.283)(.85)$$
$$+ (.034)(.19) = .73,$$

which agrees with the value computed above from the first three component-criterion correlations and individual j's first three component standard scores.

We can also compute the reduced-rank multiple correlation directly from the correlations between the criterion and the original variables, given the $\hat{\beta}_{iy}$. It is the square root of

$$R_k^2 = \hat{\beta}_{y1}r_{1y} + \hat{\beta}_{y2}r_{2y} + \cdots + \hat{\beta}_{yn}r_{ny}. \tag{12-62}$$

The criterion correlations are given just below (12-53); they are

Variable	1	2	3	4	5
Criterion correlation R_c	.483	.424	.547	.533	.398

and the $\hat{\beta}_{yi}$ are given just below (12-61). Then by (12-62) the square of the multiple correlation is

$$R_k^2 = (.166)(.483) + (.039)(.424) + (.217)(.547) + (.283)(.533)$$
$$- (.034)(.398) = .3527,$$

and

$$R_k = .594.$$

These figures agree with the figures $R_k^2 = .3528$ and $R_k = .594$, computed from the first three principal components, within rounding error.

12.6.2 Estimation of Weight-Validity

An *aggregate correlation* is the correlation between a set of N criterion standard scores and a *weighted sum* of two or more sets of N predictor standard scores. When the two or more weights are so chosen as to *maximize* the aggregate correlation, in either a population ($N \to \infty$) or a sample (N finite), this aggregate correlation becomes the *multiple correlation*. When the weights applied to the predictors in a *population* are the standard regression coefficients determined from a random *sample* of that population, the aggregate correlation in the population is the *weight-validity* of the sample: the excellence with which the sample weights enable us to predict the criterion standard scores of individuals from the population who were not members of the sample. The weight-validity of a sample is always less than the population multiple correlation because the sample regression coefficients differ from the population regression coefficients that maximize the aggregate correlation. But as the sample N increases, the weight-validity approaches the population multiple correlation, which is the *validity* of the set of two or more predictors.

An *experimentally* unbiased estimate of the weight-validity, that is, an estimate shown to be unbiased by a Monte Carlo study rather than by a mathematical proof, is given by the *cross-validity*: the aggregate correlation in a second sample drawn randomly and independently from the same population, and using as weights the standard regression coefficients from the first sample. The cross-validity is not actually an unbiased estimate of the weight-validity because the product-moment aggregate correlation in the second sample is not an unbiased estimate of its parameter, the weight-validity.

The cross-validity, moreover, is rather far from a minimum-variance estimate of the weight-validity, because it has *two* sources of sampling error. Let ρ be the population multiple correlation and ρ_c the weight-validity. Let r be the multiple correlation in the first sample, r_2 the multiple correlation in the second sample, and r_c the cross-validity: the aggregate correlation in the second sample when as weights we use the regression coefficients from the first sample. In estimating the weight-validity by r_c, the fact that we use a second sample introduces in general a larger error than the one introduced by using the weights from the first sample, that is, $r - r_2|$ is usually larger than $r_2 - r_c$. Thus if, due to sampling error, r_2 is considerably larger than r, r_c may actually exceed r, though r_c is necessarily less than r_2. Then if r is taken as an estimate of ρ and r_c as an estimate of ρ_c, we are estimating that $\rho_c > \rho$, which is impossible, as we have noted above.

The sample multiple correlation usually exceeds the population multiple correlation if it is significantly greater than zero, because the least-squares procedure as applied to the sample fits the regression function to the sampling errors as well as to the basic trends represented by the population regression equation, in maximizing the sample multiple correlation.

In a Monte Carlo study, Claudy (1978) set up 16 populations of 500. From each population he drew randomly, *with replacement* to simulate drawing without replacement from an infinite population, 100 samples of 20, 100 of 40, 100 of 80, and 100 of 160: a total of 400 from each population or 6400 all together. For each sample he computed the multiple regression and the weight validity. He found that on the average (over the 6400 samples)

$$r - \rho = \rho - \rho_c$$

to a very close approximation, that is, the weight-validity is almost exactly as far below the population multiple correlation as the sample multiple correlation is above it. From this relation

$$\rho_c = 2\rho - r. \tag{12-63}$$

Because we do not know ρ, we substitute for it $\hat{\rho}$, the unbiased estimate of ρ given r. Using his 6400 samples, Claudy found that to a close approximation

$$\hat{\rho} = \left[1 - \frac{(N-4)(1-r^2)}{N-n-1} \left(1 + \frac{2(1-r^2)}{N-n+1} \right) \right]^{1/2}. \tag{12-64}$$

The estimate of ρ_c given by (12-63), with this substitution, is

$$\hat{\rho}_c = 2\hat{\rho} - r. \tag{12-65}$$

Claudy divided each of his 6400 samples randomly into two equal subsamples, each of $N/2$ cases. For each subsample he computed the multiple correlation and the cross validity using as weights the standard regression coefficients from the other subsample. The mean-square error [mean of $(\rho_c - r_c)^2$] over the 12,800 subsamples, was greater than the mean-square error [mean of $(\rho_c - \hat{\rho}_c)^2$] over the 6400 full samples using (12-64) and (12-65). Thus, using these formulas, the full available sample can be used both to determine the sample regression coefficients and to estimate the weight-validity, with some actual *improvement* over the procedures of cross-validation.

Note that (12-65) is valid only if $\hat{\rho}$ is *significantly* greater than 0. For a very low r, $\hat{\rho}$ is not necessarily positive. Claudy advises that (12-65) not be used unless

$$2\hat{\rho} - r > 1/\sqrt{N}. \tag{12-66}$$

But this is precisely the case in which the sample regression equation would have no predictive value in any event.

It is not clear that Claudy's formula for $\hat{\rho}$ is correct when the sample multiple correlation r is estimated from the first k principal components of the predictor variables. We can recommend its use in this situation, however, if only the later *nonsalient* components have been dropped, as the best available approximation. Note that r is still based on all n of the original variables.

For the five-verbal-tests example, r^2 is the R_k^2 or $\sum_{i=1}^{k} r_{yi}^2$ of Table 12.6. From the last row of this table it can be seen that, if we retain only the first three components ($k = 3$), the multiple correlation is .594, whereas if we retain all five it is only .596, so the last two components are clearly nonsalient. Then for $k = 3$, $r^2 = .3528$, and with $N = 841$ and $n = 5$, (12-64) gives

$$\hat{\rho} = .5918;$$

and (12-65) gives

$$\hat{\rho}_c = .5896$$

as the estimate of the weight-validity. The figures $r = .5940$, $\hat{\rho} = .5918$, and $\hat{\rho}_c = .5896$ are all close together because the sample size ($N = 841$) is large.

12.7 THE DIAGONAL METHOD FOR BATTERY REDUCTION

When we use initially the principal-components procedure or the centroid-components procedure, and then use a series of Gram-Schmidt orthogonal rotations to find the $k < n$ original variables that best measure as much as possible of what all n of them measure, the computing burden is considerable. A much simpler procedure, which avoids separate rotations entirely, is the diagonal or square-root method. This method is just about as accurate as is the centroid method followed by a set of Gram-Schmidt rotations, but not quite as accurate as is the principal-components method followed by a set of Gram-Schmidt rotations. It is of the same order of accuracy as the methods described in Chapter 4 for solving simultaneous linear equations and computing inverses, and it is in fact often used for these purposes. The main reason why this method is not used for common-factor analysis is that it is a diagonal-pivot method: it pivots on the estimated communalities, thus reducing the accuracy of the results. But when we have unities on the diagonal of the correlation matrix, this difficulty does not arise.

Table 12.7 shows the computations for the five-verbal-tests example. In the first panel (panel 0) we have the correlation matrix R from Table 1.1, with unities on the diagonal. After row Σ we add a row Σr^2. Each entry in this row is the sum of squares of the entries in the corresponding column of R.

In each panel the pivotal element is the diagonal entry in the column whose Σr^2-value is largest, rather than the next in numerical order. Thus for panel 0 the largest entry in row Σr^2 is the value 2.750 in column (3). We place an asterisk in front of variable 3, and enclose its diagonal entry, 1.000, in parentheses.

TABLE 12.7
Diagonal-Component Analysis of Five Verbal Tests ($N = 841$)

Panel	Var	(1)	(2)	(3)	(4)	(5)	Σ	Ch
	(1)	1.000	.585	.658	.616	.555	3.414	
	(2)	.585	1.000	.663	.634	.689	3.571	
0	*(3)	.658	.663	(1.000)	.697	.626	3.644	
	(4)	.616	.634	.697	1.000	.598	3.545	
	(5)	.555	.689	.626	.598	1.000	3.468	
	Σ	3.414	3.571	3.644	3.545	3.468	17.642	17.642
	Σr^2	2.463	2.658	2.750	2.625	2.532		
	a	.6580	.6630	1.0000	.6970	.6260	3.6440	3.6440
	(1)	.567	.149	.000	.157	.143	1.016	1.016
	(2)	.149	.560	.000	.172	.274	1.155	1.155
1	(3)	.000	.000	.000	.000	.000	.000	.000
	(4)	.157	.172	.000	.514	.162	1.005	1.005
	*(5)	.143	.274	.000	.162	(.608)	1.187	1.187
	Σ	1.016	1.155	.000	1.005	1.187	4.363	4.363
	Σr^2	.389	.440	.000	.345	.491		
	b	.1834	.3514	.0000	.2078	.7797[4]	1.5223	1.5223
	*(1)	(.533)	.085	.000	.119	.000	.737	.737
	(2)	.085	.437	.000	.099	.000	.621	.620
2	(3)	.000	.000	.000	.000	.000	.000	.000
	(4)	.119	.099	.000	.471	.000	.689	.689
	(5)	.000	.000	.000	.000	.000	.000	.000
	Σ	.737	.621	.000	.689	.000	2.047	2.047
	Σr^2	.305	.208	.000	.246	.000		
	c	.7301[07]	.1164	.0000	.1630	.0000	1.0095	1.0095
	(1)	.000	.000	.000	.000	.000	.000	.000
	(2)	.000	.423	.000	.080	.000	.503	.503
3	(3)	.000	.000	.000	.000	.000	.000	.000
	*(4)	.000	.080	.000	(.444)	.000	.524	.524
	(5)	.000	.000	.000	.000	.000	.000	.000
	Σ	.000	.503	.000	.524	.000	1.027	1.027
	Σr^2	.000	.185	.000	.204	.000		
	d	.0000	.1201	.0000	.6663[3]	.0000	.7864	.7864
	(1)	.000	.000	.000	.000	.000	.000	.000
	*(2)	.000	(.409)	.000	.000	.000	.409	.409
4	(3)	.000	.000	.000	.000	.000	.000	.000
	(4)	.000	.000	.000	.000	.000	.000	.000
	(5)	.000	.000	.000	.000	.000	.000	.000

TABLE 12.7 (continued)

Panel	Var	(1)	(2)	(3)	(4)	(5)	Σ	Ch
	Σ	.000	.409	.000	.000	.000	.409	.409
	e	.0000	.6395[3]	.0000	.0000	.0000	.6395	.6395

Component Matrix A

Var	a	b	c	d	e
(1)	.6580	.1834	.7301	.0000	.0000
(2)	.6630	.3514	.1164	.1201	.6395
(3)	1.0000	.0000	.0000	.0000	.0000
(4)	.6970	.2078	.1630	.6663	.0000
(5)	.6260	.7797	.0000	.0000	.0000
Σa^2	2.7502	.8082	.5732	.4584	.4090
Cum Σa^2	2.7502	3.5584	4.1316	4.5900	4.9990 $\doteq$ 5
% Trace	55	71	83	92	100

In the diagonal method, a_3 is then the square root of a_{33} (here 1.0000), or in general, if the pivot row is row i,

$$a_i = \sqrt{r_{ii}}. \tag{12-67}$$

This equation is the same as equation (5-11), Section 5.5.1. Each of the other a-values is $a_j = r_{3j}(1/a_{33})$, or in general

$$a_j = r_{ij}(1/a_i) \tag{12-68}$$

where row i is the pivot row. This equation is essentially the same as equations (5-12), Section 5.5.1.

Because in this case $a_i = a_3 = 1.0000$, $\sqrt{1} = 1$, and $1/\sqrt{1} = 1$, the a-row is "free": it is simply row (3) of R. Component a accounts for all of the variance of variable 3, which was the variable having the largest initial variance (Σr_{i3}^2).

We then form the first residual matrix in the usual fashion. The values in column Ch are formed from the row sums. Thus for row (1), $3.414 - (.6580)(3.6440) = 1.016$, which agrees with the first row-sum in panel 1.

Adding a row Σr^2 to panel 1 after row Σ, we find that the largest element in this row is the .491 in column (5), so we form row b from row (5). By (12-67), b_5 is .7797, the square root of the pivotal element .608. To form its reciprocal, we carry its value to five significant figures (.77974), and the reciprocal (not shown) is 1.2825 to five significant figures. Then by (12-68) the other entries in row b are the corresponding entries in row (5) times this reciprocal. When we come to the .608 in column (5), the product is again .7797 ($\pm$.0001), which checks the computation of the square root and its reciprocal; and the check for row b is the reciprocal times the row-sum of row (5), or $(1.2825)(1.187) = 1.5223$. Component b now accounts for all of the variance of variable 5 not accounted for by component a, and variable 5 was the one having the greatest residual variance.

The other components are obtained in the same manner. For component e we do not need row Σr^2, as there is only one row [row (2)] which has a nonzero entry.

In the summary table each component-loading row (a,b,c,d,e) becomes a column; and we record for each column the sum of squares of its entries, the cumulative sum of squares, and the percent of trace (trace = 5.000).

The Bartlett test does not apply to the diagonal method, so for deciding on the number of salient components we have only the scree test. Thus

Var	Σa^2	Diff
(1)	2.7502	
		1.9420
(2)	.8082	
		.2350
(3)	.5732	
		.1148
(4)	.4584	
		.0494
(5)	.4090	

This suggests that three components are salient because the third difference (.1148) is just "substantial," whereas the fourth (.0494) is not.

The tests selected by the diagonal method are tests 3, 5, and 1, whereas those selected by the principal-components method and the Gram-Schmidt transformations (Table 12.4) were tests 1, 5, and 4. In Table 12.4 the cumulative sum of squares for the three components selected is 4.4008, and the per cent of trace is 88. In Table 12.7 the cumulative sum of squares is 4.1316 for the three components selected, and the per cent of trace is 83. The difference in the cumulative sum of squares is $4.4008 - 4.1316 = .2692$, and the difference in per cent of trace is $88 - 83 = 5$. These differences are not due entirely or even mainly to the selection of test 3 rather than test 4 by the diagonal method. If we use the diagonal method and select tests 1, 5, and 4 arbitrarily, the cumulative sum of squares is 4.1744 instead of 4.1316 for tests 3, 5, and 1, a difference of only .0428; and in both cases the per cent of trace rounds to 83, though in one case rounding up and in the other rounding down. The principal-components method picks up more of the total variance on the first three components, and this greater variance is retained in the Gram-Schmidt transformations. Thus the principal-components method followed by Gram-Schmidt transformations appears to be the best. Whether centroid–component analysis followed by Gram-Schmidt transformations would be superior to the diagonal method is not clear, but anyone who is prepared to go to the trouble of a set of Gram-Schmidt transformations would probably prefer to start from a principal-components solution in any event.

The two diagonal solutions (Table 12.7 and the 1, 5, 4 solution, not shown) suggest that in selecting three tests out of five, whether we add test 3 (Proverb Matching) or test 4 (Verbal Analogies) to tests 1 (Paragraph Meaning) and 5 (Vocabulary) makes little difference because these tests measure fairly similar functions.

Hunter (1972) discusses diagonal component analysis, which he terms maximal decomposition, in more detail than we have discussed it here, including procedures for coping with the situation in which the stepwise assumption is violated. The writers do not agree with his claim that diagonal-component analysis is a proper alternative to common-factor analysis, nor with his "common decomposition" procedure, which is based on this claim. Neither of these disagreements applies to his discussion of diagonal-component analysis (maximal decomposition) per se, which is excellent.

If, after completing a diagonal-component analysis as in Table 12.7, we wish to compute the diagonal-component scores, we can use (12-18) with A_k' the transpose of the first three columns of the summary table of Table 12.7. It will be necessary, in order to do this, to compute R^{-1} from panel 0 of Table 12.7. Equation (12-18) applies to diagonal components as well as to centroid components.

12.8 CONCLUSIONS

Component analysis is a good procedure for battery reduction when we wish to obtain a reduced battery that measures almost everything measured by the original battery. For this purpose, principal-component analysis followed by a series of Gram-Schmidt transformations is somewhat better than is diagonal analysis but entails considerably more computation.

For examining the structure of the domain represented by a battery of variables, factor analysis yields more information than does component analysis. Rotation of a reduced set of principal components provides less information and less-clear interpretation than does factor analysis.

When we wish to represent several variables by a single composite variable (as, e.g., intelligence by several psychological tests, or crop yield by the yields of several particular crops), the best weights to use in forming the composite variable are the loadings on the first principal component. The loadings on the first centroid component give an excellent approximation, and Kendall's sum-rank procedure is also quite good when N and n are small enough to make ranking feasible.

For coping with the problem of regression weights, when N is not very much larger than n, reduced-rank regression is to be preferred to stepwise regression, though the computations required are considerably greater.

The writers see only limited value in the use of component scores, as in the use of factor scores, but for different reasons. The usefulness of factor scores is limited by the fact that, although the factors are clearly interpretable, the regression estimates of the factor scores leave large parts of the total variance (the total unique variance) unaccounted for and are therefore not well determined. Component scores, on the other hand, are measured exactly in the full-rank case or estimated by regression with much less error than are factor scores when the later components are omitted; but the components themselves, even after rotation, are not as clearly interpretable as are common factors. When we wish well-determined scores on clearly interpretable composite variables, cluster scores, as described in Chapter 14, are usually to be preferred to either factor scores or component scores.

13

Factor Scores

13.1 INDETERMINACY

In a common-factor analysis we have n measured variables, from which we derive $m + n$ factors: m common factors and n unique factors. It is evident then, because we have more unknowns (factors) than measured variables, that scores on the m common factors can only be estimated, for example, by regression. The errors of estimate, moreover, are large, because they include the whole unique-factor variance. In component analysis, by contrast, when we retain only the first k components and discard the last $n - k$, the errors of estimate are smaller: they involve only the variance of the $n - k$ components discarded, and these latter components are discarded precisely because their variances are small compared to the variances of those retained.

The m common factors and the n unique factors specify a space of $m + n$ dimensions, and the n observed variables are linear combinations of the $m + n$ factors. When we reverse this situation and try to specify the $m + n$ factors as linear combinations of the n observed variables, these latter linear combinations are confined to the n-dimensional subspace of the variables and can only approximate roughly the positions of the $m + n$ factor vectors in the full $m + n$ space.

Consider two variable vectors, X_1 and X_2, in three-space with r_{12} given. The angle θ between the two vectors is $\theta = \arccos r_{12}$. Then if X_1 is regarded as fixed and is at the center of a cone whose central angle is 2θ, X_2 can lie anywhere on the surface of the cone (Fig. 13.1). As r_{12} increases, the mouth of the cone becomes smaller, and the indeterminacy in the location of X_2 relative to X_1 decreases.

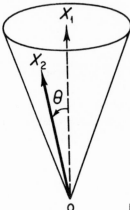

FIG. 13.1.   Locus of X_2 if X_1 is regarded as fixed and r_{12} is given.

A similar situation, but more complex, exists in common-factor analysis. The factor vectors, as estimated from the variable vectors in n-space, are free to wobble in the m additional dimensions of the $m + n$ space, subject to boundary conditions analogous to that which confined X_2, relative to X_1, to the surface of the cone in Fig. 13.1. This indeterminacy is reduced as the unique-factor variances decrease. Thus factor scores are best determined when the variables are highly reliable (decreasing the error variance) and when each common factor has a number of high loadings (decreasing the specific-factor variance).

13.2   DERIVATION

We are ordinarily interested only in estimating the scores on the m common factors, and in particular on the m *primary* factors after rotation of the F-matrix to simple structure. The following derivations parallel some of those of Sections 12.5.2 and 12.5.3 but are complete in themselves.

Let X be the n by N matrix of standard scores on the original variables, Z the m by N matrix of true (unknown) standard scores on the primary factors, $\hat{Z}$ the m by N matrix of *estimated* standard scores on these primary factors, β the m by n matrix of true regression coefficients, $\hat{\beta}$ the m by n matrix of least-squares estimates of these regression coefficients, and η the m by N matrix of residuals. Whereas the elements of Z are unknown, they are treated as true standard scores, the variance of each row being unity; and the correlations between the rows of Z and the rows of X *are* known. The rows of $\hat{Z}$, which must be estimated, have variances equal to the squares of their multiple correlations with the rows of X. The regression equations are then

$$Z = \beta X + \eta; \text{ or } \hat{Z} = \hat{\beta} X. \tag{13-1}$$

From the first equation of (13-1)

$$Z - \beta X = \eta. \tag{13-2}$$

The residuals η are present in the first equation of (13-1) because this equation represents nN inconsistent observation equations (one for each element of X) in only mN unknowns (elements of Z).

Each row of (13-2) represents one primary factor, and we can solve for the scores on each primary factor separately, by minimizing for that row the sum of squares of the residuals. For any one row, say the i-th, (13-2) becomes

$$Z_i - \beta_i X = \eta_i \qquad (i = 1, 2, \ldots, m).$$

Then

$$\eta_i \eta_i' = (Z_i - \beta_i X)(Z_i - \beta_i X)'.$$

Here η_i is a row vector of residuals, and $\eta_i \eta_i'$ is the sum of squares of these residuals, which is a scalar. Expanding this equation,

$$\eta_i \eta_i' = Z_i Z_i' - Z_i X' \beta_i' - \beta_i X Z_i' + \beta_i XX' \beta_i'.$$

Each term in this equation is a scalar, so we can write

$$\eta_i \eta_i' = Z_i Z_i' - 2\beta_i X Z_i' + \beta_i XX' \beta_i'.$$

The normal equations for $\hat{\beta}_i$, which give the solution for β_i that minimizes $\eta_i \eta_i'$ are then

$$Z_i X' = \hat{\beta}_i XX'. \tag{13-3}$$

Dividing both sides of this equation by N,

$$Z_i X'/N = \hat{\beta}_i (XX')/N. \tag{13-4}$$

The elements of Z_i are the standard scores on the i-th primary factor, and $Z_i X'/N$ represents the correlations between this i-th primary factor and the n original variables, or the i-th row of S', the transpose of the primary-factor structure, so

$$Z_i X'/N = S_i'.$$

Also $(XX')/N = R$, the matrix of correlations between the original variables, with unities on the diagonal, or

$$XX'/N = R.$$

Substituting these values, S_i' and R, into (13-4)

$$S_i' = \hat{\beta}_i R,$$

and solving for $\hat{\beta}_i$

$$\hat{\beta}_i = S_i' R^{-1}. \tag{13-5}$$

Then for all m rows

$$\hat{\beta} = S'R^{-1}. \tag{13-6}$$

Substituting into the second equation of (13-1)

$$\hat{Z} = S'R^{-1}X. \tag{13-7}$$

This is the basic equation for the estimation of factor scores.

From Table 6.3

$$S = F(\Lambda')^{-1}D = F(\Lambda^{-1})'D, \tag{13-8}$$

where D is the diagonal matrix that normalizes the columns of $(\Lambda^{-1})'$. Because D is diagonal, $D' = D$, and

$$S' = D\Lambda^{-1}F'.$$

Then from (13-7)

$$\hat{Z} = D\Lambda^{-1}F'R^{-1}X, \tag{13-9}$$

and $D\Lambda^{-1}$ is merely Λ^{-1} row-normalized.

A formula alternative to (13-7) or (13-9) can be used if we have P, the primary-pattern matrix, and R_s, the second-order correlation matrix. From Table 6.3

$$P = F\Lambda D^{-1}. \tag{13-10}$$

From (13-8)

$$S = F(\Lambda^{-1})'D,$$

which may be written

$$S = F(\Lambda D^{-1})(D\Lambda^{-1})(\Lambda^{-1})'D$$

because $(\Lambda D^{-1})(D\Lambda^{-1}) = I$. Then from (13-10)

$$S = P(D\Lambda^{-1})(\Lambda^{-1})'D.$$

In this formula, by (6-18), $D\Lambda^{-1} = T'$, so $(\Lambda^{-1})'D = T$. But by (6-22) $T'T = R_s$, and

$$S = PT'T = PR_s.$$

Then

$$S' = R_sP',$$

and substituting into (13-7)

$$\hat{Z} = R_sP'R^{-1}X. \tag{13-11}$$

We do not usually have the matrix X of standard scores on the variables, but have instead only the raw-score matrix, say Y. To obtain X from Y, we note that

$$x_{ij} = (y_{ij} - \bar{y}_i)/\sigma_i \qquad (i = 1, 2, \ldots, n; j = 1, 2, \ldots, N).$$

Then

$$X = \Sigma^{-1}(Y - M),$$

where Σ^{-1} is an n by n diagonal matrix with diagonal elements $1/\sigma_i$, and M is an n by N matrix, the elements of each row i of which are all $\bar{y}_i$. Then (13-7) becomes

$$\hat{Z} = S'R^{-1}\Sigma^{-1}(Y - M), \tag{13-12}$$

(13-9) becomes

$$\hat{Z} = D\Lambda^{-1}F'R^{-1}\Sigma^{-1}(Y - M), \tag{13-13}$$

and (13-11) becomes

$$\hat{Z} = R_s P'R^{-1}\Sigma^{-1}(Y - M). \tag{13-14}$$

It is evident that neither (13-7), (13-9), (13-11), (13-12), (13-13), nor (13-14) is suitable for desk calculation even if n is quite small, when N is large enough to warrant factor analysis in the first place. When initial factoring is done by the principal-axes method, using modified SMC communality estimates, M and Σ (the vectors of means and standard deviations) are usually given in the output along with F. R^{-1} can also be included in the output, and rotation gives Λ. With centroid factoring R^{-1} must be computed separately.

The amount of indeterminacy in each set of N factor scores (on the i-th primary factor) can be estimated from R_i, the multiple correlation between this primary factor and the n original variables. By the usual formula

$$R_i^2 = \hat{\beta}_{1i}r_{1Z_i} + \hat{\beta}_{2i}r_{2Z_i} + \ldots + \hat{\beta}_{ni}r_{nZ_i}.$$

This may be written as the vector product

$$R_i^2 = \hat{\beta}_i S_i,$$

where S_i is the vector of correlations between the i-th primary factor and the original variables. But by (13-5)

$$\hat{\beta}_i = S_i'R^{-1},$$

$$R_i^2 = S_i'R^{-1}S_i. \tag{13-15}$$

If, therefore, we form the matrix product

$$S'R^{-1}S, \tag{13-16}$$

its diagonal elements will be the squared multiple correlations between the primary factors and the original variables. By the two formulas just preceding (13-11), (13-16) can be written

$$R_s P' R^{-1} P R_s. \tag{13-17}$$

And by the formula just below (13-8), (13-16) may also be written

$$(D\Lambda^{-1}F')R^{-1}(D\Lambda^{-1}F')'. \tag{13-18}$$

Unless the multiple correlations are very high (say .99 or higher), the indeterminacy may be quite considerable [see tabulation following (13-20)].

The elements of $\hat{Z}$ do not have any given metric comparable to those of the original variables, so they are usually left in the metric of estimated standard scores. For each variable these estimated standard scores have mean 0 but variance R_i^2 (and hence standard deviation R_i).

13.3   EXAMPLE

For the five-verbal tests example, we will compute $\hat{Z}$ by (13-7):

$$\hat{Z} = S'R^{-1}X.$$

S is given in Table 6.4, along with a set of standard scores X (or X_j for the j-th individual) obtained by assuming a set of two common-factor scores A (corresponding to Z in the notation of this chapter) and a set of five unique-factor scores B. To solve for $\hat{Z}$ we require also R^{-1}, the inverse of the original correlation matrix.

To find R^{-1} we will use (5-3):

$$R = EDE',$$

where E is the matrix whose columns are the eigenvectors of R, and D is the diagonal matrix of eigenvalues of R. Then noting that E is orthonormal, so that $E^{-1} = E'$, the inverse of R is

$$R^{-1} = ED^{-1}E'. \tag{13-19}$$

The matrix E' is given at the beginning of Section 12.5.4, and the diagonal elements of D^{-1}, from the original printout, are

$$diag\ (D^{-1}) = [.28325 \quad 2.03965 \quad 2.62867 \quad 3.25521 \quad 3.42853].$$

R^{-1} is given at the top of Table 13.1 with S and X_j at its right.

$S'R^{-1}$ in the middle section of Table 13.1 is obtained by column-by-column multiplication of R^{-1} by the columns of S, and $\hat{Z} = S'R^{-1}X_j$ by row-by-column multiplication of the rows of $S'R^{-1}$ by the column vector X_j. At the right of $\hat{Z}$ we

TABLE 13.1
Computation of Estimated Factor Scores for Five Verbal Tests
$(N = 841)$

			R^{-1}				S	
Test	(1)	(2)	(3)	(4)	(5)	I	II	X_j
(1)	2.0213	−.2875	−.6832	−.4514	−.2261	.761	.685	.335
(2)	−.2875	2.4436	−.5503	−.4409	−.9160	.774	.826	−1.146
(3)	−.6832	−.5503	2.6472	−.8373	−.3981	.860	.774	1.481
(4)	−.4514	−.4409	−.8373	2.3292	−.3144	.813	.739	.588
(5)	−.2261	−.9160	−.3981	−.3144	2.1939	.731	.840	−2.007

			$S'R^{-1}$					
	(1)	(2)	(3)	(4)	(5)	$\hat{Z} = S'R^{-1}X_j$	Z^a	$Z\text{-}\hat{Z}$
I	.196	.171	.359	.259	.125	.303	1.235	.932
II	.095	.300	.173	.136	.391	−.761	−.859	−.098

	$S'R^{-1}S$		
	I	II	R_i
I	.892	.850	$R_{\mathrm{I}} = .944$
II	.850	.876	$R_{\mathrm{II}} = .936$

^{a} Vector A of Table 6.4.

show the elements of Z ($= A$ of Table 6.4): the common-factor scores assumed originally in computing the scores X_j. These X_j-scores depend also, of course, on the assumed unique-factor scores B of Table 6.4.

The first error of estimate, the first value of $(Z - \hat{Z})$, is a fairly large fraction of the unit standard deviation of the Z-scores. This first estimate is a substantial underestimate, and the second is a slight underestimate. The assumed true common and unique factor scores of Table 6.4 are not unusual, so this comparison of true and estimated common-factor scores illustrates with little bias the inaccuracies that may result when common-factor scores are estimated from real data.

In the lower section of Table 13.1 we have the matrix product $S'R^{-1}S$, whose diagonal elements (.892 and .876) are the squared multiple correlations between the primary factors and the original variables. At the right of this matrix we have these two multiple correlations R_i: $R_{\mathrm{I}} = .944$ and $R_{\mathrm{II}} = .936$. These correlations do not indicate even moderately small standard errors of estimate of the factor scores, as the previous paragraph indicates.

The standard error of estimate of a set of standard criterion scores (here primary-factor scores) is given by

$$SE_i = \sqrt{1 - R_i^2}. \tag{13-20}$$

Thus for a few high values of R_i we have

R_i	SE_i
.94	.34
.95	.31
.96	.28
.97	.24
.98	.20
.99	.14

In Table 13.1, $R_I = .944$ and $R_{II} = .936$. These multiple Rs are both close to .94, and the standard errors of estimate are $SE_I = .330$ and $SE_{II} = .352$. The individual errors of estimate are .932 for factor I and $-.098$ for factor II. The two-sided significance levels are .0012 for factor I and .195 for factor II. The value .195 is insignificant.

13.4 DISCUSSION

The method of estimating factor scores described above is termed the complete regression method. It maximizes the *validity* of the factor scores, which are in the least-squares sense as close as is possible in n-space to the true $(m + n)$-space factor scores. But by doing this it follows that these estimated factor scores are not *univocal:* their correlations are not the same as those of R_s, the correlations between the primary factors. In particular, if the factors are uncorrelated (which they very seldom are), the estimated factor scores will still be correlated. Also, as noted previously, the estimated factor scores do not have variance unity, and if they are standardized their validities are reduced.

If there is a substantial *cluster* of variables on *each* primary axis, with or without one or more clusters elsewhere, a rough approximation to factor scores may be obtained by averaging the standard scores on the variables of each such cluster. A cluster on a primary axis may be identified in the rotated factor matrix $V = F\Lambda$ by the fact that there are several variables that have one substantial loading on the same factor, with all other loadings near-zero. Cluster analysis of variables is discussed in Chapter 14.

A number of other procedures for obtaining factor scores are discussed by various writers, based mainly on the criterion of univocality (Bartlett, 1937).

Arguments in favor of such methods seem to be based primarily on the proposition that estimates of scores on orthogonal factors should be orthogonal. But primary factors based on real data are almost always oblique, in which case this argument loses some of its force. The writers prefer to minimize the indeterminacy of the solution (i.e., maximize its validity), which leads to a preference for the complete regression procedure as described above. Thomson (1951) discusses the Bartlett estimates, and more recently Mulaik (1972) discusses various types of factor scores.

14

Cluster Analysis of Variables

Cluster analysis is a larger field than is factor analysis. There are considerably more cluster analysis systems than there are factor analysis systems. We can cluster individuals as well as variables, and clustering individuals is probably more common than is clustering variables. Cluster analysis has been applied to a greater range of disciplines than has factor analysis. Its most widespread use is probably in the field of numerical taxonomy: the classification of plants and animals by mathematical procedures. It has been applied also to demography, land use, ecology, organizational structure, delinquency, medical symptomatology, the voting behavior of legislative bodies, the decisions of multijudge courts, and market selection, to name but a few. In psychology, cluster analysis methods are used in typology, clinical diagnosis, profile analysis, multidimensional scaling, and some of the procedures of test and scale construction.

It is evident, then, that we cannot attempt to cover the field of cluster analysis in one chapter. We limit the detailed discussion to three related methods for the cluster analysis of variables, and to two problems: (1) the clustering of variables as a method of battery reduction alternative to the procedures discussed in Chapter 12; (2) the clustering of a miscellaneous collection of questionnaire items to obtain scorable subsets, as in the construction of batteries of tests to measure the traits present in a set of biographical inventory items or self-report personality items.

Then, in the later sections of this chapter, we outline briefly the larger field of cluster analysis without presenting the methodological details.

14.1 CLUSTER ANALYSIS AND FACTOR ANALYSIS

We have noted that in common-factor analysis a factor is defined by a hyperplane, that is, by a subgroup of variables which do *not* measure it. The factor is *interpreted* in terms of the variables which *do* measure it: those variables whose loadings on the factor are high or fairly high. A cluster, on the other hand, is defined by a subset of variables which *do* go together, that is, by a subgroup of variables having similar factorial structures over all common factors, with variable vectors that point in roughly the same direction in the common-factor space. A cluster centroid may or may not coincide approximately with a primary factor. The number of clusters usually exceeds the number of factors, but the two numbers *may* be the same, and in fairly rare cases the number of clusters may even be less than the number of factors.

When the variables are fairly reliable, cluster analysis merely tells us which subsets of variables measure almost the same combinations of factors. But when the variables are numerous and individually quite unreliable, for example, when they are a miscellaneous collection of single items of a questionnaire, a cluster consists of a subset of items which can be scored as a test. Thus a morale questionnaire consisting of a variety of opinion items, given to the enlisted men of a military installation, yielded clusters that formed tests of attitude toward and satisfaction with military life, working conditions, communication with higher levels of command, the immediate supervisor, the management system, and the like. A miscellaneous collection of self-report items yields clusters forming tests of personality traits. A miscellaneous collection of items forming a biographical inventory, given to high school students, yields clusters measuring socioeconomic status, social maturity, attitude toward school, plans for college if any, adequacy of the school guidance program, interest in various kinds of activities, and the like.

When a variable is a single item, its unique factor is simply its error of measurement. When we have a cluster of such items forming a test, the reliability of the test can be estimated with considerable accuracy from the factor and cluster analysis data. This reliability is the mean communality of the items in the cluster, raised by the Spearman-Brown formula:

$$R_{test} = \frac{n\overline{h^2}}{1 + (n-1)\overline{h^2}}, \tag{14-1}$$

where n is the number of items in the cluster and $\overline{h^2}$ is their mean communality.

14.2 GRAPHIC CLUSTER ANALYSIS

A cluster analysis of the type we are considering starts with the initial F-matrix of a factor analysis. In the three-factor case the clusters can be observed in the extended-vector plot. Thus for the eleven WAIS subtests in the age-group 25-34, we can see in Fig. 7.2, reproduced here as Fig. 14.1 (without the lines showing the projections of the effectively bounding planes on the extended-vector plane), the locations of the clusters. In Chapter 7 we used the 3–5, 9–11, and 2–6 cluster centroids to locate the primary axes. These "corner clusters" do not locate the primary axes precisely, as we saw in Chapter 10, but they do locate them fairly well. But when we examine Fig. 14.1 we see two additional clusters that are *not* at corners of the configuration: a 1–4 cluster between the 3–5 and 2–6 clusters and closer to the latter, and a 7–10–8 cluster near the middle of the configuration.

With more than three variables there are several extended-vector plots instead of only one: one such plot for every *pair* of factors of F except the first, and it is troublesome though not impossible to locate the clusters in a set of such plots. Every true cluster of two or more variables must be observed as a cluster in *every* plot. With five or more variables there are six or more plots, and the plotting becomes tedious. We seek, therefore, a graphic method for observing clusters

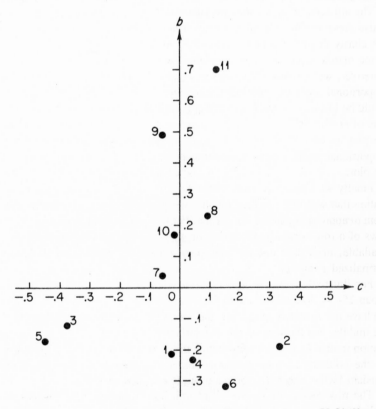

Fig.14.1.   Extended-vector plot for eleven WAIS subtests, age-group 25–34 (N = 300).

which is applicable to more than three factors and which is less time-consuming and difficult than is the method of extended vectors.

The earliest procedure for cluster analysis was proposed by Tryon (1939). He plotted each row of the correlation matrix as a profile. The abscissa was the variable number, and the ordinate was the numerical value of the correlation coefficient. He connected each row of points by a jagged line (the profile), leaving a gap at r_{ii} which would otherwise be represented by a "spike" going up to 1.000. A cluster would then be represented by a subset of approximately *parallel proportional* profiles. Figure 14.2 shows the correlation profile, from Table 5.3, for the nine-aptitude-tests problem. Parallel proportionality is hard to see when it is only approximate, and the missing point on each profile at r_{ii} makes it even more difficult. In Fig. 14.2 the profiles of tests 1, 2, and 3 are more or less horizontal to about test 5, and then drift slightly downward. Tests 4, 5, and 6 can be seen to have high correlations with one another, as can also tests 7, 8, and 9. Thus we can barely distinguish the three clusters in Fig. 14.2, though in the extended-vector picture of Exercise 7.1 they are quite clear and distinct.

The information on parallel proportionality contained in the correlation matrix is also present in the F-matrix, in any orthogonal rotation of F, and with slightly less clarity in any oblique rotation of F; and in the profile of a row-vector of a factor matrix there are only m points (with no gaps) instead of $n - 1$. If, moreover, we *normalize* the rows of F, profiles that are approximately parallel proportional become approximately *congruent*. Exactly congruent profiles would be identical, and a cluster of approximately congruent profiles consists of a set of profiles which are roughly identical: of about the same average height on the plot as well as of about the same shape; whereas approximately parallel proportional profiles are of about the same shape but may lie at different levels on the plot.

Finally we may apply to the normalized rows of F some orthogonal transformation that will more or less equalize the dispersions of the columns and bring them to approximately the same scale. For this purpose we can use profiles of the rows of a row-normalized varimax or weighted-varimax factor matrix if this is available, or if it is not we can apply a Landahl transformation to the row-normalized F-matrix.

For illustration we use again the eleven subtests of the WAIS for the age-group 25-34. Table 14.1 shows the computations. In the upper part of the table we have the F-matrix at the left, the computations of the normalizing factors in the middle, and the normalized F-matrix F_n at the right. The Landahl transformation matrix L_t is shown just below the F-matrix. Multiplying the rows of F_n by the columns of this transformation matrix we obtain the row-normalized Landahl factor matrix L_n shown at the lower right of Table 14.1.

The row-vectors of F_n are all of unit length within .0001 because the normalizing factors were computed to five decimals. The row-vectors of L_n tend to be a little large because the values .5774 of the transformation matrix, which

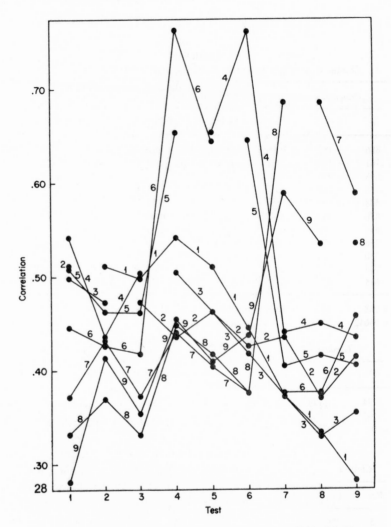

FIG. 14.2.   Correlation profiles for nine aptitude tests, from Table 5.3 ($N =$ 504).

multiply the large positive elements of column a of F_n, were rounded up to four decimals from .5773,5027. The .8165 should be .8164,9658, the $-.4082$ should be $-.4082,4829$, and the $\pm.7071$ should be $\pm.7071,0678$. But these latter rounded values, multiplying the b and c values of F_n, give products that are sometimes positive and sometimes negative, and the values in columns b and c of F_n are numerically smaller in every case than the values in column a.

The usefulness of the Landahl transformation is apparent when we compare the *ranges* of values in F_n with those of L_n. We have

TABLE 14.1
Cluster Analysis of Eleven WAIS Subtests, Age-Group 25–34 (N = 300)

	Principal Axes F			Normalization Factors			Normalized F_n			
Var	a	b	c	Σ^2	$\sqrt{\Sigma^2}$	$1/\sqrt{\Sigma^2}$	a	b	c	Σf_n^2
(1)	.886	−.183	−.029	.81933	.90517	1.10476	.9788	−.2022	−.0320	1.0000
(2)	.761	−.141	.249	.66100	.81302	1.22998	.9360	−.1734	.3063	1.0000
(3)	.698	−.085	−.262	.56307	.75038	1.33266	.9302	−.1133	−.3492	1.0000
(4)	.775	−.182	.030	.63465	.79665	1.25526	.9728	−.2285	.0377	1.0000
(5)	.588	−.098	−.263	.42452	.65155	1.53480	.9025	−.1504	−.4037	1.0001
(6)	.878	−.282	.134	.86836	.93186	1.07312	.9422	−.3026	.1438	1.0000
(7)	.657	.023	−.037	.43355	.65845	1.51872	.9978	.0349	−.0562	1.0000
(8)	.756	.176	.070	.60741	.77937	1.28309	.9700	.2258	.0898	.9999
(9)	.730	.361	−.044	.66516	.81557	1.22614	.8951	.4426	−.0540	1.0000
(10)	.744	.130	−.012	.57058	.75537	1.32385	.9849	.1721	−.0159	.9999
(11)	.615	.433	.075	.57134	.75587	1.32298	.8136	.5729	.0992	1.0000
Σ	8.088	.152	−.089	6.81897		Σ	10.3239	.2779	−.2342	
Σf^2	6.03642	.54906	.23348	6.81896 = Ch		Mean	.9385	.0253	−.0213	

	Landahl Trf L_t				Normalized Landahl L_n			
	1	2	3	Var	1	2	3	$\Sigma \ell^2$
a	.5774	.5774	.5774	(1)	.4001	.6251	.6703	1.0001
b	.8165	−.4082	−.4082	(2)	.3989	.8278	.3946	1.0001
c	0	.7071	−.7071	(3)	.4446	.3364	.8303	1.0002
				(4)	.3751	.6816	.6283	1.0000
				(5)	.3983	.2970	.8680	1.0003
	Clusters			(6)	.2970	.7692	.5659	1.0001
				(7)	.6046	.5221	.6016	1.0001
Var	Cos			(8)	.7444	.5314	.4044	1.0001
				(9)	.8782	.2980	.3743	1.0001
3–5	.998			(10)	.7092	.4872	.5097	1.0001
1–4	.997			(11)	.9375	.3061	.1658	1.0001
9–11	.976							
2–6	.978			Σ	6.1879	5.6819	6.0132	
{ 7–8	.971			Ch	6.1879	5.6820	6.0132	
7–10	.990			Mean	.5625	.5165	.5467	
8–10	.993							
{ 1–6	.979							
4–6	.991							
{ 1–2	.941							
2–4	.962							

	a, 1	b, 2	c, 3
F_n	.1842	.8755	.7100
L_n	.6405	.5308	.7022

In F_n the range in column a is much less than those in columns b and c; in L_n the ranges in columns 1, 2, and 3 are more nearly equal. In F_n, the values in column a are all positive and large, those in columns b and c vary about means close to zero. In L_n the entries are all positive, and the means do not differ greatly. Plotting profiles of the rows of L_n is much more convenient than plotting them from the rows of F_n, and in the case of F_n "how close is close" would be different in column a from columns b and c, while in L_n the ranges are near enough equal to make this consideration unnecessary in judging whether two profiles are almost congruent.

The profiles of the rows of L_n are shown in Fig. 14.3. Each profile connects three points: one for the L_n-loading on each of the factors 1, 2, and 3. With eleven profiles, we have already a bit too many to study conveniently. A better method of plotting is to set up on an 8½ by 11 inch sheet the three or more parallel scales (one for each factor), and to plot the profile of each variable on a sheet of tissue paper such as typists use for making carbon copies. In this case it is necessary to record the variable number only once, at the top of the sheet. Subsets of sheets can then be stacked and held up to the light to see if they seem to correspond to clusters, that is, to have almost-congruent profiles.

In Fig. 14.3, we have numbered the three points of each variable on each of the three factors to facilitate tracing the course of each profile.

Points 3 and 5 are close together on each of the three factors; so we can be reasonably sure these two variables form a cluster. The same is true of points 1 and 4.

Points 9 and 11 are quite close together on the scales for factors 1 and 2, but farther apart on the scale for factor 3. We call them a cluster tentatively, pending verification. The same situation holds for points 2 and 6, and we call them tentatively another cluster.

Points 7, 8, and 10 are fairly close together on the scale of factor 1, quite close together on the scale of factor 2, but moderately far apart on the scale of factor 3. We call them a cluster very tentatively, pending verification.

Point 6 might well be added to points 1 and 4 to form a cluster of three, but this would leave point 2 an *outlier*—a point not in any cluster.

In making a graphic cluster analysis it is desirable to add to the variable profiles the profiles of the primary axes. The F_n-coordinates of each primary axis are given by the elements of one row of $T = D\Lambda^{-1}$ because the normalizing matrix D makes them already of unit length. Applying the Landahl transformation to the rows of T' we obtain m (here 3) additional rows of L_n corresponding

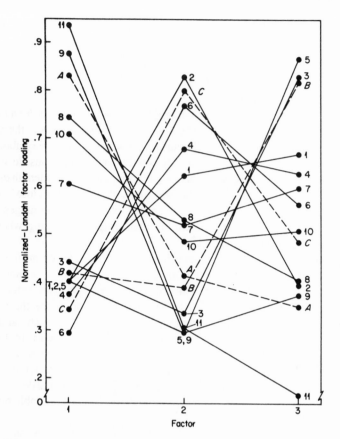

FIG. 14.3. Normalized Landah profiles for eleven WAIS subtests, age-group
25–34 ($N = 300$).

to the primary axes. These profiles enable us to see which clusters (if any) are
"corner clusters" that include a primary axis. In the extended-vector picture of
Fig. 14.1, the 3–5, 9–11, and 2–6 clusters are "corner clusters" and were used
in Chapter 7 to define the primary axes. We should be inclined not to break such
a cluster (here the 2–6 cluster) in order to form a cluster such as the 1–4–6
cluster, even though the latter includes more variables and may be a little more
compact than the "corner cluster." For the WAIS example, the matrix T is given
in Table 11.1. Then

$$
\begin{array}{cc}
T' & \qquad \textit{Landahl Trf } L_t \\
\begin{bmatrix}
.9252 & .3772 & .0427 \\
.9415 & -.1487 & -.3024 \\
.9437 & -.2440 & .2234
\end{bmatrix} &
\cdot
\begin{bmatrix}
.5774 & .5774 & .5774 \\
.8165 & -.4082 & -.4082 \\
0 & .7071 & -.7071
\end{bmatrix}
= \\
& \qquad =
\end{array}
$$

$$L_n$$

$$\begin{bmatrix} .8422 & .4104 & .3500 \\ .4222 & .3905 & .8181 \\ .3457 & .8025 & .4865 \end{bmatrix}$$

These three additional rows of L_n are labeled A, B, and C and plotted in dashed lines on Fig. 14.3. The labeling of the axes is arbitrary. On the plot, profile A is fairly close to the 9–11 cluster on the three axes, profile B is fairly close to the 3–5 cluster, and profile C is wholly contained within the 2–6 cluster but rather far from the profiles of points 1 and 4 except on axis 1.

To verify that these tentative clusters are real, we compute the cosine of the angle between each pair of test vectors for the tests presumed to lie in the same cluster. The cosine of an angle of 0° is 1, and the cosine of an angle of 90° is 0. Hence a high cosine between two test vectors indicates that they belong in the same cluster. The cosine of the angle between any two test vectors is the scalar product of these vectors after they have been normalized. We use the normalized vectors of the F_n-matrix of Table 14.1 rather than those of the L_n-matrix because these F_n values contain less rounding error. The results are shown at the lower left of Table 14.1. The 3–5 and 1–4 clusters are quite compact, with cosines .998 and .997. The 9–11 and 2–6 clusters are reasonably compact, with cosines .976 and .978. The 7–8–10 cluster is not quite so compact. Its lowest cosine, 7–8, is .971, but this is still fairly high. If we consider the alternative 1–4–6 cluster, its lowest cosine, for 1–6, is .979, which is just barely higher than the 2–6 cosine, 978. A purely numerical procedure, not using the data for the primary axes, would give us this 1–4–6 cluster, leaving variable 2 an outlier (a test not in any cluster).

Suppose we should try to combine the 1–4 cluster and the 2–6 cluster into one larger cluster: this might seem reasonable when we examine Fig. 14.1. The additional cosines would be .941 for tests 1 and 2, and .962 for tests 2 and 4. These are both lower than any of the other within-cluster cosines. On the basis of the first five clusters (and the alternative 1–4–6 cluster), we might have been inclined to set an *acceptance level* of .950, that is, to refuse to accept a set of tests as lying in the same cluster if the lowest within-cluster cosine was below .950. In this case the 1–2 cosine of .941 would prohibit the combining of the 1–4 cluster and the 2–6 cluster into one 1–4–2–6 cluster.

To interpret this cluster analysis we refer to the names of the WAIS subtests given at the beginning of Section 7.5. The 3–5 cluster consists of Arithmetic and Digit Span. It is an arithmetical or quantitative reasoning cluster, essentially the same as the corresponding factor. The 1–4 cluster consists of Information and Similarities. It is a verbal-knowledge cluster. The 9–11 cluster consists of Block Design and Object Assembly. It seems to represent some sort of visual-manipulative ability. The 2–6 cluster consists of Comprehension and Vocabulary, and might be termed verbal comprehension. When combined with the 1–4 cluster it is essentially the same as the verbal-relations factor. The 7–8–10 cluster consists of Digit Symbol, Picture Completion, and Picture Arrangement. It appears to be a visualization or visual-reasoning cluster.

The acceptance level for a reasonably compact cluster goes down as the number of factors goes up. Because obtuse structures are possible, we should consider the whole space above the "floor": the b-axis in the two-factor case or the plane orthogonal to the first axis of F in the three-factor case. Suppose we decide to set the acceptance level so as to permit no more than twice as many clusters of maximum "looseness" as the number of factors. In the two-factor case the acceptance level could not be lower than .7071, corresponding to an angle of 45°, and there could be no more than four such clusters, each contained in a 45° segment of the semicircle. In three-space the boundary is a hemisphere instead of a semicircle, and the boundary of each cluster is a cone with apex at the origin rather than a segment of a circle. We could now set the acceptance level at .5, corresponding to an angle of 60°, with five cones lying on the "floor" and the sixth with its mouth straight up. Thus as the dimensionality of the space (the number of factors) goes up, there is room for the same proportionate number of clusters (number of clusters/number of factors) at lower and lower acceptance levels.

Exercise 14:1. Do a graphic cluster analysis of the nine-aptitude-tests data. The F-matrix and T' are found in Exercise 11:1. Compare your interpretation with that of the extended-vector factors found in Exercise 7:1. Note that the plot for this exercise is much easier to interpret than is Fig. 14.3.

14.3 ELEMENTARY LINKAGE ANALYSIS

McQuitty (1957) has described a method of cluster analysis which we present here with slight modifications. This method is somewhat crude, but it is entirely numerical and is quite simple.

We have already used the within-cluster cosines to verify the results of a graphic cluster analysis. Elementary linkage analysis, as we describe it here, starts from the complete cosine matrix,

$$K = F_n F'_n. \tag{14-2}$$

The K-matrix is obtained from the F_n-matrix by forming the scalar product of every pair of rows. It is the same size as the correlation matrix and is identical with the reproduced correlation matrix ($R\dagger = FF'$) corrected for communality (Section 6.1.2). For the WAIS data, the cosine matrix is given in Table 14.2. For elementary linkage analysis we do not record the unities on the diagonal. (Each of these unities is the scalar product of one row of F_n by its own transpose.)

The general rule of elementary linkage analysis is that each test belongs in the same cluster with that test with which it has the highest cosine. We start by underlining the highest cosine in each *column*. If there are two equal highest

TABLE 14.2
Cosine Matrix for Eleven WAIS Subtests, Age-Group 25–34,
and Elementary Linkage Analysis (N = 300)

Test	(1)	(2)	(3)	(4)	(5)	(6)	(7)	(8)	(9)	(10)	(11)
(1)		.941	.945	.997	.927	.979	.971	.901	.788	.930	.677
(2)	.941		.783	.962	.747	.978	.911	.896	.744	.887	.693
(3)	.945	.783		.918	.998	.861	.944	.845	.801	.902	.657
(4)	.997	.962	.918		.897	.991	.961	.895	.768	.918	.664
(5)	.927	.747	.998	.897		.838	.918	.805	.763	.869	.608
(6)	.979	.978	.861	.991	.838		.921	.859	.702	.874	.607
(7)	.971	.911	.944	.961	.918	.921		.971	.912	.990	.826
(8)	.901	.896	.845	.895	.805	.859	.971		.963	.993	.927
(9)	.788	.744	.801	.768	.763	.702	.912	.963		.959	.976
(10)	.930	.887	.902	.918	.869	.874	.990	.993	.959		.898
(11)	.677	.693	.657	.664	.608	.607	.826	.927	.976	.898	

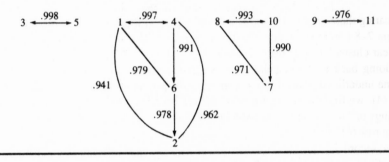

cosines in a column, we have two options: (1) compute them to more decimals to find the highest; (2) underline them both. This situation does not arise with the three-decimal cosines in Table 14.2.

If we set an acceptance level at the outset, we do not underline the highest cosine in a column if that cosine is below the acceptance level. The corresponding test becomes an *intrinsic outlier:* a test whose vector is not close enough to that of any other test to permit it to be a member of any cluster. If we set the acceptance level at .950, or even at .970, there are no intrinsic outliers in the WAIS data.

We next look along the *rows* to find the *reciprocal pairs*. Two tests, say *a* and *b*, form a rèciprocal pair if the highest cosine of *a* is with *b and* the highest cosine of *b* is with *a*. Looking along row 1, the highest cosine is with 4, and looking along row 4, the highest cosine is with 1. Tests 1 and 4 therefore form a reciprocal pair. The other reciprocal pairs are 3–5, 8–10, and 9–11. Each reciprocal pair, by the general rule, forms a *nuclear cluster*. There may or may not be other tests in the same cluster. Just below the cosine matrix we write the test numbers for the reciprocal pairs and join each pair by a double-headed arrow, with the value of the cosine written on it.

We now look along the *row* of each variable that is a member of a reciprocal pair. In each of rows (3) and (5) there is only one cosine underlined, so the 3–5 cluster is complete. The same is true for rows (9) and (11), so the 9–11 cluster is also complete. Looking along row (8), there is again only one cosine underlined. But looking along row (10), we find another highest cosine, that of test 7. We record the 7 below the 10, with a single arrow. Test 10 "brings in" test 7. Then looking along row (7), we do not find any cosine underlined: test 7 does not "bring in" any other test. The 8–10–7 cluster is therefore complete.

Suppose the 7–10 cosine had been .993 instead of .990. There would then be two equal highest cosines in column (10), both .993; and the highest cosine in column (7), row (10), would be .993 also instead of .990. We would then write below the table

$$ 7 \xleftarrow{\quad.993\quad} 10 \xleftarrow{\quad.993\quad} 8, $$

indicating that variable 10 is a member of two reciprocal pairs. Then noting that cosine 7–8 (.971) is above the acceptance level (.950 or .970) we would have a nuclear cluster of three tests: 7–10–8.

Going back to the original data, we look along row (1). There is only one cosine underlined, that of test 4 from the 1–4 reciprocal pair. But looking along row (4), we find the cosine for test 6 as well as that for test 1 underlined. Test 4 "brings in" test 6, so we record 6 below 4 with an arrow at the 6. Now looking along row (6), we find its cosine with test 2 underlined. Test 6 "brings in" test 2, so we record 2 below 6 with an arrow at 2. Looking along row (2), we find no underlines, so the cluster 1–4–6–2 is complete.

This finishes the standard elementary linkage analysis. But by the one general rule, we may have one or more "serpentine" clusters. The 1–4–6–2 cluster is one such (see Fig. 14.1). If we demand "compact" clusters, we can add an acceptance-level requirement to the basic rule. Suppose we set this acceptance level at .950. To test the 7–8–10 cluster for compactness, we draw a line without arrows from 8 to 7 and record the cosine, .971, next to it. This value also meets the acceptance level, so we accept the 7–8–10 cluster.

We complete the cosines for the 1–4–6–2 cluster by drawing the lines 1–2, 1–6, and 4–2 and recording the cosines. Cosine 1–2 is .941, which is lower than the acceptance level, so although tests 1 and 2 go together in a "serpentine" cluster, they do *not* go together in a "compact" cluster even with acceptance level .950. Test 6 goes with tests 1 and 4, because its lowest cosine in the 1–4–6 cluster (.979), is just higher than its 6–2 cosine (.978). This leaves test 2 a *forced outlier*. Though its 2–6 and 2–4 cosines are above the acceptance level, its 1–2 cosine is not, so it cannot join the 1–4–6 cluster.

If we have a bias against forced outliers, we can form a 1–4 cluster and a 2–6 cluster, with cosines .997 and .978, both above the acceptance level, though the cosine of 6 with 2 is lower than its lowest cosine with 1 or 4.

A special situation would arise if the 2–4 cosine were .997 instead of .962, the others remaining as they are. In this case we would have the picture

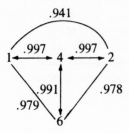

We cannot have a 1–4–2 nuclear cluster because the 1–2 cosine is below the acceptance level. Therefore we consider the 1–6 cosine (.979) and the 2–6 cosine (.978). Because the former is larger, we would form a 1–6 cluster (cosine .979) and a 2–4 cluster (cosine .997).

With these data, elementary linkage analysis gives essentially the same result as that obtained from graphic cluster analysis. This is not always the case, however.

Exercise 14:2.   Normalize the rows of the F-matrix of Exercise 14:1 and form the cosine matrix. Then do an elementary linkage analysis of these nine aptitude tests. Note that for these data the cluster analysis and the factor analysis give the same results because all of the clusters are "corner clusters."

14.4   A MORE COMPLEX SYSTEM OF CLUSTER ANALYSIS

A system of cluster analysis of the same general nature as graphic cluster analysis and elementary linkage analysis with an acceptance level is described by Cureton, Cureton, and Durfee (1970). This system is much more complex than the two described above and is impractical even for small problems without the use of an electronic digital computer. With the use of such a computer, however, it can be applied to problems involving large numbers of variables, and it does not have some of the weaknesses of these simpler systems.

We start by forming the cosine matrix, as we did for elementary linkage analysis. Then we set an acceptance level: the lowest cosine we will accept for two tests to be in the same cluster. If the objective is to build tests from subsets of items, we may also set an *exclusion level:* the lowest acceptable communality (item reliability) for an item to be included in a test (e.g., .150). The communalities are computed from the F-matrix before its rows are normalized to form F_n. Then if K is the complete cosine matrix, $K = F_n F_n'$, we delete from K

the row and column corresponding to each item whose communality is below the exclusion level, and also the row and column corresponding to each item that has no cosine above the acceptance level and is therefore an intrinsic outlier. The result is the *reduced cosine matrix* K_r. All further operations are performed on K_r.

Acceptance levels may range from as high as .95 to as low as .25, depending on the dimensionality of the space (the number of factors). The following short tabulation shows roughly the relation between angles and their cosines:

Cosine	.95	.90	.85	.80	.75	.70	.65	.60
Angle	18°	26°	32°	37°	41°	46°	49°	53°

Cosine	.55	.50	.45	.40	.35	.30	.25
Angle	57°	60°	63°	66°	70°	73°	76°

Cycle Hunt. The first cycle of the clustering system proceeds in a series of stages. At each stage, one or more of the following types of operations is possible:

1. Combine two variables, neither of which is in a cluster, to form a cluster of two.
2. Add to an existing cluster a variable not previously in any cluster.
3. Combine two clusters to form a larger cluster.

At each stage all possible operations of these types are considered. An operation of type 1 will give a single new within-cluster cosine. After an operation of type 2 there will be a lowest cosine between the added variable and one of those already in the cluster. After an operation of type 3 there will be a lowest cosine between one variable from one of the two original clusters and one variable from the other. The operation performed, among all possible operations of the three types, will be the one that leaves the new lowest within-cluster cosine highest. Whichever operation is selected, and to whichever variables and/or clusters it is applied, the lowest cosine in any cluster will be higher than it would be if any other operation had been selected, or if the given operation or either of the other two had been applied to any other variables and/or clusters. Thus at every stage in building up the clusters, all clusters are kept as compact as possible under the definition that the compactness of a cluster is the magnitude of the lowest within-cluster cosine.

At the first stage the only possible operation is an operation of type 1, and the first operation is therefore to combine into a cluster of two the two variables having the highest cosine in the entire K_r table. At the second stage operations of either type 1 or type 2 are possible. But as soon as two clusters have been formed, operations of all three types are possible.

When no further operation of either type 1 or type 2 can be performed without leading to a lowest cosine below the acceptance level, cycle Hunt terminates. Operations of type 3 might still be possible, but performing them at this time would reduce the flexibility of the second-cycle procedures and lead possibly to a "local optimum."

Note that, in cycle Hunt, when a variable has once been assigned to a cluster, it remains in that cluster. Note also that every reciprocal pair of variables with cosine above the acceptance level necessarily starts a new cluster. Because of these two points, particularly the first, the assignment of variables to clusters is usually less than optimal at the conclusion of cycle Hunt.

Cycle Change. The operations of cycle Change begin after cycle Hunt is complete.

1. For each variable in turn, including the forced outliers from cycle Hunt, find its lowest cosine with any variable in each cluster and its cosine with each forced outlier.
   a. If the highest of these is with a variable in its own cluster, leave it there.
   b. If the highest of these is with a variable in another cluster, reassign it to that cluster.
   c. If the highest of these is with a forced outlier, combine it with that forced outlier to form a new cluster of two.
   d. If the variable is itself a forced outlier, perform operation b or c only if the resulting lowest cosine is above the acceptance level.

Reassign each variable, if necessary under b or c or d, before proceeding to consideration of the next variable. When all variables have been considered and at least one change has been made, return to the first variable and repeat the entire procedure. This subcycle terminates when, after considering each variable in turn, no changes are made.

2. Consider the lowest within-cluster cosine that will result from combining each pair of clusters. Combine the *one* pair whose lowest within-cluster cosine will be highest, provided this cosine is above the acceptance level. No further combining of clusters is done at this point, even when more than one pair of clusters could be combined.

3. Repeat subcycles 1 and 2 in sequence until, at subcycle 2, no two clusters can be combined without producing a within-cluster cosine below the acceptance level. At this point the cluster analysis is finished.

Two clusters may occasionally be combined by reflecting all of the variables in one of them.

In practice it seems best to repeat the analysis using several different acceptance levels (but the same exclusion level if any), and to choose as the final result the one with the highest acceptance level that gives a "sensible" result. When the acceptance level is too high, there are too many forced outliers and too many small clusters that, from the substantive nature of the variables, ought to be combined into larger clusters. When the acceptance level is too low, some of the larger clusters become clearly heterogeneous, with obviously dissimilar variables in the same cluster.

When the number of variables is quite large and the individual variables are quite unreliable, a variable may go into the wrong one of two adjacent clusters due to its error of measurement. This situation is not uncommon when the variables are single items and we wish to form tests from the clusters. This difficulty can often be partially remedied by using a two-step procedure. The items are first clustered into a large number of small clusters and forced outliers, using a fairly high acceptance level. The cluster centroids are then computed, and these centroids, along with the forced outliers, are then clustered using a lower acceptance level. Using a procedure equivalent to this, Cureton (1970) clustered 372 variables (items of a biographical inventory), with four samples of about 4000 each. The resulting clusters were more "sensible," in terms of the substantive nature of the items, than were those obtained by clustering the 372 items just once using the lower acceptance level.

14.5 CLUSTERING TOTAL VARIANCE AND RELIABLE VARIANCE

As described in previous sections, the cosine matrix is formed from the factor matrix. But if we do not wish to lose the contributions of the unique factors, we can form the cosine matrix from a component matrix rather than from a factor matrix, either with or without deletion of the last one or a few components (without deletion if the last component is salient). The cosine matrix is then

$$K = AA' = R, \tag{14-3}$$

if no components have been deleted, because the rows of A are already of unit length. But if one or more of the later components have been deleted, the rows of A_k must be normalized to yield an A_n matrix, and

$$K = A_n A_n'. \tag{14-4}$$

The K-matrix of (14-3) or (14-4) can then be clustered by one of the methods described above.

We can also start a cluster analysis from a correlation matrix with reliability coefficients rather than either communalities or unities on the diagonal. This matrix is then factored by the principal-axes method to as many factors as appear to be salient. Call this factor matrix B. Normalize its rows to give B_n. The cosine matrix is then

$$K = B_n B_n'.$$

With this procedure we have started by factoring the total *reliable* variance, including the specific factors as well as the common factors, but not the error factors. It is, in a sense, intermediate between factor analysis, which factors only the common variance, and component analysis, which factors the total variance. Ideally the reliability coefficients should be strictly consistent with the intercorrelations, as they are in the five-verbal-tests data and very few other sets of data. But for cluster analysis, estimates of reliability which are not strictly consistent with the intercorrelations will often serve fairly well so long as every one of them is clearly higher than the corresponding communality and clearly lower than unity. And there is some "sense" to basing a cluster analysis on the total reliable variance in the system rather than on either the common variance only or the total variance, including the error variance. For if two or more tests are fairly close together in the reliable-variance space, they are *really* much alike: their alikeness is not seriously reduced by their specific-factor variances.

14.6   CLUSTER SCORES

When a clustering procedure, such as the three described above, has been used, the initial result is merely a list of the variables in each cluster and a list of the outlier variables. But the clusters can then be scored directly. A cluster score may be simply the sum of the raw scores on the variables in the cluster, or the sum of their standard scores if they are not single items and are more or less equally reliable. If we substitute one cluster score for all the variables in each cluster, the set of cluster variables plus the outlier variables becomes a reduced battery, and cluster analysis is an alternative to component analysis as a method of battery reduction.

There are two other more sophisticated methods of forming cluster scores than by merely summing the raw scores or the standard scores on the variables in each cluster. These methods, which are of most value when the variables of a cluster are quite unequally reliable and not too numerous, consist in forming a *weighted* sum of the raw scores or the standard scores on the variables in each cluster.

The first method starts by computing the loadings on the first principal component or the first centroid component of each cluster, and then using (12-7) or (12-8) to obtain the cluster scores. This is the preferred method if the variables are highly reliable, or if, when unreliable, reliability coefficients consistent with the intercorrelations cannot be obtained.

The second method is useful mainly when the variables are educational or psychological tests, and reliability coefficients consistent with the intercorrelations are available, as in the five-verbal-tests example. If the tests have all been administered on the same day, the reliability coefficients may be obtained by KR-20 (Kuder & Richardson, 1937) or by the split-half method and the Spearman-Brown formula. If they have all been administered with generous time limits, so that they are essentially power tests rather than speed tests, a good approximation to the reliability of each test (Cureton et al., 1973) is given by

$$r_{ii} = 1 - \frac{.174n_i}{\sigma_i^2} , \tag{14-5}$$

where the subscript i identifies the i-th test, n_i is the number of items in the test, and σ_i^2 is the variance of the test scores. This formula works well only when the test is of moderate difficulty for the group tested, the score is the number of right answers with no correction for guessing, every examinee answers almost every item including the last item, and there are no items to which almost all examinees give the right answer and no items for which the proportion of right answers approaches or falls short of the chance proportion. This last condition is likely to be approximated whenever the mean score on the test lies between 35% and 65% of the distance between the chance score and the perfect score.

For several tests in a cluster, each with known reliability, the appropriate weight for the i-th test in the cluster (Kelley, 1927) is given by

$$w_i = \frac{\sqrt{r_{ii}}}{\sigma_i(1 - r_{ii})} , \tag{14-6}$$

where r_{ii} is the reliability of the i-th test and σ_i is its standard deviation. If there are k tests in the cluster ($i = 1, 2, \ldots , k$), the cluster score will be

$$X = \sum_{i=1}^{k} (w_i X_i), \tag{14-7}$$

where X is the cluster score and X_i is the *raw* score on the i-th test in the cluster. There is no need to divide by k or $\sum_{i=1}^{k} w_i$, as this would affect only the *scale* of X. If $r_{ii} \doteq 1.00$ for every i; that is, if the variables are all highly reliable (e.g., physical measurements), (14-6) reduces to $w_i = 1/\sigma_i$, and this is equivalent to using standard scores on the k tests except that each score is $\bar{X}_i/\sigma_i$ larger than the standard score.

This procedure maximizes the reliability of the cluster scores, and it is therefore to be preferred to the first procedure whenever reliabilities consistent with the intercorrelations are available for all the individual tests.

In the opinion of the writers cluster scores are more generally useful than are either component scores (with or without rotation) or factor scores. They are measured directly or estimated with little error. The variables in a cluster, if the acceptance level is reasonably high, all measure almost the same combination of factors or components. The interpretation of a cluster is therefore clear: it is whatever is common to *all* the variables in the cluster. Thus the interpretation of a cluster is even clearer than is the interpretation of a factor, while the interpretation of a component (even after rotation) is considerably less clear. The only disadvantage of cluster scores is that they (like factor scores) are correlated. Unclear interpretation is usually too high a price to pay for the measurement or estimation of component scores.

14.7   TYPES OF CLUSTER ANALYSIS

As we noted at the beginning of this chapter, there are more varieties of cluster analysis than of factor analysis, even when we broaden the latter to include component analysis and analysis with reliability coefficients on the diagonal of R. The following sections represent only a sketch or outline rather than any attempt to treat the subject in any detail.

14.7.1 Indices of Association

Much of the literature on cluster analysis consists of discussions of indices of association appropriate to various problems. Correlations, cosines, overlap coefficients, coefficients of agreement of various types, covariances, Euclidean distances between standardized measures, Mahalanobis generalized distances, and other indices have been proposed in connection with various problems. Often the n-space of the original variables is first reduced to an m-space ($m < n$) by component analysis or factor analysis of preliminary indices of association, and then expanded to an n-space of derived indices of association, as we did above in going from correlations to cosines.

Most clustering procedures, including the ones described above, apply to any index of association, with the possible requirements of limited range (e.g., 0 to 1 or -1 to $+1$) and/or scale direction (higher association represented by a larger index than lower association). The variables may be measurements, ranks, or dichotomies.

14.7.2 Cluster Definitions and Cluster Compactness

We can recognize two main classes of clusters. The first may be termed compact clusters. The profiles of the variables clustered are similar in shape and often close together. The relationships are symmetrical or reciprocal, indicating resemblance.

The second class of clusters may be termed serpentine or amoeboid. They result from a single-linkage definition. The relationships may be asymmetric or complementary as well as symmetric or reciprocal. The simplest rule for single linkage is that of elementary linkage analysis without an acceptance level: every variable is in the same cluster as the variable with which its index of association is highest, and the number of clusters is equal to the number of reciprocal pairs. A diagram of a serpentine cluster might be

$$6 \longleftarrow 2 \longleftarrow 3 \longleftrightarrow 4 \longrightarrow 1 \longrightarrow 5.$$

Here 3–4 is the reciprocal pair, 4 brings in 1, 1 brings in 5, 3 brings in 2, and 2 brings in 6. The index of association for variables 6 and 5 might just possibly be the lowest in the whole table of indices. An amoeboid cluster might be represented by

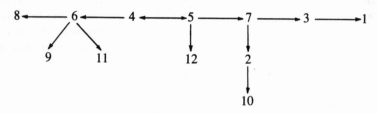

Either the 1–8, the 8–10, the 9–10, or the 11–10 index might possibly be the lowest in the table of indices. Serpentine and amoeboid clusters are sometimes facetiously termed "gerrymander" clusters, after the procedure occasionally used in clustering counties or other political units into districts in order to give some advantage to the political party in power.

For compact clusters the *coefficient of compactness* can be defined in a number of ways. In our previous discussion we defined it tacitly as the lowest within-cluster index of association (there cosine). Another is the mean or root-mean-square of the indices of pairs of variables in the cluster divided by the mean or root-mean-square of the indices of pairs of variables one of which is in the cluster while the other is not. A third is the lowest index of association of a variable with the centroid of its cluster. A fourth is the variance or standard deviation of the indices relating each variable to its cluster centroid.

14.7.3 Number of Clusters and Acceptance Levels

Some methods prespecify the number of clusters. In this case the problem is that of partitioning n variables into $k < n$ clusters in such a manner as to maximize a weighted sum of the coefficients of compactness. The weight for each cluster is ordinarily the number of variables in the cluster. Outliers may be permitted, but each such outlier must be counted as one of the k clusters (with weight one).

When the number of clusters is not prespecified, some methods require clustering of all variables, others permit outliers only when this is required by the procedure of the clustering system, and still others employ acceptance levels. The acceptance level may be either arbitrary or probabilistic. A probabilistic acceptance level is usually an alpha level for rejection of the hypothesis that if n points or vectors are distributed randomly in m-space, as many as k_i of them will fall by chance into a cluster as compact as is the i-th. In this case the acceptance level varies from cluster to cluster; a cluster of greater compactness may reject the hypothesis of randomness with smaller k_i. When there is an acceptance level, either arbitrary or probabilistic, outliers must necessarily be allowed.

Some procedures permit clusters to be adjacent; that is, they permit high indices of association between variables one of which is in one cluster and the other in a neighboring cluster. Others have a *highest* acceptance level, not to be exceeded by any index for two variables in different clusters, or alternatively not to be exceeded by the index for any two cluster centroids. Other procedures use relative rules, for example, that the lowest within-cluster index must be higher than the index for any variable in the cluster with any variable outside it, or that the lowest index for a variable and its cluster centroid must exceed the index for that variable and any variable not in its cluster. Still another rule is that the index of association for two cluster centroids must be at least p times the larger of the two coefficients of compactness, or p times the sum or average of the two coefficients of compactness (p either arbitrary or probabilistic).

14.7.4 Single-Order and Hierarchical Clustering

Some systems find clusters all of one order. Others find small clusters, then clusters of small clusters, then clusters of these larger clusters, and so on, until at the highest order there are only two clusters. Others reverse this procedure. They first partition the variable into two clusters, then partition each of these two into two more (with four at the second order), and so on, until at the lowest order there are only clusters of two and outliers. Still others use rules which do not require that all variables appear in clusters at every order: a cluster at the third order, for example, may stem directly from one at the first order, its variables not appearing in any second-order cluster. Hierarchical clustering of these types results in what are termed "tree" cluster structures.

In the WAIS data we encountered just a trace of hierarchical clustering, when the 1–4 and 2–6 clusters (or the 1–4–6 cluster and the 2 as an outlier) tended to combine to form a 1–2–4–6 cluster. If we apply elementary linkage analysis to the 3–5, 1–4, 2–6, 7–8–10, and 9–11 cluster *centroids* of Table 14.2, there is only one reciprocal pair and hence only one cluster at the second order. But with a high enough acceptance level there is one 1–2–4–6 cluster at the second order, and the 3–5, 7–8–10, and 9–11 clusters become second-order outliers.

We can now characterize the graphic procedure of Section 14.2, the elementary linkage procedure of Section 14.3, and the more complex procedure of Section 14.4.

1. They are all essentially single-order procedures.

2. When an acceptance level is used, it is arbitrary rather than probabilistic, always positive, and uniform for all clusters.

3. When an acceptance level is used, the coefficient of compactness is the lowest within-cluster index of association (cosine). When an acceptance level is not used in elementary linkage analysis, there is no coefficient of compactness and the clusters may be serpentine or amoeboid rather than compact.

4. The number of clusters is not prespecified. If an acceptance level is used, the number is determined by the coefficients of compactness. In graphic analysis the number is determined arbitrarily by the investigator's judgment. In elementary linkage analysis without an acceptance level, the number of clusters is equal to the number of reciprocal pairs.

5. Clusters may be adjacent. There is no *highest* acceptance level.

6. If there is an acceptance level, both intrinsic outliers and forced outliers may appear. If there is an exclusion rule, it generates more intrinsic outliers. In elementary linkage analysis without an acceptance level, every variable is clustered and there are no outliers.

14.8 CLUSTERING INDIVIDUALS

In many applications the individuals rather than the variables are clustered. When we cluster individuals the raw data for each individual are his scores on the n variables. These scores form a profile, so this type of analysis is often termed *profile analysis*.

When we cluster variables, the N scores on any one variable are on the same scale. When we cluster individuals, the n scores of any one individual must likewise be on the same scale. To accomplish this, the raw scores on each variable are first standardized. For a given group of individuals this puts all *variables* on the same scale.

Figure 14.4 shows the profiles of two hypothetical individuals on the standard scores of six variables. The dashed line for each individual is at his mean standard score on the six variables.

The standard-score profiles of individuals can differ in shape, in level, and in the dispersion of the profile points about their mean level. Thus, in Fig. 14.4, individual a's profile is at a high level (all standard errors positive and fairly high), with low dispersion. Individual b's profile is of a different shape, with the lines joining pairs of adjacent points not roughly parallel to those of individual a. It is at a lower level (all but two standard scores negative), and has greater dispersion than has the profile of individual a.

We could also represent the two profiles of Fig. 14.4 by two points in a space of six dimensions. The six coordinates of each point would be the standard scores

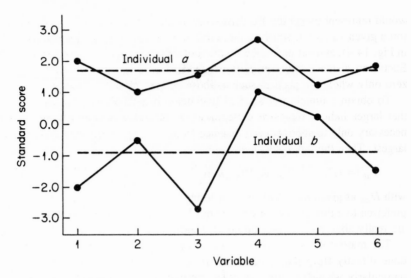

FIG. 14.4.   Profiles of two individuals: standard scores on six variables.

of the individual represented by his point in the six-space. In the general case there would be N points in n-space, for N individuals and n variables.

If we wish to consider only the *shapes* of the profiles, the appropriate index of association would be the angle between each pair of individual-vectors in the n-space, or its cosine. There would be $N(N - 1)/2$ such pairs of vectors. In Fig. 14.4 the equivalent procedure would consist in standardizing the variable-standard-scores of each *individual* (about his own mean) and then calculating the correlations between pairs of these doubly-standardized scores.

If we wish to consider both shape and dispersion but not level, the appropriate index of association would be the correlation between the variable-standard-scores of each pair of individuals. In this case the standard deviation of the n variable-standard-scores would be different for different individuals (as for individuals a and b in Fig. 14.4), but differences in level would be ignored by taking the n deviations of each individual from his own mean. These correlations would be somewhat lower in absolute value than the corresponding cosines.

If we wish to consider shape, dispersion, *and* level, the appropriate index of association is the Euclidian distance between pairs of vector termini in the n-space. By the generalized Pythagorean theorem this is

$$D_{ab} = \sqrt{\sum_{i=1}^{n} (x_{ai} - x_{bi})^2} \tag{14-8}$$

where a and b represent two individuals, and x_{ai} and x_{bi} represent their variable-standard-scores on the i-th variable ($i = 1, 2, \ldots , n$). In Fig. 14.4 this would represent taking the standard-score difference between each pair of points (on a given variable), squaring these differences, summing over the n pairs (six in Fig. 14.4), and extracting the square root. When the index of association is the Euclidean distance between pairs of standardized variables, the index will be zero only when two profiles such as those in Fig. 14.4 are identical.

To obtain a function of a set of Euclidean distances which has the property that larger indices represent closer association and with limits 0 and 1, it is necessary only to subtract each distance from the largest and then divide by the largest. Then the index becomes

$$I_{ab} = (D_{ab} - D_{ab}max)/D_{ab}max \qquad (14-9)$$

with D_{ab} as given by (14-8). For clustering individuals, D_{ab} or I_{ab} is commonly preferred to either cosines or correlations because the profiles of two individuals are really alike only as they approach identity.

The matrix of indices of association is an N by N matrix, and clustering is done directly from this matrix. But if the number of variables is large, and particularly when they are two-point variables (e.g., presence or absence of a symptom, or agree or disagree with a proposition), there may be a preliminary cluster analysis of the *variables,* usually into a fairly large number of moderately small clusters plus some outliers. The index of association for variables, in this case, is usually the cosine, computed from either a factor matrix or a component matrix, and the standard score of each individual on each variable-cluster centroid is substituted for his standard scores on all the variables in the cluster. This reduces the number of profile variables from n to k, where k is the number of variable-clusters plus the number of outlier variables. This not only reduces the number of variables from n to k; it also increases the reliabilities of the cluster-variables. The indices of association for clustering individuals are then computed for the $N(N - 1)/2$ pairs of individuals over the $k < n$ cluster-plus-outlier variable-standard-scores.

It may also be noted that indices of association between individuals can be factor-analyzed as well as cluster-analyzed. The primary factors are then the "ideal" or "pure" types of individuals. But many individuals may be of mixed types, with nonzero loadings on more than one individual-factor, just as many variables are factorially complex, with nonzero loadings on more than one variable-factor.

Blashfield and Aldenderfer (1978) review the literature of cluster analysis and give a fairly extensive bibliography of books and journal review articles. Blashfield (personal communication to Cureton) says in part, "The best of these is the article by Cormack (1971). Anderberg (1973), Sneath and Sokal (1973), and Hartigen (1975) also contain a great deal of information and are relatively non-overlapping in terms of their ideas. In addition, Everitt (1974) is a simpler introduction but is very well written."

15

Simplex Analysis

Near the end of Chapter 2 we mentioned methods of factor analysis which do not employ the linear model. Of these, simplex analysis is the method most commonly used.

Simplex analysis applies only to a limited class of problems, namely the class in which all of the variables can be arranged in an ascending or descending order of complexity and are otherwise similar. The commonest examples are those in which the variables are the successive trials or stages of a learning or growth study. Other examples might include our five-verbal-tests problem, provided we believe we can arrange these tests in an order representing verbal ability at increasing (or decreasing) levels of complexity. The procedure consists merely in fitting the simplex model to the correlation matrix of the ordered variables, and then checking to see how well the model fits.

15.1 THE SIMPLEX MODEL

15.1.1 The Superdiagonal Pattern

If a set of ordered variables represents an increasing or decreasing order of complexity of what is otherwise essentially the same process, the correlations should all be positive; those between adjacent variables in the order should in general be highest, those between variables separated by one other in the order should be next highest, . . . , and the correlation between the first variable in the order and

372

the last should be the lowest. In the upper triangular correlation matrix of the ordered variables, the correlations on the *superdiagonal* (the diagonal just above the principal diagonal) should in general be highest: they are the correlations between adjacent variables in the order. And as we go either upward in a column or to the right in a row from the superdiagonal, the correlations should decrease regularly, with the correlation at the upper right corner the lowest in the table. An upper triangular matrix of correlations between ordered variables which exhibits this last property is said to have a superdiagonal pattern.

Let us apply this idea to the example of five verbal tests. To obtain the order of complexity we might assume that variable 5 (Vocabulary) is the simplest, variable 2 (Same-Opposite) the next simplest, variable 3 (Proverb Matching) the third simplest, variable 4 (Verbal Analogies) the fourth simplest, and variable 1 (Paragraph Meaning) the most complex. Arranging the variables in this order, the upper triangular correlation matrix is

Var	(2)	(3)	(4)	(1)
(5)	.689	.626	.598	.555
(2)		.663	.634	.585
(3)			.697	.658
(4)				.616

The diagonal entries, which would all be unity, are omitted. This matrix exhibits the superdiagonal pattern, with one exception: the lower right entry, $r_{14} = .616$ is lower than the entry just above, $r_{13} = .658$, so the table is almost but not quite a perfect superdiagonal pattern.

Simplex analysis applies most clearly to variables which have a natural order that might be due to increasing or decreasing complexity, such as successive trials in a learning study, successive measurements in a growth study, and the like. In cases such as these the original order of the variables may not be changed in order to obtain a better fit of the data to the superdiagonal pattern. In other cases, such as that of the five verbal tests, we may merely *suspect* that, because they *are* all verbal tests, they *may* all measure one function (verbal ability) at increasing levels of complexity. Their order of complexity is then to be determined. Initially we merely use our best judgment, based on the substantive nature of the variables. Where this judgment is not clear, some experimentation may be necessary to see which order produces the best approximation to the superdiagonal pattern. Thus in the case of the five verbal tests there is no clear substantive reason for considering Proverb Matching less complex than Verbal Analogies. We placed Proverb Matching ahead merely because it consists of six-choice items, while Verbal Analogies consists of 30-choice items, and we happened to be right. But Paragraph Meaning, which would normally be judged more complex than either, consists of four-choice items (see Table 1.1).

We have noted that in a superdiagonal pattern the intercorrelations must all be positive. If some of these correlations are negative, and there is some reason to believe that this is due merely to scale direction, we can use preliminary reflection. Then if the matrix can be made all-positive by reflection, we reverse the *names* of the reflected variables, and these variables as renamed, along with those not reflected, might be orderable in an order of increasing or decreasing complexity such that their intercorrelations would form a superdiagonal pattern.

Large tables of intercorrelations seldom exhibit the superdiagonal pattern or the simplex form. But *portions* of such tables may do so. Thus a large table of intercorrelations among aptitude tests might include subsets of verbal tests, numerical tests, abstract reasoning tests, visual space manipulation tests, and the like, each forming a simplex. The numerical tests might include tests of addition, subtraction, multiplication, division, fractions, decimals, and arithmetic reasoning. Here, as in the case of Proverb Matching and Verbal Analogies, it might not be clear initially whether fractions or decimals are intrinsically more complex.

15.1.2 The Simplex

A simplex (Guttman, 1954b) is a special case of the superdiagonal pattern. It is specified by the equations

$$x_1 = f_1$$
$$x_2 = f_1 + f_2 \qquad\qquad\qquad (15\text{-}1)$$

$$- -$$

$$x_n = f_1 + f_2 + \cdots + f_n$$

for the case of increasing complexity, or by

$$x_1 = f_1 + f_2 + \cdots + f_{n-1} + f_n$$
$$x_2 = f_1 + f_2 + \cdots + f_{n-1} \qquad\qquad\qquad (15\text{-}2)$$

$$- - - - - - - - - - - - - - - - - - - -$$

$$x_n = f_1$$

for the case of decreasing complexity. In these sets of equations the x's are deviations from the mean scores (*not* standard scores) on the measured variables, the f's are deviations from the mean scores on the factors (*not* factor loadings), there are n measured variables and n factors, and the factors are assumed to be orthogonal. Equations (15-1) and (15-2) are essentially equivalent; they differ only in the direction of the ordering of the variables, and (15-2) gives the same correlation matrix as (15-1). When we find that a set of intercorrelations forms a simplex, the direction of complexity must therefore be inferred from the substantive nature of the variables; it is not given by the numerical data. We therefore use only (15-1) hereafter.

Each equation of (15-1) includes all of the factors of the preceding equation plus one additional factor. When we say that the simplex is a special case of the superdiagonal pattern, we mean that there are sets of equations other than those based on increasing or decreasing complexity which will also generate super-diagonal correlation patterns. One such set is

$$x_1 = f_1 \qquad\qquad + f_5 \qquad\qquad + f_8 \qquad + f_{10}$$

$$x_2 = f_1 + f_2 \qquad\quad + f_5 + f_6 \qquad + f_8 + f_9 + f_{10}$$

$$x_3 = \qquad f_2 + f_3 \quad + f_5 + f_6 + f_7 + f_8 + f_9 + f_{10}$$

$$x_4 = \qquad\quad f_3 + f_4 \quad + f_6 + f_7 + f_8 + f_9 + f_{10}$$

$$x_5 = \qquad\qquad f_4 \qquad\quad + f_7 \qquad + f_9 + f_{10}$$

Note that in this set, which is termed an open contiguity structure (Jones, 1960), there are twice as many factors as tests.

The basic equation of the simplex is

$$r_{ik} = r_{ij}r_{jk} \qquad (i < j < k), \tag{15-3}$$

where the symbol $<$ means *precedes* (in the order of the variables). To give this symbol its usual meaning ("is less than"), in the case of the five verbal tests, they would need to be renumbered in the natural order as they appear in the ordered matrix, that is, 1-2-3-4-5 instead of 5-2-3-4-1.

If we consider the partial correlation

$$r_{ik\cdot j} = \frac{r_{ik} - r_{ij}r_{jk}}{\sqrt{(1 - r_{ij}^2)(1 - r_{jk}^2)}} \qquad (i < j < k),$$

it is evident that (15-3) will hold only when $r_{ik\cdot j} = 0$. Thus if a correlation matrix forms a simplex, every partial correlation between two variables, with any variable between them in the order partialled out, must equal zero. Thus we see that the conditions for a simplex are much more restrictive than are the conditions for a superdiagonal pattern.

Note that in (15-1) the steps do *not* have to be equal. If

$$f_{i+1} = f_i + \delta_i,$$

δ_i can be different for every i from $i = 1$ to $i = n - 1$.

To derive (15-3) from (15-1), remembering that the variable-scores and factor-scores are in deviation-score form, we note first from (15-1) that

$$r_{12} = \frac{\Sigma f_1(f_1 + f_2)}{\sqrt{(\Sigma f_1^2)[\Sigma(f_1 + f_2)^2]}} = \frac{\Sigma f_1^2 + \Sigma f_1 f_2}{\sqrt{(\Sigma f_1^2)(\Sigma f_1^2 + \Sigma f_2^2 + 2\Sigma f_1 f_2)}}.$$

Then because the factors are orthogonal $\Sigma f_1 f_2 = 0$ (and in general $\Sigma f_i f_j = 0$ for all i and $j \neq i$), so

$$r_{12} = \frac{\Sigma f_1^2}{\sqrt{(\Sigma f_1^2)(\Sigma f_1^2 + \Sigma f_2^2)}} = \sqrt{\frac{\Sigma f_1^2}{\Sigma(f_1^2 + f_2^2)}} \tag{15-4}$$

Similarly

$$r_{13} = \frac{\Sigma f_1(f_1 + f_2 + f_3)}{\sqrt{(\Sigma f_1^2)[\Sigma(f_1 + f_2 + f_3)^2]}}$$

$$= \frac{\Sigma f_1^2 + \Sigma f_1 f_2 + \Sigma f_1 f_3}{\sqrt{(\Sigma f_1^2)(\Sigma f_1^2 + \Sigma f_2^2 + \Sigma f_3^2 + 2\Sigma f_1 f_2 + 2\Sigma f_1 f_3 + 2\Sigma f_2 f_3)}}$$

$$r_{13} = \sqrt{\frac{\Sigma f_1^2}{\Sigma(f_1^2 + f_2^2 + f_3^2)}} \tag{15-5}$$

And again

$$r_{23} = \frac{\Sigma(f_1 + f_2)(f_1 + f_2 + f_3)}{\sqrt{[\Sigma(f_1 + f_2)^2][\Sigma(f_1 + f_2 + f_3)^2]}}$$

$$= \frac{\Sigma f_1^2 + \Sigma f_2^2 + 2\Sigma f_1 f_2 + \Sigma f_1 f_3 + \Sigma f_2 f_3}{\sqrt{(\Sigma f_1^2 + \Sigma f_2^2 + 2\Sigma f_1 f_2)(\Sigma f_1^2 + \Sigma f_2^2 + \Sigma f_3^2 + 2\Sigma f_1 f_2 + 2\Sigma f_1 f_3 + 2\Sigma f_2 f_3)}}$$

$$= \frac{\Sigma f_1^2 + \Sigma f_2^2}{\sqrt{(\Sigma f_1^2 + \Sigma f_2^2)(\Sigma f_1^2 + \Sigma f_2^2 + \Sigma f_3^2)}}$$

$$r_{23} = \sqrt{\frac{\Sigma(f_1^2 + f_2^2)}{\Sigma(f_1^2 + f_2^2 + f_3^2)}} \tag{15-6}$$

From (15-4) and (15-6)

$$r_{12}r_{23} = \sqrt{\frac{(\Sigma f_1^2)\Sigma(f_1^2 + f_2^2)}{\Sigma(f_1^2 + f_2^2)\Sigma(f_1^2 + f_2^2 + f_3^2)}}$$

$$= \sqrt{\frac{\Sigma f_1^2}{\Sigma(f_1^2 + f_2^2 + f_3^2)}}$$

which by (15-5) is equal to r_{13}. Thus

$$r_{13} = r_{12}r_{23},$$

which is a particular case of (15-3). If in the above derivations we substitute the subscripts i, j, and k for 1, 2, and 3, we obtain (15-3) directly, so long as $i < j < k$. We can generalize (15-4), (15-5), and (15-6) to give any correlation in the matrix

$$r_{ij} = \sqrt{\frac{\Sigma(f_1^2 + f_2^2 + \cdots + f_i^2)}{\Sigma(f_1^2 + \cdots + f_i^2 + \cdots + f_j^2)}} \qquad (i < j). \tag{15-7}$$

In (15-7) and hence in (15-4), (15-5), and (15-6), remembering that the f's are deviation scores and that the factors are orthogonal, each expression under the radical is a variance ratio, and its square root is a standard deviation ratio. Thus (15-7) becomes

$$r_{ij} = \sigma_i/\sigma_j \qquad (i < j).$$

But this implies that the standard deviation increases as the complexity increases. If in place of (15-1) we write

$$x_1 = \frac{1}{c_1}f_1$$

$$x_2 = \frac{1}{c_2}(f_1 + f_2)$$

$$\text{-------------------------}$$

$$x_n = \frac{1}{c_n}(f_1 + f_2 + \cdots + f_n)$$

where $c_1, c_2, \ldots, c_n$ are scalars, then (15-7) becomes

$$r_{ij} = c_i\sigma_i/c_j\sigma_j \qquad (i < j).$$

Here σ_i and σ_j are the standard deviations of x_i and x_j, respectively. The c's express the relations between the score scales of the factors and the score scales of the measured variables (the x's), so the standard deviations of these x's need not increase with their factorial complexities. If we let $c_i\sigma_i = a_i$ and $c_j\sigma_j = a_j$, then

$$r_{ij} = a_i/a_j \qquad (i < j), \tag{15-8}$$

and a_i and a_j may be viewed as the weighted standard deviations of the variables i and j.

From (15-8)

$$r_{ik} = a_i/a_k; \ r_{ij} = a_i/a_j; \ r_{jk} = a_j/a_k \qquad (i < j < k).$$

Then from (15-3)

$$r_{ik} = r_{ij}r_{jk} = \frac{a_ia_j}{a_ja_k} = \frac{a_i}{a_k} \qquad (i < j < k),$$

which is (15-8) with the subscript k taking the place of j. Thus (15-8) is seen to be equivalent to the defining equation of the simplex (15-3). It can also be seen that a perfect simplex is defined by exactly n parameters: $a_1, a_2, \ldots, a_n$.

Note again that a simplex is a superdiagonal pattern, but a superdiagonal pattern need not be a simplex. Thus if instead of (15-8) we have

$$r_{ij} = a_j - a_i \qquad (0 \leqq a_i < a_j \leqq 1),$$

the result will again be a superdiagonal pattern but not a simplex. Dubois (1960) terms this superdiagonal pattern a pseudo-simplex.

15.1.3 Fitting a Simplex

From (15-8) we define a residual

$$r_{ij \cdot a} = r_{ij} - a_i/a_j \qquad (i < j). \tag{15-9}$$

The problem of fitting a simplex is the problem of choosing $a_1, a_2, \ldots, a_n$ so that the $n(n - 1)/2$ residuals of (15-9) will be minimized. A number of solutions have been proposed, among them those of Kaiser (1962), Schonemann (1970), and Jöreskog (1970). We propose here a simpler solution.

From (15-8)

$$a_i = r_{ij}a_j \qquad (i < j) \tag{15-10}$$

$$a_j = a_i/r_{ij} \qquad (i < j) \tag{15-11}$$

Consider a correlation matrix with empty diagonal. To the upper right section apply (15-10), and to the lower left section apply (15-11). The result (for five variables) is

$$
\begin{array}{lllll}
 & a_1 = r_{12}a_2 & a_1 = r_{13}a_3 & a_1 = r_{14}a_4 & a_1 = r_{15}a_5 \\
a_2 = a_1/r_{12} & & a_2 = r_{23}a_3 & a_2 = r_{24}a_4 & a_2 = r_{25}a_5 \\
a_3 = a_1/r_{13} & a_3 = a_2/r_{23} & & a_3 = r_{34}a_4 & a_3 = r_{35}a_5 \qquad (15\text{-}12) \\
a_4 = a_1/r_{14} & a_4 = a_2/r_{24} & a_4 = a_3/r_{34} & & a_4 = r_{45}a_5 \\
a_5 = a_1/r_{15} & a_5 = a_2/r_{25} & a_5 = a_3/r_{35} & a_5 = a_4/r_{45} &
\end{array}
$$

The $n - 1$ (here four) entries in each row are linearly independent estimates of the same a and can therefore be averaged. These a's are determined by (15-8) up to an arbitrary constant. For if $r_{ij} = a_i/a_j$, then $r_{ij} = ka_i/ka_j$ with any arbitrary k. To obtain a numerical solution, we can give any one of them an arbitrary value, and the rest are then determined numerically. Whichever a we use and whatever constant we set it equal to, the ratios of (15-8), which define the reproduced correlations, will be the same. It is most convenient to set $a_n = 1$ (here $a_5 = 1$). The other a's will then be equal to the correlations between the other variables and variable 5, as shown in the last column of (15-12), and the last row, with all entries equal to unity, need not be written. In this case (15-12) becomes

$$
\begin{array}{llll}
 & a_1 = r_{12}r_{25} & a_1 = r_{13}r_{35} & a_1 = r_{14}r_{45} & a_1 = r_{15} \\
a_2 = r_{15}/r_{12} & & a_2 = r_{23}r_{35} & a_2 = r_{24}r_{45} & a_2 = r_{25}
\end{array}
$$

$$a_3 = r_{15}/r_{13} \quad a_3 = r_{25}/r_{23} \qquad\qquad a_3 = r_{34}r_{45} \quad a_3 = r_{35} \qquad (15\text{-}13)$$
$$a_4 = r_{15}/r_{14} \quad a_4 = r_{25}/r_{24} \quad a_4 = r_{35}/r_{34} \qquad\qquad a_4 = r_{45}$$

Some writers use simply the last column of (15-13) to give estimates of the a's (e.g., Jones, 1959), but these estimates seem a bit too crude, and the writers prefer to use all of the estimates in each row of (15-13).

The elements of (15-13) are easily computed. If we set up a table with the correlations above the diagonal, their reciprocals (omitting the last row) below the diagonal, and bordered at the top by the correlations with variable n (here 5), thus

r_{15}	r_{25}	r_{35}	r_{45}	$r_{55} = 1$
	r_{12}	r_{13}	r_{14}	r_{15}
$1/r_{12}$		r_{23}	r_{24}	r_{25}
$1/r_{13}$	$1/r_{23}$		r_{34}	r_{35}
$1/r_{14}$	$1/r_{24}$	$1/r_{34}$		r_{45}

$$(15\text{-}14)$$

and then multiply the entries in each column by the entry above the upper horizontal line in this array, we will obtain the values given in (15-13). Reciprocals can be read from easily available tables or computed expeditiously on any desk or hand calculator. The estimates of the a's are then the row-averages of (15-13), the reproduced correlations are given by (15-8), and the residuals by (15-9).

Note that there is a fundamental difference between simplex analysis and common-factor analysis. Common-factor analysis is an exploratory procedure. Given a set of intercorrelations we seek a smaller set of rotated factors which account for them, and interpret these factors in terms of the variables on which they have high loadings. Simplex analysis, on the other hand, is a hypothesis-testing procedure. We hypothesize that the pattern of correlations of an ordered set of variables is a simplex pattern. We fit the simplex to the data, compute the reproduced correlation matrix and the residuals, and test the hypothesis that these residuals differ only randomly from a set of zeros. There are no loadings, and we do not know what the factors are except that they represent increasing or decreasing elements of complexity in what is otherwise essentially a single function.

15.2   THE QUASI-SIMPLEX MODEL

With real (empirical) data we are likely to have, in addition to the sampling errors, errors of measurement and specific factors; these latter two taken together make up unique factors as in common-factor analysis. Sampling errors disturb the fit of a simplex only randomly, but unique factors disturb it systematically as well. When unique factors are present, we may have a *quasi-simplex* but not a pure simplex. The quasi-simplex model corresponding to (15-1) is

$$x_1 = f_1 \qquad\qquad\qquad + u_1$$

$$x_2 = f_1 + f_2 \qquad\qquad + u_2 \qquad\qquad\qquad\qquad (15\text{-}15)$$

$$\text{-----------------------------------}$$

$$x_n = f_1 + f_2 + \cdots + f_n + u_n$$

The correlation matrix will still almost always (but not necessarily) show the superdiagonal pattern, with the largest correlations on the superdiagonal; but the drop-off as we go to the right or upward from the superdiagonal will be slower in a quasi-simplex than in a pure simplex. In a quasi-simplex the defining equations, (15-3) and (15-8), will not hold. They *will* hold, however, if we replace the raw correlation matrix by the matrix of *correlations corrected for uniqueness*

$$\rho_{ij} = \frac{r_{ij}}{\sqrt{h_i^2 h_j^2}} . \qquad\qquad\qquad\qquad (15\text{-}16)$$

Here ρ_{ij} is the corrected correlation, r_{ij} is the raw correlation, and h_i^2 and h_j^2 are the communalities.

In application we estimate the initial communalities, compute the correlations corrected for uniqueness, order these corrected correlations if they do not already have a fixed order, as in learning or growth data, fit a simplex to the ordered corrected correlations (yielding a set of estimates of the a's), compute intercorrelations by (15-8) from these a's (yielding a set of reproduced corrected correlations), de-correct these reproduced corrected correlations (yielding a set of reproduced de-corrected correlations), and compare these last with the original correlations to estimate the goodness of fit of the quasi-simplex to the data. The de-correction procedure comes from (15-16); it is

$$r\dagger_{ij} = \rho\dagger_{ij} \sqrt{h_i^2 h_j^2} = \rho\dagger_{ij} h_i h_j, \qquad\qquad\qquad (15\text{-}17)$$

where $r\dagger_{ij}$ is a reproduced de-corrected correlation, $\rho\dagger_{ij}$ is the corresponding reproduced corrected correlation, and h_i^2 and h_j^2 are the communalities.

15.3   FITTING A QUASI-SIMPLEX

In simplex analysis there is no procedure for improving the estimates of the communalities at the conclusion of the analysis, so we should use initial estimates that are as good as we can make them.

15.3.1 Estimating the Communalities

Dubois (1960) has shown that a perfect simplex can be factored into exactly $n/2$ common factors (n even) or $(n - 1)/2$ common factors (n odd). The communalities of the even-numbered variables (when ordered) are all unity, but the communality of each odd-numbered variable is the squared multiple correlation of that variable with all the others (Humphreys, 1960). This situation is to be contrasted with that of the perfect common-factor structure, where in the absence of unique factors, the communalities are *all* unity.

In the quasi-simplex, we must distinguish with some care between these communalities intrinsic to the simplex (1.00 for i even and R_i^2 for i odd) and the uniqueness communalities of the quasi-simplex, $h_i^2 = 1 - u_i^2$ of (15-15). It is only the latter which are used in correcting the correlations for uniqueness by (15-16), and later in de-correcting by (15-17).

We have noted that the number of common factors in a simplex is $n/2$ (n even) or $(n - 1)/2$ (n odd). But in direct common-factor analysis these are the upper limits for unique communalities (Section 5.5.1), and the number of salient common factors is usually appreciably less than $n/2$. The estimates of the uniqueness communalities in simplex analysis should therefore be a little higher than the estimates of the communalities in ordinary common-factor analysis.

In estimating these communalities we encounter the same difficulties that are present in ordinary common-factor analysis. Because the number of common factors is known in advance, we might use repeated refactoring; but convergence would then be to the exact sample communalities, with exact zeros instead of near-zeros on the diagonal of the residual matrix after $n/2$ or $(n - 1)/2$ factors, and there would be some probability of a Heywood or quasi-Heywood case. This procedure, moreover, would not be consistent with our effort to derive a relatively simple procedure for quasi-simplex analysis, and neither would the procedure of modified squared multiple correlation estimates described in Chapter 5.

Because matrices for simplex analysis are usually small, we describe a method of communality estimation adapted to hand and desk calculators (Cureton, 1971), with slight modifications designed to yield estimates likely to be more nearly correct when the number of factors is as large as $n/2$ or $(n - 1)/2$ for n variables, and all the correlations are positive.

We start with the matrix of correlations, with empty diagonal, between the variables in their original order.

1. Find the column sums Σ', where Σ' designates the sum of the $n - 1$ correlations in a column.
2. Find the *mean* of the n values of Σ', and call this mean $\overline{\Sigma}'$.
3. Add to each Σ' the mean $\overline{\Sigma}'$, and call the sum S.
4. In a row labeled r, record the value of the highest correlation in each column.
5. Multiply each S by the value of r just below it, and label this row rS.
6. Find the sum of the n values of r ($= \Sigma r$) and the sum of the n values of rS ($= \Sigma rS$). Find the quotient $Q = \Sigma r/\Sigma rS$.
7. Multiply each value of rS by this quotient, and call the result C.
8. The estimate of each h^2 is then either r or C, whichever is larger.

The logic behind these rules is that when a column sum is high, the highest correlation in the column is likely to be an underestimate of the communality, and when a column sum is low, the highest correlation is likely to be an overestimate. Weighting by the column sums themselves would over-correct, so we weight each r by the column sum plus the average column sum to reduce the relative variability of the weights. In common-factor analysis, the number of factors is usually less than $n/2$ or $(n - 1)/2$, so we weight only those highest r's whose weights will increase their values. The highest r's not weighted are those whose values are likely to be slight over-estimates of the communalities for the smaller number of factors of common-factor analysis, and hence more nearly correct when the number of factors is $n/2$ or $(n - 1)/2$.

15.3.2 Ordering the Variables

If the variables already have a fixed order, as in learning or growth studies, no reordering is permitted. On the other hand, a set of variables may be suspected of forming a quasi-simplex, but the investigator may not be certain that his judgment concerning the order of complexity is correct. The example of the five verbal tests is a case of this sort.

In fitting a quasi-simplex, the investigator should first order the variables according to his best judgment of their increasing or decreasing complexity. Adjustments to this preliminary order are made in terms of the correlations corrected for uniqueness: the order arrived at by considering the raw correlations may be wrong because the communalities of the variables are unequal.

Guttman (1954b) observed that, when a set of variables forming a simplex is correctly ordered, the column sums of the correlation matrix (with empty diagonal) usually increase from the beginning to the middle and then decrease from the middle to the end. This is not a sufficient rule because it does not tell us whether a given variable belongs before or after the middle, and if n is even it does not order the two middle variables. But if we have a preliminary ordering that judgment says is correct or almost correct, it does provide an approximate check, apart from the ordering of the two middle variables if n is even.

When we have an order that is almost correct, Kaiser (1962b) gives a procedure for determining whether two adjacent variables are in the correct order. Working with the *rows* of the correlation matrix corrected for uniqueness, form two rows (P_i and P_{i+1}) of the matrix P (rho), where

$$P_{ij} = \log \rho_{ij} \qquad (i < j)$$

$$P_{ij} = -\log \rho_{ij} \qquad (i > j)$$

$$P_{ij} = 0 \qquad (i = j)$$

$$P_i = \sum_j P_{ij}$$

$$P_{i+1} = \sum_j P_{(i+1)j}$$

that is, P_i and P_{i+1} are the row-sums of the elements of the i-th and the $(i+1)$-th rows of P. Exchange variables i and $(i + 1)$, if and only if

$$P_{i+1} - P_i < 2P_{(i+1)i}. \tag{15-18}$$

Note that the logarithms in the upper right section of P will be negative, while those in the lower left section with be positive. $P_{(i+1)i}$ will be the last entry before the diagonal in row $(i + 1)$.

15.3.3 Finding the *a*'s

When we have the matrix of correlations corrected for uniqueness, with the variables arranged in the correct order, we set up a matrix such as (15-14) with ρ_{ij} replacing r_{ij}. The entries in each column are then multiplied by the entry above the first horizontal line, giving a matrix such as (15-13). In this matrix each row gives $n - 1$ linearly independent estimates of a_i, where i is the row-number. To find the final estimate of each a_i, we average these $n - 1$ estimates.

There are many relations other than those used in (15-13) which could be employed to give additional linearly independent estimates of each a. But their formulas are in general more complicated than those of the elements of (15-13), and many of them involve products and/or quotients of three or more correlations. The average of $n - 1$ individual estimates, moreover, is likely to be at least as accurate as is the estimate of a communality given by the procedure of Section 15.3.1, so the overall gain from averaging more than $n - 1$ estimates would be slight.

15.3.4 Checking the Fit

As soon as we have the n a's (with $a_n = 1$), we find the $n(n - 1)/2$ values of $\rho^\dagger_{ij}$ by the equation,

$$\rho^\dagger_{ij} = a_i/a_j, \tag{15-19}$$

which comes from (15-8). This is the matrix of reproduced corrected correlations. We then use (15-17) with the estimated communalities to find the matrix $R^\dagger$ of reproduced de-corrected correlations. This is the fitted quasi-simplex. Then if R is the original correlation matrix,

$$D = R - R^\dagger \tag{15-20}$$

is the matrix of residuals.

With the method of fitting described above, we do not have any sampling theory leading to an accurate test of significance of the matrix of residuals. We can, however, devise a test that will give us a rough approximation by comparing the root-mean-square residual with the standard error of a correlation coefficient equal in magnitude to the average of the original correlations. We suggest the root-mean-square residual rather than the standard deviation of the residuals because for a perfect fit the mean residual should be zero, and any inflation of the root-mean-square residual over the standard deviation of the residuals which is due to a nonzero mean must be attributed to imperfection of fit. If the root-mean-square residual is less than the standard error, we can say that the fit is good; if it is less than 1.645 times the standard error, we can still say that the simplex or quasi-simplex hypothesis has not been rejected at roughly the .05 level.

If d is the value of one residual, the root-mean-square is

$$RMS(d) = \sqrt{\Sigma' d^2/n'}, \tag{15-21}$$

where Σ' is a summation over the $n(n - 1)/2$ residuals, and $n' = n(n - 1)/2$. Also,

$$\bar{r} = \Sigma' r/n', \tag{15-22}$$

and for a correlation equal to $\bar{r}$

$$\sigma_r = \frac{1 - \bar{r}^2}{\sqrt{N - 1}}. \tag{15-23}$$

15.3.5 Example

To illustrate the fitting of a quasi-simplex, we use again the example of five verbal tests. Table 15.1 shows at the top the original correlations as given in Table 1.1, and the computation of the estimated communalities by the method described in Section 15.3.1. Row h in the middle of the table gives the square roots of these estimated simplex communalities. At the lower left we have the products of the square roots of the communalities, $h_i h_j$, and at the lower right we have the correlations corrected for uniqueness, $\rho_{ij} = r_{ij}/h_i h_j$. The r_{ij} come from the upper right region of the correlation matrix.

The upper part of Table 15.2 shows the complete matrix of the ρ_{ij} with variables 1 and 5 interchanged so that all variables are in the correct order of complexity as indicated in Section 15.1.1. The tests for correct order should properly be applied to the corrected correlations because unequal communalities may disturb the order of the uncorrected correlations. The largest column sum is that of column (2), and those to its right decrease. Guttman's observation, which says that column (3) should have the largest sum, is violated, so we use Kaiser's test to see whether variables 2 and 3 should be interchanged in the order.

TABLE 15.1

Intercorrelations of Five Verbal Tests, Estimation of Simplex Communalities,
$h_i h_j$ Products, and Corrections for Uniqueness ρ_{ij} (N = 841)

Test	(1)	(2)	(3)	(4)	(5)	Σ	Ch (r)
1) Paragraph Meaning		.585	.658	.616	.555	2.414	.658
2) Same-Opposite	.585		.663	.634	.689	2.571	.689
3) Proverb Matching	.658	.663		.697	.626	2.644	.697
4) Verbal Analogies	.616	.634	.697		.598	2.545	.697
5) Vocabulary	.555	.689	.626	.598		2.468	.689

			(1)	(2)	(3)	(4)	(5)		
$\bar{\Sigma}' = 2.528$]		Σ'	2.414	2.571	2.644	2.545	2.468	12.642	12.642
	$\Sigma' + \bar{\Sigma}' = S$		4.942	5.099	5.172	2.073	4.996	25.282	25.284
		r	.658	.689	.697	.697	.689	3.430	3.430
$Q = \dfrac{\Sigma r}{\Sigma rS} = .19772$]		rS	3.252	3.513	3.605	3.536	3.442	17.348	17.348
	$QrS = C$		.643	.695	.713	.699	.681	3.430	3.430
	larger of r or $C = h^2$		.658	.695	.713	.699	.689	3.454	3.454
		h	.81117	.83367	.84439	.83606	.83006		

		$h_i h_j$					$\rho_{ij} = r_{ij}/h_i h_j$		
Test	(2)	(3)	(4)	(5)	Test	(2)	(3)	(4)	(5)
(1)	.6762	.6849	.6782	.6733	(1)	.8651	.9607	.9083	.8243
(2)		.7039	.6970	.6920	(2)		.9419	.9096	.9957
(3)			.7060	.7009	(3)			.9873	.8931
(4)				.6940	(4)				.8617

The second section of Table 15.2 shows this test. Rows (2) and (3) contain the logarithms of the entries in rows (2) and (3) of the first section: negative above the diagonal and positive below it. The row sums are $P_i = P_2$ and $P_{i+1} = P_3$; and $P_{(i+1)i}$ is $P_{32} = .02646$, which is enclosed in parentheses. Then $P_{i+1} - P_i > 2P_{(i+1)i}$, and by (15-18) we see that variables 2 and 3 should not be changed in the ordering. Thus Guttman's observation is not a strict rule.

The third section of Table 15.2 shows the array of (15-14), substituting ρ_{ij} for r_{ij}. Above the diagonal we have the ρ_{ij} which are above the diagonal in the first section. Below the diagonal we have the reciprocals of the ρ_{ij} which are below the diagonal in the first section, omitting the last row (1). The entries of row (1) are at the top of this section, set apart from the others by a horizontal line as in (15-14). In the fourth section we have the estimates of the a's. Each of these is the corresponding entry in the third section multiplied by the value of ρ_{ij} at the top as in (15-13). At the right of the fourth section we have the row sums and averages, the latter being the final estimates of the a's, with $a_1 = 1$.

TABLE 15.2
Ordered Corrected Correlations, Kaiser's Test of Order for Tests 2 and 3,
and Computations of a's for Five Verbal Tests ($N = 841$)

Test	(5)	(2)	(3)	(4)	(1)
			Ordered ρ_{ij}		
(5)		.9957	.8931	.8617	.8243
(2)	.9957		.9419	.9096	.8651
(3)	.8931	.9419		.8973	.9607
(4)	.8617	.9096	.8973		.9083
(1)	.8243	.8651	.9607	.9083	
Σ'	3.5748	3.7123	3.6930	3.5769	3.5584

		Test of Order for Tests 2 and 3			Σ
$i = (2)$	.00187		$-.02646$	$-.04115$	$-.06293$	$-.12867 = P_i$
$i + 1 = (3)$	.04910	(.02646)		$-.04225$	$-.01741$	$.01590 = P_{i+1}$

Order correct: .05292 $=$ $2P_{(i+1)i} < .14457 = P_{i+1} - P_i$

			ρ's and Reciprocals		
(1)	.8243	.8651	.9607	.9083	1.0000
(5)		.9957	.8931	.8617	.8243
(2)	1.0043		.9419	.9096	.8651
(3)	1.1197	1.0617		.8973	.9607
(4)	1.1605	1.0994	1.1145		.9083

			Estimates of a's				a_j
(5)		.8614	.8580	.7827	.8243	3.3264	.8316
(2)	.8278		.9049	.8262	.8651	3.4240	.8560
(3)	.9230	.9185		.8150	.9607	3.6172	.9043
(4)	.9566	9511	1.0707		.9083	3.8867	.9717
							$a_1 = 1.0000$

In Table 15.1 the variables in all of the matrices are in the original order. In Table 15.2 they are all in the revised order. Table 15.3 starts with the reproduced $\rho\dagger_{ij}$ matrix at the upper left, with the elements computed by (15-19) from the a_j in the last column of the fourth matrix of Table 15.2. These entries are still in the revised order. We can carry out the test of fit with the variables in either order. Using the original order we need only to reorder this $\rho\dagger_{ij}$ matrix, whereas if we were to use the revised order we would have to reorder both the h_ih_j matrix and the original correlation matrix of Table 15.1. At the upper right of Table 15.3 we have the reordered $\rho\dagger_{ij}$ matrix, again interchanging variables 1 and 5.

TABLE 15.3
Reproduced $\rho^\dagger_{ij}$, Reproduced $r^\dagger_{ij}$ Residuals d_{ij}, and Test of Significance
for Five Verbal Tests ($N = 841$)

Reproduced $\rho^\dagger_{ij} = a_i/a_j$					*Reordered Reproduced $\rho\dagger_{ij}$*			
Test	(2)	(3)	(4)	(1)	*Test*	(2)	(3)	(4)	(5)
(5)	.9715	.9196	.8558	.8316	(1)	.8560	.9043	.9717	.8316
(2)		.9466	.8809	.8560	(2)		.9466	.8809	.9715
(3)			.9306	.9043	(3)			.9306	.9196
(4)				.9717	(4)				.8558

Reproduced $r^\dagger_{ij} = \rho^\dagger_{ij}h_ih_j$					*Residuals: $d_{ij} = r_{ij} - r^\dagger_{ij}$*			
	(2)	(3)	(4)	(5)		(2)	(3)	(4)	(5)
(1)	.579	.619	.659	.560	(1)	.006	−.039	−.043	−.005
(2)		.666	.614	.672	(2)		−.003	.020	.017
(3)			.657	.645	(3)			.040	−.019
(4)				.594	(4)				.004

Test of Fit

$\Sigma d^2 =$	.006106	$\Sigma' r =$	6.321
$\overline{d^2} =$	.0006106	$\bar{r} =$	.6321
$\sqrt{\overline{d^2}} =$	.0247	$\bar{r}^2 =$	.39955
		$1 - \bar{r}^2 =$	.60045
		$N - 1 =$	840
		$\sqrt{N-1} =$	28.98
		$\sigma_r =$	.02072
		$1.645\,\sigma_r =$	.0341

The reproduced raw correlation matrix, $r^\dagger_{ij}$, is shown at the left center of Table 15.3. Each element is an element of the reordered $\rho^\dagger_{ij}$ matrix times the corresponding element of matrix h_ih_j from Table 15.1. The residuals d_{ij} are at the right center of Table 15.3. Each entry is an entry from the upper right region of the original correlation matrix at the top of Table 15.1, minus the corresponding entry in the reproduced $r^\dagger_{ij}$ matrix. These residuals are fairly small, the largest in absolute value being $d_{14} = -.043$.

The test of fit is given at the bottom of Table 15.3. The left column shows the computation of the root-mean-square residuals by (15-21); the right column shows the computation of the standard error of a correlation coefficient equal in magnitude to the average correlation in the original table, by (15-22) and (15-23). The last line shows that, though the root-mean-square $\sqrt{\overline{d^2}}$ is a little larger than the standard error σ_r, it is appreciably smaller than $1.645\sigma_r$. We conclude that the fit is fairly good.

Exercise 15:1. The tabulation below shows the intercorrelations among six arithmetic tests (Thurstone, 1938a).[1] Fit a quasi-simplex to these correlations; check the order of the ρ_{ij} by Guttman's rough rule; test the order of tests 3 and 4 by Kaiser's procedure; and test the fit of the simplex to the data ($N = 240$).

Test	(2)	(3)	(4)	(5)	(6)
(1) Addition	.62	.62	.54	.29	.28
(2) Subtraction		.67	.53	.38	.37
(3) Multiplication			.62	.48	.52
(4) Division				.62	.57
(5) Arithmetic Reasoning					.64
(6) Numerical Judgment					

Note. The correlations in this study are tetrachoric correlations, with each variable dichotomized at or close to the median. The standard error of a tetrachoric correlation is considerably larger than that of a product-moment correlation. For these data, $\bar{r} = .51667$ and $\sigma_r = .08146$.

[1]From Table 2, p. 111, Thurstone, 1938a. Copyright 1938 by The University of Chicago. Reprinted by permission.

16

Some Special Problems

16.1 MEASURE OF SAMPLING ADEQUACY

In the preceding chapters we have noted from time to time that certain correlation matrices were unsuitable for common-factor analysis. Guttman (1940, 1953) has shown that if a correlation matrix R is to be suitable for common-factor analysis, R^{-1} must approach a diagonal matrix as the number of variables n increases while the number of factors remains constant. For any particular correlation matrix, with n given, Kaiser and Rice (1974) proposed a measure of sampling adequacy (MSA) indicating how near R^{-1} is to a diagonal matrix. This measure is

$$MSA = \frac{\sum\sum_{i<j} r_{ij}^2}{\sum\sum_{i<j} r_{ij}^2 + \sum\sum_{i<j} q_{ij}^2},\tag{16-1}$$

where $Q = SR^{-1}S$, and $S = (diag\ R^{-1})^{-1/2}$. The term $\sum\sum_{i<j} r_{ij}^2$ is the sum of squares of the upper off-diagonal elements of the correlation matrix R. The term $\sum\sum_{i<j} q_{ij}^2$ is the sum of squares of the upper off-diagonal elements of the matrix Q. The diagonal elements of the diagonal matrix S are the square roots of the reciprocals of the diagonal elements of R^{-1}, and Q is R^{-1} with each row *and* each column multiplied by the corresponding diagonal element of S.

As MSA approaches unity, the correlation matrix becomes more and more suitable for common-factor analysis, and Kaiser and Rice suggest that if $MSA < .5$ the correlation matrix is unacceptable for factor-analytic purposes.

16.1.1 Example

For the five-verbal-tests example, R^{-1} is given in Table 13.1 and repeated at the top of Table 16.1. In Table 16.1, R^{-1} is bordered at the bottom by $(diag\ R^{-1})^{-1}$ and at the left by $diag\ S$. Each element of $(diag\ R^{-1})^{-1}$ is the reciprocal of the corresponding element on the diagonal of R^{-1}, and each element of $diag\ S$ is the square root of the corresponding element of $(diag\ R^{-1})^{-1}$.

The second section of Table 16.1 shows the matrix SR^{-1}. Each row of SR^{-1} is the corresponding row of R^{-1} times the element of $diag\ S$ at the left of that row. Only the elements of SR^{-1} on and above the diagonal are shown. This matrix is bordered at the bottom by the elements of $diag\ S$.

TABLE 16.1
Computation of *MSA* for Five Verbal Tests (N = 841)

diag S			R^{-1}		
.70337	2.0213	−.2875	−.6832	−.4514	−.2261
.63971	−.2875	2.4436	−.5503	−.4409	−.9160
.61462	−.6832	−.5503	2.6472	−.8373	−.3981
.65523	−.4514	−.4409	−.8373	2.3292	−.3144
.67514	−.2261	−.9160	−.3981	−.3144	2.1939
$(diag\ R^{-1})^{-1}$	.49473	.40923	.37776	.42933	.45581
			SR^{-1}		
	1.42172	−.20221	−.48054	−.31750	−.15903
		1.56320	−.35203	−.28205	−.58597
			1.62702	−.51462	−.24468
				1.52616	−.20600
					1.48119
diag S	.70337	.63971	.61462	.65523	.67514
			$Q = SR^{-1}S$		
	1	−.1294	−.2953	−.2080	−.1074
		1	−.2164	−.1848	−.3956
			1	−.3372	−.1652
				1	−.1391
					1

$$\sum_{i<j}\sum q_{ij}^2 = .5566; \quad \sum_{i<j}\sum r_{ij}^2 = 4.0142$$

$$MSA = \frac{4.0142}{4.0142 + .5566} = .88$$

The third section of Table 16.1 shows the matrix $Q = SR^{-1}S$. Each column of Q is the corresponding column of SR^{-1} times the element of *diag S* directly below it. The diagonal elements of Q are all unity within rounding error, which checks the computation of SR^{-1} and Q if each element of *diag S* is taken as a repeat multiplier in these computations.

The final computations for *MSA* are shown at the bottom of Table 16.1. $\sum\sum_{i<j} q_{ij}^2$ is the sum of squares of the elements of Q, exclusive of the unities on the diagonal. $\sum\sum_{i<j} r_{ij}^2$ is the sum of squares of the elements of R in Table 1.1, not including the reliabilities.

The value $MSA = .88$ indicates that the five-verbal-tests data are very well suited for common-factor analysis: this value is appreciably closer to unity than to the Kaiser–Rice critical value .5.

16.2 COMPARISON OF FACTORS

When two studies based on samples from different populations include all or a considerable number of the same variables, and when all or most of the rotated factors are interpreted similarly, we may wish to know how closely the pairs of corresponding factors resemble each other. The populations may differ in age, sex, socioeconomic status, variability of scores on the variables, and the like. For proper comparison we should note two points: (1) similar factoring procedures should be used in both studies; (2) rotation must be guided by the *simple-structure* criterion. It is advisable to use the refinement procedures of Chapter 10 to obtain the best possible simple structure for each study.

A number of procedures have been developed for factor comparison.

16.2.1 Coefficient of Congruence

This procedure is useful only when the score variabilities of the two samples are equal or very nearly equal, either originally or after some appropriate transformation. The formula is

$$CC = \frac{\sum\limits_{}^{n} \ell_1 \ell_2}{\sqrt{\left(\sum\limits_{}^{n} l_1^2\right)\left(\sum\limits_{}^{n} l_2^2\right)}} , \tag{16-2}$$

where ℓ_1 and ℓ_2 are the loadings on corresponding rotated factors from the two studies, and n is the number of variables common to these studies. This formula resembles the formula for the correlation coefficient except that the deviations are from zero rather than from the means, so that differences in average magnitude and variability of the loadings, as well as differences in relative magnitude, affect CC, and it will equal unity only if the pairs of loadings are identical.

The reference-vector structure V for the WAIS age-group 25–34 is shown in Table 11.1. This matrix is copied into the upper left section of Table 16.2 as V_y.

The WAIS was also given to a group of 150 men and 150 women ($N = 300$) from the age-group 45–54 (Wechsler, 1955, p. 17). The writers factored this correlation matrix by the principal-axes method to three factors and rotated to simple structure by the method of extended vectors. The simple structure was not good: the extended-vector picture tended toward that of Fig. 7.15, with four bounding planes instead of only three. A four-factor solution gave a better fit, but we had to retain factor d of the F-matrix with only the one highest loading, .259, higher than .167, and eigenvalue only .180. Furthermore the nonverbal reasoning factor of the three-factor solution now split into two: one with high loadings on 9 (Block Design) and 11 (Object Assembly), and the other with high loadings on 7 (Digit Symbol) and 10 (Picture Arrangement). Test 8 (Picture Completion) had low nonzero loadings (.183 and .182) on both of these factors. These two factors are not readily interpretable.

For comparison purposes, therefore, we accepted the three-factor solution, giving factors roughly comparable to those of the solution for the age-group 25–34. The reference-vector structure, V_x, is shown in the upper left middle section of Table 16.2, with the F-matrix at the far upper right.

For this comparison we did not refine the extended-vector simple structure by the methods of Chapter 10 because the comparison is used here for illustrative purposes only; and the simple structure was quite accurately determined by the extended-vector procedure even though it was intrinsically a poor simple structure from the standpoint of interpretation.

Assuming that the score variabilities are not very different in the two age-groups, and hence that the two sets of loadings are of comparable magnitudes, we compute the three coefficents of congruence by (16–2). The computations of $\Sigma \ell^2$ and $\sqrt{\Sigma \ell^2}$ for each column are shown just below the matrices V_y and V_x, and the final computations for $\Sigma \ell_x \ell_y$, $\sqrt{\Sigma \ell_x^2} \sqrt{\Sigma \ell_y^2}$, and CC in the three added lines below V_x.

It has been suggested that if corresponding factors from two studies are really the same factor, the coefficient of congruence should be at least .90. Thus we see from the CC-row of Table 16.2, below V_x, that factor I (nonverbal reasoning) is clearly the same factor in both age-groups ($CC = .96$). Factor II (numerical ability) is appreciably different in the two groups ($CC = .82$), and factor III (verbal) is similar but just fails to meet the .90 criterion ($CC = .89$). Note that it is factor I which split into two in the four-factor solution for the age-group 45–54.

16.2.2 Transformation Analysis

If the score variabilities are different in two groups, and if these differences are due to unequal variability on only one differentiating variable (e.g., age), the correlations in the group that varies more on the differentiating variable will be generally higher and more variable, and the loadings will tend to be a little higher and more variable also. We assumed equal variability for the WAIS data only because the age ranges in the two groups were equal (25–34 and 45–54). Even here the assumption may be in error: score variabilities and hence the mean values and variabilities of factor loadings might tend to increase or decrease as people grow older.

Ahmavaara (1954) suggests a procedure for dealing with this situation, which he terms transformation analysis. He regards one group as a criterion group, and performs a Procrustes transformation on the other group to make it as similar to the criterion group as is possible by means of a linear transformation. Though Ahmavaara makes the comparison graphically, by plotting pairs of corresponding loadings on the criterion factor matrix and the other transformed factor matrix, we can just as well use the coefficients of congruence to obtain numerical comparisons.

The Procrustes transformation is applied to the unrotated factor matrix F_x of the group to be transformed, with V_y, the reference-vector-structure matrix of the criterion group, taken as the hypothesis matrix. The equations are

$$L_x = (F_x'F_x)^{-1}F_x'V_y \tag{16-3}$$

$$\hat{V}_x = F_xL_x, \tag{16-4}$$

where $\hat{V}_x$ is the transformed reference-vector structure. The corresponding columns of $\hat{V}_x$ and V_y are then compared for agreement by means of the coefficient of congruence. We do *not* normalize the columns of L_x in (16-4) because the hypothesis matrix V_y is the actual matrix to be approximated by $\hat{V}_x$, and is not itself merely an approximation with columns roughly proportional to those of V_y. Thus $\hat{V}_x$ is the best approximation to V_y attainable by means of a linear transformation of F_x, and this transformation is *not* constrained to be a *rotation* of the axes of F_x.

For the WAIS data the computations of the transformation are shown in the lower portion of Table 16.2. We take V_y, the reference-vector-structure for the age-group 25–34 as the criterion matrix, and transform F_x to correspond as nearly as possible to it. Because F_x is a *principal-axes* factor matrix, $F_x'F_x = D_x$, a diagonal matrix of the eigenvalues of R_x^*. Thus (16-3) becomes

$$L_x = D_x^{-1}F_x'V_y. \tag{16-5}$$

We record these eigenvalues as *diag* D_x below V_y; they are the sums of squares of the elements in the columns of F_x. In the line below we show *diag* D_x^{-1}, whose elements are the reciprocals of those of *diag* D_x.

TABLE 16.2
Comparison of WAIS Factors for Age-Groups 25–34 and 45–54, and Transformation Analysis ($N_x = N_y = 300$)

Test	V_y I	V_y II	V_y III	V_x I	V_x II	V_x III	$\hat{V}_x = F_x L_x$ I	$\hat{V}_x = F_x L_x$ II	$\hat{V}_x = F_x L_x$ III	F_x a	F_x b	F_x c
(1)	.003	.214	.234	−.030	.326	.357	−.065	.206	.280	.881	−.226	.058
(2)	.066	−.081	.418	.044	.218	.358	.006	.132	.261	.803	−.168	−.019
(3)	.018	.380	−.045	−.030	.452	.007	.019	.346	.002	.792	−.012	.321
(4)	−.009	.141	.262	.136	.098	.413	.085	.045	.280	.782	−.128	−.131
(5)	−.018	.367	−.058	.031	.322	−.007	.075	.256	−.024	.640	.043	.236
(6)	−.066	.085	.420	−.028	.262	.484	−.096	.141	.382	.882	−.303	−.051
(7)	.152	.130	.076	.230	.057	.247	.220	.047	.122	.708	.049	−.077
(8)	.339	.003	.100	.341	−.003	.251	.339	.016	.093	.785	.138	−.120
(9)	.492	.057	−.098	.423	.011	−.017	.488	.072	−.143	.701	.369	.024
(10)	.278	.091	.055	.326	−.062	.346	.296	−.044	.174	.737	.066	−.210
(11)	.558	−.094	−.059	.416	−.011	.017	.471	−.049	−.114	.679	.342	−.009
$\Sigma \ell^2$	.7782	.3958	.5118	.6514	.5474	.9048	.7376	.2790	.4587			
$\sqrt{\Sigma \ell^2}$	.8822	.6291	.7154	.8071	.7399	.9512	.8588	.5282	.6773			
$\Sigma \ell_x \ell_y$				.6838	.3815	.6083	.7383	.2788	.4586			
$\sqrt{\Sigma \ell_x^2} \sqrt{\Sigma \ell_y^2}$				.7120	.4655	.6805	.7576	.3323	.4845			
CC				.96	.82	.89	.97	.84	.95			

$F'_x V_y$

	I	II	III
a	1.2955	.9822	1.1085
b	.4534	−.06566	−.3210
c	−.09898	.1765	−.1095

$L_x = D_x^{-1} F'_x V_y$

	I	II	III
a	.2005	.1520	.1716
b	.9680	−.1402	−.6853
c	−.4003	.6976	−.4428

	a	b	c
diag D_x	6.4604	.4684	.2473
diag D_x^{-1}	.1548	2.135	4.044

At the center we have $F'_x V_y$. Each element is the sum of products of the elements in one column of F_x and one column of V_y. There is no check more convenient than doing these computations twice.

At the lower right we have the matrix L_x as given by (16-5). The elements in each row are those in the corresponding row of $F'_x V_y$ times the element of *diag* D_x^{-1} lettered the same as that row.

At the upper right middle of Table 16.2 we have the matrix $\hat{V}_x = F_x L_x$, and below it the computations for the coefficient of congruence when we compare it to V_y. Factors I (nonverbal reasoning) and III (verbal) are clearly the same now as those of V_y, but the agreement of factor II (numerical) remains only fair. The transformation improves the agreement of factors I and II only slightly, but the agreement of factor III is improved considerably.

Ahmavaara goes on to compute a "comparison matrix"

$$L_n \Lambda_y \Delta_y^{-1}, \tag{16-6}$$

where L_n is L_x normalized by *rows*, Λ_y is defined by $F_y \Lambda_y = V_y$, and Δ_y^{-1} has diagonal elements which are the reciprocals of those of the diagonal matrix Δ_y which normalizes the columns of $(\Lambda'_y)^{-1}$. He says, however, (personal communication), that our use of the coefficients of congruence for the comparison is preferable, so we do not illustrate the use of (16-6).

We chose the WAIS age-group 25–34 as the criterion group both because the solution is "cleaner" and because further aging seemed likely to increase the score variabilities.

16.2.3 Factorial Invariance

We have seen that as people grow older their abilities (at least as these are measured by WAIS) become more specialized. In the age-group 18–19 there were only two factors. In the 25–34 group there were clearly three: the verbal-numerical factor of the younger age-group splits into separate verbal and numerical factors. In the 45–54 group there is a suggestion of a further split of the nonverbal reasoning factor into two such factors. As each group consisted half of men and half of women, an age-by-sex interaction may have contributed to this effect.

There has been some controversy concerning the effects of selection on factorial invariance. If two otherwise similar groups differ on only one variable (univariate selection), the simple-structure factors should be the same in the two groups. But if they differ on more than one variable, as seems likely with real groups, the correlations among the selection variables, which are usually not measured directly, will tend to generate additional factors in the measured variables of the group which is more variable on the selection variables. Thurstone tends to minimize the significance of these added factors; Thomson tends to emphasize them. Detailed treatments may be found in Thurstone (1947, Chapters

XVI and XIX) and in Thomson (1951, Chapters XVIII and XIX). Mulaik (1972, Chapter 14) also discusses these problems.

16.3   EXTENSION ANALYSIS

When n variables covering a specified domain are factored to obtain m rotated factors, we may have in addition one or more variables not properly a part of the domain and wish to know how they load on the factors defined by the variables of the domain. If the domain is defined, say, by a battery of aptitude tests, the additional variables may be such things as age, sex, grade-point average, or scores on a general intelligence test.

If the added variable is likely to be loaded substantially on *all* of the factors, we have described one procedure in Section 8.4: namely to include the added variable in the initial analysis, rotate first by the diagonal method so that the added variable defines a general factor, and then rotate the residuals to simple structure.

If the added variable does not define a general factor, and in some cases even if it does, its inclusion in the original analysis may enlarge the domain improperly and hence distort the results somewhat. Thus in the case of the problem of seven reasoning and perseveration tests, the inclusion of age as a variable tended to generate a small third factor. In this case we might prefer to define the reasoning-perseveration domain by the first six tests only and then extend the analysis to include the age variable without disturbing the factorial structure of the other six tests.

The intercorrelations among the six reasoning and perseveration tests were first factored by the centroid method. The correlations are shown in the first six rows and columns of Table 2.9, with test 6 reflected at the outset. With two factors the per cent of trace was 97, so refactoring was not used. The unrotated loadings are shown in rows (1)–(6) of the F-matrix at the upper left of Table 16.3. Because variable 7 (Age) is not included in this analysis, the F-matrix of Table 16.3 differs from the first six rows of both the initial and refactored two-factor matrices of Table 2.9.

To add a variable, say t, by extension, we must solve for T the normal equations (Dwyer, 1937)

$$F'FT = F'R_t, \tag{16-7}$$

where F is the unrotated factor matrix or an *orthogonal* rotation thereof, T is the vector of the m desired factor loadings of the added variable t, and R_t is the vector of correlations between the variable t and the variables initially factored.

The elements r_{it} of R_t are shown in the third column of Table 16.3. They come from column (7) of Table 2.9 after reflection and represent the variable "Youngness" (Age reversed). Note that r_{t6} ($= .340$) remains positive because variables t and 6 were both reflected. The normal equations are shown below h^2 and V in Table 16.3. The diagonal coefficients are the sums of squares of the elements in columns a and b of F, and the off-diagonal coefficients are both the sum of products of the pairs of elements of F. The constants in column 0 of these normal equations are the sums of products of the elements in columns a and b of F and the entries in column r_{it}.

The normal equations are solved in the usual manner (not shown here), and the solutions are entered in row t of the matrix F: namely .3601 and $-.0677$.

If initial factoring is done by the *principal-axes* method, the off-diagonal coefficients of the normal equations will all be zero. In this case the solution for each element of T is simply an element in column 0 divided by the diagonal element in the same row. If we assume that the off-diagonal elements .1317 are negligible in the present example, we obtain the results shown in the last row $\hat{t}$ of

TABLE 16.3
Extension Analysis: Six Reasoning and Perseveration Tests (N = 86)

		F				V		V (7)[b]	
Var	a	b	r_{it}[a]	h^2	I	II	I	II
(1)	.4548	$-.3532$	.120	.3316	$(-.056)$	.510	$(-.080)$	.478
(2)	.7965	.0802	.270	.6408	.492	.256	.403	.324
(3)	.6151	$-.0169$	.200	.3786	.314	.269	.314	.237
(4)	.7617	.3586	.180	.7088	.709	$(-.012)$	.707	$(-.021)$
(5)	.7076	.3080	.320	.5956	.638	$(.012)$	.645	$(.020)$
$-$(6)	.6879	$-.3667$	.340	.6077	$(.056)$	.618	$(-.023)$	.714
t	.3601	$-.0677$		.1343	.135	.210	$(.103)$	.234
Σ(6)[c]	4.0236	.0100		3.2631	2.153	1.653		
$\hat{t}$	.3570	.1087		Ch 3.2631	2.153	1.653		

	Λ			Normal Equations		
	I	II		a	b	0
a	.5330	.4131	a	2.7737	.1317	.9901
b	.8461	$-.9107$	b	.1317	.4894	.01432

(1) Critical Flicker Frequency
(2) Digit Symbol (WAIS)
(3) Porteus Maze
(4) Thurstone PMA Reasoning (untimed)

(5) Raven Progressive Matrices
$-$(6) Wisconsin Card Sorting (avoidance of perseverative errors)
t Age reversed ("Youngness")

[a] From Table 2.9 (reflected).
[b] From Table 2.10.
[c] Sum of first six entries.

F. The approximation to the a-loading (.3570 for .3601) is good; the approximation to the b-loading (.1087 for $-.0677$) is not so good. With a centroid factor matrix the full solution of the normal equations appears to be required.

The matrix F, including the added row t, was rotated to oblique simple structure, using only the original six rows to obtain the transformation matrix Λ. The rotation was done by the outer-centroids method, using the centroid of variables 1 and 6 for column I of Λ, the centroid of variables 4 and 5 for column II, and Fig. 2.2 (oblique case). The transformation matrix Λ is shown below the matrix F in Table 16.3, and the rotated factor matrix V at the right of column h^2. The transformation is applied to row t of F as well as to rows (1)–(6). The near-zero entries in each column of V are enclosed in parentheses.

In the last two columns of Table 16.3 we show as V (7) the rotated factor matrix of Table 2.10, in which the variable "Youngness" was included in the original analysis instead of being added by extension. Factor I is clearly reasoning and II is resistance to perseveration. The simple structure and the definitions of the factors are somewhat clearer in V than in V (7). In V the variable "Youngness" has a substantial though low loading on the reasoning factor, while in V (7) its loading on this factor is a poor near-zero (.103).

Dwyer's procedure, as described above, is the one most commonly used for adding a variable by extension. In this procedure the extension must be to an *orthogonal* factor matrix, usually an F-matrix. An alternative procedure, based on somewhat different assumptions, by which a variable may be added by extension directly to an oblique factor matrix, is given by Harman (1938). His basic assumption is slightly more logical than is Dwyer's, but requires much more computation, including the solution of a set of n simultaneous equations rather than only m, and there is no shortening of the solution when initial factoring is by the principal-axes method.

APPENDICES

1

Answers to Problems and Exercises

Problem 1.1.2:1

Alternative 1. Leadership consists of two distinct traits, consideration and structure. These two traits are fairly highly correlated.

Alternative 2. All four ratings reflect one general trait of leadership. Ratings 1 and 2 reflect an additional trait, consideration; ratings 3 and 4 reflect another additional trait, structure. The three traits are uncorrelated.

Alternative 3. Leadership consists essentially in being considerate. Ratings 1 and 2 draw more heavily on it than do ratings 3 and 4. Initiating and maintaining structure is a less general trait, accounting for the high correlation between ratings 3 and 4. The two traits are uncorrelated.

Alternative 4. Leadership consists essentially in initiating and maintaining structure in the group led. Ratings 3 and 4 draw more heavily on it than do ratings 1 and 2. Consideration is a less general trait, accounting for the high correlation between ratings 1 and 2. The two traits are uncorrelated.

Problem 1.2:1

The general factor is C.
The unique factors are U_1, U_2, U_3, and U_4.
The doublet is A.
The group factor which is not a doublet is B.

Problem 1.5.3:1

$$X_1 = a_1A + u_1U_1$$
$$X_2 = a_2A$$

$$r_{12} = \frac{SX_1X_2}{N\sigma_1\sigma_2} = \frac{S(a_1A + u_1U_1)a_2A}{N\sigma_1\sigma_2}$$

$$= \frac{a_1a_2SA^2 + u_1a_2SAU_1}{N\sigma_1\sigma_2}$$

But $SA^2/N = \sigma_A^2$; $SAU_1/N = \sigma_{AU_1} = 0$ by the basic assumption preceding (1-6). Hence

$$r_{12} = \frac{a_1a_2\sigma_A^2}{\sigma_1\sigma_2} \ .$$

But with standard scores, $\sigma_1 = \sigma_2 = \sigma_A = \sigma_A^2 = 1$, and

$$r_{12} = a_1a_2.$$

This is precisely (1-8), and by the argument following Theorem 1.1 the proposition of this problem is proved.

Problem 1.5.5:1

$$t_{123} = \frac{r_{12}r_{13}}{r_{23}} \ ; \ t_{213} = \frac{r_{12}r_{23}}{r_{13}} \ ; \ t_{312} = \frac{r_{13}r_{23}}{r_{12}}$$

$$r_{12} = .16; \quad r_{13} = .08; \quad r_{23} = .32$$

$$t_{123} = .32\overline{).0128}^{.04}; \ t_{213} = .08\overline{).0512}^{.64}; \ t_{312} = .16\overline{).0256}^{.16}$$

Theorem 1.3 is satisfied: all three triads are positive and less than 1.

$a_1 = \sqrt{.04} = .2;$	$a_2 = \sqrt{.64} = .8;$	$a_3 = \sqrt{.16} = .4$
$u_1 = \sqrt{1 - .04}$	$u_2 = \sqrt{1 - .64}$	$u_3 = \sqrt{1 - .16}$
$= \sqrt{.96}$	$= \sqrt{.36}$	$= \sqrt{.84}$
$= .9798$	$= .6$	$= .9165$

Problem 1.5.7:1

$$r_{12} = .400 \quad r_{14} = .150 \quad r_{24} = .150$$
$$r_{13} = .200 \quad r_{23} = .200 \quad r_{34} = .075$$

$$\left.\begin{array}{l} t_{1234} = r_{12}r_{34} - r_{13}r_{24} = 0 \\ t_{1243} = r_{12}r_{34} - r_{14}r_{23} = 0 \\ t_{1342} = r_{13}r_{24} - r_{14}r_{23} = 0 \end{array}\right\} \quad \text{so Theorem 1.7 holds.}$$

$a_1^2 = t_{123} = .4$	$a_2^2 = t_{213} = .4$	$a_3^2 = t_{312} = .1$	$a_4^2 = t_{412} = .05625$
$a_1^2 = t_{124} = .4$	$a_2^2 = t_{214} = .4$	$a_3^2 = t_{314} = .1$	$a_4^2 = t_{413} = .05625$
$a_1^2 = t_{134} = .4$	$a_2^2 = t_{234} = .4$	$a_3^2 = t_{324} = .1$	$a_4^2 = t_{423} = .05625$
$a_1 = .6325$	$a_2 = .6325$	$a_3 = .3162$	$a_4 = .2372$
$u_1^2 = .6$	$u_2^2 = .6$	$u_3^2 = .9$	$u_4^2 = .94375$
$u_1 = .7746$	$u_2 = .7746$	$u_3 = .9487$	$u_4 = .9715$

Problem 1.5.8:1

$$r_{12} = \quad .18 \qquad r_{14} = -.15 \qquad r_{24} = -.30$$
$$r_{13} = -.12 \qquad r_{23} = -.24 \qquad r_{34} = \quad .20$$

$$\left. \begin{array}{l} t_{1234} = r_{12}r_{34} - r_{13}r_{24} = 0 \\ t_{1243} = r_{12}r_{34} - r_{14}r_{23} = 0 \\ t_{1342} = r_{13}r_{24} - r_{14}r_{23} = 0 \end{array} \right\} \quad \text{so Theorem 1.7 holds.}$$

$a_1^2 = t_{123} = .09$	$a_2^2 = t_{213} = .36$	$a_3^2 = t_{312} = .16$	$a_4^2 = t_{412} = .25$
$(r_{12}+)$	$(r_{12}+)$	$(r_{12}+)$	$(r_{12}+)$
$a_1^2 = t_{124} = .09$	$a_2^2 = t_{214} = .36$	$a_3^2 = t_{314} = .16$	$a_4^2 = t_{413} = .25$
$(r_{12}+)$	$(r_{12}+)$	$(r_{34}+)$	$(r_{34}+)$
$a_1^2 = t_{134} = .09$	$a_2^2 = t_{234} = .36$	$a_3^2 = t_{324} = .16$	$a_4^2 = t_{423} = .25$
$(r_{34}+)$	$(r_{34}+)$	$(r_{34}+)$	$(r_{34}+)$

$$\begin{array}{llll} a_1 = \quad .3 & a_2 = \quad .6 & a_3 = -.4 & a_4 = -.5 \\ \text{or} \quad a_1 = -.3 & a_2 = -.6 & a_3 = \quad .4 & a_4 = \quad .5 \end{array}$$

$$\begin{array}{llll} u_1^2 = .91 & u_2^2 = .64 & u_3^2 = .84 & u_4^2 = .75 \\ u_1 = .9539 & u_2 = .8000 & u_3 = .9165 & u_4 = .8660 \end{array}$$

Problem 1.5.10:1

$$X_1 = a_1A + b_1B + u_1U_1$$
$$X_2 = a_2A + b_2B + u_2U_2$$
$$X_3 = a_3A + b_3B + u_3U_3$$
$$X_4 = a_4A \qquad\quad + u_4U_4$$

$$\begin{array}{ll} r_{12} = a_1a_2 + b_1b_2 & r_{14} = a_1a_4 \\ r_{13} = a_1a_3 + b_1b_3 & r_{24} = a_2a_4 \\ r_{23} = a_2a_3 + b_2b_3 & r_{34} = a_3a_4 \end{array}$$

$$\begin{aligned} t_{1234} &= r_{12}r_{34} - r_{13}r_{24} \\ &= a_1a_2a_3a_4 + a_3a_4b_1b_2 - a_1a_2a_3a_4 - a_2a_4b_1b_3 \\ &= a_3a_4b_1b_2 - a_2a_4b_1b_3 \end{aligned} \tag{1}$$

$$\begin{aligned} t_{1243} &= r_{12}r_{34} - r_{14}r_{23} \\ &= a_1a_2a_3a_4 + a_3a_4b_1b_2 - a_1a_2a_3a_4 - a_1a_4b_2b_3 \\ &= a_3a_4b_1b_2 - a_1a_4b_2b_3 \end{aligned} \tag{2}$$

$$\begin{aligned} t_{1342} &= r_{13}r_{24} - r_{14}r_{23} \\ &= a_1a_2a_3a_4 + a_2a_4b_1b_3 - a_1a_2a_3a_4 - a_1a_4b_2b_3 \\ &= a_2a_4b_1b_3 - a_1a_4b_2b_3 \end{aligned} \tag{3}$$

From (1), t_{1234} can be positive, 0, or negative according as a_3b_2 is greater than, equal to, or less than a_2b_3.

From (2), the same holds for t_{1243} with regard to a_3b_1 and a_1b_3.
From (3), the same holds for t_{1342} with regard to a_2b_1 and a_1b_2.

Problem 1.6.1:1

$t_{1234} = r_{12}r_{34} - r_{13}r_{24} = .1920$ $|R| = .2051$

$t_{1243} = r_{12}r_{34} - r_{14}r_{23} = .2658$ $N = 130$

$t_{1342} = r_{13}r_{24} - r_{14}r_{23} = \boxed{.0738}$ (smallest)

$\sigma_t^2 = \dfrac{1}{128} \left[\dfrac{131}{129} (1 - .70^2)(1 - .50^2) - .2051 \right]$

$= \dfrac{1}{128} [1.0155 (.51)(.75) - .2051]$

$= \dfrac{1}{128} [1.0155 (.3825) - .2051]$

$= \dfrac{1}{128} [.3884 - .2051]$

$= .0078125 (.1833)$

$= .001432.$

$\sigma_t = .03784$

$1.282\sigma_t = .0485 < .0738$, so Theorem 1.8 does not hold at the two-sided .20 level.

But $1.96\sigma_t = .0742 > .0738$, so Theorem 1.8 does hold at the two-sided .05 level. This suggests that Theorem 1.8 *almost* holds.

Problem 1.6.7:1

If $s_2 = 0$, then b_2^2 reaches its upper bound .092, and $b_2 = \sqrt{.092} = .303$.
Then if $b_2b_5 = .124$, $b_5 = .124/.303 = .409$, and we have

TABLE P1.6.7:1
Factor Pattern for Five Verbal Tests
When $s_2 = 0(N = 841)$

Test	Factor			
	a	*b*	*u*	h^2
(1)	.760	.000	.650	.578
(2)	.773	.303	.558	.689
(3)	.859	.000	.512	.738
(4)	.815	.000	.580	.664
(5)	.731	.409	.546	.702

Comparing the b-values with those of Table 1.4 based on the assumption that $b_2 = b_5$, we have

Values of b_2 and b_5 if

	$s_2 = s_5$	$s_2 = 0$	Absolute Difference[a]
b_2	.297	.303	.006
b_5	.420	.409	.011

[a] If we assume that $s_5 = 0$, the absolute differences will be smaller.

Thus no reasonable assumption alternative to $s_2 = s_5$ can make any substantial difference in the values of b_2 and b_5.

Exercise 1:1

TABLE E1:1a
Tetrads for Six Psychological Tests ($N = 710$)

Correlations		Tests				Tetrads				
Tests	r	a	b	c	d	$r_{ab}r_{cd}$ $-r_{ac}r_{bd}$ $(ad \text{ or } bc)^a$	$r_{ab}r_{cd}$ $-r_{ad}r_{bc}$ $(ac \text{ or } bd)^a$	$r_{ac}r_{bd}$ $-r_{ad}r_{bc}$ $(ab \text{ or } cd)^a$	Check[b]	Group Factor Location
1,2	.769	1	2	3	4	$\boxed{-.016}$	.003	.019	√	None
1,3	.671	1	2	3	5	$\boxed{-.021}$	.015	.036	√	None
1,4	.158	1	2	3	6	−.040	$\boxed{-.035}$ c	.005	√	12,36
1,5	.211	1	2	4	5	.435	.438	.002	√	12,45
1,6	.231	1	2	4	6	.441	.435	−.005	√	12,46
2,3	.681	1	2	5	6	.341	.330	−.011	√	12,56
2,4	.189	1	3	4	5	.384	.386	.002	√	13,45
2,5	.268	1	3	4	6	.393	.385	−.008	√	13,46
2,6	.242	1	3	5	6	.309	.294	−.014	√	13,56
3,4	.144	1	4	5	6	$\boxed{-.051}$d	−.063	−.012	√	14,56
3,5	.207	2	3	4	5	.384	.384	.001	√	23,45
3,6	.159	2	3	4	6	.394	.389	−.005	√	23,46
4,5	.621	2	3	5	6	.305	.297	−.007	√	23.56
4,6	.623	2	4	5	6	−.071	$\boxed{-.054}$ d	.017	√	24,56
5,6	.510	3	4	5	6	−.056	−.025	$\boxed{.030}$ c	√	35,46

Computations of $\bar{\sigma}_t$

$\Sigma r = 5.684$ $4/N = .005634$ $1 - 3\bar{r}\left(\dfrac{n-4}{n-2}\right) = .4316 = C \left(\text{because } \dfrac{n-6}{n-2} = \right.$

$\Sigma r^2 = 2.917$ $1 - \bar{r} = .6211$

$\bar{r} = .3784$ $(1 - \bar{r})^2 = .3858$ $BC = .0220$

$\bar{r}^2 = .1436$ $\bar{r}^2(1 - \bar{r})^2 = .0554 = A$ $A + BC = .0774 = D$

$\overline{r^2} = .1945$ $\overline{r^2} - \bar{r}^2 = .0509 = B$ $(4/N)D = .000436 = \bar{\sigma}_t^2$

No. r's = 15 $3\bar{r} = 1.1367$ $\bar{\sigma}_t = .0209$

TABLE E1:1a (*continued*)

$n = 6$	$\dfrac{n - 4}{n - 2} = .5$	$1.282\,\bar{\sigma}_t = .027\ (P = .20)$
$N = 710$	$3\bar{r}\left(\dfrac{n - 4}{n - 2}\right) = .5684$	$1.960\,\bar{\sigma}_t = .041\ (P = .05)$

[a] Location of group factor if $t = 0$ and the other two non-0.
[b] Sum of outer pair = middle within $\pm.001$.
[c] Marginally significant: median significant at .20; not at .05.
[d] Significant at .05.

The median tetrads for variables X–4–5–6 ($X = 1$, 2, or 3) are larger in general than those for variables 1–2–3–X ($X = 4$, 5, or 6). Two of the former are significant at .20 and the third at .05; whereas of the latter, two are not significant at .20, and the third is not significant at .05. This suggests that the group factor should lie in tests 4, 5, and 6. This suggestion is confirmed when we note that there are ten allocations to 1–2, 1–3, and 2–3, and 12 to 4–5, 4–6, and 5–6.

TABLE E1:1b
Triads, Not Including Any Two of Variables 4, 5, and 6,
for Six Psychological Tests ($N = 710$)

t	Test 1	t	Test 2	t	Test 3	t	Test 4	t	Test 5	t	Test 6
123	.758	213	.780	312	.594	412	.0388	512	.0735	612	.0727
124	.643	214	.920	314	.612	413	.0339	513	.0651	613	.0547
125	.605	215	.977	315	.658	423	.0400	523	.0815	623	.0565
126	.734	216	.806	316	.462						
134	.736	234	.894	324	.519						
135	.684	235	.882	325	.526						
136	.975	236	1.036^a	326	.447						
Σ	5.135		6.295		3.818		.1127		.2201		.1839
a^2	.7336		.8993		.5454		.03757		.07337		.06130
a	.8565+		.9483		.7385+		.1938		.2709		.2476

[a] Violates Theorem 1.3; but the computation below shows that by (1-17) this violation is not significant.

$$r_{36.2} = \frac{r_{36} - r_{23}r_{26}}{\sqrt{(1 - r_{23}^2)(1 - r_{26}^2)}} = \frac{.159 - (.681)(.242)}{\sqrt{(.5362)(.9414)}}$$

$$= -\frac{.005802}{\sqrt{.5048}} = -\frac{.005802}{.7105} = -.008166$$

$$t = .008166\,\sqrt{(707)(1 - .00007)} = .008166\,\sqrt{(707)(.99993)}$$

$$= .008166\,\sqrt{706.95} = (.008166)(26.59) = .2171 < .8416:\ n.s.$$

TABLE E1:1c
Residuals

$r_{ij\cdot a} = r_{ij} - a_i a_j$		
r	*Value*	

The first 12 of these residuals are close to zero, as they should be if the *b*-factor lies only in tests 4, 5, and 6. Each of the last three *b*-factor loadings can be obtained from a triad based on the last three residuals.

r	*Value*	
$12 \cdot a$	−.043	
$13 \cdot a$	.038	
$14 \cdot a$	−.008	
$15 \cdot a$	−.021	
$16 \cdot a$	.019	
$23 \cdot a$	−.019	$b_4^2 = (.568)(.575)/(.443) = .7372$
$24 \cdot a$	.005	
$25 \cdot a$	.011	$b_5^2 = (.568)(.443)/(.575) = .4376$
$26 \cdot a$	.007	
$34 \cdot a$	.001	$b_6^2 = (.575)(.443)/(.568) = .4485$
$35 \cdot a$	.007	
$36 \cdot a$	−.024	
$45 \cdot a$	.568	$b_4 = .8586$
$46 \cdot a$	.575	$b_5 = .6615+$
$56 \cdot a$	.443	$b_6 = .6697$

TABLE E1:1d
Factor Pattern for Six Psychological Tests
$(N = 710)$

	Factor			
Test	*a*	*b*	u^a	$(h^2)^b$
(1)	.857	.000	.516	.734
(2)	.948	.000	.317	.899
(3)	.739	.000	.674	.545
(4)	.194	.859	.475	.775
(5)	.271	.662	.699	.511
(6)	.248	.670	.700	.510

[a] From four-figure h^2 and u^2 values.
[b] From four-figure a^2 and b^2 values.

Exercise 2:1

TABLE E 2:1
Centroid Factor Analysis of Six Psychological Tests ($N = 710$)

Test	(1)	(2)	(3)	(4)	(5)	(6)	Σ	Ch
(1)	(.734)	.769	.671	.158	.211	.231	2.774	
(2)	.769	(.889)	.681	.189	.268	.242	3.048	
(3)	.671	.681	(.545)	.144	.207	.159	2.407	
(4)	.158	.189	.144	(.775)	.621	.623	2.510	
(5)	.211	.268	.207	.621	(.511)	.510	2.328	
(6)	.231	.242	.159	.623	.510	(.510)	2.275	
Σ	2.774	3.048	2.407	2.510	2.328	2.275	15.342	15.342
a	.7082	.7782	.6145+	.6408	.5943	.5808	3.9168	3.9169

Refl				1	2	3		
(1)	(.232)	.218	.236	++ .296	++ .210	++ .180	.000	1.372
(2)	.218	(.293)	.203	++ .310	++ .194	++ .210	.000	1.428
(3)	.236	.203	(.167)	++ .250	++ .158	++ .198	.000	1.212
(4)	++ .296	++ .310	++ .250	(.364)	# .240	# .251	−.001	1.711
(5)	++ .210	++ .194	++ .158	# .240	(.158)	# .165	.001	1.125
(6)	++ .180	++ .210	++ .198	# .251	# .165	(.173)	.001	1.177
Σ	1.372	1.428	1.212	1.711	1.125	1.177	8.025	8.025
b	.4843	.5041	.4278	=.6040	=.3971	=.4155−	2.8328	2.8328

Second Residual Matrix

	(1)	(2)	(3)	(4)	(5)	(6)	Σ
(1)	(−.003)	−.026	.029	.003	.018	−.021	.000
(2)	−.026	(.039)	−.013	.006	−.006	.001	.001
(3)	.029	−.013	(−.016)	−.008	−.012	.020	.000
(4)	.003	.006	−.008	(−.001)	.000	.000	.000
(5)	.018	−.006	−.012	.000	(.000)	.000	.000
(6)	−.021	.001	.020	.000	.000	(.000)	.000

Factor Matrix

Test	a	b	h^2	h_0^2
(1)	.708	.484	.736	.734
(2)	.778	.504	.859	.899
(3)	.615	.428	.561	.545
(4)	.641	−.604	.776	.775
(5)	.594	−.397	.510	.511
(6)	.581	−.415	.510	.510

Exercise 2:2

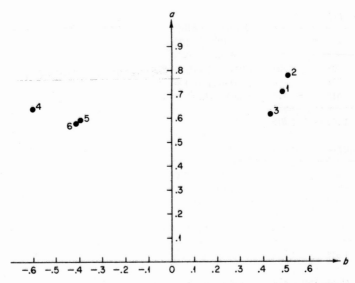

Fig. E 2:2 Plot of centroid factor loadings, from Table E 2:1, for six psychological tests ($N = 710$).

TABLE E 2:2
Alternative Rotations for Six Psychological Tests ($N = 710$)

Test	Centroid		Orthogonal $b \to$ II		Tetrad-Triad[a]	
	a	b	I	II	I	II
(1)	.708	.484	.857	−.005	.857	.000
(2)	.778	.504	.927	.017	.948	.000
(3)	.615	.428	.749	−.011	.739	.000
(4)	.641	−.604	.194	.859	.194	.859
(5)	.594	−.397	.271	.661	.271	.662
(6)	.581	−.415	.250	.669	.248	.670
Σ	3.917	.000	3.248	2.190	3.257	2.191
Ch			3.247	2.190		

TABLE E2:2 *(continued)*

Centroid (1), (2), (3)		
Test	a	b
(1)	.708	.484
(2)	.778	.504
(3)	.615	.428
Σ	2.101	1.416

$2.101^2 + 1.416^2 = 6.4193$
$\sqrt{6.4193} = 2.5336$
$1/2.5336 = .39470$
$(.39470)(2.101) = .829 = (IIa)$
$(.39470)(1.416) = .559 = (IIb)$
Check: $(IIa)^2 + (IIb)^2 = 1.000$

Centroid (4), (5), (6)		
Test	a	b
(4)	.641	−.604
(5)	.594	−.397
(6)	.581	−.415
Σ	1.816	−1.416

$1.816^2 + (−1.416)^2 = 5.3029$
$\sqrt{5.3029} = 2.3028$
$1/2.3028 = .43425$
$(.43425)(1.816) = .789 = (Ia)$
$(.43425)(−1.416) = −.615 = (Ib)$
Check: $(Ia)^2 + (Ib)^2 = 1.001$

	Orthogonal a → I		Oblique	
Test	I	II	I	II
(1)	.261	.817	.817	−.005
(2)	.304	.876	.876	.017
(3)	.222	.716	.716	−.011
(4)	.877	−.082	−.082	.859
(5)	.713	.052	.052	.661
(6)	.714	.030	.030	.669
Σ	3.091	2.409	2.409	2.190
Ch	3.091	2.409	2.409	2.190

[a] From Exercise 1:1.

Problem 3.2.2:1

1. If A is of order n by m, then A' is of order m by n. This follows from the definition of a transpose, because each row (column) of A becomes a column (row) of A'.

2. If $A \pm B = C$, then $A' \pm B' = C'$. The elements of the rows of A are the same as those of the columns of A', and the rows of B are the same as those of the columns of B'. When we add or subtract, it follows that the elements of the rows of C are the same as those of the columns of $(A' \pm B')$, so by the definition of a transpose, $A' \pm B' = C'$.

3. $(A')' = A$. If we make the rows of A into the columns of A', and then

make the rows of A' into the columns of $(A')'$, we have merely reversed the initial operation, and $(A')' = A$.

4. Let $(A \pm B) = C$. Then $(A \pm B)' = C'$. But by 2, above, $C' = A' \pm B'$, so $(A \pm B)' = A' \pm B'$.

Problem 3.2.3:1

$$\begin{array}{cccc} B' & \cdot & A & = c \end{array}$$

$$[1 \quad 2 \quad 3] \cdot \begin{bmatrix} 2 \\ 3 \\ 4 \end{bmatrix} = 20$$

For either $A'B$ or $B'A$, the sum of products is the same, here $1 \cdot 2 + 2 \cdot 3 + 3 \cdot 4 = 20$.

$$\begin{array}{ccccc} B & \times & A' & = & BA' \end{array}$$

$$\begin{bmatrix} 1 \\ 2 \\ 3 \end{bmatrix} \times [2 \quad 3 \quad 4] = \begin{bmatrix} 2 & 3 & 4 \\ 4 & 6 & 8 \\ 6 & 9 & 12 \end{bmatrix} = C'$$

where C' is the transpose of C in the matrix product example of Section 3.2.3.

Problem 3.2.6:1

$$\begin{array}{ccccc} B & \cdot & A & = & BA \end{array}$$

$$\begin{bmatrix} b_{11} & b_{12} \\ b_{21} & b_{22} \end{bmatrix} \cdot \begin{bmatrix} a_{11} & a_{12} \\ a_{21} & a_{22} \end{bmatrix} = \begin{bmatrix} b_{11}a_{11} + b_{12}a_{21} & b_{11}a_{12} + b_{12}a_{22} \\ b_{21}a_{11} + b_{22}a_{21} & b_{21}a_{12} + b_{22}a_{22} \end{bmatrix}$$

$$\begin{array}{ccc} BA & \cdot & X \end{array}$$

$$\begin{bmatrix} b_{11}a_{11} + b_{12}a_{21} & b_{11}a_{12} + b_{12}a_{22} \\ b_{21}a_{11} + b_{22}a_{21} & b_{21}a_{12} + b_{22}a_{22} \end{bmatrix} \cdot \begin{bmatrix} x_1 \\ x_2 \end{bmatrix}$$

$$\begin{array}{ccc} BA \cdot X & = & Z \end{array}$$

$$= \begin{bmatrix} (b_{11}a_{11} + b_{12}a_{21})x_1 + (b_{11}a_{12} + b_{12}a_{22})x_2 \\ (b_{21}a_{11} + b_{22}a_{21})x_1 + (b_{21}a_{12} + b_{22}a_{22})x_2 \end{bmatrix} = \begin{bmatrix} z_1 \\ z_2 \end{bmatrix}$$

This matrix equation is clearly the same as equations (3-8).

Problem 3.2.6:2

This is a verification. The answer is given by the numerical matrix product immediately above the statement of the problem in the text.

Problem 3.2.6:3

1. The matrix A is 2 by 3, B is 2 by 3, and C is 3 by 2. The matrices that do not exist are therefore:

    c. $A + C$ (different orders)

    d. $A - C$ (different orders)

e. *AB* (no common order)

h. *A* + *B'* (different orders)

ℓ. *AC'* (no common order)

2.
$$A' = \begin{bmatrix} 6 & 10 \\ 9 & 4 \\ 3 & 6 \end{bmatrix} \quad B' = \begin{bmatrix} 5 & 6 & 8 & 2 \\ 4 & 7 & 4 & 0 \\ 3 & 8 & 2 & 1 \end{bmatrix} \quad C' = [6 \quad 5 \quad 2]$$

3.
$$\begin{bmatrix} 5 & 6 & 3 \\ 9 & 10 & 2 \\ 3 & 8 & 3 \end{bmatrix} \cdot \begin{bmatrix} x_1 \\ x_2 \\ x_3 \end{bmatrix} = \begin{bmatrix} 7 \\ 4 \\ 10 \end{bmatrix}$$

4. In the set of two equations the coefficients and constant of the second are all twice those of the first. In the set of three equations the sum of the first and second is equal to the third.

5. $\bar{X}_1 = 3; \bar{X}_2 = 8; N = 5$. Hence

a. $Y = \begin{bmatrix} 0 & 1 & 2 & -1 & -2 \\ 2 & 1 & -1 & -2 & 0 \end{bmatrix}$

b. From Y, $\quad \Sigma y_1^2/5 = 10/5 = 2 = \sigma_1^2$

$\Sigma y_2^2/5 = 10/5 = 2 = \sigma_2^2$

$\Sigma y_1 y_2/5 = 1/5 = .2 = \sigma_{12}$

$$\frac{YY'}{5} = \frac{1}{5} \begin{bmatrix} 0 & 1 & 2 & -1 & -2 \\ 2 & 1 & -1 & -2 & 0 \end{bmatrix} \cdot \begin{bmatrix} 0 & 2 \\ 1 & 1 \\ 2 & -1 \\ -1 & -2 \\ -2 & 0 \end{bmatrix}$$

$$= \frac{1}{5} \begin{bmatrix} 10 & 1 \\ 1 & 10 \end{bmatrix} = \begin{bmatrix} 2 & .2 \\ .2 & 2 \end{bmatrix} = \begin{bmatrix} \sigma_1^2 & \sigma_{12} \\ \sigma_{12} & \sigma_2^2 \end{bmatrix}$$

the last two of which are the variance-covariance matrix: numerical and symbolic. But

$$\frac{Y'Y}{5} = \frac{1}{5} \begin{bmatrix} 0 & 2 \\ 1 & 1 \\ 2 & -1 \\ -1 & -2 \\ -2 & 0 \end{bmatrix} \cdot \begin{bmatrix} 0 & 1 & 2 & -1 & -2 \\ 2 & 1 & -1 & -2 & 0 \end{bmatrix}$$

$$= \frac{1}{5} \begin{bmatrix} 4 & 2 & -2 & -4 & 0 \\ 2 & 2 & 1 & -3 & -2 \\ -2 & 1 & 5 & 0 & -4 \\ -4 & -3 & 0 & 5 & 2 \\ 0 & -2 & -4 & 2 & 4 \end{bmatrix}$$

$$= \begin{bmatrix} .8 & .4 & -.4 & -.8 & 0 \\ .4 & .4 & .2 & -.6 & -.4 \\ -.4 & .2 & 1 & 0 & -.8 \\ -.8 & -.6 & 0 & 1 & .4 \\ 0 & -.4 & -.8 & .4 & .8 \end{bmatrix}$$

which is entirely different.

c. If $\sigma_1^2 = \sigma_2^2 = 2$, the matrix D is

$$D = \begin{bmatrix} 1/\sqrt{2} & 0 \\ 0 & 1/\sqrt{2} \end{bmatrix}$$

Then $D \dfrac{YY'}{5} D = \begin{bmatrix} 1/\sqrt{2} & 0 \\ 0 & 1/\sqrt{2} \end{bmatrix} \cdot \begin{bmatrix} 2 & .2 \\ .2 & 2 \end{bmatrix} \cdot \begin{bmatrix} 1/\sqrt{2} & 0 \\ 0 & 1/\sqrt{2} \end{bmatrix}$

$$= \begin{bmatrix} 2/\sqrt{2} & .2/\sqrt{2} \\ .2/\sqrt{2} & 2/\sqrt{2} \end{bmatrix} \cdot \begin{bmatrix} 1/\sqrt{2} & 0 \\ 0 & 1/\sqrt{2} \end{bmatrix}$$

$$= \begin{bmatrix} 1 & .1 \\ .1 & 1 \end{bmatrix}$$

The correlation $r_{12} = \sigma_{12}/\sigma_1 \sigma_2 = .2/(\sqrt{2}\,\sqrt{2}) = .2/2 = .1$, and the correlation matrix is

$$R = \begin{bmatrix} 1 & r_{12} \\ r_{12} & 1 \end{bmatrix} = \begin{bmatrix} 1 & .1 \\ .1 & 1 \end{bmatrix}$$

which is the same as $D \dfrac{YY'}{5} D$.

Problem 3.2.7:1

1. The symmetric matrices are B and D.
2. For the matrix A

$$AA' = \begin{bmatrix} 4 & 3 & 2 \\ 2 & 4 & 3 \\ 3 & 2 & 4 \end{bmatrix} \cdot \begin{bmatrix} 4 & 2 & 3 \\ 3 & 4 & 2 \\ 2 & 3 & 4 \end{bmatrix} = \begin{bmatrix} 29 & 26 & 26 \\ 26 & 29 & 26 \\ 26 & 26 & 29 \end{bmatrix}$$

$$A'A = \begin{bmatrix} 4 & 2 & 3 \\ 3 & 4 & 2 \\ 2 & 3 & 4 \end{bmatrix} \cdot \begin{bmatrix} 4 & 3 & 2 \\ 2 & 4 & 3 \\ 3 & 2 & 4 \end{bmatrix} = \begin{bmatrix} 29 & 26 & 26 \\ 26 & 29 & 26 \\ 26 & 26 & 29 \end{bmatrix}$$

For the matrix C

$$CC' = \begin{bmatrix} 5 & 2 & 3 \\ 2 & 5 & 4 \\ 4 & 3 & 5 \end{bmatrix} \cdot \begin{bmatrix} 5 & 2 & 4 \\ 2 & 5 & 3 \\ 3 & 4 & 5 \end{bmatrix} = \begin{bmatrix} 38 & 32 & 41 \\ 32 & 45 & 43 \\ 41 & 43 & 50 \end{bmatrix}$$

$$C'C = \begin{bmatrix} 5 & 2 & 4 \\ 2 & 5 & 3 \\ 3 & 4 & 5 \end{bmatrix} \cdot \begin{bmatrix} 5 & 2 & 3 \\ 2 & 5 & 4 \\ 4 & 3 & 5 \end{bmatrix} = \begin{bmatrix} 45 & 32 & 43 \\ 32 & 38 & 41 \\ 43 & 41 & 50 \end{bmatrix}$$

Although in *general* $AA' \neq A'A$ unless A is symmetric, this relation *can* hold in some cases other than the case of symmetry. Here $AA' = A'A$, but $CC' \neq C'C$.

Problem 3.2.8:1

Let A be the variance-covariance matrix with elements σ_{ij}. The diagonal elements (where $i = j$) are the variances ($\sigma_{ii} = \sigma_i^2$); their square roots are the standard deviations σ_i; and the off-diagonal elements are the covariances $\sigma_{ij} = \sigma_{ji}$. Thus

$$A = \begin{bmatrix} \sigma_1^2 & \sigma_{12} & \cdots & \sigma_{1n} \\ \sigma_{21} & \sigma_2^2 & \cdots & \sigma_{2n} \\ \hline \sigma_{n1} & \sigma_{n2} & \cdots & \sigma_n^2 \end{bmatrix}$$

If we premultiply A by the matrix D with elements $1/\sigma_i$, each *row* of A is divided by σ_i for that row, so that

$$DA = \begin{bmatrix} \sigma_1^2/\sigma_1 & \sigma_{12}/\sigma_1 & \cdots & \sigma_{1n}/\sigma_1 \\ \sigma_{21}/\sigma_2 & \sigma_2^2/\sigma_2 & \cdots & \sigma_{2n}/\sigma_2 \\ \hline \sigma_{n1}/\sigma_n & \sigma_{n2}/\sigma_n & \cdots & \sigma_n^2/\sigma_n \end{bmatrix}$$

And if we now postmultiply DA by D, each *column* of DA is divided by σ_j for that column, so that

$$DAD = \begin{bmatrix} \sigma_1^2/\sigma_1^2 & \sigma_{12}/\sigma_1\sigma_2 & \cdots & \sigma_{1n}/\sigma_1\sigma_n \\ \sigma_{21}/\sigma_2\sigma_1 & \sigma_2^2/\sigma_2^2 & \cdots & \sigma_{2n}/\sigma_2\sigma_n \\ \hline \sigma_{n1}/\sigma_n\sigma_1 & \sigma_{n2}/\sigma_n\sigma_2 & \cdots & \sigma_n^2/\sigma_n^2 \end{bmatrix}$$

The diagonal elements are all unity, and the off-diagonal elements are all $\sigma_{ij}/\sigma_i\sigma_j = r_{ij}$, so

$$DAD = \begin{bmatrix} 1 & r_{12} & \cdots & r_{1n} \\ r_{21} & 1 & \cdots & r_{2n} \\ \hline r_{n1} & r_{n2} & \cdots & 1 \end{bmatrix} = R,$$

the correlation matrix (symmetric, as is also A, so that $r_{ij} = r_{ji}$).

Problem 3.4.1:1

The first two rows of the orthonormal matrix are those of

$$A = \begin{bmatrix} 2/3 & 2/3 & 1/3 \\ 1/\sqrt{2} & -1/\sqrt{2} & 0 \\ a_{31} & a_{32} & a_{33} \end{bmatrix}$$

If A is orthogonal, the scalar product of rows 2 and 3 must be 0. This scalar product is

$$a_{31}/\sqrt{2} - a_{32}/\sqrt{2} = 0,$$

so a_{31} must be equal to a_{32}. Hence the third row must be of the form $[x \quad x \quad y]$.

If A is orthogonal, the scalar product of the first and third rows must also be 0. Thus

$$\begin{aligned} (2/3)x + (2/3)x + (1/3)y &= 0 \\ (4/3)x + (1/3)y &= 0 \\ 4x + y &= 0 \\ y &= -4x \end{aligned}$$

and the third row is $[x \quad x \quad -4x]$. The sign of x may be either positive or negative.

If A is orthonormal, the sum of squares of the elements of the third row must be unity:

$$\begin{aligned} x^2 + x^2 + 16x^2 &= 1 \\ 18x^2 &= 1 \\ x^2 &= 1/18 \\ x &= \pm\sqrt{1/18} = \pm 1/\sqrt{18} \end{aligned}$$

Thus the orthonormal matrix is

$$A = \begin{bmatrix} 2/3 & 2/3 & 1/3 \\ 1/\sqrt{2} & -1/\sqrt{2} & 0 \\ \pm 1/\sqrt{18} & \pm 1/\sqrt{18} & \mp 4/\sqrt{18} \end{bmatrix}$$

Hence there are two solutions, one for x positive and one for x negative.

Problem 3.4.2:1

Taking the matrices of the first row and then those of the second in order from left to right, the ranks are as follows:

1. 2 (row 3 = 2 × row 1)
2. 2 (row 1 + row 2 = row 3)
3. 2 (2 × row 2 − row 1 = row 3)
4. 1 (2 × row 1 = row 2; 3 × row 1 = row 3)
5. 2 (col. 2 + col. 3 = col. 1)
6. 2 (row 1 + row 2 = row 3)
7. 1 (col. 2 all 0; 2 × col. 1 = col. 3)

Alternative Solutions
1. 2 (5 × col. 1 − col. 2 = col. 3)
2. 2 (5 × col. 1 − col. 2 = col. 3)

3.   2 (2 × col. 2 − col. 1 = col. 3)
4.   1 (2 × col. 2 = col. 3; 3 × col. 2 = col. 1)
5.   2 (2 × row 2 − row 1 = row 3)
6.   2 (col. 1 + col. 3 = col. 2)
7.   1 (2 × row 2 = row 1; 3 × row 2 = row 3)

Problem 3.4.3:1

$$
\begin{array}{ccccc}
A & \cdot & A' & = & B
\end{array}
$$

$$
\begin{bmatrix} 2 \\ 3 \\ 4 \end{bmatrix} \cdot [2 \quad 3 \quad 4] = \begin{bmatrix} 4 & 6 & 8 \\ 6 & 9 & 12 \\ 8 & 12 & 16 \end{bmatrix}
$$

B is symmetric; it is equal to the product AA'; and hence it is Gramian.

Problem 3.4.3:2

$$
G = \begin{bmatrix} .13 & .14 & .05 \\ .14 & .20 & .06 \\ .05 & .06 & .02 \end{bmatrix}
$$

If $A' = [.2 \quad .4 \quad .1]$, then

$$
AA' = \begin{bmatrix} .2 \\ .4 \\ .1 \end{bmatrix} \times [.2 \quad .4 \quad .1] = \begin{bmatrix} .04 & .08 & .02 \\ .08 & .16 & .04 \\ .02 & .04 & .01 \end{bmatrix}
$$

$$
G - AA' = \begin{bmatrix} .09 & .06 & .03 \\ .06 & .04 & .02 \\ .03 & .02 & .01 \end{bmatrix} \quad \text{(first residual matrix)}
$$

Then if $B' = [.3 \quad .2 \quad .1]$,

$$
BB' = \begin{bmatrix} .3 \\ .2 \\ .1 \end{bmatrix} \times [.3 \quad .2 \quad .1] = \begin{bmatrix} .09 & .06 & .03 \\ .06 & .04 & .02 \\ .03 & .02 & .01 \end{bmatrix}
$$

which is equal to $G - AA'$, so that the second residual matrix, $G - AA' - BB'$, will consist entirely of zeros.

If we combine A and B to form the factor matrix F,

$$
FF' = \begin{bmatrix} .2 & .3 \\ .4 & .2 \\ .1 & .1 \end{bmatrix} \cdot \begin{bmatrix} .2 & .4 & .1 \\ .3 & .2 & .1 \end{bmatrix} = \begin{bmatrix} .13 & .14 & .05 \\ .14 & .20 & .06 \\ .05 & .06 & .02 \end{bmatrix} = G
$$

Problem 4.2.2:1

Set 1

$$
\begin{bmatrix} (4) & 2 \\ 6 & -1 \end{bmatrix} \begin{bmatrix} 2 \\ 1 \end{bmatrix} \quad \begin{array}{c} \text{Using (4-4)} \\ \text{and (4-5),} \end{array} \quad \begin{bmatrix} 1 & 1/2 \\ 0 & (-4) \end{bmatrix} \begin{bmatrix} 1/2 \\ -2 \end{bmatrix}
$$

Using (4-7) $\begin{bmatrix} 1 & 0 \\ 0 & 1 \end{bmatrix} \begin{bmatrix} 1/4 \\ 1/2 \end{bmatrix} \begin{matrix} x_1 = 1/4 \\ x_2 = 1/2 \end{matrix}$
and (4-8),

Check: $\begin{cases} 4/4 + 2/2 = 2 \\ 6/4 - 1/2 = 3/2 - 1/2 = 1 \end{cases}$

Set 2

$$\begin{bmatrix} (1) & 1 & -1 \\ 1 & 2 & -1 \\ 0 & 2 & 2 \end{bmatrix} \begin{bmatrix} 3 \\ 5 \\ 8 \end{bmatrix}$$

Using (4-4) $\begin{bmatrix} 1 & 1 & -1 \\ 0 & (1) & 0 \\ 0 & 2 & 2 \end{bmatrix} \begin{bmatrix} 3 \\ 2 \\ 8 \end{bmatrix}$
and (4-5),

Using (4-7) $\begin{bmatrix} 1 & 0 & -1 \\ 0 & 1 & 0 \\ 0 & 0 & (2) \end{bmatrix} \begin{bmatrix} 1 \\ 2 \\ 4 \end{bmatrix}$
and (4-8),

Using (4-10) $\begin{bmatrix} 1 & 0 & 0 \\ 0 & 1 & 0 \\ 0 & 0 & 1 \end{bmatrix} \begin{bmatrix} 3 \\ 2 \\ 2 \end{bmatrix} \begin{matrix} x_1 = 3 \\ x_2 = 2 \\ x_3 = 2 \end{matrix}$
and (4-11),

Check: $\begin{cases} 3 + 2 - 2 = 3 \\ 3 + 4 - 2 = 5 \\ 0 + 4 + 4 = 8 \end{cases}$

Problem 4.2.4:1

$$A = \begin{bmatrix} (1) & 0 & 1 \\ 0 & 1 & 0 \\ 0 & 0 & 1 \end{bmatrix} \begin{bmatrix} 1 & 0 & 0 \\ 0 & 1 & 0 \\ 0 & 0 & 1 \end{bmatrix}$$

Using (4-4) and (4-5),

$$\begin{bmatrix} 1 & 0 & 1 \\ 0 & (1) & 0 \\ 0 & 0 & 1 \end{bmatrix} \begin{bmatrix} 1 & 0 & 0 \\ 0 & 1 & 0 \\ 0 & 0 & 1 \end{bmatrix}$$

Using (4-7) and (4-8),

$$\begin{bmatrix} 1 & 0 & 1 \\ 0 & 1 & 0 \\ 0 & 0 & (1) \end{bmatrix} \begin{bmatrix} 1 & 0 & 0 \\ 0 & 1 & 0 \\ 0 & 0 & 1 \end{bmatrix}$$

Using (4-10) and (4-11),

$$\begin{bmatrix} 1 & 0 & 0 \\ 0 & 1 & 0 \\ 0 & 0 & 1 \end{bmatrix} \begin{bmatrix} 1 & 0 & -1 \\ 0 & 1 & 0 \\ 0 & 0 & 1 \end{bmatrix} = A^{-1}$$

$$
\begin{array}{ccc}
A & \cdot & A^{-1} & = & I
\end{array}
$$

$$
\begin{bmatrix} 1 & 0 & 1 \\ 0 & 1 & 0 \\ 0 & 0 & 1 \end{bmatrix} \cdot \begin{bmatrix} 1 & 0 & -1 \\ 0 & 1 & 0 \\ 0 & 0 & 1 \end{bmatrix} = \begin{bmatrix} 1 & 0 & 0 \\ 0 & 1 & 0 \\ 0 & 0 & 1 \end{bmatrix}
$$

$$
A = \begin{bmatrix} (3) & 2 & 6 \\ 2 & 2 & 5 \\ 1 & 1 & 2 \end{bmatrix} \begin{bmatrix} 1 & 0 & 0 \\ 0 & 1 & 0 \\ 0 & 0 & 1 \end{bmatrix}
$$

Using (4-4) and (4-5),

$$
\begin{bmatrix} 1 & 2/3 & 2 \\ 0 & (2/3) & 1 \\ 0 & 1/3 & 0 \end{bmatrix} \begin{bmatrix} 1/3 & 0 & 0 \\ -2/3 & 1 & 0 \\ -1/3 & 0 & 1 \end{bmatrix}
$$

Using (4-7) and (4-8),

$$
\begin{bmatrix} 1 & 0 & 1 \\ 0 & 1 & 3/2 \\ 0 & 0 & (-1/2) \end{bmatrix} \begin{bmatrix} 1 & -1 & 0 \\ -1 & 3/2 & 0 \\ 0 & -1/2 & 1 \end{bmatrix}
$$

Using (4-10) and (4-11),

$$
\begin{bmatrix} 1 & 0 & 0 \\ 0 & 1 & 0 \\ 0 & 0 & 1 \end{bmatrix} \begin{bmatrix} 1 & -2 & 2 \\ -1 & 0 & 3 \\ 0 & 1 & -2 \end{bmatrix} = A^{-1}
$$

$$
\begin{array}{ccc}
A & \cdot & A^{-1} & = & I
\end{array}
$$

$$
\begin{bmatrix} 3 & 2 & 6 \\ 2 & 2 & 5 \\ 1 & 1 & 2 \end{bmatrix} \cdot \begin{bmatrix} 1 & -2 & 2 \\ -1 & 0 & 3 \\ 0 & 1 & -2 \end{bmatrix} = \begin{bmatrix} 1 & 0 & 0 \\ 0 & 1 & 0 \\ 0 & 0 & 1 \end{bmatrix}
$$

Problem 4.3.1:1

TABLE P4.3.1:1
Solution of Equations and Computation of Determinant[a]

Panel	Eq	\<Variable\>(1)	(2)	(3)	\<Constant\>(4)	Σ	Ch
0	(1)	(.4)	.1	−.3	−.2	0.0	−.2
	(2)	.1	.3	.2	.5	1.1	.5
	(3)	.2	.2	.3	.9	1.6	.9
1	(2)		(.275)	.275	.550	1.100	1.100
	(3)		.150	.450	1.000	1.600	1.600
	(1)	1	.250	−.750	−.500	.000	.000

(*continued*)

TABLE P4.3.1:1 (*continued*)

Panel	Eq	Variable (1)	(2)	(3)	Constant (4)	Σ	Ch
	(3)			(.3000)	.7000	1.0000	1.0000
2	(1)	1		−1.0000	−1.0000	−1.0000	−1.0000
	(2)		1	1.0000	2.0000	4.0000	4.0000
	(1)	1			1.3333	2.3333	2.3333
3	(2)		1	$X =$	−.3333	.6667	.6667
	(3)			1	2.3333	3.3333	3.3333

[a] Determinant of coefficients = .033.

Problem 4.3.3:1

TABLE P4.3.3:1
Computation of Inverse

Panel	Eq	Variable (1)	(2)	(3)	Variable (1)	(2)	(3)	Σ + 1	Ch
	(1)	(.26)	.19	−.12				1.33	
0	(2)	−.10	.45	.16	$= A$			1.51	
	(3)	.15	−.14	.27				1.28	
	(2)		(.5231)	.1138	.3846			2.0215	2.0216
1	(3)		−.2496	.3392	−.5769			.5127	.5127
	(1)		.7308	−.4615	3.8462			5.1155	5.1154
	(3)			(.3935)	−.3934	.4772		1.4773	1.4773
2	(1)			−.6205	3.3089	−1.3971		2.2913	2.2914
	(2)			.2175	.7352	1.9117		3.8644	3.8645
	(1)				2.6886	−.6446	1.5769	4.6209	4.6208
3	(2)		$A^{-1} =$		.9527	1.6478	−.5530	3.0475	3.0478
	(3)				−.9997	1.2127	2.5413	3.7543	3.7543

Problem 4.5.1:1

TABLE P4.5.1:1
Solution of Equations: Almost-Singular Case[a]

Panel	Eq	Variable (1)	(2)	(3)	Constant (4)	Σ	Ch
	(1)	(.2256)	.3552	.2320	.1632	.9760	.1632
0	(2)	.3552	.5684	.3640	.2584	1.5460	.2583
	(3)	.2320	.3640	.2400	.1680	1.0040	.1680

TABLE P4.5.1:1 (*continued*)

Panel	Eq	Variable (1)	Variable (2)	Variable (3)	Constant (4)	Σ	Ch
	(2)		(.0091)	−.0013	.0014	.0092	.0093
1	(3)		−.0013	.0014	.0002	.0003	.0003
	(1)	1	1.5745	1.0284	.7234	4.3263	4.3262
	(3)			(.0012)	.0004	.0016	.0016
2	(1)	1		1.2534	.4812	2.7346	2.7346
	(2)		1	−.1429	.1538	1.0109	1.0110
	(1)	1			.0634	1.0634	1.0634
3	(2)		1	X =	.2014	1.2014	1.2014
	(3)			1	.3333	1.3333	1.3333

a These equations were constructed by premultiplying

$$\begin{bmatrix} .4 & .6 & .4 \\ .2 & .4 & .2 \\ .16 & .22 & .2 \end{bmatrix} \begin{bmatrix} .28 \\ .16 \\ .12 \end{bmatrix}$$

by the transpose of the coefficient matrix. The third equation is *approximately* the first minus the second.

Problem 4.6.1:1

TABLE P4.6.1:1
Normalization

Mean Method						Σ
X	1	2	3	4	5	
f	71	137	181	53	58	500 = N
p	.142	.274	.362	.106	.116	1.000
pc	.142	.416	.778	.884	1.000	
y	.225	.390	.298	.195	.000	
yd	−.225	−.165	.092	.103	.195	.000
z	−1.6	−.6	.3	1.0	1.7	
T	34	44	53	60	67	

Midpoint Method						Σ
X	1	2	3	4	5	
f	71	137	181	53	58	500 = N
2fc	71	279	597	831	942	1000
pr	.071	.279	.597	.831	.942	1.000
z	−1.5	−.6	.2	1.0	1.6	
T	35	44	52	60	66	

Problem 6.1:1

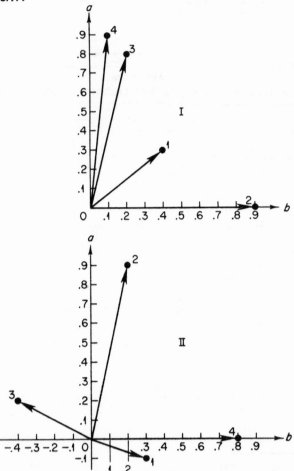

Fig. P6.1:1   Plots of two sets of points.

Problem 6.3.2:1

If Λ is orthonormal, $\Lambda' = \Lambda^{-1}$. Then

$$(\Lambda')^{-1} = (\Lambda^{-1})^{-1} = \Lambda.$$

But by (6-20), $T = (\Lambda')^{-1}D$. Substituting from the above,

$$T = \Lambda D.$$

But Λ is already normal by columns (as well as by rows), so $D = I$, and

$$T = \Lambda.$$

Then if $V = F\Lambda$, and by (6-21) $S = FT$, it follows that

$$S = F\Lambda = V.$$

Exercise 6:1

TABLE E6:1
Structures and Patterns for Six Psychological Tests ($N = 710$)

Test	F a	F b	$V = F\Lambda$ I	$V = F\Lambda$ II	$W = FY$ I	$W = FY$ II	$S = FT$ I	$S = FT$ II	$P = FQ$ I	$P = FQ$ II
(1)	.708	.484	.817	−.005	.902	.274	.857	.261	.860	−.006
(2)	.778	.504	.876	.017	.975	.320	.927	.304	.922	.018
(3)	.615	.428	.716	−.011	.788	.234	.749	.222	.753	−.012
(4)	.641	−.604	−.082	.859	.204	.923	.194	.877	−.087	.904
(5)	.594	−.397	.052	.661	.285	.750	.271	.713	.055	.695
(6)	.581	−.415	.030	.669	.263	.751	.250	.714	.031	.704
Σ	3.917	.000	2.409	2.190	3.417	3.252	3.248	3.091	2.534	2.303
Ch			2.409	2.190	3.416	3.251	3.247	3.091	2.534	2.303

	Λ I	Λ II	$Y = (\Lambda')^{-1}$ I	$Y = (\Lambda')^{-1}$ II	$T = (\Lambda')^{-1}D$ I	$T = (\Lambda')^{-1}D$ II	$Q = \Lambda D^{-1}$ I	$Q = \Lambda D^{-1}$ II
a	.615	.559	.872	.830	.829	.789	.647	.588
b	.789	−.829	.588	−.647	.559	−.615	.830	−.872

	I	II
diag D^{-1}	1.052	1.052
diag D	.9506	.9506

Test	h^2	$1 - h^2$	u
(1)	.7355	.2645	.514
(2)	.8593	.1407	.375
(3)	.5614	.4386	.662
(4)	.7757	.2243	.474
(5)	.5104	.4896	.700
(6)	.5098	.4902	.700

$$
\begin{array}{ccc}
P & \cdot & A \quad + \\
\begin{bmatrix} .860 & -.006 \\ .922 & .018 \\ .753 & -.012 \\ -.087 & .904 \\ .055 & .695 \\ .031 & .704 \end{bmatrix} & \cdot \begin{bmatrix} .782 \\ -.431 \end{bmatrix} + &
\end{array}
$$

(continued)

TABLE E6:1 (*continued*)

$$
\begin{array}{ccc}
U & & B
\end{array}
$$

$$
\begin{bmatrix}
.514 & 0 & 0 & 0 & 0 & 0 \\
0 & .375 & 0 & 0 & 0 & 0 \\
0 & 0 & .662 & 0 & 0 & 0 \\
0 & 0 & 0 & .474 & 0 & 0 \\
0 & 0 & 0 & 0 & .700 & 0 \\
0 & 0 & 0 & 0 & 0 & .700
\end{bmatrix}
\cdot
\begin{bmatrix}
.613 \\
-.729 \\
.212 \\
.314 \\
-.456 \\
-.824
\end{bmatrix}
$$

$$
=
\begin{array}{ccc}
PA & + & UB & = & X
\end{array}
$$

$$
=
\begin{bmatrix}
.675 \\
.713 \\
.594 \\
-.458 \\
-.257 \\
-.279
\end{bmatrix}
+
\begin{bmatrix}
.315 \\
-.273 \\
.140 \\
.149 \\
-.319 \\
-.577
\end{bmatrix}
=
\begin{bmatrix}
.990 \\
.440 \\
.734 \\
-.309 \\
-.576 \\
-.856
\end{bmatrix}
\begin{array}{l}
= x_1 \\
= x_2 \\
= x_3 \\
= x_4 \\
= x_5 \\
= x_6
\end{array}
$$

Problem 7.1.4:1

TABLE P7.1.4:1
Extended-Vector Rotation for Artificial Data

Var	F-Matrix a	b	c	F-Extended a	b	c	Rotated $V = F\Lambda$ I	II	III
(1)	.60	−.06	−.12	1	−.1	−.2	.249	.155	.000
(2)	.80	.08	−.16	1	.1	−.2	.221	.345	.000
(3)	.70	.14	−.14	1	.2	−2	.145	.363	.000
(4)	.80	.24	.00	1	.3	.0	.000	.415	.157
(5)	.60	.12	.06	1	.2	.1	.000	.233	.176
(6)	.70	.07	.14	1	.1	.2	.000	.181	.275
(7)	.80	−.16	.16	1	−.2	.2	.166	.000	.314
(8)	.60	−.18	.00	1	−.3	.0	.249	.000	.118
Σ	5.60	.25	−.06			Σ	1.030	1.692	1.040
						Ch	1.028	1.692	1.039

Panel	Eq	Variable (1)	(2)	(3)	Variable (1)	(2)	(3)	Σ + 1	Ch
0	(1)	(1)	−.4	−.2				1.4	
	(2)	1	.5	−.2	= E'			2.3	
	(3)	1	−.1	.4				2.3	
1	(2)		(.9)	.0	−1			.9	.9
	(3)		.3	.6	−1			.9	.9
	(1)		−.4	−.2	1			1.4	1.4

TABLE P7.1.4:1 (continued)

Panel	Eq	Variable			Variable			Σ + 1	Ch
		(1)	(2)	(3)	(1)	(2)	(3)		
	(3)			(.6000)	−.6667	−.3333		.6000	.6000
2	(1)			−.2000	.5556	.4444		1.8000	1.8000
	(2)			.0000	−1.1111	1.1111		1.0000	1.0000
	(1)				.3333	.3333	.3333	1.9999	2.0000
3	(2)			$(E')^{-1} =$	−1.1111	1.1111	.0000	1.0000	1.0000
	(3)				−1.1111	−.5556	1.6667	1.0000	1.0000
				Σ^2	2.58025	1.65432	2.88889		
				$\sqrt{\Sigma^2}$	1.60632	1.28620	1.69967		
				$1/\sqrt{\Sigma^2}$	.62254	.77748	.58835	$= diag\ (\Delta^{-1}D)$	
				$\Lambda =$	.207	.259	.196		
					−.692	.864	.000		
					−.692	−.432	.981		
				Σ^2	1.001	1.000	1.001		

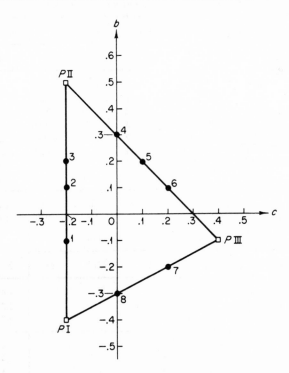

Fig. P7.1.4:1 Extended-vector plot for artificial data.

Exercise 7:1

TABLE E7:1
Extended-Vector Rotation for Nine Aptitude Tests ($N = 504$)

Test	Principal Axes F			F-Extended			Rotated[a] $V = F\Lambda$		
	a	b	c	a	b	c	I	II	III
(1)	.645	−.185	−.319	1	−.29	−.49	.487	.029	−.085
(2)	.639	−.004	−.293	1	−.01	−.46	.423	−.054	.088
(3)	.619	−.106	−.259	1	−.17	−.42	.407	.024	−.003
(4)	.826	−.285	.201	1	−.35	.24	.053	.540	.005
(5)	.746	−.216	.035	1	−.29	.05	.179	.350	.005
(6)	.765	−.307	.304	1	−.40	.40	−.054	.616	−.005
(7)	.692	.483	−.004	1	.70	−.01	.058	−.090	.630
(8)	.658	.438	.080	1	.67	.12	−.020	−.008	.601
(9)	.645	.305	.124	1	.47	.19	−.037	.098	.485
Σ	6.235	.123	−.131				1.496	1.505	1.721
Ch							1.496	1.506	1.720
(1) + (2) + (3)	1.903	−.295	−.871	1	−.1550+	−.4577			
(4) + (6)	1.591	−.592	.505	1	−.3721	.3174	= E'		
(7) + (8) + (9)	1.995	1.226	.200	1	.6145	.1003			

Panel	Eq	Variable			Variable			$\Sigma + 1$	Ch
		(1)	(2)	(3)	(1)	(2)	(3)		
0	(1)	(1) −.1550	−.4577		= E'			1.3873	
0	(2)	1	−.3721	.3174				1.9453	
0	(3)	1	.6145	.1003				2.7148	
1	(2)		(−.2171)	.7751	−1			.5580	.5580
1	(3)		.7695	.5580	−1			1.3275	1.3275
1	(1)		−.1550	−.4577	1			1.3873	1.3873
2	(3)			(3.3053)	−4.5445	3.5445		3.3053	3.3053
2	(1)			−1.0111	1.7140	−.7140		.9889	.9889
2	(2)			−3.5703	4.6062	−4.6062		−2.5703	−2.5703
3	(1)				.3238	.3703	.3059	2.0000	2.0000
3	(2)		$(E')^{-1} =$		−.3026	−.7774	1.0800	1.0000	1.0000
3	(3)				−1.3749	1.0724	.3025	1.0000	1.0000
	Σ^2				2.0868	1.8915	1.3515		
	$\sqrt{\Sigma^2}$				1.4446	1.3753	1.1625		
	$1/\sqrt{\Sigma^2}$				.69223	.72711	.86022	= diag $(\Delta^{-1}D)$	

TABLE E7:1 (*continued*)

Panel	Eq	Variable			Variable			Σ + 1	Ch
		(1)	(2)	(3)	(1)	(2)	(3)		
				Λ =	.224	.269	.263		
					−.209	−.565	.929		
					−.952	.780	.260		
				Σ²	1.000	1.000	1.000		

[a] Factor I is a quantitative-reasoning factor.
  Factor II is a verbal-relations factor.
  Factor III is a visual-space-manipulation factor.

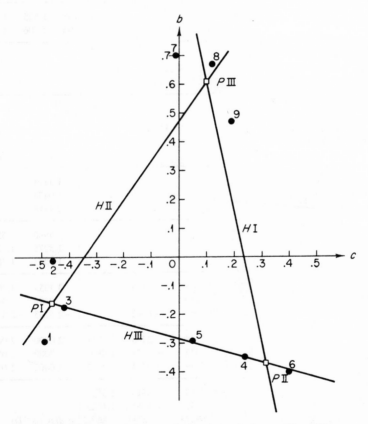

Fig. E7:1   Extended-vector plot for nine aptitude tests ($N = 504$).

Problem 8.3:1

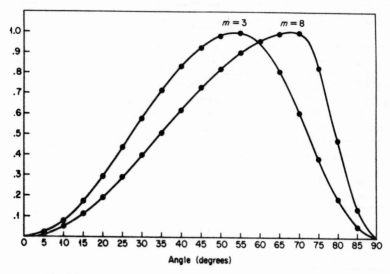

Fig. P8.3:1   Relation between w_i and $\cos^{-1}a_{i1}$ for $m = 3$ and $m = 8$.

Exercise 8:1

TABLE E8:1
Orthogonal Rotation of WAIS Factor Matrix for Age-Group 25–34 ($N = 300$)

Test	Principal Axes F			General Factor G			Transformed V			h_v^2	h^2
	a	b	c	$g = 1$	2	3	$g = $ I	II	III		
(1)	.886	−.183	−.029	.759	.493	.014	.759	.358	.339	.819	.819
(2)	.761	−.141	.249	.666	.388	−.260	.666	.091	.458	.662	.661
(3)	.698	−.085	−.262	.612	.351	.254	.612	.428	.069	.562	.563
(4)	.775	−.182	.030	.658	.447	−.045	.658	.284	.348	.635	.635
(5)	.588	−.098	−.263	.506	.324	.254	.506	.409	.049	.426	.425
(6)	.878	−.282	.134	.721	.570	−.156	.721	.293	.513	.869	.868
(7)	.657	.023	−.037	.620	.219	.039	.620	.182	.127	.434	.434
(8)	.756	.176	.070	.770	.105	−.056	.770	.035	.114	.607	.607
(9)	.730	.361	−.044	.809	−.068	.073	.809	.004	−.100	.664	.665
(10)	.744	.130	−.012	.740	.149	.022	.740	.121	.090	.570	.571
(11)	.615	.433	.075	.732	−.186	−.040	.732	−.160	−.103	.572	.571
Σ	8.088	.152	−.089	7.593	2.792	.099	7.593	2.045	1.904	6.820	6.819
Ch				7.593	2.791	.101	7.593	2.044	1.904		

TABLE E8:1 (*continued*)

| *Normalized Centroid Vector of Rows* | *Residual* Λ_0 | |
| (8) + (9) + (10) + (11) | II | III |

				II	III
$\Sigma = [2.845$	1.100	$.089]$	2	.7071	.7071
$\Sigma(\Sigma^2) = 9.3119$			3	.7071	$-.7071$
$\sqrt{\Sigma(\Sigma^2)} = 3.0515$					
$1/\sqrt{\Sigma(\Sigma^2)} = .32771$					
$X_1' = [.9323$	$.3605$	$.0292]$			
$\Sigma(X_1')^2 = 1.000$					

Factor I is the general (reasoning) factor
Test 1 (Comprehension) has a high loading also.

$k_2 = \sqrt{1 - .9323^2} = .36169$
$1/k_2 = 2.7648$
$-ab = -.33609$
$-ac = -.02722$

Factor II is the numerical or quantitative reasoning factor. It is not as clear-cut a group factor here as is factor I of Table 7.1.

$$Y_3 = \Lambda_g'$$

Factor III is the verbal factor. It is just about as clear a group factor as is factor III of Table 7.1.

	a	b	c
1	.9323	.3605	.0292
2	.3617	$-.9292$	$-.0753$
3	0	.0807	$-.9967$

Problem 8.4.2:1

TABLE P8.4.2:1
Landahl Transformation for Data of Table E8.1

	Landahl $L = FL_t$				*Landahl Trf* L_t		
Test	1	2	3		1	2	3
(1)	.362	.566	.607	a	.5774	.5774	.5774
(2)	.324	.673	.321	b	.8165	$-.4082$	$-.4082$
(3)	.334	.252	.623	c	0	.7071	$-.7071$
(4)	.299	.543	.501				
(5)	.259	.194	.565				
(6)	.277	.717	.527				
(7)	.398	.344	.396				
(8)	.580	.414	.315				
(9)	.716	.243	.305				
(10)	.536	.368	.385				
(11)	.709	.231	.125				
Σ	4.794	4.545	4.670				
Ch	4.794	4.545	4.671				
$\Sigma\ell^2$	2.378	2.221	2.220				

Exercise 9:1

TABLE E9:1
Procrustes Rotation for Nine Aptitude Tests ($N = 504$)

Test	Principal Axes F			FE^{-1}			Hypothesis H		
	a	b	c	a	b	c	I	II	III
(1)	.645	−.185	−.319	.148	−.236	−.777	1	0	0
(2)	.639	−.004	−.293	.147	−.005	−.714	1	0	0
(3)	.619	−.106	−.259	.142	−.135	−.631	1	0	0
(4)	.826	−.285	.201	.189	−.363	.490	0	1	0
(5)	.746	−.216	.035	.171	−.275	.085	0	1	0
(6)	.765	−.307	.304	.175	−.391	.741	0	1	0
(7)	.692	.483	−.004	.159	.615	−.010	0	0	1
(8)	.658	.438	.080	.151	.558	.195	0	0	1
(9)	.645	.305	.124	.148	.388	.302	0	0	1
Σ	6.235	.123	−.131	1.430	.156	−.319			
E	4.3594	.7858	.4105	1.430	.157	−.319			
E^{-1}	.2294	1.273	2.436						

Ch

	L				Rotated V_p			Extended Vectors[a] V		
	I	II	III	Test	I	II	III	I	II	III
a	.437	.535	.458	(1)	.468	.066	−.087	.487	.029	−.085
b	−.376	−1.029	1.561	(2)	.411	−.023	.085	.423	−.054	.088
c	−2.122	1.316	.487	(3)	.391	.057	−.005	.407	.024	−.003
				(4)	.019	.570	.019	.053	.540	.005
$\Sigma\ell^2$	4.835	3.077	2.884	(5)	.152	.381	.013	.179	.350	.005
				(6)	−.089	.642	.012	−.054	.616	−.005
$\sqrt{\Sigma\ell^2}$	2.199	1.754	1.698	(7)	.059	−.075	.630	.058	−.090	.630
				(8)	−.021	.004	.603	−.020	−.008	.601
$1/\sqrt{\Sigma\ell^2}$	.4548	.5701	.5889	(9)	−.043	.111	.490	−.037	.098	.485
				Σ	1.347	1.733	1.760			
				Ch	1.346	1.731	1.759			

	Λ_p		
	I	II	III
a	.199	.305	.270
b	−.171	−.587	.919
c	−.965	.750	.287
$\Sigma\lambda^2$	1.000	1.000	1.000

Hyperplane Counts				
	I	II	III	Σ
Procrustes	5	5	6	16
Extended Vector	5	6	6	17

TABLE E9:1 (continued)

| | | Absolute Sums | | | |
		I	II	III	Σ
The extended-vector solution is slightly better on both the hyperplane counts and absolute sums.	Procrustes	.231	.336	.221	.788
	Extended Vector	.222	.303	.191	.716

[a] From Exercise 7:1.

Exercise 9:2

TABLE E9:2
Procrustes Rotation for Six Psychological Tests ($N = 710$)

Test	Centroid F a	Centroid F b	FE^{-1} a	FE^{-1} b	Hypothesis H I	Hypothesis H II	Procrustes V_p I	Procrustes V_p II	Outer Centroids[a] V I	Outer Centroids[a] V II
(1)	.708	.484	.274	.354	1	0	.818	−.004	.817	−.005
(2)	.778	.504	.301	.369	1	0	.877	.019	.876	.017
(3)	.615	.428	.238	.313	1	0	.716	−.009	.716	−.011
(4)	.641	−.604	.248	−.442	0	1	−.080	.860	−.082	.859
(5)	.594	−.397	.230	−.291	0	1	.054	.662	.052	.661
(6)	.581	−.415	.225	−.304	0	1	.032	.670	.030	.669
Σ	3.917	.000	1.516	−.001			2.417	2.198		
E	2.586	1.366	1.515	.000			2.417	2.197		
E^{-1}	.3867	.7321								

Ch (under FE^{-1})   Ch (under Procrustes V_p)

	L I	L II	Procrustes Λ_p I	Procrustes Λ_p II
a	.813	.703	.617	.561
b	1.036	−1.037	.787	−.828
$\Sigma \ell^2$	1.7343	1.5696	1.000	1.000
$\sqrt{\Sigma \ell^2}$	1.3169	1.2528		
$1/\sqrt{\Sigma \ell^2}$	.7594	.7982		

[a] From Exercise 2:2.

Exercise 10:1

TABLE E10:1
Single-Hyperplane Rotations of Factor I for WAIS Age-Group 25–34 ($N = 300$)

Panel	Eq	Variable (1)	(2)	(3)	Constant Λ_{02}	Σ	$Ch\,(\Lambda_{12})$	Test V_{12}		Test $[V_{12}]$	
0	(1)	(3.3861)	.4047	.3652	.1620	4.3180	(.133)	(1)	.187	(3)	.365
	(2)	.4047	.4651	−.0456	−.2380	.5862	(−.226)	(2)	−.107	(5)	.354
	(3)	.3652	−.0456	.0925	−.9580	−.5459	(−.965)	(3)	.365	(1)	.187
1	(2)		(.4167)	−.0893	−.2573	.0701	.0701	(4)	.115	(7)	.118
	(3)		−.0892	.0531	−.9755	−1.0116	−1.0116	(5)	.354	(4)	.115
	(1)	1		.1195	.1079	.0478	1.2752	1.2752	(6)	.051	(10)	.081
2	(3)			(.0340)	−1.0306	−.9966	−.9966	(7)	.118	(9)	.058
	(1)	1		.1335	.1216	1.2551	1.2551	(8)	−.007	(6)	.051
	(2)		1	−.2143	−.6175	.1682	.1682	(9)	.058	(8)	−.007
3	(1)	1			4.1683	5.1683	5.1683	(10)	.081	(11)	−.088
	(2)		1	$U_{02} =$	−7.1134	−6.1134	−6.1134	(11)	−.088	(2)	−.107
	(3)			1	−30.3120	−29.3120	−29.3120	Σ	1.127		
								Ch	1.127		

$$\Sigma\Sigma(f_{02}f_{02}) = 5.3923; \quad Ch = 5.3924 \quad | \quad r_{m1}^2 = 31.41; \quad r_{m2}^2 = 31.41$$

$$\Sigma u_{02}^2 = 986.79; \quad \sqrt{\Sigma u_{02}^2} = 31.416; \quad 1/\sqrt{\Sigma u_{02}^2} = .03183; \quad \Sigma\lambda_{12}^2 = 1.000$$

Try weight 2 on variable 2.

Panel	Eq	Variable (1)	(2)	(3)	Constant Λ_{12}	Σ	$Ch\,(\Lambda_{22})$	Test V_{22}		Test $[V_{22}]$	
0	(1)	(3.9652)	.2974	.5547	.1330	4.9503	(.155)	(1)	.215	(3)	.380
	(2)	.2974	.4850	−.0807	−.2260	.4757	(−.272)	(2)	−.080	(5)	.368
	(3)	.5547	−.0807	.1545	−.9650	−.3365	(−.950)	(3)	.380	(1)	.215
1	(2)		(.4627)	−.1223	−.2360	.1044	.1044	(4)	.141	(4)	.141
	(3)		−.1223	.0769	−.9836	−1.0290	−1.0290	(5)	.368	(7)	.131
	(1)	1		.0750	.1399	.0335	1.2484	1.2484	(6)	.085	(10)	.091
2	(3)			(.0446)	−1.0460	−1.0014	−1.0014	(7)	.131	(6)	.085
	(1)	1		.1597	.0718	1.2315	1.2315	(8)	.003	(9)	.057
	(2)		1	−.2643	−.5100	.2257	.2256	(9)	.057	(8)	.003
3	(1)	1			3.8173	4.8173	4.8173	(10)	.091	(2)	−.080
	(2)		1	$U_{12} =$	−6.7087	−5.7087	−5.7087	(11)	−.094	(11)	−.094
	(3)			1.	−23.4534	−22.4534	−22.4534	Σ	1.297		
								Ch	1.297		

$$\Sigma\Sigma(f_{12}f_{12}) = 6.1475; \quad Ch = 6.1476 \quad | \quad r_{m1}^2 = 24.66; \quad r_{m2}^2 = 24.66$$

$$\Sigma u_{12}^2 = 609.64; \quad \sqrt{\Sigma u_{12}^2} = 24.691; \quad 1/\sqrt{\Sigma u_{12}^2} = .04050; \quad \Sigma\lambda_{22}^2 = 1.001$$

$.094 - .091 = .003$, so this completes the refinement.

Exercise 11:1

TABLE E11:1
Primary Factors and Second-Order Analysis for Nine Aptitude Tests ($N = 504$)

Test	F (Exercise 7:1)			$V = F\Lambda$			$P = VD^{-1}$		
	a	b	c	I	II	III	I	II	III
(1)	.645	−.185	−.319	.487	.029	−.085	.781	.044	−.116
(2)	.639	−.004	−.293	.423	−.054	.088	.679	−.083	.121
(3)	.619	−.106	−.259	.408	.025	−.003	.655	.038	−.004
(4)	.826	−.285	.201	.054	.540	.005	.087	.827	.007
(5)	.746	−.216	.035	.179	.350	.005	.287	.536	.007
(6)	.765	−.307	.304	−.054	.617	−.005	−.087	.945	−.007
(7)	.692	.483	−.004	.058	−.090	.630	.093	−.138	.863
(8)	.658	.438	.080	−.020	−.008	.601	−.032	−.012	.823
(9)	645	.305	.124	−.037	.098	.486	−.059	.150	.666
Σ	6.235	.123	−.131	1.498	1.507	1.722	2.404	2.307	2.360
Ch				1.497	1.507	1.721	2.403	2.307	2.358

Λ (Exercise 7:1)

	I	II	III
a	.2242	.2692	.2631
b	−.2095	−.5653	.9290
c	−.9518	.7797	.2602
Σ^2	1.0001	1.0000	1.0000

	(1)	(2)	(3)	Σ^2	$\sqrt{\Sigma^2}$	$1/\sqrt{\Sigma^2}$
(1)	1	−.1550	−.4577	1.23351	1.110635	.900386
$E' = $ (2)	1	−.3721	.3174	1.23920	1.113194	.898316 $\}$ diag Δ
(3)	1		.6145	.1003	1.38767	1.177994	.848901

	(1)	(2)	(3)		
(1)	.9004	−.1396	−.4121	1.0000	
$T' = $ (2)	.8983	−.3343	.2851	1.0000	$= \Sigma t^2$
(3)	.8489	.5216	.0851	.9999	

$R_s = T'T$

	I	II	III
(1)	1.0000	.7380	.6565
(2)	.7380	1.0000	.6125
(3)	.6565	.6125	1.0000

diag $(\Delta^{-1}D)$ .69223   .72711   .86022 (From Exercise 7:1)
diag D .62327   .65317   .73024 $= (diag\ \Delta)\ [diag\ (\Delta^{-1}D)]$
diag D^{-1} 1.6044   1.5310   1.3694 $= 1/diag\ D$

Second-Order Triad Analysis

$$r_{12} = .7380$$
$$r_{13} = .6565$$
$$r_{23} = .6125$$
$$t_{123} = r_{12}r_{13}/r_{23} = .7910 = h_1^2$$
$$t_{213} = r_{12}r_{23}/r_{13} = .6885 = h_2^2$$
$$t_{312} + r_{13}r_{23}/r_{12} = .5449 = h_3^2$$
$$g_1^2 + s_1^2 = 1.0001$$

$$g_1 = \sqrt{h_1^2} = .8894$$
$$g_2 = \sqrt{h_2^2} = .8298$$
$$g_3 = \sqrt{h_3^2} = .7382$$
$$s_1 = \sqrt{1 - h_1^2} = \sqrt{.2090} = .4572$$
$$s_2 = \sqrt{1 - h_2^2} = \sqrt{.3115} = .5581$$
$$s_3 = \sqrt{1 - h_3^2} = \sqrt{.4551} = .6746$$
$$\left. \right\} = G$$

$$g_2^2 + s_2^2 = 1.0000 \qquad\qquad g_3^2 + s_3^2 = 1.0000$$

Exercise 11:2

TABLE E11:2
Hierarchical Orthogonal Solution for Nine Aptitude Tests ($N = 504$)

Factor	Matrix G				diag D^{-1}	Matrix $T_g = D^{-1}G$			
	g	s_1	s_2	s_3		g	s_1	s_2	s_3
I	.8894	.4572	0	0	1.6044	1.4270	.7335	0	0
II	.8298	0	.5581	0	1.5310	1.2704	0	.8545	0
III	.7382	0	0	.6746	1.3694	1.0109	0	0	.9238

Test	Matrix $H = VT_g{}^a$					Communalities		
	g	gr_1	gr_2	gr_3	u	h_h^2	h_f^2	$h_f^2 - h_h^2$
(1)	.646	.357	.025	−.079	.669	.552	.552	.000
(2)	.624	.310	−.046	.081	.711	.494	.494	.000
(3)	.611	.299	.021	−.003	.733	.463	.461	−.002
(4)	.768	.040	.461	.005	.443	.804	.804	.000
(5)	.705	.131	.299	.005	.629	.604	.604	.000
(6)	.702	−.040	.527	−.005	.477	.772	.772	.000
(7)	.605	.043	−.077	.582	.536	.713	.712	−.001
(8)	.569	−.015	−.007	.555	.607	.632	.631	−.001
(9)	.563	−.027	.084	.449	.688	.526	.524	−.002
Σ	5.793	1.098	1.287	1.590		5.560	5.554	−.006
Ch	5.793	1.099	1.288	1.591				

[a] g = general intelligence;
 gr_1 = quantitative reasoning;
 gr_2 = verbal relations;
 gr_3 = visual space manipulation.

Exercise 12:1

TABLE E12:1
Centroid Component Analysis of Six Psychological Tests ($N = 710$)

Test	(1)	(2)	(3)	(4)	(5)	(6)	Σ	Ch
(1)	(1.000)	.769	.671	.158	.211	.231	3.040	
(2)	.769	(1.000)	.681	.189	.268	.242	3.149	
(3)	.671	.681	(1.000)	.144	.207	.159	2.862	
(4)	.158	.189	.144	(1.000)	.621	.623	2.735	
(5)	.211	.268	.207	.621	(1.000)	.510	2.817	
(6)	.231	.242	.159	.623	.510	(1.000)	2.765	
Σ	3.040	3.149	2.862	2.735	2.817	2.765	17.368	17.368
a	.7294	.7556	.6867	.6563	.6759	.6635−	4.1674	4.1675
Refl				1	3	2		
(1)	(.468)	.218	.170	╫ .321	╫ .282	╫ .253	.000	1.712
(2)	.218	(.429)	.162	╫ .307	╫ .243	╫ .259	.000	1.618
(3)	.170	.162	(.528)	╫ .307	╫ .257	╫ .297	— .001	1.721
(4)	╫ .321	╫ .307	╫ .307	(.569)	╪ .177	╪ .188	— .001	1.869
(5)	╫ .282	╫ .243	╫ .257	╪ .177	(.543)	╪ .062	.000	1.564
(6)	╫ .253	╫ .259	╫ .297	╪ .188	╪ .062	(.560)	.001	1.619
Σ	1.712	1.618	1.721	1.869	1.564	1.619	10.103	10.103
b	.5386	.5090	.5414	= .5880	= .4921	= .5094	3.1785	3.1785
Refl	2	4		3	1			
(1)	(.178)	⊕ .056	╫ .122	╪ .004	╪ .017	╫ .021	.000	.286
(2)	⊕ .056	(.170)	╫ .114	╪ .008	⊕ .007	.000	.001	.229
(3)	╫ .122	╫ .114	(.235)	╫ .011	╫ .009	.021	.000	.512
(4)	╪ .004	╪ .008	╫ .011	(.223)	⊕ .112	╫ .112	.000	.246
(5)	╪ .017	⊕ .007	╫ .009	⊕ .112	(.301)	╫ .189	.001	.397
(6)	╫ .021	.000	.021	╫ .112	╫ .189	(.301)	.000	.644
Σ	.286	.229	.512	.246	.397	.644	2.314	2.314
c	= .1880	= .1505+	.3366	.1617	.2610	= .4234	1.5212	1.5212
Refl					1	2		
(1)	(.143)	— .084	.059	— .026	╫ .032	╫ .059	.001	.183
(2)	— .084	(.147)	.063	— .016	╫ .046	╫ .064	.000	.220
(3)	.059	.063	(.122)	— .043	╫ .079	╪ .122	.000	.402
(4)	— .026	— .016	— .043	(.197)	╫ .154	= .044	.002	.222
(5)	╫ .032	╫ .046	╫ .079	╫ .154	(.233)	╫ .078	.000	.622
(6)	╫ .059	╫ .064	╫ .122	= .044	╪ .078	(.122)	— .001	.401
Σ	.183	.220	.402	.222	.622	.401	2.050	2.050
d	= .1278	= .1537	.2808	.1550	= .4344	.2801	1.4318	1.4318

(*continued*)

TABLE E12:1 (*continued*)

Refl	3		1	2				
(1)	(.127)	+.104	.023	+.046	+.024	.023	−.001	.347
(2)	+.104	(.123)	=.020	⊕.040	⊕.021	=.021	−.001	.125
(3)	.023	=.020	(.043)	+.087	+.043	.043	−.001	.219
(4)	+.046	⊕.040	+.087	(.173)	+.087	+.087	.000	.440
(5)	+.024	⊕.021	+.043	+.087	(.044)	+.044	−.001	.221
(6)	.023	=.021	.043	+.087	+.044	(.044)	.000	.220
Σ	.347	.125	.219	.440	.221	.220	1.572	1.572
e	=.2768	.0997	.1747	=.3509	.1763	.1755−	1.2539	1.2538

Refl	2	1						
(1)	(.050)	+.076	+.025	+.051	+.025	+.026	−.001	.253
(2)	+.076	(.113)	+.037	+.075	+.039	+.038	.000	.378
(3)	+.025	+.037	(.012)	.026	.012	.012	.000	.124
(4)	+.051	+.075	.026	(.050)	.025	.025	.000	.252
(5)	+.025	+.039	.012	.025	(.013)	.013	−.001	.127
(6)	+.026	+.038	.012	.025	.013	(.013)	−.001	.127
Σ	.253	.378	.124	.252	.127	.127	1.261	1.261
f	.2253	=.3366	.1104	=.2244	.1131	.1131	1.1229	1.1229

Centroid Component Matrix A

Test	a	b	c	d	e	f
(1)	.7294	.5386	−.1880	−.1278	−.2768	.2253
(2)	.7556	.5090	−.1505	−.1537	.0997	−.3366
(3)	.6867	.5414	.3366	.2808	.1747	.1104
(4)	.6563	−.5880	.1617	.1550	−.3509	−.2244
(5)	.6759	−.4921	.2610	−.4344	.1763	.1131
(6)	.6635	−.5094	−.4234	.2801	.1755	.1131
Σa^2	2.9023	1.6897	.4448	.4100	.3021	.2522
Cum Σa^2	2.9023	4.5920	5.0368	5.4468	5.7489	6.0011 ≐ 6.0000
% Trace	48	77	84	91	96	100

Exercise 14:1

TABLE E14:1
Cluster Analysis of Nine Aptitude Tests ($N = 504$)

	T'			Landahl Trf L_t			L_n		
	(1)	(2)	(3)	(1)	(2)	(3)	I	II	III
(1)	.9004	−.1396	−.4121	.5774	.5774	.5774	.4059	.2855	.8683
(2)	.8983	−.3343	.2851	.8165	−.4082	−.4082	.2457	.8567	.4535
(3)	.8489	.5216	.0851	0	.7071	.7071	.9160	.3374	.2171

		F			Normalization Factors			F_n	
Test	a	b	c	Σ^2	$\sqrt{\Sigma^2}$	$1/\sqrt{\Sigma^2}$	a	b	c
(1)	.645	−.185	−.319	.55201	.74297	1.34595	.8681	−.2490	−.4294
(2)	.639	−.004	−.293	.49419	.70299	1.42250	.9090	−.0057	−.4168
(3)	.619	−.106	−.259	.46148	.67932	1.47206	.9112	−.1560	−.3813
(4)	.826	−.285	.201	.80390	.89660	1.11532	.9213	−.3179	.2242
(5)	.746	−.216	.035	.60440	.77743	1.28629	.9596	−.2778	.0450
(6)	.765	−.307	.304	.77189	.87857	1.13821	.8707	−.3494	.3460
(7)	.692	.483	−.004	.71217	.84390	1.18497	.8200	.5723	−.0047
(8)	.658	.438	.080	.63121	.79449	1.25867	.8282	.5513	.1007
(9)	.645	.305	.124	.52443	.72418	1.38087	.8907	.4212	.1712
Σ	6.235	.123	−.131	5.55568			7.9788	.1890	−.3451
Σf^2	4.35938	.78576	.41052	5.55566					

Clusters		Normalized Landahl L_n			
Test	Cosine	Test	1	2	3
1–2	.969	(1)	.2979	.2993	.9065
1–3	.994	(2)	.5202	.2325	.8219
2–3	.988	(3)	.3988	.3202	.8594
		(4)	.2724	.8203	.5032
		(5)	.3272	.6993	.6357
4–5	.982	(6)	.2175	.8900	.4007
4–6	.991	(7)	.9408	.2365	.2432
5–6	.948	(8)	.9283	.3244	.1820
		(9)	.8582	.4634	.2213
7–8	.994	Σ	4.7613	4.2859	4.7739
7–9	.971	Ch	4.7613	4.2858	4.7738
8–9	.987	Mean	.5290	.4762	.5304

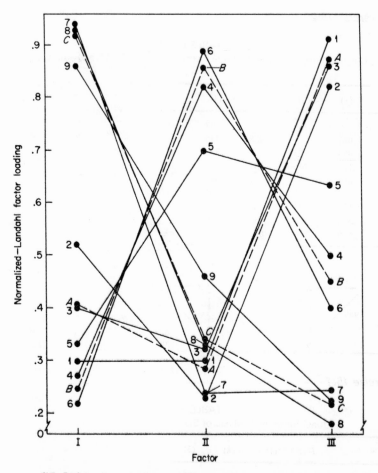

FIG. E14:1   Normalized Landahl profiles for nine aptitude tests ($N = 504$).

Exercise 14:2

TABLE E14:2
Cosine Matrix for Nine Aptitude Tests, and Elementary Linkage Analysis
($N = 300$)

Test	(1)	(2)	(3)	(4)	(5)	(6)	(7)	(8)	(9)
(1)		.969	.994	.783	.883	.694	.571	.538	.595
(2)	.969		.988	.746	.855	.649	.744	.708	.736
(3)	.994	.988		.804	.901	.716	.660	.630	.681
(4)	.783	.746	.804		.982	.991	.572	.610	.725
(5)	.883	.855	.901	.982		.948	.628	.646	.745
(6)	.694	.649	.716	.991	.948		.512	.563	.688
(7)	.571	.744	.660	.572	.628	.512		.994	.971
(8)	.538	.708	.630	.610	.646	.563	.994		.987
(9)	.595	.736	.681	.725	.745	.688	.971	.987	

Exercise 15:1

TABLE E15:1
Quasi-Simplex Analysis of Six Arithmetic Tests ($N = 240$)

Test	(1)	(2)	(3)	(4)	(5)	(6)	Σ	$Ch\ (r)$
(1)		.62	.62	.54	.29	.28	2.35	.62
(2)	.62		.67	.53	.38	37	2.57	.67
(3)	.62	.67		.62	.48	.52	2.91	.67
(4)	.54	.53	.62		.62	.57	2.88	.62
(5)	.29	.38	.48	.62		.64	2.41	.64
(6)	.28	.37	.52	.57	.64		2.38	.64

		(1)	(2)	(3)	(4)	(5)	(6)		
$[\overline{\Sigma}' = 2.583]$	Σ'	2.35	2.57	2.91	2.88	2.41	2.38	15.50	15.50
	$\Sigma' + \overline{\Sigma}' = S$	4.933	5.153	5.493	5.463	4.993	4.963	30.998	30.998
	r	.62	.67	.67	.62	.64	.64	3.86	3.86
$\left[Q = \dfrac{\Sigma r}{\Sigma rS} = .1935\right]$	rS	3.058	3.453	3.680	3.387	3.196	3.176	19.950	19.950
	$QrS = C$	.59	.69	.71	.66	.62	.61	3.88	3.86
larger of r or $C = h^2$		.62	.69	.71	.66	.64	.64		
	h	.7874	.8307	.8426	.8124	.8000	.8000		

(*continued*)

TABLE E15:1 (continued)

		$h_i h_j$						$\rho_{ij} = r_{ij}/h_i h_j$				
Test	(2)	(3)	(4)	(5)	(6)	Test	(1)	(2)	(3)	(4)	(5)	(6)
(1)	.6541	.6635	.6397	.6299	.6299	(1)		.9479	.9344	.8441	.4604	.4445
(2)		.6999	.6749	.6646	.6646	(2)	.9479		.9573	.7853	.5718	.5567
(3)			.6845	.6741	.6741	(3)	.9344	.9573		.9058	.7121	.7714
(4)				.6499	.6499	(4)	.8441	.7853	.9058		.9540	.8771
(5)					.6400	(5)	.4604	.5718	.7121	.9540		1.0000
						(6)	.4445	.5567	.7714	.8771	1.0000	

Σ' 3.6313   3.8190   4.2810   4.3663   3.6983   3.6497

Test of Order for Tests 3 and 4

Test	(1)	(2)	(3)	(4)	(5)	(6)	Σ
(3)	.02947	.01895		$-.04297$	$-.14746$	$-.14272$	$-.28473 = P_i$
(4)	.07361	.10496	(.04297)		$-.02045$	$-.05695$	$.14414 = P_{i+1}$

Order correct: $.08494 = 2P_{(i+1)i}$ $<$ $.42887 = P_{i+1} - P_i$

p's, Reciprocals, and Estimates of a's

Test	(1)	(2)	(3)	(4)	(5)	(6)		
(6)	.4445	.5567	.7714	.8771	1.0000	1.0000		
(1)		.9479	.9344	.8441	.4604	.4445		
(2)	1.0550		.9573	.7853	.5718	.5567		
(3)	1.0702	1.0446		.9058	.7121	.7714		
(4)	1.1847	1.2734	1.1040		.9540	.8771		
(5)	2.1720	1.7489	1.4043	1.0482		1.0000	Σ	a_i
(1)		.5277	.7208	.7404	.4604	.4445	2.8938	.5788
(2)	.4689		.7385	.6888	.5718	.5567	3.0247	.6049
(3)	.4757	.5815		.7945	.7121	.7714	3.3352	.6670
(4)	.5266	.7089	.8516		.9540	.8771	3.9182	.7836
(5)	.9655	.9736	1.0833	.9194		1.0000	4.9418	.9884

$a_6 = 1.0000$

TABLE E15:1 *(continued)*

	Reproduced $\rho^\dagger_{ij} = a_i/a_j$						Reproduced $r^\dagger_{ij} = \rho^\dagger_{ij} h_i h_j$				
Test	(2)	(3)	(4)	(5)	(6)	Test	(2)	(3)	(4)	(5)	(6)
(1)	.9569	.8678	.7386	.5856	.5788	(1)	.6259	.5758	.4725−	.3689	.3646
(2)		.9069	.7719	.6120	.6049	(2)		.6347	.5210	.4067	.4020
(3)			.8512	.6748	.6670	(3)			.5826	.4549	.4496
(4)				.7928	.7836	(4)				.5152	.5093
(5)					.9884	(5)					.6390

	Residuals $d_{ij} = r_{ij} - r^\dagger_{ij}$					Test of Fit
Test	(2)	(3)	(4)	(5)	(6)	$\Sigma d^2 = .044762 \qquad \sigma_r = .08146$
(1)	−.006	.044	.068	−.079	−.085	$\overline{d^2} = .002984$
(2)		.035	.009	−.027	−.032	
(3)			.037	.025	.070	$\sqrt{\overline{d^2}} = .0546$
(4)				.105	.061	
(5)					.001	

2 Computer Programs

The methods of factor analysis described and recommended in this book have been programmed in FORTRAN IV. The manual is: Durfee, R. C. and Cureton, E. E., *Manual for Seven Factor Analysis Programs*, Oak Ridge National Laboratory Report ORNL/CSD-107, 1982. Copies, either printed or microfiche, may be obtained from the National Technical Information Service, U.S. Department of Commerce, 5285 Port Royal Road, Springfield, VA 22161. The additional code for the printed copy is A-10. The seven programs are (1) PRINAX, (2) ROTATE, (3) FACTOR [combines (1) and (2) with interpolated subroutine for the number of factors], (4) REFINE, (5) PRIFAC (gives primary factor-pattern matrix and second-order correlation matrix), (6) HIRARC (gives hierarchical orthogonal solution), (7) FSCORE (gives factor scores). There is also a program for single-order cluster analysis as described in Chapter 14, with a separate leaflet manual.

Any of these programs (and the cluster analysis leaflet) may be obtained by sending a blank tape (9 track, 800 SPI), along with return postage, to the University of Tennessee Computing Center, Knoxville, Tennessee, attention User Service.

Several of the standard packages of statistical software include factor analysis programs. The accompanying tabulation shows some of the main characteristics of the four programs with which the writers are most familiar. The manuals are:

440

Characteristics	BMD	SPSS	OSIRIS	SAS
Initial factoring				
Principal axes	X	X	X	X
Iterated principal axes	X	X		X
Maximum likelihood	X			X
Canonical		X		
Image analysis	X[1]	X		X
Alpha factor analysis		X		X
Communality estimates				
Unities (principal components)	X	X	X	X
SMC's	X	X	X	X
$|r|max$'s	X	X		X
Specified		X	X	X
Number of factors				
No. of eigenvalues greater than specified constant	X			X
No. of eigenvalues greater than unity in principal components solution		X	X	X
No. of eigenvalues to account for specified per cent of trace			X	X
No. specified	X	X		X
Rotation				
Varimax	X	X	X	X
Quartimax	X	X		X
Equamax	X	X		X
Oblimin (including direct oblimin)	X	X	X	
Orthoblique (Little Jiffy only)	X[1]			
Promax with power specified				X
Factor scores	X	X	X	X

[1]Kaiser second-generation Little Jiffy (1970).

BMD.   Frane, J. & Jennrich, R. Factor analysis. In J. W. Dixon (Series ed.) & M. B. Brown (Ed. 1977 ed.) *Biomedical computer programs,* P-series (BMDP-77). Berkeley: University of California Press, 1977, 656–684.

SPSS.   Kim, J-O. Factor analysis. In N. H. Nie, C. H. Hull, J. G. Jenkins, K. Steinbrenner, & D. H. Bent. (Eds.), *Statistical package for the social sciences* (2nd ed.). New York: McGraw-Hill, 1975, 468–514.

OSIRIS.   Miller, A. H., Barge, S. J., & Wang, S. Factor analysis and multidimensional scaling. In S. J. Barge & G. A. Marks (Eds.), *OSIRIS III System and program description* (Vol. I). Ann Arbor, Michigan: Center for Political Studies, Survey Research Center ISR, 1973, 597–675.

SAS.   Sall, J. P. Factor. In J. T. Helwig & K. A. Council (Eds.), *SAS Users Guide* (1979 ed.). Raleigh, N.C.: SAS Institute, 1979, 203–210.

References

This list contains only the references cited in the text. Fairly extensive bibliographies are contained in Harman (1976), Mulaik (1972), and Rummel (1970).

Ahmavaara, Y. Transformation analysis of factorial data. *Annales Academiae Scientiarum Fennicae*, 1954 (Series B 88, 2).

Albert, A. A. The matrices of factor analysis. *Proceedings of the National Academy of Sciences*, 1944, *30*, 90–95. (a)

Albert, A. A. The minimum rank of a correlation matrix. *Proceedings of the National Academy of Sciences*, 1944, *30*, 144–148. (b)

Anderberg, M. R. *Cluster analysis for applications*. New York: Academic Press, 1973.

Baker, B. O., Hardyck, C. D., & Petrinovich, L. F. Weak measurement *vs* strong statistics: An empirical critique of S. S. Stevens. *Educational and Psychological Measurement*, 1966, *26*, 291–309.

Bargmann, R. *A study of independence and dependence in multivariate normal statistics*. (Institute of Statistics, Mimeographed Series No. 186.) Chapel Hill: University of North Carolina Press, 1957.

Bargmann, R., & Brown, R. H. *IBM 650 programs for factor analysis*. Blacksburg: Virginia Polytechnic Institute, 1961. (Mimeographed)

Bartlett, M. S. The statistical conception of mental factors. *British Journal of Psychology*, 1937, *28*, 97–104.

Bartlett, M. S. Tests of significance in factor analysis. *British Journal of Psychology, Statistical Section*, 1950, *3*, 77–85.

Bartlett, M. S. A further note on tests of significance in factor analysis. *British Journal of Psychology, Statistical Section*, 1951, *4*, 1–2.

Bentler, P. M. Factor simplicity index and transformations. *Psychometrika*, 1977, *42*, 277–295.

Blashfield, R. K., & Aldenderfer, M. S. The literature of cluster analysis. *Multivariate Behavior Research*, 1978, *13*, 271–295.

Burket, G. R. A study of reduced rank models for multiple prediction. *Psychometric Monographs*, 1964 (No. 12).

Butler, J. M. Simplest data factors and simple structure in factor analysis. *Educational and Psychological Measurement*, 1964, *24*, 755-763.

Carroll, J. B. An analytic solution for approximating simple structure in factor analysis. *Psychometrika*, 1953, *18*, 23-38.

Carroll, J. B. Biquartimin criterion for rotation to oblique simple structure in factor analysis. *Science*, 1957, *126*, 1114-1115.

Cattell, R. B. The scree test for the number of factors. *Multivariate Behavioral Research*, 1966, *1*, 245-276.

Claudy, J. G. Multiple regression and validity estimation in one sample. *Applied Psychological Measurement*, 1978, *2*, 595-607.

Comrey, A. L. The minimum residual method of factor analysis. *Psychological Reports*, 1962, *11*, 15-18.

Comrey, A. L., & Ahumadra, A. An improved procedure and program for minimum residual factor analysis. *Psychological Reports*, 1964, *15*, 91-96.

Comrey, A. L., & Ahumadra, A. Note and FORTRAN program for minimum residual factor analysis. *Psychological Reports*, 1965, *17*, 446.

Cormack, R. M. A review of classification. *Journal of the Royal Statistical Society* (Series A), 1971, *134*, 321-367.

Cureton, E. E. A note on factor analysis: Arbitrary orthogonal transformations. *Psychometrika*, 1959, *24*, 169-174.

Cureton, E. E. *A factor analysis of Project TALENT tests and four other test batteries.* (Interim Report No. 4 to the U.S. Office of Education, Cooperative Research Project No. 3051.) Palo Alto: American Institutes for Research and University of Pittsburgh, 1968.

Cureton, E. E. Communality estimation in factor analysis of small matrices. *Educational and Psychological Measurement*, 1971, *31*, 371-380.

Cureton, E. E. Studies of the Promax and Optres rotations. *Multivariate Behavioral Research*, 1976, *4*, 449-460.

Cureton, E. E., Cook, R. T., Fischer, R. T., Laser, S. A., Rockwell, N. J., & Simmons, J. W., Jr. Length of test and standard error of measurement. *Educational and Psychological Measurement*, 1973, *33*, 63-68.

Cureton, E. E., Cureton, L. W., & Durfee, R. C. A method of cluster analysis. *Multivariate Behavioral Research*, 1970, *5*, 101-116.

Cureton, E. E., et al. *Verbal abilities experiment: Analysis of new word meaning and verbal analogies tests* (Personnel Research Section, AGO, PRS Report No. 548). Arlington, Va.: War Department, 1944. (Mimeographed)

Cureton, E. E., & Mulaik, S. A. On simple structure and the solution of Thurstone's "invariant" box problem. *Multivariate Behavioral Research*, 1971, *6*, 375-387.

Cureton, E. E., & Mulaik, S. A. The weighted varimax rotation and the Promax rotation. *Psychometrika*, 1975, *40*, 183-195.

Cureton, L. W. *Early identification of behavior problems*, Vol. I. (Final Report to the National Institutes of Mental Health, Grant No. MH-07274.) Silver Spring, Md.: American Institutes for Research, 1970. (Available from American Institutes for Research, Palo Alto, Ca.)

Davis, F. B. Research in comprehension in reading. *Reading Research Quarterly*, 1968, *3*, 499-546.

Dubois, P. H. An analysis of Guttman's simplex. *Psychometrika*, 1960, *25*, 173-182.

Dwyer, P. S. The determination of factor loadings of a given test from the known factor loadings of other tests. *Psychometrika*, 1937, *2*, 173-178.

Dwyer, P. S. *Linear computations.* New York: Wiley, 1951.

Eber, H. E. Maxplane meets Thurstone's "invariant" box problem. *Multivariate Behavioral Research*, 1968, *3*, 249-254.

Edgerton, H. A., & Kolbe, L. E. The method of minimum variation for the combination of criteria. *Psychometrika*, 1936, *1*, 183-187.

Everitt, B. S. *Cluster analysis*. London: Halstead Press, 1974.

Ferguson, G. A. The concept of parsimony in factor analysis. *Psychometrika*, 1954, *19*, 281-290.

Garnett, J. C. M. On certain independent factors in mental measurement. *Proceedings of the Royal Society of London*, 1919, *46*, 91-111.

Gitter, A. G., D'Agostino, R. B., & Graffman, R. A. *Quality of army life: The effects of military leadership* (Army Research Institute for Behavioral and Social Sciences Report DAHC 19-74-C-0020). Arlington, Va.: Department of the Army, 1975.

Guttman, L. Multiple rectilinear prediction and the resolution into components. *Psychometrika*, 1940, *5*, 75-99.

Guttman, L General theory and methods of matric factoring. *Psychometrika*, 1944, *9*, 1-16.

Guttman, L. Image theory for the structure of quantitative variables. *Psychometrika*, 1953, *18*, 277-296.

Guttman, L. Some necessary conditions for common-factor analysis. *Psychometrika*, 1954, *19*, 149-161. (a)

Guttman, L. A new approach to factor analysis: The radex. In P. F. Lazarsfeld (Ed.), *Mathematical thinking in the social sciences*. Glencoe, Ill.: Free Press, 1954, 258-348. (b)

Hakstian, A. R. Optimizing the resolution between salient and non-salient factor pattern coefficients. *British Journal of Mathematical and Statistical Psychology*, 1972, *25*, 229-245.

Hamaker, H. C. Approximating the cumulative normal distribution. *Applied Statistics*, 1978, *27*, 76-77.

Harman, H. H. Extensions of factorial solutions. *Psychometrika*, 1938, *3*, 75-84.

Harman, H. H. *Modern factor analysis* (3rd ed). Chicago: University of Chicago Press, (1st ed.) 1960, (2nd ed.) 1967, (3rd ed.) 1976.

Harman, H. H., & Jones, W. H. Factor analysis by minimizing residuals (minres). *Psychometrika*, 1966, *31*, 351-368.

Harris, C. W. Some Rao-Guttman relationships. *Psychometrika*, 1962, *27*, 247-263.

Harris, C. W., & Kaiser, H. F. Oblique factor analytic solutions by orthogonal transformations. *Psychometrika*, 1964, *29*, 347-362.

Hartigan, J. *Clustering algorithms*. New York: Wiley, 1975.

Hastings, C. *Approximations for digital computers*. Princeton: Princeton University Press, 1955.

Hendrickson, A. E., & White, P. O. Promax: A quick method of rotation to oblique simple structure. *British Journal of Statistical Psychology*, 1964, *17*, 65-70.

Heywood, H. B. On finite sequences of real numbers. *Proceedings of the Royal Society of London*, 1931, *134*, 486-501.

Holzinger, K. J., & Harman, H. *Factor analysis*. Chicago: University of Chicago Press, 1941.

Horst, P. Obtaining a composite measure from a number of different measures of the same attribute. *Psychometrika*, 1936, *1*, 53-60.

Horst, P. Matrix reduction and approximation to principal axes. *Psychometrika*, 1962, *27*, 169-178.

Horst, P. *Matrix algebra for social scientists*. New York: Holt, Rinehart & Winston, 1963.

Horst, P. *Factor analysis of data matrices*. New York: Holt, Rinehart & Winston, 1965.

Hotelling, H. Analysis of a complex of statistical variables into principal components. *Journal of Educational Psychology*, 1933, *24*, 417-441, 498-520.

Hotelling, H. Simplified calculation of principal components. *Psychometrika*, 1936, *1*, 27-35.

Humphreys, L. G. Investigations of the simplex. *Psychometrika*, 1960, *25*, 313-323.

Hunter, J. E. Maximal decomposition: An alternative to factor analysis. *Multivariate Behavioral Research*, 1972, *7*, 243-268.

Hurley, J. R., & Cattell, R. B. The procrustes program: Producing direct rotation to test a hypothesized factor structure. *Behavioral Science*, 1962, *7*, 258-262.

Jennrich, R. I., & Sampson, P. F. Rotation for simple loadings. *Psychometrika*, 1966, *31*, 313–323.

Jones, M. B. *Simplex theory*. Pensacola: U.S. Naval School of Aviation Medicine, 1959.

Jones, M. B. *Molar correlational analysis*. Pensacola: U.S. Naval School of Aviation Medicine, 1960.

Jöreskog, K. G. Estimation and testing of simplex models. *British Journal of Mathematical and Statistical Psychology*, 1970, *23*, (Part 2), 121–145.

Kaiser, H. F. The varimax criterion for analytic rotation in factor analysis. *Psychometrika*, 1958, *23*, 187–200.

Kaiser, H. F. Formulas for component scores. *Psychometrika*, 1962, 27, 83–87. (a)

Kaiser, H. F. Scaling a simplex. *Psychometrika*, 1962, 27, 155–162. (b)

Kaiser, H. F. A second-generation Little Jiffy. *Psychometrika*, 1970, *35*, 401–415.

Kaiser, H. F. A note on the equamax criterion. *Multivariate Behavioral Research*, 1974, *9*, 501–503.

Kaiser, H. F. Review of *Factor analysis as a statistical method* (2nd ed.) by D. N. Lawley & A. E. Maxwell. *Educational and Psychological Measurement*, 1976, *36*, 586–588.

Kaiser, H. F., & Caffrey, J. Alpha factor analysis. *Psychometrika*, 1965, *30*, 1–14.

Kaiser, H. F., & Rice, J. Little Jiffy, Mark IV. *Educational and Psychological Measurement*, 1974, *34*, 111–117.

Kelley, T. L. *Statistical method*. New York: Macmillan, 1923.

Kelley, T. L. *Interpretation of educational measurements*. Yonkers-on-Hudson: World Book, 1927.

Kelley, T. L. *Crossroads in the mind of man*. Stanford: Stanford University Press, 1928.

Kendall, M. G. The geographical distribution of crop productivity in England. *Journal of the Royal Statistical Society*, 1939, *102*, 21–48.

Kendall, M. G. *Rank correlation methods* (2nd ed.). New York: Hafner, 1955.

Kendall, M. G. *A course in multivariate analysis*. (Griffin Statistical Monographs and Courses No. 2.) London: Charles Griffin, 1957.

Kuder, G. F., & Richardson, M. W. The theory of the estimation of test reliability. *Psychometrika*, 1937, 2, 151–160.

Landahl, H. D. Centroid orthogonal transformations. *Psychometrika*, 1938, *3*, 219–223.

Lawley, D. N. The estimation of factor loadings by the method of maximum likelihood. *Proceedings of the Royal Society of Edinburgh*, 1940, *60*, 64–82.

Lawley, D. N. Further investigations in factor estimation. *Proceedings of the Royal Society of Edinburgh*, 1941, *61*, 176–185.

Lawley, D. N., & Maxwell, A. E. *Factor analysis as a statistical method*. London: Butterworth, 1963.

Longley, J. W. An appraisal of least squares programs for the electronic computer from the point of view of the user. *Journal of the American Statistical Association*, 1967, *62*, 819–841.

Lord, F. M. Some relations between Guttman's principal components of scale analysis and other psychometric theory. *Psychometrika*, 1958, *23*, 291–296.

McQuitty, L. L. Elementary linkage analysis isolating orthogonal and oblique types and typal relevancies. *Educational and Psychological Measurement*, 1957, *17*, 207–229.

Meyer, E. P. A measure of the average intercorrelation. *Educational and Psychological Measurement*, 1975, *35*, 67–72.

Misiak, H., & Loranger, A. W. Cerebral dysfunction and intellectual impairment in old age. *Science*, 1961 (10 Nov), *134*, 1518–1519.

Mosier, C. I. Determining a simple structure when loadings for certain tests are known. *Psychometrika*, 1939, *4*, 149–162.

Mulaik, S. A. *The foundations of factor analysis*. New York: McGraw-Hill, 1972.

Murdoch, D. C. *Linear algebra for undergraduates*. New York: Wiley, 1957.

Neuhaus, J. O., & Wrigley, C. The quartimax method: An analytical approach to orthogonal simple structure. *British Journal of Statistical Psychology*, 1954, *7*, 81–91.

Pearson, E. S., & Hartley, H. O. *Biometrika tables for statisticians* (Vol. I). Cambridge, England: Cambridge University Press, 1954.

Pearson, K. On lines and planes of closest fit to systems of points in space. *Philosophical Magazine*, 1901, *2* (Series 6), 559–572.

Pearson, K., & Moul, M. The mathematics of intelligence. I. The sampling errors in the theory of a generalized factor. *Biometrika*, 1927, *19*, 246–291.

Peters, C. C., & Van Voorhis, M. A. *Statistical procedures and their mathematical bases*. New York: McGraw-Hill, 1940.

Rao, C. R. Estimation and tests of significance in factor analysis. *Psychometrika*, 1955, *20*, 93–111.

Rummel, R. J. *Applied factor analysis*. Evanston: Northwestern University Press, 1970.

Saunders, D. R. *An analytic method for rotation to orthogonal simple structure* (Research Bulletin 53-10, Educational Testing Service). Princeton, N.J.: Educational Testing Service, 1953.

Saunders, D. R. Trans-varimax. *American Psychologist*, 1962, *17*, 395.

Schonemann, P. H. Fitting a simplex symmetrically. *Psychometrika*, 1970, *35*, 1–21.

Sneath, P. H. A., & Sokal, R. R. *Numerical taxonomy*. San Francisco: Freeman, 1973.

Spearman, C. General intelligence, objectively determined and measured. *American Journal of Psychology*, 1904, *15*, 201–293.

Spearman, C. *The abilities of man: Their nature and measurement*. New York: Macmillan, 1927.

Spearman, C., & Holzinger, K. J. The sampling error in the theory of two factors. *British Journal of Psychology*, 1924, *15*, 17–19.

Spearman, C., & Holzinger, K. J. Note on the sampling error of tetrad differences. *British Journal of Psychology*, 1925, *16*, 86–88.

Spearman, C., & Holzinger, K. J. The average value for the probable error of tetrad differences. *British Journal of Psychology*, 1929, *20*, 368–370.

Swineford, F. A study in factor analysis: The nature of the general, verbal, and spatial bi-factors. *Supplementary Educational Monographs* (published in conjunction with *The School Review* and *The Elementary School Journal*). Chicago: University of Chicago Press, 1948 (No. 67).

ten Berge, J. M. F., & Nevels, K. A general solution to Mosier's oblique Procrustes problem. *Psychometrika*, 1977, *42*, 593–600.

Thomson, G. H. *The factorial analysis of human ability* (5th ed.) New York: Houghton Mifflin, 1951.

Thurstone, L. L. Primary mental abilities. *Psychometric Monographs*, 1938 (No. 1). (a)

Thurstone, L. L. A new rotational method in factor analysis. *Psychometrika*, 1938, *3*, 199–218. (b)

Thurstone, L. L. Current issues in factor analysis. *Psychological Bulletin*, 1940, *37*, 189–236.

Thurstone, L. L. *Multiple factor analysis*. Chicago: University of Chicago Press, 1947.

Thurstone, L. L. An analytic method for simple structure. *Psychometrika*, 1954, *19*, 173–182.

Thurstone, L. L., & Thurstone, T. G. Factorial studies of intelligence. *Psychometric Monographs*, 1941 (No. 2).

Tryon, R. C. *Cluster analysis*. Ann Arbor: Edwards Brothers, 1939.

Waugh, F. V., & Dwyer, P. S. Compact computation of the inverse of a matrix. *Annals of Mathematical Statistics*, 1945, *16*, 259–271.

Webb, E. Character and intelligence. *British Journal of Psychology Monograph Supplement*, 1915 (No. 3).

Wechsler, D. *WAIS manual: Wechsler Adult Intelligence Scale*. New York: Psychological Corporation, 1955.

Wherry, R. J., & Winer, B. J. A method for factoring large numbers of items. *Psychometrika*, 1953, *18*, 161–179.

Wilkinson, J. H. *The algebraic eigenvalue problem*. New York: Oxford University Press, 1965.

Wishart, J. Sampling errors in the theory of two factors. *British Journal of Psychology*, 1928, *19* (Part II), 181–187.

Author Index

447

Subject Index